Dimensions of Macroeconomics: A Book of Readings

D0721585

S. Mittra

Dimensions of Macroeconomics

A Book of Readings

RANDOM HOUSE, New York

FOR
BANI,
RITA,
AND
AJIT

Preface

"Macro-theory," wrote Fritz Machlup a decade ago, "so far as it is not econo-metric, seems simpler than micro-theory." This is no longer the case. During the last three or four decades, economists have been discovering with considerable excitement many new dimensions to macroeconomics, all of which have great exploratory potential.

Macroeconomic theory, as any other scientific theory does, establishes cause-and-effect relationships between key independent and dependent variables. An understanding of these relationships helps the theorist develop strategies for using macro tools in his efforts to achieve the predetermined goals of full employment, price stability, balance-of-payments equilibrium, and economic growth. The application of these strategies may be called the "long view" of macro theory. On the other hand, when macro tools are used to "solve" such economic problems as unemployment, poverty, inflation, and low income, these applications may be considered the "short view" of macro theory.

Leading macroeconomic textbooks on the market today do not, for obvious reasons, cover all the aspects of both the long and short views of macroeconomic theory. A good supplement to these books has long been needed, and it is my hope that this collection of readings I have assembled will fill this void.

I wish to point out that this volume contains materials from domestic and inter-national journals as well as materials from official reports, unpublished papers, and books dealing with macroeconomics. The coverage is thus broad and varied.

Before I began my search for material for this book, I realized my task was going to be an arduous one. I had become aware of the fact that a wide variety of topics and economic problems that had not been traditionally considered as strictly falling within the scope of macroeconomics had come to be treated as an integral part of this branch of economics. Also, in recent years an increasing number of economists had been turning their attention to macroeconomic problems and as a result the list of articles dealing with macroeconomics had greatly increased. To keep my selections within manageable limits, I decided to choose only those articles that either (1) had clarity of exposition, (2) had made a new contribution to theory or had extended existing theory, (3) provided empirical support to hypotheses, or (4) discussed critical issues. The articles/monographs that met one or more of these criteria greatly exceeded the limit my publisher had imposed upon me. I resolved this problem by using the following approach. First, I divided the chosen articles into fourteen chapters, each chapter covering one aspect of macroeconomics. I then divided each chapter into three sections. In the first section I put articles to be reprinted in full. In the second section I included summaries of important articles that could not be reprinted because of space limitation. In the third section I listed references to valuable articles that were either too long to be reprinted or too diffi-cult to summarize without doing an injustice to the authors.

Generally macro readings books are classified into sections on general equi-librium, the Keynesian theory, consumption and investment, monetary and fiscal theory, income fluctuations, international trade, economic policy, etc. In addition to these topics, this book also covers those subjects that macroeconomics has come to emphasize in recent years: macro-methodology, economic models, macro-measurement, distribution and expectation, and planning and growth.

My acknowledgments are many and varied. The following people gave generously of their help: Dr. Leonall C. Anderson (Federal Reserve Bank of St. Louis), Professors William J. Baumol (Princeton), El. N. Botsas (Oakland), Karl Brunner (Ohio State), Carl F. Christ (Johns Hopkins), Thomas F. Dernburg (Oberlin), Dudley Dillard (Maryland), George Horwich (Purdue), Harry G. Johnson (Chicago), Dale W. Jorgenson (Harvard), Kenneth K. Kurihara (State University of New York at Binghamton), Wassily Leontief (Harvard), John H. Lindauer (Claremont), Fritz Machlup (Princeton), Hyman P. Minsky (Washington), Robert A. Mundell (Chicago), Barry N. Siegel (Oregon), Robert M. Solow (MIT), Harold M. Somers (UCLA), Jan Tinbergen (Netherlands), Henry C. Wallich (Yale), and Dr. William H. White (IMF). However, the customary professional disclaimer is in order here. I am also grateful to Professor Richard Thorn, Consulting Editor for Random House, for his many helpful suggestions, to Barbara Conover, Senior Manuscript Editor, and to Christopher Benz, Acquiring Editor, for their smooth handling of the entire publishing operation. In addition, I am most grateful to the various authors and publishers who so readily gave permission for their material to be reprinted in this collection.

I wish here to give special thanks to all the members of my office staff for the excellent assistance they gave me in the preparation of my book for the press.

Editing a book of readings in macroeconomics is not an end in itself. The real payoff comes to an editor of such a book only if students and teachers find it helpful in acquiring a comprehensive knowledge of macroeconomic theory and policy. It is in this spirit that I offer this book of readings to these students and teachers.

Oakland University   S. Mittra
January 30, 1971

Contents

Dimensions of Macroeconomics: A Book of Readings

1
MACRO-METHODOLOGY

We have come a long way toward understanding the inner workings of our economic system since Lord Keynes focused the economist's attention on what is known today as macroeconomic theory. Much theoretical and empirical work has been done in this area over the past twenty or more years, and many general equilibrium models have been constructed by theoretical economists so as to assist policy makers in their task of formulating effective public policies.

Four articles are included in this part. In the first three—all of which are short—Baumol, Haavelmo, and Tinbergen discuss, respectively, the nature of consolidation in economics, the reasons for enlarging the scope of economics, and the need for supporting economic theory with empirical studies. In the fourth article, Weintraub makes an eclectic study of the numerous articles on theoretical economics that have appeared in economic literature.

The Present State of Economic Theory
W. J. Baumol

The last few decades in economic theory have seen very significant changes in the nature of its most outstanding and most productive efforts. The period may be said to have begun with the general acceptance, among economists, of the Keynesian resolution. At that time much of our theoretical work was devoted to further exploration, elucidation, and the infusion of rigour into the system. Thus the primary preoccupation was with macroeconomic analysis which was directly or ultimately applicable to public policy.

However, during this period the increasing interest in mathematical eco-

William J. Baumol, "Thoughts on the Present State of Economic Theory," *Indian Economic Journal*, 14 (September 1968), pp. 69–70.

nomics and econometrics was already beginning to manifest itself. The early postwar period exhibited several major theoretical breakthroughs all involving a degree of mathematical sophistication beyond that which had previously characterized any widespread movement in economic analysis. These developments included the theoretical applications of mathematical programming—notably activity analysis, and the econometric theory of systems involving simultaneous relationships—the theory of identification and of estimation in such systems.

These results have colored many subsequent developments. General equilibrium theory, the theory of the firm, growth theory, and welfare economics were all heavily affected in their analytic methods, though few really startling new theorems were produced. The developments in econometrics have aroused new and widespread interest in the marriage of theory and empirical materials, and many of the brightest young economists have turned to this area for their research.

The last decade has been a period of consolidation in economic theory. There have been no revolutions, no startling new discoveries, no major reorientations in method. Economic theorists have become increasingly concerned with verification, testing, and application. Work has, for example, turned from the theory of welfare economics to its application in cost-benefit analysis. Theorists have begun increasingly to advise government agencies and business firms. They have turned their efforts to operations analysis, which can be described as the application to business and government of rigorous microeconomic theory. From this all participants have been learning. Businessmen and administrators have learned how much rigorous analysis can help them, while the economists have gotten new ideas for their theory out of their opportunities to observe reality more closely.

Meanwhile, the technical training of our graduate students has increased enormously. The quality of workmanship of their research and their degree of mastery of the subject has risen spectacularly. They have, consequently, become prime contributors to the period of consolidations which promises to be with us for some time to come.

The Need for Widening the Scope of Economic Theory
Trygve Haavelmo

During the last twenty or thirty years economic theory had made great progress in clarifying the laws and principles that govern a market economy. Classical theorems have been made more stringent and new ones have been discovered. Theoretical models of a centrally planned economy have, of course, also been studied, in the search for different ways of reaching essentially the same kind of economic results as those which could be produced by a market economy under ideal conditions.

There is, however, one feature that is strikingly common to nearly the whole

Trygve Haavelmo, "Some Thoughts on the Need for Widening the Scope of Economic Theory," *Indian Economic Journal*, 14 (September 1968), pp. 70–71.

existing body of economic thought, and that is the very restricted meaning of the word realism in connection with economic models. A "realistic" model seems to be regarded as nearly identical with a model which simulates either what actually is, or what is just around the corner, as far as economic policy is concerned. The thinking of economists in this respect seems to be rather different from that of scientists and experts working on technological development. Modern engineers and technicians work out an enormous variety of models and projects, most of which are probably never seen in practical use. The models and schemes that are discarded are not necessarily "unrealistic" in the sense that they could not be constructed and used in practice. They are discarded as a result of a process of comparison and choice.

Why are not economists much more curious about investigating radically different ways of organizing the economy? It is not certain that people would prove to be so stubbornly fond of what is if alternatives could be spelled out with convincing clarity. It is undoubtedly true that there are economic systems which are feasible, but which are such that we are sure we would not like to live with them. Other systems may, a priori, appear somewhat far fetched. But would it be so dangerous just to take a look? An economist cannot fail to see that much of the economy of a country depends on institutions that are man-made rather than given by Nature. How about a little more of the "engineering approach" in the study of economic system?

To be more specific I should like to mention two directions in which it may be interesting to consider a radical change of fundamental assumptions.

One of these directions has to do with the growing importance of social—rather than hedonistic—preferences. The possibility of so-called interdependent utilities has, of course, already been strongly emphasized by many economists, but we know as yet very little about how to construct economic systems in which the production incentives are set up in a sensible way to match such preferences. The situation now prevailing in many countries, where the incentives to produce or to earn income are based largely on self-interest while at the same time high taxation aims at making everybody one big happy family, is approaching the point of being ridiculous.

The other direction I have in mind also concerns basic assumptions regarding preferences, but has to do with the question of stability or permanence. We may not like to hear this but it is, I think, obvious to everybody that individual preferences are to a growing extent acquired, taught, or even imposed, rather than innate. If this old element of invariance is no longer reliable as a foundation for developing economic systems and for judging their efficiency, we shall have to start looking for something else as the pivot of economic theory.

Balance Between Theory and Measurement
J. Tinbergen

On assuming the development of economic thinking during the last thirty years my main impressions are the following:

In the first place, some methods of theorizing have been more productive than others. I feel that theories using measurable or measured relationships have been much more productive than theories using

Jan Tinbergen, "Balance Between Theory and Measurement," *Indian Economic Journal*, 14 (September 1968), pp. 84–85.

qualitative concepts and hardly measurable relationships mainly. To quote a few examples, I think considerable progress has been made in the theory of business cycle policy, the theory of development policy, the theory of production, the theory of consumption decisions, and the theory of investment decisions. On the other hand, areas where not much progress has been made are the theory of imperfect competition, welfare-economics-old-style, the theory of the business cycle, and the theory of international trade, often because there was no possibility to test theories. It seems vital to the development of any science that there is a continual interplay between theory and observation. Theories using all sorts of "curves" that can hardly be measured remain hanging in the air.

Secondly, there has been a clear orientation towards applied economic theory. This is already partly reflected in the above, where several of the areas considered to have been successful are areas of applied theory (theories of policy and planning).

Thirdly, there has been some extension of the "territory" where economic theory has been applied; I am thinking of the application of economic theory to education and to other "social" activities, including the appraisal of "social projects."

Among the subjects where progress has been remarkable I mention the input–output method, the establishment of Cobb–Douglas or CES production functions, activity analysis, the theory of the flexible accelerator, the theory of demand for durable goods, and the theory of decision making and of decision strategy.

I consider as relatively less successful the attempts at refining the theory of imperfect competition, and the theory of international trade, where mostly phenomena or relationships have been discussed which we are not able to measure, for lack of data. In a way it may be said that here theory is too much ahead of measurement and then too speculative. There should be some balance between theory and observation. The theory of the business cycle is no longer interesting, since we now know more or less how to avoid it.

Looking at the future, the best thing I think I can do is to enumerate some subjects which it is desirable to tackle, because they concern urgent issues in many countries and because it seems possible to have a balance between (new) theory and (new) measurement. Among such subjects are the following:

1. To establish production functions in which the quality of labour is introduced rather than the quantity. We have regulation of the quantity of labour, in most countries, but we are able to vary the quality. Moreover we have growing material about the quality of labour in the form of job evaluation figures.

2. To establish production functions for agriculture, bringing out, above all, the complicated complementarities between the various inputs.

3. To establish social welfare functions. For purposes of planning there is an outspoken need to specify the "objective function" (in the language of programmers) for the economy as a whole, which is some type of social welfare function (in the language of economists).

4. The theory of income distribution and redistribution and the influence of the latter on productivity should be further developed.

5. Developing the theory of international trade along manageable lines so as to deal with a very large number of commodities and of countries and a large number of production factors, in order that it can be used to analyse the optimal division of labour among a large number of countries.

6. Formulation of welfare economics in such a way that light can be shed on the optimal organization of the economy, for instance on the problem of the most desirable degree of decentralization of a number of decisions.

Theoretical Economics
Sidney Weintraub

This article seeks to offer some guide to the flow of studies of the last few years in theoretical economics.* Completeness is disavowed. Space limitations permit only a clue to the essential content; those who want the detail will have recourse to the original sources of the ascribed views, which are merely spotlighted here.

DEMAND THEORY

Ivor Pearce has produced a readable, balanced, and comprehensive book on demand theory, leaning more than a bit on utility concepts.[1] Deep issues are raised concerning the homogeneity of the utility function when savings and expected price changes are included in the demand function. Communal indifference curves and market independence–interdependence ("neutral" want-association) are also extensively explored.

Peter Newman has provided a rigorous companion volume on demand and ex-

Sidney Weintraub, "Theoretical Economics," *The Annals of the American Academy of Political and Social Science*, 352 (March 1964), pp. 145–162.

* The period covered is, roughly, 1964–1967. A previous survey by the present author appeared in *The Annals* (March 1964). This constitutes some updating of the earlier article. Note that because of the numerous references to economic journals, they are numbered according to the following key:

[1] *American Economic Review*
[2] *Economica*
[3] *Economic Journal*
[4] *Econometrica*
[5] *Journal of Political Economy*
[6] *Oxford Economic Papers*
[7] *Quarterly Journal of Economics*
[8] *Review of Economic Studies*
[9] *Review of Economics and Statistics*
[10] *Southern Economic Journal*
[11] *International Economic Review*
[12] *Kyklos*

change theory.[2] "Comparability," "consistency," and "selection" are described as the general axioms of ordinal demand theory, with "dominance," "continuity," "convexity," and "continuity of substitution" serving as special postulates. The welfare implications of market exchange are meticulously staked out.[3]

Clarkson has argued that theories of utility-maximization are "*ex post facto* rationalizations*,*" arguing for recasting the theory in terms of "decision-making" behavior.[4] A sign of the extent of current specialization is the book-length treatment of generally familiar demand ideas in Wu and Pontney.[5]

For an empirical study of demand and consumption outlays, interested readers will want to consult the important volume by Houthakker and Taylor.[6] International comparisons of consumption are presented in an informative article by Yang.[7]

The various demand curves, depending on whether money or real income, or neither, is held constant, are considered by Usher.[8] Undoubtedly, too little attention is accorded to this question. Bierwag and Grove, in a more traditional spirit, extend indifference analysis to asset choice, based on whether individuals tend to accept or avert risk.[9] Consumer's surplus engages Winch, who hopes to reconcile "Marshallian simplicity with the purist's insistence on precision."[10] While Winch is sanguine that the measure is often suitable, the revelation of 36 separate results from policy changes is hardly reassuring. Lerner is also receptive to consumer's surplus; Lerner, however, is less alarmed at "value" judgments.[11]

Lancaster has injected some fresh thoughts into demand theory.[12] Likening a consumer to a firm buying inputs, Lancaster argues that consumers buy a collection of attributes: "even a single good will possess more than one characteristic" (pp. 133–134). The approach offers some promise for handling new goods within the utility function.

Gorman has expanded the utility function to include the influence of *habit*, or past choices, on current tastes.[13] Frisch proposed reinstating cardinal utility for considering choice over time under uncertainty; Morishima and Pollak maintained that only ordinal elements were involved.[14]

Mathematical statements of the theory of consumer behavior occupy Sonnenschein and Richter.[15] Liviatan has sought to simplify the theory of long-run consumption plans through a "composite-commodity" approach; Green and Thompson explore further the intertemporal dimensions of the utility function."[16]

Definitional aspects of complementarity and substitution have reappeared in articles by Kamien and Hadar. Lerner has endeavored to simplify Hicks's now commonplace indifference approach through some new definitional categories.[17]

PRODUCTION

The literature on the theory of production has become vast.

For the theory of the firm, two books are especially worthy of note, namely, those by Frisch and Danø.[18] Professor Frisch, who did so much to shape the modern theory, has gathered together his mature reflections in a major work which includes the time dimensions of the problem, involving depreciation and reinvestment decisions, along with multiple product aspects. Danø pays more attention to programming models, quality variation, multiple plant, multiple product, and vertical integration aspects. Managerial economics should draw heavily on this work.

For macro-theory and econometric measurement, a volume sponsored by the National Bureau of Economic Research contains the reminiscences of former Senator Paul Douglas on his pioneering work in developing the Cobb–Douglas function involving linear and homogeneous input–output relations.[19] Solow's contribution is largely concerned with the problems of technical change, and the complexities of measuring factor inputs.[20] Marc Nerlove analyzes CES (constant elasticity of substitution) production functions, of which the Cobb–Douglas function is a special case.[21]

On the same problems, Murray Brown offers detailed contrasts of the Cobb–Douglas and CES functions.[22] Hildebrand and Liu are concerned primarily with measuring industry production relations.[23] A new book by Edwin Mansfield deals comprehensively with matters of technological change.[24] Walters has summarized the mounting literature on the econometrics of the production problem.[25]

There has also been a protracted debate on the proper form of *the* production function for the firm, albeit based on *a priori* ideas rather than empiric findings. Nutter, on the basis of a textbook account, disputed the view that marginal products had to fall monotonically given a linear and homogeneous function. Summing up, Nutter restated the controversy to signify: (1) the marginal product of one factor could be negative if the marginal exceeded the average product for the other factor; (2) both marginal products could not be negative, while the average product could increase for only one factor; and that (3) convexity entailed marginal and average products moving in the same direction. Rowe questioned whether the search for a symmetrical total product function was appropriate.[26]

Related is a very lucid article by Professor Danø, arguing that, where the fixed factor was divisible, we can dispense with that part of the production function where the average product of the variable factor was rising, for firms would discard units of the divisible fixed factor to ensure *constant* average returns to the variable agent.[27]

Tangri explored the implications for the fixed factor in the several regions of the production function where average product was rising, reaching its peak, subsequently declining to zero.[28] Tangri, also doubting the symmetry features, observes that Region I for one input is Region III for another, and develops the bivalued variable cost phenomena implicit in the usual drawings. This treatment was long overdue; the usual presentation had scarcely been altered since Cassels' fine study over thirty years ago.[29] The spacing of isoquants, involving the elasticity of productivity and returns to scale, has also been explained, but less conclusively.[30]

Leibenstein has raised the more substantive issue of whether "given" inputs lead to "given," and "maximum," outputs. Describing what he terms "X-Efficiency," Leibenstein writes: "It is conceivable that in practice a situation would arise in which managers are exceedingly poor, that is, others are available . . . who would be very much superior," and that, in underdeveloped countries especially, "managers determine not only their own productivity but the productivity of all cooperating units in the organization."[31] He concludes that "in a great many instances, the amount to be gained by increasing allocative efficiency is trivial while the amount to be gained by increasing X-Efficiency is frequently significant" (p. 413). This is a proposition with far-reaching implications for the neat mathematization of input–output relations which omit the past history or the human relationship.[32]

Shapley and Shubik argue that "the simple concept of property implicit in many classical models of a competitive economy is . . . an insufficiently basic representation of the phenomenon of ownership."[33] They consider, briefly, feudal systems, village communes, landless peasants, and the like. The cases would lend themselves to closer study; they have relevance in many parts of the world.

In a reconsideration of Marshallian functional time periods, De Alessi has sought a more conscious clock-time formulation.[34] The shorter the time interval from disturbance to adjustment, the higher the cost of a change in output and the fewer the inputs that can be varied—a fairly familiar Marshallian conclusion. But Alessi, like Borts and Mishan, argues that temporarily the firm may even use *excessive* amounts of factors.[35] It is also argued that average cost curves involving larger-scale plants tend to be "wider and shallower," enlarging the range of minimum average cost, than with smaller plants.[36]

Lucas considers the joint determination of output and investment decisions to situations in which resources are drawn from current output to facilitate the investment level, so that current production falls and prices rise.[37] Buchanan considers a situation in which "externalities are classified as one subcategory of joint supply," so that in producing more of one output, other outputs (or well-being) may be enhanced in a manner not consciously intended: the well-tended garden of one individual enhances the well-being of his neighbors. Buchanan observes that the "optimal" output level, or its "precise statement, becomes a formidable undertaking" (p. 413).[38]

For "reasonable" values of CES production functions, involving elasticities of substitution between 0.5 and 10.0, Nelson asserts that even a 45 per cent increase in capital per man-hour leads to an output increase that ranges from 10.3 to 13.3 per cent. Hence he defends the serviceability of the Cobb–Douglas function.[39]

CONSERVATION

For the conservation aspect of the theory of production, Keynes' concept of user cost, involving links between present actions and future consequences, is vital. Journal articles by Gordon, relevant to minerals, timber, fisheries, and the like, and on the fishery problem, by Turvey, may be noted.[40] A more optimistic view on technological advance overpowering depletion was a theme advanced by Barnett and Morse.[41]

THE FIRM AND MARKETS

J. K. Galbraith's work undoubtedly created the largest stir on the theory of the firm and the trends of our economic order.[42] Its lucidity, insights, and phrase-making, and the sin of large sales, led to its frequent condemnation by economists who take a dim view of these qualities. But Galbraith's stress on technology and the expert—the "technostructure"—and his understanding of managerial capitalism and the firm's objectives of profits and growth, of advertising, of government spending, and employment-income control, of the military complex, and of some dubious educational accommodations, should assure the book of a life and vitality for several years to come.

Robin Marris covers some of the same ground, often in a quasi-mathematical way and with more emphasis on the firm's profit and growth objectives and its financial value for takeovers and mergers: "managerial capitalism" is having a new vogue.[43] Optimistic in outlook, and re-counting the evolution of the welfare state, with some glimpse of the future, is Shonfield's *Modern Capitalism*.[44]

Technical textbooks include Vickers' efforts to weave financial aspects into the theory of the firm, Hadley's and Whitin's analysis of inventory control, and Ferguson's play on J. M. Clark's ideas on "workable competition," reinterpreted in a macropolicy setting.[45] Several Carnegie-

Mellon University works on behavioral aspects of the firm also bowed.[46] A critique of Chamberlinian theory, scoring several good points but without erecting a new structure, is a short book by Andrews.[47]

Reviewing the Berle and Means findings, in their influential *Modern Corporation and Private Property*, Larner reports that management-controlled corporations have increased from 88 in 1929 to about 169 in 1963, among the largest two hundred firms.[48] Shorey Peterson, nonetheless, argued that the corporation still remains subject to market restraints and competitive forces almost as in a simpler day; A. A. Berle and Carl Kaysen responded skeptically to this view.[49] Williamson, in a more theoretical contribution, argued that as organizations grow, "control loss occurs between successive hierarchical levels," placing limitations on the size of firms and involving "ultimately diminishing returns to scale."[50] Monsen and Downs assert that managers "desire to maximize their own lifetime incomes" (p. 236) and that large size fosters imperfectly controlled bureaucratic structures.[51]

Fritz Machlup, from whom we have come to expect consistent fealty to "marginalism," makes some overtures to behavioral approaches in his presidential address to the American Economic Association, remarking that the marginal approach based on profit-maximization

is suitable where (1) *large groups* of firms are involved and nothing has to be predicted about particular firms, (2) the effects of a *specified change* in conditions upon prices, inputs, and outputs are to be explained or predicted rather than the values of these magnitudes . . . and (3) only *qualitative answers* . . . about directions of change, are sought rather than numerical results.[52]

The vexing problems of duopoly and bilateral monopoly continued to invite study. A slender book by Thin summarized some earlier literature.[53] Ferguson, for differentiated products, developed an Edgeworth contract-curve solution; Cross argued that bargaining-costs hastened solutions in bilateral monopoly sequences, extending these to domestic and international politics; Bishop stressed the time aspects of negotiations while Saraydar was concerned with the limits of the bargaining process.[54]

Some appreciation of Chamberlin's theory of monopolistic competition appeared in several articles.[55] A less sympathetic flaying of the "tangency" solution and the "excess-capacity" theorem occupied Demsetz.[56] In his view, his criticism renders "the monopolistic competition model empty with respect to empirically testable content" (p. 622). One may predict that Chamberlin's general views will retain their hold. Stigler, formulating a theory of oligopoly, argues that collusion to maximize joint profits is restricted because of "the problem of policing a collusive agreement, which proves to be a problem in the theory of information."[57]

The Bain–Sylos argument of "limit-prices" to forestall entry—which was earlier offered by Harrod—also received attention.[58] Osborne argued that in several industries, limit-prices were ineffective, though his data was challenged.[59] According to Wenders, based on considerations of demand elasticity, even collusive oligopolists would have to accept prices below the monopoly level.[60] A game-theory approach advanced the view that potential entrants tended to *raise* the limit-price.[61]

ADVERTISING

The late Professor Chamberlin sought to clarify the blurred distinction between production and selling costs: costs to fulfill whatever was "transferred" were "production" costs while outlays to raise the price, or sell more units, were selling costs.[62] Empirically, Comanor and Wilson concluded that "industries with high advertising outlays" experience nearly "a 50 per cent increase in profit rates."[63] Their conclusions "are precisely the opposite of the conclusions reached by Telser" (p. 423). Telser had found "little empirical support for an inverse association between advertising and competition," asserting instead that "advertising is frequently . . . a sign of competition" and "an important source of information" (p. 558).[64]

Simon, linking advertising outlays to sales and revenue probabilities, doubted "simple, general, determinate rules" following changes in the number of firms or products.[65] Williamson examined the influence of selling costs as a barrier to entry.[66] The effect of elasticity on market structure was also viewed as of some importance.[67] Gilani extended the idea of plant flexibility to the notion of "product flexibility," involving quality changes.[68]

LESS CONVENTIONAL ANALYSES OF THE FIRM

In a potentially significant analysis, John Williamson distinguished between output behavior of the firm under (1) profit-maximization, (2) sales-maximization, and (3) hypotheses of growth-maximization: both (2) and (3) follow Baumol's lead. While many difficulties remain with this argument, the introduction of the influence of time is a salutory aspect of the theory.[69] Scott examined constantly changing demand and supply conditions which may leave "large differences in profitability and pockets of excess or deficient capacity which persist for a long time."[70]

More offbeat is an often witty account of professional sports by Neale.[71] Ginzberg (and others), writing *The Pluralistic Economy*, call attention to nonenterprise activities by government, philanthropic, religious, educational, and other institutions.[72]

ANTITRUST

While antitrust and corporate regulation is off our track, in an article which contains references to recent literature, Bork argues that "the introduction of goals other than consumer welfare into antitrust is destructive of antitrust as law."[73] Comanor examines the regulatory obscurities of mergers.[74]

PEAK-LOAD PRICING

Uneven demands involving high peak-hour use, such as in electric power, transportation, bridge traffic, telephone use, and the like, pose interesting and intricate issues. Buchanan affirmed that in any pricing decision "the allocational decision cannot be isolated from the distributional decision" (p. 469), signifying that real income division as well as output magnitudes will be affected.[75] Other views are perhaps overly optimistic on the optimality of price = marginal cost arrangements.

UNCERTAINTY

Uncertainty, which colors decisions and affects the content of economic activity, occasioned several writings. Ozga's book contains a valuable survey of the problems and an assessment of the literature, as well as contributing to it.[76] Kenneth Arrow followed an earlier major article with a small monograph declaring that "the immediate basis for a special theory of behavior under uncertainty is the subjective sensation that an *action* may not uniquely determine the consequences to the agent" and that "it is possible to attach numbers called utilities to consequences in such a way that the expected value of utility measures the preference for an action."[77] For investment under uncertainty, Hirshleifer argues that "precise beliefs as to the probabilities of these alternative states are assumed."[78] A mathematical approach to the theory of uncertainty is offered by Pratt.[79]

THE COST OF CAPITAL

Following the path-breaking article by Modigliani and Miller, a fine expository article by Baumol and Malkiel remarks "that the market value of the firm . . . is totally independent of the firm's capital structure—the ratio between its debt and equity" (p. 550), neglecting tax phenomena favoring bonds, and transactions cost-associated with altering the financial structure; ideally "the financing decision makes absolutely no difference at all" (p. 549).[80]

GENERAL EQUILIBRIUM

Morishima, an outstanding practitioner of the mathematical mode, has produced a book extending Leontief models to efficient growth paths.[81] The general equilibrium approach is detailed in a new book by Quirk and Saposnik; less formidable is the book by Kuenne.[82] Jones offers a simplified account of the major relations.[83] The stability issue, and an interpretation of the Walrasian *tâtonnement*, have been presented in substantially literary fashion.[84] Allen, with accustomed clarity, has prepared a book on macro-theory.[85]

THE THEORY OF MONEY

New attention has been devoted to the theory of money; while the argument and the estimating techniques are highly sophisticated, it is doubtful if the conclusions differ from a qualified Quantity Theory stance.

Among Keynesians, Tobin has considered the relation of money to growth, though the important linkage of money supplies to wage levels has been excluded.[86] Stein has argued that "the long-run marginal product of capital is negatively related to the proportionate rate of growth in the money supply" (p. 463), suggesting thereby that monetary policy will affect the course of development.[87] Brownlee and Scott contend that: "Debt management could be concerned with the size of GNP [gross national product] and ignore the interest costs with little loss to the economy."[88]

The Keynesian "liquidity-trap" attracted further, inconclusive debate.[89] Cagan's book on the supply of money will undoubtedly become an important reference source.[90] A lengthy article by Teigen contends that through member-bank borrowing, the demand for money is at least partly endogenous, while "transactions requirements form the only rational basis for demanding cash balances" and that this is "interest-responsive" (p. 506).[91]

For Horwich the Quantity Theory is very much alive, though often in the background in the concentration on the asset structure; Pesek and Saving, in some departure from the Gurley–Shaw theme, acknowledge that banks *produce* money, an object of demand in the economy.[92]

Meltzer is dubious of economies of scale in the demand for money as transactions grow; he concludes that "the simple quantity theory of money predicts the money demand by business firms reasonably well" (p. 420).[93] Miller and Orr also argue that "a doubling of prices will double the quantity of money" (p. 426) demanded by firms.[94] Meltzer also finds that the demand function for money "is stable for several alternative definitions of money" (p. 244), though he favors excluding time deposits from the money category. Also, "that the long-run demand function is consistent with the quantity theory of money" (p. 227), with some concession to the "liquidity-trap" in a "deep depression" (p. 243).[95]

A puzzling but generally remarkable article by Allais deserves particular attention; two major conclusions can be reported here. He remarks that "there is a proportional relationship between the price level and the quantity of money. But the coefficient of proportionality is not constant; its value at each moment depends on the past historical development of total outlay," though "from the dynamic standpoint of causality," it may be "that the price level is proportional to the ratio of the quantity of money to the level of activity; or it may mean that the quantity of money is proportional to the product of the price level and the level of economic activity" (p. 1153).[96] He cites *wage inflation as yielding to the latter interpretation.* This literally turns monetary theory around (correctly in my view), to making the demand for money a function of the accomplished wage-price-employment facts, rather than as quantity theorists would have it.

Laidler declares that the stability of the demand function for money is improved by including time-deposits in money, and that "permanent income is a better explanatory variable for the demand for money" (p. 55).[97] Also that "the hypothesis of the liquidity trap ... appears to be refuted" (pp. 550–551), and that the short-rate of interest "is relevant for money-holding" (p. 554). To Chow, "current income is more important in short-run *changes* in the demand for money" and that "permanent income is a better explanatory variable than both wealth and current income" in the long-run demand function.[98] Hamburger writes that "interest rates appear to be the most important determinants of the short-run movements in households' money balances."[99] The precautionary demand for money is explored by Whalen.[100]

MONETARY POLICY

On monetary policy, Modigliani concludes "that (1) on the whole the evidence supports the use of discretion over a rule, but that (2) there is room for some limitations in the use of discretion, particularly in the form of spelling out more precisely the goals to which the discretionary powers should be directed, and the procedure by which these goals are to be changed" (p. 244).[101] Also: "At best, therefore, rules can only provide a rough guide for monetary management."

Professor Milton Friedman, who has led much of the current research into monetary phenomena, maintains the contrary view, promulgating it often and cogently. In his presidential address to the American Economic Association, he again called for the Federal Reserve's "setting itself a steady course and keeping to it," and that "the precise rate of growth [in the money supply] is less important than the adoption of some stated and known rate. I myself have argued ... for something like a 3 to 5 per cent per year rate of growth in currency plus all commercial bank deposits."[102] Recently, the Joint Economic Committee of Congress has announced a predilection toward this view; the Federal Reserve people undoubtedly prefer the Modigliani thesis.

THE STRUCTURE OF INTEREST RATES

An active discussion on the structure of interest rates, surrounding the publication of Meiselman's small monograph, also developed. Following Hicks, who largely argued (*Value and Capital*, Oxford, 1939) that long rates were some average of expected short rates, Meiselman declared that "forward rates are unbiased estimates of expected rates."[103] Subsequent discussion involved the facts and their interpretation, and inquired whether the different markets were substantially interdependent or independent, that is, "segmented," as well as whether concentrations of securities in special sectors would influence the rate pattern.[104] A more neutral

and tentative note is struck in an article by Telser.[105]

THE THEORY OF INFLATION

Inflation theory, and the inflation problem, seem always to be with us. The one new alternate set of views involving *incomes policy*, or wages policy primarily, received some new impetus through Prime Minister Wilson's program this past spring in England, even while our guidepost policy languished. The important article by Professor Lerner may yet induce other prominent Keynesian economists to reconsider their views.[106] Meanwhile, a literature on this theory and policy is developing alongside the more conventional monetary views.[107]

For the inflated earlier inflation literature, see the survey article of Bronfenbrenner and Holtzman.[108] A comprehensive analytic and econometric volume has been published by Ball.[109] A reinterpretation of the great German inflation after World War I, in terms of the wage-price chain, occupies a slim volume by Laursen and Pedersen.[110] More theoretically, Phelps argued that whether *anticipated* inflation affects investment and growth depends significantly on the use made of fiscal and monetary controls.[111]

PHILLIPS CURVE

Phillips-curve literature, embodying arguments on an inverse relation between unemployment and money-wage changes, accumulated.[112] Hines, a critic, insisted that "the rate of change of unionisation is closely associated with the rate of change of money wage rates" (p. 242).[113] Perry introduced profits as a parameter, yielding a *family* of Phillips curves.[114] Eagley has argued that the "quit-rate," rather than unemployment, explains wage changes better than unemployment.[115] The special influence of "frictional" unemployment has also been examined; Rees and Hamilton question much of the empirical work "because the data are of poor quality for much of the early part of the period" (p. 70).[116]

Phelps has introduced *shifting* Phillips curves, involving higher rates of wage and price changes with any given amount of unemployment as inflation progresses and further inflation is anticipated; thus, inflation breeds more inflation "as expectations are continually revised upwards."[117] This entails the disquieting thought of a rising unemployment-inflation tradeoff for those who are reluctant to accept some form of incomes policy.

Kuh, in contrast to Phillips-curve proponents, argues that for the United States, "the unemployment level does not provide a powerful explanation of wage changes" (p. 334), holding the effect of labor productivity on the demand for labor to be more significant.[118] Professor Klein, with customary skill, outlines the econometric relations of wage-price determination emerging from his studies of several countries, with employment implications.[119]

GROWTH THEORY

Growth theory has achieved its own path of enormous growth since Sir Roy Harrod prepared his famous essay some thirty years ago. An 111-page survey article by Hahn and Matthews lists approximately 250 items in an 11-page bibliography.[120]

Of more recent contributions, Professor Phelps' work on Golden Rules might be cited as a sequel to Mrs. Robinson's Golden Age, in which labor force, capital stock, and output grow apace. For Phelps, there is the "fundamental notion of a 'commanding' growth path ... which gives uniformly higher consumption through time than any other path parallel to it in some respects" (p. ix).[121]

Tobin concludes that "government can affect the growth of the economy," and inquires whether it should (p. 10). He reiterates the important theme that "the rates of growth of productivity per man and of consumption per capita are in the long run controlled by the rate of advance of technology" (pp. 8–9). In the interests of "unborn generations," and on "a reasonable set of social time preferences" (p. 17), Tobin advocates a conscious growth policy.[122] Hicks, reverting to John Stuart Mill and his vision of improvement in the moral and aesthetic qualities of man, raises some pithy questions on growing income, or affluence.[123] His recent book also expresses skepticism of the concept of an "optimal" growth rate. A related theme occupies Koopmans: revisions of decisions by successive generations, decisions on population growth, and the unforeseen changes in technology are the big hurdles in specifying an optimal growth path.[124]

INCOME DISTRIBUTION

Perhaps the most important theoretical discussion of all in recent years concerned the theory of income-distribution. For about a decade, Professors Joan Robinson and Nicholas Kaldor, joined more recently by Pasinetti, have advanced the view that aggregate profits, the profit share, and the rate of profits depend crucially on the level of (gross) investment, the savings propensities of "capitalists," including business or corporate saving, and the considerably lower savings ratios of wage-earners.[125] Samuelson and Modigliani, in a defense of marginal productivity explanations of factor prices and factor shares, profess that the same results can be derived under the more traditional framework, while they "confess to most serious qualms on the empirical relevance of these [recent] assumptions—notably that relating to the existence of identifiable classes of capitalists and workers" (p. 271). Their qualms, however, as Kaldor pointed out, did not extend to their own assumptions involving stationary conditions, continuous production functions, pure competition, profit-maximization, a homogeneous stock of capital, or the analysis of a case where "the capitalists' share of total wealth will approach zero while the workers' share . . . will approach unity" (p. 277). These hypotheses will hardly pass a test of "empirical relevance."[126]

Among other articles, Rothschild modifies the Kaldor view by assuming that unions resist a reduction in the wage share, or insist on a given real wage; both hypotheses would reduce investment levels, barring a rise in entrepreneurial savings.[127] Ferguson expresses satisfaction with neoclassical smooth production functions and the inverse relation of the capital-labor ratio to the rate of interest (apparently ignoring the "reswitching" controversy, noted below), and regards marginal productivity theory generally as a "useful and satisfactory approximation to reality" (p. 500).[128]

A review of some of the theoretical work appears in an article by Marjorie Turner; some attempt to link the wage share to wage levels and investment magnitudes is made by Gallaway.[129] Davidson considers the demand for securities as an aspect of the savings propensities and the income distribution.[130]

but thought this a *curiosum*. Piero Sraffa, in his volume on *Production of Commodities by Means of Commodities* (1960), had perceived the same possibility. Now, Pasinetti and others agree that capital per head does not bear "an inverse monotonic relationship to the rate of profit" or interest. That is, capital-labor ratios profitable at high interest may become uneconomical as interest rates fall, and economical again as interest rates fall lower, so that "switches of techniques due to changes in the rate of profit do not allow us to make any general statement on changes in the 'quantity of capital' per unit of labor" (pp. 513–514).

Effectively, the neoclassical production function which relates the demand for capital to the rate of interest becomes "stepped" or discontinuous. Garegnani underscores the theoretical consequences, inasmuch as "the dominant [marginal productivity] theory of distribution" has been erected on the inverse monotonic relationship (p. 575). To compound matters, Bruno, Burmeister, and Sheshinski show that "it is *not* true that steady state consumption always *rises* as the rate of interest falls" (p. 528); thus, savings also evidence some "reswitching." Samuelson observes that the one valid conclusion remaining seems to be that a lower rate of interest will signify a higher real wage.[131]

Traditional views will be altered by this discussion.

CAPITAL RESWITCHING

There are profound implications for the theory of distribution in the series of articles on "reswitching." Briefly, it was generally thought that a fall in the rate of interest would render production more capital-using. Mrs. Robinson, in her *Accumulation of Capital* (1956), had pointed up a situation in which a fall in the rate of interest had the *contrary* effect,

INDUCED INVENTION

A rise in the relative price of labor, say, should foster a substitution of capital for labor. With a given production function, the substitution should proceed in a determinate way, according to the "state of the arts." Those who frown on the production-function concept, and Robinson and Kaldor have also led this point of view, would go beyond this, to suggest that the higher real wage would initiate a search for *newer*, less capital-using techniques, that the pressure of a higher real wage leads entrepreneurs to uncover *new* input-output relations, so that the production function is a very amorphous concept.

This is at the bottom of the theory of *induced* invention. Further, as the relative shares of labor and capital tend to remain fairly fixed, the production-function *substitution* approach is unable to account significantly for this constancy.

Kennedy thus argues that entrepreneurs seek to reduce the use of that factor whose income share is highest, to restore relative shares thereby when real wages, say, rise, and that the innovation aspect need not be disentangled from substitution: "Since this question is in principle unanswerable, there is some advantage in not having to ask it" (p. 546).[132]

WELFARE ECONOMICS

Mishan describes welfare economics as "in a quandary right now" for "we do not seem to know quite what we are doing when we are 'maximizing welfare,'" and that we may merely be maximizing "gross productive power, or human population on this planet" (p. xv).[133] Elsewhere, considering many actions that invade the privacy of others, he suggests "alterations in the legal framework that would promote Pareto improvements unattainable under the existing system" (p. 281).[134]

On another level, cost-benefit analyses for public improvements such as flood control, reforestation, highways, education, air pollution, and the like, have been pushed rather actively. A lengthy article reviews the present state of this analysis.[135]

The theory of "second-best," concerned with the optimal adaptation in one sector when other sectors deviate from the Pareto optimum, received further (inconclusive) attention.[136]

Considering that the New Welfare Economics sanctions policy only when someone can be made better off without injury to others, and that this rarely is possible, there is some new concern with democratic principles. It is doubtful if rigorous results will be found on this line, despite the stimulus to some incisive articles on the theory of democracy or social order generally.[137]

Some asymmetrical aspects of externalities, where A can influence the well-being of B, but not vice versa, are considered by Buchanan and Kafoglis.[138] Buchanan also considers the theory of clubs, and their optimal size.[139]

Disability insurance has also been examined in terms of marginal gains and losses.[140] Externalities reached by either market action or administrative processes are examined by Wellisz.[141] In a most interesting, and potentially important, article, Foldes demonstrates the lack of coincidence in decisions to pay some "real" income, and the consequences of presumed equivalent money payments.[142]

An optimistic view of the prospect of "social welfare functions" is the subject of a paper by Coleman.[143] Tullock infers that the Arrow "impossibility" theorem for group choice is largely irrelevant, for "majority voting will choose the alternative which is closest to the optima of the majority of voters" (p. 263).[144]

An interesting situation is outlined by Kahn, who argues that changes are often accomplished through a series of small decisions, so that we are not faced with a choice in the aggregate, such as in car-styling, decisions to abandon a railway spur, or in various similar services, so that these disappear, or never appear, although they could command support.[145]

NOTES

1 Ivor F. Pearce, *A Contribution to Demand Analysis* (New York: Oxford University Press, 1964).

2 Peter Newman, *The Theory of Exchange* (Englewood Cliffs, N.J.: Prentice-Hall, 1965). The book contains a rather full set of bibliographical references.

3 Although it transcends the scope of this survey, note might be made of the important work, also complete in its bibliographical aspects, of Murray Kemp, *The Pure Theory of International Trade* (Englewood Cliffs, N.J.: Prentice-Hall, 1964).

4 Geoffrey P. E. Clarkson, *The Theory of Consumer Demand: A Critical Appraisal* (Englewood Cliffs, N.J.: Prentice-Hall, 1963), p. 85.

5 Shih-Yen Wu and Jack Pontney, *An Introduction to Modern Demand Theory* (New York: Random House, 1967).

6 H. S. Houthakker and Lester D. Taylor, *Consumer Demand in the United States, 1929–1970* (Cambridge, Mass.: Harvard University Press, 1966).

7 Charles Yneu Yang, "An International Comparison of Consumption Functions," [9], August 1964.

8 Dan Usher, "The Derivation of Demand Curves from Indifference Curves," [6], March 1965.

9 G. O. Bierwag and M. A. Grove, "Indifference Curves in Asset Theory," [3], June 1966.

10 David M. Winch, "Consumer's Surplus and the Compensation Principle," [1], June 1965.

11 A. P. Lerner, "Consumer's Surplus and Micro-Macro," [5], February 1963.

12 K. Lancaster, "A New Approach to Consumer Theory," [5], April 1966, and "Change and Innovation in the Technology of Consumption," [1], May 1966. See also W. J. Baumol, "Calculation of Optimal Product and Retailer Characteristics: The Abstract Product Approach," [5], October 1967.

13 W. M. Gorman, "Tastes, Habits and Choice," [11], June 1967.

14 Ragnar Frisch, "Dynamic Utility," [4], July 1964; Michio Morishima, "Should Dynamic Utility Be Cardinal?"; and Robert Pollak, "Dynamic Utility: A Comment," [4], October 1965.

15 Hugo Sonnenschein, "The Relationship Between Transitive Preference and the Structure of the Choice Space," [4], July 1965; and Marcel K. Richter, "Revealed Preference Theory," [4], July 1966.

16 Nissan Liviatan, "Multiperiod Future Consumption as an Aggregate," [1], September 1966; H. A. John Green,

"Intertemporal Utility and Consumption," [6], March 1967; Earl A. Thompson, "Intertemporal Utility Functions and the Long-Run Consumption Function," [4], April 1967.

17 M. I. Kamien, "Note On Complementarity and Substitution," [11], 1964; J. Hadar, "The Substitution Term Is Ambiguous," with replies by E. Mishan and R. G. D. Allen, [2], 1967. Also, A. P. Lerner, "The Analysis of Demand," [1], September 1962.

18 Ragnar Frisch, *Theory of Production* (Chicago: Rand McNally, 1965); and Sven Danø, *Industrial Production Models* (New York: Springer-Verlag, 1966).

19 Paul H. Douglas, "Comments on the Cobb–Douglas Production Function," in Murray Brown (ed.), *The Theory and Empirical Analysis of Production* (New York: National Bureau of Economic Research, 1967).

20 Robert M. Solow, "Some Recent Developments in the Theory of Production," *ibid.* An earlier article argued that long-run substitutability of capital and labor yields results for heterogeneous capital similar to those for capital homogeneity— "Heterogeneous Capital and Smooth Production Functions: An Experimental Study," [4], October 1963.

21 Marc Nerlove, "Recent Empirical Studies of the CES and Related Production Functions," *ibid.*

22 Murray Brown, *On the Theory and Measurement of Technological Change* (New York: Cambridge University Press, 1966).

23 George H. Hildebrand and Ta-Chung Liu, *Manufacturing Production Functions in the United States, 1957* (Ithaca, N.Y.: Cornell University Press, 1965).

24 Edwin Mansfield, *The Economics of Technological Change* and *Industrial Research amd Technological Innovation* (New York: W. W. Norton, 1968).

25 A. A. Walters, "Production and Cost Functions: An Econometric Survey," [4], 1963.

26 All of the items appeared in the *American Economic Review*: G. Warren Nutter, "Diminishing Returns and Linear Homogeneity" (December 1963). Comments subsequently by H. Liebhavsky, Ryuzo Sato, and John W. Rowe, Jr., Dieter Schneider, Patrick De Fontenay, and a reply by G. Warren Nutter (September 1964). Also, John W. Rowe, Paul Van

Moeseke, and G. Warren Nutter (June 1965). Paresh Challepadhyay and Robert Piron, Jr. (March 1966). Edward Saraydar (June 1967) and reply by Robert Piron, *ibid.*

27 Sven Danø, "Diminishing Returns and the Cost Functions: A Reconsideration," *Zeitschrift für Weltwirtschaftliches Archiv*, Band 97, Heft 1, 1966.

28 Om P. Tangri, "Omissions in the Treatment of the Law of Variable Proportions," [1], June 1966.

29 J. M. Cassels, "The Law of Variable Proportions," in *Explorations in Economics: Essays in Honor of Frank W. Taussig* (New York: McGraw-Hill, 1936).

30 A. M. Levenson and Babette Solon, "Returns to Scale and the Spacing of Isoquants," [1], June 1966, and comment by F. W. McElroy, [1], March 1967.

31 Harvey Leibenstein, "Allocative Efficiency vs. X-Efficiency," [1], June 1966, p. 397.

32 See the comments by P. J. McNulty and J. P. Shelton. The latter argues from data on managerial performance in restaurants, compared to that of franchised owners, that the latter are much superior in performance, suggesting thus an institutional aspect as conducive to higher productivity.—[1], December 1967.

33 L. S. Shapley and Martin Shubik, "Ownership and the Production Function," [7], February 1967, p. 33.

34 Louis De Alessi, "The Short Run Revisited," [1], June 1967.

35 G. H. Borts and E. J. Mishan, "Exploring the 'Uneconomic Region' of the Production Function," [8], October 1962.

36 H. P. Gray and P. B. Trescott, "Drawings on an Old Envelope: Short-Run and Long-Run Average Cost Curves," [1], December 1967.

37 Robert E. Lucas, "Adjustment Costs and the Theory of Supply," [5], August 1967.

38 James M. Buchanan, "Joint Supply, Externality and Optimality," [2], November 1966.

39 Richard R. Nelson, "The CES Production Function and Economic Growth Projections," [9], August 1965. See also his earlier article on "Aggregate Production Functions and Medium-Range Growth Projections," [1], September 1964.

40 R. Gordon, "A Reinterpretation of the Pure Theory of Exhaustion," [5], June 1967; and Ralph Turvey, "Optimization

and Suboptimization in Fishery Regulation," [1], March 1964.

41 H. J. Barnett and C. Morse, *Scarcity and Growth: The Economics of Natural Resource Availability* (Baltimore: Johns Hopkins Press, 1963).

42 John Kenneth Galbraith, *The New Industrial State* (Boston: Houghton Mifflin, 1967).

43 Robin Marris, *The Economic Theory of "Managerial" Capitalism* (New York: Free Press, 1964).

44 Andrew Shonfield, *Modern Capitalism* (New York: Oxford University Press, 1965).

45 Douglas Vickers, *The Theory of the Firm: Production, Capital, and Finance* (New York: McGraw-Hill, 1968); G. Hadley and T. M. Whitin, *Analysis of Inventory Systems* (Englewood Cliffs, N.J.: Prentice-Hall, 1963); Charles E. Ferguson, *A Macroeconomic Theory of Workable Competition* (Durham, N.C.: Duke University, 1964).

46 Richard M. Cyert and James G. March, and Others, *A Behavioral Theory of the Firm* (Englewood Cliffs, N.J.: Prentice-Hall, 1963); Oliver E. Williamson, *The Economics of Discretionary Behavior: Managerial Objectives in a Theory of the Firm* (Englewood Cliffs, N.J.: Prentice-Hall, 1964). A textbook in price theory under the same auspices is Kalman J. Cohen and Richard M. Cyert, *Theory of the Firm: Resource Allocation in a Market Economy* (Englewood Cliffs, N.J.: Prentice-Hall, 1965).

47 P. W. S. Andrews, *On Competition in Economic Theory* (New York: The Macmillan Company, 1964).

48 Robert J. Larner, "Ownership and Control in the 200 Largest Nonfinancial Corporations, 1929 and 1963," [1], September 1966.

49 Shorey Peterson, "Corporate Control and Capitalism," Adolf A. Berle, "The Impact of the Corporation on Classical Economic Theory," and Carl Kaysen, "Another View of Corporate Capitalism"—all in [7], February 1965.

50 Oliver E. Williamson, "Hierarchical Control and Optimum Firm Size," [5], April 1967, pp. 123, 125.

51 R. Joseph Monsen, Jr., and Anthony Downs, "A Theory of Large Managerial Firms," [5], June 1965.

52 Fritz Machlup, "Theories of the Firm: Marginalist, Behavioral, Managerial," [1], March 1967, p. 31.

53 Tun Thin, *Theory of Markets* (Cambridge, Mass.: Harvard University Press, 1960).

54 C. E. Ferguson, "Cournot Points and the Conflict Curves," [8], February 1962; John G. Cross, "A Theory of the Bargaining Process," [1], March 1965; Robert L. Bishop, "A Zeuthen–Hicks Theory of Bargaining," [4], July 1964; Edward Saraydar, "Zeuthen's Theory of Bargaining: A Note," [4], October 1965.

55 Articles on *The Theory of Monopolistic Competition After Thirty Years*, by Joe S. Bain, Robert L. Bishop, and William J. Baumol—all in [1], May 1964.

56 H. Demsetz, "The Welfare and Empirical Implications of Monopolistic Competition," [3], September 1964, with comment by G. C. Archibald, and reply by Demsetz, *ibid.* (June 1967). For some well-taken remarks on the "tangency" solution, see also Milton Friedman. "More on Archibald versus Chicago," [8], February 1963, esp. p. 67.

57 George J. Stigler, "A Theory of Oligopoly," [5], February 1964, p. 44. See also Robert McKinnon's suggestions of rules to detect price-cutting by rivals.—*Ibid.*, June 1966.

58 Joe S. Bain, *Barriers to New Competition* (Cambridge, Mass.: Harvard University Press, 1956); Paolo Sylos Labini, *Oligopoly and Technical Progress* (Cambridge, Mass.: Harvard University Press, 1962); R. F. Harrod, *Economic Essays* (New York: Harcourt, Brace, 1952), Essay 8.

59 Dale K. Osborne, "The Role of Entry in Oligopoly Theory," [6], August 1964. Also, the comment by Michael Mann, Paul Haas, and John Walgreen and reply, *ibid.*, August 1964.

60 John T. Wenders, "Entry and Monopoly Pricing," [5], October 1967.

61 Roger Sherman and Thomas D. Willett, "Potential Entrants Discourage Entry," [5], August 1967.

62 E. H. Chamberlin, "The Definition of Selling Costs," [8], January 1964.

63 William S. Comanor and Thomas A. Wilson, "Advertising, Market Structure and Performance," [9], November 1967, p. 437.

64 Lester G. Telser, "Advertising and Competition," [5], December 1964.

65 Julian L. Simon, "The Effect of the Competitive Structure Upon Expenditures for Advertising," [7], November 1967.

66 Oliver E. Williamson, "Selling Expense as a Barrier to Entry," [7], February 1963.

67 A. C. Johnson, Jr., and Peter Helmberger,

"Price Elasticity of Demand as an Element of Market Structure," [1], December 1967.

68 S. J. Gilani, "The Cost of Product Variation," [6], July 1964.

69 John Williamson, "Profit, Growth and Sales Maximization," [2], February 1966.

70 M. F. G. Scott, "Supply and Demand Refurbished," [6], July 1967, p. 162.

71 Walter C. Neale, "The Peculiar Economics of Professional Sports," [7], February 1964.

72 Eli Ginzberg, Dale L. Hiestand, and Beatrice G. Reubens, *The Pluralistic Economy* (New York: McGraw-Hill, 1965).

73 Robert H. Bork, "The Goals of Antitrust Policy," [1], May 1967, p. 253.

74 William S. Comanor, "Vertical Mergers, Market Powers, and Antitrust Laws," *ibid.*

75 James M. Buchanan, "Peak-Loads and Efficient Pricing: Comment," [7], August 1966. Also, a supplementary note by André Gabor, *ibid.* Other articles are by Oliver Williamson, favoring marginal cost-pricing, "Peak-Load Pricing and Optimal Capacity Under Indivisibility Constraints," [1], September 1966; a criticism of Federal Power Commission rate policy leaning to the marginal rule, by Lawrence C. Rosenberg, "Natural-Gas-Pipeline Rate-Regulation: Marginal-Cost Pricing and the Zone-Allocation Problem," [5], April 1967; also, Lawrence H. Officer, "The Optimality of Pure Competition in the Capacity Problem," with a comment by Buchanan, and a reply—all in [7], November 1966, 1967. For some reconsideration of the entire approach to public utility rate-making, see my article, "Utility Pricing and Incentive Rate-Making," *Public Utilities Fortnightly* (April 1968).

76 S. Andrew Ozga, *Expectations in Economic Theory* (Chicago: Aldine, 1965).

77 Kenneth J. Arrow, *Aspects of the Theory of Risk-Bearing* (Helsinki: Yrjo Jahnsson, 1964), pp. 12, 18.

78 J. Hirshleifer, "Investment Decisions Under Uncertainty: Choice-Theoretic Approaches," [7], November 1965. Also, on applications of his approach, *ibid.*, May 1966.

79 John W. Pratt, "Risk Aversion in the Small and in the Large," [4], January–April 1964.

80 William J. Baumol and Burton G. Malkiel, "The Firm's Optimal Debt-Equity

Combination and the Cost of Capital," [7], November 1967. A bibliography of much of the literature can be found here. For the original article of Franco Modigliani and Merton Miller, see "The Cost of Capital, Corporation Finance and the Theory of Investment," [1], June 1958, and "Some Estimates of the Cost of Capital to the Electric Utility Industry," *ibid.*, June 1966.

81 Michio Morishima, *Equilibrium, Stability, and Growth* (New York: Oxford University Press, 1964).

82 James Quirk and Rubin Saposnik, *Introduction to General Equilibrium Theory and Welfare Economics* (New York: McGraw-Hill, 1968), and Robert E. Kuenne, *Microeconomic Theory of the Market Mechanism: A General Equilibrium Approach* (New York: The Macmillan Company, 1968).

83 Ronald W. Jones, "The Structure of Simple General Equilibrium Models," [5], December 1965.

84 Martin J. Beckman and James P. Wallace, "Marshallian versus Walrasian Stability," [12], Fasc. 4, 1967; William Jaffé, "Walras' Theory of *Tâtonnement:* A Critique of Recent Interpretations," [5], February 1967.

85 R. G. D. Allen, *Macroeconomic Theory* (The Macmillan Company, 1967).

86 James Tobin, "Money and Economic Growth," [4], October 1965. See a forthcoming article by Paul Davidson, "Money, Portfolio Balance, Capital Accumulation and Economic Growth," to appear in the October 1968 issue of the same journal. Also, by Paul Davidson, an emphasis on the "finance-motive," and a reinterpretation of Keynes of the Treatise, in "The Demand and Supply of Securities and Economic Growth and Its Implications for the Kaldor–Pasinetti versus Samuelson–Modigliani Controversy," [1], May 1968, and "Keynes' Finance Motive," [6], November 1965, and "The Importance of the Demand for Finance," [6], July 1967.

87 Jerome L. Stein, "Money and Capacity Growth," [5], October 1966.

88 O. H. Brownlee and I. O. Scott, "Utility, Liquidity, and Debt-Management," [4], July 1963, p. 362.

89 Robert Eisner, "Another Look at Liquidity Preference," [4], July 1963, with rejoinder by M. Bronfenbrenner and Thomas Mayer, and Allen H. Meltzer, *ibid.*

90 Phillip Cagan, *Determinants and Effects of Changes in the Stock of Money, 1875–1960* (New York: National Bureau of Economic Research, 1965). See also the review article by Meltzer, [5], April 1967.

91 Ronald L. Teigen, "Demand and Supply Functions for Money in the United States: Some Structural Estimates," [4], October 1964.

92 George Horwich, *Money, Capital, and Prices* (Homewood, Ill.: Richard D. Irwin, 1964); and Boris P. Pesek and Thomas R. Saving, *Money, Wealth, and Economic Theory* (New York: The Macmillan Company, 1967).

93 Allan H. Meltzer, "The Demand for Money: A Cross-Section Study of Business Firms," [7], August 1963.

94 Merton H. Miller and Daniel Orr, "A Model of the Demand for Money by Firms," [7], August 1966.

95 Allan H. Meltzer, "The Demand for Money: The Evidence from the Time Series," [5], June 1963. Meltzer also declares that "interest rates have played the predominant role in determining the level of velocity" (p. 244).

96 Maurice Allais, "A Restatement of the Quantity Theory of Money," [1], December 1966.

97 David Laidler, "Some Evidence on the Demand for Money," [5], February 1966, and "The Rate of Interest and the Demand for Money—Some Empirical Evidence," *ibid.*, December 1966.

98 Gregory C. Chow, "On the Long-Run and Short-Run Demand for Money," [5], April 1966.

99 Michael J. Hamburger, "The Demand for Money by Households, Money Substitutes, and Monetary Policy," [5], December 1966, p. 621.

100 Edward L. Whalen, "A Rationalization of the Precautionary Demand for Cash," [7], May 1966. A more extensive treatment of uncertainty aspects is provided in R. C. O. Matthews. "Expenditure Plans and the Uncertainty Motive for Holding Money," [5], June 1963.

101 Franco Modigliani, "Some Empirical Tests of Monetary Management and of Rules Versus Discretion," [5], June 1964.

102 Milton Friedman, "The Role of Monetary Policy," [1], March 1968, pp. 16–17. Some other recent articles in which Professor Friedman advocated a monetary approach to economic stabilization, in lieu of some Keynesian-type alternatives, include his reply, with David Meiselman,

to Donald Hester, "Keynes and the Quantity Theory: A Comment on the Friedman–Meiselman CMC Paper," [9], November 1964, and a similar pairing against Albert Ando and Franco Modigliani, "Velocity and the Investment Multiplier," as well as Michael De Prano and Thomas Mayer, "Autonomous Expenditures and Money," [1], September 1965.

103 David Meiselman, *The Term Structure of Interest Rates* (Englewood Cliffs, N.J.: Prentice-Hall, 1962), p. 60.

104 The following articles may be cited for the interested reader: J. A. G. Grant, "Meiselman on the Structure Interest Rates: A British Test," [2], February 1964; Robert Haney Scott, "Liquidity and the Term Structure of Interest Rates," [7], February 1965; James Van Horne, "Interest-Rate Risk and the Term Structure of Interest Rates," [5], August 1965; and the exchange between Richard Roll and Van Horne, *ibid.*, December 1966. Also, A. Buse, "Interest Rates, the Meiselman Model, and Random Numbers," [5], February 1967, and his "The Structure of Interest Rates and Recent British Experience: A Comment," [2], August 1967, involving a reply to Douglas Fisher on "Expectations, the Term Structure of Interest Rates, and Recent British Experience," [2], August 1966. Also, John H. Wood, "The Expectations Hypothesis, the Yield Curve, and Monetary Policy," [7], August 1964, and Van Horne and Wood, *ibid.*, November 1965. For a segmented market theory, see Franco Modigliani and Richard Sutch, "Debt-Management and the Term Structure of Interest Rates: An Empirical Analysis of Recent Experience," [5], August 1964 (Supplement), with comments by N. Wallace and Reuben A. Kessel.

105 L. G. Telser, "A Critique of Some Recent Empirical Research on the Explanation of the Term Structure of Interest Rates," [5], August 1964 (Supplement), with informative comments by Burton G. Malkiel and David I. Rand.

106 A. P. Lerner, "Employment Theory and Employment Policy," [1], May 1967.

107 E.g., Ronald G. Bodkin, *The Wage-Price-Productivity Nexus* (Philadelphia: University of Pennsylvania Press, 1966); George L. Perry, *Unemployment, Money-Wage Rates, and Inflation* (Cambridge, Mass.: M.I.T. Press, 1966); John Sheahan,

The Wage-Price Guideposts (Washington, D.C.: Brookings Institution, 1967). See also my article on "Guideposts," in A. Phillips and O. E. Williamson (eds.), *Prices: Issues in Theory, Practice, and Public Policy* (Philadelphia: University of Pennsylvania Press, 1968).

108 Martin Bronfenbrenner and F. D. Holtzman, "Survey of Inflation Theory," [1], September 1963.

109 R. J. Ball, *Inflation and the Theory of Money* (Chicago: Aldine, 1964).

110 Karsten Laursen and Jørgen Pedersen, *The German Inflation, 1918–1923* (Amsterdam: North-Holland, 1964).

111 Edmund S. Phelps, "Anticipated Inflation and Economic Welfare," [5], February 1965.

112 For the original discussion, see A. W. Phillips, "The Relation Between Unemployment and the Rate of Changes of Money Wage Rates in the United Kingdom," [2], November 1958.

113 A. G. Hines, "Trade Unions and Wage Inflation in the United Kingdom," [8], October 1964.

114 G. L. Perry, "The Determinants of Wage Rate Changes and the Inflation-Unemployment Trade-Off for the United States," *ibid.*

115 Robert V. Eagley, "Market Power as an Intervening Mechanism in Phillips Curve Analysis," [2], February 1965.

116 Albert Rees and Mary T. Hamilton, "The Wage-Price-Productivity Perplex," [5], February 1967, a review article of the Bodkin book.

117 Edmund S. Phelps, "Phillips Curves, Expectations of Inflation, and Optimal Unemployment Over Time," [2], August 1967, p. 255.

118 E. Kuh, "A Productivity Theory of Wage Levels—An Alternative to the Phillips Curve," [8], October 1967.

119 Lawrence Klein, "Wage and Price Determination in Macroeconomics," in Phillips and Williamson (eds.), *Prices: Issues in Theory, Practice, and Public Policy, loc. cit.*

120 F. H. Hahn and R. C. O. Matthews, "The Theory of Economic Growth: A Survey," [3], December 1964.

121 Edmund S. Phelps, *Golden Rules of Economic Growth* (New York: W. W. Norton, 1966).

122 James Tobin, "Economic Growth as an Objective of Government," [1], May 1964.

123 J. R. Hicks, "Growth and Anti-Growth,"

[6], November 1966. Also, his *Capital and Growth* (New York: Oxford University Press, 1965).

124 Tjalling C. Koopmans, "Objectives, Constraints and Outcomes in Optimal Growth Models," [4], January 1967. Other technical articles are: C. von Weizsacker, "Existence of Optimal Programs of Accumulation for an Infinite Time Horizon," [8], April 1965; Mordecai Kurz, "Optimal Paths of Capital-Accumulation Under the Minimum Time Objective," [4], January 1965; William Fellner, "Measures of Technological Progress in the Light of Recent Growth Theories," [1], December 1967; Murray C. Kemp and Pham Chi Thanh, "On a Class of Growth Models," [4], April 1966; and R. M. Solow, P. Tobin, C. von Weizsacker, and M. Yaari, "Neoclassical Growth with Fixed Factor Proportions," [8], April 1964.

125 For some account of these writings, see my *Employment Growth and Income Distribution* (Philadelphia: Chilton, 1966), chap. vii.

126 P. A. Samuelson and F. Modigliani, "The Pasinetti Paradox in Neoclassical and More General Models," [8], October 1966. Also, Luigi L. Pasinetti, "New Results in an Old Framework," *ibid.;* Joan Robinson, "Comment on Samuelson and Modigliani," *ibid.;* and Nicholas Kaldor, "Marginal Productivity and the Macroeconomic Theories of Distribution," *ibid.*

127 K. W. Rothschild, "Theme and Variations: Remarks on the Kaldorian Distribution Formula," [12], Fasc. 4, 1965.

128 C. E. Ferguson, "Neoclassical Theory of Technical Progress and Relative Factor Shares," [10], April 1968.

129 Marjorie S. Turner, "A Comparison of Some Aspects of the Cambridge Theory of Wages and Marginal Productivity Theory," *Journal of Economic Issues* (September 1967). Lowell E. Gallaway, "The Theory of Relative Shares," [7], November 1964. Also, comment by F. W. Bell, and reply by Gallaway, *ibid.*, November 1965.

130 Davidson, "The Demand and Supply of Securities and Economic Growth and Its Implications . . .," *loc. cit.*

131 The immediate literature, with some earlier references, appears in the symposium on *Paradoxes in Capital Theory*, [7], November 1966, with articles by Luigi L. Pasinetti, "Changes in the Rate of Profit and Switches of Techniques"; by David Levhari and P. A. Samuelson, "The Nonswitching Theorem is False"; by M. Morishima, "Refutation of the Nonswitching Theorem"; by Michael Bruno, Edwin Burmeister, and Eytan Sheshinski, "Nature and Implications of the Reswitching of Techniques"; by P. Garegnani, "Switching of Techniques"; and by P. A. Samuelson, "A Summing Up."

132 Charles Kennedy, "Induced Bias in Innovation and the Theory of Distribution," [3], September 1964. Also, see W. E. G. Salter, *Productivity and Technical Change* (New York: Cambridge University Press, 1960); and P. A. Samuelson, "A Theory of Induced Innovation along Kennedy–Weizsacker Lines," [9], November 1965, for the production-function point of view. Also, the discussion between Kennedy and Samuelson, *ibid.*, November 1966. Further, Syed Ahmad, "On the Theory of Induced Invention," [3], June 1966, with reply and rejoinder by Kennedy and Ahmad, *ibid.*, December 1967. Ahmad had argued in terms of shifting production functions, and Kennedy replied that this procedure really made substitution and innovation indistinguishable.

133 E. J. Mishan, *Welfare Economics* (New York: Random House, 1964).

134 E. J. Mishan, "Pareto Optimality and the Law," [6], November 1967.

135 A. R. Prest and Ralph Turvey, "Cost-Benefit Analysis," [3], December 1965. See also applications to supersonic transport, work-experience programs, and subsidized housing, by Stephen Enke, Worth Battman, and William Ross, [1], May 1967.

136 O. A. Davis and A. B. Whinston, "Welfare Economics and the Theory of Second Best," [8], January 1965, and responses by P. Bohm, T. Negishi, M. McManus, and Davis and Whinston, *ibid.*, July 1967.

137 See H. Leibenstein, "Notes on Welfare Economics and the Theory of Democracy," [3], June 1967, and responses by P. Pattanaik, R. Saposnik, and Leibenstein, *ibid.*, June 1963 and December 1967.

138 J. M. Buchanan and M. Z. Kafoglis, "A Note on Public Goods Supply," [1], June 1963.

139 J. M. Buchanan, "An Economic Theory of Clubs," [2], February 1965. See also M. V. Pauly, "Clubs, Commonality, and the Core: An Integration of Game

Theory and the Theory of Public Goods," *ibid.*, August 1967.

140 O. E. Williamson, Douglas G. Olson, and August Ralston, "Externalities, Insurance, and Disability Analysis," [2], August 1967.

141 S. Wellisz, "On External Diseconomies and the Government-Associated Invisible Hand," [2], November 1964.

142 Lucius Foldes, "Income-Redistribution in Money and in Kind," [2], February and May 1967. Also, the interchange of Buchanan, Mishan, Kurt Klappolz, and Foldes, *ibid.*, May 1968. On the negative income tax to aid the poor, Buchanan commented on the lack of social concern "for the prudent poor whose lives are well-ordered and stable" (p. 189). The replies focused on implications of this view.

143 James S. Coleman, "The Possibility of a Social Welfare Function," [1], December 1966, with comments and reply by R. F. Park, D. C. Mueller, and Coleman, *ibid.*, December 1967. See also K. Inada, "On the Economic Welfare Function," [4], July 1964.

144 Gordon Tullock, "The General Irrelevance of the General Impossibility Theorem," [7], May 1967.

145 Alfred E. Kahn, "The Tyranny of Small Decisions: Market Failures, Imperfections, and the Limits of Economics," [12], Fasc. 1, 1966.

Summaries

Fritz Machlup, "Micro- and Macro-Economics: Contested Boundaries and Claims of Superiority," in *Essays on Economic Semantics* (Englewood Cliffs, N.J.: Prentice-Hall, Inc., 1963), pp. 97–144.

The terms micro-theory and macroeconomics are widely used by economists, and their meanings are generally understood by them. However, their respective boundaries are not always clearly defined, nor has the superiority of one over the other been established. Machlup addresses himself to the tasks of defining the boundaries of micro- and macro-economics and undertaking an in-depth analysis of the problem of determining whether microeconomics provides us with a theory superior to the macroeconomics theory.

In an effort to carve out contested boundaries, he delves into the past (from Quesnay's *Tableau Economique* of 1758 to Keynes' *General Theory* of 1936) and skillfully brings out the hidden relationships between micro- and macro-theory.

Machlup asserts that, ever since the emergence of economics as a recognized body of knowledge, macro- and micro-theory have existed harmoniously side by side and that this relationship will in all likelihood continue in the future. Since each is needed by the economist, neither theory can be superior to the other. Machlup, however, does imply that macro-theory is inferior to micro-theory in all respects but one. He states that it "seems simpler, and the intellectually under-equipped student is more likely to pass examinations successfully if he has only macro-theory questions to answer."

Joan Robinson, "What Are the Rules of the Game?" in *Economic Philosophy* (Chicago: Aldine Publishing Co., 1962), pp. 124–147.

Joan Robinson, a leading British socialist economist, exposes the reader to the dogmatic content of economic orthodoxy. "In the midst of all the confusion," says Mrs.

Robinson, "there is one solid unchanging lump of ideology that we take so much for granted that it is rarely noticed—that is, nationalism."

Mrs. Robinson begins by claiming that such a celebrated economic doctrine as free trade is right for those nations that practice this doctrine, but not necessarily right for the rest of the world. She discusses the concepts of full employment, utility, imperfect competition, and efficient distribution of gains, and concludes that in each case individualism and nationalism play dominant roles and that a genuinely universalistic point of view is almost nonexistent. Summing up her views, the author says, "The first essential for economists, arguing amongst themselves, is to 'try very seriously . . . to avoid talking at cross purposes' and, addressing the world, reading their own doctrines aright, to combat, not foster, the ideology which pretends that values which can be measured in terms of money are the only ones that ought to count."

Bibliography

L. A. Boland, "Economic Understanding and Understanding Economics," *South African Journal of Economics*, 37 (June 1969), pp. 144–160.

A. W. Coats, "Is There a 'Structure of Scientific Revolutions' in Economics?" *Kyklos*, 22 (1969), pp. 289–294.

M. J. Fores, "No More General Theories," *Economic Journal*, 79 (March 1969), pp. 11–22.

W. Leontief, "The New Outlook in Economics," *Indian Economic Journal*, 14 (September 1968), pp. 71–77.

Fritz Machlup, "Statics and Dynamics: Kaleidoscopic Words," in *Essays on Economic Semantics* (Englewood Cliffs, N.J.: Prentice-Hall, Inc., 1963), pp. 13–22, 33–37.

Henry Margenau, "What Is a Theory?" in Sherman Roy Krupp (ed.), *The Structure of Economic Science* (Englewood Cliffs, N.J.: Prentice-Hall, Inc., 1968), pp. 25–38.

2
MODELS

The art of model building is not new to theoretical economists. For instance, Quesnay's *Tableau Economique* (1758) is one of the most remarkable macro models ever developed. What is new in the field of model building is the frequency with which large-scale mathematical and econometric macro models are being constructed.

In the first selection, Harrod examines the true nature of a macro model. In the next article, White discusses the usefulness of econometric models and some of the problems encountered in constructing them. In the concluding selection, Tinbergen demonstrates how models can be used to assist policy makers in formulating national policies.

What Is a Model?
Roy Harrod

In recent years the word "model" has come to besprinkle the page of learned articles and books on economics, and, even more so, the examination papers of candidates for degrees in that subject. I have the impression that, for the word "model," some specific meaning can be formulated, although this meaning is subtle and elusive, and has, to my knowledge, been so far nowhere defined. If the word "model," which has its aroma of implications, is applied to formulations which are not in fact "models" in any meaningful sense that may be found for that word, then the implications can lead to false conclusions in relation to those formulations.

In my own case this problem happens

Reprinted from J. N. Wolfe, ed.: *Value, Capital, and Growth* (Edinburgh: Edinburgh University Press, 1968); copyright © Edinburgh University Press, 1968.

to come right home. Many years after I had made certain formulations in the field of growth theory and after Professor Domar had made similar formulations, there began to be references to the "Harrod–Domar model." I found myself in the position of Le Bourgeois Gentilhomme who had been speaking prose all his life without knowing it. I had been fabricating "models" without knowing it. It may be, and I suspect it to be the case, that the word "model" can, in a meaningful sense, be applied to some of the Harrod–Domar formulations; I also think that to some of those formulations the word "model" cannot be applied appropriately. I shall return to this theme later in this article.

To make sense of *some* references in the literature to "model," one has to take the view that it is a substitute for the words "general proposition." The number of letters in "model" is five, whereas that in "general proposition" is eighteen; thus, if we could take "model" to be synonymous with ($\equiv$) "general proposition," that would be economical. But, if there is indeed some subtle and elusive meaning in "model," as implied by its more sophisticated users, there would be a loss of discrimination, if it came to be accepted that it meant precisely the same as "general proposition."

It may serve to focus thought to ask, at the outset, certain questions.

1. Does a "model" contain one or more propositions that have the character of being "true or false"? Modern logic undergoes kaleidoscopic changes, and it is a hard task for a layman to keep pace with these. The "truth table" continues, surely, to be of fundamental importance in logic, and applies, as I understand it, to any group of symbols that contain a connective, whatever that may mean. If there is a connective in the group of symbols, then the "T or F" attribute applies.

It may be that a "model" can be constituted by a group of symbols with no connective. Thus one might write "rate of growth of the G.D.P.," "capital/output ratio," "savings ratio." These symbols might be juxtaposed without any connective.

I have noticed that the word "useful" is often applied to "models," in a pragmatic spirit. Thus it might be deemed "useful" to write the symbols, say G, C, and s for the magnitudes mentioned in the last paragraph. There need be no "connective." The idea would be that the contemplation of these symbols in juxtaposition might lead on to some worthwhile intellectual process. Perhaps my own "growth model" might be interpreted in that sense. It grouped together in a small space certain symbols which it would be worthwhile for a thinking agent to dwell on simultaneously. The "model" would not be "useful" if the simultaneous contemplation of the symbols bore no intellectual

fruit. This minimal interpretation of what is meant by a "model" is attractive; but I doubt if it is what is actually meant by a "model" as commonly used in economics; it is less than what is meant in other disciplines; it is also much less than what I meant and, I believe, than what Professor Domar meant, in our formulations.

2. What is the relation of a model to a hypothesis or to a theory? To get down to brass tacks, but still in the realm of preliminary skirmishing, I would suggest that in this kind of context a "model" is a formulation that has adjustable parameters.

A digression is necessary here. There is a cloud of ambiguity, I fear, around the word "parameter." My own idea is that it can be exemplified as follows:

$$\dot{W} = A + B(x_2)^b + C(x_3)^c + D(x_4)^d + \cdots + N(x_n)^n$$

where $\dot{W}$ is the rate of increase of wages, $A, B, C, \ldots, N$ and $b, c, \ldots, n$ are constants, x_2 is the rate of increase in the cost of living, x_3 is the rate of increase in trade union membership, x_4 is the level of unemployment, etc. In my view $A, B, C, D, \ldots, N$ and $a, b, c, d, \ldots, n$ are the adjustable parameters. When one has set up this equation, econometric studies may suggest specific values for $A, B, C, D, \ldots, N$ and for $b, c, d, \ldots, n$. Once this is done, these parameters cease to be "adjustable."

One might take the line that, when these parameters cease to be "adjustable," owing to econometric studies, the formulation in question has become a hypothesis. This, of course, does not mean that the hypothesis is known to be true. I may insert here that very often in studies that I have read the number of observables in ratio to the number of "adjustable parameters" has been too small to give more than a very low probability to the specific hypotheses claimed to be established by the observations.

How does one classify the terms? Is a statement in which the parameters remain adjustable to rank as a "model" while one with specific numbers inserted is a hypothesis? Or can one enlarge the scope of the sense of a hypothesis, to include, as a weaker form of it, a model in which the parameters are still "adjustable"? In that case some hypotheses would also be models. And can we also go the other way and include in our category of "models" hypotheses in which the parameters have already been fixed (provisionally) by econometric studies?

I would ask a further question here. If the expression "adjustable parameter" is meaningful, what is an "unadjustable parameter"? I would suggest that the meaning of the latter expression relates to a state of intellectual enquiry, whether due to econometric studies or laboratory experiments, in which the "adjustable parameters" have been given specific values in the hope that these are true, at least in the area of observation to which the specific formulae are supposed to apply.

But among learned discussants I have found the view that "the parameters of a system" are constituted by the determining variables. This view seems to make complete nonsense of the idea of a "parameter." There is no doubt that the coefficients and indices are "adjustable" parameters. How can variables possibly be identified with parameters? Surely a variable can neither be "adjustable" nor "unadjustable."

On the word "parameter" it seemed expedient to have resort to the *Oxford English Dictionary*. The definition is:

A quantity which is constant (*as distinct from the ordinary variables*) in a particular case, but which varies in different cases; esp. a constant occurring in the equation of a curve or surface, by the variation of which the equation is made to represent a *family* of such curves or surfaces. (Italics mine.)

This definition seems to be, possibly, applicable to the case of wage determination cited above. The model would hypothetically specify the determining variables for all countries, leaving the parameters (indices and coefficients) to be adjusted from country to country. The model would embody the hope that in a particular country, at least for a certain phase of history, including the near future, the adjustable parameters could be replaced, in consequence of econometric study, by specific numbers. But the influence of any variable such as Trade Union membership, might differ from country to country and its parameters would need adjustment accordingly. Thus the bare model, with its parameters still adjustable would be applicable to all countries, at least for a certain period of history. If a variable that seemed to be one of the determinants in one or more countries, such as the potency of the effective head of state, was deemed to have no influence at all in other countries, for those the coefficient could simply be written as zero. This account seems to make sense; but it is not certain that it expresses what is now meant in all cases, when the word "parameter" is used.

I would suggest that "parameter," like "model," has become something of a show-off word, and that serious economists should be careful in regard to both these words.

It is now expedient to dig deeper, by reference to traditional usage, and to present usages outside economics.

In Bourton-on-the-Water there is a model of that village of considerable size. As the model is inside the village it can, by the Dedekind paradox, never be made complete, however fine the materials available for its construction. The model contains, surely enough, a rough model of itself; but there the matter stops. For completeness there would have to be a model of the model of the model, and so ad infinitum. This model of the village can be said also to be a "copy" of it, in the sense that the model and the village are, as near as may be, structurally identical.

While each is in that sense a copy of the other, it is more natural to apply the word "copy" to the model, rather than the other way round. The village itself may be regarded as a "reality" in its own right. In many of the varied uses of the word model, these two features seem to re-appear, namely (i) that there are two related objects similar to each other and (ii) that one of the two objects is an independent "reality," while the other has been fabricated as a copy of it. It may also be a feature common to most users that the model is an approximate, or rough, copy only.

In the case of Bourton-on-the-Water the "original," to use another word, ante-dates the model. But in some cases it is the other way round. One may make a model of a projected university building or factory. If it is intended to be helpful, and not something devised for public relations only, one may call it a "working model." Again the two features appear, namely, that the model and what it is supposed to be a model of have similar structures, and that the factory is destined to have a "reality" in some sense that is lacking to the model. We cannot in this case, how-ever, say that the factory is the "original."

It may be convenient to make a digres-sion from the main theme here, and refer to a rather different, but still allied, use. One may think of the working model of a factory as something that *ought* to be copied and rendered into a reality. Per-haps the failure to make a correct copy in certain respects might be detrimental to the quality of the factory itself. One some-times talks of a model husband, or a model farm. Here, what is a model is, so to say, a living reality. But, as with the model of the factory, it is something that *ought* to be copied. As with the model factory, certain objectives will be achieved, only if every husband has a structural similarity in his behaviour to the model husband.

Carrying the analogy still further,

Gladstone, in his culminating Free Trade Budget (1860), expressed the hope, quot-ing Milton, that it

Might serve as a model for the mighty world
And be the fair beginning of a time.

The word "model" has long been used for a person who poses for students in an art school. Here there seems to be an inversion of the relation noted above, which will reappear later; one would say that the live person was the "reality," while the likenesses painted upon the canvases of the students were copies of the reality. It is not clear, however, whether there is really an inversion here. One might take the painting to be the substantive reality, while the live person is a mere instrument, like the working model of a factory, for the achievement of the grand design, which is the picture itself.

This comes out more clearly when, as in the old days of representative painting, the painter has some large composition, like the Rape of the Sabine Women, and employs models for the various figures. The models are clearly tools to aid him in his achievement.

The matter becomes more subtle in the case of portraiture. Here at least it would seem that the sitter himself, say a King or Prime Minister, is the substantial reality, and the painting a subordinate object, a mere likeness of the great man. But this fact is perhaps itself expressed by a subtle variation of usage. When the Prime Minister himself comes to the studio to give a sitting, he is not said to be a "model," but "the sitter." Only when some other person comes and puts on the garter robe for the benfit of the painter—the great man having no time for such details—do we use the word model. In relation to the hireling, it is the picture that is the substantial reality and the hire-ling the model; but in the case of the great man, it is he who is the substantial reality in relation to the picture, although we do not call it a model, but a likeness.

The foregoing sense of model has presumably led on to the use of the word that is now far the commonest in popular speech, namely for a lady who is used to display clothes in a shop. She is like the person who puts on the garter robe for the painter's convenience. There does not seem to be much of the copy idea left in this case. It may be that the model is conceived as such because her figure has a similar structure to that of the grand lady destined to buy the dress. And in this case too the model is the subordinate partner in the copy relation.

I believe that Bohr's model of the atom may have played a crucial part in introducing that word into physics. The idea was, as I understand it, that if one could magnify an atom a billionfold, or by whatever was requisite, one would have a visual object of structural similarity to a model of the solar system correspondingly reduced. It would not be necessary actually to construct such a model, but a visual image might be helpful in advancing thought. The structure of this image would be specified in certain functional equations relating to the mass, etc., of the protons and electrons.

As physics advanced, it became doubtful whether an atom, however much magnified, would really look like a solar system to the naked eye. But the structure of Bohr's equations, as suitably modified in consequence of further experiments, lived on. It was this structure that became the "model" in our modern more recondite sense.

The old features remained. The structural features displayed in the functional equations were taken to resemble, or anyhow to have a 1 to 1 relation to, the structure of the atom itself. Again, the atom is the "reality," while the functional equations constitute a tool, enabling one, hopefully, to apprehend the reality.

At this point it may be interesting to note a certain contrariety in usage, as between mathematics and physics. As I understand the matter, a model has the following sense in mathematics.[1] One may write down a number of symbolic expressions, along with rules of interpretation and deduction. These may be said to be in the realm of the highest conceivable abstraction. Then one may come down to earth and contemplate something that is still, of course, abstract, as it must be in mathematics, but is concrete relatively to the formulae previously set out. One might take the row of natural numbers. If concrete is the wrong word, one might at least call this row a "hard fact." If the row of natural numbers exemplifies the relations that are set out in the abstract formulations, so that they can be said to be true of it, then the row of natural numbers is a model.

This does seem to be an inversion of usage. In physics the group of functional equations is the model, and it is hoped that real atoms will, by their behaviour as evidenced at second or nth hand in experimental data, exemplify the relations set out in the model. In mathematics the position seems to be inverted. It is that which exemplifies in hard fact the relations set out in a series of formulae that is the model. The relation of the similarity of the model to what it is a model of remains, but in mathematics it seems to be the model that is the substantial reality.

In biological science the meaning appears to shift again. It seems that the word model is applied to a system of functional equations specifying a behaviour pattern, only when this system is taken over from another science, such as physics. A behaviour pattern in physics as expressed in functional equations may give a key for the formulation of laws about bacteriological behaviour. It is this key, taken over from physics, that is the model, while the formulations relating specifically to bacteriological behaviour and expressed in appropriate terms are hypotheses. Thus the equations in physics serve as a model for a similar system of equations that one hopes will prove a correct specification for bacteriological processes.

It is expedient to consider physics a little more closely. It may be that there also a model is distinguished from a set of hypotheses in that there are still adjustable parameters. It is also suggested that a model may not give a full and final account of the reality with which it is concerned, but only pick out certain important features. In this respect the usage of physics may not be far from that of economics.

It may be valuable, for the progress of thinking and investigation, to concentrate on what are hypothetically taken to be the more important determining variables, leaving fringe influences on one side. If one gets approximate verifications for these admittedly incomplete formulations, that may be significant. Modifications in the equations required for fringe influences may be brought in later. It still remains a little difficult to distinguish between a model and a group of hypotheses. Surely an incomplete formulation, viz. omitting fringe influences, would be called an hypothesis. Could one cut through this tangle of terminological inexactitudes (*not* in the Churchillian sense!) by saying that a model is nothing more than a group of hypotheses? That would surely be too simple a solution. It would not accord with the sense in which "model" is often used in economics. I do not think that this word, as generally employed in economics, *essentially* implies a group of equations, as contradistinguished from a single equation.

There remains one important question to be considered in relation to physics, which makes physics unlike economics. Physics is concerned with entities of which we have (and can have) no direct observation and the question must be asked whether the use of the word model in physics has not some relation to this fact. If this were so, then it would be wrong to think that the use of the word "model" in economics is analogous to, or authorized by, its use in physics.

We may make a working model of a factory not yet built; we cannot at the outset compare the model with the factory, to see how closely they resemble one another, because the factory does not yet exist. In physics one can *never* compare the model with the reality because one has no direct access to the reality.

Physicists may posit that there is a kind of entity to be named an electron. Certain structural properties are then specified in a series of equations. It is not correct to say that the "electron" is *defined* by these equations.

Positing an entity, to which the name "electron" is given, has, in physics, unlike mathematics, the implication that the existence of this entity will somehow show up in and influence the nature of our experience. We just posit that there is a kind of entity to which certain functional equations apply. By a chain of deductions from the equations we build up more complex structures. By carrying on with the deductions to a sufficient extent, we get a structure which ought to have similarity with an empirical structure, as observed in instrument readings or lines on a photographic plate. Having got certain readings, we can argue by a backward deductive process, to show that our readings are consistent with the fundamental structural equations specifying the nature of the posited entity, viz. the "electron." Some sort of linkage between the structural equations specified as describing properties of the posited entity and actual observations is an essential part of the definition of that entity. This constitutes the difference between *positing* that there exists an entity to which the functional equations apply and *defining* an entity as being just anything to which the functional relations might apply. Furthermore, if the observations would be consistent, by the deductive chain, not with the functional equations, as originally formulated, but with a modified version of those equations, we are ready to modify them in an appropriate manner. This shows that the original equations should not be taken as a definition, in the proper sense of that word.

It may be objected that I have used the word "posit" without attempting to define it. I quail before such an attempt, since it would take me into uncharted logical seas. I believe that a perceptive reader will gain an insight into its proposed meaning from the context, even if the ultimate definition is still absent. "Positing," as used here, is first cousin to "postulating," or, alternatively, perhaps is a species of "postulating." A postulate usually contains two groups of symbols on either side of a connective, both of which are already defined. We "posit" when we say that "an entity (or type of entity) exists which is . . . ." On the right hand of "is" stands a group of symbols, representing properties, which may have to be further specified in a whole series of equations. Some philosophers object to the word "exist" altogether; in this paper I can explore the matter no further.

I cannot resist the impression that the use of the word "model" in physics is somehow connected with the fact that it is dealing with a real world of posited entities, none of which can ever be directly observed. And indeed these posited entities may eventually be discarded, like the ether. One cannot exactly say that the ether does not exist because, from the beginning, it was only a posited entity, like the electron or the neutrino. What one can say is that a model which posits ether and then sets up a number of equations specifying its properties is not "useful." The legitimacy of using the word "useful" rather than "true" in relation to a series of equations is intimately connected with the fact that the entities to which the equations relate are merely posited entities.

Mr. Richard Wayne, the physicist, who has been good enough to comment on this paper, has written the following, which provokes thought:

I wonder whether you are right in stating that the concept of "ether" did not prove "useful." Clerk-Maxwell would not have been able to derive his laws of electro-magnetic radiation at that time without the prop of the ether. Nor would Faraday have been able to make the correlations between his various observations on electric and magnetic phenomena without his concept of "lines of force." Faraday's ideas led in turn to Clerk-Maxwell's formulations, and these are, perhaps, the only important remnant of classical physics to be taken over intact into modern physics. Although the ether was discarded, the equations derived from assuming its existence remain; so I think that the concept was no less "useful" than the Bohr model of the atom, which served a similar purpose.

Here we have a double idea in regard to posited entities, namely (a) that they may be genuinely "useful," but only for a time, and (b) that they may also be regarded as having the status of being "useful" for all time since, during their period of their—what shall we say?—"active" usefulness, certain advances in thought, valid for all time, were made, that could not have been made at the time in question without their assistance. Whether they could have been made by some more devious route is a matter of historical judgment. One may tremble to wonder whether the Harrod–Domar model, if it has to be downgraded into the category of "useful" only, will finally be judged to have the better status described under (b)—or, of course, perhaps no status at all.

There still remains the difference between systems that posit certain entities and those that do not. Euclidean geometry may be a case in point. I do not believe that it "posits" any entities that are *in principle* unobservable. Physicists in the past postulated that the system of relations set out in Euclidean geometry is exemplified in the physical world of what we call space. It is true that in fact a straight line may nowhere exist in the physical world, but it is not, like the electron, a "posited" entity; its properties may be specified without residue by deduction from its definition; not so the properties of an electron. Euclidean geometry has obviously been highly "useful" ((b) category of usefulness), and will long continue to be so as an approximative specification of the spatial relations of our world. But we can also affirm that its system of propositions, as deduced from its postulates, has eternal Platonic "truth," even if they do not apply to our observable world. They could apply to some other world that conformed to the postulates. This can hardly be said of a system containing "posited" entities, whose properties are not specified by deduction only *without residue.*

Thus it does seem that the boundary line between systems, the maximum claim of which is that they are "useful," and those that can also claim "truth," is that which divides systems that comprise posited entities from those that do not.

In economics we are not, I believe, concerned with any entities that are merely posited; all the entities with which economics deals are, in principle at least, directly observable.

My own dynamic equations take a number of forms. The basic one, $G = s/C$, is self-evident. G is the increment of income in a period divided by income, s the fraction of income saved, and C the capital accumulation during the period divided by the increment of income. I have been content to describe this as a "tautology." This need not be regarded as a belittling description. Possible tautologies are infinite in number, and merit may be assigned to the selection of one likely to be fruitful in stimulating thought. Perhaps the electronic computers that we have inside our skulls winnow through millions of tautologies before selecting one for presentation to the conscious mind, just as, so it is said, they go through all permutations of letters when one is trying

to remember a name; we give the computer an especially hard task when we wrongly believe that we remember the first letter of the name.

It may be that, when one selects a tautology out of the myriads, one can be held to be presenting a "model." But this seems to give that word an inappropriate coverage. In a tautology there can be no adjustable parameters. Nor can there be any question of what is stated being a rough approximation, or one which, while it claims to present the most important determining variables, leaves others out of the formulation as being of minor influence.

I am not, however, happy with the word "tautology." It came into favour in my youth in consequence of that movement in logic which discarded the possibility of *a priori* synthetic judgements and divided all statements into tautologies (or deductions therefrom in accordance with arbitrary rules) and those susceptible to empirical test. This movement was due as much to the downfall of Euclidean geometry as to the cogitations of the symbolic logicians. I have been content to use this word during a lifetime of teaching, for example in relation to monetary equations. In the early days it was a smart thing to do; later one became lazy-minded.

I doubt if anyone has a clear idea as to what a tautology is. The conceptual foundations of symbolic logic, as expressed in meta-language, remain very insecure. Progress towards greater refinement and perfection in the techniques of this logic have not, I believe, been accompanied by any improvement in its philosophical position.

I can illustrate one of my difficulties from the Fisherine and Cambridge monetary equations, both, in common parlance, said to be tautological. (Would they have been called "models," if enunciated at a later date?) The Cambridge equation is *more* tautological than the Fisher equation. Can there be degrees of tautologicality? That does not seem very proper. Both equations are, of course, self-evident.

The value of the four variables in the Fisher equation ($MV = \sum pq = PT$) can in principle be independently ascertained for a given period.[2] It may be objected that it is rather difficult to ascertain the value of V (velocity of circulation of money) in practice. It may be replied that the practical difficulty is irrelevant, or, alternatively, that the Fisher equation can be reduced to three terms, by treating MV as a single term, for the value of which it should not be difficult to obtain a rough approximation, e.g. from clearing house returns. We can infer from the equation that, if the observations do not accord with its requirement, then the observations must be wrong. Some fringe definitions may be needed, such as how to deal with loans and gifts. But the main variables in the equation do not have to be defined. Thus the equation may be used to detect errors and omissions, just as the necessary equality of debits and credits in a country's balance of external payments may be used. If we use index numbers, as with the notation PT (rather than $\sum pq$), then the constituents of the index numbers must be correctly weighted; otherwise we shall get a discordant result.

With the Cambridge equation the whole scene is transformed. We may take the simplest version, $n = pk$, where n is the quantity of money, p is the price of a basketful of goods, and k is the number of such basketfuls that the money held by people will purchase. This equation cannot be used to check any statistical data, and it does not matter what index number is used for p. The equation will always be verified by the data, however defective they may be in fact. The reason is that in this equation there are not three values that can be independently ascertained by observation, but two only. k is simply n/p; there is no possible way of evaluating k except by dividing n by p.

This is not to deny that the Cambridge equation has interest. Tautologies often have interest. I hold that it is in some respects more illuminating than the less tautological Fisher equation. Incidentally, it would be quite wrong to say that k is *defined* as n/p. The idea of the amount of value (purchasing power) that people hold in money form is intelligible in its own right.

The fact remains that the Cambridge equation is more utterly tautological than the Fisher equation, although the latter also is self-evident. Until we can have a good definition of degrees of tautologicality, I shall view that word with suspicion.

It might be said that, to give more life to the Cambridge equation, we can substitute for "the amount of value that people hold in money form" the words "the amount of value that people *desire* to hold in money form." But then the equation is no longer self-evident and may be false. If one adds the postulate that people always hold what they desire to hold—a very unsafe proposition—we are back where we were.

My basic equation can be interpreted *either* in the Fisher *or* the Cambridge manner. Cambridgewise we could deduce s from observations of the two values G and C. Or we might have independent statistics for s, as in the combined capital account of national income statistics, and use the formula to check errors in our statistical data.

For the reasons already given (no adjustable parameter and no possibility of empirical verification) it does not seem that this equation should be regarded as a "model." The matter may be different when we move on to the variant $G_w = s_d/C_r$, where G_w stands for what I called a warranted growth rate, s_d stands for the fraction of income that people desire to save, and C_r for the Capital required to effectuate the extra output.

We may consider the right-hand side first. The question arises whether what people desire to save is a meaningful concept. We are not discussing the determinants of what people desire to save, which may include the rate of interest, but rather the deeper question of whether they have a desire to save anything in particular. They might just take things as they come. Therefore it would seem that at this point some investigation of a psychological kind is needed. s_d might turn out to be a band within which people were indifferent. One would like to assume provisionally that people do have some definite propensity to save, which would cause an adjustment of behaviour if actual s deviated from s_d, an adjustment by persons in their amount of spending and by companies in their dividend distributions or in their capital outlays.

It would seem that one might be readier to take the meaningfulness of C_r for granted. People do not want to have money locked up in idle capital (except as an adaptation to short-term fluctuations) nor to be short of such capital as is required for efficient production. The value of C_r depends of course on the price of capital disposal and, more importantly, on the relative values of the various kinds of input required to create capital.

C_r is a relation between capital formation and output growth. C_r might be regarded as not meaningful if the output of some capital is nil. Even in the case of public parks and museums, however, one may surely suppose that there is an output of amenity, to which some value could be putatively assigned, even although it is not reckoned as part of the G.N.P. Be it noted that the distinction here referred to, between capital that has no output and capital that has output, is not the same as the distinction between induced and autonomous investment as strongly stressed by Hicks; the latter distinction relates to the sensitivity of current investment plans to current events.

It might be argued, I suppose, that the act of postulating that these two concepts are meaningful is tantamount to setting up a model.

I have long since admitted that there is some difficulty in regard to the status of G_w in this equation.

One way of treating the matter would be to regard the equation as definitional, in which case no question of its truth would arise and it could not be verified (or falsified). G_w would be *defined* as that rate of growth, which, if it took place, would be consistent with people saving what they desired to save and with additional capital being furnished in accordance with requirements. By the basic equation (the so-called tautology) only one rate of growth is consistent with the realization of s_d and C_r. In the unlikely event of s_d and C_r continuing to have the same value through time G_w would be steady. In practice of course there are likely to be variations, particularly in C_r.

Unfortunately there was another concept involved in my original formulation, namely an implication that G_w was a rate of growth which, if achieved, was self-sustaining because proving satisfactory to entrepreneurs. Thus G_w was taken by me to constitute a dynamic equilibrium, although not a stable equilibrium—but it is not necessary to discuss my "instability principle" here. The idea was that if everything was turning out well in regard to the size of their stocks and the degree of utilization of their equipment, the entrepreneurs would be content to continue happily in their growth path.

However, at an early date I felt bound to concede to Professor Alexander that this might not be so (Harrod, 1951). If one takes s_d/C_r, to be the definition of G_w, then the growth path so specified *may* not represent an entrepreneurial equilibrium. In the article referred to, I felt bound to redefine G_w otherwise than as being simply the quantity that is equal to s_d/C_r. But then we have to leave the happy hunting ground of "tautologies" and definitions and make empirical investigations into the behavioural parameters (if it is right to use that word) of the representative entrepreneurs. Deeper doubts were expressed in a much later article

(Harrod, 1964), to the effect that the behavioural parameters might be such that steady growth could, in a market economy, be sustained only by inflationary doses (or, in other cases, by deflation).

Whether those particular doubts are true or not, we are left with the conclusion that this set-up of equations (model?) calls for empirical investigations into the behavioural parameters of representative entrepreneurs.

I pass to another variant, $s_0 = G_n C_r$. Once again we have to ask whether a concept is meaningful, in this case G_n, the "natural" rate of growth. We now move right away from the idea of progress being trammelled by what people choose or desire to save. s_0, optimal saving, becomes a desiderand for the economy. The equation assumes that, relatively to it, the natural growth rate is exogenously determined—by population increase and technical progress. (This determination may not be altogether exogenous relatively to *other* variables in the economy.) The difficulty here lies not in the concept of natural growth, but in making a statistical forecast of it.

s_0, optimal saving, is a welfare optimum concept. If it is assumed that, from an economic welfare point of view, output should grow at the greatest feasible rate (making all proper allowances, of course, for an optimal increase of leisure and subject to a correct evaluation of C_r), then this equation seems to be self-evident. There are no adjustable parameters, and no investigation could verify or falsify it.

But there are some behind-the-scenes troubles. One is the optimal rate of interest, or, better, the optimal minimum acceptable rate of return on capital, which may have some influence on the value of C_r. This optimum depends in turn on the prospective growth rate (thereby simultaneous equations are involved) and on the elasticity of the marginal utility of income schedule. The determination of this elasticity requires econometric study. It has already received some, but not

enough; and there may be very great difficulties. If one inserted a tentative guess for this elasticity, say one half, on the basis that likely errors in this could not have much practical effect, then the set-up as a whole would become rather model-like.

There is a further constraint. In certain circumstances the value of s_0, as determined by $G_n C_r$, may reduce consumption to a lower level than is required from an incentive point of view in a growing economy. Here again statistical work, and also field work, are required.

While in very poor economies this constraint may have an important effect on C_r (but this must not be exaggerated, since there are far more important constraints on capital-intensive methods operating there, such as insufficient cadres of qualified personnel and balance of payments troubles), I would suppose that in mature countries it has an insignificant influence. The relative values of inputs and the availabilities of the various kinds of inputs (e.g. inputs of highly specialized technological or managerial man-hours)—we must never forget that the factor market is an imperfect one—are far more important in determining C_r than the acceptable rate of return on capital. Incidentally, it must not be assumed that the ready availability of plenty of technologists and technologically orientated managers always tends to raise C_r; it may sometimes reduce C_r.

Economists, if one may judge, as one now has to, from a small sample of the literature only, too often proceed to this kind of problem by setting up a two-factor model—the word slips out—by choosing capital and labour for their two factors, and by then discussing movements along the production function. No doubt what they say is correct in theory. Some of us have treated this theme in lectures designed to help examination candidates for nearly half a century. Journal articles that seek to advance the subject are a different matter. Even for a class-room it would be much better to choose technologico-manager man-hours and unskilled labour man-hours as the two factors in a two-factor model. This dictum applies even more importantly to international trade theory. This is so, not only because the relative availability of these two factors is probably more important for movements along the production function than the availability of capital and "labour," but also because capital is a very peculiar kind of factor with special properties, and in a general exposé of production functions one should seek to avoid capital, as being likely to bog one down in problems irrelevant to the central theme.

Associated with this, I detect a continuing tendency to hold that dynamic theory can be regarded as a sort of offshoot of, or an appendix to, static theory. In my opinion, dynamic theory brings into consideration influences that have no place at all in static theory. It must always be remembered that John Stuart Mill failed in precisely this respect; he stated dynamic theory, which had played so potent a part in the work of Adam Smith and Ricardo, in what was, in effect, no more than a series of corollaries to static theory. Thereby in my judgement he killed dynamic theory for a century. This murder, or temporary entombment, was assisted by the new lease of life given to static theory by Jevons, Menger, and Walras.

To sum up. I should have preferred that in science, including social science (as distinct from references to model husbands, fair ladies, etc.), the word "model" should have been confined to formulae relating to posited entities, viz. to entities that we can never directly observe and about the very existence of which we cannot be sure. Such posited entities include not only those of modern physics, but also, by a profounder philosophy, macroscopic entities, like chairs and tables. Locke postulated that these entities of the real world had a structural resemblance to our perceptions of them in respect of primary qualities, like configuration and number. But as regards the secondary qualities of our perceptions, colour, light, etc., all that we can say of the real world is that it has "powers" that cause these sensations in us, "powers" with which we can never gain direct acquaintance, but in reference to which we have built up a great structure of equations—the theory of light waves, etc.

There would not, by this restriction, be much scope for models in the social sciences, but some. The unconscious mind is a posited entity, with which we can never have direct acquaintance. The laws of its behaviour, as framed by Freud, would constitute a model. Jung provided an alternative model, judged by many to be inferior. Economists are not much concerned with such entities, although perhaps they should be more so. The Freudian model might make them better able to understand (and predict?) the actions of the British economic authorities.

The fact that the subject matter of this kind of model is posited only, gives a meaning to the pragmatic flavour of that word. The fact that we never have acquaintance with these entities means that they can be scrapped if, like the ether, they do not eventually prove "useful" in explaining the phenomena with which we do have acquaintance. The sense-datum, red, or, indeed, what we call money, cannot be scrapped in that way. Those are things with which we do have direct acquaintance.

If we want to bring "models" into economics, but to keep them meaningful, we might confine the term to a system of equations, not all of which are tautologies. Some at least might have adjustable parameters. It might be made a condition for the use of the word that some equations explicitly omit to take account of fringe influences. In this sense my system might be called a model, but only if it is taken to include those equations containing adjustable parameters, like the behavioural parameter of the representative entre-preneur or the marginal utility of income schedule.

Whether a single equation, like that cited above about wage increases, should be called a "model," even if it does include adjustable parameters, is more doubtful. We have the word "hypothesis." Perhaps "model" is appropriate if the equation explicitly excludes fringe influences?

Then we get down to self-evident truths (tautologies), like my basic equation in the form in which it is most often quoted. At this point I have a proprietary feeling. It seems to be downgraded by the appella-tion "model," which surely implies either uncertainty or incompleteness or, perhaps, both. If a single tautology can be called a "model," then that word becomes synony-mous with general proposition; such a usage would do violence to our sense that,

despite much mishandling, the word still retains a connotation of its own.

Can a respectable economist refer to his model (or models) if he has one? I think that he can, if, unlike Ph.D. candidates, he does so with selectivity and discrimina-tion. *Not* every time he sits down to dinner!

NOTES

1 I am indebted to Mr. John Bell at this point.
2 In case any noneconomists read this book, I should define. M is the quantity of money existing in a given region in a given period, V the average number of times that each unit of money is used in exchange in that period, q is the quantity of each valuable that is exchanged for money, p is the value in money terms of each unit of each of the valuables, P is the general price level, and T is the quantum of valuables that are exchanged for money.

Econometric Models: General Considerations
William H. White

Economists have long been trying to pro-vide the policymaker with guidance on what kinds of economic policy to adopt; recently they have been attempting to provide more precise guidance on how strong the policy measures should be. For success in economic planning in the de-veloping countries and in minimizing unemployment and maintaining reason-able stability in the rate of economic growth in developed countries—and for other purposes as well—this is potentially an important advance. The means of providing this advice are based on the derivation of mathematical formulas,

William H. White, "How Useful Are Econometric Models?" *Finance and Develop-ment*, 6 (March 1969), pp. 23–29; "The Use-fulness of Econometric Models for Policy-makers," 6 (September 1969), pp. 8–13.

analogous to those expressing the laws of physics. These formulas, or "models," represent the operation of the most im-portant economic cause-and-effect rela-tionships—the laws (or rules) of economic behavior—and show the chains of reac-tions which are initiated by changes in particular causal factors. Econometric models are relatively new; they have only recently been developed and are now constantly being refined.

Success in the development of such mathematical models depends on the ability to measure the strength of the current influence of the various causal factors. Because it is patterns of human behavior rather than mechanical laws of physics that must be measured, the economic laws will never be known with the accuracy of the laws of physics.

Nevertheless, the prospect now exists for improving the guidance offered to economic policymakers beyond the guidance provided by their own experience or the judgments of premodel era economists.

WHAT IS AN ECONOMETRIC MODEL?

Although it may help those who have a knowledge of physics to think of an econometric model as resembling one of the laws of physics (e.g., Boyle's law), yet econometrics differs from physics in two ways. (1) It is impossible (with some exceptions) to conduct controlled laboratory experiments in which different amounts of the causal factors of special interest can be introduced, while the strength of all other factors is held unchanged, so that the effect of each factor can be directly measured. (2) The laws of classical physics are known with certainty: for given amounts of cause, the same effect will always be produced. This rigidity of physical laws reflects the mechanical nature of the physical relationships. In contrast, economic "laws" involve the rather flexible reactions of human behavior to a cause. Here the relationship between cause and effect cannot be either rigid or precise: the laws of behavior can be verified therefore only in an approximate sense; they are probabilities rather than certainties. They will tend to be accurate on the *average* over time (unless the passage of time has caused a change in the strength of the human reactions), but they will not be completely accurate at any single time.[1] Where the inaccuracy found proves to be sufficiently small, the information derived from the econometric model will be useful; often, however, it will have to be considered merely as a best guess that carries with it a large margin of error, and frequently the margin of error will be so large that the econometrician will not issue any finding at all for the use of the policymaker or even as a guide to further econometric research.

DISCOVERING THE MODEL WITHOUT BENEFIT OF LABORATORY EXPERIMENT

The econometrician usually meets the first disadvantage in the discovery of economic laws—the inability to conduct controlled laboratory experiments—through the use of series of statisical data on likely candidates as causal factors which are collected *over time*.

In a primitive way, this sort of extraction of economic cause-and-effect relationships was used even before the development of econometrics. If, for example, it was observed that after a 20 per cent reduction of the price of bread, consumers began spending 10 per cent less for bread, the economist would offer as his best-guess estimate that any change in the price of bread would affect the amount of money spent for bread in the same direction (less money spent when the price was cut, more when the price was raised) and by an amount which was roughly half the amount of the change in the price. The confidence with which such a conclusion could be reached would be improved, of course, if later on the price returned to its original level and it was observed that the amount of money spent also rose to roughly its original level.

Usually, however, even the pre-econometrician had to try to deal with more complex relationships than this. For example, the price of bread might fall at a time when personal incomes were also falling, so that the economist had to try to distinguish the depressing effect of the price decline on the amount spent from that depressing effect which was presumably exerted by a decline in the consumer's spendable income. If there was one time at which either the price of bread or the income level was different from the initial value while the level of the other factor was *not* different from its initial level, then the pre-econometrician still had a chance to distinguish the influence of the two causal factors, consumer income level and price, in the amount of money spent for bread. Ordinarily, however, he could not count on having measured the influences of these two factors accurately, because the influence of other factors which he could not take into account (the price of alternative food products such as potatoes, change in the average age of the population or in its concern about being overweight) would have exerted differing influences on the total spent between the observations made at the three different times. In more general terms, the fact that even the true strengths of causal influences are—as described earlier—only *probable* relationships, valid on the average but not valid at any particular point of time, had to be allowed for. It meant that any inference drawn from comparing the sizes of causes with the sizes of their apparent effects on behavior at only a few points of time was very likely to yield estimates of the strength of effects which misrepresented the true (i.e., true on average) strength of effect. With *several* sets of three observation periods—each set containing three observations of the two factors (bread price, consumer income) and of the behavior which they had influenced (spending for bread)—the economist might have been able to find such an average value for the influence of each of the two factors on the third; but these results are likely to be very difficult to obtain, and run the risk of being distorted by subjective judgment or other influences. Of course, if the several estimates for each of the two factors turned out to be close to each other, the method could be accepted, but such good results cannot be routinely expected. Also, as the number of factors included increases, the procedure is less feasible and reliable. Moreover, it may then become necessary to allow for "feedbacks"—the elaborate interconnections among economic events which make the size of some causal factors in part the result of the size of other causal factors or even of the size of the very effect under study. And the problems increase further when it is necessary to compare the results of alternative "models" which use different sets of causal factors to see which gives the best results.

To be able to derive results that are at all worthy of serious consideration, the economist has had to turn to the econometrician, a specialist in applying the mathematical techniques developed by the statistician. With these techniques he can quickly extract estimates of the influence of various relevant causal factors which are a sort of average of the influences which would have been derived from separate sets of observations. Moreover, this procedure yields objective measurements of how closely the estimated effects of the movements of the several causal factors add up to the actual, observed movements over time for the behavior under study (the spending for bread). If, for example, the model succeeds in deriving estimated values for the amount of expenditure on bread which are reasonably close to the expenditures actually observed during each of the separate months, quarters, or years which constitute the separate observations, then the achievement of a successful model may be assured.

USES OF AN ECONOMETRIC MODEL

If an econometric model can help in forecasting economic events, its value to policymakers is obvious. For example, in some countries, the government wants to improve farmers' incomes through buying enough of each grain harvest until the grain price is pushed up to a level which yields the desired money income. The question of how much money the government should plan to spend to purchase grain then becomes an important one. The change in the price of grain can be converted into the associated change in the price of bread, and knowledge of the effect of the change in bread price on the amount the public spends for bread (described earlier) is easily used to show the government how much money it must spend in buying up the grain which the public will stop buying when the price rises. If we consider for simplicity only the bread price, government attempts to raise the bakers' receipts from the sale of bread by 20 per cent would require a 20 per cent rise in the selling price on the pre-existing quantities of bread sales. But we know that the public will raise its spending by only 10 per cent when the price rises 20 per cent. Hence, to achieve the desired 20 per cent rise in the proceeds to bakers, the government will itself have to spend the missing 10 per cent for the purchase of bread. With this kind of information, the government can judge better whether aiming at a given improvement in the prices that farmers receive will be too costly for its budget; alternatively, it can prepare its budgetary requests with a greater degree of accuracy.

In countries where the necessary statistical data exist, the policymaking uses of the econometric models will of course extend far beyond the question of the price of a given product. The amount of a necessary exchange devaluation may be better estimated with the use of that part of a model's results which shows the influence of a change in the price foreigners pay for the country's exports upon the quantity of those exports they buy, and the comparable effect of changes in the cost of imports on the country's own imports. When expenditure on goods and services within the country is foreseen to be larger than the capacity to produce goods and services, the appropriate strength of measures to restrict expenditures—such as raising interest rates (to restrict expenditures for business investment) or raising taxes on consumer income (to restrict consumer spending)—becomes of major concern to the government policymaker. Models which show how and how much interest rates and taxes affect investment and consumption

expenditures therefore are of great importance to the authorities.

In questions of economic development, also, the effect of increases in taxes on consumers is of great interest. For example, the extent to which taxes cause them to reduce their savings rather than their consumption expenditure is important because the savings are necessary for financing the investment which will lead to economic development. Guidance on what export industries should be established can be found in forecasts of the growth of world demand for various products and in the amount that will be bought of particular products when different prices are charged. Similarly, the amount of addition to total productive capacity which investment expenditures will produce obviously is important, and knowledge about it too can be obtained from observation of past experience with growth in production as affected by the size and the industrial distribution of total investment spending. Finally, the faster the rate of development, the faster is the growth in incomes and hence in the portion of incomes which is saved and can finance further investment for development. Because of this relationship between income growth and growth in the financeable level of investment spending, information on the effect of income growth on savings would also be extremely valuable for development planning.

THE PROBLEM OF LAGS

The reader will already suspect that information as valuable as this is not easily obtained—and he is right. One of the major difficulties is that a cause may not exert its effects until some time has passed, as when a reduction in taxes which leaves consumers with more spendable income leads them at first to spend only a small part of the extra resources; the consumer may require some time to adjust his standard of living to meet the new possibilities in full. The pre-econome-trician had very little hope of making proper allowance for the presence of these so-called lags, but the econometrician has been able to test efficiently models which provide a variety of alternative lags and select the one which yields the best results (the estimated values for the effect which on average came closest to the observed values of the effect). In this way, very complex lag patterns have been derived, consumption in the current quarter of the year being found to be influenced rela-tively little by spendable income in the current quarter, with most of the influence being assigned to the spendable income of, e.g., the preceding 12-month period and the 12 months before that.

The fact that economic causes produce their effects with such lags gives the econometric model real advantage as a device for forecasting economic develop-ments. To know how much consumer spending is likely to rise from the current quarter to the next one, it need not be very important to know what the spend-able income will be in that next quarter. From what has just been said, the infor-mation on spendable income in the current and preceding quarters is (almost) com-pletely sufficient for a good forecast of next-quarter consumption. And since con-sumption accounts for the greater part of spending on the country's production of goods and services, this information carries us a long way toward having a forecast of the levels of gross national product (GNP), employment, etc., in the near future. With similar lagging causal factors being important in the determina-tion of other major segments of the GNP total—e.g., fixed investment and exports —a forecast of most of the total of near-future GNP can be made without need for accurate estimates of the strengths of the various factors that will be found to exist during that future period.

Government spending (or the size of the government budget surplus or deficit) —another important factor in the GNP—

cannot be so readily forecast by use of lags. However, since the future values of the government factor are (at least ideally) under the control of the policymakers, no forecast of this factor is necessary. For example, the combination of the forecast levels of consumption, investment, and exports plus, e.g., the same figure for the government budget as the current one might yield an unsatisfactory level of GNP. But the combination of the fore-cast for the private sector and the as-sumed value for government expenditure has provided a guide to policy. If the forecast GNP derived under the assump-tion that the current level of government spending will continue in the future is too high, the policymakers can adjust the budgeted future expenditure until the forecast results yield a suitable level.

VALIDITY OF GROUP BEHAVIOR FORECASTS

Another problem related to econo-metric models which may occur to many readers is whether the erratic, "lawless" economic behavior of the individuals making up a society can permit the con-duct of the whole group to conform sufficiently to such a model. The ap-parently erratic behavior of each individual may be considered a reflection of the influence of many causal factors—eco-nomic and noneconomic—which cannot be considered strong ones for all members of the community taken together and which therefore cannot be easily measured. If those various secondary factors could be considered as more or less self-neutral-izing in their net effect on the behavior of an economic group, the plausibility of stable aggregate behavior despite erratic individual behavior would be established. And at least a tendency for such self-cancellation among the secondary factors can in fact be established, provided that one condition is satisfied: these factors must be more or less random. Random-ness exists when no one strength (including zero strength) for a particular factor is more likely to be experienced among the individuals in the group than any other; and all strengths of any particular factor are equally likely to be experienced by an individual, regardless of the strength of the other factors affecting him at the same time. While it is not possible to prove that the neglected secondary factors will always satisfy the randomness requirement sufficiently well, it is nevertheless reasonable to assume that in many instances most of the secondary factors producing deviations from a supposed norm will be distributed among the population in a sufficiently close-to-random way. It will be noted that imposing the above randomness condition will yield stable behavior in spite of the fact that it *exaggerates* the difficulty of establishing stable group behavior in one important respect, namely, its requirement that any given factor yield equal frequencies of strong and weak distorting effects. In reality, just as huge distorting influences are not expected at all from secondary factors, so also relatively large influences are expected to occur with relatively low frequency.

To illustrate the operation of the various secondary factors, assume two influences on the rate of bread consumption which may cause the rate to deviate from the norm and which seem reasonably likely to be randomly distributed: differing amounts of increase of current physical exertion, starting from no increase, which will raise bread consumption by 0 per cent, 1 per cent, 2 per cent, or 3 per cent; different amounts of recent tendency for increases in the individual's weight which will again have no effect (zero weight increase) or reduce bread consumption by 1 per cent, 2 per cent, or 3 per cent. Given our crucial assumption that these changes occur randomly—each one having as much chance to be experienced as any other and any combination of changes in the two factors together being as likely to

Table 1. Combinations of Two Random Factors Influencing Bread Consumption

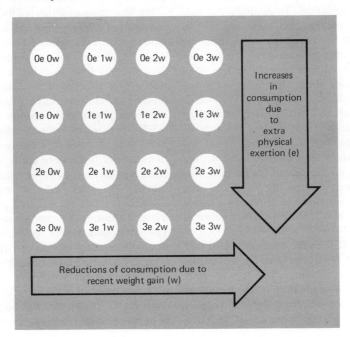

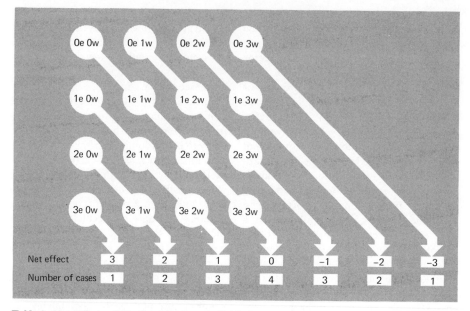

Table 2. Net Effects of the Combinations in Table 1

be experienced as any other combination —there are just 16 possible combinations of distorting factors, all of which are assumed to be equally likely to affect individuals making up the bread-consuming population. To simplify, we can, therefore, assume that there are just 16 individuals in the population, one for each possible combination of strengths of the random factors—see Table 1.

The tables show that from these assumptions it follows that most individuals will be clustered in the neighborhood of zero deviation from the normal rate of bread consumption, with relatively few having extreme deviations. Moreover, the deviations on one side of the norm will be just counterbalanced by those on the other side, so that the group as a whole shows a zero deviation from normal behavior.

Why is it that the randomly distorted cases tend to cluster around the undistorted, normal value? The logical basis for so neat a result from a set of random factors can be seen from Table 2. There is only one possible instance of the two

maximum divergences from norm—those when the 3 per cent effect from one factor are accompanied by a zero effect from the other, offsetting factor—but there are four possible cases of zero deviation from norm —the four cases in which the four possible strengths of one factor are accompanied by equal opposite strengths of the other factor. Thus, it is seen that opposing random factors must tend to coincide in a relatively large proportion of cases, thereby holding a relatively large proportion of individuals close to the norm.

This demonstration may seem limited because it assumes that the two illustrative random factors are either neutral or counterbalancing but never reinforce each other's distorting effects. Reinforcing distortions could be expected to produce more disruption of the average result. The interested reader can construct a three-dimensional version of Table 1, that is to say a set of tables like Table 1 but each allowing for a different size of the influence of another factor affecting food consumption, such as the ages of the population. With the age factor starting at neutral and then reducing bread consumption by three successive 1 percentage-point steps, the three new tables would stand behind Table 1 but would be shifted successively to the right by one step. When this is done and the totals for each size of net deviation from norm taken (as in the bottom row of Table 2), it is found, as expected, that the maximum deviations from norm are larger than before ($4\frac{1}{2}$ per cent instead of just 3 per cent); the bread consumption norm itself is also depressed to a somewhat lower figure; but the same clustering of cases around the (new) norm is found, with again only a single case at the extreme "corners," and the same counterbalancing of deviations from the norm remains. (Instead of the distribution of cases among the various sizes of net effect found in Table 2—1, 2, 3, 4, 3, 2, 1 —we find the symmetrical "bell-shaped-curve" distribution of probability theory: 1, 3, 6, 10, 12, 12, 10, 6, 3, 1.)

QUALIFICATIONS

These examples represent ideal cases. The laws of random chance require that every possible combination of ignored, random factors *tend* to be influencing the average (and making that average conform to the norm). But they also recognize the existence of a certain probability that on some occasions certain of the 16 combinations of factors will be absent while others will be overrepresented, so that the observed average result for the whole population will at times differ from the underlying norm. It is only when several observations of the population's behavior are used that the results taken together can be counted on to approximate to the symmetrical distributions described above; only then will the average result for all the individuals in the population approximate the norm.

The number of observations does not, on the other hand, have to be extremely large, for, analogously with the clustering of individuals around the norm described

above, large deviations of a group's behavior at a given time from the underlying group norm tend to be relatively infrequent, with small deviations occurring the greater part of the time. However, a further need for including additional observations before a trustworthy estimate of the norm can be reached is created by the fact that economic life is subjected from time to time to unpredictable shocks (such as climatic or political disturbance) which cause a substantial proportion of the population to depart in the same direction from its normal behavior pattern. Comparable distortions must be expected from time to time because of errors in the statistics themselves. If enough separate observations of society's behavior are made, either the observations which include the influence of such shocks or errors will not have a chance to dominate the results, or else the distortions created by several such shocks will tend to be in opposite directions and therefore counterbalancing.

In recent years, the increasing availability of the varieties of economic data necessary for estimating econometric models and the increasing availability of electronic computers to perform the otherwise almost impossible task of making the estimates (and making them for a large variety of lag patterns, of alternative selections of causal factors, etc., in order to see which ones yield good results) has led to great optimism about the possibilities for producing sufficiently reliable models. Nevertheless, it remains true that the estimates must be taken at best as merely probabilities—the most likely value given the information available, but a value which is correct only in a probabilistic sense: if all goes well and the patterns of human behavior remain unchanged, the effects estimated through the models will be correct on average, although at any given point of time they will not be correct. By some scale of size, small errors in the indicated effects will be quite frequent, and large errors quite infrequent. But for the economist's purposes even the small error may be too large to permit the model's finding to be relied on, or the medium-size errors may be so serious that even their moderate frequency of occurrence will be excessive. In these conditions the model will be of little more use to the policymaker than the "educated guesses" he had to rely on before the recent flowering of econometric models. Some use may exist even here because, even at the worst, models can be used to show the ultimate effects of policy actions under a plausible range of *assumed* values for the strengths of factors; and sometimes the range of results found will exclude certain outcomes which otherwise would have seemed to be plausible ones.

In spite of the limitations, the results now being derived from econometric models are often an improvement over the other information available to the policymaker, and refinement of techniques and of standards of reliability will assure that increasingly the policymaker will be presented with usable results. For the present, however, the policymaker should be placed in a position to evaluate correctly the econometrician's measures of the reliability of the results presented; even if they are clearly an improvement over those obtainable by educated guessing, these results will commonly still have sufficient margin of error that the policymaker may want to adopt a compromise, "safety first" policy rather than the one for which the model evidence would call if it could be taken at its face value.

•   •   •

In the making of economic policies for economic growth, maintaining full employment, avoiding inflation, adjusting the rate of exchange, and so on, it is necessary to decide how much of a particular policy measure should be applied. To reduce consumer expenditure during the year by 1 million pesos, it is necessary to remove some amount from consumer income through taxes. But an increase in income tax will also reduce savings, which serve to finance part of the country's development. The policymaker must ask: how much tax to activate a desired result (reducing consumer expenditure)? How little to avoid an undesired one (damage to the savings program)?

To come close to an estimate of the quantitative effect of given amounts of measures, the policymaker can study past experience, looking for occasions on which similar changes occurred and trying to determine what their effects were, although the reaching of conclusions will be made difficult because differing amounts of other factors will be found to have been influencing the effect at the same time as the factor under study. The econometric model provides a means of inferring from the amounts of causes and effects observed (and measured) over a period of time the amount of effect separately attributable to, say, a 1 per cent change in each of the causal factors. Using mathematical techniques developed by the statistician, the econometrician can "fit" to the data on past events a formula or model which gives the appropriate cause/effect law. The numerical strengths of the various causal factors found in the deriving of the law will tell us—if the model used in the derivation of the law was properly made—what, on average, the effects of a particular amount of a given cause will be.

Because the law takes into consideration only the major causes of the behavior at issue, it cannot be accurate at all times; it will overestimate consumer spending some times and underestimate it at others. If the numerous neglected factors operate on individual consumers in a random or chance way, their influences will tend to cancel each other out, with their net, uncanceled influences on total consumer spending being relatively small at most points of time. However, it is· possible that even then the average amount of distortion of consumer spending from the amount given by the law would be large from the point of view of the policymaker.

MEASUREMENT OF ACCURACY

Before the policymaker can use such a law of behavior, he must know how trustworthy the whole law and, in particular, its estimate of the strength of the influence of the policy factor is. The question of accuracy is reduced to two issues: first, the extent to which the observed effect on any given occasion is likely to be distorted through the operation of random factors from the average effect given by the law and, second, the accuracy with which the true, underlying normal law of behavior was estimated.

Information on the first aspect of accuracy—the accuracy of the law's estimates of behavior at particular points of time—is provided by the "standard error of estimate." This is a sort of average of the discrepancies found be-

tween the model's estimates of the effect (of the amount of consumer spending) at the various points of time for which data were employed in the deriving of the model, and the effects actually observed. But the standard error is not the customary average of the errors: rather it is computed so that errors smaller than itself can be expected two thirds of the time, larger errors being expected, of course, one third of the time. Since large random distortions must be less frequent than small ones, distortions greater than twice the standard error would be expected to be rather infrequent; in fact, they occur only 5 per cent of the time, and distortions more than two and a half times the standard error occur only 1 per cent of the time. These values for the probabilities of increasingly large random distortions can be found from the "normal probability distribution" that was derived in an approximate way in my previous article. Figure 1 shows the normal distribution.

The size of the standard error can be made most meaningful when the error is presented as a fraction of the average amount of effect (for example, the

Figure 1. Normal Dispersion of Observed Effect Around the Average Effect Caused by Random Factors
Numbers represent the deviation, measured in terms of standard errors, from the average effect. Percentages are the proportions of observed results that should be found within the stated distances from the average. Sixty-eight per cent of the results should fall within one standard-error of the average, so that 32 per cent will fall further away than 1 standard error.

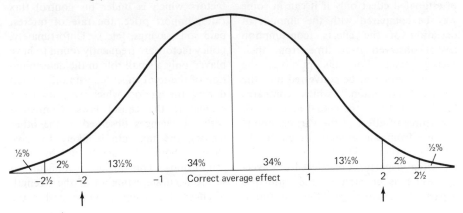

average amount of consumer spending) actually observed. The policymaker who thinks it may be necessary to restrict consumption by 2 per cent through raising tax rates will be more cautious about doing so when he finds that there is a one-third probability, whether the taxes are adjusted or not, that actual consumption will be either, say, over 4 per cent smaller or over 4 per cent larger than expected. In fact, since one year's consumption is normally within 5 per cent of the preceding year's consumption (increases in the money value of consumption that are due to price increases aside), he might conclude that his correct normal law of consumer behavior was made almost worthless by the severity of the random distortions of actual behavior from the norm. And if it happened that the difference between the highest and the lowest consumption observed over the past decade was only, say, 7½ per cent he would probably have to conclude that the 4 per cent standard error made his estimated causal law of consumption inferior to an assumed "law" which said that any year's consumption was simply equal to the average level observed in the past. The maximum error that could result from using that arbitrarily assumed "law" (3¾ per cent) would have to be smaller than the 4 per cent standard error of his estimated causal law.

It follows that the standard error provides adequate information on accuracy of estimated effect only if it can in some way be compared with the amount of deviation of the effects (consumption levels) observed over time from their average level. For this purpose, the standard error can be converted into the related "correlation," which compares the estimated and the actual amounts of departures of effect at the various points of time from the amount of effect observed on average. The greater the part of the actual departures of effect from average which is covered by the estimated departures from average at the same times,

the higher is the correlation. A correlation of 1.00 would imply perfect conformity between the estimated and the actual effects. Published econometric models commonly show a quite good correlation such as 0.90, which implies that 81 per cent of the observed difference from average amount of effect is explained by —or, more cautiously, matched by—the divergences from average shown by the estimated influences of the set of causal factors used. A correlation of 0.80 implies a less satisfactory explanation of 64 per cent, 36 per cent of the observed departures from the average size of effect being unaccounted for. A rather unsatisfactory 0.70 correlation would imply that 51 per cent of the observed deviations were left unexplained.

A low correlation—under 0.70—or a high standard error of estimate—e.g., 10 per cent—are evidence of limited usefulness for a model which may be a basically correct one (or which may itself be somewhat untrustworthy).

INADEQUACY OF THE CORRELATION

When a model proves to have a low standard error of estimate and a high correlation, so that estimated and actual effects have been close to each other, the results may still be considered unreliable for the policymaker's purposes. The policymaker will be especially interested in the accuracy of that one of the causal factors which is under his control (tax rates, import price, the rate of interest paid on savings, etc.). Unfortunately, policy factors are frequently found to have played only a small role in the determination of the total effect (consumption, etc.) during the period which was used for estimating the causal laws. Compared with the changes observed in the other factors, the tax rate is likely to have changed both infrequently and by small proportions. This makes it difficult to secure accurate estimates of the strength of effect of a change in taxes, and at the same time it permits misestimation of the influences of taxes to be consistent with high correlations and low standard errors; the correct estimation of the influences of the other factors which were important in the past is sufficient to produce good over-all accuracy.

Sometimes the policy factor has been of substantial importance. But here a second obstacle to discovery of reliable laws may exist: it is often found that the movements of this factor and those of another important factor tended to be synchronized (as over the business cycle, where many factors tend to change at the same time).

Here it may not be possible to distinguish the comparative influences of the two factors reliably; if they vary together most of the time, very little indication is available of the effects each would have in isolation. Thus, it is plausible that a very high correlation will be found, but the influences estimated for particular causal factors are unreliable ones. Given the plausibility of such a result, the policy-maker must know, in addition to the correlation, the reliability of the estimated strength of the particular causal factors with which he is concerned.

STANDARD ERROR OF THE REGRESSION COEFFICIENT

Our law of consumer behavior may be represented by a formula or equation which states that consumption will be equal to the sum of the effects of the various other factors (the level of consumer incomes, the rate of new marriages) *minus* a certain fraction of the taxes which the government takes away from the incomes of the consumers. Let us assume that taking $1\frac{3}{4}$ million units in taxes reduces consumption by just 1 million; it follows from this—in a first approximation—that the imposition of taxes will reduce consumption by four sevenths of the amount of the taxes ($\frac{4}{7} = 1 \div 1\frac{3}{4}$). To find the effect on consumption of any

specified amount of tax collection, we multiply the amount of taxes by the coefficient $\frac{4}{7}$. Because the average law of behavior fitted to the data is called a "regression" relationship, the coefficient is fully identified by the prevalent but intrinsically meaningless term, "regression coefficient." (The existence of this awkward term illustrates the possibilities for sentiment within science. A perfecter of the technique of fitting mathematical laws to observed causes and effects adopted the term as a tribute to a pioneer of the subject, Sir Francis Galton. In the mid-nineteenth century Galton had derived from data on a large number of families a law of hereditary regression: offspring of exceptional parents reflect the parental characteristics only in part, tending to "regress" toward the average characteristics of the population.)

The customary measure of the reliability of an estimated regression coefficient as a reflection of its normal, undistorted value is its standard error. In this instance the standard error is a measure of the plausible range of variation among the several estimates of the regression coefficient which might have been derived if several sets of data on observed amounts of causes and effects had been separately available. These several randomly distorted estimates of the regression coefficient will have an average which approximates the true, undistorted regression coefficient, given that random distortions tend on average to be self-canceling. Hence, even though we do not know that true average value, we can still judge that our estimate is a good one if we know that the range of variation among several estimates will be a narrow one. And we can obtain an approximation to that range by use of the known amounts of random distortions *within* the one set of observations of causes and effects which we have at our disposal. This approximation is called the standard error of the estimated regression coefficient.

As with the standard error of estimate discussed earlier, our particular estimate of the regression coefficient (four sevenths) is highly unlikely to prove to be as far as two and a half standard errors from its true but unknown value and rather unlikely to be as much as two standard errors from the true value. The reasoning here may be verified by reference to Figure 1. With the true value as shown, estimated values more remote than the arrows at two standard errors would turn up only 5 per cent of the time: 2½ per cent of the time the estimate would be more than two standard errors larger than the true value and another 2½ per cent of the time it would be found more than two standard errors smaller than the true value. Similarly, estimates in excess of or below the true value by more than one standard error would each appear 16 per cent of the time, so that there is a total probability of 32 per cent of divergences greater than one standard error.

If the standard error actually found for the estimated regression coefficient were a small fraction of the coefficient, the knowledge that we could almost certainly exclude the possibility of errors larger than two and a half or twice the standard error would be reassuring. But if one standard error constitutes a large fraction of the regression coefficient (e.g., more than one seventh out of the four sevenths), then the ability to rule out mistakes larger than two standard errors is not worth very much. Estimates that had a now serious divergence from the true value of a little more than one standard error could *not* be ruled out, for they would retain a fairly high probability of being found. Even with a standard error of just one seventh, there would be a 32 per cent probability of having derived the four-sevenths estimate even if the true value was outside the range three sevenths to five sevenths. While this result may constitute an improvement over the impressionistic estimates which the policymaker might otherwise have to use, it

clearly must be considered an imprecise result.

Unfortunately the standard errors of regression coefficients for policy factors such as taxes are commonly larger than a fourth of the coefficient, and errors as large as half of the coefficient (as large as two sevenths in our example) are not uncommon. There we must recognize that there is a 32 per cent probability of having found our estimate (four sevenths) even when the true value was more than 50 per cent larger or more than 50 per cent smaller (i.e., when the actual value lay outside the range two sevenths to six sevenths). In these instances the econometric findings will be of limited use to the policymaker. Reliance on such findings would involve a substantial risk that the policy adopted was more than 50 per cent weaker or 50 per cent stronger than called for.

REJECTING THE HYPOTHESIS OF 100 PER CENT ERROR IN THE RESULT

It has become the practice among econometricians to consider useful their estimated influences for factors which have this rather high probability of 50 per cent or more error, and to be quite confident of the results when the error is just a little smaller than half of the regression coefficient (i.e., when the 32 per cent chance of errors refers to errors equal to at least 40 per cent of the estimated regression coefficient).

The policymaker who uses econometric guidance may be surprised to find that what is called "good" econometric evidence has so very wide a margin for error, but those who were puzzled by the continuous discoveries of precise laws of behavior by groups made up of individualistic human beings will be reassured. (The surprise and the reassurance will both be increased when attention is drawn to a further exaggeration of the accuracy of results which has crept into econometric practice.)

The reason why econometricians have underemphasized the degree of unreliability in their results lies, paradoxically, in the very self-critical approach they began to use in evaluating the accuracy of their findings. They began by deciding that all regression coefficients must be assumed completely worthless if there was even a small probability that the supposed factor (taxes) had no influence at all on the effect under study (consumption). They therefore tested the possibility that the regression coefficients they actually found could have been derived as a result of random chance distortions when the true average relationship was zero—*no* influence of the supposed cause on the effect at issue. To do this the econometricians hypothesized that the true, average value of the regression coefficient is in fact zero and saw what is the probability that the one they derived (four sevenths) could have been derived by chance as the result of random distorting factors. Here Figure 1 would show the value zero at the center and the value four sevenths somewhere to the right. If it was as far to the right as the arrow marking two standard errors, they could conclude that there was only an inconsequential 2½ per cent probability of their having found a value of four sevenths or more if the true value was as low as zero. The hypothesis that the true value was in fact zero could then be rejected and the regression coefficient accepted as a valid one.

Whether the econometricians find that their regression coefficient is as much as two standard errors above zero obviously depends on the size of the standard error. A standard error of two sevenths in their regression coefficient of four sevenths, for example, would meet this test. Here they can be almost certain that the true value is not 100 per cent smaller than their estimate. But while the test might have successfully ruled out the need to cut

down their estimate by 100 per cent, they continue to face the 32 per cent chance of having to reduce or increase their estimate by at least one standard error; and, by their assumption, one standard error equals 50 per cent of the estimate. Here the policymaker may share the econometrician's enthusiasm for having achieved results so good that 100 per cent errors are unlikely, but he will also have to regret that the results are so extremely poor that 50 per cent or larger errors must be expected 32 per cent of the time.[2]

INCREASE IN PROBABILITY OF ERROR CAUSED BY TESTING ALTERNATIVE MODELS

There are a variety of other rather technical problems which may cause the goodness of the econometric evidence to be further exaggerated—problems which warn of their technical character by wearing names such as heteroscedasticity, identification problem, time trend, serial correlation, autocorrelation, or lagged endogenous variables. The alert econometrician will avoid these as far as possible, but there is another serious source of exaggeration of the goodness of the results created in recent years by the availability of the electronic computer; this is difficult to avoid and has until recently been too new to be widely recognized. The sinister role played by the electronic computer is the consequence of the computer's high speed and efficiency. These make it quite easy, and customary, for the investigator to test a large variety of alternative models in order to find one which yields high correlations and high values for regression coefficients in comparison with their standard errors. Since he does not have any firm guidance from economic theory about what model is the best representation of the laws of human behavior, he is of course fully entitled to test a large variety of models. For example, when faced with causes which exert their effects only with delays, he has no basis for preferring one pattern of delay in effects (an increase in personal income tax rates will reduce consumer spending not at all in the first three months, by one seventh of the extra taxes in the second three months, by two sevenths in the next, and by four sevenths in the following and all later periods) against any other pattern (a three-sevenths cut of consumption in the initial three months and a four-sevenths cut thereafter, etc.). With the computer he can test an enormous variety of patterns of delay in effects; he can also quickly test the effects on the goodness of the results of including or excluding various alternative or additional causal factors in the model, of allowing for various kinds of interactions among the factors (the factors being multiplied rather than added together), etc.

This searching for the model which yields the best results (called "fishing" by the statistician and "data mining" by econometricians) may be logically the proper thing to do—the only way of finding what is the best set of cause/effect relationships—but its benefits are secured at a price which econometricians all too often overlook. The econometrician is correct in pointing out that there was only a $2\frac{1}{2}$ per cent or even just a $\frac{1}{2}$ per cent probability that he would have found such a high value for the correlation or for the regression coefficient relative to its standard error when the true value of the regression coefficient was zero. But those low probabilities refer to the percentage probabilities of getting so high a result in a *single attempt*, and the electronic computer has led to the making of a large number of different attempts simultaneously. If we can speak in terms of three different attempts, the probabilities of finding just one model which yields so high a value for the regression coefficient relative to the standard error when the true average coefficient is zero are themselves multiplied by three (to $7\frac{1}{2}$ per cent and $1\frac{1}{2}$ to 3 per cent, respectively). These

probabilities of 100 per cent error are still quite small ones, and that makes it easy to see why econometricians continued the convention of reporting their error probabilities as if they referred to only a single test.[3] But once the focus of attention is shifted to the much larger probabilities of a 50 per cent or 40 per cent error, probabilities such as 16 per cent or 32 per cent, it will become quite obvious that multiplying the probability even by two must very greatly increase the policymaker's skepticism about his econometric evidence.

At times the policymaker might be able to avoid this barrier to the finding of reliable results by restricting his econometrician to testing only one or two alternative models on the computer. But if the econometrician has been able to get statistically good results from only two tries there is a likelihood that many more models were in fact tested: the econometrician either continued on from the models already tested by others and found to be unsatisfactory or else he studied charts of the data on the effect and on the various candidates for causal factors, made some rough tests in his head, and eliminated some of the candidates which seemed unpromising. Thus it remains true that evidence which would normally be considered reliable will often be made suspect by the presence of multiple testing.

The only hope for discovering the true reliability of such models is to wait for a year or so and see how well the estimated regression coefficients perform in estimating the newly observed values for the actual effect. Since there is ground for suspicion that the model itself had been tailored to fit certain observed effects, it therefore can be verified only by seeing how well its estimated effects conform to subsequently observed effects when the appropriate (subsequent) values of the causes are used. Many of the supposedly reliable models will fail this test, and one or possibly even two successes will often be insufficient to establish that the model is reliable and even less useful in establishing the reliability of the particular factor within the model (taxes) which is of interest to the policymaker. Most of the rest of the model may be fairly accurate and the whole model may therefore yield good estimates, but the estimated effect attributed to the tax factor alone may still be unreliable.

CONCLUSION

The policymaker will very often be obliged to consider that econometric evidence considered of good quality under the conventional criteria is actually not much better than the evidence obtainable from, for example, surveys of the views of a sample of the group whose activities are of interest (how much did you reduce your weekly savings as a result of last year's 10 peso increase in your weekly tax payment?). The econometric evidence might even lose its claim to superiority over the policymaker's own informal estimates. Instead of accepting regression coefficients which are at the conventionally accepted minimum of two to two and a half times their standard errors, he will have to consider suspect the large proportion of the results for which the coefficients are less than—to give an illustrative example —five times their standard errors. Even the models which fail to meet this degree of reliability will, of course, yield some amount of guidance; and on important questions an additional source of guidance is always worth having even if it cannot contribute very much toward narrowing the range of choices. Nevertheless, the weight the policymaker places on such guidance will depend on how accurate it is: recognition that the econometric evidence of this quality, even if the best evidence available, is itself not much different from an informal estimate may lead the policymaker to adopt other kinds of policy measures—e.g., partial use of two alternative policies rather than full

use of the one policy measure which would have been preferred if the econometric estimate of the strength of its effects could have been considered accurate.

ADDENDUM: EXAGGERATION OF RELIABILITY BECAUSE OF LAXNESS OF TEST FOR SERIAL CORRELATION

A frequent cause of understatement of the size of the standard error of a regression coefficient is correlation of the discrepancies between the actual and estimated values of the dependent variable at successive points of time. This "serial correlation of residuals" is reflected in sequences of estimated values for the dependent variable that diverge in the same direction from the actual values of the variable. For example, for four successive dates the estimate might exceed the actual and for another three, four, or five it might fall short of the actual. (The existence of such a pattern may be explainable by the neglect of the role of an additional independent variable which tended to depress the value of the dependent variable during the first set of observations and raise it during the second, depress it during the third set, etc.) Where such serial correlation exists, the values of the regression coefficients may be somewhat distorted and their standard errors substantially understated. If these biasing effects of serial correlation are not eliminated, there must exist a strong further cause of apparent but spurious reliability of econometric results.

Recently it has become customary to test for the existence of serial correlation and, when found, to carry out approximately the corrections called for, including enlargement of the reported standard error. The test applied is analogous to that of rejecting the null hypothesis when there is anything over a (supposedly) $2\frac{1}{2}$ per cent chance that the estimated value could have been found even though the true value was zero. However, the popular test for serial correlation (that of Durbin and Watson) is presented so as to be an extremely lax test; it makes it probable that the existence of serial correlation and the associated understatement of standard errors will often be denied when it actually is present.

Whereas the null-hypothesis test requires the presumption of crippling unreliability even if there is only just over a $2\frac{1}{2}$ per cent chance of the given result being found when the true result is zero, the Durbin–Watson test as actually applied requires that the results be presumed free of serial-correlation bias even where the evidence of its presence is so strong that there is only just over a 5 per cent chance that that evidence could have been found when the true underlying relationship was free of serial correlation. In simpler terms, serial correlation is *assumed* to be *absent* when there is anything more than a small, 5 per cent chance that it is absent.[4]

While the preceding may make it unlikely that the given results could have been found if the true amount of serial correlation was zero, it is nevertheless possible that the results are consistent with a comfortable over-50-per cent chance of being found when the true amount of serial correlation was greater than zero but still low enough to prevent serious understatement of standard errors. But even where true, this argument cannot be used, for it cuts two ways: The same possibility of being consistent with substantially *less* serial correlation than what the first step of the test itself indicates holds also for substantially *more* serial correlation than the test indicates. In short, the indicated value for the serial correlation is the best estimate of the value we have, and the fact that it has even a moderate chance of being consistent with a smaller amount of correlation does not justify our departing from that best estimate value.

It will be noted that the downward bias of standard errors due to neglected serial correlation has a multiplicative rather than merely an additive effect on the upward adjustments of standard errors already proposed. For example, a reported $\frac{1}{2}$ per cent probability of 100 per cent error (where that standard error is $\frac{4}{10}$ of its regression coefficient) must be raised to a 16 per cent probability of need to cut the estimated regression coefficient 40 per cent or more and then raised further to a 32 per cent probability of that need because of the multiple testing of alternative hypotheses. But the finding of need for an enlargement of the original standard-error figure itself by, say, one quarter (from $\frac{4}{10}$ to $\frac{5}{10}$ of the regression coefficient) would mean that our final 32 per cent probability of need to cut the coefficient referred to a 50 per cent or greater cut rather than to just a 40 per cent or greater cut. Under these conditions the probability of the original 40 per cent-plus cut would be raised from 32 per cent to 43 per cent.

NOTES

1 On a determinist view, this inaccuracy of the laws of human behavior could be construed simply as a lack of sufficient information on all the causal factors operating on the kind of human action at issue. The laws derived are imprecise ones simply because it has not been possible to measure —or even to identify—the influence of a very large number of very weak factors which participate in the determination of human action. Without necessarily accepting the determinist philosophy, econometricians usually do believe that they are likely to be able to reduce the degree of inaccuracy of laws of behavior they derive through developing statistics on additional factors which up to now have been unavailable or of too low quality to be trustworthy.

2 The econometrician feels more confident of the acceptability of his regression coefficient if it is two and a half times, rather than just twice, its standard error, for then (cf. Figure 1) there is only a $\frac{1}{2}$ to 1 per cent chance of its having been found when the true, average value was zero or less. But

even here the 32 per cent probability would refer to a still serious 40 per cent error. (If the coefficient was three times its error, the 32 per cent probability would refer to a still somewhat serious $33\frac{1}{3}$ per cent error.)

3 A further reason for the neglect of this adjustment is that the separate models tested usually include many of the same causal factors and to that extent are not fully equivalent to the separate tests, each of which added the same probability of error. And in the absence of a suitable formula for converting the number of models into the appropriate—smaller—multiple of truly separate tests, it has not been difficult to suppose that the multiple would be quite small. In any case, our illustrative number, 3, seems a reasonably low multiple, one that ought not exceed and may be below what is actually justified, given the very many models that are usually tested.

4 A clue to the fact that the Durbin–Watson test is the reverse of the null-hypothesis test is provided by the presentation of one writer which indicates that the 1 per cent criterion, instead of being a stricter one, is a laxer criterion (Carl Christ, *Econometric Models and Methods*, New York, 1966, p. 524, and table referred to found on page 672). But Christ does not take an explicit stand on the adequacy of either of these two criteria, stating neutrally: "Suppose that 95 per cent [i.e., the 5 per cent criterion] has been chosen as the best significance level for the test." However, the fact that he publishes only the generally available 1 per cent, $2\frac{1}{2}$ per cent, and 5 per cent tables, without mentioning the need indicated in the present discussion for, say, 10 per cent and 20 per cent tables, implies endorsement of the present standards. (It is possible that Christ wanted to discourage use of the correction for serial correlation except where the bias in the uncorrected form was extremely large, because of distortions which the correction procedure itself can introduce. But such reasoning still requires recognition that the uncorrected equations probably do contain serial correlation and the associated understatement of standard errors.)

A Policy Model for an Open Economy
Jan Tinbergen

4.221   PROBLEM 161. MODEL 16
[EQUATIONS (1)–(17)]

Targets: "full" employment,
  balance of payments equilibrium,
  a given volume of investment,
  a given distribution of income between workers and independents;

meaning that the target variables are a, D, j, and λ;

it depends on the initial situation which numerical values these variables have to assume.

Jan Tinbergen, "Multiple Target Policies for Open Economies," in *Economic Policy: Principles and Design* (Amsterdam: North-Holland Publishing Company, 1967), pp. 116–124, 255- 259.

Instruments: government expenditure C, wage rate l, indirect tax rate τ, and direct tax rate θ.

Comments: this problem is chosen as an example of modern policy, with two targets of a short-run character and the two others representing long-term targets: a given volume of investment being a prerequisite for a certain rate of development and a given distribution being part of a policy of social equilibrium.

4.222.   Evidently we have to solve the system of equations for the values of X_0, l, τ, and θ. Since this problem will be shown—for this model—to be insoluble, it is worth while to go into the process in some detail, using various methods of presentation.

As a first method we use an "arrow

system" constructed in an intuitive way: starting with data and given values of target variables we try to find out which of the irrelevant variables and of the instrument variables (forming, together, our unknowns) can be determined. And it appears that the structure is such as to permit us to go a long way with this "method."

Starting with equation (9) we see that the given value of a enables us to find v; equation (8) then yields i; equation (13) I; together with the given value for D, equation (15) then supplies E. According to (14) and (6)—here we have to combine two equations in order to find our way—they may be written

$$E = (\bar{e} - \varepsilon_1)p \qquad (4201)$$

from which we can find p, and with (6), e. Next, (7) now yields l, our first instrument variable. Also, we can now deduce Y, since equation (1) may be given a somewhat different form in this model, namely,

$$Y = v + \bar{v}p - I \qquad (1')$$

and all the right-hand side members are known.

Remembering now that j is also given, we find from equation (12) the value of J and from v, j, and e, equation (16), the value of c. From (10) C^F can then be calculated. Taking up l again, and com-

bining it with a, according to equation (2), we deduce L; Z can now be found with the help of equation (3).

4.223. Here our first important result emerges: now that we know both L and Z, *we cannot prescribe a ratio λ between them*, as equation (17) and our fourth target would require us to do: this social equilibrium target is not therefore compatible with the other targets so far used to find Z and L, i.e. only a and D. Of course this incompatibility only applies to the specific model now considered, including the choice of instruments. With one more instrument intervening in one of the relations so far used, it would be possible to reconcile the targets a, D, and λ.

4.224. The second important result is the counterpart of the first one; it is that the two instruments not yet calculated, namely C_0 and τ, *cannot be calculated separately*. This is most easily seen if we eliminate C from our equations by substituting (11) into (4):

$$\bar{c}(p + \tau) + (1 + \bar{\tau})c \\ = C_0 + \gamma(1 - \bar{\theta})Z - \gamma\bar{Z}\theta + L \quad (4')$$

Having eliminated C we do not need equation (11) any more in our system and (4') is now the only equation left in which both the unknowns τ and C_0 appear. It follows that one of them can be chosen

Figure 4.225. Logical Structure of Problem 161
Symbols in fully drawn squares indicate data; those in fully drawn circles are targets and those in dotted circles (unknown) instrument values. Simon ordering is indicated below.

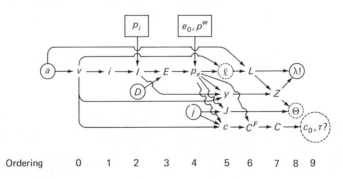

Ordering   0   1   2   3   4   5   6   7   8   9

Table 4.225. Equations for Problem 161

EQ. ↓	VAR.: →	v	i	I	E	p	e	l	Y	J	c	L	C^F	Z	θ	τ	C_0
9	$a =$	αv															
8	$0 =$	w	$-i$														
13	$0 =$		i	$-I$													
15	$D =$			I	$-E$												
14	$0 =$				E	$-\bar{e}p$	$-e$										
6	$0 =$					$+\varepsilon_1 p$	$+e$										
7	$0 =$	$\pi_1 v$				$-p$		$+\pi_2 l$									
1′	$0 =$	v				$+\bar{v}p$			$-Y$								
12	$j =$			$-I$		$-jp$				$+J$							
16	$j =$	v															
2	$La =$						$-e$	$-\bar{L}l$									
10	$0 =$					$\bar{c}p$					$-c$	$+L$					
3	$0 =$										$+c$	$+L$	$-C^F$	$+Z$			
5	$0 =$								$-Y$	$-J$	$+c$	$+L$		$+(1-\gamma)(1-\theta)Z + \lambda Z$	$-(1-\gamma)\bar{Z}\theta$		
17	$0 =$											$-L$		$\gamma(1-\theta)Z$			
4	$0 =$					$-\bar{c}p$					$-(1+\bar{\tau})c$	$+L$			$\gamma\bar{Z}\theta$	$-\bar{c}\tau$	$+C_0$

freely, and only then can the other be derived. The phenomena just discovered may also be formulated thus. If we had eliminated all the irrelevant variables and thus retained only four equations in the four unknown instruments, we would have found that in three of these four equations the values of the two instruments l and θ only would have occurred, whereas in the fourth equation only the two others, τ and C_0, would have occurred. This has the two consequences just stated; on the one hand the first three equations cannot be satisfied at the same time, meaning that the targets cannot all be reached at the same time, whereas the fourth equation is not sufficient to yield us the two remaining instruments.

4.225. The logical structure just discussed can be symbolized in the arrow scheme of Figure 4.225. Here the symbols are those used in the equations; target variables are indicated by a fully drawn circle; data have been indicated by a square (these data do not occur in model 16, but might have easily been added in the same way as in model 12).

4.226. As another presentation of the same state of affairs we use Herbert Simon's causal ordering, which primarily comes down to writing the equations in another order: (see p. 57).

4.227. From this presentation it is easily seen that the matrix of the system of equations is almost triangular; the exception being that in equation (14) a term $-e$ appears; and the implication being that, with that exception, every unknown can be calculated in succession from the others. This is, however, not possible with the unknowns τ and C_0, since these only occur in the last equation; they cannot be calculated separately. In [return] the last-but-one equation (17) only contains variables (L and Z) that have already been determined and that will then satisfy equation (17) only by pure coincidence. Simon's "ordering" can be

read from Table 4.225. Variables v, i, I, and E are of orders 0, 1, 2, and 3, respectively; variables p and e of order 4. Variables l, Y, J, and c are of the order 5. In our arrow scheme this is brought out by their being placed in one (vertical) column. Similarly, L and C^F are of order 6, Z is of order 7, θ of order 8, and $-c\tau + C_0$ of order 9.

4.228. One last remark, one of *economic interpretation*, may be made. Upon closer consideration it will be clear that in this model and with the targets and instruments chosen, the instrument τ is irrelevant by itself; it only influences the internal price level for consumer goods; if it is raised, private consumption will fall but it may do so without changing anything else if only C_0, public consumption, is raised accordingly. It is only the two types of consumption together that matter for the balance of payments, for employment, or for incomes.

4.231 PROBLEM 162. MODEL 16 [EQUATIONS (1)–(16) AND (17′)]

Targets: "full" employment,
balance of payments equilibrium,
a given volume of investment,
a given internal price level.
Instruments: public expenditure,
the wage rate,
the indirect tax rate,
the direct tax rate.

Comments: by a slight change in the problem we have now presented a soluble problem. In addition, this problem may be considered a good example of modern economic policy, the emphasis now being laid on a somewhat different aspect of social policy: the protection of fixed incomes and of savings. (We already stated that the aim of a certain distribution of income between workers and independents might also have been brought in, but would have required the introduction of another instrument.)

4.232. After what has been said about the solution of problem 161 we may be brief here and only reproduce both the arrow scheme and the Simon arrangement of the equations (cf. Figure 4.232[1] and table 4.232).

4.233. We will now proceed to the *numerical solution* in order to be able to discuss the orders of magnitude of the changes in instruments necessary to attain the targets. Using the values of the coefficients and constants indicated in model 16 we will obtain, in the order of Table 4.232, the expressions of the instrument and the irrelevant variables in terms of the targets:

Solutions of problem 162:

$$v = \quad 2.5\ a \qquad (4202)$$
$$i = \quad 0.84a \qquad (4203)$$
$$I = \quad 0.84a \qquad (4204)$$
$$E = \quad 0.84a - \qquad D \qquad (4205)$$
$$p = -1.68a + 2 \quad D \qquad (4206)$$
$$e = \quad 1.68a - 2 \quad D \qquad (4207)$$
$$*l = -5.8\ a + 6 \quad D \qquad (4208)$$
$$Y = -0.86a + 3 \quad D \qquad (4209)$$
$$J = -0.16a + 0.2\ D + \quad j \qquad (4210)$$
$$c = \quad 0.82a + 2 \quad D - \quad j \qquad (4211)$$
$$L = -2.41a + 3 \quad D \qquad (4212)$$
$$C^F = -0.70a + 3.8\ D - \quad j \qquad (4213)$$

$$C = -0.90a + 2.2\ D - 1.1j$$
$$+ 0.9p' \qquad (4214)$$
$$Z = \quad 1.55a \qquad (4215)$$
$$*\theta = \quad 3.27a - 1.33D - 6.7j \qquad (4216)$$
$$*\tau = \quad 1.68a - 2 \quad D$$
$$+ \quad p' \qquad (4217)$$
$$*C_0 = \quad 3.71a - 1.27D - 3.4j$$
$$+ 0.9p' \qquad (4218)$$

4.234. The solutions with an asterisk refer to *instruments* and hence are of particular interest. They enable us to compute, for whatever change in targets we desire, the necessary values of the instrument variables. In order to illustrate their use let us suppose that a country finds itself faced with a deficit in the balance of payments of 10 per cent of current items, i.e. $D = 0.05$; if it is desired to eliminate this deficit while maintaining employment, the rate of investment, and the internal price level, our targets will be $D = -0.05$, $a = j = p' = 0$; and we easily deduce that $l = -0.3$, $\theta = +0.07$, $\tau = 0.1$, and $C_0 = 0.06$, a very drastic programme indeed: the wage rate should be reduced by 30 per cent, direct taxes increased from 0.3 to 0.37, i.e. by some 23 per cent, indirect taxes from 0.1 to 0.2, i.e. doubled, and public expenditure be increased from 0.25 to 0.31, i.e. by some 25 per cent.

Figure 4.232. Logical Structure of Problem 162 (For explanation cf. Figure 4.225.)

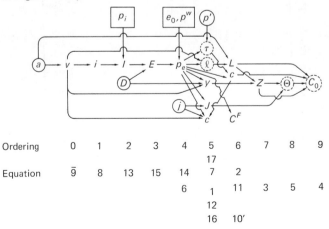

Ordering	0	1	2	3	4	5	6	7	8	9
						17				
Equation	$\bar{9}$	8	13	15	14	7	2			
					6	1	11	3	5	4
						12				
						16	10'			

Table 4.232. Equations for Problem 162

EQ. ↓	VAR. →	v	i	I	E	p	e	l	Y	J	c	L	C^F	Z	θ	τ	C_0
9	$a =$	αv															
8	$0 =$		$w - i$														
13	$0 =$		i	$- I$													
15	$D =$			I	$- E$												
14	$0 =$				E	$- \bar{e}p$	$- e$										
6	$0 =$					$+ \varepsilon_1 p$	$+ e$										
7	$0 =$	$\pi_1 v$				$- p$		$+ \pi_2 l$									
1'	$0 =$	v				$+ \bar{v}p$			$- Y$								
12	$j =$	v		$- I$													
16	$j =$	v				$- jp$	$- e$			$+ J$							
2	$La =$						$- e$	$- \bar{L}l$									
10	$0 =$					$\bar{c}p$					$- c$	$+ L$					
3	$0 =$										$+ c$		$- C^F$				
5	$0 =$								$- Y$		$+ c$	$+ L$		$+ (1 - \gamma)(1 - \theta)Z$	$- (1 - \gamma)\bar{Z}\theta$	$+ \tau$	
17'	$p' =$					p				$- J$							
4	$0 =$					$- \bar{c}p$					$- (1 + \bar{\tau})c$	$+ L$		$+ \gamma(1 - \theta)Z$	$- \gamma\bar{Z}\theta$	$- \bar{c}\tau$	$+ C_0$

60

4.235. This programme would, in most countries, be *politically impossible*; in our terminology, *boundary conditions* would be transgressed and a less ambitious programme should be accepted. Our formulae enable us to investigate a large number of possibilities. There are some remarkable further conclusions to be drawn: if, in particular, the huge reduction in wage rate should, rightly, be deemed impossible, the only change in targets that can help to overcome this difficulty is either a change in the balance of payments target or a change in the employment target: the other target variables to not enter into (4208). For each per cent less employment 6 per cent less wage reduction could be "bought." Surely this statement does not apply to real wage rates; they can be easily calculated to be

$$l^R = l - p' = -5.8a + 6D - p'$$

and evidently depend on the internal price target as well; still not, however, on the investment target.

4.236. Suppose now we choose the targets $D = -0.03$, $a = -0.01$, $j = 0$,

and $p' = -0.05$; we find $l = -0.12$, $\theta = 0.01$, $\tau = -0.007$, and $C_0 = -0.044$; implying that real wage rates will now have to be down 7 per cent "only." The striking feature is the very important place taken in these problems by the wage rate.

4.237. The reader should be aware of the simple structure of the solution now discussed; in particular it should be mentioned that for this same model the analytical method would be much more cumbersome: the matrix of the system of equations then becomes far from triangular and the causal ordering much less simple. This is not an incidental property of the example chosen; it is closely related to the role played by the two main targets, full employment and balance of payments equilibrium. Had a and D been among the unknowns, the interrelations between the unknowns would have been much more complicated.

NOTES

1 This graph was constructed independently by B. Hansen (cf. *Finanspolitikens ekonomiska teori*, p. 364).

Model 16. Open, Static, Micro, Money, Product and Factor Flow, and Public Finance Model

---

ACTORS	*Number:*	4, wage earners, independents, government, and "rest of the world."
	Income:	*wage earners:* total wages; supply of labour inelastic;
		independents: net national income minus wages; supply of products not inelastic;
		government: direct and indirect tax receipts minus expenditure;
		rest of the world: not specified.
	Spending habits:	*wage earners* spend all income on consumer goods;
		independents spend all income after direct tax, in a fixed proportion between consumer and investment goods;
		government spending is independent of tax receipts (but if exact balance of payments equilibrium is a target of policy it follows that there will be equality between income and expenditure);
		rest of the world: demand for export products not inelastic.

Model 16.—*continued*

MARKETS

Number: 5, consumer goods and investment goods sold at home; export goods sold abroad, import commodity, and labour.

TECHNICAL RELATIONS

Imports and labour assumed to be linearly dependent on volume of production.

EQUATIONS

All variables are deviations from initial situation.

Income formation: total income:

$$Y = C^F + J + E - I \tag{1}$$

Because of the distinction made between consumer and investment goods the term X in previous models has now been split into $C^F + J$. Because of the existence of indirect taxes (only levied from home-sold consumer goods) a distinction between the value of home-sold consumer goods at market prices C and at factor cost C^F has to be made. The relation between these two variables is given by eqs. (10) and (11).

wages: $L = \bar{L}(a + l)$ (2)

The form of this equation differs from equations like (8)–(10) in model 12 (where they first appeared), because a is not measured in the same way as e.g. x in equation (8) in model 12; $\bar{a}$ is an index number of employment with its base value $\bar{a} = 1$.

independents' income: $Z = \bar{Y} - L$ (3)

Demand: consumer goods at home market: $C = C_0 + \gamma(1 - \hat{\theta})Z - \gamma\bar{Z}\theta + L$ (4)

In this equation the first term represents government expenditure and the last term consumer expenditure by workers. The two remaining terms derive from the expression for consumption expenditure by independents C_z of which the absolute amount is given by

$$\bar{C}_z = \gamma(1 - \hat{\theta})\bar{Z}$$

i.e. the proportion γ of income after direct tax. The assumptions involved are relatively simple, e.g. a proportionate tax on $\bar{Z}$ and a fixed average propensity to consume. It would not be difficult to generalize these assumptions; this may be left to the reader.

investment goods at home market: $J = (1 - \gamma)(1 - \hat{\theta})Z - (1 - \gamma)\bar{Z}\theta$ (5)

This equation expresses that the remainder of income after tax $\bar{Z}(1 - \hat{\theta})$, after deducting consumption from income, is invested.

Model 16.—*continued*

$$\text{export goods: } e = -\varepsilon_1 p \tag{6}$$

Here the autonomous component in export demand e_0 has been assumed to be unchanged ($e_0 = 0$); further it is assumed that prices of all products (consumer goods, investment goods, and export goods) are the same ("national price level" p) and that no indirect taxes are paid on export goods.

$$\text{Supply: price fixation equation: } p = \pi_1 v + \pi_2 l \tag{7}$$

Since foreign prices and the exchange rate are assumed not to vary, this equation takes its simplest form. It would not be difficult to introduce equations with different coefficients for consumer goods, investment goods, and export goods.

$$\text{Technical: } i = w \tag{8}$$

$$a = \alpha v \tag{9}$$

These equations express proportionality between changes in production volume on the one hand, and imports as well as volume of labour employed on the other hand.

$$\text{Definition: } C^F = \bar{c}p + c \tag{10}$$

$$C = \bar{c}(p + \tau) + (1 + \bar{\tau})c \tag{11}$$

$$J = jp + j \tag{12}$$

$$I = i \tag{13}$$

$$E = \bar{e}p + e \tag{14}$$

$$D = I - E \tag{15}$$

$$v = c + j + e \tag{16}$$

$$\text{Social equilibrium coefficient: } L = \lambda Z \tag{17}$$

This equation expresses the fact that a certain preconceived ratio between increases in labour income and "non-labour" income may be aimed at.

Alternatively this equation will be replaced by another defining the home price level for consumer goods:

$$p' = p + \tau \tag{17'}$$

The numerical values of the coefficients and constants will be chosen in a way similar to the one followed with model 14, but slightly different only where the simpler structure of 16 makes this necessary. This refers primarily to the neglect of the difference between home prices and export prices, as to their response to competing prices abroad. Apart from this feature, short-term reaction coefficients have been chosen for a country with imports normally equal to one-half of net national income. Model 16 is more complicated than model 14 as regards the fiscal structure; accordingly some new assumptions as to this sector have been necessary. All price indices are equal to 1 in the base period.

We have chosen $\bar{L} = \bar{Z} = \bar{e} = 0.5$, meaning that in the base period net national income at factor cost $\bar{Y} = 1$ and is distributed in equal parts between workers and independents; in addition, exports (and imports $\bar{i}$) = 0.5. The factor value of consumption $\bar{C}^F = \bar{c} = 0.9$, that of investment $\bar{j} = 0.1$. The tax rates are $\bar{\tau} = 0.1$, meaning an indirect tax of some 11 per cent on home consumption and $\bar{\theta} = 0.3$, meaning a tax of 30 per cent on non-labour income. Taxes on labour income are taken as zero. The marginal propensity to consume γ for independents, calculated on the basis of income *after* tax, = 0.7, and the marginal propensity to invest = 0.3, almost equal to the average propensity in the base period:

$$\frac{0.1}{0.7 \times 0.5}$$

The elasticity of demand for export products has again been taken = 2, making $\varepsilon_1 = 1$; the flexibility of the home price level is taken as 0.15, equivalent with $\pi_1 = 0.1$; the wage coefficient in prices, $\pi_1 = 0.33$, exactly corresponds to the average labour quota in the base period:

$$\frac{\bar{L}}{\bar{v}} = \frac{0.5}{1.5}$$

The marginal import quota ι has also been taken to equal the average quota:

$$0.33 \left(= \frac{0.5}{1.5} \right)$$

Finally, the marginal labour quota in equation (9) has been taken less than the average labour quota, actually about 0.55 times that quota, in accordance with numerous investigations[1]; $a = 0.40$ seems to be a fair estimate. That the wage coefficient in prices is nevertheless equal to the average labour quota probably has to be explained by the custom of calculating some of the entrepreneurial income on the basis of the prevailing wage level.

NOTES

1 P. J. Verdoorn, *Praeadvies 1952 voor de Vereniging voor de Staathuishoudkunde*, where a slightly lower figure has been chosen. Our figure has to be considered as a round figure.

Summary

Gerhard Tintner, "Some Thoughts About the State of Econometrics," in Sherman Roy Krupp (ed.), *The Structure of Economic Science* (Englewood Cliffs, N.J.: Prentice-Hall, Inc., 1968), pp. 114–128.

The author surveys the entire field of econometrics and related sciences (input–output, linear programing models, demand function, supply function, and inventory models).

Tintner first defines econometrics as the application of mathematical statistics to models constructed with the help of mathematical economic theory. He then traces the interrelationship of econometrics and economic theory. He states that most econometric models are static, and adds that those few that are dynamic neglect the most realistic models of risk and uncertainty. He goes on to say that macro models are needed for dealing with really crucial problems of policy. He feels, however, that the aggregation problem has not been fully solved so far and that this must be done before a successful macro model can be built.

Tintner also discusses the statistical problems connected with the verification of econometric models, and he develops a proposal for stochastic models.

Bibliography

Paul A. Samuelson, "Dynamic Process Analysis," in Howard S. Ellis (ed.), *A Survey of Contemporary Economics* (Homewood, Ill.: Richard D. Irwin, Inc., Vol. I, 1945), pp. 352–357

J. Tinbergen, *Centralization and Decentralization in Economic Policy* (Amsterdam: North Holland Publishing Company, 1954), pp. 1–44.

3
GENERAL EQUILIBRIUM OF INCOME AND EMPLOYMENT

One of the greatest contributions Lord Keynes made to the body of economic knowledge was his concept of general equilibrium. Since the appearance of the *General Theory* on the economic scene, much theoretical work has been done by economists in their efforts to determine not only how general equilibrium can be achieved but also those factors which might cause economic disturbances once such an equilibrium is reached.

In the first article in this part, Shackle discusses the nature of general equilibrium in economic theory. His article is followed by Patinkin's, in which the author analyzes in highly theoretical terms the effects of changes in the level of an economy's prices.

The Concept of Equilibrium
G. L. S. Shackle

Why study equilibrium? Why investigate minutely the bearings and interpretation of an idea seemingly so artificial and remote from experience? This question may simply mean: Why have a theory at all? A theory or a model, as we sought to show, is intentionally and designedly phantasmal and is of set purpose constructed with only a minute percentage of the immense assortment of impressions that life supplies. If we do not care to see the wood, but are only interested in the trees, we need make no effort to select a viewpoint, to marshal the scene into a composition, to have some control over the army of observations or records. If we

G. L. S. Shackle, "Equilibrium," in *A Scheme of Economic Theory* (Cambridge: Cambridge University Press, 1965), pp. 23–26.

are content to gulp the stream of conscious life down without seeking in it any general structure or orderliness beyond its obvious small-scale stereotypes of action and effect which we recognize and use for living from minute to minute, we need no general theory. To seek insight is to theorize. But beyond this general challenge to theorizing itself, what of the efficacy, efficiency, and value of this particular specimen of theory, the concept of equilibrium? Two main propositions together compose the case in its favour. First, it reveals coherence and single-mindedness in the complex conduct of the individual. He is seen by all of us to do all sorts of things with all sorts of means, materials, and tools. Does this mean that he is aimless or hopelessly confused by distracting and conflicting stimuli or pressures? On the contrary, we are well convinced that he or she is seeking the maximum possible fulfilment of a unified plan of life, even if this plan is not explicit in the individual's mind. The measure as well the nature of this fulfilment is a state of mind, but the degree to which this state is attained depends on a fine balance of technically diverse uses of basic resources limited in quantity. Equilibrium shows the action-chooser as endeavouring to "get the most" out of his limited strength, skill, and material possessions. He has a purpose and pursues it with the nearest approach to rationality which is open to him. Secondly, the equilibrium model makes the simplest and most natural assumption about the "rules of the game" within which this attempt takes place, namely, that these rules are the same for all the players. It does not assume that these players all have equal strength and skill, equally ample and excellent equipment.

Equilibrium is a paradox, for in it each rival interest serves itself by offering advantages to all the others. These advantages consist essentially of knowledge, knowledge for each man of what alternative results he can attain for himself by this or that action of his own. He buys this knowledge about his own environment by contributing his own conditional promise to the general pool. Equilibrium is action subject to rules which ensure the essential communication. Because of these rules, freedom is not perfect, but because of them also, it is *equal*, and because of them, finally, *knowledge* is (relevantly) perfect and therefore also equal. Only endowment can be unequal, and the consequence of this possible inequality we shall consider below.

In the paradox of equilibrium the members of society, acting in equality of freedom each in pursuit of his own interest, yet compose a coherent whole. This coherence of action amongst uncoerced individuals arises from coherence of knowledge. Certain facts are public and correct and are taken account of by all individuals. When we confine ourselves to the economic model, this publicly available and general basis for choice consists in the prices of all goods, which prices signal to all members of society the fact and implications of particular conduct on the part of others. Upon this all-pervasive web of communication rests the most important single fact which economics has to convey, namely, the universal interdependence of the conduct of human beings: my conduct has, in however slight degree, consequences for everyone else, and what results I have the power to bring about depend upon what actions are chosen by others.

Equilibrium, as we have here interpreted this term, is the set of actions chosen by the members of the society in equal freedom and equal and perfect relevant knowledge. But these two equalities imply nothing as to tastes, capacities, or means. How much a man possesses and how much he can enjoy whatever he possesses are questions not connected in any simple way with the questions of what he knows and whether the formal "rules of the game" are identical for all people including himself. Thus what we have discerned as to the nature and meaning of equilibrium does not directly talk to us of *welfare* when that word is applied, legitimately or not, to the whole of the society. To complete our discussion of equilibrium we must make an excursion into so-called *welfare economics*.

If general equilibrium gives to each person the best that his circumstances allow, when we include in those circumstances the results of the equal freedom which it accords to every other person to strive for his best position; then it is natural to ask whether this equality of freedom and of knowledge, and this perfect adjustability of all elements, such as prices and quantities exchanged, which are the defining conditions and the necessary foundation of equilibrium, ensure in some sense an absolute best position for the people of the society all taken together? Though this question is natural, it cannot be answered until we have sorted out its implications. The solution, the specified set of actions for all the people of the economy, which in the timeless exchange economy means simply the quantities of some goods given up and of others received by each person, will be different if we start with a different initial situation, this initial situation consisting in the means of action possessed by person A, by person B, and so on. It is natural that a different problem should have a different answer. Thus we have to ask whether one distribution of means of action, of goods initially possessed, is better than another. There may be sense in the statement that if *everybody* has larger means in position R than in position S, position R is better; though this statement ought really to be interpreted as meaning: "No matter whom you ask, he will say that, for him, position R is better." But we cannot make any sense of a claim that R is better because, although some people are worse off in R than in S, this fact is outweighed by the fact that others are better off. There

is no meaning in a comparison between one person's happiness and another's. Let us not confuse this statement with another which is concerned with two possible states of happiness of *one and the same person*, who, therefore, is in a position to judge between them: "Your happiness, when I see plain evidence of it, makes me happy. And thus if your evident happiness increases enough, this will more than make good a deterioration in the rest of my circumstances." The latter statement involves only one person's judgement and preferences, and so it is meaningful and self-consistent. We can no more add together judgements made by different individuals, each, necessarily, from that individual's own, perculiar, special viewpoint and constructed with his own inimitable private, personal criteria, than we can make an intelligible perspective drawing, partly from one and partly from another viewpoint. When we ask whether situation R, in which each separate person has more goods than he has in situation S, is the better of the two, we can answer: "Everyone thinks so." But if we then go on to ask: "Do they, then, all think the same?" the answer is that the question really means nothing.

Price Flexibility and Full Employment[*]
Don Patinkin[†]

At the core of the Keynesian polemics of the past ten years and more is the relationship between price flexibility and full

Don Patinkin, "Price Flexibility and Full Employment," in F. A. Lutz and Lloyd W. Mints (eds.), *Readings in Monetary Theory* (Homewood, Ill.: Richard D. Irwin, Inc., 1951), pp. 252–283.

** Originally published in *American Economic Review*, 38 (1948), 543–564. Reprinted, by the courtesy of the publisher and the

employment. The fundamental argument of Keynes is directed against the belief that price flexibility can be depended upon to generate full employment automatically. The defenders of the classical tradition, on the other hand, still insist upon this automaticity as a basic tenet.

During the years of continuous debate on this question, the issues at stake have been made more precise. At the same time, further material on the question of flexibility has become available. This paper is essentially an attempt to incorporate this new material, and, taking advantage of the perspective offered by time, to analyze the present state of the debate.

In Part I, the problem of price flexibility and full employment is presented from a completely static viewpoint. Part II then goes on to discuss the far more important dynamic aspects of the problem. Finally, in Part III, the implications of the discussion for the Keynesian–classical polemic are analyzed. It is shown that over the years these two camps have really come closer and closer together. It is argued that the basic issue separating them is the rapidity with which the economic system responds to price variations.

I. STATIC ANALYSIS

1. The traditional interpretation of Keynesian economics is that it demonstrates the absence of an automatic mechanism assuring the equality of desired savings and investment at full

---

author. (Advantage has been taken of this reprinting to correct and modify several parts of the article. The major changes are the following: the addition of the latter part of the last paragraph of § 5, as a result of discussions with Milton Friedman; the addition of paragraphs three and four of § 6, as a result of comments by Donald Gordon, Franco Modigliani, and Norman Ture; the correction of the last paragraph of § 6 and Table 1 of § 11 in accordance with Herbert Stein's comment on the original article in the *American Economic Review*, 39 (1949), 725–726; and the addition of the last three paragraphs of § 14, in the attempt to clarify some points left ambiguous in the original article. All significant additions are enclosed in brackets.)

† In the process of writing this paper the author acknowledges having benefited from stimulating discussions with Milton Friedman, University of Chicago, and Alexander M. Henderson, University of Manchester.

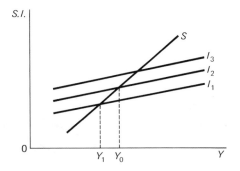

Figure 1

employment. The graphical meaning of this interpretation is presented in a simplified form in Figure 1. Here desired real savings (S) and investment (I) are each assumed to depend only on the level of real income (Y). I_1, I_2, and I_3 represent three possible positions of the investment schedule. Y_0 is the full employment level of real income. If the investment desires of individuals are represented by the curve I_1, desired savings at full employment are greater than desired investment at full employment. This means that unemployment will result: the level of income will drop to Y_1, at which income desired savings and investment are equal. Conversely, if I_3 is the investment curve, a situation of overemployment or inflation will occur: people desire to invest more at full employment than the amount of savings will permit.Only if the investment schedule happened to be I_2 would full employment, desired investment, and savings be equal. But since investment decisions are independent of savings decisions, there is no reason to expect the investment schedule to coincide with I_2. Hence there is no automatic assurance that full employment will result.

2. The classical answer to this attack is that desired savings and investment depend on the rate of interest, as well as the level of real income; and that, granted flexibility, variations in the interest rate

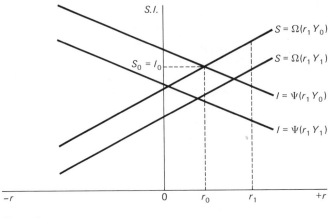

Figure 2

serve as an automatic mechanism insuring full employment.

The argument can be interpreted as follows: the savings and investment functions (representing what people desire to do) are written as

$$S = \Omega(r, Y)$$
$$I = \Psi(r, Y)$$

where r represents the rate of interest.

Consider now Figure 2. On this graph there can be drawn a whole family of curves relating savings and investment to the rate of interest—one pair for each level of real income. In Figure 2, these pairs of curves are drawn for the full employment income, Y_0, and for the less than full employment income, Y_1. On the assumption that for a given rate of interest people will save and invest more at a higher level of income, the investment curve corresponding to $Y = Y_0$ is drawn above that corresponding to $Y = Y_1$; similarly for the two savings curves. The curves also reflect the assumption that, for a given level of real income, people desire to save more and invest less at higher rates of interest.

Consider now the pair of curves corresponding to the full employment income Y_0. If in Figure 2 the interest rate were r_1,

then it would be true that individuals would desire to save more at full employment than they would desire to invest. But, assuming no rigidities in the interest rate, this would present no difficulties. For if the interest rate were to fall freely, savings would be discouraged, and investment stimulated until finally desired full employment savings and investment would be equated at the level $S_0 = I_0$. Similarly, if at full employment desired investment is greater than desired savings, a rise in the interest rate will prevent inflation. In this way variations in the rate of interest serve automatically to prevent any discrepancy between desired full employment investment and savings, and thus to assure full employment.

This argument can also be presented in terms of Figure 1: assume for simplicity that desired investment depends on the rate of interest as well as the level of real income, while desired savings depends only on the latter. Then downward variations in the interest rate can be counted on to raise the investment curve from, say, I_1 to I_2. That is, at any level of income people can be encouraged to invest more by a reduction in the rate of interest. Similarly, upward movements of the interest rate will shift the investment curve from, say, I_3 to I_2. Thus desired full employment savings and investment will always be equated.

3. The Keynesian answer to this classical argument is that it greatly exaggerates the importance of the interest rate. Empirical evidence has accumulated in support of the hypothesis that variations in the rate of interest have little effect on the amount of desired investment. (That savings are insensitive to the interest rate is accepted even by the classical school.) This insensitivity has been interpreted as a reflection of the presence of widespread uncertainty.[1] The possible effect of this insensitivity on the ability of the system automatically to generate full employment is analyzed in Figure 3. For simplicity the savings functions corresponding to different levels of income are reproduced from Figure 2. But the investment functions are now represented as being much less interest-sensitive than those in Figure 2. If the situation in the real world were such as represented in Figure 3, it is clear that interest rate variations could never bring about full employment. For in an economy in which there are negligible costs of storing money, the interest rate can never be negative.[2] But from Figure 3 we see that the only way the interest rate

can equate desired full employment savings and investment is by assuming the negative value r_2. Hence it is impossible for the full employment national income Y_0 to exist: for no matter what (positive) rate of interest may prevail, the amount people want to save at full employment exceeds what they want to invest. Instead there will exist some less than full employment income (say) Y_1 for which desired savings and investment can be brought into equality at a positive rate of interest (say) r_3 (cf. Figure 3).

Thus once again the automaticity of the system is thrown into question. Whether the system will generate full employment depends on whether the full employment savings and investment functions intersect at a positive rate of interest. But there is no automatic mechanism to assure that the savings and investment functions will have the proper slopes and positions to bring about such an intersection.[3]

4. Sometimes attempts are made to defend the classical position by arguing that the investment function is really higher (or the savings function lower) than represented by the Keynesians—so that desired full employment savings and investment can be equated at a positive rate of interest (cf. Figure 3). But this is beside

Figure 3

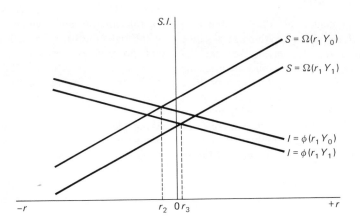

the point. [The fundamental disagreement between Keynesian and classical economics lies in the former's denial of the automaticity of full employment posited by the latter.] Hence a successful restatement of the classical position must demonstrate the existence of some automatic mechanism which will always bring about full employment. Thus to argue that *if* the investment or saving function is at a certain level, full employment will be brought about is irrelevant; what must be shown is that there exist forces which will *automatically* bring the investment or saving functions to the required level. In other words, the issue at stake is not the *possible*, but the *automatic*, generation of full employment.

5. [To the Keynesian negative interest rate argument replies have been made by both Haberler and Pigou.[4] Just as the crude Keynesian argument of § 1 was answered by introducing a new variable— the rate of interest—into the savings function, so the more refined argument of § 3 is countered by the introduction of yet another variable—the real value of cash balances held by the individuals in the economy. Thus, denoting the amount of money in the economy M_1 (assumed to remain constant) and the absolute price level by p, Pigou's saving schedule is written as

$$S = \Gamma\left(r, \, Y, \frac{M_1}{p}\right)\Big]$$

His argument is as follows: if people would refuse to save anything at negative and zero rates of interest, then the desired savings schedule would intersect the desired investment schedule at a positive rate of interest regardless of the level of income (cf. Figure 3). The willingness to save even without receiving interest, or even at a cost, must imply that savings are not made solely for the sake of future income (i.e., interest) but also for "the desire for possession as such, conformity to tradition or custom and so on."[5] But

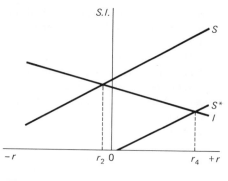

Figure 4

the extent to which an individual wishes to save out of current income for reasons other than the desire of future income is inversely related to the real value of his cash balances.[6] If this is sufficiently large, all his secondary desires for saving will be fully satisfied. At this point the only reason he will continue to save out of current income is the primary one of anticipated future interest payments. In other words, if the real value of cash balances is sufficiently large, the savings function becomes zero at a positive rate of interest, regardless of the income level.

A graphical interpretation of this argument is presented in Figure 4. Here S and I are the full-employment savings and investment curves of Figure 3 (i.e., those corresponding to $Y = Y_0$), and r_2 is again the negative rate of interest at which they are equal. Pigou then argues that by increasing the real value of cash balances, the full employment savings curve shifts to the right until it is in such a position that no savings are desired except at positive rates of interest. This is represented by the savings curve S^*, which becomes zero for a positive rate of interest. (In fact, S^* shows dissaving taking place for sufficiently low rates of interest.) The full employment savings curve S^* clearly intersects the full employment investment curve I at the positive rate of interest r_4. Thus by changing the real value of cash balances, desired full employment savings and investment can always be equated at a positive rate of interest.

How can we be sure that real cash balances will automatically change in the required direction and magnitude? Here Pigou brings in his assumptions of flexible wage and price levels, and a constant stock of money in circulation. If full employment saving exceeds investment, national income begins to fall, and unemployment results. If workers react to this by decreasing their money wages, then the price level will also begin to fall. As the latter continues to fall, the real value of the constant stock of money increases correspondingly. Thus, as the price level falls, the full employment saving function continuously shifts to the right until it intersects the full employment investment function at a positive rate of interest.[7]

This is the automatic mechanism on which Haberler and Pigou rely to assure full employment. It is essential to note that it will operate regardless of the interest-elasticities of the savings and investment functions—provided they are not both identically zero. [It should also be emphasized, as Haberler does, that although this argument has been presented above as an answer to Keynes, it is of much older origin. In particular, it is implicit in classical theorizing on the quantity theory of money. The crucial step in this analysis, it will be recalled, comes at the point where it is argued that as a result of increasing the amount of money in the economy, individuals' cash balances are larger than desired at the existing price level, so that they will attempt to reduce these real balances by increasing their money expenditures. The main contribution of Haberler and Pigou is to show how this set of forces must, and can, be introduced into the Keynesian analytical apparatus.]

6. The inner mechanism and distinctive characteristic of the Pigou analysis can be laid bare by considering it from a larger perspective. It is obvious that a price reduction has a stimulating effect on creditors. But, restricting ourselves to the private sector of a closed economy, to every stimulated creditor there corresponds a discouraged debtor. Hence from this viewpoint the net effect of a price reduction is likely to be in the neighborhood of zero. The neatness of the Pigou approach lies in its utilizing the fact that although the private sector considered in isolation is, on balance, neither debtor nor creditor, when considered in its relationship to the government, it *must be* a net "creditor." This is due to the fact that the private sector always holds money, which is a (non-interest bearing) "debt" of government. It we assume that government activity is not affected by the movements of the absolute price level,[8] then the net effect of a price decline must always be stimulatory.[9] The community gains at the "expense" of a gracious government, ready, willing, and able to bear the "loss" of the increased value of its "debt" to the public.

More precisely, not every price decline need have this stimulating effect. For we must consider the effect of the price decline on the other assets held by the individual. If the decline reduces the real value of these other assets (e.g., houses and other forms of consumer capital; stock shares; etc.) to an extent more than offsetting the increased value of real cash balances,[10] then the net effect will be discouraging. But the important point is that no matter what our initial position, *there exists* a price level sufficiently low so that the total real value of assets corresponding to it is greater than the original real value. Consider the extreme case in which the value of the other assets becomes arbitrarily small.[11] Clearly even here the real value of the fixed stock of money can be made as large as desired by reducing the price level sufficiently. Thus, to be rigorous, the statement in the preceding paragraph should read: "There always exists a price decline such that its effect is stimulatory." From this and the analysis of the preceding section, we can derive another statement which succinctly summarizes the results of the Pigou analysis: "In the static classical model, regardless of the position of the investment schedule, there always exists a sufficiently low price level such that full employment is generated." In any event, it is clearly sufficient to concentrate (as Pigou has done) on cash balances alone.[12]

[This analysis is subject to at least two reservations, neither one of which has been considered by Haberler or Pigou. First of all, we have tacitly been assuming that the depressing effect of a price decline on a debtor is roughly offset by its stimulating effect on a creditor; hence the private sector, being on balance a creditor with respect to the government, can ultimately be stimulated by a price decline. But allowance must be made for the possibility of a differential reaction of debtors and creditors. That is, if debtors are discouraged by a price decline much more than creditors are encouraged, it may be possible that there exists no price decline which would have an encouraging effect on expenditures. In brief, the Keynesian aggregative analysis followed by Pigou overlooks the possibility of microeconomic "distribution effects."

Secondly, we have so far considered only the effects of a change in real balances on household behavior; that is, on the consumption (or, its counterpart, the savings) function. It seems only natural to extend the analysis to include the influence of real cash balances on firms, and, hence, on the investment function as well. However, this extension cannot be made automatically, inasmuch as the respective motivations of firms and households are not necessarily the same. Nevertheless, it does seem reasonable to assume that investment decisions of firms are favorably influenced by a higher level of real balances. Once we take account of firms, the differential

reactions mentioned in the preceding paragraph become increasingly significant. If firms are, on balance, debtors with respect to households and government, then a persistent price decline will cause a wave of bankruptcies. This will have a seriously depressing effect upon the economy which may not be offset by the improved status of creditors. Furthermore, in most cases of bankruptcy the creditors also lose. For these reasons it is not at all certain that a price decline will result in a positive net effect on the total expenditures (consumption plus investment) function. On this point much further investigation—of a theoretical as well as an empirical nature—is required.]

From the preceding analysis we can also see just exactly what constitutes the "cash balance" whose increase in real value provides the stimulatory effect of the Pigou analysis. This balance clearly consists of the net obligation of the government to the private sector of the economy. That is, it consists primarily of the total interest- and non-interest-bearing government debt held outside the treasury and central bank [plus the net amount owed by the central bank to member banks]. Thus, by excluding demand deposits and including government interest-bearing debt and member bank reserves, it differs completely from what is usually regarded as the stock of money.

These same conclusions can be reached through a somewhat different approach. Begin with the ordinary concept of the stock of money as consisting of hand-to-hand currency and demand deposits. Consider now what changes must be made in order to arrive at the figure relevant for the Pigou analysis. Clearly, government interest-bearing debt must be added, since a price decline increases its value. Now consider money in the form of demand deposits. To the extent that it is backed by bank loans and discounts, the gains of deposit holders are offset by the losses of bank debtors.[13] Thus the net effect of a price decline on demand deposits is reduced to its effect on the excess of deposits over loans, or (approximately) on the reserves of the banks held in the form of hand-to-hand currency [and deposits in the central bank]. Finally, hand-to-hand currency held by individuals outside the banking system is added in, and we arrive at exactly the same figure as in the preceding paragraph.

For convenience denote the stock of money relevant for the Pigou analysis by M_1. Note that this is completely different from M_0 of footnote 7: for M_0 is defined in the usual manner as hand-to-hand currency plus demand deposits. This distinction is of fundamental importance. [One of its immediate implications is that central bank open-market operations which do not change the market price of government bonds affect the economic system only through the liquidity preference equation.] Since such operations merely substitute one type of government debt (currency) for another (bonds), they have no effect on M_1 and hence no direct effect on the amount of savings. [Even when open-market purchases do cause an increase in the price of government bonds, the changes in M_0 and M_1 will not, in general, be equal. The increase in M_0 equals the total amount of money expended for the purchase of the bonds; the increase in M_1 equals the increase in the value of bonds (both of those bought and those not bought by the central bank) caused by the open-market operations.[14] Corresponding statements can be made for open-market sales.]

7. How does the Pigou formulation compare with the original classical theory?[15] Although both Pigou and the "classics" stress the importance of "price flexibility," they mean by this term completely different things. The "classics" are talking about flexibility of relative prices; Pigou is talking about flexibility of absolute prices. The classical school holds that the existence of long-run unemployment is

prima facie evidence of rigid wages. The only way to eliminate unemployment is, then, by reducing *real* wages. (Since workers can presumably accomplish this end by reducing their *money* wage, this position has implicit in it the assumption of a constant price level—[or at least one falling relatively less than wages].) Pigou now recognizes that changing the relative price of labor is not enough, and that the absolute price level itself must vary. In fact, a strict interpretation of Pigou's position would indicate that unemployment can be eliminated even if real wages remain the same or even rise (namely, if the proportionate fall in prices is greater than or equal to that of wages); for in any case the effect of increased real value of cash balances is still present.[16]

The Pigou analysis also differs from those interpretations of the classical position which, following Keynes, present the effect of a wage decrease as acting through the liquidity preference equation to increase the real value of M_0 and thereby reduce the rate of interest; this in turn stimulates both consumption and investment expenditures—thus generating a higher level of national income. To this effect, Pigou now adds the direct stimulus to consumption expenditures provided by the price decline and the accompanying increase in real balances. Consequently, even if the savings and investment functions are completely insensitive to changes in the rate of interest (so that the effect through the liquidity equation is completely inoperative), a wage decrease will still be stimulatory through its effect on real balances and hence on savings.

8. Before concluding this part of the paper, one more point must be clarified. The explicit assumption of the Pigou analysis is that savings are directly related to the price level, and therefore inversely related to the size of real cash balances. This assumption by itself is, on *a priori* grounds, quite reasonable; [indeed, in a money economy it is a direct implication

of utility maximization (above, note 15)]. But it must be emphasized that even if we disregard the reservations mentioned in the preceding sections, this assumption is insufficient to bring about the conclusion desired by Pigou. For this purpose he *implicitly* makes an additional, and possibly less reasonable, assumption. Specifically, in addition to postulating explicitly the direction of the relationship between savings and the price level, he also implies something about its *intensity*.

The force of this distinction is illustrated by Figure 5. Here S and I are the full employment savings and investment curves of Figure 3 (i.e., those corresponding to $Y = Y_0$) for a fixed price level, p_0. The other savings curves, S_1, S_2, S_3, S_4, represent the full employment savings schedules corresponding to the different price levels p_1, p_2, p_3, p_4, respectively. In accordance with the Pigou assumption, as the price level falls, the savings function shifts over to the right. (That is, p_1, p_2, p_3, p_4 are listed in descending order.) But it may well be that as the real value of their cash balances continues to increase, people are less and less affected by this increase. That is, for each successive increase in real balances (for each successive price level decline) the savings function moves less and less to the right, until eventually it might respond only infinitesimally, no matter how much prices fall. In graphical terms, as the price decline continues, the savings function might reach S_3 as a limiting position. That is, no matter how much the price level might fall, the savings function would never more to the right of S_3.[17] In such an event the declining price level would fail to bring about full employment. The validity of the Pigou argument thus depends on the additional assumption that the intensity of the inverse relationship between savings and real cash balances is such that it will be possible to shift over the savings function to a position where it will intercept the investment function at a positive rate of interest: say, S_4 (cf. Figure 5).

What is at issue here is the reaction of individuals with already large real balances to further increases in these balances. Consider an individual with a cash balance of a fixed number of dollars. As the price falls, the increased real value of these dollars must be allocated between the alternatives of an addition to either consumption and/or real balances.[18] How the individual will actually allocate the increase clearly depends on the relative marginal utilities of these two alternatives. If we are willing to assume that the marginal utility of cash balances approaches zero with sufficient rapidity relative to that of consumption, then we can ignore the possibility of the savings curve reaching a limiting position such as in Figure 5. That is, we would be maintaining the position that by increasing the individual's balances sufficiently, he will have no further incentive to add to these balances; hence he will spend any additional real funds on consumption, so that we can make him consume any amount desired. If, on the other hand, we admit the possibility that, for sufficiently large consumption, the decrease in the marginal utility of cash balances is accompanied by a much faster decrease in the marginal utility of consumption, then the individual will continuously use most of the additional real funds (made available by the price decline) to add to his balances. In this event, the situation of Figure 5 may well occur.

9. I do not believe we have sufficient evidence—either of an *a priori* or empirical[19] nature—to help us answer the question raised in the preceding paragraph. The empirical evidence available is consistent with the hypothesis that the effect of real balances on savings is very weak. But even granted the truth of this hypothesis, it casts no light on the question raised here. What we want to know is what happens to the effect of real balances

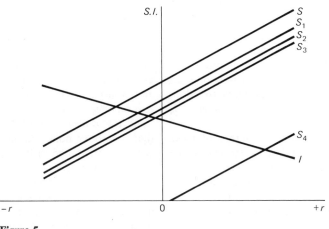

Figure 5

on savings as these real balances increase in size. Even if the effect were arbitrarily small, but remained constant regardless of the size of real balances, there could be no convergence of savings functions like that pictured in Figure 5. In the face of this lack of evidence, we have to be satisfied with the conclusion that, subject to the [reservations of §§ 6 and 8, Haberler and Pigou have] demonstrated the automaticity of full employment within the framework of the classical static model[20] —the main mechanism by which this is brought about being the effect of a price decline on cash balances.

The statement of this conclusion immediately raises the interesting question of how this set of forces [emphasized by Haberler and Pigou] could have been overlooked by Keynesian economists, in general, and Keynes himself, in particular. Questions of this type can rarely be answered satisfactorily—and perhaps should not even be asked. Nevertheless, I think it is both possible and instructive to trace through the exact chain of errors in Keynes's reasoning which caused him to overlook these factors.

I submit the hypothesis that Keynes recognized the influence of assets on saving (consumption), but unfortunately

thought of this influence only in terms of physical capital assets. This was his fundamental error.[21] From it immediately followed that in his main discussion of the (short-run) consumption function, where he assumed a *constant* stock of capital, the possible influence of assets was not (and could not) even be considered.[22] But as soon as Keynes discussed a period sufficiently long for noticeable capital growth, the influence of assets on savings was immediately recognized.[23] Even here, Keynes could not come to the same conclusion as Pigou. For Keynes restricted himself to physical assets, and thus rightfully pointed out that it would be "an unlikely coincidence" that just the correct amount of assets should exist—i.e., that amount which would push over the savings function to such a position where full employment could be generated. Compare this with the determinate process by which just exactly the "correct amount" of real cash balances is brought into existence in the Pigou analysis. (See above, § 5, paragraph 4.)

This exclusion of physical assets from the short-run consumption function was subconsciously extended to all kinds of assets. Here was the last link in the chain of errors. For later when Keynes began to examine the effects of increased real cash balances (brought about either by price declines or increases in the amount of money), he did not even consider their possible influence on consumption. Instead, he concentrated exclusively on their tendency, through the liquidity function, to lower interest rates.[24] (Cf. above, § 7, last paragraph.)

Looking back on the nature of these errors, we cannot but be struck by the irony that they should have emanated from the man who did most to demonstrate the fundamental inseparability of the real and monetary sectors of our economy.

II. DYNAMIC ANALYSIS: THE QUESTION OF POLICY

10. [The Haberler–Pigou analysis discussed in Part I makes two contributions. First, in its emphasis on the effects of a price on savings via its effects on real balances, it introduces into the Keynesian analytical apparatus a set of forces hitherto overlooked by the latter. (For convenience this will be referred to as the Pigou effect—though, as mentioned at the end of § 5 above, it is of much older origin.) Secondly, it proceeds to draw the implications of this set] of forces for static analysis, and summarizes its results in the following theorem (cf. §§ 5 and 6): *There always exists a sufficiently low price level such that, if expected to continue indefinitely,*[25] *it will generate full employment.*[26] (For convenience this will be referred to as the Pigou Theorem.) The purpose of this part of the paper is to accomplish a third objective: viz., to draw the implications of the Pigou effect for dynamic analysis and policy formulation. It must be emphasized that the Pigou Theorem tells us nothing about the dynamic and policy aspects which interest us in this third objective. (This point is discussed in greater detail in § 12.)

Specifically, consider a full employment situation which is suddenly terminated by a downswing in economic activity. The question I now wish to examine is the usefulness of a policy which consists of maintaining the stock of money constant, allowing the wage and price levels to fall, and waiting for the resulting increase in real balances to restore full employment.

At the outset it must be made clear that the above policy recommendation is *not* to be attributed to Pigou. His interest is purely an intellectual one, in a purely static analysis. As he himself writes: "... The puzzles we have been considering ... are academic exercises, of some slight use perhaps for clarifying thought, but with very little chance of ever being posed on the chequer board of actual life."[27]

In reality, Pigou's disavowal of a deflationary policy (contained in the paragraph from which the above quotation is taken) is not nearly as thoroughgoing as might appear on the first reading. The rejection of a price decline as a practical means of combatting unemployment may be due to: (a) the conviction that dynamic considerations invalidate its use as an immediate policy, regardless of its merits in static analysis; (b) the conviction that industrial and labor groups, sometimes with the assistance of government, prevent the price flexibility necessary for the success of a deflationary policy. A careful reading of Pigou's disclaimer indicates that he had only the second of these alternatives in mind; i.e., that he felt that the policy would not work because it would not be permitted to work. What I hope to establish in this part of the essay is the first alternative: namely, that even granted full flexibility of prices, it is still highly possible that a deflationary policy will not work, due to the dynamic factors involved.

Nevertheless, nothing in this part of the paper is intended (or even relevant) as a criticism of Pigou, since the latter has clearly abstained from the problem of policy formulation. If sometimes the terms "Pigou effect" and "Pigou Theorem" are used in the following discussion, they should be understood solely as shorthand notations for the concepts previously explained.

11. The analysis of this section is based on the following two assumptions: (a) One of the prerequisites of a successful anti-depression policy is that it should be able to achieve its objective rapidly (say, within a year). (b) Prices cannot fall instantaneously; hence, the larger the price level fall necessary to bring about full employment via the Pigou effect, the longer the time necessary for the carrying out of the policy. (If no price fall can bring about full employment, then we can say that an infinite amount of time is necessary for the carrying out of the policy.)

There are at least two factors which act toward lengthening the period necessary to carry out a policy based on the Pigou effect. The first is the possibility that the effect of an increase in cash balances on consumption is so small, that very large increases (very great price declines) will be necessary. [Certainly there is a burden of proof on the supporters of a policy of absolute price flexibility to show that this is not so;] that the economic system is sufficiently responsive to make the policy practical. So far no one has presented the required evidence.

The second factor is a result of the price decline itself. In dynamic analysis we must give full attention to the role played by price expectations and anticipations in general. It is quite possible that the original price decline will lead to the expectation of further declines. Then purchasing decisions will be postponed, aggregate demand will fall off, and the amount of unemployment increased still more. In terms of Figures 1 and 3, the savings function will rise (consumption will be decreased) and the investment function fall, further aggravating the

problem of achieving full employment. This was the point on which Keynes was so insistent.[28] Furthermore, the uncertainty about the future generated by the price decline will increase the liquidity preference of individuals. Thus if we consider an individual possessing a fixed number of dollars, and confronted with a price decline which increases the real value of these dollars, his uncertainty will make him more inclined to employ these additional real funds to increase his real balances, than to increase his expenditures.[29] In other words, the uncertainty created by the price decline might cause people to accumulate indefinitely large real cash balances, and to increase their expenditures very little if at all. [Finally, the bankruptcies caused by the inability of creditors to carry the increased real burden of their debt (above, § 6) will strengthen the pessimistic outlook for the future. The simultaneous interaction of these three forces] will further exacerbate these difficulties. For as the period of price decline drags itself out, anticipations for the future will progressively worsen, and uncertainties further increase. The end result of letting the Pigou effect work itself out may be a disastrous deflationary spiral, continuing for several years without ever reaching any equilibrium position. Certainly our past experiences should have sensitized us to this danger.

Because of these considerations I feel that it is impractical to depend upon the Pigou effect as a means of policy: the required price decline might be either too large (factor one), or it might be the initial step of an indefinite deflationary spiral (factor two).

On this issue, it may be interesting to investigate the experience of the United States in the 1930's. In Table I, net balances are computed for the period 1929–1932 according to the definition of § 6. As can be seen, although there was a 19 per cent *increase* in real balances from 1930 to 1931, real national income during this

Table I

YEAR	MONEY IN CIRCULATION OUTSIDE TREASURY AND FEDERAL RESERVE SYSTEM	MARKET VALUE OF GOVERNMENT INTEREST-BEARING DEBT HELD OUTSIDE GOVERNMENT AGENCIES AND THE FEDERAL RESERVE SYSTEM	MEMBER BANK DEPOSITS IN THE FEDERAL RESERVE SYSTEM	NON-MEMBER BANK DEPOSITS IN THE FEDERAL RESERVE SYSTEM	OTHER FEDERAL RESERVE ACCOUNTS	RESERVE BANK CREDIT OUTSTANDING EXCLUDING THAT BASED ON RESERVE BANK HOLDINGS OF U.S. GOVERNMENT SECURITIES	TREASURY DEPOSITS IN MEMBER AND NON-MEMBER BANKS	POSTAL SAVINGS	NET BALANCES (M_1) $(1)+(2)$ $+(3)+(4)$ $+(5)-(6)$ $-(7)+(8)$	COST OF LIVING INDEX (p)	NET REAL BALANCES $\frac{M_1}{p}$ $(9)\div(10)$	REAL NATIONAL INCOME
	(1)	(2)	(3)	(4)	(5)	(6)	(7)	(8)	(9)	(10)	(11)	(12)
1929	4.5	14.5	2.4	0.0	0.4	1.3	0.4	0.2	20.2	1.22	16.6	89.9
1930	4.2	13.9	2.4	0.0	0.4	0.5	0.3	0.2	20.4	1.19	17.1	76.3
1931	4.7	15.1	2.3	0.1	0.4	0.6	0.4	0.6	22.1	1.09	20.3	66.3
1932	5.3	16.0	2.1	0.1	0.4	0.6	0.4	0.9	23.7	0.98	24.2	54.2

All money figures are in billions of dollars.

Data for series (1), (3), (4), (5), (6) were obtained from *Banking and Monetary Statistics*, p. 368. On pp. 360–367 of this book their inter-relationships are discussed. For (7) see *ibid.*, pp. 34–35. For (8) see the following procedure: Total outstanding government debt at face value was classified according to maturities (0–5 years, 5–10, and over 10) on the basis of *Banking and Monetary Statistics*, p. 511. These classifications were multi-plied by price indexes for government bonds with maturities of more than 3 and less than 4 years, more than 6 and less than 9, and more than 10, respectively (Standard and Poor, *Statistics: Security Price Index Record*, 1948 edition, pp. 139–144). The sum of these products was used as an estimate of the market value of the total government debt. The ratio of this to the face value of the total debt was computed, and this ratio applied to the face value of government debt held outside the Treasury and Federal Reserve System (*Banking and Monetary Statistics*, p. 512) to yield an estimate of the required series.

Series (10): Bureau of Labor Statistics, cost of living index, *Survey of Current Business*, Supplement, 1942, p. 16.

Series (12): National income in billions of 1944 dollars. J. Dewhurst and Associates, *America's Needs and Resources* (New York, The Twentieth Century Fund, 1947), p. 697.

period *decreased* by 13 per cent. Even in the following year, when a further increase of 19 per cent in real balances took place, real income proceeded to fall by an additional 18 per cent. For the 1929–1932 period as a whole there was an increase in real balances of 46 per cent, and a decrease in real income of 40 per cent.

It will, of course, be objected that these data reflect the presence of "special factors," and do not indicate the real value of the Pigou effect. But the pertinent question which immediately arises is: To what extent were these "special factors" necessary, concomitant results of the price decline itself! If the general feeling of uncertainty and adverse anticipations that marked the period is cited as one of these "special factors," the direct relationship between this and the decline in price level itself certainly cannot be overlooked. Other proposed "special factors" must be subjected to the same type of examination. The data of the preceding table are not offered as conclusive evidence. But they are certainly consistent with the previously stated hypothesis of the impracticability of using the Pigou effect as a means of policy; and they certainly throw the

burden of proof on those who argue for its practicality.

12. The argument of the preceding section requires further explanation on at least one point. In the discussion of the "second factor" there was mentioned the possibility of an indefinitely continuing spiral of deflation and unemployment. But what is the relation between this possibility and the Pigou Theorem (cf. § 10) established in Part I? The answer to this question may be expressed as follows:

On the downswing of the business cycle it might be interesting to know that there exists a sufficiently low price level which, if it were expected to continue existing indefinitely, would bring about full employment. Interesting, but, for policy purposes, irrelevant. For due to perverse price expectations and the dynamics of deflationary spirals, it is impossible to reach (or, once having reached, to remain at) such a position.

The implication of these remarks can be clarified by consideration of the cobweb theorem for the divergent case. Assume that a certain market can be explained in terms of the cobweb theorem. It is desired to know whether (assuming

Figure 6

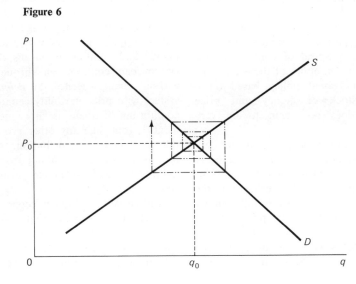

unchanged demand and supply curves) the designated market will ever reach a stationary position; that is, whether it will settle down to a unique price that will continue indefinitely to clear the market. This question is clearly divided into two parts: (a) does there exist such a price, and (b) if it does exist, will the market be able to attain it? In the case of the cobweb presented in Figure 6 it is clear that such a price does exist. For if the price p_0 had always existed and were expected to exist indefinitely, it would continuously clear the market. But Figure 6 represents the case of a divergent cobweb; hence the market will never be able to reach the price p_0. In brief, even though p_0 exists, it is irrelevant to the workings of the market. The analogy to the argument of the preceding paragraph is obvious.[30]

III. CONCLUSIONS

13. The conclusions of this paper can be summarized as follows: in a static world with a constant stock of money,[31] price flexibility assures full employment. (I abstract here again from the difficulties raised in §§ 6 and 8.) But in the real dynamic world in which we live, price flexibility with a constant stock of money might generate full employment only after a long period; or might even lead to a deflationary spiral of continuous unemployment. On either of these grounds, a full employment policy based on a constant stock of money and price flexibility does not seem to be very promising.

All that this means is that our full employment policy cannot be the fairly simple one of maintaining a constant stock of money and waiting for the economic system to generate full employment automatically through price declines. Other policies will be required. One possible alternative policy can be inferred from the Haberler–Pigou analysis itself:

there are two ways to increase real balances. One is to keep the money stock constant and permit prices to fall. An equally effective way is to maintain the price level constant, and increase the stock of money by creating a government deficit.[32] This method of increasing real balances has the added advantage of avoiding one of the difficulties encountered previously (§ 11), for a policy of stabilizing the price level by increasing money stocks avoids some of the dangers of uncertainty and adverse anticipation accompanying general price declines. Nevertheless, there still remains the other difficulty—that individuals may not be very sensitive to increases in real balances. If this turned out to be true, we would have to seek still other policies.

14. [On the basis of the analysis presented in this paper it is possible to reexamine the question which has been a favorite one of economists these past years: namely,] What is the distinctive characteristic of Keynesian analysis? It certainly cannot be the claim to have demonstrated the possibility of the coexistence of underemployment equilibrium and flexible prices. This, in its day, served well as a rallying cry. But now it should be definitely recognized that this is an indefensible position. For flexibility means that the money wage falls with excess supply, and rises with excess demand; and equilibrium means that the system can continue on through time without change. Hence, *by definition*, a system with price flexibility cannot be in equilibrium if there is any unemployment[33]; [but, like any other proposition that must be true by definition, this one, too, is uninteresting, unimportant, and uninformative about the real problems of economic policy].

Nor should Keynesian economics be interpreted as asserting that just as an underemployment equilibrium is impossible, so, too, in a static system may a full-employment equilibrium be impossible. That is, the static system may be at neither an underemployment equilibrium, nor a full-employment equilibrium. In other words, the static system may be inconsistent. (This is the negative interest rate argument of § 3.) For Pigou's and Haberler's discussion of the effect of a declining price level of real balances shows how this inconsistency is removed. It is, of course, still possible to maintain this interpretation of Keynes on the basis of the reservations of §§ 6 and 8. But I think this is neither necessary nor advisable. For the real significance of the Keynesian contribution can be realized only within the framework of *dynamic* economics. Whether or not an underemployment equilibrium exists; whether or not full employment equilibrium always will be generated in a static system —all this is irrelevant. The fundamental issue raised by Keynesian economics is the *stability of the dynamic system*: its ability to return automatically to a full-employment equilibrium within a reasonable time (say, a year) if it is subjected to the customary shocks and disturbances of a peacetime economy. In other words, what Keynesian economics claims is that the economic system may be in a position of underemployment *dis*equilibrium (in the sense that wages, prices, and the amount of unemployment are continuously changing over time) for long, or even indefinite, periods of time.

But this is not sufficient to characterize the Keynesians. Everyone agree thats there exist dynamic systems which will not automatically generate full employment. What distinguishes one economic school from the other is the system (or systems) to which this lack of automaticity is attributed. If the Keynesian message is applied to an economic system with no monetary policy (if such a thing is possible to define), then it is purely trivial. For few would claim automaticity of full employment for such a system. Keynesian theory acquires mean-

ing only when applied to systems with more intelligent monetary policies. Here an element of arbitrariness is introduced; for what is termed "Keynesian" depends entirely on the choice of the monetary policy to be used as a criterion.

On the basis of Keynes' writings, I believe it is clear that he was primarily interested in attacking the policy of assuring full employment by manipulation of the interest rate through open-market operations.[34] But to Keynes, this policy was equivalent to one of wage flexibility[35]; for (he erroneously thought) the only effect of a wage decline was to increase the real value of the stock of money (in the M_0, not M_1, sense; cf. above, last paragraph of § 6) and thereby decrease the rate of interest—just as in open-market operations. As we have pointed out above (end of §§ 6 and 7), these policies are really not equivalent. For open-market operations may change only M_0, whereas a wage and price decline change the real value of M_1 as well. Hence, open-market operations may act only through the liquidity preference equation, whereas a policy of price flexibility acts also through the savings function (cf. above, footnote 7 and end of §§ 6 and 7).

Let us now assume that even if Keynes had recognized the distinction between open-market and wage flexibility policies (i.e., if he had recognized the Pigou effect) he still would have continued to reject the latter as a means of assuring full employment. This is not an unreasonable assumption; for most of the objections cited above (§ 11) against the use of a policy based on the Pigou effect are the very same ones that Keynes uses in arguing against open-market operations.[36]

Granted this assumption, I believe it is useful to identify the Keynesian position against one which maintains that full employment can be automatically achieved via the Pigou effect by maintaining a constant stock of money, and providing for wage and price flexibility. It is now possible to delineate three distinct theoretical formulations of the Keynesian position—differing in varying degrees from the classical one: (a) Most opposed to the classical position is the Keynesian one which states that even if there were no problem of uncertainty and adverse anticipations (that is, even if there were a static system), and even if we were to allow an infinite amount of time for adjustment, a policy of price flexibility would still not assure the generation of full employment. (This is the negative interest rate argument of §§ 3 and 8; [or the argument based on differential creditor-debtor responses of § 6].)

(b) Then there is the position which states that, in a static world, price flexibility would always assure full employment. But in a dynamic world of uncertainty and adverse anticipations, even if we were to allow an infinite adjustment period, there is no certainty that full employment will be generated. That is, we may remain indefinitely in a position of underemployment disequilibrium. (c) Finally, there is the Keynesian position, closest to the "classics," which states that even with uncertainty full employment would eventually be generated by a policy of price flexibility; but the length of time that might be necessary for the adjustment makes the policy impractical.

Although these positions are quite distinct theoretically, their policy implications are very similar. (In what way would the policies of a man advocating position (a) differ from those of a man advocating (c) and stating that the adjustment would take ten years?) The policies would in general be directed at influencing the consumption and investment functions themselves, in addition to manipulating the amount of money. Thus the policies may advocate tax reductions to stimulate consumption and investment (the Simons–Mints school); or may insist on direct government investment to supplement private investment (Hansen, *et al.*). In this way we could cross-classify Keynesian positions according to their advocated policies, as well as their theoretical foundations.

[Finally, it should be noted that none of the preceding three formulations of the Keynesian position is dependent upon the assumption of wage rigidities. This assumption is frequently, and erroneously, attributed to Keynesian economics as a result of two related misconceptions as to its nature. First of all, as we have seen, the attempt to interpret Keynes' analysis of unemployment within a static equilibrium framework makes it mandatory, by definition, to assume the existence of wage rigidities. The dynamic approach followed in this paper obviates this necessity.

A second implication of restricting ourselves to static equilibrium analysis is that *involuntary* unemployment can, *by definition*, exist only if there are wage rigidities. For if there were no wage rigidities, the wage level could assume any value; and for each such value there would be a corresponding, and presumably different, amount of labor supplied. Thus at the intersection point of the demand and supply curves—the only point of interest in static equilibrium analysis—workers are providing all the labor they wish to at the equilibrium wage. There can be no question of involuntary unemployment. Only if there are wage rigidities—a minimum wage w_0, below which the workers refuse to go—can the situation be different. For then the supply curve of labor is parallel to the quantity axis at the height w_0 until a certain point (say) N_1 is reached; only afterwards does the curve begin to rise. If the demand curve is now assumed to intersect the supply curve in its horizontal portion at, say, the quantity N_0, then we can say that *involuntary* unemployment to the extent $N_1 - N_0$ exists; for at the equilibrium wage rate, w_0, workers desire to provide a maximum of N_1 units of labor, and are instead providing only N_0.

However, once we throw off the restrictions of static equilibrium analysis, we also free ourselves of the necessity of assuming wage rigidity as a necessary precondition of involuntary unemployment. For, during any given period of time, the dynamic workings of the system may well keep the workers at a point *off their supply curve*. In this departure from the supply curve lies the *involuntariness* of the unemployment. The important point here is that this situation can exist regardless of the shape of the supply curve; that is, even if wages are not rigid. One's view on the length of time such a situation can continue clearly depends on one's choice of the three alternative Keynesian positions delineated above. All this has been dealt with at length elsewhere,[37] and there is no need for any further repetition here.[38]]

NOTES

1 Cf. Oscar Lange, *Price Flexibility and Employment* (Bloomington, Indiana, Principia Press, 1945), p. 85 and the literature cited there. For an excellent theoretical discussion of this insensitivity, cf. G. L. S. Shackle, "Interest Rates and the Pace of Investment," *Economic Journal*, LVI (1946), 1–17.

2 Note that in a dynamic world of rising prices, the effective rate of interest may become negative. But even here the *anticipated* effective rate cannot be negative. For in that event there would again be an infinite demand for money.

3 I have discussed this whole question of the contrast between the classical and Keynesian positions in greater detail elsewhere. Cf. "Involuntary Unemployment and the Keynesian Supply Function," *Economic Journal*, LIX (1949), 376–378.

4 [G. Haberler, *Prosperity and Depression* (League of Nations, Geneva, 1941), 3rd ed., pp. 242, 389, 403, 491–503.]
A. C. Pigou, "The Classical Stationary State," *Economic Journal*, LIII (1943), 343–351; "Economic Progress in a Stable Environment," *Economica*, n. s.

XIV (1947), 180–190. Although these articles deal only with a stationary state, their basic argument can readily be extended to the case in which net investment is taking place.
[In the subsequent text, I shall follow the exposition of Pigou; but the argument holds also with respect to Haberler.]

5 *Ibid.*, p. 346.

6 And all his other assets too. But the introduction of these other assets does not change Pigou's argument; while concentration on money assets brings out its (the argument's) basic aspect. Cf. § 6.

7 The exact price level is determined when to our preceding four equations is added the liquidity preference equation, $M_0 = (r, Y, p)$, where M_0 represents the given amount of money in the system. (As will be shown in the next section, the "stock of money" relevant for the liquidity equation is completely different from the "stock of money" relevant for the Pigou analysis of the savings function; hence the use of two different symbols—M_0 and M_1.) We then have the complete system of five equations in five variables:

$$I = \Phi(r, Y)$$
$$S = \Gamma\!\left(r, Y, \frac{M_1}{p}\right)$$
$$I = S$$
$$Y = Y_0$$
$$M_0 = \Lambda(r, Y, p)$$

Under the Pigovian assumptions this system is consistent; its equations are satisfied for a positive rate of interest.
[The workings of a more general system of equations under the Pigovian assumption are described in detail in Parts IV and V of the reference cited in footnote 3. In this more detailed treatment, the full employment level, Y_0, is not arbitrarily defined—as is done in the present paper—but emerges instead from the economic behavior functions themselves.]

8 Pigou makes this assumption when he writes the investment function (which presumably also includes government expenditure) as independent of the absolute price level. Cf. footnote 7.

9 It must be emphasized that I am abstracting here from all dynamic considerations of the effect on anticipations, etc. These will be discussed in Part II of the paper.

10 A necessary (but not sufficient) condition for this to occur is that the price level of assets falls in a greater proportion than the general price level.

11 I am indebted to M. Friedman for this example.

12 Cf. footnote 6. Another possible reason for Pigou's emphasis on cash balances to the exclusion of other assets is that the relative illiquidity of the latter makes them less likely to be used as a means of satisfying the "irrational" motives of saving. Hence the inverse relationship between other assets and savings out of current income might not be so straightforward as that between real cash balances and savings.

13 Cf. M. Kalecki, "Professor Pigou on 'The Classical Stationary State'—A Comment," *Economic Journal*, LIV (1944), 131–132.

14 [It might be argued that through its effect on the interest rate, open-market purchases affect the value of assets other than government securities; hence, this change in value should also be included in the change in M_1. This is a point which deserves further investigation. The main question is whether there exists an offset to this improvement in the position of bondholders of private corporations.]

15 Pigou, of course, introduces the absolute price level into the analysis of the real sector of the economy, whereas classical economics insists that this sector must be considered on the basis of relative prices alone. [As I have shown elsewhere, on this point classical economics is definitely wrong. For, in a money economy, the demand for any good must, in general, depend on the absolute price level, as well as on relative prices. This is a direct result of utility maximization. Cf. "Money in General Equilibrium Theory: Critique and Reformulation," *Econometrica*, XVIII (1950), and references cited there.]

16 The role of real wages in Pigou's system is very ambiguous. At one point (p. 348, bottom) he assumes that reduced money wages will also decrease real wages. At another (p. 349, lines 20–38) no such assumption seems to be involved. "As money wage-rates fall ... prices fall and go on falling." *Ibid.*

17 Mathematically this may be stated as follows. Write the savings function as

$$S = \Gamma(r, p, Y)$$

(Cf. footnote 7, above.) Pigou's explicit assumption is

$$\Gamma_p(r, p \ Y) > 0$$

where Γ_p is the partial derivative of S with respect to p. Let $Y = Y_0$ represent the full employment income. Then the argument here is that the savings function, Γ, may still be of a form such that

$$\lim_{p \to 0} \Gamma(r, p, Y_0) = \Gamma^*(r, Y_0)$$

for any fixed r—where Γ^* is any curve which intersects the investment curve at a negative rate of interest. (In the argument of the text, Γ^* is taken to be S_2 in Figure 5.) Pigou tacitly assumes that the savings function approaches no such limit; or that if it does, the limiting function intersects the investment function at a positive rate of interest.

18 I am abstracting here from the possible third alternative, investment.

19 Empirical studies on the effect of real balances on savings have been made by L. R. Klein, "The Use of Econometric Models as a Guide to Economic Policy," *Econometrica*, XV (1947), 122–125. Klein's procedure was incorrect in that he used a series of M_0, instead of M_1, in fitting his equations (cf. last paragraph of § 6).

20 It must be re-emphasized that this conclusion holds only for static analysis. The modifications that must be introduced once dynamic factors enter are discussed in Part II.

21 Note that there are really two distinct errors involved here. The first is the obvious one of the exclusion of monetary assets. The second is that what is relevant for the influence on saving is not the *physical* asset, but its *real* value in terms of some general price level.

22 J. M. Keynes, *The General Theory of Employment, Interest, and Money* (New York, Harcourt, Brace, and Co., 1936), Chap. 8. See especially pp. 91–95, where Keynes considers the possible influence of other factors besides income on consumption, and does not even mention assets.

23 *Ibid.*, p. 218, second paragraph.

24 *Ibid.*, pp. 231–234, 266. The following passage is especially interesting: "It is, therefore, on the effect of a falling wage- and price-level on the *demand for money* that those who believe in the self-adjusting quality of the economic system must rest the weight of their argument; though I am not aware that they have done so. If the quantity of money is itself a function of the wage- and price-level, there is, indeed, nothing to hope for in this direction. But if the quantity of money is virtually fixed, it is evident that its quantity in terms of wage-units can be indefinitely increased by

a sufficient reduction in money wages...."
(*Ibid.*, p. 266. Italics not in original.)

25 This qualifying phrase incorporates in it the restriction of the Pigou argument to static analysis.

26 I am overlooking here the reservations discussed in §§ 6 and 8.

27 "Economic Progress in a Stable Environment," *Economica*, n.s. XIV (1947), 188.

28 See his discussion of changes in money wages, *op. cit.,* pp. 260–269, especially p. 263. Cf. also J. R. Hicks, *Value and Capital* (Oxford, Oxford University Press, 1939), and O. Lange, *op. cit.*

29 Cf. § 8, last paragraph.

30 The distinction of this section can be expressed in rigorous mathematical form using the dynamic system which has become familiar through the work of Samuelson and Lange (P. A. Samuelson, "The Stability of Equilibrium: Comparative Statics and Dynamics," *Econometrica*, IX (1941), 97–120; Lange, *op. cit.*, pp. 91 ff.). Consider a single market and let D, S, and p represent the demand, supply, and price of the particular good, respectively. Let t represent time. Then we can write this system as

$$D = f(p) \qquad \text{demand function} \quad \text{(a)}$$

$$S = g(p) \qquad \text{supply function} \quad \text{(b)}$$

$$\frac{dp}{dt} = h(D - S) \qquad \begin{array}{l}\text{market adjusting} \\ \text{function}\end{array} \quad \text{(c)}$$

The last equation has the property that

$$\text{sign } \frac{dp}{dt} = \text{sign } (D - S) \qquad \text{(d)}$$

i.e., price rises with excess demand and falls with excess supply. Consider now the static system identical with (a) − (c), except that it replaces (c) by

$$D = S \qquad \text{(e)}$$

As long as (e) is not satisfied, we see from (d) that the system will not be in stationary equilibrium, but will continue to fluctuate. Thus the existence of a solution to the static system (a), (b), (e) (i.e., the consistency of (a), (b), (e)) is a *necessary* condition for the existence of a stationary solution for the dynamic system (a), (b), (c). But this is not a sufficient condition. For the static system (a), (b), (e) may have a consistent solution which, if the dynamic system is not convergent, will never be reached.

Thus Pigou has completed only half the task. Setting aside the difficulties of § 8, we can accept his proof of the *consistency* of the *static* classical system. But that still leaves completely unanswered the question of whether the classical *dynamic* system will converge to this consistent solution. In this and the preceding section I have tried to show why such convergence may not occur in the real world. (I have discussed these issues in greater detail elsewhere. Cf. footnote 3.)

31 Throughout Part III, unless otherwise indicated, "stock of money" is to be understood in the M_1 sense of the last paragraph of § 6.

32 Considered from this perspective, the Pigou analysis presents in a rigorous fashion part of the theoretical framework implicit in the fiscal-monetary policy of the Simons–Mints position. Cf. the recently published collection of essays of Henry C. Simons, *Economic Policy for a Free Society* (Chicago, University of Chicago Press, 1948); and Lloyd W. Mints, "Monetary Policy," *Revue of Economic Statistics*, XXVIII (1946), 60–69.

33 This can be expressed mathematically in the following way: let N^S and N^D be the amounts of labor supplied and demanded, respectively; w, the money wage rate; and t, time. Then a flexible dynamic system will, by definition, contain an equation of the general type

$$\frac{dw}{dt} = f(N^D - N^S)$$

where

$$\text{sign } \frac{dw}{dt} = \text{sign } (N^D - N^S)$$

If by equilibrium is meant a situation such that

$$\frac{dw}{dt} = 0$$

then clearly this system cannot be in equilibrium unless

$$N^D - N^S = 0$$

i.e., unless there is full employment.

34 Cf. Keynes, *op. cit.*, pp. 231–234, 266–267.

35 "There is, therefore, no ground for the belief that a flexible wage policy is capable of maintaining a state of continuous full employment;—any more than for the belief that an open market monetary policy is capable, unaided, of achieving this result. The economic system cannot

be made self-adjusting along these lines."
(*Ibid.*, p. 267.)

36 Cf. the passages cited in footnote 34.

37 Cf. reference cited in footnote 3.

38 It might be added that in the light of Chapter 19 of the *General Theory*—the chapter which provides the climax to Keynes' argument, and which explicitly examines the effects of wage flexibility—it is difficult to understand how wage rigidities can be considered a basic assumption of the Keynesian theory of unemployment. From this chapter it is quite clear that wage rigidities are *not* an *assumption* of Keynes' analysis, but rather a policy conclusion that follows from his investigation of the probable effects of *wage flexibility*.

Further explicit evidence that Keynes, in his theory of unemployment, was concerned with a regime of flexible prices is provided by the following passage from the *General Theory* (p. 191): "in the extreme case where money wages are assumed to fall without limit in face of involuntary unemployment ... there will, it is true, be only two possible long period positions—full employment and the level of employment corresponding to the rate of interest at which liquidity preference becomes absolute (in the event of this being less than full employment)."

Summaries

Arthur M. Okun, "The Gap Between Actual and Potential Output," in Edmund S. Phelps *et al.* (eds.), *Problems of the Modern Economy* (New York: W. W. Norton & Company, Inc., 1966), pp. 287–296.

One of the difficult questions policy makers consistently face is: How can output be maximized under conditions of full employment? This question cannot be answered satisfactorily until we develop an acceptable technique for measuring potential GNP. Okun discusses the problem of defining "potential" GNP and measuring a nation's productivity with some degree of accuracy.

Okun discusses the numerous problems connected with the task of forecasting GNP. Although not clearly evident, he says forecasting a country's potential GNP is primarily dependent upon that country's unemployment target rate. But who is to say in periods of inflation what is the highest rate of unemployment that would be acceptable? And even if such a consensus could be reached, the problem of measuring the productivity of, say, 96 per cent of the labor force would still remain, for much would depend upon contractual commitments, technological factors, transaction costs, acquired skills, and morale factors.

Okun's conclusion is not a surprising one: "Still, I shall feel much more satisfied with the estimate of potential output when data and analysis have advanced to the point where the estimate can proceed step by step and where the capital factor can explicitly be taken into account. Meanwhile, the measure of potential must be used with care and any specific figure must be understood as the center of a range of plausible estimates."

O. H. Brownlee, "The Theory of Employment and Stabilization," *Journal of Political Economy*, 58 (October 1950), pp. 412–424.

Following a decade of excitement over Keynes' formulation of the general equilibrium theory, several writers (especially Patinkin, Friedman, Pigou, and Tobin) turned their attention to the development of the static theory of employment, to output, and to the subject of the general level of prices. More importantly, these and other economists include "assets"—physical and monetary (cash and government)—as one of the variables in the aggregate consumption function. In this article, Brownlee compares the static theory with the "Keynesian" theory, which postulates that real consumption expenditure (and hence real savings) is a function of real income and that real investment is a function of the rate of interest. Also, Brownlee examines certain policy implications of the "Keynesian" position, particularly those relating to wage policy, secular stagnation, and the impacts of monetary and debt operations.

According to Brownlee, "the important policy problem which has been raised by the alternative [classical or Keynesian] theory is not whether wage flexibility should be employed as a means of achieving full employment or what the appropriate fiscal and monetary instruments are for economic stabilization. Policy proposals with a stable general price level as the objective could not propose wage flexibility as the only requisite policy. The important policy problem is whether action should be discretionary or automatic." Brownlee examines this policy problem in great detail in his article and comes to the conclusion that the Keynesians prefer discretionary action, whereas the proponents of the classical theory favor built-in flexibility. He then concludes that "the alternative [classical] theory is superior to the 'Keynesian' theory [partly because the former theory provides us with built-in flexibility]. . . This alone, however, does not establish a firm case against discretionary action."

Bibliography

Ronald Britto, "A Study in Equilibrium Dynamics in Two Types of Growing Economies," *Economic Journal*, 78 (September 1968), pp. 624–634.

Everett E. Hagen, "The Classical Theory of the Level of Output and Employment," in *Six Chapters on the Theory of Output, Income, and the Price Level* (mimeographed, 1949).

Alvin Hansen, "The General Theory," in Seymour E. Harris (ed.), *The New Economics* (New York: Alfred A. Knopf, Inc., 1947), pp. 133–144.

4
POST-KEYNESIAN ECONOMICS

"We are all Keynesians now." So said Milton Friedman, the best-known Quantity theorist in the country. There is a good deal of truth to this statement. We seem no longer to discuss economic theory except by using terminology developed by Keynes, such as "general equilibrium," "national income," "consumption function," "the multiplier," "acceleration," and so on.

The articles in this part present a fairly comprehensive survey of post-Keynesian economics. The first selection, by Somers, integrates the Keynesian, Robertsonian, and Swedish theories of income determination. In the second article, Leijonhufvud discusses the effectiveness of the Keynesian theory in solving monetary problems. In the third selection, Tobin constructs a macro growth model. Using Keynesian tools, he considers factors in variable proportions. He also analyzes monetary factors associated with growth. In the final selection, Kurihara surveys the major contributions of the Keynesian theory and points out some of its limitations.

A Theory of Income Determination
Harold M. Somers

It is not unusual for a writer who tries valiantly to conduct a study of income determination along Keynesian lines to slip involuntarily into a Robertsonian period analysis or introduce surreptitiously one or two Swedish concepts. The result is hard on the reader's patience and the writer's conscience. Students of income determination have long recognized the need for an integration of Keynesian,

Harold M. Somers, "A Theory of Income Determination," *Journal of Political Economy*, 58 (December 1950), pp. 523–541. *The Journal of Political Economy* is published by the University of Chicago Press.

Robertsonian, and Swedish income analysis, and a decade ago Lerner issued a call for someone to invent "a way of using nonequilibrium *ex ante* process analysis".[1] Hansen's and Hicks's penetrating discussion of some of the issues involved has recently emphasized the continued importance of the problem.[2] This paper makes suggestions for the integration of the three approaches through the use of the concept of "realized surprise." It discusses the relation between the various approaches and indicates how they may form mutually consistent and complementary parts of a workable model.

I. KEYNESIAN EQUATIONS

The Keynesian equations are:

$$Y = C + I$$
$$S = I$$

where Y is income, C consumption, I investment, and S saving. Numerous interpretations of the Keynesian equations are extant. In our interpretation both equations refer to *ex post* or realized magnitudes and cover the same period of time. To indicate this unambiguously, we rewrite the equations as follows:

$$Y_{r_t} = C_{r_t} + I_{r_t} \qquad (1)$$

$$S_{r_t} = I_{r_t} \qquad (2)$$

where the subscript r represents an *ex post* or realized magnitude and the subsubscript t refers to the period t.

Since it follows from (1) that

$$Y_{r_{t-1}} = C_{r_{t-1}} + I_{r_{t-1}}$$

and these magnitudes, referring as they do to period $t - 1$, have a known value for any analysis of the period t, we may rewrite equation (1) as follows:

$$Y_{r_t} - \bar{Y}_{r_{t-1}} = C_{r_t} - \bar{C}_{r_{t-1}} + I_{r_t} - \bar{I}_{r_{t-1}}$$

where the barred symbols represent magnitudes which may be considered given for the evaluation of the endogenous variables of the current period. This equation may be rewritten

$$\Delta Y_{r_t} = \Delta C_{r_t} + \Delta I_{r_t}$$

or

$$\Delta Y_{r_t} = \Delta I_{r_t} \frac{1}{1 - \dfrac{\Delta C_{r_t}}{\Delta Y_{r_t}}} \qquad (1')$$

The term $(\Delta C_{r_t})/(\Delta Y_{r_t})$ is the "instantaneous marginal propensity to consume," and the term

$$\frac{1}{1 - \dfrac{\Delta C_{r_t}}{\Delta Y_{r_t}}}$$

is the "instantaneous multiplier." This lengthy way of arriving at this well-known result (which was demonstrated at an early date by Haberler)[3] is used here to emphasize the fact the the "instantaneous marginal propensity to consume" and the "instantaneous multiplier" are derived directly from definitional equation (1) with nothing added. It is important to emphasize this because it means that the Keynesian definitional propensity to consume, which, as Ohlin suggested, might have been called the "realized consumption ratio,"[4] must be entirely consistent with any "behaviour" consumption function we may wish to assume, such as the Robertsonian. This will be explored more fully later. A realization of this is an important first step in integrating the so-called "timeless" system of Keynes with the "period" analysis of Robertson.

Equation (2) represents the *ex post* equality of saving and investment. They are stated here simply as realized magnitudes. The question whether they may be regarded as functions of income or anything else will be considered after we have set up several additional relationships.

The term I_{r_t} in equation (1) represents all forms of investment which are part of the national income, including private investment of all kinds (plant, equipment, and inventories of capital and consumption goods), the government contribution at all levels of government, and the foreign balance. If we wished to explore these separately, we could add the following equation:

$$I_{r_t} = P_{r_t} + G_{r_t} + F_{r_t}$$

where P represents private investment, G governmental contribution, and F foreign balance. Each component may be subdivided further for particular problems. In the analysis of inventory cycles, for instance, P would be broken down into capital equipment and inventories and a definite determining relationship for the latter established, as in the case of

Metzler's "inventory accelerator."[5] The governmental segment may be sub-divided to take account of the several levels of government.[6] The foreign-trade element may be analyzed in detail.[7] More general forms may also be established.[8] In case I is broken down along these lines, a subsidiary set of equations will have to be added to our model, except for the components that are assumed to have been given exogenously. No particular difficulty will be involved.

One caution must be sounded, however, in connection with all these sub-divisions of "investment" in multiplier analysis. Where investment as a whole is assumed to be "given," it is not assumed that each component of investment remains unchanged but rather that the components of investment constantly arrange themselves so as to keep the magnitude of I constant. For instance, if we begin with a certain amount of increased investment in equipment, it is likely that many changes will take place in other investment components, such as inventories, net government contribution, and foreign trade. Yet if our multiplier analysis assumes investment given, all these internal changes do not affect the investment item in the multiplier formula.[9]

These two equations, (1) and (2), do not, of course, do justice to the Keynesian system, which has important things to say about the causal determinants of consumption and investment. In the case of the consumption function, however, the Robertsonian analysis provides an essential contribution; and, in the case of the inducement to invest, the Swedish approach formulates a very useful set of relationships. In both cases the overall non-Keynesian formulation provides greater power than the Keynesian while not being inconsistent with it. The consumption function and the inducement to invest are, therefore, discussed in subsequent sections of this paper. The extent to which the Keynesian tools, such as the marginal propensity to consume, the marginal efficiency of capital, and the rate of interest, may be utilized in our model is indicated in those sections.

II. ROBERTSONIAN EQUATIONS

The Robertsonian system accepts the relationships between realized magnitudes expressed in equations (1) and (2) but adds the equations

$$Y_{t-1} = C_t + S_t$$

and

$$C_t = f(Y_{t-1})$$

The question whether the terms in these equations are to be designated as "realized" magnitudes is now to be considered. It can be shown that not all terms can represent "realized" (i.e., actual or *ex post*) magnitudes. The term Y_{t-1}, representing last period's income, must be taken as given for the current period. It may also be assumed that consumers accomplish whatever consumption they undertake during the current period. Hence C_t is "realized." If S_t were also "realized," it would be equal to I_{r_t} by equation (2). Hence a comparison of equations (1) and (3) would lead to the conclusion that Y_{t-1} and Y_t are equal. The system of equations would then permit no income changes from period to period. Hence S_t cannot be regarded as a realized magnitude. Although it represents the full amount of last period's income which people do not currently spend on consumption, hence "save," it cannot represent the full amount that actually constitutes saving in the current period. The realized saving may be different from the currently nonconsumed portion of last period's income because of unexpected changes in the current income which do not affect consumption but increase or decrease saving. To make clear these necessary distinctions, we rewrite the Robertsonian equations as follows:

$$\bar{Y}_{r_{t-1}} = C_{r_t} + S_{p_t} \qquad (3)$$

$$C_{r_t} = f(\bar{Y}_{r_{t-1}}) \qquad (4)$$

The subscript p represents planned (i.e., intended or *ex ante*, in the sense of a single magnitude rather than a schedule) saving. In this respect our interpretation of Robertsonian saving conforms to that of Lutz and disagrees with that of Lerner. The fact that the funds involved in Robertsonian saving come from the previous period does not preclude their use in determining the planned saving of the current period, nor does the fact that Robertsonian saving is measured in relation to income of the previous period prevent it from being the planned component of the realized saving and income of the current period.[10]

Although these distinctions sound "Swedish," they are implicit in the Robertsonian system and essential to it. The Swedish contribution lies in formulating the distinctions explicitly and setting up a complete system based on them. The source of the funds represented by S_{p_t} is last period's income, but the decision as to how much saving to plan for during the current period (S_{p_t}) is made with a view to the plans of the current period. The consumption function reflects those plans, and S_{p_t} is an expression of them.

It should be pointed out that equation (4) represents the consumption function. It is not inconsistent with the "instantaneous marginal propensity to consume,"

$$\frac{\Delta C_{r_t}}{\Delta Y_{r_t}}$$

which was derived from equation (1). Equation (4) tells us how much consumption there will be in the current period. Equation (1) and the instantaneous marginal propensity to consume merely tell us how the amount of current consump-

tion, which was determined by equation (4) or otherwise determined, compares in magnitude with investment and income of the current period. Just as equations (1) and (4) are different from, independent of, and yet consistent with each other, so the instantaneous marginal propensity to consume is different from, independent of, and consistent with the consumption function. There are various possible alternatives to equation (4). One alternative which may be considered as the Keynesian consumption function is

$$C_{r_t} = f_1(Y_{r_t}) \qquad (4')$$

For C_{r_t} and Y_{r_t} in equation (1) to be the same as the corresponding magnitudes in equation (4'), $f_1(Y_{r_t})$ must be equal to $Y_{r_t} - I_{r_t}$, which means that equation (4') and definitional equation (1) must be consistent with each other. For instance, if (4') tells us that C_{r_t} is some fraction, a, of Y_{r_t}, then the magnitudes in (1) must conform. The value of I_{r_t} in (1) then automatically sets the values of C_{r_t} and Y_{r_t}. Equation (4') is not a consumption function in the sense of giving us an absolute amount of current consumption: it merely tells us the ratio of the current consumption to current income. The actual amounts of consumption and income are determined by investment—hence the controlling role of investment in the Keynesian system. With equation (4), however, we have a "true" consumption function which gives us an absolute amount of current consumption regardless of the current level of investment.

Equation (3) provides for the "expenditure lag." In this case, the income of one period is spent in the next. A lag of several periods could readily be substituted. There are many studies—such as those of Duesenberry, Katona, and Modigliani—which indicate that a lagged relationship is appropriate or, at any rate, that a simple concurrent relationship is not appropriate.[11] Studies of available data by Metzler and by Tinbergen and Polak, however, point to a short-run correspondence between current income and current consumer expenditure in the United States.[12] In the case of annual data, Haavelmo has shown that the preceding year's income may be given some part in the consumption function.[13]

Any lag between the production and payment of income is not taken into account here. The output of goods creates income which accrues to the income recipients. If, perchance, some of the accruals are not paid out and thus do not become available for disposal by consumers, the result will presumably be to affect the level of consumption. Hence any "income payments" lag will show its effects through the consumption function, equation (4). In so far as the retention of business earnings also affects the inducement to invest, the "income payments" lag will also show its effects in the magnitude of investment in equation (1) the determinant of which is introduced at a later state (in equations [7]–[10]).

The relation between the" instantaneous" and "normal" marginal propensity to consume (hence multiplier) may now be demonstrated through the use of equations (1′) and (4). Suppose that income, consumption, and investment have grown proportionately for some years and the ratio $(\Delta C_{r_t})/(\Delta Y_{r_t})$ has been the same year after year, say at 4/5, and that we call this the "normal" value. Specifically in period t, $(\Delta C_{r_t})/(\Delta Y_{r_t})$ is 4/5. The reason why the two rose proportionately may be that consumers foresaw fully the effects of increments of investment. Now suppose that in period $t + 1$ there is an increment of investment $\Delta I_{r_{t+1}}$ which, departing from earlier experience, is not foreseen by consumers, who make no adjustment whatever. According to (1), however, income will rise by the amount of increase in investment. Hence $(\Delta C_{r_{t+1}})/(\Delta Y_{r_{t+1}})$ will be less than $(\Delta C_{r_t})/(\Delta Y_{r_t})$, which equaled the normal value. This has come about because of a lag in the response of

consumption to an increase in income, as in equation (4). Under equation (4), however,

$$C_{r_{t+2}} = f(Y_{r_{t+1}})$$

Therefore the increase in realized income $\Delta Y_{r_{t+1}}$ will be reflected in the consumption of the next period, $\Delta C_{r_{t+2}}$. Thus $(\Delta C_{r_{t+2}})/(\Delta Y_{r_{t+1}})$ will be greater than $(\Delta C_{r_{t+1}})/(\Delta Y_{r_{t+1}})$ and will be closer to the normal value representd by $(\Delta C_{r_t})/(\Delta Y_{r_t})$. This rise in the direction of the normal value continues indefinitely. Thus for each period when we have income changes unforeseen by consumers, we shall have a different "instantaneous" $(\Delta C_r)/(\Delta Y_r)$, but after a sufficient length of time, or after consumers foresee and adjust to the new pattern of income changes, the "instantaneous" multiplier for some period, say, $t + m$, will attain or approach the normal value.

III. SWEDISH EQUATIONS

The differences which exist among Swedish writers such as Wicksell, Myrdal, Lundberg, and Ohlin make it difficult to characterize the Swedish school in any simple manner. Nevertheless, the general though not universal Swedish emphasis has been on the contrast between planned and unplanned magnitudes. Perhaps it is correct to say (analytically, not chronologically) that Robertson has emphasized planned magnitudes, Keynes has stressed realized magnitudes, and the Swedish writers have accented the relation between the two.

The Swedish system has contributed the following equations:

$$S_{r_t} = S_{p_t} + S_{u_t} \tag{5}$$

$$I_{r_t} = I_{p_t} + I_{u_t} \tag{6}$$

where the subscript u represents unplanned (i.e., unexpected or unintended) magnitudes. The Swedish analysts can readily make assumption (4), which, when stated in terms of expectations, could be interpreted to mean that consumers expect their income to remain stable. If they choose, they may, instead, consider consumption as being determined by expectations based on other variables within the system (i.e., endogenous to the model) or even totally outside the system (i.e., exogenous to the model). In the latter case, we should have

$$C_{r_t} = \bar{C}_{r_t} \qquad (4'')$$

In place of (4) or (4'') a more complicated consumption function taking account of past peak income, trough income, or any other income (or other variables within the system) might be used.

IV. ADDITIONAL EQUATIONS

The additional equations which are needed to complete our system deal with the inducement to invest—hence draw heavily on Keynesian, Robertsonian, and Swedish analyses, to mention only a few. Emphasis is placed on "expectation-formation" and "realized surprise," concepts which will be explained in due course.

The planned investment of the current period may be determined by the unplanned changes of the preceding period, which are emphasized in the Swedish analysis.[14] In that case we might have

$$I_{p_t} = g(\bar{S}_{u_{t-1}}, \bar{I}_{u_{t-1}}, \bar{i}_t) \qquad (7)$$

where g represents some functional relationship and $\bar{i}_t$ is the rate of interest set by the monetary authority. This equation may be interpreted in terms of expectations, in which case we may say that the unintended changes of the preceding period govern current expectations and output decisions.

The Keynesian investment function which is based on the marginal efficiency of capital in relation to the rate of interest (and is comparable although not identical to the Wicksellian relation between the

natural and market rates of interest) is implicit in equation (7).[15] The marginal efficiency of capital is an expression of entrepreneurial expectations concerning the profitability of investment. Although Keynes did not himself tie those expectations closely into past experiences, equation (7) suggests that the significant factors determining those expectations are the unintended saving and investment of the previous period, since they imply the making of unexpected profits or losses. Other factors could be included, but most of the factors that come to mind are redundant in that the unintended saving and investment are derived from them. As for the rate of interest, it has been included as being given exogenously by the banking system. The interest rate is thus treated as a given magnitude for the current period. We may also make the rate of interest an endogenously determined variable and incorporate the Keynesian theory of interest into the model if we wish. In that case we would substitute the following three equations for (7):

$$I_{p_t} = g_1(\bar{S}_{u_{t-1}}, \bar{I}_{u_{t-1}}, i_t) \qquad (7'a)$$

$$i_t = g_2(M_{d_t}, \bar{M}_{s_t}) \qquad (7'b)$$

$$M_{d_t} = g_3(Y_{r_t}, i_t) \qquad (7'c)$$

where $\bar{M}_{s_t}$ is an exogenously determined amount of money supplied by the monetary authority and M_{d_t} is the demand for money, here assumed to be related to realized income and the interest rate. The loanable funds theory might be used instead. In that case we would have

$$i_t = g_4(\bar{B}_{d_t}, B_{s_t}) \qquad (7'b')$$

$$B_{s_t} = g_5(I_{p_t}, i_t) \qquad (7'c')$$

in place of (7'b) and (7'c), where $\bar{B}_{d_t}$ is the demand for securities, here assumed to be determined (in the aggregate) by the banking system, and B_{s_t} is the supply of securities, here assumed to be related to planned investment and the rate of interest. More elaborate assumptions may be introduced in the case of both theories.

Similarly, equations could be established for the production function and the demand and supply of labor. Since these matters take us far afield, they are not incorporated in the model, but it would not be difficult to provide a place for them.

The planned investment of the current period could be determined by expectations based on other variables within the system through some other investment function, of which one example would be the acceleration principle which forms the basis of Lundberg's study.[16] The complicated nature of the accleration relationship, however, imposes serious difficulties on the explicit inclusion of the principle in the present model.[17] The level of planned investment could also be determined by exogenously given expectations. In that case we would have

$$I_{p_t} = \bar{I}_{p_t} \tag{7''}$$

The next step is to determine the unplanned investment. Here we have the most interesting implications of the Swedish emphasis on unplanned saving and investment. We may designate by C_{m_t} and I_{m_t} the current output of goods produced for consumption and investment (in excess of replacement requirements), respectively. The entire amount will contribute to the employment and income of the period, although some of the goods may not sell and may, instead, accumulate in inventories, thereby constituting part of the realized investment of the period. Thus we derive the equation

$$I_{u_t} = (C_{m_t} - C_{r_t}) + (I_{m_t} - I_{p_t}) \tag{8}$$

which tells us that unplanned investment consists of consumption and capital goods which were intended to be sold within the period but were not sold, hence were unexpectedly added to inventories (or, alternatively, sales might exceed production with the result that inventories are depleted). All unplanned investment is included under I_{u_t}, whether in the form of inventories of capital or consumption goods. The two types of inventories might be distinguished and separate relationships established for them.

In order to appreciate the meaning of C_{m_t} and I_{m_t}, we need some understanding of the concept of "expected income." "Expected income" may have four meanings in this context:[18] (a) the income which consumers expect and on which they form their consumption plans; by equation (4) this expected income is last period's income, and by (4″) it is not based on any past experience embodied in the model; (b) the total sales of capital and consumption goods expected by producers of such goods; this is embodied in our equations (9) and (10); (c) the income level expected by those who make investment decisions; this is embodied in our equation (7); and (d) the sum of planned consumption and planned investment, i.e., the sum of C_{r_t} (since we are assuming consumption plans are realized) and I_{p_t}; this is the income which an economist would "expect" if he surveyed consumers and investors, and it would be realized, too, if only producers would consult him and produce accordingly.

It may seem that the distinction between I_{m_t} and I_{p_t} is an unnecessary one, since I_{m_t} consists of capital goods, which must contribute to realized investment, I_{r_t}, in one way or another—either as planned investment, I_{p_t}, if the capital goods are sold or intentionally added to inventories, or as I_{u_t}, if they unexpectedly remain unsold and are thus unexpectedly added to the producers' inventories of goods on hand. It is true that the current value of I_{r_t} would not be affected if we assumed I_{m_t} to be identical with I_{p_t}. The resulting magnitude of I_{u_t} derived from equation (7) would not, however, reflect the full amount of unplanned investment and would thus impair its usefulness as a determinant of subsequent changes.

The need for the distinction between C_{m_t} and C_{r_t} is even greater. In this case we cannot tell whether the consumption goods produced reached consumers, thus constituting C_{r_t}, or remained unsold, thus being added to investment in inventories. In the latter case the investment in inventories may be planned (in which case part of C_{m_t} becomes I_{p_t}) or unplanned (in which case part of C_{m_t} becomes I_{u_t}). This leads to the suggestion that it may be desirable to distinguish also between consumption planned by consumers and that realized by them. In that case planned consumption would appear in place of realized consumption in equation (8) and in several of the earlier equations. The rationale of this would be that unexpected income changes might result in a greater or smaller consumption than had been planned by consumers. If this distinction is made, the consumption planned by consumers must not be confused with C_{m_t}, i.e., the consumption goods produced by producers in the expectation of sale to consumers or for inventory accumulation.

Equation (8) represents the "output-sales" gap. The discrepancy is between *current* output and *current* sales, hence the term "gap" is used here instead of "lag." The latter term may not be entirely inappropriate, however, in that an excess of current sales over current output involves the sale of past output, while an excess of current output over current sales involves the accumulation of goods for future sale. However, the mere fact that inventories are depleted affords no reason to believe that they will be restored unless expectations are favorable.[19]

In order to complete the determination of I_{u_t} in equation (8), we need determinants of C_{m_t} and I_{m_t}. There are provided by the following equations.

$$C_{m_t} = \phi(\bar{S}_{u_{t-1}}, \bar{I}_{u_{t-1}}) \tag{9}$$

$$I_{m_t} = \psi(\bar{S}_{u_{t-1}}, \bar{I}_{u_{t-1}}) \tag{10}$$

The production of both consumption and capital goods is assumed to be influenced (but possibly in different ways) by the unexpected events of the previous period, i.e., unintended saving and investment. Again, a variety of other, more complicated relationships may be assumed.

We have defined C_{m_t} and I_{m_t} in such a way that

$$Y_{r_t} = C_{m_t} + I_{m_t} \tag{D-1}$$

But we cannot include this as an independent structural equation unless we leave out one of the other equations, since it may be derived from (8), (6), and (1) and would make the system over-determined. Nevertheless, it may well be asked why we bother at all with equations (1)–(8). If we had a model consisting of (D-1), (9), and (10) alone, we would have a complete self-sufficient system which would determine income of the current period for us. All we would have to feed into this system would be the unplanned saving and investment of the previous period. But then how would we determine the unplanned saving and investment of the current period, t, for use in the next period, $t + 1$? The complete set of equations is necessary for that purpose. In a sequence analysis using the above assumptions, the income, unplanned saving, and unplanned investment of each period are required in order to determine the income of the following period, etc. Equations (D-1), (9), and (10) would give us income of the current period. But that would be the end of it. We would have no way of going on to the next period (on the assumptions made).

VI. AN INTEGRATED MODEL

The complete model consisting of ten equations and ten endogenous variables follows. The model is broken down into Keynesian, Robertsonian, Swedish, and "additional" segments.

Keynesian segment:

$$Y_{r_t} = C_{r_t} + I_{r_t} \tag{1}$$

$$S_{r_t} = I_{r_t} \tag{2}$$

Robertsonian segment:

$$\bar{Y}_{r_{t-1}} = C_{r_t} + S_{p_t} \tag{3}$$

$$C_{r_t} = f(\bar{Y}_{r_{t-1}}) \tag{4}$$

Swedish segment:

$$S_{r_t} = S_{p_t} + S_{u_t} \tag{5}$$

$$I_{r_t} = I_{p_t} + I_{u_t} \tag{6}$$

Additional segment:

$$I_{p_t} = g(\bar{S}_{u_{t-1}}, \bar{I}_{u_{t-1}}, i_t) \tag{7}$$

$$I_{u_t} = (C_{m_t} - C_{r_t}) + (I_{m_t} - I_{p_t}) \tag{8}$$

$$C_{m_t} = \phi(\bar{S}_{u_{t-1}}, \bar{I}_{u_{t-1}}) \tag{9}$$

$$I_{m_t} = \psi(\bar{S}_{u_{t-1}}, \bar{I}_{u_{t-1}}) \tag{10}$$

The subscripts are: r, realized magnitudes; p, planned magnitudes; u, unplanned magnitudes; m, goods produced; t, period of time. The variables are: Y, income; C, consumption; I, investment; S, saving; and i, interest rate.

We may trace through the process of income determination in this model. Given last period's unplanned saving and investment, equations (10) and (9) supply us with the volume of capital goods and consumption goods produced. Given last period's income, we obtain consumption in (4). With this information and planned investment in (7), we obtain unplanned investment in (8). Adding them together in (6), we get the realized investment. With the realized investment we obtained from (6) and the realized consumption we obtained from (4), we obtain realized income in (1). Then, using the realized investment from (6) again, we obtain realized saving from (2). And using realized consumption from (4) again, we obtain planned saving in (3). Using these in (5), we obtain unplanned saving. In this way we obtain income, unplanned saving, and unplanned investment.

Another way of describing the function performed by the various equations is to say that the Keynesian segment establishes the relationships that exist between realized income, consumption, investment, and saving; the Robertsonian segment contributes consumption and planned saving; the Swedish segment defines the relation between planned and unplanned magnitudes; and the added segment gives us the determination of planned and unplanned investment. Combining these segments and using the model as a whole, we can determine income from period to period.

VI. PRICES AND PROFITS

The reader may be disturbed by the fact that prices and profits do not appear explicitly in the above model. The variables are stated in monetary terms using current dollars. This probably creates no problem in connection with the functional relationships for planned investment (g) and for output (ϕ and ψ), since behavior in these cases is likely to be in response to the monetary rather than the real magnitudes. If wages were included as a determining variable, a more difficult question would arise here. As for the consumption function (f), there is a greater likelihood that a stable relationship requires the use of real magnitudes or at least some explicit allowance for price fluctuations. Even then there would be a serious question as to the effect of a changing income distribution on the stability of the relationship.[20] From any point of view, a more elaborate consumption function seems to be indicated. It is not required, however, for the present limited purpose of setting up a broad framework for various approaches to income determination.

Nevertheless, the prominent place given to price fluctuations and concomitant profits or losses in Swedish, particularly Wicksellian, analysis dictates a further examination of the model. We measure output (Y_{r_t}, C_{m_t}, and I_{m_t}) at market prices. This means that any additions to or subtractions from inventories, whether planned or not, are also measured at market prices, a procedure which is consistent with some current accounting practices. Any positive amount of unplanned investment in inventories in any period would exert a downward pressure on prices and profits in the next period (a pressure which might, of course, be offset by either exogenous or endogenous changes). Similarly, any negative amount of unplanned investment would exert an upward pressure. Unplanned savings might have similar effects but with opposite signs: positive unplanned saving in the current period might have a stimulative effect in the next period, while unplanned dissaving in the current period might have a restrictive effect in the next. Thus it seems reasonable to assume that changes in unplanned saving and investment are indicative of changes in prices and profits in so far as they provide the stimulus for a cumulative movement along Wicksellian lines.

VII. CONDITIONS FOR STABILITY OF INCOME OVER TIME

There is now an interesting derived equation to be obtained. From (1), (2), (3), and (5) we have

$$Y_{r_t} - \overline{Y}_{r_{t-1}} = S_{r_t} - S_{p_t} = S_{u_t} \qquad \text{(D-2)}$$

Unplanned savings thus consist simply of the change in income from one period to the next. It will be noted that this derived equation is obtained without the use of (4), hence is independent of the particular consumption function we adopt.[21]

Several important conditions concerning the stability of income over time may

be derived. From (D-2) if follows that the condition for the "equilibrium" of income is that realized saving shall equal planned saving, i.e., that unplanned saving shall be zero. In other words,

$$Y_{r_t} = Y_{r_{t-1}}$$

when

$$S_{r_t} = S_{p_t}$$

i.e., when

$$S_{u_t} = 0$$

The condition $S_{r_t} = S_{p_t}$ (or $S_{u_t} = 0$) is both *necessary* and *sufficient* for unchanging income. Planned investment and the relation between planned saving and planned investment do not enter into the condition. The question arises, though, whether realized investment must equal planned investment (i.e., whether unplanned investment must be zero) when there is equilibrium. In other words, does $I_{u_t} = 0$ when $S_{u_t} = 0$?

Equation (6) tells us

$$I_{u_t} = I_{r_t} - I_{p_t} \qquad \text{(6)}$$

Substituting (2) and (5), we have

$$I_{u_t} = S_{p_t} + S_{u_t} - I_{p_t} \qquad \text{(D-3)}$$

Putting $S_{u_t} = 0$, we have

$$I_{u_t} = S_{p_t} - I_{p_t}$$

which will ordinarily not be zero, since S_{p_t} and I_{p_t} are determined independently, the one by the consumption function (4) and the other by the investment function (7). Yet, by (D-1), there is stability of income over time.

Does the equality of planned saving and planned investment insure equilibrium? If we put $S_{p_t} = I_{p_t}$ in (D-3), we have

$$I_{u_t} = S_{u_t}$$

There is no reason to believe that this will be zero and hence no reason to believe that there will be equilibrium over time.

Does the equality of realized investment and planned investment insure equilibrium? If realized investment and planned investment are equal, $I_{u_t} = 0$. Substituting this in (D-3), we have

$$S_{p_t} + S_{u_t} - I_{p_t} = 0$$

or

$$S_{u_t} = I_{p_t} - S_{p_t}$$

which is ordinarily not equal to zero.

A rigorous analysis of the necessary and sufficient conditions for the stability of income over time gives us the following conclusions:

I. *The equality of realized and planned saving is sufficient and necessary for an equilibrium of income over time.*

II. *The equality of realized investment (saving) and planned investment is neither sufficient nor necessary for an equilibrium of income over time.*

III. *The equality of planned saving and planned investment is neither sufficient nor necessary for the equilibrium of income over time.*

IV. *The combination of conditions II and III is sufficient but not necessary for the equilibrium of income over time.*[22]

Since these conclusions may strike the reader as being incorrect, it is suggested that he try out several numerical examples. For this purpose it should be recalled that there are two behavior functions (4) and (7) from which values of C_{r_t} and I_{p_t}, respectively, may be obtained and two additional behavior functions (9) and (10) from which values of C_{m_t} and I_{m_t}, respectively, may be obtained. Limitations of space prevent the use of illustrative examples here.

It should be emphasized that neither (II) nor (III) taken by itself is either sufficient or necessary to achieve equilibrium over time but that the combination of the two is sufficient although not necessary. Conclusion (IV) reduces algebraically to (I); but if (II) and (III) were revised to state inequalities of equal magnitude, a combination of the revised (II) and (III) would also reduce to (I).

Therefore (IV) is merely sufficient and not necessary.

This analysis leads to some important conclusions. The fact that investment plans may be realized is neither an assurance nor a necessary concomitant of income stability (condition II). The same may be said of the fact that investment plans match saving plans (condition III). Income stability may be achieved even if investment plans are not realized. It may also be achieved even if investment plans do not match saving plans, i.e., the compatibility of saving and investment plans is neither sufficient nor necessary for equilibrium of income over time. The compatibility of *production* plans with other plans holds the key to stability.

It is true that income stability will be achieved whenever investment plans are realized and also match saving plans (condition IV), but a stable income may also be attained if these conditions are not met. The realization of saving plans (condition I), however, is both sufficient and necessary to accomplish the stability of income. If saving plans are not realized, income will change. Another way of stating the equilibrium condition is to say that income remains stable whenever the extent of the disappointment of investment plans equals the extent to which those plans fail to match saving plans. This makes it clear once more that the condition for stability is that the realized investment (saving) should equal planned saving, for then planned investment will necessarily be equidistant from both realized investment and planned saving. It does not matter how far off the investment plans are as long as saving plans are realized. Still another way of saying this is that it does not matter for this purpose whether the realized investment of any period was planned or unplanned. As long as total investment matches planned saving, the income of the period will be the same as that of the preceding period. Thus Robertson's first thought was the right one—it is the equality of actual (not planned) investment and planned saving which holds the complete key (both necessary and sufficient) to a stable income.[23]

What is the use, then, of our equations which distinguish planned and unplanned investment? Similarly, do we need equation (6), which gives us unplanned saving? The answer lies in our expectational assumptions. We need this period's unplanned saving and investment to determine the surprises of the period, hence next period's income.

VIII. SAVINGS AND INVESTMENT AS FUNCTIONS OF INCOME

We may now return to the question whether S_{r_t} and I_{r_t} in equation (2) should be regarded as functions of income, as Klein has emphasized.[24] We cannot, of course, simply add two equations

$$S_{r_t} = h_1(Y_{r_t}) \tag{2a}$$

$$I_{r_t} = h_2(Y_{r_t}) \tag{2b}$$

since this evidently would make the system overdetermined in view of the other equations of the model which determine values for S_{r_t} and I_{r_t}. The only meaningful way to make S and I functions of income is to assume inventories to be negligible or to define investment to exclude undesired inventory changes, thereby eliminating most of the other equations. In the latter case the equation $S = I$ could be regarded as an "equilibrium condition," in the sense that undesired inventory changes are excluded, as Koopmans has suggested.[25]. This would mean that I is defined as planned investment, I_p, and S is presumably defined as realized saving, S_r. The equilibrium condition is then $S_r = I_p$. In other words, $I_u = 0$ is taken as the equilibrium condition. This must be the rationale of Klein's use of $S(Y) = I(Y)$ as an equilibrium condition,

for he says that "...the rate of change of income varies inversely with unintended inventory accumulation."[26] The condition $I_u = 0$ is not an equilibrium condition, however, in the sense of insuring stability of income over time. It was shown above that income could change, i.e., $Y_{r_t} - Y_{r_{t-1}} \neq 0$ even though $I_{u_t} = 0$. Alternatively, if $S = I$ means $S_p = I_p$, it was shown above that there is no assurance of stability of income over time. Only if $S = I$ means $S_p = I_r$, i.e., $S_u = 0$, do we have stability of income over time. But this condition, $S_p = I_r$ or $S_u = 0$, is derived from our system (eq. [D-2]), and to add it as a separate equation would make the system overdetermined. In short, $S(Y) = I(Y)$ cannot be added to our present model; but this is not to deny that saving, investment, and income are interrelated through the set of equations as a whole.

IX. EXPENDITURE LAG VERSUS OUTPUT LAG

The stability condition derived in Part VII seems to place emphasis on the "expenditure lag" which expresses itself in equations (3) and (4) and tells us how much planned saving we can expect for the current period. (In so far as there is an "income payments lag" it will also be expressed in equation [4], as pointed out earlier, but this does not affect the present point.) If there were no expenditure lag, there could be no discrepancy between realized investment (saving) and planned saving, but neither would there be a link between current and past income. If there is a zero expenditure lag, we can only say that current income is what it is. A zero expenditure lag, and consequent equality of planned saving and realized investment (saving), would not, however, mean stability of income. If $Y_{r_{t-1}}$ in equation (3) were written Y_{r_t}, then S_{p_t} would have to be identical with I_{r_t} in equation (1).

Equations (1) and (3) would be one and the same, and we would not be able to compare Y_{r_t} with $Y_{r_{t-1}}$. Thus the stability condition, $S_{r_t} = S_{p_t}$, is operative only as long as there is an expenditure lag.

The statistical findings on the existence of such a lag are inconclusive. Although Metzler's and Tinbergen's studies suggest a close short-run correspondence between current income and current consumer expenditures in the United States, the studies by Duesenberry, Katona, and Modigliani suggest that it would be wise to retain some sort of expenditure lag for the present.

So much for the planned saving component of the stability condition. What of the other component, realized investment (saving)? Granted that the stability condition directs attention to total investment rather than its planned and unplanned components, is it not important to examine the formation of these components on the assumption that the whole grows if its parts grow? In other words, is not the "output lag" important in determining the magnitude of current realized investment, hence the relation between current realized investment (saving) and planned saving, hence the fluctuations of national income? Certainly equation (6) and the planned investment relation (7) and unplanned investment relation (8)—to say nothing of the studies of Metzler and Lundberg— would give the impression that the "output lag" is important. Yet there is the possibility that it is the total of investment that has causal primacy and that the breakdown between planned and unplanned investment is a subsidiary and secondary operation which may be interesting for some purposes but is of no concern for income stability. If we combine equations (6) and (8), we shall have

$$I_{r_t} = C_{m_t} + I_{m_t} - C_{r_t} \qquad (D\text{-}4)$$

All three terms on the right-hand side are based on data outside the system or per-taining to previous periods through equations (9), (10), and (4), respectively. Thus our suspicions are confirmed. The output lag, i.e., the breakdown between planned and unplanned investment, does not help us to determine the realized investment of the current period. It does not affect the relationship between realized investment (saving) and planned saving and hence does not determine whether income this year is equal to, greater than, or less than last year's. The realized amount of investment depends on the expectations of *producers*, not investors, in relation to decisions of *consumers*. The investors make plans which will determine what component of the produced goods will be classified (if anyone is interested) as "planned" investment. Consumers decide how much they want to consume. All the rest of the goods produced, whether originally designed for investment or consumption, becomes classified as "unplanned" investment. The current "output lag" may then be computed, but its causal significance for the current period's investment and income is nil.

This conclusion is substantiated from another point of view. If we assumed for the moment that the "expenditure lag" and the "income payments lag" were negligible, then income produced would fluctuate with consumption without lead or lag. But since investment is the difference between income and consumption, it too could neither lead nor lag behind income or consumption. Hence the "output lag" could merely determine the internal composition of investment but have no significance for the timing relation of income and investment. If the relation between income and consumption were stable, the relation between income and investment would also have to be stable. If income rises and consumption rises proportionately, investment must also rise proportionately. Any growth of inventories would have to be at the expense of other components of investment. The absence of an "output lag" would affect the composition of realized investment but not the magnitude of investment. This conforms to our earlier analysis, which showed (Part VII) that zero inventory accumulation (therefore zero "output lag") is neither necessary nor sufficient for income stability.

The question of lags is the other side of the question of reaction speeds and unit periods. If we give the period t some definite chronological length, say, three months, we are assuming that a period of three months is representative (or is some sort of average) of the many decision-making components of the economy concerned with consumption, investment, and production. However, if we get to the point of specifying the chronological length of the period, we can make use of statistical studies which will give us the macro-equivalent of the diverse micro-periods. Nor is it necessary to assume that reaction speeds (hence time lags) in consumption, investment, and production decisions are all the same. The consumption lag could be two periods of t length each, the investment lag one such period, the production lag three, or any other combination. However, if we use a lag of more than one period, we may end up with more than one sequence.[27] This complicates the analysis but does not present any insuperable barrier.

X. EQUILIBRIUM VERSUS SEQUENCE VERSUS ECONOMETRIC ANALYSIS

The fact that the Keynesian system is an equilibrium system and the Swedish a nonequilibrium system concerned with cumulative sequences[28] does not mean that the two are incompatible. As in the foregoing model, the two may exist side by side in peace and harmony. In fact, they supplement each other. The Keynes-

ian relationships have been used in many "dynamic" studies (in the Samuelsonian[29] rather than Harrodian[30] sense). In the above model, consumption is dynamized along Robertsonian lines and investment along Swedish lines. At the same time, equilibrium may exist in the Swedish system, as indicated in the foregoing analysis of the conditions for stability. The formal Keynesian system describes a balance of forces in a state of rest, while the Robertsonian and Swedish systems (and less formal aspects of Keynesian analysis) show how these forces react upon one another when they are not in balance. Thus the dilemma posed by Hicks does not exist: "One of the greatest economic questions which remains to be settled is whether the trade cycle is more easily to be explained in terms of mechanical periodicities which can be expressed by difference equations, or whether a temporary equilibrium theory of the Keynesian type is ultimately the more potent."[31] Each approach increases the potency of the other.

It should perhaps be mentioned that the above is a theoretical model and is not amenable to statistical analysis in its present form. The main remaining task would be to state explicitly the assumed nature of the functional relationships. Once these modifications are made in the equations, the model is ready for statistical analysis along econometric lines. Reduced forms can be derived linking current to past magnitudes along the lines of Tinbergen's studies. Thus the proposed model may provide a link between Keynesian equilibrium analysis, Robertsonian–Swedish sequence analysis, and contemporary econometric analysis.

XI. THE ROLE OF "REALIZED SURPRISE" IN THE FORMATION OF EXPECTATIONS

A major feature of this system is that the income of any period is determined by the degree of "realized" surprise. This is not like Shackle's "potential" surprise,[32] which is a device for describing the structure of existing expectations. We are trying to explain the *formation* of expectations by anchoring our expectations firmly in the surprises of the last period—the actual amounts of unplanned saving and unplanned investment. We assume that these surprises determine our expectations regarding the future, hence our output decisions. Perhaps it would be correct to say that realized surprise is an important determinant of any structure of expectations, whether in the form of a probability distribution or a "potential surprise function." The "realized surprise" thus plays a role in the formation of expectations.

Surprisingly enough, that "prince of expectation merchants,"[33] Hicks, denies the importance of realized magnitudes in decision formation. He says:

The income *ex post* of any particular week cannot be calculated until the end of the week, and then it involves a comparison between present values and values which belong wholly to the past. On the general principle of "bygones are bygones," it can have no relevance to present descisions. The income which is relevant to conduct must always exclude windfall gains; if they occur, they have to be thought of as raising income for future weeks (by the interest on them) rather than as entering into any effective sort of income for the current week. Theoretical confusion between income *ex post* and *ex ante* corresponds to practical confusion between income and capital.[34]

Here Hicks is confining his attention to the effect of realized surprise of any period on the decisions which took effect during that period. He neglects the effect which such surprise has on the formation of expectations for the decisions to be taken concerning future periods. Granted that current and recent experience should not have a controlling effect on current decisions concerning the future, how can

it fail to color expectations in practice? If experience is no guide to conduct, how are expectations formed at all? The economist's injunction to the businessman that "bygones are bygones" means that the businessman should not be *controlled* by the past; it does not mean that he should not allow his past experience to assist him in making decisions. Otherwise there would be no way of selecting any of the myriad universes of possibilities in any situation, as to which are likely to occur and which not; which are ridiculous and which reasonable; which (as a practical matter) should be included and which excluded from the range of possibilities. In other words, we may rephrase the advice to read "bygones are gone but not forgotten; nor should they be." The use to which the "bygones" in the form of "realized surprise" are put in our model is indicated more clearly below.

XII. THE MODEL REARRANGED

Our model is rearranged here to show more conveniently how the "realized surprise" elements are obtained and how they are used. The numbers employed previously are shown on the right. The only change is that derived equation (D-1) is used instead of equation (8).

Determination of national income:

(i) $\quad Y_{r_t} = C_{m_t} + I_{m_t}$ \hfill (D-1)

(ii) $\quad C_{m_t} = \phi(\bar{S}_{u_{t-1}}, \bar{I}_{u_{t-1}})$ \hfill (9)

(iii) $\quad I_{m_t} = \psi(\bar{S}_{u_{t-1}}, \bar{I}_{u_{t-1}})$ \hfill (10)

Determination of unplanned investment:

(iv) $\quad I_{u_t} = I_{r_t} - I_{p_t}$ \hfill (6)

(v) $\quad I_{r_t} = Y_{r_t} - C_{r_t}$ \hfill (1)

(vi) $\quad C_{r_t} = f(\bar{Y}_{r_{t-1}})$ \hfill (4)

(vii) $\quad I_{p_t} = g(\bar{S}_{u_{t-1}}, \bar{I}_{u_{t-1}}, i_t)$ \hfill (7)

Determination of unplanned saving:

(viii) $S_{u_t} = S_{r_t} - S_{p_t}$ (5)

(ix) $S_{r_t} = I_{r_t}$ (2)

(x) $S_{p_t} = \overline{Y}_{r_{t-1}} - C_{r_t}$ (3)

In our first group of equations we substitute (ii) and (iii) in (i) to obtain Y_{r_t}. We could stop there, since we have attained our main goal, the national income. But this does not give us the magnitudes we need to determine the income of the next period, namely, the "realized surprise" elements, unplanned saving and investment. The next group of equations gives us unplanned investment by substituting (i) and (vi) in (v) and then (v) and (vii) in (iv). The third group of equations gives us unplanned saving by substituting (v) in (ix) and then (x) and (ix) in (viii). This model then determines income from period to period in unending sequence.

XIII. AN ABBREVIATED MODEL

We conclude with an abbreviated model which may prove to be a workable substitute for the ten-equation system presented above. It takes a number of short cuts and streamlines the equations as follows:

(I) $Y_{r_t} = \mu(\overline{Y}_{r_{t-1}}, \overline{I}_{u_{t-1}})$
        [mainly combines (i), (ii), and
        (iii)]

(II) $I_{u_t} = Y_{r_t} - C_{r_t} - I_{p_t}$
        [combines (iv) and (v)]

(III) $C_{r_t} = f(\overline{Y}_{r_{t-1}})$ (vi)

(IV) $I_{p_t} = \eta(\overline{I}_{u_{t-1}}, i_t)$
        [adapted from (vii)]

Unplanned saving does not appear at all, on the assumption that its importance in determining expectations is very small compared with that of unplanned investment. The fact that current unplanned saving provides a means of stating the stability condition does not imply anything whatever regarding the role of past unplanned saving in influencing current expectations and current decisions. Equation (I) assumes that the output of all goods is determined by expectations whose determining influences are last period's income and the "realized surprise" in the form of unplanned investment. That gives us all we need for the determination of the current national product. For this purpose the usual breakdown of national income into consumption and investment is not required. However, in order to determine next period's income we need the current period's unplanned investment. Equation (II) defines unplanned investment as total output less consumption less planned investment. Equation (III) determines consumption on the basis of expectations of which the endogenous determinant is last period's income. Equation (IV) determines planned investment on the basis of expectations, of which the endogenous determinant is last period's "realized surprise" in the form of unplanned investment, in relation to the current interest rate. The total of realized investment, if needed for any purpose, can be derived from II and IV. There are four equations and four unknowns.

This simplified model recognizes the fact that the output, hence income, of any period is determined by the expectations of those who make production decisions and not merely by those who make investment or consumption decisions. Even in the limiting case where definite advance orders are given to producers, there is an expectational factor to some extent in the possibility of cancellation. The accumulation of large backlogs of orders also suggests that orders alone are not sufficient to determine the rate of current production; producers' expectations, among other factors, are involved in the decision as to the rate at which to use up the backlog.

The investors and consumers are important, however, in determining the extent of the "realized surprise" experienced by the producers, and this in turn influences producers' expectations and decisions for the following period.

NOTES

1 A. P. Lerner, "Some Swedish Stepping Stones in Economic Theory," *Canadian Journal of Economics and Political Science*, November, 1940, p. 590. See the important contribution made along these lines in A. Smithies, "Process Analysis and Equilibrium Analysis," *Econometrica*, January, 1942, pp. 26–38.

2 Alvin H. Hansen, "The Robertsonian and Swedish Systems of Period Analysis," *Review of Economics and Statistics*, February, 1950, pp. 24–29, and "A Note on Savings and Investment," *Review of Economics and Statistics*, February, 1948, pp. 30–33; J. R. Hicks, *A Contribution to the Theory of the Trade Cycle* (Oxford: Clarendon Press, 1950), chap. iii, "Saving, Investment, and the Multipler."

3 Gottfried Haberler, "Mr. Keynes' Theory of the 'Multipler': A Methodological Criticism," *Zeitschrift für National-ökonomie*, 1936, pp. 299–305 (reprinted in *Readings in Business Cycle Theory* [Philadelphia: Blakiston Co., 1944], pp. 193–202).

4 Bertil Ohlin, "Some Notes on the Stockholm Theory of Savings and Investment," *Economic Journal*, 1937 (reprinted in *Readings in Business Cycle Theory*, p. 125).

5 See Lloyd A. Metzler, "Factors Governing the Length of Inventory Cycles," *Review of Economic Statistics*, XXIX (1947), 1–15, and "The Nature and Stability of Inventory Cycles," *ibid.*, XXIII (1941), 113–129.

6 See Harold M. Somers, "The Multiplier in a Tri-Fiscal Economy," *Quarterly Journal of Economics*, LXIII (1949), 258–272.

7 See, e.g., Fritz Machlup, *International Trade and the National Income Multiplier* (Philadelphia: Blakiston Co., 1943).

8 For two different approaches to the problem of generalizing the multiplier, see John S. Chipman, "The Generalized Bi-System Multiplier," *Canadian Journal of Economics and Political Science*, May, 1949, pp. 176–189; Richard M. Goodwin, "The Multiplier as Matrix," *Economic Journal*, December, 1949, pp. 536–555; and papers presented by both authors at the meeting of the Econometric Society in New York City, December, 1949, subsequently abstracted in *Econometrica*, July, 1950, pp. 286–288.

9 See Harold M. Somers, "The Instantaneous Theory of the Multiplier: A Comment [on a note by Clarence L. Barber in the February, 1950, issue]," *Canadian Journal of Economics and Political Science*, May, 1950, pp. 239–240.

10 See Friedrich A. Lutz, "The Outcome of the Saving-Investment Discussion," *Quarterly Journal of Economics*, Vol. LII (1937–1938) (reprinted in *Readings in Business Cycle Theory*, pp. 138–150); and Abba P. Lerner, "Saving and Investment: Definitions, Assumptions, Objectives," *Quarterly Journal of Economics*, Vol. LIII (1938–1939) (reprinted in *Readings in Business Cycle Theory*, p. 160, n. 2).

11 For a review of earlier studies on this subject see Harold M. Somers, *Public Finance and National Income* (Philadelphia: Blakiston Co., 1949), chap. iv, pp. 39–64. For recent studies see James S. Duesenberry, *Income, Saving and the Theory of Consumer Behavior* (Cambridge: Harvard University Press, 1949), esp. chaps. v and vi; George Katona, "Effect of Income Changes on the Rate of Saving," *Review of Economics and Statistics*, May, 1949, pp. 95–103, and "Analysis of Dissaving," *American Economic Review*, June, 1949, p. 673–688; Franco Modigliani, "Fluctuations in the Saving-Income Ratio: A Problem in Economic Forecasting," *Studies in Income and Wealth* (New York: National Bureau of Economic Research, 1949), XI, 371–443; and Roy C. Cave, "Prewar-Postwar Relationship between Disposable Income and Consumption Expenditures," *Review of Economics and Statistics*, May, 1950, pp. 172–176.

12 Lloyd Metzler, "Three Lags in the Current Flow of Income," in *Income, Employment and Public Policy: Essays in Honor of Alvin H. Hansen* (New York: Norton, 1948), pp. 1–32, esp. pp. 21–24; and Jan Tinbergen and J. J. Polak, *The Dynamics of Business Cycles* (Chicago: University of Chicago Press, 1950), chap. xiii, pp. 159–232, esp. 182–191. Contrast Robert V. Rosa, "Use of the Consumption Function in Short Run Forecasting," *Review of*

Economics and Statistics, May, 1948, pp. 91–105.

13 Trygve Haavelmo, "Methods of Measuring the Marginal Propensity to Consume," *Journal of the American Statistical Association*, March, 1947, pp. 105–122, esp. p. 120 n.

14 However, Ohlin seems to be willing to make planned investment an exogenous variable, since he refers to the use of questionnaire surveys to obtain the necessary estimates (Bertil Ohlin, *The Problem of Employment Stabilization* [New York: Columbia University Press, 1949], pp. 117–118). Presumably estimates of the sort made by the U.S. Department of Commerce would be useful in this connection. See Lawrence Bridge and Bernard Beckler, "Capital Investment Programs and Sales Expectations in 1950," *Survey of Current Business*, April, 1950.

15 As Tarshis has pointed out, the effect of disappointment on the marginal efficiency of capital can readily be taken into account if the knowledge is available. See Lorie Tarshis, review of Bertil Ohlin, *The Problem of Employment Stabilization*, in *Journal of Political Economy*, LVII (1950), 359.

16 Erik Lundberg, *Studies in the Theory of Economic Expansion* (London: P. S. King & Son, Ltd., 1937).

17 See Somers, *Public Finance and National Income*, pp. 65–116; see also Lundberg, *op. cit.*, p. 243 n.

18 The first two are proposed by Hansen, "The Robertsonian and Swedish Systems of Period Analysis," *op. cit.*, p. 26.

19 Contrast the assumptions made in Metzler, "Factors Governing the Length of Inventory Cycles," *op. cit.*, and "The Nature and Stability of Inventory Cycles," *op. cit.*

20 For a clear exposition of this problem see Erich Schneider, "A Note on the Consumption Function," *Nordisk Tidsskrift for Teknisk Økonomie*, 1948, pp. 223–227.

21 It should be emphasized that we are using the term "stability of income," in the restrictive sense of "no change over time," the sense in which it is used by the authors cited in this section.

22 Contrast: "The condition of equilibrium requires *both* that intended investment shall be equal to designed saving *and* that actual investment shall be equal to intended investment" (Hansen, "The Robertsonian and Swedish Systems of Period Analysis," *op. cit.*, p. 26). This suggests that the joint condition is neces- sary, whereas our analysis indicates that it is not necessary.

23 Contrast: "So it is equality of *designed*, or *intended* 'investment,' not of actual 'investment,' with designed saving that can be regarded as a condition of equilibrium" (D. H. Robertson, *Money* [New York and London: Pitman, 1948], p. 210). Hansen ("The Robertsonian and Swedish Systems of Period Analysis," *op. cit.*) refers to this quotation as stating a necessary but not sufficient condition. According to our analysis, it is neither necessary nor sufficient.

24 Lawrence R. Klein, *The Keynesian Revolution* (New York: Macmillan, 1947), pp. 110–117. Cf. his "Theories of Effective Demand and Employment," *Journal of Political Economy*, April, 1947, p. 262.

25 Tjalling C. Koopmans, "Identification Problems in Economic Model Construction," *Econometrica*, April, 1949, p. 137, n. 9.

26 *The Keynesian Revolution*, p. 114. Samuelson's approach is similar: "...an excess of actual savings-investment over intended investment would tend to make income fall" (Paul A. Samuelson, *Foundations of Economic Analysis* [Cambridge: Harvard University Press, 1947], p. 278).

27 J. Marschak, "Lectures in Econometrics: Lectures Delivered at the University of Buffalo, March–May, 1948" (mimeographed).

28 See Sidney D. Merlin, *The Theory of Fluctuations in Contemporary Economic Thought* (New York: Columbia University Press, 1949), pp. 59–120.

29 Paul A. Samuelson, "Dynamic Process Analysis," in *A Survey of Contemporary Economics*, pp. 352–387, ed. H. S. Ellis (Philadelphia and Toronto: Blakiston, 1948).

30 R. F. Harrod, *Towards a Dynamic Economics* (London: Macmillan, 1948), "Lecture One" (pp. 1–34).

31 J. R. Hicks, *Value and Capital* (2d ed.; Oxford: Clarendon Press, 1946), p. 337.

32 See G. L. S. Shackle, *Expectation in Economics* (Cambridge: Cambridge University Press, 1949).

33 To add a second principality to that already conferred on Hicks by Robertson, who called him "prince of liquidity merchants" (D. H. Robertson, "A Revolutionist's Handbook," *Quarterly Journal of Economics*, February, 1950, pp. 1–14).

34 *Value and Capital*, p. 179.

Keynes and the Effectiveness of Monetary Policy
Axel Leijonhufvud*

The Keynesian tradition in macro-economics, particularly in the United States, has been associated with a decided preference for fiscal over monetary stabilization policies. In the development of this school of thought, certain arguments to the effect that monetary policy is generally ineffective have historically played a large role. By no means all the major contributors to the Keynesian tradition can be tarred with this brush. But, of those who have been outspokenly pessimistic about the usefulness of monetary policy, the vast majority would certainly be popularly identified as "Keynesians." Since the proposition that monetary policy is ineffective has in this way become associated with his name, it is of some interest to examine the case originally made by Keynes.

Since abounding faith in fiscal measures and a withering away of interest in monetary policy was one of the most dramatic aspects of the so-called "Keynesian Revolution," there is, I believe a tendency to impute these views, as well as the analytical tools with which they were propounded, to the *General Theory*. It is of course true that this work, on the one hand, expressed doubts about the efficacy of banking policy and, on the other, argued for public works programs and for

Axel Leijonhufvud, "Keynes and the Effectiveness of Monetary Policy," *Western Economic Journal*, 6 (March 1968), pp. 97–111.

* The material of this paper, as well as that of an earlier paper [12], has been drawn from a lengthier manuscript, *On Keynesian Economics and the Economics of Keynes*, to be published by Oxford University Press in the fall of 1968. I am deeply indebted to the Relm Foundation for making possible my work on this article.

"a somewhat comprehensive socialization of investment" [8, p. 378]. But Keynes' position on the issue was a good deal less clearcut than one would gather from standard textbook expositions of the "Keynesian system." The position on these policy-issues advocated in the *General Theory*, moreover, was not at all "revolutionary" in the sense of making a distinct break with Keynes' own past ideas. On the scales of his personal judgment, there had been only a subtle shift away from reliance on monetary policy and in favor of direct government measures. The extent of this shift has been much exaggerated.

The exaggerated popular view of the extent to which Keynes' *magnum opus* downgraded the usefulness of monetary policy reflects an oversimplified and mechanical interpretation of his contribution which is deeply embedded in the "Keynesian" tradition. This paper seeks to restore some perspective on the issue. The motive for this attempt is the one common to most doctrine-historical essays: Misconceptions of where one has been and of the path followed to the present most often mean ignorance of where one is, and where one is going.

Sections I and II below are of a purely doctrine-historical nature. The continuity of Keynes' thought on matters of "Applied Theory" is emphasized, and some of the reasons why this continuity has not been more apparent to his readers are discussed. Sections III and IV continue the doctrine-historical documentation of the assertions made about Keynes' views but deal mainly with some theoretical issues that, while neglected in the Keynesian literature, should still be of interest for their own sake. Section III considers Keynes' diagnosis of the disequilibrium characterizing a persistent unemployment state. Section IV relates the alternative cures of monetary expansion and fiscal deficit to his diagnosis of the unemployment problem.

I

Today, the *General Theory* is remembered chiefly as signaling a revolution in professional thinking and popular attitudes on stabilization policy. Among modern economists, Keynes' reputation derives chiefly from the book's impact on practical affairs, for the outcome of the "Keynes and the Classics" debate represents the rejection of his claims to being a major theoretical innovator. The fact is however that, while Keynes' earlier *Treatise on Money* [10] gave equal space to "Applied Theory" and "Pure Theory," the *General Theory* was written as a treatise on pure theory. Its sundry reflections on policy-matters appear in passages scattered as the progression of the theoretical argument dictates. There are no separate chapters on stabilization policy, corresponding to the systematic treatment of the subject given by modern textbooks on "Keynesian macroeconomics."

One must recall, therefore, that the main corpus of fiscal policy theory identified with the "New Economics" was constructed by later Keynesians. "Balanced Budget Multipliers," for example, belong to a later period. The once-popular idea that the maintenance of full employment requires ever-increasing government expenditures also came into fashion first with the later incorporation of the accelerator in Keynesian models. Similarly, the standard "Keynesian" argument *against* monetary policy is simply not to be found in the *General Theory* but was a later development about which Keynes expressed the deepest reservations.[1]

In an earlier paper [12], I have argued that, contrary to the conclusions embodied in the so-called Neoclassical "synthesis," Keynes was indeed justified in claiming that his 1936 work presented a more "general" theory than that of the Classics.[2] That, however, applies to the *General Theory* as "Pure" theory. When we turn to Keynes' comments on alternative stabilization policies, we have to deal with his "Applied Theory," and here such a sweeping claim for generality cannot be upheld.

This observation is particularly pertinent to the issue of the effectiveness of monetary policy. The usual textbook discussion of the issue proceeds in terms of the properties of a static simultaneous equation model. It makes no reference to past states of the system, nor to a specific historical and political real world context. Consequently, the conclusions tend to emerge as if they were universally valid: "The interest-elasticity of investment is for various reasons quite low. Hence, monetary policy is not a very useful stabilization instrument." This familiar type of argument does not rely on specific conditions obtaining at a particular time and place.

Keynes' judgment on the issue as it gradually developed to the position voiced in the *General Theory* was based on a number of considerations. These were, on the one hand, assumptions about how unemployment disequilibria generally develop and about the nature of the monetary transmission mechanism. The empirical status of these hypotheses was certainly not settled by his casual empiricism and some of them, at least, must still be regarded as in doubt at this late date. On the other hand, his discussion of monetary policy drew on his personal diagnosis of the nature of the problems facing Britain in the interwar period and also on his judgments with regard to the kinds of policy that were politically feasible in that context. These time- and place-bound considerations naturally cannot without further ado be invoked in judging the effectiveness of monetary policy, say, in the United States of the sixties. Finally, the interest-inelasticity of investment—the pivotal argument in the New Economics position of the issue—was not involved in Keynes' analysis at all.

To Keynes' American readers, in particular, the doubts as to the efficacy of monetary policy expressed in the *General Theory* must nonetheless have been one of the book's most dramatic features. His two previous major works (the *Tract on Monetary Reform* and the *Treatise*) had both dealt almost exclusively with monetary issues, and it was on these books that his theoretical reputation outside Britain chiefly rested. Not only had the *Treatise* been devoted wholly to explaining how monetary policies worked and should be used; its most controversial feature had been the theory that income disequilibria generally had monetary "causes"[3]—for which, consequently, monetary remedies were appropriate.

Comparisons between the *Treatise* and the *General Theory* will easily give an exaggerated impression of the change in Keynes' policy-views also for another reason. The *Treatise* had next to nothing to say about fiscal measures. But in his efforts as a financial journalist, Keynes had consistently argued for public works ever since 1924.[4] There were two parts to this advocacy. On the one hand, the government was urged to subsidize or directly to undertake investment in certain sectors as a matter of longer-run growth policy. Underlying this recommendation was Keynes' judgment that capital outflow from Britain would otherwise lead to too little domestic long-term investment. In the *Treatise*, this theme received but brief mention—it is significant that it was put under the heading of "International Complications" [10, Vol. II, p. 376]. Following Britain's return to

gold at the old parity, maintenance of employment under conditions of an overvalued currency became the main ground on which Keynes advocated this policy. On the other hand, he also argued for public works as a supplement to monetary policy in combatting the short-run "Credit Cycle." His testimony before the Macmillan Committee makes it clear that, in this context, he saw public works as a "pump-priming" device[5]—i.e., as a method of jolting a disorganized economy back towards equilibrium, not as a continuing measure needed to close an otherwise inexorable "deflationary gap."[6] On both counts, then, he differed from the policy-prescriptions later propounded on the basis of closed-system, comparative static models.

The *General Theory* added very little to this. What mainly made his position more radical in that work was the fact that the "socialization of investment" was there argued with little explicit reference to the International Complications that had initially prompted him to advance this recommendation. It is hard to judge to what extent this represents merely the omission of part of the supporting argument. But there can be little doubt that his increasing pessimism with regard to the efficacy of the monetary policies that Central Banks could be persuaded to pursue made him state the case for fiscal policies in a more uncompromising fashion.

II

A superficial comparison of the analytical frameworks utilized in the *Treatise* and in the *General Theory* respectively may easily reinforce the impression that, in the later work, Keynes suddenly scuttled monetary policy. These eye-catching differences in analytical approach therefore deserve some comments.

What are the major differences between the two works? Many economists are likely to think first of the changed definition of saving. Because of the trouble caused readers, much space in the early discussion was devoted to unraveling the implications of this. But such definitional changes were made as a matter of analytical expediency and do not reflect changes in the substance of the underlying theory.

The switch from the "Fundamental Equations" of the *Treatise* to the investment-multiplier of the *General Theory* as the expository device, whereby Keynes sought to compress a complicated and sophisticated theory in a nutshell, is more significant. Yet, it must not be misinterpreted. The "Multiplier" does indeed summarize the two major changes in his model, i.e., (*i*) the idea that the system responds to disturbances by quantity-adjustments and not simply by price-level adjustments (while remaining at full employment), and (*ii*) the idea that initial disturbances are amplified through the consumption-income relation.[7]

In another respect, however, this switch of expository devices can very easily be misleading. The Fundamental Equations were recognizable descendants of the traditional Equation of Exchange.[8] In the *Treatise*, the Quantity Theory lineage is still very evident—the various factors affecting income are still analyzed in terms of their impact on the excess demands for the assets and liabilities of the banking system [10, Vol. I, pp. 142–144, 182–184]. The multiplier-analysis, in contrast, focuses directly on the demand for and supply of commodities. This switch in the immediate focus of the analysis from the excess demand (supply) of "money" to the excess supply (demand) of commodities has probably contributed heavily to the widespread impression that the *General Theory* represented a clean break with Keynes' "monetary" past and an attempt to approach macroeconomics

practically from scratch—and from the "real" side. But it does *not* reflect any basic change in Keynes' views of the processes generating changes in money income and of the role of financial markets in such processes. This cannot be too strongly emphasized. If the further discussion of the *General Theory*'s appraisal of monetary policy is to make any sense at all, one must first be free of the notion that it was based on some newfound conviction that "money is unimportant."

The development of Keynes' views relevant here did not take place between the *Treatise* and the *General Theory* but between the *Tract* and the *Treatise*. By and large, the *Tract* respected the traditional boundary between monetary theory and value theory, whereby the former field deals with the demand for output in general and the value of money, and the latter with relative prices. In the interval between the two books, Keynes—very much under the influence of D. H. Robertson—had come to the conviction that it was necessary to relinquish this traditional compartmentalization in order to explain the disequilibrium processes producing changes in money income and price-levels and, in particular, to explain the *modus operandi* of monetary policy. The disaggregation of total output into consumer-goods and investment-goods was a *sine qua non* of the process-analysis presented in the *Treatise*, which invoked systematic changes in the relative price and in relative rates of output of the two in explaining how money income moves from one short-run "equilibrium" level to another.[9] The trouble with the Fundamental Equations was that they still incorporated a variable purporting to represent the total physical volume of output, in the way of the traditional Equation of Exchange, and thus were inconsistent with the verbal explanation of the processes studied.

In the *General Theory*, the Fundamental Equations—and mathematical ambitions generally—were given up. All a bit ironic, for Keynes' successors immediately reverted to an algebraic model devoid of relative prices and with only a single commodity-aggregate. Through the glasses of this standard model, Keynes' claim to having brought "the theory of prices as a whole back to close contact with the theory of value" [8, p. 293] looks incomprehensible. In fact, it has not been widely comprehended. In any case, the *General Theory* retained all the essentials of the theory of the *Treatise*, although its dramatic extension to account for sustained unemployment drew attention away from its older elements.

It is important to understand clearly the nature of the two commodity aggregates with which Keynes worked. The consumption-good is "Liquid"—when looking for an illustration in the *Treatise*, he hit on bananas: "ripe bananas will not keep for more than a week or two" [10, Vol. I, p. 178]. Investment, on the other hand, is in very durable "Fixed Capital," illustrated by "Land, Buildings, Roads and Railways." These are the types of capital-assets for which he advocated some "socialization of investment"— not a very radical recommendation from today's standpoint. Two notes on this definition of the investment-variable need be made.

First, the "short run" of Keynes' theoretical model of fluctuations in investment is not so short in terms of calendar time as we are likely to think. We are exceedingly familiar with "Keynesian" models of inventory-cycles à la Metzler. The *Treatise* did contain a good discussion of variations in stocks of Liquid Capital but explicitly argued that they were of interest as an amplifying and not as an initiating factor in business fluctuations. In the *General Theory*, the "minor miscalculations" underlying inventory cycles rate only a bare mention [8, p. 322]. The modern ambition is to stabilize employment on a year-by-year or even quarter-by-quarter basis. Keynes' perspective, however, was not that of the Kitchin-cycle but rather that of the Juglar or, perhaps, the "Long Swing," to use the not entirely appropriate terminology of Business Cycle Theory. Mere questions of short-run "business conditions" held little interest for him. He dealt with problems in which he saw a threat to the civilization of his time.

Secondly, "the sensitiveness of these activities even to small changes in the long-term rate of interest, though with an appreciable time-lag, is surely considerable" [10, Vol. I, p. 364]. The determination of the price of the representative "Fixed Capital" asset, Keynes handled as an ordinary present value problem. On the one side, the price depends upon entrepreneurial expectations of the earnings stream in prospect. These expectations were discussed in terms of certainty-equivalents, and such certainty-equivalent streams he treated as perfect substitutes for bond-streams of comparable time-profile. On the other side, the rate of interest for the appropriate maturity-class of bonds is the discount rate by which the present value of prospective earnings is to be evaluated.[10]

Within this framework, *if* the price of long-term bonds can be raised by the monetary authority, there will be a proportional rise in the demand-price for Fixed Capital. In Keynes' language, "a decline in the interest rate" *means* "a rise in the market prices of capital goods, equities, and bonds." Thus control over long rate means control over investment and, thereby, money income and employment. The later dogma of interest-inelasticity of investment as the bane of monetary policy originated, not in Cambridge, but in Oxford. The problem with monetary policy, in Keynes' view, is that the required changes in the rate of interest may not be "practicable" [8, p. 164].

III

In the previously cited paper, I argued that Keynes never departed from the "Classical" presumption that a hypothetical vector of nonnegative prices will exist which, if once established, would permit all traders to carry out their corresponding transactions-plans, including the desired sales of labor services· Price-incentives are effective so that it is possible, in principle, to control individual activities so as to make them mesh. When coordination fails, it is because the requisite information is not generated and transmitted, a state of affairs reflected in the persistence of a price-vector different from the one conducive to full employment.

When dealing with Keynes' views, one cannot very well divorce the question of the appropriateness and efficacy of monetary measures from the perceived problem that they are designed to correct. Keynes' diagnosis of the social malady, for which monetary policy was one of the cures to be considered, is best discussed in terms of the relationship between the actual and the "equilibrium" price-vector. It is not necessarily true that only one vector of spot prices is consistent with full employment in the current period, but for simplicity of exposition we shall assume this to be the case in what follows.

Spot-Prices: Wages Versus Asset-Prices

It is tempting to start with the sweeping assertion that in Keynes' eyes wages were "always right." For this aspect of his position has been utterly lost sight of in the interminable literature on the Pigou-effect which seems generally to presume that, if there is unemployment, wages are *ipso facto* above the level consistent with equilibrium. Whereas Keynes obviously recognized unemployment as the most serious of the symptoms of deflationary

disequilibrium, his diagnosis of the malady blamed too low asset-prices. But the generalization is somewhat too broad. There was, as Wright has noted "another Mr. Keynes...though admittedly a junior partner. *He* is the man who points out that money wages can be too high" [14, p. 19].

Three notes on this will suffice: (1) the possibility that the monetary authority will have to deal with a disequilibrium caused by "spontaneous" wage-push is indeed recognized in the *Treatise* [10, Vol. 1, pp. 166 ff.]. But the discussion is fairly perfunctory and the problem soon fades from view. (2) There was one period in which Keynes found himself forced to grapple with a situation in which "too high wages" were the crux of the problem, namely the years of Britain's ill-starred relapse to gold at the old parity [5, esp. p. 411]. Even so, he would have prescribed a low interest policy if not deterred by the prospect of increased capital outflow, and the partial socialization of long-term investment was not his only scheme for avoiding the pains of wage-deflation.[11] Here, however, "too high wages" translate simply into "overvaluation of currency" and this case is therefore of limited relevance in the usual closed system context. (3) His attitude toward the gold standard incident was an instance of a more general value-judgment on which he differed profoundly from Wicksell. For, if a Wicksellian inflation had once been permitted, he argued, the monetary authority should live with its past mistakes and try to stabilize prices (or employment) at the prevailing level of wages.[12] In effect, the Central Bank ought to act *as if* the actual wage-level were the "proper" one.

This, then, leaves "too low" demand prices for augmentable assets as the problem to be dealt with in a situation of deflation and/or unemployment. The issue provides a fair illustration of the characteristic mix of "Pure" theory, casual but shrewd empiricism, and personal value-judgments of which Keynes' "Applied Theory" is composed.

Intertemporal Values: Entrepreneurial Expectations Versus Market Rate

There are two broad reasons why asset prices may be wrong: (*i*) entrepreneurial expectations may be unduly pessimistic or optimistic in relation to the returns in prospect, were the system to follow a hypothetical equilibrium path. Since savers do not place forward orders for consumption goods, the market mechanisms are lacking that would provide entrepreneurs with adequate information on the future demand conditions presently to be reckoned with. (*ii*) Long-term market rates may be too high or too low. Only in the very long run need they conform to the underlying intertemporal transformation possibilities and saving propensity. In the "short-run"—which in terms of calendar time may be measured in years—speculation in securities markets will make them diverge from the levels that would obtain under conditions of full information.

This distinction, I believe, provides the key to the considerations that led Keynes to take a dimmer view of the prospects for effective monetary policy in the *General Theory* than he had done in the *Treatise*.

By the time that Keynes was writing the *General Theory*, Britain was again off gold, and the constraints due to "International Complications" discussed at length in the *Treatise* were no longer of current relevance. Consequently, we may now disregard these complications in appraising the *Treatise*. Looking only at the closed-system arguments, the bulk of the work presumes that *entrepreneurial expectations are roughly right*. But it is also assumed that entrepreneurs generally tend to over-react. "The real prospects do not suffer such large and quick changes as does the spirit of enterprise" [10, Vol. II, p. 362]. This characteristic Keynesian

assumption is not generally accepted.[13] It means, however, that implicitly, the *Treatise*'s analysis of how monetary policy should be conducted in the current short period presumes that the system already has a history of appropriate monetary policies up to the present time. Otherwise, the expectations ruling at the outset of the period might just as well be wildly inaccurate as roughly right, since entrepreneurs would have over-reacted to past experiences of excessive or deficient aggregate demand.

The normative force of the main prescription of the *Treatise* derives from this assumption.[14] If expectations are not approximately right, there is nothing "natural" about the natural rate. The recommendation that the monetary authority cause market rate to move in such a manner as to maintain the demand-prices for augmentable assets inherited from last period presumes that this long rate will generally be an "equilibrium" rate. Whenever investment starts to rise or fall, thereby threatening inflation or deflation, the *Treatise* treats this as evidence of an inappropriate level of market rate. Consequently, the appropriate cure consists of a monetary policy designed to correct market rate. It is this presumption that Hayek attacked in criticizing Keynes' neglect of "real" causes of business fluctuations. Keynes' views, of course, flew in the face of the widespread contemporary opinion that the cause of depression were often to be found in the "excesses" of the preceding boom.[15] In Keynes' position that one should never resign oneself to a depressed but supposedly salutary period in which past mistakes were to be "weeded out," one again perceives his characteristic mixture of empirical hypothesis and personal value-judgment.

On this issue, I believe that the relinquishing of the Wicksellian apparatus in the *General Theory* reflects a further development of Keynes' theoretical views, although with no change in his value-judgments towards the "purgatory" views indicated above. The reasons for relinquishing the natural rate-market rate apparatus are but perfunctorily sketched in the *General Theory* however [8, pp. 242–244]. The crux of the matter one finds implicit already in the important penultimate chapter of the *Treatise* in which the assumption that entrepreneurs are right was finally dispensed with. But before turning to that pivotal case, we should consider the difficulties which Keynes saw in the way of conducting an appropriate monetary policy under the simpler conditions when, save for minor miscalculations, the entrepreneurs are right.

Keynes' views of the "normal" difficulties facing Central Bankers must be seen in relation to his diagnosis of the objective situation to be dealt with in the interwar period. He ascribed the prosperity of the early twenties primarily to a Schumpeterian concatenation of war-induced innovations promising quick and high profits. The consequent investment boom had pulled long rate up to a level that, in historical perspective, was exceptionally high [10, Vol. II, esp. pp. 378 ff.]. As the new industries caught up with demand, and war damage and investment backlogs from the war were made good, the abnormal levels of interest rates would no longer be "natural." Over the longer term, the problem facing the monetary authority was that of ensuring that market rate kept pace with the downward trend of natural rate.

In the *Treatise*, there is no question but that the monetary authority can do it— if it only keeps at it continuously. A steady chastisement of bearish speculators might be needed, but the banking system "can by the terms of credit influence *to any required extent* the volume of investment.[16]

There is still a major problem in the execution of the proper policy: "we have *not* claimed that the banking system can produce any of these effects instantaneously; or that it can be expected always to foresee the operation of nonmonetary factors in time..." [10, Vol. II, p. 346]. We have already quoted Keynes on the "appreciable time-lag" between changes in long rates and changes in the rate of output of capital goods. But the lag that mainly concerned him was that inherent in the traditional Bank Rate *cum* Bills Only mode of operation to which Central Banks were addicted— unfortunately and unnecessarily so, in Keynes' opinion. One of the reforms most emphatically urged in the *Treatise*, and echoed in the *General Theory*, was that the monetary authority should operate directly in the long end and not "leave the price of long-term debts to be influenced by belated and imperfect relations from the price of short-term debts" [8, p. 206]. The dangers inherent in this lag were forcefully, if not altogether tastefully, illustrated by his bismuth–castor oil analogy [10, Vol. II, pp. 223–224].

By the time of the *General Theory*, Keynes had reason to be less sanguine about this lag-problem. The Macmillan Committee had given him the best possible platform from which to press this reform on the authorities—but he had found them unwilling to listen [5, p. 413 ff.]. This experience must be taken into account in judging his reasons for being "now somewhat sceptical of the success of a merely monetary policy directed towards influencing the rate of interest" [8, p. 164]. But his own views on the long-term problem had also darkened, quite apart from what the Bank of England could be made to do. He seemed to be looking forward to an indefinite period of deflationary pressure from which "socialization of investment" was well-nigh the only salvation. These were the passages that the Stagnationists fastened upon and enlarged into an elaborate doctrine. Keynes' position at this time was based on two assumptions.

Against one of them one must surely object[17]—the idea that a state of capital saturation and zero marginal efficiency of capital would be reached within a generation if full employment was maintained [8, pp. 420, 375 ff.]. Against the other most economists would hold grave reservations —Keynes' conviction that the long rate will only come down at a most excruciatingly slow pace. There are arguments in favor of his pessimism with regard to manipulating the long rate deftly enough over the "Credit Cycle,"[18] but surely the *General Theory* drew an exaggerated picture of both the obstinacy and the power of the Bear army. When he states that the long rate "may fluctuate *for decades* about a level which is chronically too high" [8, p. 204 (italics added)] one should take into account the historical background of "obstinate maintenance of misguided monetary policies" [10, Vol. II, p. 384] that he painted. But his position on the inflexibility of long rates still seems extreme.

While the Liquidity Trap "might become important in the future," Keynes in 1936 knew "no example of it hitherto" [8, p. 207]. The future envisaged in this passage is one in which capital saturation is so near that the "objective" marginal efficiency of capital would have crept below the margin necessary to cover lender's risk and the cost of intermediation. The diagnosis of the American thirties as an illustration of the static Liquidity Trap came into Keynesian economics with Alvin Hansen and others. Keynes' own stagnationist fears were based on propositions that must be stated in terms of time-derivatives. Modern economies, he believed, were such that, at a full employment rate of investment, the marginal efficiency of capital would always tend to fall *more rapidly* than the long rate of interest [8, pp. 219, 228]. As an inherent tendency of capitalistic civilization, this chronic disparity between the two time-derivatives seems a doubtful proposition. But it sums up a considerable proportion of the passages in which Keynes vented his later doubts on the efficacy of monetary policy.

IV

Through the better part of the *Treatise*, the technical prescriptions for the conduct of monetary policy presume, explicitly, an inherited situation of full employment, and implicitly, the prevalence of entrepreneurial expectations of future demand such as will be by and large fulfilled if only the market rate is brought into correspondence with the natural rate. These beneficial bequests of the past imply, in effect, that past monetary policy has successfully followed the guidelines that Keynes proceeded to prescribe. The conduct of monetary policy in such circumstances poses a relatively easy task, even if we admit that Keynes made light of the practical target-indicator problems involved in keeping track of the unobservable, and supposedly volatile, natural rate with the help of instruments afflicted with seriously lagged effects. In all fairness, he repeatedly acknowledged that the preservation of good health cannot be the end-all of medical practice: "It is much easier to preserve stability than to restore it quickly, after a serious state of disequilibrium has been allowed to set in" [10, Vol. II, pp. 351, 352]. But in the *Treatise*, Chapter 37 was the only one wholly devoted to the cure of the already ill, thereby foreshadowing the main concerns of the *General Theory*.

Consider, then, a depressed situation in which entrepreneurial expectations are attuned to a continuous slump. This is reflected in the current market-values of Fixed Capital assets. Again, asset demand-prices can be raised if only long rates can be brought down—there is no problem of interest-inelasticity of investment. As always with Keynes, the interest-elasticity of the demand for savings-deposits associated with the Speculative Supply of long-term securities is the Central Bank's main problem. To restore a full employment rate of investment, market rate has to be brought down much further than would be needed if entrepreneurial expectations had not already been adversely affected. But, the Keynes of the *Treatise* concluded, this makes no difference in principle. The prescription indicated will not be so much a different policy as more of the same—an "extraordinary" dosage of open-market purchases "to the point of satisfying to saturation the desire of the public to hold savings-deposits" [10, Vol. II, p. 370].

To demand the execution of this "monetary policy *à outrance*" means to "*impose on the Central Bank the duty of purchasing bonds up to a price far beyond what it considers to be the long-period norm*" [10, Vol. II, p. 373]. This is made clearer if we explicitly assume that the initial undervaluation of assets is due entirely to the pessimism of entrepreneurs and that the actually prevailing long rate is exactly the one that would enter into a hypothetical full information state equilibrium vector. The holders of securities are right and entrepreneurs wrong, instead of *vice versa* as in the previous case. The policy recommended is thus one of dragging the righteous through purgatory for the salvation of the unbeliever. For, if the Central Bank succeeds in raising asset demand-prices and making a full employment rate of output of augmentable assets profitable, entrepreneurs will find their pessimistic forecasts falsified by reviving aggregate demand. With the consequent revival of the "spirit of enterprise," the demand prices of capital goods and equities will shortly shoot up *above* the level consistent with continuing stability, if market rate is maintained at the level reached. Having bought high, the Central Bank will therefore be obliged to sell low and thus to "show a serious financial loss" [10, Vol. II, p. 373].

At this point, obviously, Keynes has arrived on the verge of a "Keynesian" policy. For, surely, the step is not long from recommending Central Bank losses to advocating government deficits. If, in fact, orthodox prudence is to be defined, the most promising tack to take may well be to insult the fiscal prudence of elected politicians rather than the financial prudence of self-sufficient central bankers. Keynes, of course, had no success at all in selling this idea to the Bank of England; but, then, the *Treatise's* scarcely veiled intimations that the Central Bank's losses would be its Just Desert for letting the contraction get under way were presumably of little help.

The Central Bank would not be the only loser. Although Keynes makes no mention of it, speculators content to go along with the Central Bank will also have their fingers burned—to the elbow, if they collaborated vigorously. Keynesian bond-holders are notable for long memory; this learning-experience would swell the Bear army and make the Central Bank's task harder the next time a monetary policy *à outrance* is tried. Thus, if the actual market rate is already at the level that would obtain in a hypothetical full employment state, the case for a massive assault on securities markets to drive yields down is not self-evidently a strong one.

The alternative would be a policy of government deficit spending designed to "correct" entrepreneurial demand-forecasts. Direct expenditures on commodities will prevent the self-fulfillment of pessimistic prophecies. By falsifying the forecasts, a rise of asset-values should be obtained at the going market rate of interest. This is a "pump-priming" case, for as full employment is approached the government spending-program may be phased out without throwing the system back into depression.

In the *General Theory*, the whole context of the discussion of short-run problems was one in which entrepreneurial expectations were "depressed," as in Chapter 37, and not objectively right, as in the bulk of the *Treatise*. Keynes recommended continuing government intervention to deal with the long-term threat of stagnation and with the long-term consequences of being committed to maintaining an over-valued currency, as we have seen in previous sections. This should be carefully distinguished from the fiscal measures that he found appropriate for dealing with the shorter-term problem of internal business fluctuations. His Macmillan Committee testimony was explicit on the transitory nature of the injections he deemed needed: "Government investment will break the vicious circle .... I believe you have first of all to do something to restore profits and then rely on private enterprise to carry the thing along."[19]

Further reflection on the case of Chapter 37 may well have contributed significantly to Keynes' new-found favor for fiscal "pump-priming" over the monetary stabilization measures he had previously advocated. In the *Treatise* and the *General Theory*, evidence bearing directly on this point is sparse, however, and this suggestion must therefore be a matter more of speculation than of straight-forward exegesis. Somewhere, one would think, in Keynes' oral testimonies before official bodies, letters, memoranda, and vast printed output, there should be further evidence bearing on the question. Quite possibly, however, he never did carry the explicit analysis of this particular issue beyond the point reached at the end of the *Treatise*.[20] On points of technique, Keynes, after all, was hardly the contemporary master of process-analysis. But questions concerning the extent to which Keynes successfully developed his mode of analysis will today only excite doctrine-historians. His basic approach, however, is still of more than historical interest. The Keynesian tradition, with its biases towards static analysis, against price-theory, and against monetary policy, has not preserved all the worthwhile elements in Keynes' thought, nor has it discarded only his analytical errors and most ill-considered empirical hunches. The standard simultaneous equation model generally accepted as embodying "the Keynesian System" does not represent the successful realization of Keynes' theoretical aims. It is not even a promising point of departure for the development of a rigorous body of analysis which could cope systematically with the type of disequilibrium problems informally sketched in Sections III and IV.

V

All Keynes' arguments, of course, dissolve entirely under the eyes of anyone convinced that, when everything is said and done, the fact remains that the improvement or augmentation of "Land, Buildings, Roads and Railroads" are *not* activities highly sensitive to changes in the rate of interest. If the major components of aggregate expenditures are in fact highly interest-inelastic, that would pretty well settle the matter and one's interest in the more complicated case made by Keynes would then be merely "academic." Among the "elasticity-optimists," furthermore, some may well feel that his theoretical framework is not the most appropriate one for organizing the empirical questions bearing on the substantive issue, or even that it tends to be positively misleading for such purposes. Those, finally, who both tend to agree with Keynes on the interest-elasticities and find his theoretical framework useful, will presumably disagree with his empirical or political judgment on several of the points discussed above. The substantive issues, of course, remain untouched by the clarification of Keynes' views on them attempted here.

We may conclude that Keynes weighed fiscal vs. monetary policies on the basis of a more complex set of considerations than is apparent from the standard "Keynesian" textbook discussion and also that his views were quite different. It is especially important to consider carefully the nature of the case for government spending and against Central Bank action that emerges from the analysis of Section IV. It is a case against reliance on monetary policy for the pursuit of certain objectives under certain conditions, i.e., in this instance, for the reversal of a "cumulative" process triggered by a disequilibrium diagnosed as being of a particular type. It is *not* a case for the general uselessness of monetary policy. On the contrary, the analysis makes very clear the great power for good or evil that monetary policy is seen to retain within Keynes' theoretical framework. For it is still as vital as ever that the Central Bank acts vigorously so as to hold market rate continuously in the near neighborhood of an appropriately defined natural rate. The main prescription of the *Treatise* is not affected by the finding that there are conditions to the correction of which fiscal measures are better fitted than monetary measures. In the context of Keynes' theory, the diagnosis of disequilibria, on the lines sketched in Sections III and IV, is thus seen as a prerequisite for the choice of an appropriate mix of fiscal and monetary policies in a particular situation.

NOTES

1 Cf. the letter of Keynes quoted by L. R. Klein [11, pp. 66–67].
2 Put briefly, Classical general equilibrium theory assumes that transactors have perfect information on market opportunities. The characteristic implications of Keynes' theory flow from its rejection of the Classical treatment of the information-problem.
3 Its neglect of "real" causes had been severely criticized, especially by F. A. von Hayek [6]. The sense in which "cause" is used here will become fully clear only in the context of Sections III and IV. Briefly, the present usage is designed to emphasize that a movement in the natural rate (regarded in the *Treatise* as due to "real" factors) is not a sufficient condition for the emergence of an income disequilibrium. Instead, the strategic factor lies in the failure of market rate to adjust, and it is on this inadequacy of the endogenous adjustment-mechanisms that Keynes focused in both the *Treatise* and the *General Theory*.
4 [5, esp. pp. 345–351 and 411–424]. Again, these efforts were of course less known in the United States than in Britain.
5 Harrod's *Life* [5, p. 417]. For a fuller background on the development of Keynes' views prior to the *General Theory*, on his work on and testimony before the Macmillan Committee, Harrod's biography is indispensable.
6 Compare Section IV.
7 Cf. Leijonhufvud [12, pp. 402–403].
8 [10, Vol. I, Ch. 10:iv, and Ch. 14]. The Fundamental Equations sought to marry Keynes' saving-investment analysis to the Equation of Exchange by incorporating the difference between saving and investment as a determinant of changes in velocity in the latter. For present-day appraisals of this apparatus, cf. Burstein [3, Ch. 12, App. A] and Hicks [7, Ch. 11].
9 The basic contention here is that a monetary injection, for example, will not impinge with the same force on all markets and all prices and that an understanding of the *modus operandi* of monetary policy therefore requires an analysis of the disequilibrium process which descends at least one step from the ultimate level of aggregation of both the Cambridge-Equation and the Equation of Exchange. (This idea was later all but buried in the avalanche of static, one-commodity models produced first by the Keynesian Revolution and then by the Neo-Classical Resurgence.) When all is serene once more, of course, only the new level of nominal values remains as an "unreal" monument to past Central Bank efforts. Keynes' repeated acknowledgments of the validity of the Quantity Theory in the long run show that he understood quite clearly that this traditional tool was sufficient in order to

obtain comparative static results, just as his criticisms of Quantity Theories reveal his understanding of what witnesses to the later "Neutrality"-debate know only too well, namely that comparative static analysis can tell us nothing about the "real" powers of a Central Bank or of how they should be used in different circumstances.

10 Cf., e.g., *Treatise*, Vol. I, p. 180.

11 The present interest-equalization scheme is just the sort of thing Keynes would come up with—as long as he could not see any prospect of flexible rates being adopted.

12 Wicksell, of course, spent much of the 1920s trying to persuade the Swedish authorities to reverse the World War I inflation.

13 Cf., e.g., Arthur F. Burns' criticism of this assumption [2, pp. 231–235].

14 At the same time its practical relevance is thereby circumscribed. The task set for the Applied Theory of the *Treatise* is for the most part too easy: when the curtain goes up for Keynes' usual one-act Morality Play, the Laborers are fully employed and the Entrepreneurs regard the future with firm and sober realism. The Moral of that tale is simple and is preached in no uncertain terms. But what if unemployment is rampant and entrepreneurial expectations have become seriously distorted?

15 For example, *Treatise*, Vol. I, pp. 178–179. For a recent reappraisal of Hayek's position, cf. Hicks, "The Hayek Story," in [7].

16 [10, Vol. II, p. 346 (italics added)]. In practice, as Keynes sternly pointed out, the Federal Reserve System did exactly the opposite of what was required. Predictably, the decline of long rates was associated with a drastic upward revaluation of the shares of public utilities and similar "semi-monopolistic" enterprises [10, Vol. II, p. 381]. The speculation on the trend, which this required change in the level of equity-values set off, caused the System to adopt a contractionary policy at the time when its proper objective was still that of helping to nudge down the market rate. This could only restrict the "Industrial Circulation" with little direct effect on the "Financial Circulation" and thus served to trigger the decline in output and prices.

17 For the objections, cf., e.g., Samuelson [13, p. 584] or Bailey [1, pp. 107–114, 123–130]. The classical statement is that of Cassel [4, *passim*].

18 Cf. Section IV.

19 Quoted by Harrod [5, p. 417].

20 It should be recalled that the whole of *General Theory*, Chapter 12, is devoted to painting a lurid picture of the Games that People Play on the Stock Exchanges ("Snap, Old Maid, Musical Chairs"), i.e., of the kind of speculative activity which in Keynes' opinion was principally responsible for preventing the adjustment of "the" rate of interest to its "natural" level. The language is in fact even stronger than in the corresponding passages of the *Treatise*. This would seem to indicate that Keynes still regarded a "too high" rate of interest as the *main* cause of persistent deflationary pressures. Then, however, the case for attacking the rate of interest with a monetary policy "to the point of saturation" would remain unimparied.

REFERENCES

1. M. J. Bailey, *National Income and the Price Level*. New York 1962.
2. Arthur F. Burns, *The Frontiers of Economic Knowledge*. Princeton 1954.
3. M. L. Burstein, *Money*. Cambridge 1963.
4. Gustav Cassel, *The Nature and Necessity of Interest*. London 1903.
5. Sir Roy Harrod, *The Life of John Maynard Keynes*. London 1951.
6. F. A. von Hayek, "Reflections on the Pure Theory of Money of Mr. J. M. Keynes," Pt. I-II, *Economica*, August 1931 and February 1932, *11*, 270–295, *12*, 22–44.
7. Sir John Hicks, *Critical Essays in Monetary Theory* (forthcoming).
8. John Maynard Keynes, *The General Theory of Employment, Interest and Money*. London 1936.
9. ———, *Tract on Monetary Reform*. London 1924.
10. ———, *Treatise on Money*, Vol. I: "The Pure Theory of Money," Vol. II: "The Applied Theory of Money." London 1930.

11. L. R. Klein, *The Keynesian Revolution.* New York 1947.
12. Axel Leijonhufvud, "Keynes and the Keynesians: A Suggested Interpretation," *Am. Econ. Rev.*, May 1967, *57*, 401–410.
13. P. A. Samuelson, *Economics*, 6th ed. New York 1963.
14. David McCord Wright, "Comment," *Am. Econ. Rev.*, May 1961, *51*, 19–20.

A Dynamic Aggregative Model
James Tobin

Contemporary theoretical models of the business cycle and of economic growth typically possess two related characteristics: (1) they assume production functions that allow for no substitution between factors, and (2) the variables are all real magnitudes; monetary and price phenomena have no significance. Because of these characteristics, these models present a rigid angular picture of the economic process: straight and narrow paths from which the slightest deviation spells disaster, abrupt and sharp reversals, intractable ceilings and floors. The models are highly suggestive, but their representation of the economy arouses the suspicion that they have left out some essential mechanisms of adjustment.

The purpose of this paper is to present a simple aggregative model that allows both for substitution possibilities and for monetary effects. The growth mechanism in the model is not radically different from the accelerator mechanism that plays the key role in other growth models. But it is unlike the accelerator mechanism in that there is not just one tenable rate of growth. As in accelerator models, growth is limited by the availability of factors other than capital. But here these limitations do not operate so abruptly, and they

James Tobin, "A Dynamic Aggregative Model," *Journal of Political Economy*, 63 (April 1955), pp. 103–115. *The Journal of Political Economy* is published by The University of Chicago Press.

can be tempered by monetary and price adjustments that the accelerator models ignore.

The cyclical behavior of the model is similar to the nonlinear cyclical processes of Kaldor, Goodwin, and Hicks.[1] But the cycle in the present model depends in an essential way on the inflexibility of prices, money wages, or the supply of monetary assets.

Furthermore, the model to be described here does not restrict the economic process to two possibilities, steady growth or cycles. An alternative line of development is continuing underemployment—"stagnation"—during which positive investment increases the capital stock and possibly the level of real income. This outcome, like the cycle, depends on some kind of price or monetary inflexibility.

In Part I the structure of the model will be described, and in Part II some of its implications will be examined.

I

The building blocks from which this model is constructed are four in number: (1) the saving function; (2) the production function; (3) asset preferences; and (4) labor-supply conditions.

The Saving Function

At any moment of time output is being produced at a rate Y, consumption is occurring at a rate C, and the capital stock, K, is growing at the rate $\dot{K}$, equal to $Y - C$. The saving function tells how output is divided between consumption and net investment:

$$\dot{K} = S(Y) \tag{1}$$

This relationship is assumed to hold instantaneously. That is, consumption is adjusted without lag to the simultaneous level of output; any output not consumed is an addition to the capital stock. Whether or not it is a welcome addition is another matter, which depends on the asset preferences of the community, discussed below.

Of the saving function, it is assumed that $S'(Y)$ is positive and that $S(Y)$ is zero for some positive Y. Otherwise the shape of the saving function is not crucial to the argument. Variables other than Y—for example, W, total real wealth—could be assumed to affect the propensity to save without involving more than inessential complications.

The Production Function

The rate of output, Y, depends jointly on the stock of capital in existence, K, and the rate of input of labor services, N:

$$Y = P(K, N) \tag{2}$$

The production function is assumed to be linear homogeneous. It follows that the marginal products are homogeneous functions of degree zero of the two factors; in other words, the marginal products depend only on the proportions in which the two inputs are being used. The real wage of labor, w, is equated by competition to the marginal product of labor; and the rent, r, per unit of time earned by ownership of any unit of capital is equated to the marginal product of capital:

$$w = P_N(K, N) \tag{3}$$

$$r = P_K(K, N) \tag{4}$$

If labor and capital expand over time in proportion, then output will expand in the same proportion, and both the real wage and the rent of capital will remain constant. If capital expands at a faster rate than labor, its rent must fall, and the real wage must rise.

A production function with constant returns to scale, both at any moment of time and over time, is a convenient beginning assumption. In judging the appropriateness of this kind of production function to the model, it should be remembered that, if it ignores technical improvement, on the one hand, it ignores limitations of other factors of production, "land," on the other. In the course of the argument the consequences of technological progress will be briefly discussed.

Asset Preferences

Only two stores of value, physical capital and currency, are available to owners of wealth in this economy. The own rate of return on capital is its rent, r, equal to its marginal product. Currency is wholly the issue of the state and bears an own rate of interest legally and permanently established. This rate will be assumed to be zero. The stock of currency, M, is exogenously determined and can be varied only by budget deficits or surpluses. The counterpart of this "currency" in the more complex asset structure of an actual economy is not money by the usual definition, which includes bank deposits corresponding to private debts. It is, for the United States, currency in circulation plus government debt plus the gold stock.[2]

If p is the price of goods in terms of currency, the community's total real wealth at any moment of time is

$$W = K + \frac{M}{p} \tag{5}$$

Given K, M, and p, the community may be satisfied to split its wealth so that it holds as capital an amount equal to the available stock, K, and as currency an amount equal to the existing real supply, M/p. Such a situation will be referred to as "portfolio balance."

Portfolio balance is assumed to be the necessary and sufficient condition for price stability ($\dot{p} = 0$). If, instead, owners of wealth desire to hold more goods and less currency, they attempt to buy goods with currency. Prices are bid up ($\dot{p} > 0$). If they desire to shift in the other direction, they attempt to sell goods for currency ($\dot{p} < 0$). These price changes may, in turn, be associated with changes in output and employment; but that depends on other parts of the model, in particular on the conditions of labor supply.

What, then, determines whether an existing combination of K and M/p represents a situation of portfolio balance or imbalance? Portfolio balance is assumed in this model to be defined by the following functional relationship:

$$\frac{M}{p} = L(K, r, Y) \qquad (6)$$

$$L_K \gtrless 0 \qquad L_r < 0 \qquad L_Y > 0$$

Requirements for transactions balances of currency are assumed, as is customary, to depend on income; this is the reason for the appearance of Y in the function. Given their real wealth, W, owners of wealth will wish to hold a larger amount of capital, and a smaller amount of currency, the higher the rent on capital, r. Given the rent on capital, owners of wealth will desire to put some part of any increment of their wealth into capital and some part into currency. It is possible that there are levels of r (e.g., negative rates) so low that portfolio balance requires all wealth to be in the form of currency and that there is some level of r above which wealth owners would wish to hold no currency. But the main argument to follow in Part II concerns ranges of r between those extremes.

The assumption about portfolio balance has now been stated, and the reader who is

more interested in learning its consequences than its derivation can proceed to the next section. But since this is the one of the four building blocks of the model that introduces possibly unconventional and unfamiliar material into the structure, it requires some discussion and defense.

The theory of portfolio balance implicit in most conventional aggregative economic theories of investment implies that rates of return on all assets must be equal. Applied to the two assets of the mythical economy of this paper, this theory would go as follows: Owners of wealth have a firm, certain, and unanimous expectation of the rate of price change, $\dot{p}_e$. This may or may not be the same as the actual rate of price change $\dot{p}$ at the same moment of time.[3] The rate at which a unit of wealth is expected to grow if it is held in the form of currency is, therefore, $-\dot{p}_e/p$. Similarly, owners of wealth have a firm and unanimous view of the rate at which wealth will grow if it is held as physical capital. This rate is r_e, the expected market rent, which may or may not be the same as r. Owners of wealth will choose that portfolio which makes their wealth grow at the fastest rate. If $-\dot{p}_e/p$ were to exceed r_e, they would desire to hold all currency and no capital; if r_e were greater than $-\dot{p}_e/p$, they would desire to hold all capital and no currency. Only if the two rates are equal will they be satisfied to hold positive amounts of both assets; and, indeed, in that case, they will not care what the mix of assets is in their portfolios. On this theory of asset preferences the relative supplies of the assets do not matter. Whatever the supplies, portfolio balance requires that the real expected rates of return on the assets be equal. In particular, if $r_e = r$ and $\dot{p}_e = 0$, equilibrium requires that $r = 0$.

Keynes departed from this theory in his liquidity-preference explanation of the choice between cash balances and interest-bearing monetary assets. He was able to show that, given uncertainty or lack of unanimity in the expectations of wealth owners, the rate of interest that preserves portfolio balance between cash and "bonds" is not independent of the supplies of the two kinds of assets. But he did not apply the same reasoning to the much more important choice between physical goods or capital, on the one hand, and monetary assets, on the other. His theory of investment was orthodox in requiring equality between the marginal efficiency of capital and the rate of interest.

The assumptions behind the portfolio-balance equation in the present model, equation (6), may be briefly stated. Each owner of wealth entertains as possibilities numerous values of both r_e and $-\dot{p}_e/p$, and to each possible pair of values he attaches a probability. The expected value of r_e, that is, the mean of its marginal probability distribution, is assumed to be r. The expected value of $-\dot{p}_e/p$ is assumed to be zero. In other and less precise words, the owner of wealth expects *on balance* neither the rent of capital nor the price level to change. But he is not sure. The dispersions of possible rents and price changes above and below their expected values constitute the risks of the two assets.

Owners of wealth, it is further assumed, dislike risk. Of two portfolios with the same expected value of rate of return, an investor will prefer the one with the lower dispersion of rate of return.[4] The principle of "not putting all your eggs in one basket" explains why a risk-avoiding investor may well hold a diversified portfolio even when the expected returns of all the assets in it are not identical. For the present purpose it explains why an owner of wealth will hold currency in excess of transactions requirements, even when its expected return is zero and the expected return on capital is positive. It also explains why, given the risks associated with the two assets, an investor may desire to have more of his wealth in capital the larger is r. The higher the

prospective yield of a portfolio, the greater is the inducement to accept the additional risks of heavier concentration on the more remunerative asset.[5]

Labor Supply

The behavior of the model depends in a crucial way on assumptions regarding the relations of the supply of labor to the real wage, to the money wage, and to time. It will be convenient, therefore, to introduce alternative assumptions in the course of the argument of Part II.

II

Stationary Equilibrium

The model would be of little interest if its position of stationary equilibrium were inevitably and rapidly attained, but, for the sake of completeness, this position will be described first. There are any number of combinations of labor and capital that can produce the zero-saving level of output. To each combination corresponds a marginal productivity of labor, to which the real wage must be equal; this marginal productivity is higher the more capital-intensive the combination. Suppose there is a unique relation between the supply of labor and the real wage. An equilibrium labor-capital combination is one that demands labor in an amount equal to the supply forthcoming at the real wage corresponding to that combination. The equilibrium absolute price level is then determined by the portfolio-balance equation. Given the rent and amount of capital in the equilibrium combination and the supply of currency, portfolio balance must be obtained by a price level that provides the appropriate amount of real wealth in liquid form.

Balanced Growth

Proportional growth of capital, income, and employment implies, according to the assumed production function, constancy of capital rent, r, and the real wage, w. Maintenance of portfolio balance requires, therefore, an increase in M/p. Given the supply of currency, the price level must fall continuously over time. Balanced growth requires an expanding labor supply, available at the same real wage and at an ever decreasing money wage.

Growth With Capital Deepening

In this model, unlike those of Harrod, Hicks, and others, failure of the labor supply to grow at the rate necessary for balanced growth does not mean that growth at a slower rate is possible. If the real wage must rise in order to induce additional labor supply, the rent of capital must, it is true, fall as capital grows. Portfolio balance requires, therefore, that a given increment of capital be accompanied by a greater price decline than in the case of balanced growth. But there is some rate of price decline that will preserve portfolio balance, even in the extreme case of completely inelastic labor supply. Although the rate of price decline per increment of capital is greater the less elastic the supply of labor with respect to the real wage and with respect to time, the time rate of price decline is not necessarily faster. The growth of income, saving, and capital is slower when labor is less elastic, and it takes longer to achieve the same increment of capital.

Technological Progress and Price Deflation

The preceding argument has assumed an unchanging production function with constant returns to scale. In comparison with that case, technological progress is deflationary to the extent that a more rapid growth of income augments transactions requirements for currency. But technological progress has offsetting inflationary effects to the extent that it raises the marginal productivity of capital corresponding to given inputs of capital

and labor. Conceivably technical improvement can keep the rent on capital rising even though its amount relative to the supply of labor is increasing. This rise might even be sufficient to keep the demand for real currency balances from rising, in spite of the growth of the capital stock and of transactions requirements. At the other extreme, it is possible to imagine technological progress that fails to raise or even lowers the marginal productivity of capital corresponding to given inputs of the two factors. Progress of this kind contains nothing to counteract the deflationary pressures of a growing capital stock, declining capital rent, and increasing transactions needs.

Monetary Expansion as an Alternative to Price Deflation

Growth with continuous price deflation strains the assumption that wealth owners expect, on balance, the price level to remain constant. The process itself would teach them that the expected value of the real return on currency is positive, and it would perhaps also reduce their estimates of the dispersion of possible returns on currency. This lesson would increase the relative attractiveness of currency as a store of value and thus force an ever faster rate of price decline.

An alternative to price deflation is expansion of the supply of currency. As noted above, monetary expansion cannot, in this model, be accomplished by monetary policy in the conventional sense but must be the result of deficit financing.[6] Assume that the government deficit $\dot{M}$ takes the form of transfer payments. Then equation (1) must be changed to read:

$$\dot{K} + \frac{\dot{M}}{p} = S\left(Y + \frac{\dot{M}}{p}\right) \qquad (7)$$

The normal result is that consumption will be a larger and investment a smaller share of a given level of real income. Thus, the greater is $\dot{M}$, the slower will be the rate of

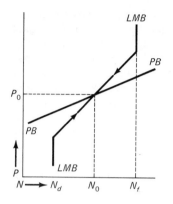

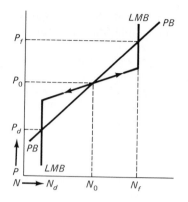

Figure 1. *A*—Stable. *B*—Unstable

capital expansion. At the same time the growth of the currency supply meets growing transactions requirements and satisfies the desire of wealth owners to balance increased holdings of capital, possibly yielding lower rents, with enlarged holdings of liquid wealth.

That there is a time path of M compatible with price stability may be seen by considering the inflationary consequences of large values of $\dot{M}$. There is presumably a value of $\dot{M}$ large enough so that the desire of the community to save at the disposable income level $Y + \dot{M}/p$ would be satisfied by saving at the rate $\dot{M}/p$. Then the capital stock would remain constant, its marginal product would stay constant, and transactions requirements would remain unchanged. Portfolio balance could then be maintained only by inflation at the same rate as $\dot{M}/M$. Somewhere between this value of M and zero there is a rate of growth of the currency supply compatible with price stability.

Wage Inflexibility as an Obstacle to Growth

If the currency supply grows too slowly, the necessity that price deflation— probably an ever faster price deflation— accompany growth casts considerable

doubt on the viability of the growth processes described above. This doubt arises from the institutional limits on downward flexibility of prices, in particular money wage rates, characteristic of actual economies. The purpose of this and the two following sections is to analyze the behavior of the system when money wage rates are inflexible.

For this analysis it is convenient to work with two relationships between the price level, p, and employment of labor, N. Both relationships assume a constant capital stock, K. The first, called the "labor market balance" (LMB) relation, gives for any level of employment, N, the price level, p, that equates the marginal productivity of labor to the real wage. Given the money wage, this p is higher for larger values of N, because the marginal product of labor declines with employment with a given capital stock. This relation is shown in Figure 1 as curve LMB. The level of employment N_f is the maximum labor supply that can be induced at the given money wage. At that level of employment the money wage becomes flexible upward. If the money wage is raised or lowered, the LMB curve will shift up or down proportionately. If the capital stock is expanded, the LMB

curve will shift downward, because an addition to capital will raise the marginal product of labor at any level of employment.

The second relation between the same two variables, p and N, is the "portfolio balance" relation PB, also shown in Figure 1. As the name indicates, it shows for any level of employment the price level required for portfolio balance between the given stock of capital K and the given supply of currency M. Its slope may be either positive or negative. The marginal productivity of the given stock of capital, and hence the rent of capital, is greater the higher the volume of employment. Currency is thus a relatively less attractive asset at higher levels of employment; so far as this effect is concerned, the price level must be higher at higher levels of employment in order to reduce the real supply of currency. The transactions relation of demand for currency to the level of real income works, however, in the opposite direction. Whatever its slope, the PB curve will, for obvious reasons, shift upward if currency supply M is expanded, and downward if capital expands.

It is not possible to establish a priori which curve, LMB or PB, has the greater slope. The two possibilities are shown in Figures 1A and 1B. In Figure 1A the LMB curve has the greater slope; both curves are drawn with positive slopes, but the PB curve could equally well have a negative slope. In Figure 1B the PB curve has the greater slope. As indicated by the arrows, the intersection (p_0, N_0) is a stable short-run equilibrium in Figure 1A but an unstable one in Figure 1B. This follows from the assumption that $\dot{p}$ will be positive, zero, or negative, depending on whether wealth owners regard their currency holdings as too large, just right, or too small.[8] In Figure 1B (p_f, N_f) is a stable short-run equilibrium. And there may be another stable intersection (p_d, N_d). Here N_d would be a level of employment so low and, correspondingly, a real wage so high that the rigidity of the money wage breaks down.

Capital expansion shifts both the LMB and the PB curve downward. How does capital expansion affect the point (p_0, N_0)? The following results are proved in the Appendix: When the intersection (p_0, N_0) is an unstable point (Fig. 1B), capital expansion increases both N_0 and p_0. The PB curve shifts more than the LMB curve, and their intersection moves northeast. The qualitative effect of capital expansion may be depicted graphically by imagining the PB curve to shift downward while the LMB curve stays put. The same argument shows that capital accumulation moves a point like (p_f, N_f) or (p_d, N_d) in Figure 1B downward, while capital decumulation moves it upward. When the intersection (p_0, N_0) is a stable point (Fig. 1A), the argument of the Appendix indicates that capital expansion necessarily lowers p_0 but may either increase or decrease N_0; the intersection may move either southeast or southwest. It is, in other words, not possible to say which curve shifts more as a consequence of a given change in the capital stock.

These results permit consideration of the question whether growth with full employment of labor is compatible with a floor on the money wage rate. Except in the case where labor supply grows as rapidly as capital or more rapidly, the growth process brings about an increase of the real wage. A certain amount of price deflation is therefore compatible with rigidity of the money wage. But, according to the results reported in the previous paragraph, certainly in the unstable case and possibly in the stable case, too, the amount of price deflation needed to maintain portfolio balance is too much to enable employment to be maintained at a rigid money wage. Capital growth shifts the PB curve down more than the LMB curve. However, it is also possible in the stable case that the LMB curve shifts more than the PB curve, so that employment could be maintained and even increased while the money wage remains rigid and prices fall. But even this possibility depends on the assumption that wealth owners balance their portfolios on the expectation that the price level will remain the same. As noted above, it is only realistic to expect that a process of deflation would itself teach owners of wealth to expect price deflation rather than price stability. Such expectations would inevitably so enhance the relative attractiveness of currency as an asset that the process could not continue without a reduction of the money-wage rate.

Wage Inflexibility and Cyclical Fluctuations

It is the situation depicted in Figure 1B that gives rise to the possibility of a cycle formally similar to those of Kaldor, Goodwin, and Hicks. Suppose the economy is at point (p_f, N_f). Capital expansion will sooner or later cause this point to coincide with (p_0, N_0) at a point like R in Figure 2. This day will be hastened by any inflation in the money-wage floor fostered by full employment; it may be that, once having enjoyed the money wage corresponding to (p_f, N_f) in Figure 1B, labor will not accept any lower money wage. Once R is reached, any further capital expansion will require a price decline

Figure 2

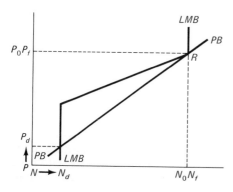

that will push the real wage of labor, given that the money wage cannot fall, above its marginal productivity. Employers will therefore contract employment. But this does not obviate the necessity of price deflation. Indeed, it aggravates it, because the reduction of employment lowers the marginal productivity of capital. Balance cannot be restored both in the labor market and in wealth holdings until a level of employment is reached at which the wage rate becomes flexible downward (N_d in Fig. 2).

The permanence of this "floor" equilibrium depends upon the saving function. If positive saving occurs at the levels of income produced by labor supply N_d, capital expansion will continue; and so also will price and wage deflation. Increase of employment then depends on the willingness of labor to accept additional employment at the low level to which severe unemployment has driven the money wage. Willingness to accept additional employment at this money wage may be encouraged by the increase in the real wage due to continued capital accumulation. A sufficient lowering of the money-wage rate demanded for increased employment would result in a situation like that represented by point S in Figure 3, and full employment could be restored.

Alternatively, the "floor" may correspond to a level of income at which there is negative saving. The gradual attrition of the capital stock will then move the PB curve up relative to the LMB curve. As capital becomes scarcer, its marginal product rises; and for both reasons its attractiveness relative to that of currency increases. Whatever happens to the money-wage terms on which labor will accept additional employment, the decumulation of capital will eventually lead to a position like S in Figure 3.

Once S is reached, any further reduction in the money wage, or any further decumulation of capital, will lead to an expansion of employment. But increasing

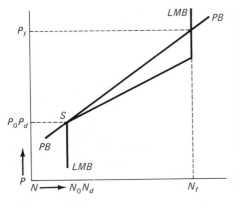

Figure 3

employment only enhances the relative attractiveness of the existing stock of capital, causing the price level to rise and employment to be still further increased. As Figure 3 shows, the only stopping point is (p_f, N_f). Once N_f is reached, the money wage becomes flexible upward and follows the price level upward until portfolio balance is restored at the price level p_f. The cycle then repeats itself.

The floor in this model is provided by a level of employment so low, and a real wage correspondingly so high, that money-wage rates become flexible downward. The breakdown of money-wage rigidity may also be interpreted as a function of time; as Leontief has suggested, money-wage rigidity may not reflect any persistent "money illusion" on the part of workers and their organizations but only a lag in their perception of the price level to use in reckoning their real wage.[9] Trouble occurs at full employment, even when real wages are increasing, because the time rate of price deflation becomes too fast in relation to this lag. Likewise, contraction of employment can be stopped and even reversed when money-wage demands have had time to catch up with what has been happening to the price level.

In this discussion of the floor it has been assumed that the rate of capital decumulation is controlled by the saving function. An interesting question arises when the saving function indicates dissaving at a rate higher than that at which the capital stock can physically decumulate. In the models of Goodwin and Hicks, in fact, the floor is the level of income at which dissaving equals the maximum possible rate of capital decumulation.

A physical limit on the rate of capital decumulation cannot really be handled within the framework of an aggregative model that takes account of only one industry, one commodity, and one price level. Such a model assumes that the output of the economy is essentially homogeneous and can equally well be consumed or accumulated in productive stocks, from which it can be withdrawn at will. If capital goods and consumers' goods are regarded as less than perfect substitutes, it is necessary to imagine that they have different price levels. Encountering a Goodwin–Hicks floor would then mean that the two price levels diverge. At any lower level of income the community would be unable to consume capital at the rate at which it wished to dissave. Consequently, the community would dissave from its holdings of currency. This would stop the fall in the price level of consumption goods and make the Goodwin–Hicks floor an equilibrium level of employment and income. The price of capital goods would continue to fall as owners of wealth attempted to convert capital into either currency or consumption. This fall in the value of capital goods would restore portfolio balance—even though consumers' goods prices ceased to fall and money-wage rates remained rigid —by making capital a smaller proportion of the community's wealth.

With the model thus amended, the physical limit on capital decumulation provides a floor that will stop and eventually reverse a contraction even if the money-wage rate is intractable. But the contraction need not proceed to this extreme, if the wage-flexibility floor described above occurs at a higher level of employment and output.

Wage Inflexibility and Stagnation

The cycle just described arises from the situation depicted in Figure 1*B*. But the situation of Figure 1*A*, where the *LMB* curve has an algebraically greater slope than the *PB* curve and the intersection (p_0, N_0) is a stable equilibrium, also is a possibility. In this case the intersection may move to the left as the capital stock increases. Growth of capital is accompanied by reduction of employment, so long as the money-wage rate is maintained. This process may end in a stationary equilibrium position if it entails such a reduction in output (or, if wealth is relevant to the saving function, such an increase in wealth) as to reduce saving to zero. But it is also possible that a process with positive saving, growth of capital, and increasing unemployment will continue indefinitely.

SUMMARY

The simple aggregative model that has been presented here differs from others used in discussions of growth and cycles in two main respects. The production function allows for substitution between capital and labor. The willingness of the community to hold physical capital depends on its rate of return and on the value of the liquid wealth held by the community. These two assumptions provide a link, generally absent in other models, between the world of real magnitudes and the world of money and prices. This link provides the model with some adjustment mechanisms ignored in other growth and cycle models. The following conclusions result:

1. Growth is possible at a great variety of rates and is not necessarily precluded

when the labor supply grows slowly or remains constant.

2. The course of the price level as capital grows depends on (a) the accompanying rate of expansion of the labor force, (b) the rate at which the supply of currency is augmented by government deficits, and (c) the rate of technological progress. The first two factors are both inflationary. Technological progress has mixed effects. In the absence of monetary expansion and technological progress, price deflation is a necessary concomitant of growth even when the labor supply is increasing just as rapidly as capital. In these circumstances, therefore, growth with stable or increasing employment cannot continue if the money-range rate is inflexible downward.

3. Given wage inflexibility, the system may alternate between high and low levels of employment and, concurrently, between periods of price inflation and deflation. The ceiling to this cyclical process is provided by inelasticity of the labor supply. The floor may be provided either by the breakdown of the rigid money wage or by physical limits on the rate of consumption of capital. Alternatively, the system may "stagnate" at less than full employment, quite conceivably with capital growth and reduction of employment occurring at the same time. Whether the system behaves in this manner or with cyclical fluctuations depends on the relation between the conditions of portfolio balance and the rate of return on capital. The greater the shift in portfolios that owners of wealth wish to make when the rate of return on capital changes, the more likely it is that the system will have a cyclical solution.

APPENDIX

The equation of the labor-market-balance curve, for given K, is

$$pP_N(K, N) = w_0 \qquad (1)$$

where w_0 is the rigid money-wage rate. The slope of this curve is

$$\left(\frac{dp}{dN}\right)_{LMB} = \frac{-p^2 P_{NN}}{w_0} \tag{2}$$

Since $P_{NN} < 0$, this slope is positive.

The equation of the portfolio-balance curve, for given K and M, is

$$\begin{aligned} M &= pL(K, r, Y) \\ &= pL(K, P_K(K, N), P(K, N)) \end{aligned} \tag{3}$$

The slope of this curve is

$$\left(\frac{dp}{dN}\right)_{PB} = \frac{-p^2}{M}(L_r P_{KN} + L_Y P_N) \tag{4}$$

Since $L_r < 0$, $P_{KN} > 0$, and $L_Y > 0$, this slope may be either positive or negative.

The point (p_0, N_0) is determined by the intersection of (1) and (3). The problem is to find the changes in p_0 and N_0 associated with an increase in K.

Differentiating (1) and (3) with respect to K gives

$$\frac{\partial p_0}{\partial K}\left(\frac{w_0}{p_0}\right) + \frac{\partial N_0}{\partial K}(p_0 P_{NN}) = -p_0 P_{NK} \tag{5}$$

$$\frac{\partial p_0}{\partial K}\left(\frac{M}{p_0}\right) + \frac{\partial N_0}{\partial K}(p_0 L_r P_{KN} + p_0 L_Y P_N)$$

$$= -p_0 L_K - p_0 L_r P_{KK} - p_0 L_Y P_K \tag{6}$$

NOTES

1 N. Kaldor, "A Model of the Trade Cycle," *Economic Journal*, L (March, 1940), 78–92; R. Goodwin, "The Nonlinear Accelerator and the Persistence of Business Cycles," *Econometrica*, XIX (Jan. 1951), 1–17, and "Econometrics in Business Cycle Analysis," in A. H. Hansen, *Business Cycles and National Income* (New York: W. W. Norton & Co., 1951), chap. 22; J. R. Hicks, *A Contribution to the Theory of the Trade Cycle* (Oxford: Oxford University Press, 1950).

2 This is the same concept developed in connection with discussions of the "Pigou effect"; see Herbert Stein, "Price Flexibility and Full Employment: Comment," *American Economic Review*, XXXIX (June 1949), 725–726, and Don Patinkin, "Price Flexibility and Full Employment: Reply," *American Economic Review*, XXXIX (June 1949), 726–728.

3 An individual may be assumed to know the historical course of prices $p(t)$ up to the present (for $t \lesseqgtr t_0$) and to expect a future course of prices $p_e(t)$ (for $t \gtreqless t_0$). Presumably the expected course starts at the same price at which the historical course ends $[p(t_0) = p_e(t_0)]$. But there is no reason that one should start with the same slope with which the other ends: $p'(t_0)$, referred to in the text as $\dot{p}$, is not necessarily the same as $p_e'(t_0)$, referred to in the text as $\dot{p}_e$.

4 Risk aversion in this sense may be deduced from the assumption of generally declining marginal utility of income. Here, however, it is not necessary to go into the question of the usefulness of the concept of cardinal utility in explaining behavior under uncertainty.

5 There is an "income effect" working in the opposite direction. The portfolio-balance function, equation (6), assumes the substitution effect to be dominant.

6 The implications of the approach of this paper concerning the effects of conventional monetary policy are left for discussion elsewhere. Clearly such a discussion requires the introduction of additional types of assets, including bank deposits and private debts.

7 Employment has been assumed always to be at the point where the marginal product of labor equals the real wage. But the conclusions on the stability of (p_0, N_0) in the two parts of Figure 1 would not be altered if it were assumed instead that N is positive, zero, or negative depending on whether the marginal product of labor exceeds, equals, or is less than the real wage.

8 W. Leontief, "Postulates: Keynes' *General Theory* and the Classicists," in S. E. Harris (ed.), *The New Economics* (New York: Alfred A. Knopf, 1947), chap. 19.

Contributions and Limitations of Keynesian Theory
Kenneth K. Kurihara

My general purpose in this essay[1] is to delineate the essential contributions of Keynes' *General Theory* and its fundamental limitations,[2] with a specific view to indicating the nature and direction of theoretical advance in the field of macrodynamic economics for greater generality and applicability.

I. THE CONTRIBUTIONS

There are, in my view, seven contributions and seven limitations to be outlined here. The numerical symmetry is accidental, but the controversial juxtaposition of contributions and limitations is intentional. Let us begin with the contributions of Keynesian theory.

The Investment-Saving Discrepancy and Underemployment Equilibrium

One of the lasting contributions of the *General Theory* is the simple yet revolutionary notion that *ex ante* investment and *ex ante* saving represent two different sets of activities and motives on the part of two independent groups of individuals, as far as a market economy is concerned. In Keynesian jargon, the inducement to invest may be greater or smaller than the propensity to save:

$$I \lessgtr S(Y) \qquad \text{or} \qquad I(Y) \lessgtr S(Y) \quad (1.1)$$

where Y is national income, I investment, I autonomous investment, and S saving.

The inequalities expressed by (1.1) are revolutionary in effect, for two reasons. First, they have invalidated Say's law that

Kenneth K. Kurihara, "Contributions and Limitations of Keynesian Theory," *Economic Studies Quarterly*, 20 (April 1969), pp. 34–49.

supply creates its own demand: $Y \equiv C + I$ or $I \equiv S$, where Y stands for supply and $C + I$ denotes demand, implying that general overproduction and mass unemployment are theoretical impossibilities so as to justify laissez-faire. Keynes not only succeeded where Malthus and Marx failed in their attempts to repudiate Say's law, but also established the following condition of equilibrium to be satisfied (preferably by design):

$$Y - [C(Y) + I] = 0 \qquad I - S(Y) = 0 \quad (1.2)$$

where C and I represent respectively consumption-demand and investment-demand. Second, and what is more, the general equilibrium condition specified by (1.2) is, when satisfied, likely to be associated with less than full employment in a peacetime market economy:

$$I = S(Y_u) \qquad Y = Y^0 = Y_u < Y_f \quad (1.3)$$

where Y^0 is equilibrium income, Y_u underemployment income, and Y_f full-employment income. The relations expressed by (1.3) imply the full-employment equilibrium condition to be satisfied:

$$\bar{I}_f - S(Y_f) = 0 \qquad Y = Y^0 = Y_f \quad (1.4)$$

where $\bar{I}_f$ is autonomous investment in conditions of full employment.

The Basic Mechanism of Income-Employment Fluctuations

Another theoretical contribution with important practical implications is the predictable and controllable multiplier mechanism of the basic form

$$\Delta Y = s^{-1} \Delta \bar{I} = k \Delta \bar{I}$$
$$\Delta N = v \Delta Y = vk \Delta \bar{I} \quad (1.5)$$

where N is the macro labor-input demanded or simply employment, s the marginal propensity to save, k the investment multiplier, and v the marginal labor-output ratio (reciprocal of marginal labor productivity), the other variables being the same as before.

The policy implications of the relations expressed by (1.5) can be brought out by making the investment multiplicand the unknown:

$$\Delta I = k^{-1} \Delta Y = (Y_f - Y_a)/s^{-1} \qquad (1.6)$$

where Y_f is potential full-employment income, Y_a actual income, and ΔY the income gap to be wiped out in order to attain full employment. Equation (1.6) enables the policy-makers to know how much more investment is needed to close the gap between potential full-employment income and actual income, when the saving ratio remains constant. Moreover, the burden on the extra autonomous investment to be found is reduced if induced investment is also present, for we have the "super multiplier" of the form $k' = (s - v)^{-1}$, where v is the positive marginal propensity to invest. Econometric parameter-estimation of s and v could help forecast the exact amount of autonomous investment needed at some future time:

$$\Delta I_{t+n} = \Delta Y_t/(s - v)^{-1} \qquad (n \geqq 1) \quad (1.7)$$

We know that the basic equations given by (1.5)–(1.7) can be expanded to embrace the foreign-trade multiplier in an open economy, the government-expenditure multiplier in a mixed economy, and the price multiplier in a full-employment economy. Keynes credited R. F. Kahn with the discovery of the multiplier principle, but it was Keynes who put the idea across for general acceptance and universal practice. Be that as it may, Keynes' multiplier principle made classical (if unorthodox) murmurs about "commercial crises" and other cylical disturbances operationally significant for both analysis and policy.

The Static Investment-Saving Equilibrium Condition as a Preliminary to the Dynamic Counterpart

Another basic contribution lies in the restrospective fact that Keynes' static investment-saving equilibrium condition paved the way to Harrod's dynamic counterpart, that is, Harrod's "dynamised version of Keynes' excess or deficiency of aggregate effective demand"[3] running in terms of ratios:

$$\frac{I}{Y} - \frac{S}{Y} = 0 \qquad (1.8)$$

$$\frac{I}{Y} = \frac{I}{\Delta Y}\frac{\Delta Y}{Y} \qquad \left(\frac{I}{\Delta Y} \equiv C_r, \frac{\Delta Y}{Y} \equiv G_w\right) \qquad (1.9)$$

The investment-saving equilibrium condition in terms of ratios (instead of levels) specified by (1.8) does not in itself reveal its dynamic nature, but Harrod has made the net investment ratio the product of one dynamic variable (G_w or the "warranted" rate of growth of income) and one parameter (C_r = const.).[4] Substituting (1.9) in (1.8) yields

$$\left(\frac{I}{\Delta Y}\frac{\Delta Y}{Y}\right) - \frac{S}{Y} = 0$$

$$C_r G_w = s \qquad \left(s \equiv \frac{S}{Y}\right) \qquad (1.10)$$

which tells us that the marginal "capital coefficient" (C_r) times the "warranted" rate of growth (G_w) must, in equilibrium, equal the average saving ratio (s) if the economy's inducement to invest is to be in harmony with its propensity to save in terms of ratios. Equation (1.10) implies that the rate of growth of effective demand necessary for the full utilization of capital is given by

$$\frac{\Delta Y}{Y} = \frac{\dfrac{S}{Y}}{\dfrac{I}{\Delta Y}}$$

$$G_w = \frac{s}{C_r} \qquad (s,\, C_r = \text{const.}) \qquad (1.11)$$

which indicates the possibility of the required rate of growth of effective demand changing directly with the saving ratio and inversely with the capital coefficient. Since Harrod holds s and C_r constant, G_w given by (1.11) signifies the line of "steady advance," albeit with "involuntary unemployment."[5] Failure to satisfy the dynamic equilibrium condition expressed by (1.10) would impliedly entail an inflationary tendency over time (t) due to $(I/Y)_t - (S/Y)_t > 0$ or a stagnationary tendency due to $(I/Y)_t - (S/Y)_t < 0$.

The Dynamic Investment-Saving Relation and Global Economic Development

Keynes' static investment-saving equilibrium condition for a closed economy has also led to a dynamic post-Keynesian formula for narrowing the standard-of-living gap between the advanced and the underdeveloped economies. Keynes' remark that "a wealthy community will have to discover much ampler opportunities for investment if the saving propensities of its wealthier members are to be compatible with the employment of its poorer members"[6] can be paraphrased to read: "The world economy will have to provide a mechanism whereby the excess saving of its advanced sectors is utilized by its underdeveloped sectors, to the mutual benefit of the former's stable growth and the latter's rapid growth." Such a mechanism on a "purely technical and non-political" basis was suggested in Keynes' proposal for a World Bank for Reconstruction and Development.[7] Instead of leaving global economic development to the vagaries of laissez-faire capital movements, Keynes would have us provide autonomous and anonymous developmental capital free from traditional political strings.

Accordingly, a dynamic extension of Keynes' static investment-saving equilibrium condition to an open economy can be shown in two ways:

$$g_u \equiv \frac{\Delta K}{K} = \frac{I}{K} = \frac{S + \bar{B}}{K} = \frac{s Y_u + \beta Y_u}{b Y_u}$$
$$= \frac{(s + \beta) Y_u}{b Y_u} = \frac{s + \beta}{b} \qquad (1.12)$$

on the assumptions that $I = \Delta K$, $I = S + \bar{B}$, $s \equiv S/Y_u$, and $b \equiv K/Y_u$, $\beta \equiv \bar{B}/Y_u$;

$$\frac{I}{\Delta Y_a} \frac{\Delta Y_a}{Y_a} = \frac{I}{Y_a} = \frac{S}{Y} - \frac{\bar{L}}{Y_a} = \frac{s' Y_a}{Y_a} - \frac{\lambda Y_a}{Y_a}$$
$$= \frac{(s' - \lambda) Y_a}{Y_a} = s' - \lambda$$

or $\quad b' g_a = s' - \lambda \qquad (1.13)$

on the assumption that $I + \bar{L} = S$, $g_a \equiv \Delta Y_a/Y_a$, $s' \equiv S/Y_a$, $b' \equiv I/\Delta Y_a$, and $\lambda \equiv \bar{L}/Y_a$.

Here Y_u is an underdeveloped economy's productive capacity, Y_a an advanced economy's effective demand, K real capital, I net investment, S domestic saving, $\bar{B}$ autonomous net foreign borrowing (representing capital imports), $\bar{L}$ autonomous net foreign lending (representing capital exports), g_u the rate of growth of capital, g_a the rate of growth of effective demand, b or b' the average-marginal capital coefficient, s or s' the domestic saving ratio, β the ratio of autonomous foreign borrowing to domestic productive capacity, and λ the ratio of autonomous foreign lending to domestic effective demand. Equation (1.12) is for the rapid growth of capital in an underdeveloped open economy, while equation (1.13) is for the stable growth of effective demand in an advanced open economy. It is to be noted that (1.12) involves $I = S + \bar{B}$ as the "investment-saving" equilibrium condition to be satisfied by an underdeveloped economy, and that (1.13) includes $I + \bar{L} = S$ as the counterpart to be satisfied by an advanced economy. To the former economy foreign borrowing (β) is a force tending to accelerate its capital formation; to the latter economy foreign lending (λ) is a force tending to stabilize its effective demand (by serving as an additional offset to its excess saving in terms of ratios).

Flexible Fiscal-Monetary Policy Parameters

Keynes made it possible to include what J. Tinbergen calls "instrument variables" in relevant behavioral functions so as to promote economic stability or growth.[8] Specifically he made powerful suggestions about the possibility and desirability of manipulating government expenditure and income taxes in a manner that compensates for destabilizing private consumption and investment activities, as A. P. Lerner's "functional finance" and A. H. Hansen's "compensatory fiscal policy," and more recently W. Heller's *New Dimensions of Political Economy* attest.

Thus we can now have the government-expenditure multiplier equation of the expanded form thus:

$$\Delta Y = c(\Delta Y - \Delta T + \Delta \bar{R}) + i(\Delta Y - \Delta T' + \Delta \bar{R}') + \Delta \bar{G} \tag{1.14}$$

dividing which equation through by ΔY yields

$$1 = c(1 - t + r) + i(1 - t' + r') + \frac{\Delta \bar{G}}{\Delta Y} \tag{1.15}$$

solving which equation for ΔY gives the government-expenditure multiplier equation in question:

$$\Delta Y = [1 - c(1 - t + r) - i(1 - t' + r')]^{-1} \Delta \bar{G} \tag{1.16}$$

Here Y is national income, T personal income taxes, $\bar{R}$ autonomous consumer

subsidies, T' corporate income taxes, $\bar{R}'$ autonomous business subsidies, $\bar{G}$ autonomous government expenditure, $t = \Delta T/\Delta Y$ or the marginal personal-income tax rate, $t' = \Delta T'/\Delta Y$ or the marginal corporate-income tax rate, $r = \bar{R}/\Delta Y$ or the government transfer payments ratio for the consumers, $r' = \Delta \bar{R}'/\Delta Y$ or the government transfer payments ratio for the producers, c the marginal propensity to consume out of disposable income, and i the marginal propensity to invest out of disposable income. Equation (1.16) derived from (1.14) and (1.15) included s t, t', r, and r' as manipulative fiscal-policy parameters to influence private consumption expenditure and investment, as well as flexible $\Delta \bar{G}$—albeit subject to the parliamentary constraint.

Moreover, Keynes' marginal efficiency of capital theory and liquidity-preference theory have, between them, inspired a "cheap money" or "dear money" policy as a countercyclical measure. For we have from these theories

$$r(L, \bar{M}) - e(I) = 0$$
$$(\partial I/\partial e > 0, \partial I/\partial r < 0, e \equiv y/c) \tag{1.17}$$

implying:

If $r - e < 0$ (cheap money policy), then $\Delta I(t) > 0$.

If $r - e > 0$ (dear money policy), then $\Delta I(t) < 0$.

Here I is real investment (in contradistinction to financial investment in securities), L the demand for money or liquidity-preference, $\bar{M}$ the autonomous supply of money (via central bank policy), r the rate of interest, e the marginal efficiency of capital, y the annual yield of capital in general, c the replacement cost of that capital, and t time. Equation (1.17) expresses the equilibrium investment condition to be satisfied by the producers of capital goods in a money economy with a positive rate of interest.

Income as the Central Variable and the Strategic Division of Aggregate Demand

The substitution of income for price as the key variable and the division of aggregate demand into consumption-demand and investment-demand constitute Keynes' permanent methodological contribution to macro analysis and policy. For these methodological innovations sharply and fundamentally distinguish the Keynesian theory of macro equilibrium from the classical Walrasian general equilibrium system and the neoclassical quantity theory of money. Compare the following three constitutions of general equilibrium:

$$Y - (C + I) = 0 \qquad I(Y) - S(Y) = 0$$
$$(Y < Y_f) \quad (1.18)$$

$$\sum_{i=0}^{n} p_i D_i - \sum_{i=0}^{n} p_i S_i = 0$$
$$(p_i \neq const.) \quad (1.19)$$

$$pQ - vM = 0 \qquad (Q, v = const.) \quad (1.20)$$

Here Y is national income, Y_f full-employment income, C consumption-demand, I investment-demand, S saving, D_i the i-th good demanded, S_i the i-th good supplied, Q constant output (on the the assumption of $Y = Y_f$), M the total supply of money, p_i the price of the i-th good demanded and supplied, p the index of general prices, and v the velocity of circulation of money. The equations expressed by (1.18) are familiarly the Keynesian crosses I and II. Two things deserve special attention, namely, (a) variable income at less than full employment as compared with constant full-employment income assumed by Walras to justify variable price as the equilibrating factor, and (b) consumption expenditure and investment regarded as the most strategic components of total demand.[9] System of equations (1.19) expresses Walras' general equilibrium condition inferentially involving $D_i = \phi_i(p_1, p_2, \ldots, p_n)$ and $S_i = \Psi_i(p_1, p_2, \ldots, p_n)$ (where $i = 1, \ldots, n$). This system is an improve-

ment over Say's law, to be sure, but it implies the pious hope that milliards of individual demand and supply equations would be equilibrated through laissez-faire price change (as in the absence of government intervention and monopolistic or oligopolistic market rigidities). By contrast, Keynes makes income change as the *modus operandi* of the whole economy, and also specifies consumption expenditure and investment as predictable and controllable components of aggregate demand (irrespective of market conditions).

As for equation (1.20), we need not belabor it beyond reminding ourselves of the catch-all nature of vM that represents total money expenditure or demand and the unrealistic constancy assumption about v (in a short period) and Q (even in a longer period). The monetary counterpart of equation (1.18) is of greater theoretical significance and practical importance for the study and control of general prices:

$$pY = Y_m = c_m Y_m + i_m Y_m$$
$$p = \frac{c_m Y_m + i_m Y_m}{Y} \qquad (Y \geq Y_f) \quad (1.21)$$

where Y_m is money national income, Y_f constant or variable full-employment real income, c_m the marginal propensity to consume out of money income, i_m the marginal propensity to invest out of money income, and p the general price index. Equation (1.21) would enable the policy-makers to stabilize general prices by influencing or/and controlling the cyclical behavior of c_m and i_m instead of by estimating the parametric value of v alone relatively to Y, Q, and M.

The Full Employment Inelasticity of Output as the Criterion of Demand-Pull Inflation[10]

The last contribution to be mentioned here is Keynes' conceptual provision of an unequivocal criterion by which to judge whether rising general prices do or do not constitute "true inflation"[11] in a fairly short period with the given size of population and the given state of technology. And that criterion is the full-employment inelasticity of output with respect to aggregate demand:

$$\frac{\partial(\log\ Y(N))}{\partial(\log D)} = 0$$

$$(Y = \bar{Y}_f, D = C + I, \Delta N(t) = 0) \quad (1.22)$$

where Y is output from full employment, N labor-input, D total demand comprising real consumption-demand (C) and real investment-demand (I), Y_f constant full-employment real income, and t time. The partial derivatives in equation (1.22) suggest the reservation that even in a relatively short period total output from full employment might conceivably increase if labor productivity affecting $Y(N)$ or total population affecting N could be supposed to rise significantly.

Given the demand inelasticity of output in conditions of full employment expressed by (1.22), general prices will, *cet. par.*, rise in a truly inflationary manner according to the mechanism of the form

$$p(t) = \frac{Y_m(t)}{\bar{Y}_f}$$

$$(p(0) = 1, t = 0, 1, \ldots, n, n < \infty) \quad (1.23)$$

as equation (1.18) implies. Equation (1.23) indicates that general prices can rise at the same rate as the rate at which money national income increases:

$$\frac{\Delta p(t)}{p(t)} = \frac{\dfrac{\Delta Y_m(t)}{Y_f}}{p(t)} = \frac{\dfrac{\Delta Y_m(t)}{\bar{Y}_f}}{\dfrac{Y_m(t)}{\bar{Y}_f}} = \frac{\Delta Y_m(t)}{Y_m(t)}$$

$$(Y_f = Y_f(t) = \bar{Y}_f) \quad (1.24)$$

Equations (1.23) and (1.24) show the possibility of general prices rising in a genuinely inflationary way as a consequence of increasing money national income (which, in equilibrium, equals total demand or expenditure in money

terms: $Y_m - (C_m + I_m) = 0$, $Y_m = p\,\bar{Y}_f$) respectively in terms of levels and in terms of rates. These equations represent a Keynesian antidote for the "anti-inflation obscurantism" of those who are alarmed by every small rise of general prices irrespective of whether total output can or cannot be increased to meet the increasing demand for goods and services, and who are therefore blindly biased in favor of deflationary measures even at the risk of provoking a recession.

II. THE LIMITATIONS

Turning now to the limitations of Keynesian theory, I might preface the subsequent discussions by making the observation that post-Keynesian economists including myself have been more or less aware of those limitations and have made various attempts to begin where Keynes left off. For those limitations are a reflection of historical circumstances in which Keynes lived and worked, circumstances that historically delimited the generality and applicability of the *General Theory*. To point up the limitations of Keynesian theory here or elsewhere is not to slight its contributions as some readers might suppose, but to stress the need for imaginative and perceptive extensions of a Master Economist's seminal insights[12] in such a way as to render the economic discipline increasingly serviceable to all mankind and the rapidly changing world.

Overaggregative Income-Expenditure Variables

The first limitation of Keynesian theory to be mentioned consists in the methodological inadequacy of income-expenditure aggregates. The basic equation of the form $Y = C + I$, while it is a pedagogically useful simplification, nevertheless is inadequate for the specific purpose of singling out inefficient units which militate against overall stability and growth. For that purpose W. W. Leontief's multisectoral approach[13] is more helpful. Let Leontief's intermediate demand supplement Keynes' final demand, while at the same time letting Keynes' endogenous expenditure variables serve to close Leontief's open model. The result is the transformation of the Leontief system of equations

$$Y_i = \sum_{j=1}^{n} a_{ij} Y_j + D_i \qquad (i = 1, \ldots, n)$$

$$(2.1)$$

into the general equilibrium form

$$\sum_{i=1}^{n} Y_i = \sum_{i=1}^{n} \sum_{j=1}^{n} a_{ij} Y_j + \sum_{i=1}^{n} \sum_{j=1}^{n} b_{ij} \, \varDelta Y_j$$

$$+ \sum_{i=1}^{n} c_i Y_i + \sum_{i=1}^{n} g_i Y_i$$

$$+ \sum_{i=1}^{n} e_i Y_i \qquad (2.2)$$

Here Y_i is the i-th sector's output, Y_j the j-th sector's output, D_i the final demand for the i-th sector's output, a_{ij} the j-th sector's input coefficient, b_{ij} the j-th sector's capital coefficient, c_i the i-th sector's average propensity to consume, g_i the ratio of autonomous government expenditure to the i-th sector's output, and e_i the ratio of autonomous exports to the i-th sector's output.

System (2.1) expresses Leontief's open model in which the i-th sector's output must, in equilibrium, equal the sum of intermediate interindustry demand (under the summation) and final household demand (exogenously given). This system is more disaggregative than Keynes' aggregative theory in which interindustry demand is completely submerged, but it suffers from the subsumption of component final demands under one set of exogenously given variables (D's). By contrast, equation (2.2) expresses the condition of general equilibrium to be satisfied by the whole economy, that is,

the requirement that total output must, in equilibrium, equal total input-output demand (under the first double summation) plus total net investment-demand (under the second double summation) plus total consumption-demand plus total government expenditure plus total exports. Inclusion of the net capital formation sector makes this multisectoral model *substantively dynamic*, and paves the way for multisectoral growth analysis.[14] Furthermore, the breakdown of final demand into *endogenously determined* investment-demand, consumption-demand, government expenditure, and exports facilitates the control and prediction of sectoral and intersectoral activities for stabilization purposes.

The Linear Investment Function and One-Sided Investment

The next limitation to be noted is two-fold, namely, the incompleteness of Keynes' linear investment function for business-cycle analysis and that of his demand-generating investment for growth analysis. Keynes' linear investment function ($I = i + iY, i \geq 0, i \leq 0$ or $I = \bar{I}$), together with his linear saving function, is in and by itself incapable of producing a mixed model of stable-unstable equilibria to explain cyclical movements, as the reader of N. Kaldor's contribution knows.[15] J. R. Hicks' attempt to impose exogenous constraints (a ceiling and a floor) on a linear system resulted in a rather unsatisfactory "billard-ball" model of cycles.[16] M. Kalecki before the *General Theory* and R. Goodwin thereafter[17] provided the pioneering suggestion that investment is a decreasing function of capital, a suggestion which proved essential to the explanation of investment non-linearity.

Thus we can now have an endogenous model of the self-limiting cycle with a constant amplitude (neither explosive nor damped) but without artificial exogenous constraints. That we can have via the *nonlinear* investment function of the form

$$I = f(Y) - \eta K \qquad \left(\frac{\partial I}{\partial Y} > 0, \frac{\partial I}{\partial K} < 0\right) \tag{2.3}$$

and the linear (or nonlinear *à la* Kaldor) saving function of the form

$$S = \bar{s} + sY \qquad (s = \text{const.}, s \lessgtr 0) \tag{2.4}$$

Here I is investment-demand as an increasing function of income and a decreasing function of capital, Y income, K capital, S saving, η a positive constant, s the marginal saving ratio, and $\bar{s}$ a zero or negative intercept. (2.3) and (2.4) can, between them, give rise to oscillatory movements of a self-limiting nature,[18] though those equations would have to be duly modified for the analysis of *cyclical growth*.[19]

Moreover, Keynes, while quite aware of it, nevertheless ignored the capacity-increasing aspect of investment as if the production of all durable capital goods were of the pyramid-building variety that merely generates demand. For any long-run analysis the supply side of investment must be thrown into bold relief, as Keynes' own digressive chapter on capital implied.[20] In this respect, E. D. Domar's stress on "the dual character of investment"[21] and R. F. Harrod's implicit production function[22] stand out as a post-Keynesian rehabilitation of classical capital theory for long-run purposes:

$$\frac{\Delta I}{\alpha} = \sigma I \qquad \Delta Y^d = \frac{\Delta I}{\alpha}$$

$$\Delta Y^s = \sigma I = \sigma \Delta K \qquad \Delta K = \sigma^{-1} \Delta Y^s \tag{2.5}$$

$$Y^s = \min\left(\frac{K}{C_r}, \frac{N}{\lambda}\right) \qquad Y^s = C_r^{-1} K$$

$$\Delta Y^s = C_r^{-1} \Delta K = C_r^{-1} I \quad \text{when}$$

$$\frac{K}{C_r} = \min \tag{2.6}$$

Here Y^d is effective demand, Y^s productive capacity, I net investment, K capital (fixed

or/and circulating), N labor-input, α the marginal saving ratio, σ the marginal productivity of capital (Domar's "sigma effect"), C_r Harrod's "required capital coefficient," and λ the average-marginal labor-output ratio. (2.5) gives Domar's basic equation representing the demand and supply sides of a growing economy, a representation that synthesizes the Keynesian multiplier theory and the classical theory of capital productivity. (2.6) expresses Harrod's implicit one-factor production function when capital rather than labor is considered the scarce limiting factor of production. Thus viewed, is it surprising to hear: "Since capital is the most scarce factor in most underdeveloped economies, the model which suits our purpose best is the Harrod–Domar model"?[23]

The Gap Analysis and "Cost-Push" Inflation

Keynes' "Principle of Effective Demand" is incapable of explaining the anomalous postwar phenomenon of "cost-push" inflation that occurs even at less than full employment. Let us grant that the inflation gap analysis, which Keynes made in his *How to Pay for the War* as a sequel to his *General Theory*, is still useful to those economies which are committed to full-employment policy and therefore exposed to the constant threat of "demand-pull" inflation. Thus we can express the inflation gap to be wiped out by fiscal-monetary measures in the expanded form

$$(I_f + \bar{G}_f + \bar{X}_f)$$
$$- [S(Y_f) + T(Y_f) + M(Y_f)] > 0 \tag{2.7}$$

where $\bar{I}_f$, $\bar{G}_f$, and $\bar{X}_f$ are respectively autonomous investment, government expenditure, and exports in conditions of full employment, while $S(Y_f)$, $T(Y_f)$, and $M(Y_f)$ are respectively saving, taxes, and imports out of full-employment income—all in real terms.

However, the difficulty with (2.7) is that it has nothing to say about the structure of costs which exists independently of the behavior of effective demand. The cost structure of a market economy is predetermined by such trend forces as technology, business monopolism, and labor unionism. There is not yet a coherent or cogent theory of "cost-push" inflation, most arguments being one-sidedly against "big business" or "big labor" as an explanatory dummy variable.[24] We are left with the dismal impression that the coexistence of "demand-pull" and "cost-push" inflation is here to stay without there being any practicable experiment with either low enough costs to isolate "demand-pull" inflation or low enough demand to isolate "cost-push" inflation.

Be that as it may, a modest start in the direction of an operationally significant model of "cost-push" inflation can be seen thus[25]:

$$p_t Y_t = w_t N_t + (\pi_t + r_t) q_t K_t \qquad (2.8)$$

solving which equation for p yields

$$p_t = \frac{w_t N_t + (\pi_t + r_t) q_t K_t}{Y_t} \qquad (2.9)$$

which, by putting $Y/N = \rho$ and $K/N = \theta$, can in turn be rewritten as

$$p_t = \frac{w_t + (\pi_t + r_t) q_t \theta_t}{\rho_t} \qquad (2.10)$$

Here Y is real income, N labor-input, K capital-input, p the general-price index, w the money-wage rate, π the net profit rate, r the interest rate, q the unit price of capital-input, ρ labor productivity, θ the capital-labor ratio, and t time. Equation (2.10), which is derived from (2.8) and (2.9), indicates the possibility of general prices varying directly with various cost elements and the capital-labor ratio and inversely with labor productivity at time t. The cost elements involved are w as the unit price of labor-input, π as the real cost of risk and uncertainty (or as a target rate

of return on investment for the normal utilization of capital), r as the cost of money (or the index of capital charges), and q as the unit price of capital-input. On the other hand, ρ and θ are technological variables which are more difficult to control than the cost variables. Theorists would have to make some plausible assumptions about the expected behavior of all these variables affecting the cost structure and the state of technology in order to facilitate a reliable forecasting model at time $t + n$ ($n \geq 1$).

Structural Underemployment due to Capital Scarcity and Ethnic Discrimination

Another limitation of Keynesian theory can be seen in its inability to account for those kinds of underemployment which arise from the persistent shortage of capital to equip a large and growing labor force and from the anachronistic relic of discrimination against racial minorities. The widespread existence of "disguised unemployment" in *capital-poor* economies attests the former type of structural underemployment, while the drive for a national "fair employment practice law" in *race-conscious* economies reflects the stubborn persistence of the latter type. Keynes' formula for "full employment" through increased effective demand is obviously inapplicable to the case of what Joan Robinson calls "Marxian unemployment," which "expands and contracts as the growth of population runs faster or slower than the rate of capital accumulation."[26] As for underemployment due to ethnic discrimination, we are painfully reminded of L. R. Klein's epilogue: "A complete economic theory must tell us how to get both fair and full employment"[27]; and Gov. Nelson Rockefeller's plea: "We must eliminate racial discrimination. In addition to its moral indefensibility, such discrimination prevents the nation from making full use of the skills of a significant portion of the population—and therefore —retards growth."[28]

Thus we are prodded to ponder over ways and means of satisfying some such *new* conditions of full *and* fair employment equilibrium as

$$L(P) - N(K) = 0$$

$$\left(\frac{dL}{dP} > 0, \frac{dN}{dK} > 0\right) \qquad (2.11)$$

$$\bar{L} - N(Y, \varepsilon) = 0$$

$$\left(L = \text{const.}, \frac{\partial N}{\partial Y} > 0, \frac{\partial N}{\partial \varepsilon} > 0\right) \qquad (2.12)$$

where

$$\varepsilon = \frac{\partial(\log N^m)}{\partial(\log Y)} \qquad (2.13)$$

Here L is the labor force, N total employment, N^m racial-minority employment, P total population, K capital when fully utilized, Y real income or output, and ε the elasticity of racial-minority employment with respect to output.[29] The full-employment equilibrium condition expressed by (2.11) is applicable to underdeveloped economies,[30] while the fair and full-employment equilibrium condition expressed by (2.12) is relevant to race-conscious economies (whether advanced or underdeveloped). The exploratory employment functions involved in (2.11) and (2.12) stand in sharp contrast with the Keynesian variant, which makes employment a unique function of income ($N = N(Y)$), and which takes the stock of capital and the structure of society as given.

Technology and Population as Determinants of Employment and Growth

Another limitation of Keynesian theory lies in the deliberate neglect of technological change and population growth for short-run purposes.[31] But even in a relatively short period a technologically advancing economy can experience "technological unemployment" on a scale that cannot be dismissed simply as "fractional." Also, in such a period total population may be growing fast enough to increase the labor force relatively to existing employment opportunities and so to entail mass unemployment.

Suppose that automation is the preponderant type of technological advance. Then the marginal labor-input ratio (reciprocal of marginal labor productivity) will fall so as to give us a flatter employment curve via

$$N_t = \bar{n} + n_t Y_t \qquad (\Delta n(t) < 0, \bar{n} = 0)$$
$$(2.14)$$

which is the dynamic linear employment function with a smaller numerical slope due to the parenthesized technological assumption that $\Delta n(t) < 0$. Equation (2.14) implies that unless output increases to offset the decreasing impact of automation on employment relatively to the given labor force, technological unemployment becomes the inevitable result.[32]

Suppose, alternatively, that total population is rapidly growing without accompanying technological advance. Then the macro supply of labor curve can bodily shift upward relatively to any given macro demand for labor curve via

$$L_t = \bar{L}_t \qquad (\Delta \bar{L}(t) = \alpha \, \Delta P(t)) \qquad (2.15)$$

which is the autonomous supply of labor function based on the parenthesized demographical assumption that it shifts upward over time and at all levels of output by an amount equal to $\Delta \bar{L}(t) = \alpha \, \Delta P(t)$ (where P is population and α the constant manpower coefficient). Equation (2.15) with the attendant demographical indicator implies that unless output increases over time to offset the increasing impact of population growth on the labor force relatively to the given demand for labor, an unemployment gap becomes wider (as before full employment) or reappears (as after full employment).

Thus we see that Keynes' full-employment equilibrium condition $\bar{I}_f - S(Y_f) = 0$ is not sufficient (though necessary) condition to be satisfied even in the short run if rapid technological advance and population growth are taken into account. Moreover, as Harrod has indicated, the rate of growth of potential output is determined by what "the increase of population and technological improvements allow."[33] So we are led to the post-Keynesian growth equation of the reduced form[34]:

$$g^p \equiv \frac{\Delta Y^p}{Y^p} = \lambda + \pi$$

$$\left(\lambda \equiv \frac{\Delta N}{N}, \pi \equiv \frac{\Delta \rho}{\rho} \right) \qquad (2.16)$$

which, if realized, would guarantee full employment of a growing population with an increasing productivity. Here g^p is the rate of growth of potential output (or the "natural" growth rate in Harrod's terminology), y^p potential output, λ the rate of growth of full-employed labor population, π the rate of growth of labor productivity, and ρ the technologically given average productivity of labor. It is with the growth rate given by (2.16) that we must compare the rate of growth of actual output co-determined by the saving ratio and the capital-output ratio ($g^a = s/b$ or $G_w = s/C_r$ is Harrod's symbolism)—if we are to wipe out any gap between the potential and the actual rate of growth ($g^p - g^a > 0$) for a "golden-age" state of dynamic equilibrium with full utilization of *both* labor and capital. Thus it is necessary to go beyond Keynes' static theory of employment, which precludes technological and demographical considerations.

The Unstable Multiplier and Consumption-Led Fluctuations

Another limitation has to do with Keynes' "fundamental psychological law" of consumption on which "the stability of

the economic system essentially depends."[35] That law is expressible as the less than unitary marginal propensity to consume ($0 < \Delta C/\Delta Y < 1$) that entails the finite multiplier ($k < \infty$) and hence non-explosive income-employment fluctuations. Moreover, this latter "investment multiplier" is supposed to be as stable as the presumably constant marginal propensity to consume, so that economic fluctuations may be considered primarily due to a change in the investment multiplicand ($\pm \Delta \bar{I}$). However, the predictive value of Keynes' "investment multiplier" theory is thrown into question as soon as we take into acount the *highly volatile* demand for *consumer durables*, which nowadays makes up a quantitatively significant part of total consumption-demand in an increasingly "gadget-happy" advanced economy *with extensive and vagarious consumer-credit facilities* (to finance the purchases of automobiles, refrigerators, TV sets, washing machines, furniture, and other consumer durables).

We may see the destabilizing effect of the demand for consumer durables thus:

$$\delta = \frac{\Delta C^d(t)}{\Delta \bar{D}(t)} \qquad (\delta \neq \text{const.}) \quad (2.17)$$

$$\bar{\beta} = \frac{\Delta C^p(t)}{\Delta Y((t)} \qquad (\beta = \text{const.}) \quad (2.18)$$

$$\gamma = \frac{\Delta \bar{D}(t)}{\Delta Y(t)} \qquad (\gamma \neq \text{const.}) \quad (2.19)$$

$$\begin{aligned} \Delta Y(t) &= \Delta C^p(t) + \Delta C^d(t) + \Delta \bar{I}(t) \\ &= \bar{\beta} \Delta Y(t) + \delta \Delta \bar{D}(t) + \Delta \bar{I}(t) \end{aligned} \qquad (2.20)$$

$$1 = \bar{\beta} + \delta \gamma + \frac{\Delta \bar{I}}{\Delta Y} \qquad (2.21)$$

$$k = \frac{\Delta Y(t)}{\Delta \bar{I}(t)} = (1 - \bar{\beta} - \delta \gamma)^{-1}$$

$$\neq \text{const.} \qquad (2.22)$$

$$k = \infty \qquad \text{if} \quad \bar{\beta} + \delta \gamma = 1 \qquad (2.23)$$

Here Y is income, C^p perishable or nondurable consumption-demand, C^d durable consumption-demand, $\bar{I}$ autonomous investment-demand, $\bar{D}$ autonomous consumer credits, δ the cyclically variable marginal propensity to consume durables out of credit, $\bar{\beta}$ the constant marginal propensity to consume nondurables out of income, γ the cyclically variable marginal ratio of autonomous credits (extended by banks and firms) to income, k the "investment multiplier" in question, and t time. Equation (2.20), which is the discrete differentiation of an implicit equation of the form $Y = C^p + C^d + \bar{I}$ in light of (2.17)–(2.19) and over time, is divided through by $\Delta Y(t)$ to yield equation (2.21). The resulting "Investment multiplier" expressed by (2.22) is as unstable as the cyclically variable values of δ and γ despite a stable β. Equation (2.23) indicates the conceivable case of an explosive multiplier ($k = \infty$) where the marginal propensities to consume durables and nondurables out of national income are assumed to equal unity ($\bar{\beta} + \delta\gamma = 1$, where $\delta\gamma$ represents the marginal propensity to consume durables out of *income*, since dividing $\Delta C^d = \delta \Delta \bar{D}$ by ΔY yields $\Delta C^d/\Delta Y = \delta(\Delta D/\Delta Y) = \delta\gamma$). This formal demonstration via (2.17)–(2.23) strongly suggests the possibility of a "gadget-happy" economy with highly developed consumer-credit arrangements experiencing consumption-led fluctuations of an extremely large amplitude.

Income Distribution Both as a Determinant and as a Determinate

The last, but not the least, limitation of Keynesian theory to be mentioned here is its neglect of income distribution both as an independent variable and as a dependent variable in the macro model. Keynes, while stressing the importance of income distribution in the concluding chapter of the *General Theory*,[36] nevertheless took as given "the social structure including the forces... which determine the distribution of the national income."[37] This caused

post-Keynesian economists to make fragmentary attempts[38] to synthesize distribution theory, income-employment theory, and growth theory. Most of those attempts have treated income distribution as an independent variable, however. Considering income distribution as a dependent variable, as it should be in a macro distribution theory, look, for example, at Kaldor's static distribution equation of the simplified form

$$\frac{Q}{Y} = \frac{1}{s}\frac{I}{Y} \qquad \left(\frac{W}{Y} = 1 - \frac{Q}{Y}\right) \qquad (2.24)$$

which is derived from $I/Y = s(Q/Y)$. Here Y is full-employment income, Q profit-income, W wage-income, I investment, and s the marginal propensity to save out of profit-income (that of wage-income being assumed to be zero for simplicity). Equation (2.24) implicitly makes a profit-income distribution ratio (Q/Y) an increasing function of the investment ratio (I/Y), given the constant marginal propensity to save ($s = \bar{s}$). Kaldor seems to imagine that he has dispensed with the classical "marginal productivity" variable in macro income distribution.

However, once we take a long view and remember the Harrodian investment equation of the form $I/Y = (I/\Delta Y)(\Delta Y/Y)$, we can see the dynamic role of the marginal productivity of net investment in macro income distribution. For the marginal capital coefficient ($I/\Delta Y$) is nothing but the reciprocal of capital productivity ($\Delta Y/I = (I/\Delta Y)^{-1}$). Substituting the above Harrodian equation in equation (2.24), we have

$$\frac{Q}{Y} = \frac{1}{s}\frac{g}{\sigma} \qquad \left(g \equiv \frac{\Delta Y}{Y}, \sigma \equiv \frac{\Delta Y}{I}\right) \qquad (2.25)$$

which indicates the possibility of the profit-income distribution ratio rising as a consequence of a higher rate of growth of income ($\Delta g(t) > 0$) when the saving ratio and capital productivity remain constant

$(\Delta s(t), \Delta \sigma(t) = 0)$. It also indicates that a larger productivity of capital $(\Delta \sigma(t) > 0)$ would decrease the profit-income distribution ratio when the saving ratio and the growth rate remain constant. Thus in a technologically dynamic economy with an increasing productivity of capital, the net investment ratio tends to fall via $I(t)/Y(t) = g(t)/\sigma(t)$ and the profit-income distribution ratio with it—unless the rate of growth of income is kept increasing over time so as to require an increasingly larger net investment ratio $(\Delta g(t) > 0$ and hence $\Delta (I/Y)_t > 0$ via $I/Y = (I/\Delta Y)(\Delta Y/Y))$. This brief discussion is indicative of the desirability of exploring further the Keynesian investment variable in terms of levels or the Harrodian investment variable in terms of ratios as a possible determinant of macro income distribution—as well as such levels and ratios regarded as determinants in macro income and growth models.

NOTES

1 The substance of this essay was given in my luncheon address before the New York State Economic Association Convention at Oneonta, New York, April 27, 1968.
2 For controversial views, see S. E. Harris (ed.), *The New Economics*, 1948; A. C. Pigou, *Keynes' General Theory*, 1950; R. F. Harrod, *The Life of John Maynard Keynes*, 1951; K. K. Kurihara (ed.), *Post Keynesian Economics*, 1954; W. Fellner, "Keynesian Economics After Twenty Years," *American Economic Review*, May 1957; D. Dillard, "The Influence of Keynesian Economics on Contemporary Thought," *ibid.*; H. C. Wallich, "Keynes Re-Examined: The Man, The Theory," *New York Times Magazine*, April 20, 1958; K. K. Kurihara, "Prof. Hansen on America's Economic Revolution," *Economic Journal*, September 1958; H. G. Johnson, A. P. Lerner, L. R. Klein, and D. M. Wright, "The General Theory After Twenty-Five Years," *American Economic Review*, May

1961; H. L. McCracken, "Keynesian Economics and the Future" in *Keynesian Economics in the Stream of Economic Thought*, 1961; A. Murad, "Evaluation and Criticism of the General Theory" in *What Keynes Means*, 1962; G. Schwartz, "The Keynes Formula Sweeps on," *New York Times Magazine*, September 8, 1963; K. K. Kurihara, "The Keynesian Impact on American Economic Thinking and Policy," Michigan State University *Centennial Review*, Vol. 7, No. 1, 1963; R. Lekachman (ed.), *Keynes' General Theory: Reports of Three Decades*, 1964; A. H. Hansen, "Keynes After Thirty Years," *Weltwirtschaftliches Archiv*, Vol. 97, No. 1, 1966; W. Heller, *New Dimensions of Political Economy*, 1967; and L. A. Hahn, "End of the Era of Keynes?," *Kyklos*, Vol. XX, 1967, Fasc. 1, as translated by W. E. Kuhn, *Nebraska Journal of Economics and Business*, Vol. 7, No. 1, 1968.
3 R. F. Harrod, "Domar and Dynamics," *Economic Journal*, September 1959.
4 R. F. Harrod, *Towards a Dynamic Economics*, 1948.
5 *Ibid.*, p. 87.
6 *General Theory*, p. 31.
7 The Keynes Plan advocating, among other things, an "International Investment or Development Corporation" (reprinted in S. E. Harris (ed.), *The New Economics*, p. 339).
8 For applications to a growing economy see J. G. Gurley, "Fiscal Policy in a Growing Economy," *Journal of Political Economy*, December 1953; my "Growth Models and Fiscal-Policy Parameters," *Public Finance*, No. 2/1956; A. T. Peacock, "The Public Sector and the Theory of Economic Growth," *Scottish Journal of Political Economy*, February 1959; and R. Musgrave, *The Theory of Public Finance*, 1960.
9 Keynes may have tacitly borrowed from Marx the idea of dividing total demand into consumption and investment (the Marxian counterparts being Departments I and II). See in this respect, a symposium on "Das Kapital: a Centenary Appreciation," *American Economic Review*, May 1967 (including such participants as P. A. Samuelson, E. D. Domar, and M. Bronfenbrenner).
10 Cost-push inflation will be discussed in Part II.
11 *General Theory*, p. 119, p. 303.
12 Cf. J. A. Schumpeter, *Ten Great Economists: From Marx to Keynes*, 1954. Schumpeter himself is fittingly considered

as one of such great economists in doctrinal history.

13 Leontief, *The Structure of American Economy: 1919–1939—An Empirical Application of Equilibrium Analysis*, 1953.

14 For various growth applications, see my *Macroeconomics and Programming*, 1964 (esp. Part II).

15 Kaldor, "A Model of the Trade Cycle," *Economic Journal*, March 1940.

16 Hicks, *A Contribution to the Theory of the Trade Cycle*, 1950.

17 Kalecki, "A Macrodynamic Theory of Business Cycles," *Econometrica*, III, 1935; and Goodwin, "The Non-Linear Accelerator and the Persistence of Business Cycles," *Econometrica*, January 1951.

18 See S. Ichimura, "Toward a General Nonlinear Macrodynamic Theory of Economic Fluctuations," in K. K. Kurihara (ed.), *Post Keynesian Economics* (Ch. 8).

19 See my "An Endogenous Model of Cyclical Growth," *Oxford Economic Papers*, October 1960.

20 *General Theory* (Ch. 16 on "Sundry Observations on the Nature of Capital").

21 Domar, *Essays in the Theory of Economic Growth*, 1957 (esp. Ch. IV).

22 Harrod, *Towards a Dynamic Economics* (Lecture 3).

23 S. Ichimura, "Macro-Economic Models" in United Nations, *Programming Techniques for Economic Development*, 1960 (appendix to Ch. II).

24 Cf. A. W. Phillips, "The Relation between Unemployment and the Rate of Change of Money Wage Rates in the United Kingdom, 1861–1957," *Economica*, November 1958; P. A. Samuelson and R. M. Solow, "Analytical Aspects of Anti-Inflation Policy," *American Economic Review*, May 1960; G. Means, *Administrative Inflation and Public Policy*, 1959; G. Ackley, "Administered Price and the Inflationary Process, *American Economic Review*, May 1959.

25 For details see my "A Note on 'Cost-Push' Inflation" (appendix to Ch. 4) in *National Income and Economic Growth*, 1961.

26 J. Robinson, "Mr. Harrod's Dynamics," *Economic Journal*, March 1949.

27 Klein, *The Keynesian Revolution*, 1947, p. 186.

28 Rockefeller, *Accelerated Economic Growth —A Key to the American Future*, 1960, p. 18.

29 The rate of growth of racial-minority employment can be measured by estimating the prevailing elasticity of racial-minority employment with respect to output (ε) and the prevailing rate of growth of output ($\Delta Y/Y$):

$$\frac{\Delta N^m}{N^m} = \varepsilon \frac{\Delta Y}{Y} \quad \text{since} \lim \frac{\Delta N^m}{N^m} \Big/ \frac{\Delta Y}{Y}$$

$$= \frac{Y}{N^m} \frac{\partial N^m}{\partial Y} = \frac{\partial(\log N^m)}{\partial(\log Y)} = \varepsilon$$

30 Cf. my "Dual Unemployment in Underdeveloped Economies" (Ch. 6) in *The Keynesian Theory of Economic Development*, 1959.

31 *General Theory*, p. 245.

32 Cf. The National Commission on Technology, Automation, and Economic Progress (headed by H. R. Bowen), *Technology and the American Economy* (U.S. Government Printing Office, Washington, D.C.), Vol. 1, February 1966.

33 Harrod, *Towards a Dynamic Economics*, p. 87.

34 For a rigorous derivation of g^p from exponential functions (on the simplifying assumption of $t = 0, 1$) see my *National Income and Economic Growth*, pp. 153–155.

35 *General Theory*, pp. 96–97.

36 *General Theory*, p. 372ff.

37 *Ibid.*, p. 245.

38 N. Kaldor, "Alternative Theories of Distribution," *Review of Economic Studies*, XXIII, 1955/1956 (reprinted in his *Essays on Value and Distribution*, 1960); S. Weintraub, *A General Theory of the Price Level Output, Income Distribution and Economic Growth*, 1959; J. Robinson, *The Accumulation of Capital*, 1956; J. Vibe-Pedersen, *National Income and Aggregate Income Distribution*, 1964; and my "Distribution, Employment and Secular Growth" in *Post Keynesian Economics*, and "The Redistributive Role in Economic Development" in *The Keynesian Theory of Economic Development*.

Summaries

Lawrence R. Klein, "The Keynesian Revolution Revisited," *Economic Studies Quarterly*, 15 (November 1964), pp. 1–24.

Lawrence Klein interprets some of the more important empirical findings relating to consumption, investment, liquidity preference functions, and national macroeconomic models. As a basis for his discussion, Klein examines critically the true meaning of the expression, *The Keynesian Revolution*. In his view, this revolution is based upon the invention by Keynes of (1) a theory of the determination of total income, (2) a theoretical explanation of the possibility of underemployment equilibrium, (3) a group of doctrines in public policy about how to control the economy at desired levels of economic activity, and (4) a long-run view on the historical trend of capitalism. Since most of the empirical work centers around (1) and (2), Klein concentrates on these aspects of Keynesian theory in this article.

Klein mentions that one of the most important statistical studies on the theory of consumption has been directed toward estimating the consumption coefficient. Another area of exploration is the propensity to invest. Statisticians have also studied the liquidity preference function and the production and labor demand functions, and have attempted to estimate their relevant parameters and coefficients.

Robert A. Mundell, "An Exposition of Some Subtleties in the Keynesian System," *Weltwirtschaftliches Archiv*, 93 (1964), pp. 301–312.

"The introduction of supply conditions into the Keynesian system and their integration with the theory of income and interest rate determination," says Robert Mundell, "pose one of the more formidable subjects for the student of income theory to master." With this student in mind, Mundell attempts a generalized exposition in this article of some of the less-known aspects of the Keynesian system. He limits his exposition to a discussion of the working of the Keynesian system under four assumptions: (1) that prices and wages are both flexible, (2) that prices are flexible and wages are rigid, (3) that wages are flexible and prices are rigid, and (4) that both prices and wages are rigid. The distinction he makes among the four cases hinges on whether or not firms are prevented from maximizing profits and workers are impeded in their pursuit of maximum utility.

Mundell uses simple algebra and a set of two-dimensional graphs to discuss "wealth effects" and "dichotomies in the pricing process." Mundell analyzes each of the four cases mentioned above. In the end, he summarizes his findings in the following words: "(1) Flexible wages and prices imply profit maximization of firms and utility maximization of labor. The system settles at a full employment equilibrium in which the real values of the variables are independent of the quantity of money. (2) Any rigidity in the system means that the interest rate, income, employment and the real wage rate are all affected by changes in the quantity of money. If money wages are rigid and prices are flexible, firms can maximize profits but there is full employment only at a unique level of the quantity of money. (3) If prices are rigid and money wages are flexible, there is automatic full employment, but firms produce at outputs where marginal cost differs from the fixed price, except when the supply of money is at a unique equilibrium level. (4) If both wages and prices are fixed, the general case is one where the marginal disutility of labor differs from the real wage, and marginal cost differs from the fixed price level."

Bibliography

Paul Davidson, "A Keynesian View of Patinkin's Theory of Employment," *Economic Journal*, 77 (September 1967), pp. 559–577.

Wassily Leontief, "Postulates: Keynes's *General Theory* and the Classicists," in S. Harris (ed.), *The New Economics* (New York: Alfred A. Knopf, Inc., 1948), pp. 232–242.

Paul P. Streen, "Keynes and the Classical Tradition," in Kenneth K. Kurihara (ed.), *Post Keynesian Economics* (New Brunswick, N.J.: Rutgers University Press, 1954), pp. 345–364.

5

CONSUMPTION AND INVESTMENT

It is agreed among most professional economists that the consumption and investment theories are two of the most important contributions Lord Keynes made to macroeconomic theory. Both of these have been given wide attention in economic literature, and a great amount of empirical and econometric work has been done in these two areas.

In the first selection in this part, Friedman explains the nature of the long-run consumption function. He first develops the permanent income hypothesis. Then, utilizing the concepts of permanent consumption and permanent income, he proves that, in the long run, consumption and income are proportional to each other. In the second article, Jorgenson concerns himself with the theory of investment behavior within a neoclassical framework. He establishes a direct relationship between the stock of capital and the investment theory. He also points out the differences between the neoclassical investment theory and other theories of investment behavior.

The Permanent Income Hypothesis
Milton Friedman

The magnitudes termed "permanent income" and "permanent consumption"* that play such a critical role in the theoretical analysis cannot be observed directly for any individual consumer unit. The

Milton Friedman, *A Theory of Consumption Function*, National Bureau of Economic Research (Princeton, N.J.: Princeton University Press, 1957), pp. 20–37. Reprinted by permission of Princeton University Press.

* [In *A Theory of the Consumption Function* (NBER; Princeton: Princeton University Press, 1957), Friedman states:

"The designation of current receipts as 'income' in statistical studies is an expedient enforced by limitations of data. On a theoretical level, income is generally defined as the amount a consumer unit could consume

most that can be observed are actual receipts and expenditures during some finite period, supplemented, perhaps, by some verbal statements about expectations for the future. The theoretical constructs are *ex ante* magnitudes; the empirical data are *ex post*. Yet in order to use the theoretical analysis to interpret empirical data, a correspondence must be established between the theoretical constructs and the observed magnitudes.

The most direct way to do so, and the one that has generally been followed in similar contexts, is to construct estimates of permanent income and permanent consumption for each consumer unit separately by adjusting the cruder receipts and expenditure data for some of their more obvious defects, and then to treat the adjusted *ex post* magnitudes as if they were also the desired *ex ante* magnitudes. Cash expenditures during a particular time period that are regarded as expenses of earning income can be deducted from cash receipts during the corresponding time period; accrual methods of accounting can be substituted for cash accounting for some or all income items; expenditures on durable consumer goods can be regarded as capital expenditures and only the imputed value of services rendered included as consumption; and so on. These adjustments clearly reduce the difference between the statistical estimates and the theoretical constructs and are therefore highly desirable. But even when they are carried as far as is at all

feasible, the resulting magnitudes, interpreted as estimates of permanent income and permanent consumption, are not consistent with equation (2.6)*: measured consumption turns out to be a smaller fraction of measured income for high than for low measured incomes even for groups of consumer units for whom it does not seem reasonable to attribute this result to differences in the values of *i*, *w*, or *u*.

We are thus driven either to reject equation (2.6), which is what earlier workers have done, or to resort to more indirect means of establishing a correspondence between the theoretical constructs and the observed magnitudes, which is what I propose to do. One indirect means is to use evidence for other time periods and other consumer units to interpret data for one consumer unit for one period. For example, if Mr. A's measured income fluctuates widely from year to year while Mr. B's is highly stable, it seems reasonable that Mr. A's measured income is a poorer index of his permanent income than Mr. B's is of his. Again, suppose Mr. A's measured income in any period is decidedly lower than the average measured income of a group of individuals who are similar to him in characteristics that we have reason to believe affect potential earnings significantly—for example, age, occupation, race, and location. It then seems reasonable to suppose that Mr. A's measured income understates his permanent income.

The following formalization of the relation between the theoretical constructs

---

(or believes that it could) while maintaining its wealth intact. (The well-known problems raised by this definition are not relevant to the analysis that follows. For a discussion of some of them see J. R. Hicks, *Value and Capital*, Oxford: Oxford University Press, 1939, pp. 171–188.) In our analysis, consumption is a function of income so defined....

"A similar problem arises about the meaning of 'consumption.' We have been using the term consumption to designate the value of the *services* that it is *planned* to consume during the period in question, which, under conditions of certainty, would also equal the value of the services actually consumed. The term is generally used in statistical studies to designate actual expenditures on goods and services. It therefore differs from the value of services it is planned to consume on two counts: first, because of additions to or subtractions from the stock of consumer goods, second, because of divergencies between plans and their realization.

"Let us use the terms 'permanent income' and 'permanent consumption' to refer to the concepts relevant to the theoretical analysis, so as to avoid confusion with the frequent usage of income as synonymous with current receipts and consumption as synonymous with current expenditures, and let us designate them by y_p and c_p respectively, with an additional numerical subscript to denote the year in question." (pp. 10–11)—*Eds.*]

* [Equation (2.6) is

$$c_p = k(i, w, u)y_p = k(i, w, u)iW$$

where *w* stands for the ratio of nonhuman wealth to permanent income: *u* for utility factors such as age, family composition, and the like as well as any objective factors that affect anticipations; *i* for the rate of interest; and *W* for wealth of a consumer unit. All variables refer to the same point in time. See Friedman, *op cit.*, p. 17—*Eds.*]

and observed magnitudes is designed to facilitate the use of such evidence. Its central idea is to interpret empirical data as observable manifestations of theoretical constructs that are themselves regarded as not directly observable.

1. THE INTERPRETATION OF DATA ON THE INCOME AND CONSUMPTION OF CONSUMER UNITS

Let y represent a consumer unit's measured income for some time period, say a year. I propose to treat this income as the sum of two components: a permanent component (y_p), corresponding to the permanent income of the theoretical analysis, and a transitory component (y_t),[1] or

$$y = y_p + y_t \qquad (3.1)$$

The permanent component is to be interpreted as reflecting the effect of those factors that the unit regards as determining its capital value or wealth: the nonhuman wealth it owns; the personal attributes of the earners in the unit, such as their training, ability, personality; the attributes of the economic activity of the earners, such as the occupation followed, the location of the economic activity, and so on. It is analogous to the "expected" value of a probability distribution. The transitory component is to be interpreted as reflecting all "other" factors, factors that are likely to be treated by the unit affected as "accidental" or "chance" occurrences, though they may, from another point of view, be the predictable effect of specifiable forces, for example, cyclical fluctuations in economic activity.[2] In statistical data, the transitory component includes also chance errors of measurement; unfortunately, there is in general no way to separate these from the transitory component as viewed by the consumer unit.

Some of the factors that give rise to transitory components of income are specific to particular consumer units, for example, illness, a bad guess about when to buy or sell, and the like; and, similarly, chance errors of measurement. For any considerable group of consumer units, the resulting transitory components tend to average out, so that if they alone accounted for the discrepancies between permanent and measured income, the mean measured income of the group would equal the mean permanent component, and the mean transitory component would be zero. But not all factors giving rise to transitory components need be of this kind. Some may be largely common to the members of the group, for example, unusually good or bad weather, if the group consists of farmers in the same locality; or a sudden shift in the demand for some product, if the group consists of consumer units whose earners are employed in producing this product. If such factors are favorable for any period, the mean transitory component is positive; if they are unfavorable, it is negative.[3] Similarly, a systematic bias in measurement may produce a nonzero mean transitory component in recorded data even though the transitory factors affecting consumer units have a zero effect on the average.

Similarly, let c represent a consumer unit's expenditures for some time period, and let it be regarded as the sum of a permanent component (c_p) and a transitory component (c_t), so that

$$c = c_p + c_t \qquad (3.2)$$

Again, some of the factors producing transitory components of consumption are specific to particular consumer units, such as unusual sickness, a specially favorable opportunity to purchase, and the like; others affect groups of consumer units in the same way, such as an unusually cold spell, a bountiful harvest, and the like. The effects of the former tend to average out; the effects of the latter produce positive or negative mean transitory components for groups of consumer units; the same is true with chance and systematic errors of measurement.

It is tempting to interpret the permanent components as corresponding to average lifetime values and the transitory components as the difference between such lifetime averages and the measured values in a specific time period. It would, however, be a serious mistake to accept such an interpretation, for two reasons. In the first place, the experience of one unit is itself but a small sample from a more extensive hypothetical universe, so there is no reason to suppose that transitory components average out to zero over the unit's lifetime. In the second place, and more important, it seems neither necessary nor desirable to decide in advance the precise meaning to be attached to "permanent." The distinction between permanent and transitory is intended to interpret actual behavior. We are going to treat consumer units *as if* they regarded their income and their consumption as the sum of two such components, and *as if* the relation between the permanent components is the one suggested by our theoretical analysis. The precise line to be drawn between permanent and transitory components is best left to be determined by the data themselves, to be whatever seems to correspond to consumer behavior.

Figure 1 is designed to bring out more explicitly the wide range of possible interpretations of permanent income. This figure refers to a single consumer unit, the head of which is assumed to be 30 years of age on the date in 1956 for which the figure is drawn. We may suppose the unit to have been formed when the head was aged 20. Measured income experience from 20 to 30, as recorded in the solid jagged line, is a datum; so also, of course, are other items not recorded in the figure, such as the amount of nonhuman wealth possessed, the occupation of the head and

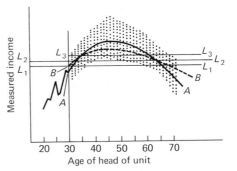

Figure 1. Illustration of Alternative Interpretations of Permanent Income. Lifetime Income Experience as Viewed in 1956 by a Consumer Unit with Head Aged 30

of other members of the unit, location, and so on. Future measured income experience is uncertain. The scatter of dots for later ages is intended to represent the possibilities as *viewed* by the unit; for each future date, there is some anticipated probability distribution of measured income. Because of the limitations of a two-dimensional figure, this scatter diagram seriously misrepresents the situation in one important respect. It suggests that the probability distributions at different ages are independent, whereas in general they might be expected to be interdependent. The distribution anticipated for age 40, for example, if a high measured income is realized at age 31 would presumably be different from the distribution expected if a low measured income is realized.[4] But this defect of the figure is not serious for our present limited purpose.

The scatter in the figure should not be confused conceptually with the corresponding scatter that would be generated by plotting the contemporaneous incomes of a large number of units with heads of different age. The scatter in the figure is the anticipated experience of one unit, not the realized experience of many. In forming its anticipations, the one unit may well take into account the contemporaneous experience of units which are of different age but alike in respect to other factors such as occupation, nonhuman wealth, etc.; and it may for some purposes usefully be regarded as doing so by simply accepting the contemporaneous differences as describing its own future possibilities. On the conceptual level, however, there is no need to foreclose the possibility that the unit will take other information into account as well.[5]

The solid curve AA in Figure 1 is the mean of the probability distributions anticipated for future years. It is one possible interpretation of the permanent income to which consumption is adapted. The horizontal line L_1L_1 is the mean lifetime income as anticipated at age 20; L_2L_2, as anticipated at age 30, taking into account realized experience from age 20 to age 30; L_3L_3, mean income anticipated at age 30 for the remaining lifetime of the unit. Each of these is another possible interpretation of permanent income, and almost at the opposite extreme of the spectrum from AA. No one of these has very great intuitive appeal as *the* permanent income to which consumption is adapted; AA, because it implies an exceedingly short time horizon; L_1L_1, L_2L_2, and L_3L_3, not only because they imply an extremely long time horizon, but also because they imply that units can borrow on the basis of anticipated receipts from both human and nonhuman wealth at the same interest rate at which they can lend accumulated nonhuman wealth. L_3L_3 has the further objection that it supposes no carry-over into the present of past adaptations. The dashed curve BB is an intermediate interpretation, intended to be something of an average of AA and L_1L_1 or L_2L_2. Something like this seems intuitively the most plausible interpretation, but intuitive plausibility gives little guidance to the exact kind of average, or length of horizon. For this, we must rely on the empirical evidence.

Figure 1 is drawn for a particular date. There is nothing about the concept of permanent income that requires the relevant parts of the figure to remain the same for any later date. Aside from the point already made, that in advance the probability distribution for any future date depends on the measured income actually experienced, the whole joint probability distribution may be shifted by occurrences that were entirely unanticipated at the date in question. In our empirical work, we shall sometimes find it desirable to suppose that permanent income, or the age pattern of permanent income, remains unchanged over a period of years, but it should be clear that this is an empirical specialization of a more general concept.

2. A FORMAL STATEMENT OF THE PERMANENT INCOME HYPOTHESIS

In its most general form our hypothesis about the consumption function, which we shall hereafter refer to as the permanent income hypothesis, is given by the three equations (2.6), (3.1), and (3.2):

$$c_p = k(i, w, u)y_p \tag{2.6}$$

$$y = y_p + y_t \tag{3.1}$$

$$c = c_p + c_t \tag{3.2}$$

Equation (2.6) defines a relation between permanent income and permanent consumption. It specifies that the ratio between them is independent of the size of permanent income but does depend on other variables, in particular: (1) the rate of interest (i) or sets of rates of interest at which the consumer unit can borrow or lend; (2) the relative importance of property and nonproperty income, symbolized by the ratio of nonhuman wealth to income (w); and (3) the factors symbolized by the portmanteau variable u determining the consumer unit's tastes and preferences for consumption versus additions to wealth. The most significant of the latter factors probably are (a) the number of members of the consumer unit and their characteristics, particularly their ages, and (b) the importance of transitory factors affecting income and consumption, measured, for example, by the "spread" or standard deviation of the probability distributions of the transitory components relative to the size of the corresponding permanent components. Equations (3.1) and (3.2) define the connection between the permanent components and the measured magnitudes.

In this most general form the hypothesis is empty, in the sense that no empirical data could contradict it. Equations (3.1) and (3.2) are purely definitional; they add two equations but also two additional unknowns, the transitory components. There are a variety of ways to specialize the hypothesis so that it is capable of being contradicted by observed data. The one I shall use is to specify some of the characteristics of the probability distributions of the transitory components. A particularly simple specification, yet one that seems adequate to explain existing evidence, is to suppose that the transitory components of income and consumption are uncorrelated with one another and with the corresponding permanent components, or

$$\rho_{y_t y_p} = \rho_{c_t c_p} = \rho_{y_t c_t} = 0 \qquad (3.3)$$

where ρ stands for the correlation coefficient between the variables designated by the subscripts.

The assumptions that the first two correlations in (3.3)—between the permanent and transitory components of income and of consumption—are zero seem very mild and highly plausible. Indeed, by themselves, they have little substantive content and can almost be regarded as simply completing or trans-

lating the definitions of transitory and permanent components; the qualitative notion that the transitory component is intended to embody is of an accidental and transient addition to or subtraction from income, which is almost equivalent to saying an addition or subtraction that is not correlated with the rest of income. The merging of errors of measurement with transitory components contributes further to the plausibility that these correlations are zero.

For a group of individuals, it is plausible to suppose that the absolute size of the transitory component varies with the size of the permanent component: that a given random event produces the same percentage rather than the same absolute increase or decrease in the incomes of units with different permanent components. This may make more convenient an alternative definition of transitory component that is suggested below; it is not, however, inconsistent with zero correlation. Zero correlation implies only that the *average* transitory component— the algebraic average in which positive and negative components offset one another—is the same for all values of the permanent component. For example, suppose that the transitory component is equally likely to be plus or minus 10 per cent of the permanent component. The average transitory component is then zero for all values of the permanent component, although the average absolute value, which disregards the sign of the components, is directly proportional to the permanent component.

The plausibility of taking our definition of transitory components to imply a zero correlation for a group of consumer units depends somewhat on the criteria determining membership in the group. The clearest example is a classification of units by the size of their measured income. For each such group, the correlation between permanent and transitory components is necessarily negative, since with a common measured income the permanent component can be relatively high only if the transitory component is relatively low, and conversely.[6]

The assumption that the third correlation in (3.3)—between the transitory components of income and consumption—is zero is a much stronger assumption. It is primarily this assumption that introduces important substantive content into the hypothesis and makes it susceptible of contradiction by a wide range of phenomena capable of being observed. The ultimate test of its acceptability is of course whether such phenomena are in fact observed, and most of what follows is devoted to this question. It is hardly worth proceeding to such more refined tests, however, unless the assumption can pass—or at least not fail miserably—the much cruder test of consistency with casual observation of one's self and one's neighbors, so some comments on the intuitive plausibility of the assumption are not out of order.

The common notion that savings, or at least certain components of savings, are a "residual" speaks strongly for the plausibility of the assumption. For this notion implies that consumption is determined by rather long-term considerations, so that any transitory changes in income lead primarily to additions to assets or to the use of previously accumulated balances rather than to corresponding changes in consumption.

Yet from another point of view, the assumption seems highly implausible. Will not a man who receives an unexpected windfall use at least some part of it in "riotous living," i.e., in consumption expenditures? Would he be likely to add the whole of it to his wealth? The answer to these questions depends greatly on how "consumption" is defined. The offhand affirmative answer reflects in large measure, I believe, an implicit definition of consumption in terms of purchases, including durable goods, rather than in terms of the value of services. If the latter definition is adopted, as seems highly desirable in applying the hypothesis to empirical data—though unfortunately I have been able to do so to only a limited extent—much that one classifies offhand as consumption is reclassified as savings. Is not the windfall likely to be used for the purchase of durable goods? Or, to put it differently, is not the timing of the replacement of durable goods and of additions to the stock of such goods likely to some extent to be adjusted so as to coincide with windfalls?

Two other considerations argue for the plausibility of the assumption that transitory components of income and consumption are uncorrelated. First, the above identification of a windfall with transitory income is not precise. Suppose, for example, inheritances are included in a particular concept of measured income. Consider a consumer unit whose receipts remain unchanged over a succession of time periods except that it receives an inheritance in the final period. If the inheritance was expected to occur some time or other, it will already have been allowed for in permanent income; the transitory component of income is only the excess of the inheritance over this element of permanent income. There seems no reason why the receipt of the inheritance should make consumption in the final period different from that of preceding periods, except through inability to borrow in advance on the strength of the inheritance. But this implies that the receipt of the inheritance changes w (the ratio of wealth to income) in (2.6); it is therefore already taken into account in the hypothesis. There is no essential difference if the inheritance is unexpected. The effect of the inheritance is then to increase the permanent income of the unit, and this will justify a higher consumption in the final period; again the transitory component is only the excess of the windfall over this element of permanent income, and it is no longer intuitively obvious that it should lead to an increase in current consumption.[7] The second consideration is that just as there are instances in which one would expect a transitory increase in income to produce a transitory increase in consumption, so also there are instances in which one would expect the reverse. The simplest example is when a transitory increase in income reduces opportunities for consumption as when it is obtained by working longer hours or going to a backward country. Such negative and positive correlations will tend to offset one another.

The preceding remarks abstract from errors of measurement. Yet, as noted, in any statistical analysis errors of measurement will in general be indissolubly merged with the correctly measured transitory components. The effect on the correlation between statistically recorded transitory components of income and consumption depends critically on how the statistical data are obtained. If income and consumption are measured independently, the errors of estimate might be expected to be independent as well and therefore to contribute toward a small or zero observed correlation between transitory components of income and consumption. On the other hand, if consumption is estimated, as it frequently is, by measuring independently savings and income and subtracting the former from the latter, then measured consumption and measured income have common errors of measurement. This tends toward a positive observed correlation between transitory components of income and consumption.

The purpose of these remarks is not to demonstrate that a zero correlation is the *only* plausible assumption—neither evidence like that alluded to nor any other can justify such a conclusion. Its purpose is rather to show that common observation does not render it absurd to suppose that a hypothesis embodying a zero correlation can yield a fairly close approximation to observed consumer behavior. The assumption that the correlation between transitory components of income and consumption is zero could, of course, be replaced by the less restrictive assumption that it is a positive number between zero and unity, but this would greatly weaken the hypothesis and reduce its potential usefulness for predicting behavior. It seems highly undesirable to do so until and unless a significant contradiction arises between the stronger hypothesis and empirical evidence on consumer behiavor.

A particulary simple special case of the hypothesis arises if, in addition to (3.3), it is assumed that the mean transitory components of consumption and income are zero, or

$$\mu_{y_t} = \mu_{c_t} = 0 \qquad (3.4)$$

where μ stands for the mean of the variable designated by its subscript. This assumption is eminently reasonable if the probability distribution in question is sufficiently comprehensive. In general, however, we shall want to use conditional probability distributions, for example, the distribution of transitory components in a particular year, or for members of a particular group. In such cases, it will generally be undesirable to assume that (3.4) holds, just as for the single consumer unit viewed *ex post* it is undesirable to assume that the transitory components themselves are necessarily zero.

It may be desirable or necessary to impose additional conditions on the probability distributions to facilitate the estimation of the parameters of the system from observed data. I shall, however, largely neglect the problem of statistical estimation, and so we need not go into such conditions.

A more important qualification is that, for simplicity of exposition, equations

(3.1) and (3.2) express the relation between observed income and its permanent and transitory components as additive. The form of the relation is important because it may affect the empirical validity of such specifications of the characteristics of the probability distributions as (3.3) and (3.4), as well as the validity of using specifications of other characteristics of the distribution that are convenient statistically. From this point of view, I conjecture that a multiplicative specification is preferable for income and consumption data. If we let capital letters stand for the logarithms of the variables designated by the corresponding lower case letters, the equations defining the hypothesis then take the following alternative form:

$$C_p = K(i, w, u) + Y_p \qquad (2.6')$$

$$Y = Y_p + Y_t \qquad (3.1')$$

$$C = C_p + C_t \qquad (3.2')$$

$$\rho_{Y_t Y_p} = \rho_{C_t C_p} = \rho_{Y_t C_t} = 0 \qquad (3.3')$$

Many of the results that follow apply equally to both forms of the hypothesis, requiring only that the same symbol be interpreted in one case as an absolute value, in the other, as a logarithm. For any significant results for which this is not true, the logarithmic expressions are given in footnotes.

3. THE RELATION BETWEEN MEASURED CONSUMPTION AND MEASURED INCOME

Suppose we have observations on consumption and income for a number of consumer units, for all of whom the k of equation (2.6) can be taken to be numerically the same. Let us proceed, as is usually done in family budget studies, to estimate from these data a relation between consumption and income. For simplicity,

let the relation to be estimated be linear, say:

$$c = \alpha + \beta y \qquad (3.5)$$

where c is to be interpreted as the mean consumption for a given value of y, it being understood that the consumption of individual units deviates from this value by chance.[8] The least squares estimates of α and β (call these a and b), computed from the regression of c on y, are

$$b = \frac{\sum (c - \bar{c})(y - \bar{y})}{\sum (y - \bar{y})^2} \qquad (3.6)$$

$$a = \bar{c} - b\bar{y} \qquad (3.7)$$

where $\bar{c}$ and $\bar{y}$ stand for the mean consumption and income respectively of the group of consumer units, and the summation is over the group. In the numerator of the expression for b, replace y and c by the right-hand sides of (3.1) and (3.2), and $\bar{y}$ and $\bar{c}$ by the corresponding sums of means. This gives

$$\begin{aligned}
\sum (c &- \bar{c})(y - \bar{y}) \\
&= \sum (c_p + c_t - \bar{c}_p - \bar{c}_t) \\
&\quad \times (y_p + y_t - \bar{y}_p - \bar{y}_t) \\
&= \sum (c_p - \bar{c}_p)(y_p - \bar{y}_p) \\
&\quad + \sum (c_p - \bar{c}_p)(y_t - \bar{y}_t) \\
&\quad + \sum (c_t - \bar{c}_t)(y_p - \bar{y}_p) \\
&\quad + \sum (c_t - \bar{c}_t)(y_t - \bar{y}_t)
\end{aligned} \qquad (3.8)$$

From (2.6),

$$c_p = k y_p \qquad (2.6)$$

Inserting (2.6) in (3.8) yields

$$\begin{aligned}
\sum (c - \bar{c})(y - \bar{y}) &= k \sum (y_p - \bar{y}_p)^2 \\
&\quad + k \sum (y_p - \bar{y}_p)(y_t - \bar{y}_t) \\
&\quad + \frac{1}{k} \sum (c_t - \bar{c}_t)(c_p - \bar{c}_p) \\
&\quad + \sum (c_t - \bar{c}_t)(y_t - \bar{y}_t)
\end{aligned} \qquad (3.9)$$

Given the zero correlations specified in (3.3), the final three terms will differ from zero only because of sampling fluctuations: they will approach zero as the sample size is increased, or average zero over many similar samples. Since our present concern is not with the problem of statistical estimation but with the interpretation of the results, let us suppose the sample to be sufficiently large so that sampling error can be neglected. In that case

$$b = k \frac{\sum (y_p - \bar{y}_p)^2}{\sum (y - \bar{y})^2} = k \cdot P_y \qquad (3.10)$$

where P_y is the fraction of the total variance of income in the group contributed by the permanent component of income. More generally, of course, b can be regarded as an estimate of the righthand side of (3.10).[9]

The algebraic relation in (3.10) lends itself directly to meaningful interpretation in terms of the permanent income hypothesis. The regression coefficient b measures the difference in consumption associated, on the average, with a one dollar difference between consumer units in measured income. On our hypothesis, the size of this difference in consumption depends on two things: first, how much of the difference in measured income is also a difference in permanent income, since only differences in permanent income are regarded as affecting consumption systematically; second, how much of permanent income is devoted to consumption. P_y measures the first; k, the second; so their product equals b. If P_y is unity, transient factors are either entirely absent or affect the incomes of all members of the group by the same amount; a one dollar difference in measured income means a one dollar difference in permanent income and so produces a difference of k in consumption; b is therefore equal to k. If P_y is zero, there are no differences in permanent income; a one dollar difference in measured income means a one dollar difference in the transitory component of income, which is taken to be uncorrelated with consumption; in consequence, this difference in measured income is associated with no systematic difference in consumption; b is therefore zero. As this explanation suggests, P_y, though *defined* by the ratio of the variance of the permanent component of income to the variance of total income, can be *interpreted* as the fraction of any difference in measured income that on the average is contributed by a difference in the permanent component. This point is developed more fully below.

Substitute (3.10) in (3.7), replace $\bar{c}$ by $\bar{c}_p + \bar{c}_t$, $\bar{y}$ by $\bar{y}_p + \bar{y}_t$, and $\bar{c}_p$ by $k\bar{y}_p$. The resulting expression can then be written:

$$a = \bar{c}_t - kP_y\bar{y}_t + k(1 - P_y)\bar{y}_p \qquad (3.11)$$

The elasticity of consumption with respect to income at the point (c, y) is

$$\eta_{cy} = \frac{dc}{dy} \cdot \frac{y}{c} = b \cdot \frac{y}{c} = kP_y \cdot \frac{y}{c} \qquad (3.12)$$

Suppose that the mean transitory components of both income and consumption are equal to zero, so that $\bar{y} = \bar{y}_p$, $\bar{c} = \bar{c}_p$. In this special case

$$\frac{\bar{y}}{\bar{c}} = \frac{1}{k} \qquad (3.13)$$

It follows that if the elasticity is computed at the point corresponding to the sample mean:

$$\eta_{cy} = P_y \qquad (3.14)$$

Consider, now, the regression of y on c, say

$$y = a' + b'c \qquad (3.15)$$

By the same reasoning it can be shown that, sampling errors aside,

$$b' = \frac{1}{k} P_c \qquad (3.16)$$

where P_c is the fraction of the variance of consumption contributed by the permanent component, and

$$a' = \bar{y}_t - \frac{1}{k} P_c\bar{c}_t + \frac{1}{k}(1 - P_c)\bar{c}_p \qquad (3.17)$$

The elasticity of consumption with respect to income computed from this regression is

$$\eta'_{cy} = \frac{dc}{dy} \cdot \frac{y}{c} = \frac{1}{b'} \cdot \frac{y}{c} = \frac{k}{P_c} \cdot \frac{y}{c} \qquad (3.18)$$

Again, if $\bar{y}_t = \bar{c}_t = 0$,

$$\eta'_{cy} = \frac{1}{P_c} \qquad (3.19)$$

if evaluated at the point corresponding to the sample mean.[10]

Some of these results are presented in graphic form in Figure 2 for the special case in which the mean transitory components of income and consumption are zero.

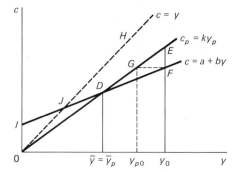

Figure 2. Hypothetical Relation Between Measured Consumption and Measured Income (Mean Transitory Components Equal Zero)

Consider the consumer units with a particular measured income, say y_0, which is above the mean measured income for the group as a whole. Given zero correlation between the permanent and transitory components of income, the average permanent income of these units is less than y_0; that is, the average transitory component is positive. These units have been classified together precisely because their measured income is a certain amount *above* the average income of the group; such a relatively high measured income could have been received despite unfavorable transitory effects; clearly, it is more likely to have been received because of favorable transitory effects; the winners in any particular set of races may well be better on the average than the losers but they are also likely to have had more than their share of good luck. Put more rigorously, the transitory component of income is positively correlated with the sum of itself and a variable (the permanent component) with which it is itself uncorrelated.[11] What about the average transitory component of consumption for these units? The corresponding component of their income is positive because the transitory component of income helped to determine which units had a

measured income of y_0 and so were classified together; given, however, that the transitory components of income and consumption are uncorrelated, a classification by income is random with respect to transitory components of consumption; in consequence, the latter tend to average out to the average for the group as a whole, which is assumed to be zero. The average consumption of units with a measured income y_0 is therefore equal to their average permanent consumption. On our hypothesis, this is k times their average permanent income. If y_0 were not only the measured income of these units but also their permanent income, their mean consumption would be ky_0 or y_0E. Since their mean permanent income is less than their measured income, their average consumption, y_0F, is less than y_0E.

By the same reasoning, for consumer units with an income equal to the mean of the group as a whole, or $\bar{y}$, the average transitory component of income as well as of consumption is zero, so the ordinate of the regression line is equal to the ordinate of the line OE which gives the relation between permanent consumption and permanent income. For units with an income below the mean, the average transitory component of income is negative, so average measured consumption is greater than the ordinate of *OE*. The regression line therefore intersects *OE* at *D*, is above it to the left of *D*, and below it to the right of *D*.

Let us return to the income class y_0. Draw a horizontal line through *F*. The abscissa of the point *G*, where this line intersects *OE*, is the permanent income associated with a permanent consumption y_0F. This income, labelled y_{p0} on the figure, is therefore the average permanent component of the income of the members of the income class y_0, and $(y_0 - y_{p0})/(y_0 - \bar{y})$ is the fraction of the deviation of their average income from the average for the group attributable to the transitory component. If this fraction is the same for all income classes, *IF* is a straight line, and the common value of the fraction is $1 - P_y$.[12] The higher this fraction, the flatter *IF* and conversely. At one extreme, if P_y is zero, that is, if all members of the group have the same permanent component, average consumption is the same for all income classes and *IF* is horizontal. At the other extreme, if $P_y = 1$, so transitory components are all zero, *IF* coincides with *OE*.

If *k* is less than unity, permanent consumption is always less than permanent income. As is clear from the figure, however, it does not follow that measured consumption is necessarily less than measured income. The line *OH* on the figure is a 45 degree line along which $c = y$. The vertical distance between this line and *IF* is average measured savings. Point *J* is the "break even" point at which average measured savings are zero. To the left of *J*, average measured savings are negative, to the right, positive; as measured income increases, so does the ratio of average measured savings to measured income. Our hypothesis thus yields a relation between measured consumption and measured income that reproduces the broadest features of the corresponding regressions that have been computed from observed data.

For the special case for which Figure 2 is drawn, *k* could be readily computed from observed data on the measured consumption and measured income of a group of consumer units, since average measured consumption and average measured income then equal the corresponding average permanent components. The line *OE* in the figure therefore goes through the point describing the mean income and consumption of the group, so $k = \bar{c}/\bar{y}$. P_y could then be computed from the relation between the regression of *c* on *y* (the line *IF*) and the line *OE*, and P_c from the corresponding relation between the regression of *y* on *c* and the line *OE*.[13]

If the mean transitory component of consumption is not zero, the curve *IF* is shifted vertically by a corresponding amount—upwards, if the mean transitory component is positive, downwards, if it is negative. Clearly, there is no way of distinguishing such a shift from a change in *k*. Similarly, a positive mean transitory component of income shifts *IF* to the right, a negative mean, to the left. For a straight line, there is no way of distinguishing such horizontal shifts from vertical shifts produced by a mean transitory component of consumption. It follows that, if the mean transitory components cannot be set equal to zero, data for one group for one time period are inadequate to estimate all the parameters. Some other source of information is required as well.

Our hypothesis gives a major role to certain features of the income distribution generally neglected in consumption studies. It asserts that some of the most strikingly uniform characteristics of computed regressions between consumption and income are simply a reflection of the inadequacy of measured income as an indicator of long-run income status. In consequence, differences among various groups of consumer units in observed marginal propensities to consume may not reflect differences in underlying preferences for consumption and wealth at all; they may reflect primarily the different strength of random forces, including errors of measurement, in determining measured income. Fortunately, considerable evidence is available on the importance of transitory components of income from studies of changes over time in the relative income status of individuals or consumer units. One of the attractive features of our hypothesis is that it enables us to bring this independent body of evidence to bear on the interpretation of consumption behavior; such evidence can provide some of the additional information required when transitory components of income and consumption cannot be supposed to be zero.

Before examining these data, however, we shall first examine the consistency of the hypothesis with some of the major general findings of empirical studies of consumption behavior and its relation to the relative income hypothesis suggested by Brady and Friedman, Duesenberry, and Modigliani. This will serve the double purpose of bringing out more fully the implications of the hypothesis and of suggesting the evidence that recommends its acceptance as a provisional working hypothesis.

NOTES

1 The terminology, and much of the subsequent analysis, is taken from Friedman and Kuznets, *Income from Independent Professional Practice* [New York: National Bureau of Economic Research, 1945], pp. 325–338, 352–364.
2 This division is, of course, in part arbitrary, and just where to draw the line may well depend on the particular application. Similarly, the dichotomy between permanent and transitory components is a highly special case. See *ibid.*, pp. 352–364, for a generalization to a larger number of components.
3 Note the difference from *ibid.*, p. 326, where the mean transitory component can be taken to be zero without loss of

generality. The difference reflects a narrower definition of transitory component in *ibid.* plus the use of the concept to compare the same group in two years.
4 The most general description would be in terms of a probability distribution of alternative age-measured-income values. It should be noted that the generalized analytical formulation in *ibid.*, pp. 352–364, allows fully for interdependence.
5 For example, in sec. 3 of Chap. 4 below [Friedman, *op. cit.*], the unit is interpreted as modifying contemporaneous experience by information on the secular trend of income.
6 See [Friedman and Kuznets, *op. cit.*,] pp. 326 and 327.
7 I owe this point to Modigliani and Brumberg, "Utility Analysis and the Consumption Function [An Interpretation of Cross-Section Data]," [*Post-Keynesian Economics*, ed. by Kenneth K. Kurihara (New Brunswick: Rutgers University Press)], 1954, pp. 405–406. ...
8 On our hypothesis, the relation between the mean value of c and y will be linear only under special conditions. For example, it will be if y_p, y_t, and c_t are distributed according to a trivariate normal distribution. See ·D. V. Lindley, "Regression Lines and the Linear Functional Relationship," *Journal of the Royal Statistical Society, Supplement*, IX (1947), 218–244.
9 In the special case of the preceding footnote, $\beta = kP_y$.
10 For the logarithmic alternative described by (2.6′), (3.1′), (3.2′), and (3.3′) the analogues to the results given in the text are

$$B = P_Y \tag{3.10'}$$

$$A = K + \bar{C}_t - \bar{Y}_t P_Y + \bar{Y}_P(1 - P_Y) \tag{3.11'}$$

$$\eta_{cy} = \frac{dC}{dY} = B = P_Y \tag{3.12'}$$

$$B' = P_C \tag{3.16'}$$

$$A' = -K + \bar{Y}_t - \bar{C}_t P_C + \bar{C}_P(1 - P_C) \tag{3.17'}$$

$$\eta'_{cy} = \frac{1}{P_C} \tag{3.19'}$$

These results are in some ways simpler and more appealing than those in the text, since the elasticity of consumption with respect to income is the same everywhere and hence equal to P_Y or $1/P_C$ without the necessity of assuming the mean transitory components to be zero.

11 See Friedman and Kuznets, *op. cit.*, pp. 327–332, esp. footnotes 10 and 13.

12 See *ibid.* pp. 332–336, 358. Figure 2 is essentially the same as Chart 28 on p. 333.

13 The estimation problem is the classical one of "mutual regression" or regression when "both variables are subject to error." See D. V. Lindley, *op cit.*, for an excellent analysis of the problem and survey of the literature. Many of our equations duplicate equations in his paper. As Lindley points out, there are no efficient statistics for estimating all the parameters in the model from sample data. The method described in the text is therefore not statistically efficient. The usual solution is to assume the ratio of the variance of y_t to the variance of c_t known, in which case efficient statistical procedures do exist.

The Theory of Investment Behavior
Dale W. Jorgenson

1. INTRODUCTION

Business investment behavior is one of the areas of modern economic research that is being studied most intensively; empirical studies are accumulating rapidly,[1] and at the same time important developments in the economic theory of investment behavior are taking place.[2] As yet, there is very little common ground between the empirical and theoretical approaches to this subject. From a certain point of view this is a desirable state of affairs.[3] Econometric studies of investment behavior date back no more than thirty years.[4] Only recently have data on investment expenditures suitable for analysis by econometric methods become available. If empirical studies are forced prematurely into a theoretical straitjacket, attention may be diverted from historical and institutional considerations that are essential to a complete understanding of investment behavior. On the other hand, if theoretical work is made to conform to "realistic"

Dale W. Jorgenson, "The Theory of Investment Behavior," in Robert Ferber (ed.), *Determinants of Investment Behavior* (New York: National Bureau of Economic Research, 1967), pp. 129–155. [Footnotes expanded—Eds.]

assumptions at too early a stage in the development of empirical work, the door may be closed to theoretical innovations that could lead to improvements in empirical work at a later stage.

While there is some surface plausibility in the view that empirical and theoretical research are best carried out in isolation from each other, this view is seriously incomplete. Econometric work is always based on highly simplified models. The number of possible explanations of investment behavior, which is limited only by the imagination of the investigator, is so large that, in any empirical investigation, all but a very few must be ruled out in advance. Insofar as the necessary simplifications restrict the possible explanations of investment behavior, these simplifications constitute, at least implicitly, a theory of investment behavior. Such theories can be compared with each other most expeditiously by reducing each to its basic underlying assumptions, after which empirical tests to discriminate among alternative theories can be designed. Far from forcing empirical studies into a theoretical straitjacket, judicious use of a theoretical framework is essential to the proper direction of empirical work.

The view that theoretical and empirical

research should be carried out in isolation is incomplete in a second respect. The use of economic theory as a source of possible explanations for investment behavior frees econometric work from reliance on empirical generalizations that have not been subjected to rigorous econometric tests. There is a very real danger that econometric models of investment behavior may be made to conform prematurely to assumptions that are "realistic" by the standards of empirical work not based on econometric methods. Just as premature reliance on "realistic" assumptions may be stultifying to the development of economic theory, so reliance on historical and institutional generalizations may restrict the development of econometric models unduly. The paramount test for "realism" of an econometric model is its performance in econometric work. If a model does not perform satisfactorily by the standards of econometrics, it must be rejected, however closely it parallels historical and institutional accounts of the same economic behavior.

The point of departure for this paper is that progress in the study of investment behavior can best be made by comparing econometric models of such behavior within a theoretical framework. Ideally, each model should be derived from a common set of assumptions about the objectives of the business firm. Differences among alternative models should be accounted for by alternative assumptions about the behavior of business firms in pursuing these objectives. It will undoubtedly be surprising to some that a theoretical framework is implicit in the econometric models of investment behavior currently under study. The objective of this paper is to make this framework explicit in order to provide a basis to evaluate evidence on the determinants of investment behavior. This objective can only be attained by a thoroughgoing reconstruction of the theory of investment.

Once the theory of investment is placed in a proper setting, the arguments advanced for pessimism about combining theoretical and empirical work largely evaporate.

In providing a framework for the theory of investment behavior, the first problem is to choose an appropriate basis for the theory. Two alternative possibilities may be suggested. First, the theory of investment could be based on the neoclassical theory of optimal capital accumulation. There are three basic objections to this possibility, the first of which is that a substantial body of noneconometric work on the motivation of business firms, mainly surveys of businessmen, suggests that "marginalist" considerations are largely irrelevant to the making of business decisions. This evidence has been subjected to careful scrutiny by White,[5] who concludes that the data accumulated by the surveys are so defective, even by the standards of noneconometric empirical work, that no reliance can be placed on conclusions based on them. A second objection is that previous attempts to base the study of investment on neoclassical economic theory have been unsuccessful,[6] but this argument will not withstand critical scrutiny. First, none of the tests of the neoclassical theory reported in the early literature was based on a fully rigorous statement of the theory. Secondly, the assumptions made about the lag between changes in the demand for capital services and actual investment expenditures were highly restrictive. Frequently, the lag was assumed to be concentrated at a particular point or to be distributed over time in a very simple manner. Tests of the neoclassical theory were carried out prior to the important contribution of Koyck to the analysis of distributed lags and investment behavior.[7] Despite these deficiencies, the pioneering tests of the neoclassical theory reported by Tinbergen reveal substantial effects for the price of investment goods, the change in this price, and the rate of interest.[8]

Similarly, tests reported by Roos reveal substantial effects for the price of investment goods and rate of interest.[9] Klein's studies of investment in the railroad and electric power industries reveal substantial effects for the rate of interest.[10]

A third and more fundamental objection has recently been restated by Haavelmo, who argues that a demand schedule for investment goods cannot be derived from neoclassical theory[11]:

What we should reject is the naive reasoning that there is a demand schedule for investment which could be derived from a classical scheme of producers' behavior in maximizing profit. The demand for investment cannot simply be derived from the demand for capital. Demand for a finite addition to the stock of capital can lead to any rate of investment, from almost zero to infinity, depending on the additional hypothesis we introduce regarding the speed of reaction of capital-users. I think that the sooner this naive, and unfounded, theory of the demand-for-investment schedule is abandoned, the sooner we shall have a chance of making some real progress in constructing more powerful theories to deal with the capricious short-run variations in the rate of private investment.

We will show that it is possible to derive a demand function for investment goods based on purely neoclassical considerations. While it is true that the conventional derivation of such a demand schedule, as in Keynes' construction of the marginal efficiency of investment schedule,[12] must be dismissed as naive, there is a sense in which the demand for investment goods can be taken to depend on the cost of capital; such a theory of investment behavior can be derived from the neoclassical theory of optimal capital accumulation.

A second possible basis for the theory of investment is the assumption that business firms maximize utility defined more broadly than in the characterization of objectives of the firm in the neoclassical theory of optimal capital accumulation.

This basis has been suggested by Meyer and Kuh[13]:

Partial recognition of institutional changes has led in recent years to shift the theory of the firm, and consequently of plant and equipment investment, from a profit maximization orientation to that of utility maximization. Primarily, this move represents a growing belief that profit maximization is too narrow to encompass the full scope of modern entrepreneurial motives, particularly once the previously assumed objective conditions are released from *ceteris paribus*, and the theory seeks to explain a much wider range of behavioral responses.

This position has recently been supported with much force by Simon:

...I should like to emphasize strongly that neither the classical theory of the firm nor any of the amendments to it or substitutes for it that have been proposed have had any substantial amount of empirical testing. If the classical theory appeals to us, it must be largely because it has a certain face validity... rather than because profit maximizing behavior has been observed.[14]

In putting forward this view, Simon ignores the entire econometric literature on cost and production functions, all of which is based on the neoclassical theory of the firm. A recent survey of this literature by Walters[15] enumerates 345 references, almost all presenting results of econometric tests of the neoclassical theory of the firm which are overwhelmingly favorable to the theory. The evidence is largely so favorable that current empirical research emphasizes such technical questions as the appropriate form for the production function and the appropriate statistical specification for econometric models of production based on this theory. We conclude that Simon's statement that the alternatives to the neoclassical theory of the firm have had no substantial amount of empirical testing is correct. However, his characterization of the empirical evidence on the neoclassical theory is completely erroneous.

One possible reaction to a proper assessment of the support for the neoclassical theory of the firm from econometric studies of cost and production functions is to reject out of hand studies of investment behavior not based explicitly on the neoclassical theory, such as the study of Meyer and Kuh. In fact, the theoretical basis for the econometric model of investment behavior proposed by Meyer and Kuh is consistent with the neoclassical theory of optimal capital accumulation. Their appeal to a less narrow view of entrepreneurial objectives is not essential to the interpretation of the empirical results they present. We conclude that the objections to the neoclassical theory of the firm as a basis for the theory of investment behavior are ill-founded. Furthermore, the appeal to a broader view of entrepreneurial objectives than that which underlies this theory is not required by evidence either from econometric studies of cost and production functions or from studies of investment behavior. The neoclassical theory of optimal accumulation of capital is a far more powerful theory than the "broader view" suggested by Simon and others in the sense that a much narrower range of conceivable behavior is consistent with it than with the amorphous utility-maximizing theory. Accordingly, we will employ a theoretical framework based on the neoclassical theory of the firm for constructing a theory of investment behavior.

The objective of explaining investment behavior on the basis of the neoclassical theory of the firm cannot be described as novel. This objective is clearly in evidence in Tinbergen's pioneering monograph, *Statistical Testing of Business Cycle Theories*. Subsequently, a similar objective was adopted by Roos and by Klein.[16] In these early studies of investment behavior, the neoclassical theory was employed to provide a list of possible explanatory variables for investment expenditures. The rate of interest, the level of stock prices, the price of investment goods, and changes in the price of investment goods were used along with other variables such as profits, output, and changes in output. Little attention was paid to the manner in which the rate of interest and the price of investment goods enter the demand for capital services or the demand for investment goods. Both variables enter only through the *user cost* of capital services.[17] There is no effect of the price of investment goods except in combination with the rate of interest and vice versa. We conclude that, although the objective of explaining investment behavior on the basis of the neoclassical theory of the firm is not new, this objective remains to be fully realized.

2. THE NEOCLASSICAL FRAMEWORK

In formulating a theory of investment behavior based on the neoclassical theory of optimal capital accumulation, a great number of alternative versions of the theory could be considered. Reduced to its barest essentials, the theory requires only that capital accumulation be based on the objective of maximizing the utility of a stream of consumption. This basic assumption may be combined with any number of technological possibilities for production and economic possibilities for transformation of the results of production into a stream of consumption. In selecting among alternative formulations, a subsidiary objective must be borne in mind. The resulting theory of capital accumulation must include the principal econometric models of investment behavior as specializations, but the theory need not encompass possibilities for the explanation of investment behavior not employed in econometric work.

The essentials of a theory of optimal

capital accumulation that meets this basic objective are the following: The firm maximizes the utility of a consumption stream subject to a production function relating the flow of output to flows of labor and capital services. The firm supplies capital services to itself through the acquisition of investment goods; the rate of change in the flow of capital services is proportional to the rate of acquisition of investment goods less the rate of replacement of previously acquired investment goods. The results of the productive process are transformed into a stream of consumption under a fixed set of prices for output, labor services, investment goods, and consumption goods. These prices may be considered as current or "spot" prices together with forward prices for each commodity or, alternatively, as current and future prices together with a normalization factor, which may be identified with current and future values of the rate of time discount or interest rate. Both current and forward prices are taken as fixed by the firm. Alternatively, current and future prices together with current and future values of the rate of interest are taken as fixed. Under these conditions, the problem of maximizing utility may be solved in two stages. First, a production plan may be chosen so as to maximize the present value of the productive enterprise. Secondly, consumption is allocated over time so as to maximize utility subject to the present value of the firm. In view of our concern with the theory of business investment behavior, we will consider only the first of these problems. It should be noted that, under the assumption of fixed prices, the choice of a production plan is independent of the subsequent allocation of consumption over time. Two firms with different preferences among alternative consumption streams will choose the same plan for production.

This version of the neoclassical theory of the firm is not the only one available in the literature on capital theory. From a certain point of view, the objective of maximizing the present value of the firm is only one among many possible objectives for the firm. In a recent survey paper on the theory of capital, Lutz remarks that "It is one of the surprising things about capital theory that no agreement seems to have been reached as to what the entrepreneur should maximize."[18] Alternative criteria discussed in the literature include maximization of the average internal rate of return, maximization of the rate of return on capital owned by the firm, investment in any project with an internal rate of return greater than the ruling market rate of interest, and so on. None of these criteria can be derived from maximization of the utility of a stream of consumption under the conditions we have outlined. Maximization of the present value of the firm is the only criterion consistent with utility maximization. This approach to the theory of optimal capital accumulation was originated by Fisher and has recently been revived and extended by Bailey and by Hirshleifer.[19] The essential justification for this approach is summarized by Hirshleifer, as follows:

Since Fisher, economists working in the theory of investment decision have tended to adopt a mechanical approach—some plumping for the use of this formula, some for that. From a Fisherian point of view, we can see that none of the formulas so far propounded is universally valid. Furthermore, even where the present-value rule, for example, is correct, few realize that its validity is conditional upon making certain associated financing decisions as the Fisherian analysis demonstrates. In short, the Fisherian approach permits us to define the range of applicability and the short-comings of all the proposed formulas—thus standing over against them as the general theoretical solution to the problem of investment decision under conditions of certainty.[20]

A second controversial aspect of the version of the neoclassical theory outlined above is the assumption that the set of technological possibilities confronted by the firm can be described by a production function, where the flow of output is a function of flows of labor and capital services and the flow of capital services is proportional to the stock of capital goods obtained by summing the stream of past net investments.[21] The concept of capital service is not essential to the neoclassical theory. A production function relating output at each point of time to inputs of labor and capital services at that point of time may be replaced by a production function relating output at every point of time to inputs of investment goods at every point of time; this description of the set of production possibilities is employed by Fisher; moreover, it may be characterized abstractly so that even the notion of a production function may be dispensed with, as is done by Malinvaud.[22] The description of the set of technological possibilities by means of a production function as presented by Fisher is a specialization of the description given by Malinvaud. The further assumption that the relationship between inputs of investment goods and levels of output may be reduced to a relationship between output at each point of time and a corresponding flow of capital services involves a specialization of the description of technological possibilities given by Fisher.

In the neoclassical literature, two basic models of the relationship between flows of investment goods and flows of capital services have been discussed, namely, a model of inventories and a model of durable goods. At the level of abstraction of Fisher's description of the set of production possibilities, no distinction between inventories and durable goods is required. For both inventories and durable goods, the acquisition of a stock of productive goods may be represented as an input to the productive process at the time of acquisition. For inventories, the

individual items "used up" at different points of time may be represented as the output of a subprocess representing the holding of stocks; these outputs may be inputs into other subprocesses. For durable goods, the outputs of the corresponding stockholding process are the services of the goods rather than the individual items of the stock; the services of the durable goods may be inputs into other parts of the productive process.

The basis for the distinction between inventories and durable goods lies in the relationship among the initial input and the various outputs from the stockholding process. For inventories, the outputs provided by the stockholding process are customarily treated as perfect substitutes. For each item held in stock, the ultimate consumption of that item can occur at one and only one point in time. By contrast, the outputs provided by durable goods are treated as if they were perfectly complementary. The output of the service of a durable good at any point of time is assumed to bear a fixed relation to the output of the same service at any other point of time. The assumptions that outputs provided by a given input of investment goods are perfectly complementary or perfectly substitutable are highly restrictive. Nevertheless, the simplification of the neoclassical theory for these limiting cases and the practical importance of these cases are very great. A far more substantial proportion of the literature on capital theory is devoted to these two limiting cases than to the theory of production at the level of abstraction of the descriptions of technology given by Fisher or by Malinvaud. In the following we assume that the conventional neoclassical description of a durable good is appropriate for each investment good considered.

A second assumption required for a relationship between output at each point of time and the corresponding flow of capital services is that the services of investment goods acquired at different points of time are perfect substitutes in production. Accordingly, the flow of capital services from each investment good is proportional to the stock of capital that may be obtained by simply adding together all past acquisitions less replacements. This assumption is highly restrictive; the assumption can be justified primarily by the resulting simplification of the neoclassical theory. We discuss only a single investment good. Under the assumptions outlined above, there is only a single capital service. This simplification is also completely inessential to neoclassical theory.

Finally, we assume that the flow of replacement generated by a given flow of investment goods is distributed over time in accord with an exponential distribution. This assumption implies that the flow of replacement investment at any point of time is proportional to the accumulated stock of investment goods. Again, this assumption is only one among many possibilities. Alternative assumptions employed in practice include the following: First, replacement is equal to investment goods acquired at some earlier point in time; second, replacement is equal to a weighted average of past investment flows, with weights derived from studies of the "survival curves" of individual pieces of equipment.[23] For empirical work the exponential distribution of replacements is of special interest. While empirical studies of "survival curves" for individual pieces of equipment reveal a wide variety of possible distributions, there is a deeper justification for use of the exponential distribution. This justification arises from a fundamental result of renewal theory, namely, that replacement approaches an amount proportional to the accumulated stock of capital whatever the distribution of replacements for an individual piece of equipment, provided that the size of the capital stock is constant or that the stock is growing at a constant rate (in the probabilistic sense).[24] This asymptotic result may be used as the basis for an approximation to the distribution of replacements; for any investment good, the stream of replacements eventually approaches a stream that would be generated by an exponential distribution of replacements. Accordingly, the exponential distribution may be used as an approximation to the distribution of replacements for the purpose of estimating the stream of replacements. A simple indirect test of the validity of this approximation has been carried out by Meyer and Kuh.[25] For any distribution of replacements except the exponential distribution, one would expect to observe an "echo effect" or bunching of replacements at lags corresponding to points of relatively high density in the conditional distributions of replacements for individual types of equipment. Meyer and Kuh report no evidence for such an effect.

To summarize, we consider a version of the neoclassical theory in which the objective of the firm is maximization of its present value. This may be derived from the objective of maximizing the utility of a consumption stream subject to a fixed set of production possibilities and to fixed current and future prices and interest rates. Since the choice of a production plan is entirely independent of the corresponding choice of a consumption stream, two individuals with different preferences among consumption streams will choose the same production plan. Secondly, we consider a description of technological possibilities in which output at each point of time depends on the flow of labor and capital services at that point of time, the flow of capital services is proportional to the stock of capital goods, and replacements are also proportional to the stock of capital goods. This description of technology is a specialization of the descriptions given by Malinvaud and by Fisher. The essential justification for this specialization is that the resulting theory of optimal capital accumulation is sufficiently broad to include the principal econometric models of investment behavior as special cases.

3. OPTIMAL CAPITAL ACCUMULATION

To develop the theory of investment behavior in more detail, we must first define the present value of the firm. For simplicity, we limit the analysis to a production process with a single output, a single variable input, and a single capital input. Where Q, L, and I represent levels of output, variable input, and investment in durable goods, and p, w, and q represent the corresponding prices, the flow of net receipts at time t, say $R(t)$, is given by:

$$R(t) = p(t)Q(t) - w(t)L(t) - q(t)I(t) \quad (1)$$

Present value is defined as the integral of discounted net receipts; where $r(s)$ is the rate of time discount at time s, net worth (W) is given by the expression:

$$W = \int_0^\infty e \exp\left[-\int_0^t r(s)\, ds\right] R(t)\, dt \quad (2)$$

For purposes of the following discussion, we may assume that the time rate of discount is a constant without loss of generality. Accordingly, the present value of the firm may be represented in the simpler form:

$$W = \int_0^\infty e^{-rt} R(t)\, dt$$

Present value is maximized subject to two constraints. First, the rate of change of the flow of capital services is proportional to the flow of net investment. The constant of proportionality may be interpreted as the time rate of utilization of capital stock, that is, the number of units of capital service per unit of capital stock. We will assume that capital stock is fully utilized so that this constant may be taken to be unity. Net investment is equal to total investment less replace-

ment; where replacement is proportional to capital stock, this constraint takes the form:

$$\dot{K}(t) = I(t) - \delta K(t) \quad (3)$$

where $\dot{K}(t)$ is the time rate of change of the flow of capital services at time t. This constraint holds at each point of time so that $\dot{K}$, K, and I are functions of time; to simplify notation, we will use K in place of $K(t)$, I in place of $I(t)$, and so on. Secondly, levels of output and levels of labor and capital services are constrained by a production function:

$$F(Q, L, K) = 0 \quad (4)$$

We assume that the production function is twice differentiable with positive marginal rates of substitution between inputs and positive marginal productivities of both inputs. Furthermore, we assume that the production function is strictly convex.

To maximize present value (2) subject to the constraints (3) and (4), we consider the Lagrangian expression:

$$\mathcal{L} = \int_0^\infty [e^{-rt}R(t) + \lambda_0(t)F(Q, L, K) \quad (5)$$
$$+ \lambda_1(t)(\dot{K} - I + \delta K)]\, dt$$
$$= \int_0^\infty f(t)\, dt$$

where

$$f(t) = e^{-rt}R(t) + \lambda_0(t)F(Q, L, K)$$
$$+ \lambda_1(t)(\dot{K} - I + \delta K)$$

The Euler necessary conditions for a maximum of present value subject to the constraints (3) and (4) are:

$$\frac{\partial f}{\partial Q} = e^{-rt}p + \lambda_0(t)\frac{\partial F}{\partial Q} = 0 \quad (6)$$

$$\frac{\partial f}{\partial L} = -e^{-rt}w + \lambda_0(t)\frac{\partial F}{\partial L} = 0$$

$$\frac{\partial f}{\partial I} = -e^{-rt}q - \lambda_1(t) = 0$$

$$\frac{\partial f}{\partial K} - \frac{d}{dt}\frac{\partial f}{\partial \dot{K}} = \lambda_0(t)\frac{\partial F}{\partial K} + \delta\lambda_1(t)$$
$$- \frac{d}{dt}\lambda_1(t) = 0$$

and also:

$$\frac{\partial f}{\partial \lambda_0} = F(Q, L, K) = 0 \tag{7}$$

$$\frac{\partial f}{\partial \lambda_1} = \dot{K} - I + \delta K = 0$$

Combining the necessary conditions for labor and output, we obtain the marginal productivity condition for labor services:

$$\frac{\partial Q}{\partial L} = \frac{w}{p} \tag{8}$$

Of course, output, labor, wages, and prices are all functions of time. The difference between this marginal productivity condition and the corresponding condition of the "static" theory of the firm is that condition (8) holds at every point of time over the indefinite future whereas the marginal productivity condition of the "static" theory of the firm holds only at a single point in time. A similar marginal productivity condition for capital services may be derived. First, solving the necessary conditions (6) for $\lambda_1(t)$:

$$\lambda_1(t) = -e^{-rt}q$$

the necessary condition for capital services may be written:

$$\lambda_0(t) \frac{\partial F}{\partial K} - \delta e^{-rt}q - re^{-rt}q + e^{-rt}\dot{q} = 0$$

Combining this condition with the necessary condition for output, we obtain the marginal productivity condition for capital services:

$$\frac{\partial Q}{\partial K} = \frac{q(r + \delta) - \dot{q}}{p} = \frac{c}{p} \tag{9}$$

where:

$$c = q(r + \delta) - \dot{q} \tag{10}$$

Again, output, capital, prices, and the rate of time discount are functions of time so that these conditions hold at every point of time over the indefinite future.

Expression (10) defines the implicit rental value of capital services supplied by the firm to itself. This interpretation of the price $c(t)$ may be justified by considering the relationship between the price of capital goods and the price of capital services. First, the flow of capital services over an interval of length dt beginning at time t from a unit of investment goods acquired at time s is:

$$e^{-\delta(t-s)} dt$$

If $c(t)$ is the price of capital services at time t, then the discounted price of capital services is $e^{-rt}c(t)$, so that the value of the stream of capital services on the interval dt is:

$$e^{-rt}c(t)e^{-\delta(t-s)} dt$$

Similarly, if $q(s)$ is the price of capital goods at time s, then the discounted price of capital goods is $e^{-rs}q(s)$, so that the value of a unit of investment goods acquired at time s is:

$$e^{-rs}q(s)$$

But the value of investment goods acquired at time s is equal to the integral of the discounted value of all future capital services derived from these investment goods:

$$e^{-rs}q(s) = \int_s^\infty e^{-rt}c(t)e^{-\delta(t-s)} dt$$

$$= e^{\delta s} \int_s^\infty e^{-(r+\delta)t}c(t) dt$$

Solving for the price of capital goods, we obtain:

$$q(s) = e^{(r+\delta)s} \int_s^\infty e^{-(r+\delta)t} c(t) dt$$

$$= \int_s^\infty e^{-(r+\delta)(t-s)}c(t) dt$$

To obtain the price of capital services implicit in this expression, we differentiate with respect to time:

$$\dot{q}(s) = [r(s) + \delta]q(s) - c(s)$$

so that:

$$c = q(r + \delta) - \dot{q}$$

which is expression (10) given above for the implicit rental value of capital services.

The conditions describing the neoclassical model of optimal capital accumulation may also be derived by maximization of the integral of discounted profits, where profit at each point of time, say, $P(t)$, is given by:

$$P(t) = p(t)Q(t) - w(t)L(t) - c(t)K(t) \tag{11}$$

The integral of discounted profits, say, W^+, is given by the expression:

$$W^+ = \int_0^\infty e^{-rt}P(t)\,dt \tag{12}$$

The side condition for investment may be disregarded, since investment does not enter into the definition of profit (11); substituting the side condition for the shadow price of capital services into the profit function, we obtain:

$$W^+ = \int_0^\infty e^{-rt}[p(t)Q(t) - w(t)L(t) \\ - \{q(t)[r(t) + \delta] - \dot{q}(t)\} \\ \times K(t)]\,dt$$

To maximize this function subject to the production function, it suffices to maximize profit at each point of time subject to the production function. But this yields the marginal productivity conditions (8) and (9) and the production function (4) itself. Reintroducing the side conditions (3) and (10), we obtain the complete neoclassical model of optimal capital accumulation.

The integral of discounted profits is not the same as the integral defining present value of the firm. The difference between

the two is given by:

$$\begin{aligned} W - W^+ &= \int_0^\infty e^{-rt}[R(t) - P(t)]\,dt \\ &= \int_0^\infty e^{-rt}[\{q(t)[r(t) + \delta] \\ &\quad - \dot{q}(t)\}K(t) - q(t)I(t)]\,dt \\ &= \int_0^\infty e^{-rt}[q(t)\delta K(t) \\ &\quad + q(t)r(t)K(t) \\ &\quad - \dot{q}(t)K(t) - q(t)\dot{K}(t) \\ &\quad - q(t)\delta K(t)]\,dt \\ &= q(0)K(0) \end{aligned}$$

which is the value of capital stock on hand at the initial point of time. The present value of the firm is the sum of the integral of discounted profits and the market value of the assets of the firm. Since the market value of the assets of the firm is fixed, maximization of the integral of discounted profits results in the same path for accumulation of capital as maximization of present value of the firm. To summarize, the neoclassical model of optimal capital accumulation may be derived by maximizing present value of the firm, by maximizing the integral of discounted profits of the firm, or simply by maximizing profit at each point of time.

In taking maximization of profit as the objective of the firm, profit is defined in a special sense, namely, net receipts on current account less the implicit rental value of capital services. This concept of profit would agree with the usual accounting definition of profit only in rather unusual circumstances, for example, where the firm actually rents all the capital services it employs. The price of capital services is then a market price and the rental value of the services is an actual outlay. Where the firm supplies capital services to itself, the implicit rental value of capital services $c(t)$ is a shadow price which may be used by the firm in the computation of an optimal path for capital accumulation. For optimal capital accumulation, the firm should charge itself a price for capital services equal to the implicit rental value and should then maximize profit at each point of time in the usual way. It is very important to note that the conditions determining the values of each of the variables to be chosen by the firm—output, labor input, and investment in capital goods—depend only on prices, the rate of interest, and the rate of change of the price of capital goods for the current period. Accordingly, in the neoclassical theory of optimal capital accumulation, the firm behaves at each point of time as in the "static" theory of the firm, provided that the price of capital services is taken to be equal to the corresponding implicit rental value. Of course, in the "static" theory the marginal productivity condition (9) holds only at a single point in time.

The complete neoclassical model of optimal capital accumulation consists of the production function (4) and the two marginal productivity conditions (8) and (9):

$$F(Q, K, L) = 0 \qquad \frac{\partial Q}{\partial L} = \frac{w}{p} \qquad \frac{\partial Q}{\partial K} = \frac{c}{p}$$

and the two side conditions (3) and (10):

$$I = \dot{K} + \delta K$$
$$c = q(r + \delta) - \dot{q}$$

The production function and marginal productivity conditions hold at each point of time. The side conditions are differential equations also holding at each point of time. Combined, these conditions determine the levels of output, labor input, and capital input, together with the level of investment and the shadow price for capital services.

The interpretation of condition (3) determining the level of investment is the source of some difficulty in the literature. If the level of investment is bounded, the derivative of the level of capital services must be bounded. But this implies that the level of capital services itself must be continuous. Since we have assumed that the production function is twice differentiable, a sufficient condition for continuity of the level of capital services is continuity of the prices—w, p, c.

One interpretation of condition (3) is that the initial value of the level of capital services may be chosen arbitrarily. This interpretation has been suggested by Haavelmo and by Arrow.[26] If the initial level of capital services is derived from the production function and the marginal productivity conditions and if the initial value of capital is fixed arbitrarily, optimal capital accumulation may require an unbounded initial level of investment. In management science, this interpretation of the problem may be of some interest, though even there the interpretation seems somewhat forced, as Arrow points out.[27] For empirical work this interpretation is completely artificial since firms are viewed as making new decisions to invest continuously over time. To maximize present value at each point of time, a firm following an optimal path for capital accumulation must maximize present value subject to the initial condition given by the optimal path up to that point. But this results in a new optimal path which is precisely the same as the old from that point forward. Accordingly, if the optimal path for capital accumulation is continuous, the initial value of the level of capital services may not be chosen arbitrarily in the maximization of the present value of the firm. At each point it is precisely that for which the initial level of investment is bounded, namely, the level of capital services derived from the production function and the marginal productivity conditions. A possible objection to this view is that firms must begin to accumulate capital at some point in time. But at such a point the initial level of capital services is not given arbitrarily; the initial level must be zero with a positive derivative.

4. THE THEORY OF INVESTMENT BEHAVIOR

Beginning with the neoclassical model of optimal capital accumulation, we may derive differentiable demand functions for labor and capital services and a differentiable supply function for output, say:

$$L = L(w, c, p)$$
$$K = K(w, c, p)$$
$$Q = Q(w, c, p) \tag{13}$$

The problem of deriving the demand for investment goods as a function of the rate of interest is a subtle one. Haavelmo expresses the view that the demand for investment goods cannot be derived from the profit-maximizing theory of the firm. This is a consequence of his interpretation of the demand function for capital services and condition (3) determining the level of investment from replacement and the rate of change of demand for capital services. According to this interpretation, finite variations in the rate of interest with all other prices held constant result in finite changes in the demand for capital services. As the rate of interest varies, demand for investment goods assumes only three possible values—negatively infinite, positively infinite, or the value obtained where the initial level of capital services is precisely equal to the demand for capital services. Investment demand has a finite value for only one rate of interest. In this interpretation, the demand function for capital services is analyzed by means of comparative statics, that is, by comparing alternative production plans at a given point of time. Any attempt to derive the demand for investment goods as a function of the rate of interest by such comparisons leads to nonsensical results, as Haavelmo correctly points out.

However, an alternative interpretation of the demand function for capital services and condition (3) determining the level of investment is possible. Under the hypothesis that the firm is following an optimal path for capital accumulation and that the optimal path is continuous, the initial level of capital is always equal to the demand for capital services. By imposing this condition at the outset, the demand for investment goods as a function of the rate of interest at any point of time may be analyzed by means of comparative dynamics, that is, by comparing alternative paths of capital accumulation, each identical up to that point of time and each continuous at that point. The demand for investment goods is given by condition (3):

$$I = +\delta K$$

where the level of capital services, K, is fixed; but from the demand function for capital services (13), this condition implies that for fixed values of the price of output and the price of labor services, the implicit price of capital services must remain unchanged. Holding the price of investment goods constant, the rate of change of the price of investment goods must vary as the rate of interest varies so as to leave the implicit price of capital services unchanged. Formally, the condition that variations in the rate of interest leave the implicit price of capital services unchanged may be represented as:

$$\frac{\partial c}{\partial r} = 0$$

holding the price of investment goods constant, this condition implies that the own-rate of interest on investment goods, $r - \dot{q}/q$, must be left unchanged by variations in the rate of interest.

We assume that all changes in the rate of interest are precisely compensated by changes in the rate of change of the price of current and future investment goods so as to leave the own-rate of interest on investment goods unchanged. Under this condition the discounted value of all future capital services, which is equal to the current price of investment goods, is left unchanged by variations in the time path of the rate of interest. The condition that the time path of the own-rate of interest on investment goods is left unchanged by a change in the time path of the rate of interest implies that forward prices or discounted future prices of both investment goods and capital services are left unchanged by variations in the rate of interest. For a constant rate of interest, this condition may be represented in the form:

$$\frac{\partial^2 e^{-rt}c(t)}{\partial r \partial t} = 0$$

Like the previous condition, this condition holds at every point of time.

To derive the demand for investment goods as a function of the rate of interest, we first differentiate the demand for capital services with respect to time, obtaining:

$$\dot{K} = \frac{\partial K}{\partial w} \cdot \frac{\partial w}{\partial t} + \frac{\partial K}{\partial c} \cdot \frac{\partial c}{\partial t} + \frac{\partial K}{\partial p} \cdot \frac{\partial p}{\partial t}$$

For simplicity, we consider only the case in which $\partial w/\partial t = \partial p/\partial t = 0$, that is, the price of output and the price of labor services are not changed. In this case, we obtain:

$$\dot{K} = \frac{\partial K}{\partial c} \cdot \frac{\partial c}{\partial t}$$

Differentiating the implicit price of capital services with respect to time, we have:

$$\frac{\partial c}{\partial t} = \frac{\partial q}{\partial t}(\delta + r) + q\frac{\partial r}{\partial t} = \frac{\partial^2 q}{\partial t^2} \qquad (14)$$

To derive the demand for investment goods, we combine expression (14) for the rate of change of capital services with condition (3) for the rate of investment, obtaining:

$$I = \frac{\partial K}{\partial c}\left[\frac{\partial q}{\partial t}(\delta + r) + q\frac{\partial r}{\partial t} - \frac{\partial^2 q}{\partial t^2}\right] + \delta K$$

which depends on the rate of interest and the price of investment goods through the rate of change of capital services. Differentiating this investment demand function with respect to the rate of interest, we obtain:

$$\frac{\partial I}{\partial r} = \frac{\partial^2 K}{\partial c^2} \cdot \frac{\partial c}{\partial r} \cdot \frac{\partial c}{\partial t} + \frac{\partial K}{\partial c} \cdot \frac{\partial^2 c}{\partial t \partial r} + \delta \frac{\partial K}{\partial c} \cdot \frac{\partial c}{\partial r}$$

But $\partial c/\partial r = 0$, since changes in the rate of interest are compensated by changes in the rate of change of the price of investment goods so as to leave the implicit price of capital services unchanged. This condition implies that:

$$\frac{\partial^2 q}{\partial t \partial r} = q$$

Secondly, $\partial^2 e^{-rt}c(t)/\partial r \partial t = 0$, since changes in the time path of the rate of interest leave the time path of forward or discounted prices of capital services unchanged. This condition implies that:

$$\frac{\partial^2 c}{\partial t \partial r} = c$$

Combining these two conditions, we obtain:

$$\frac{\partial I}{\partial r} = \frac{\partial K}{\partial c} \cdot c < 0$$

so that the demand for investment goods is a decreasing function of the rate of interest.

We conclude that it is possible to derive the demand for investment goods as a function of the rate of interest on the basis of purely neoclassical considerations. However, the demand for investment goods depends on the rate of interest through a comparison of alternative paths of capital accumulation, each continuous and each depending on a time path of the rate of interest. Although this conclusion appears to be the reverse of that reached by Haavelmo, his approach to the demand for investment goods is through comparative statics, that is, through comparison of alternative production plans at a given point of time. The demand function for investment goods cannot be derived by means of such comparisons. As a proposition in comparative statics, any relation between variations in the rate of investment and changes in the rate of interest is nonsensical.

To summarize, the complete neoclassical model of optimal capital accumulation consists of the production function (4), the two marginal productivity conditions (8) and (9), and the side condition (10). An alternative form of this model consists of the demand functions for capital and labor services, the supply function for output:

$$L = L(w, c, p) \qquad K = K(w, c, p)$$
$$Q = Q(w, c, p)$$

and the demand function for investment goods:

$$I = \frac{\partial K}{\partial c} \frac{\partial c}{\partial t} + \delta K$$
$$= I\left(w, c, p, \frac{\partial c}{\partial t}\right)$$

The demand for investment goods depends on the change in the demand for capital with respect to a change in the implicit price of capital services, the time rate of change in the price of capital services, and the level of replacement demand. Where the time rates of change of the price of labor services and the price of output are not zero, the demand function for investment goods may be rewritten:

$$I = \frac{\partial K}{\partial w} \frac{\partial w}{\partial t} + \frac{\partial K}{\partial c} \frac{\partial c}{\partial t} + \frac{\partial K}{\partial p} \cdot \frac{\partial p}{\partial t} + \delta K$$
$$= I\left(w, c, p, \frac{\partial w}{\partial t}, \frac{\partial c}{\partial t}, \frac{\partial p}{\partial t}\right)$$

5. ALTERNATIVE THEORIES OF INVESTMENT BEHAVIOR

The neoclassical theory of demand for investment goods just outlined may be contrasted with the theory current in the literature. Most recent accounts of the theory of demand for investment are based on Keynes' *General Theory*, in which the criterion for optimal investment behavior is that any project with an internal rate of return greater than the ruling rate of interest is undertaken.[28] An investment demand schedule is constructed by varying the rate of interest and plotting the quantities of investment undertaken for each value of the rate of interest. The criterion for optimal investment behavior used by Keynes is inconsistent with maximization of the present value of the firm, as Alchian and Hirshleifer have pointed out.[29] Nevertheless, a substantial portion of the current literature on the investment demand function is based on a straightforward reproduction of Keynes' derivation. Alchian lists a number of examples from the literature prior to 1955; examples from the current literature are provided by the recent work of Duesenberry and Tarshis.[30] Keynes' construction of the demand function for investment must be dismissed as inconsistent with the neoclassical theory of optimal capital accumulation.

An alternative construction of the demand function for investment goods has been suggested by Fisher.[31] In Fisher's theory any project with positive present value is undertaken. Keynes appears to have identified his construction of the marginal efficiency of capital schedule with that of Fisher, as Alchian points out.[32] There are two difficulties with Fisher's construction. First, the construction is carried out by means of comparative statics so that the resulting schedule may be interpreted as a theory of demand for capital services for which no demand function for investment goods exists. Second, the construction is not internally consistent in a second sense pointed out by Alchian, since "... we cannot in full logical consistency draw up a demand curve for investment by varying only the rate of interest (holding all other prices in the impound of *ceteris paribus*)."[33] The relevant prices are forward prices of all commodities; but altering the rate of interest amounts to altering certain forward prices. It is inconsistent to vary the rate of interest while holding such prices fixed. This inconsistency may be eliminated by stipulating that variations in the rate of interest must be precisely compensated by changes in the time rate of change of the price of investment goods. The price of investment goods at a given point of time is held fixed; the rate of change of the price of investment goods varies with the rate of interest. The construction of the demand function for investment goods involves a comparison among alternative paths of optimal capital accumulation; all paths are identical up to the point of time for which the investment function is constructed. Such a theory of investment behavior is internally consistent and may be derived by means of comparative dynamics.

Klein has attempted to derive a demand function for investment goods on the basis of profit maximization. His treatment, though suggestive, is marred by a number of inconsistencies. In his first attempt, the stock of investment goods is defined as the integral of past flows of investment, but the flow of investment is employed as a stock in the production function and in the definition of "discounted profit."[34] A second attempt involves the identification of the flow of capital services with the flow of depreciation.[35] In both attempts, quantities measured as rates of capital service per unit of time are added to quantities measured as rates of investment per unit of time, which is self-contradictory. This inconsistency

carries over to the empirical implementation of the resulting investment function, where the price of investment goods is identified with the price of capital services.[36] An internally consistent treatment of the theory of investment along the lines suggested by Klein leads to a comparative statics theory of demand for capital services in which no demand function for investment goods exists.

Another branch of the current literature is based on the view that no demand function for investment goods exists. We have already cited Haavelmo's support of this position. A similar view may be found in Lerner's *Economics of Control*. Lerner argues that, under diminishing returns, the firm has a downward sloping demand curve for capital services but that, except where there is no net investment, the rate of investment is unbounded[37]:

... there is no limit to the rate per unit of time at which [the individual] can acquire assets by buying them, borrowing money for the purpose if he has not enough of his own. This indefinitely great rate of "investment" means that he can move at once to the position ... which makes the (private) marginal productivity of capital equal to the rate of interest. Once he gets there, there is no tendency for further expansion....

This view is the same as that expressed by Haavelmo. A recent restatement of this position has been given by Witte, who concludes, with Lerner and Haavelmo, that "... the continuous function relating the rate of investment to the rate of interest at the micro level has no foundation in the ordinary theory of the firm."[38] We have demonstrated that it is possible to derive the demand for investment goods from the comparative dynamics applied to the ordinary neoclassical theory of the firm. The conclusion reached by Haavelmo, Lerner, and Witte concerning a demand function for investment goods derived on the basis of comparative statics is, of course, correct.

An attempt has been made by proponents of the view that the demand function for investment goods does not exist to rehabilitate the Keynesian marginal efficiency of investment schedule. Alternative versions of this rehabilitation are presented by Haavelmo, Lerner, and Witte.[39] The essentials of the argument are that, at a given rate of interest, a certain price for investment goods is required to equate the marginal productivity of capital with the implicit price of capital services; but the higher this price the lower the rate of interest, so that a rising supply curve for investment goods implies that the amount of investment goods produced will increase as the rate of interest falls. A fundamental difficulty with this view is that it fails to account for the purchase of new investment goods by the users of capital equipment.[40] Witte summarizes this consequence of the view as follows: "... the rate-of-investment decision is the rate-of-output decision of supplying enterprises and not the rate-of-input decision of capital-using firms."[41] In the same vein Haavelmo writes, "... it is, actually, not the users of capital who demand investment, it is the producers of capital goods who determine how much they want to produce at the current price of capital."[42] A further attempt along these lines of the rehabilitation of the Keynesian marginal efficiency of investment schedule has been presented by Clower.[43] His argument follows that of Haavelmo, Lerner, and Witte in assuming that demand for capital services is equal to supply. However, Clower introduces a demand for investment goods which is not necessarily equal to the supply of investment goods. The excess or deficiency of demand over supply is net accumulation of capital. This view also fails to account for the purchases of new investment goods by the users of capital equipment.

For internal consistency, the rehabilitation of the Keynesian marginal efficiency of investment schedule requires either a changing rate of interest, as suggested by Haavelmo, or a changing price of capital goods, as suggested by Lerner.[44] For if the rate of interest and the price of investment goods are fixed over time and the marginal productivity of capital is equal to the implicit price of capital services, the firm's demand for investment is determinate; this demand is precisely equal to replacement demand so that net investment is zero. Under these circumstances, the rate of investment demand by users of capital equipment is independent of the rate of interest so that the price of investment goods must be that at which this rate of investment will be supplied by investment goods producers. But then if the marginal productivity of capital is to be equal to the implicit price for capital services, the rate of interest is uniquely determined, which is inconsistent with variations in the rate of interest from whatever source.

To complete the rehabilitation of the Keynesian marginal efficiency of investment schedule, interpreted as the level of investment resulting from a market equilibrium in investment goods corresponding to a given rate of interest, market equilibrium must be studied in a fully dynamic setting. The demand for investment goods must be derived from a comparison among alternative paths of optimal capital accumulation. It remains to be seen whether such a rehabilitation can be carried out in an internally consistent way.

NOTES

1 A very detailed review of the literature through 1960 has been provided by R. Eisner and R. Strotz, "The Determinants of Business Investment," in D. B. Suits, et al., *Impacts of Monetary Policy* (Englewood Cliffs, [N.J.: Prentice-Hall,] 1963), pp. 60–338. A more concise review of developments through 1962 has been presented by E. Kuh, "Theory and

Institutions in the Study of Investment Behavior," *American Economic Review*, [LIII] May 1963, pp. 260–268. Empirical studies published since 1962 include: S. Almon, "The Distributed Lag between Capital Appropriations and Expenditures," *Econometrica*, [XXXIII] Jan. 1965, 178–196; W. H. L. Anderson, *Corporate Finance and Fixed Investment* (Boston: [Harvard Business School,] 1964); A. Bourneuf, "Investment, Excess Capacity, and Growth," *American Economic Review*, [LIV] Sept. 1964, pp. 607–625; R. Eisner, "Investment: Fact and Fancy," *American Economic Review*, [LIII] May 1963, pp. 237–246; Eisner, "Capital Expenditures, Profits, and the Acceleration Principle," *Models of Income Determination*, Studies in Income and Wealth 28, Princeton University Press for National Bureau of Economic Research, 1964, pp. 137–176; Eisner, "Realization of Investment Anticipations," in J. S. Duesenberry, E. Kuh, G. Fromm, and L. R. Klein, eds., *The Brookings Quarterly Econometric Model of the United States* (Chicago: [Rand McNally,] 1965); E. Greenberg, "A Stock-Adjustment Investment Model," *Econometrica*, [XXXII] July 1964, pp. 339–357; B. Hickman, *Investment Demand and U.S. Economic Growth* (Washington: [The Brookings Institution] 1965); D. W. Jorgenson, "Capital Theory and Investment Behavior," *American Economic Review*, [LIII] May 1963, pp. 247–259; Jorgenson, "Anticipations and Investment Behavior," in *Brookings Quarterly Econometric Model;* E. Kuh, *Capital Stock Growth: A Micro-Econometric Approach* (Amsterdam: [North Holland Publ. Co.,] 1963); J. R. Meyer and R. R. Glauber, *Investment Decisions, Economic Forecasting and Public Policy* (Boston: [Harvard Business School,] 1964); G. J. Stigler, *Capital and Rates of Return in Manufacturing Industries*, Princeton for NBER, 1963.

2 See, for example, the following papers: K. J. Arrow, "Optimal Capital Policy, The Cost of Capital, and Myopic Decision Rules," *Annals of the Institute of Statistical Mathematics*, 1964, pp. 21–30; "Optimal Capital Adjustment," in K. J. Arrow, S. Karlin, and H. Scarf, eds., *Studies in Applied Probability and Management Science* (Stanford, [Calif.: Stanford University Press,] 1962); K. J. Arrow, M. Beckmann, and S. Karlin, "Optimal Expansion of the Capacity of the Firm,"

in K. J. Arrow, S. Karlin, and H. Scarf, eds., *Studies in the Mathematical Theory of Inventory and Production* (Stanford, [Calif.: Stanford University Press,] 1958); A. S. Manne, "Capacity Expansion and Probabilistic Growth," *Econometrica*, [XXIX] Oct. 1961, pp. 632–649; E. Zabel, "Efficient Accumulation of Capital for the Firm," *Econometrica*, [XXXI] Jan.-April 1963, pp. 131–150; and the following books: T. Haavelmo, *A Study in the Theory of Investment* (Chicago: [University of Chicago Press,] 1960); F. A. Lutz and D. G. Hague, eds., *The Theory of Capital* (London: [Macmillan & Co.,] 1961); P. B. D. Massé, *Optimal Investment Decisions* (Englewood Cliffs, [N.J.: Prentice-Hall,] 1962); V. L. Smith, *Investment and Production*, Cambridge, [Mass.: Harvard University Press,] 1961; B. Thalberg, "A Keynesian Model Extended by Explicit Demand and Supply Functions for Investment Goods," *Stockholm Economic Studies*, Pamphlet Series, No. 3, 1964.

3 This point of view has been put forward by K. Borch, "Discussion," *American Economic Review*, [LIII] May 1963, pp. 272–274.

4 J. Tinbergen, *Statistical Testing of Business Cycle Theories*, Part I, "A Method and its Application to Investment Activity," Geneva, 1939.

5 W. H. White, "Interest Inelasticity of Investment Demand," *American Economic Review*, [XLVI] Sept. 1956, pp. 565–587.

6 J. Meyer and E. Kuh, *The Investment Decision* (Cambridge, Mass.: [Harvard University Press,] 1957), pp. 7–14.

7 L. M. Koyck, *Distributed Lags and Investment Analysis* (Amsterdam, 1954).

8 Tinbergen, *Statistical Testing, op. cit.*, see also the discussion of Tinbergen's results by T. Haavelmo, "The Effect of the Rate of Interest on Investment: A Note," *Review of Economic Statistics*, [XXIII] Feb. 1941, pp. 49–52.

9 C. F. Roos and V. S. Von Szeliski, "The Demand for Durable Goods," *Econometrica*, [XI] April 1943, pp. 97–122; Roos, "The Demand for Investment Goods," *American Economic Review*, [XXXVIII] May 1948, pp. 311–320; Roos, "Survey of Economic Forecasting Techniques," *Econometrica*, [XXIII] Oct. 1955, pp. 363–395.

10 L. R. Klein, "Studies in Investment Behavior," in *Conference on Business Cycles* (New York: National Bureau of Economic Research, 1951).

11 Haavelmo, *Theory of Investment, op. cit.*, p. 216.

12 J. M. Keynes, *The General Theory of Employment, Interest and Money* (New York: [Harcourt, Brace & Co.,] 1936), esp. Chapter 11, pp. 135–146.

13 Meyer and Kuh, *Investment Decision, op. cit.*, p. 9.

14 H. A. Simon, "New Developments in the Theory of the Firm," *American Economic Review*, [LII] May 1962, p. 8.

15 A. A. Walters, "Production and Cost Functions: An Econometric Survey," *Econometrica*, [XXXI] April 1963, pp. 1–66.

16 See footnotes 9 and 10. See also L. R. Klein, *The Keynesian Revolution* (New York: [The Macmillan Co.,] 1947), esp. pp. 62–68, pp. 196–199; Klein, "Notes on the Theory of Investment," *Kyklos*, II, Fasc. 2 (1948), 97–117; Klein, *Economic Fluctuations in the United States, 1921–1941* (New York: [John Wiley & Sons, Inc.,] 1950), esp. pp. 14–40.

17 A complete discussion of the concept of user cost has been given by W. A. Lewis, "Depreciation and Obsolescence as Factors in Costing," in J. L. Meij, ed., *Depreciation and Replacement Policy*, Amsterdam, 1961, pp. 15–45. See also Keynes, *General Theory, op. cit.*, pp. 66–73; A. P. Lerner, "User Cost and Prime User Cost," *American Economic Review*, [XXXIII] March 1943, pp. 131–132; F. A. Lutz and V. Lutz, *The Theory of Investment of the Firm* (Princeton: [Princeton University Press,] 1951); A. D. Scott, "Notes on User Cost," *Economic Journal*, [LXIII] June 1953, pp. 364–384.

18 F. A. Lutz, "The Essentials of Capital Theory," in Lutz and Hague, *Theory of Capital, op. cit.*, p. 6.

19 I. Fisher, *The Theory of Interest* (New York: [The Macmillan Co.,] 1930). M. J. Bailey, "Formal Criteria for Investment Decisions," *Journal of Political Economy*, [LXVII] Oct. 1959, pp. 476–488. J. Hirshleifer, "On the Theory of the Optimal Investment Decision," in E. Solomon, ed., *The Management of Corporate Capital* (Glencoe, [Ill.: Free Press,] 1959), pp. 205–228.

20 *Ibid.*, p. 228.

21 For a discussion of this assumption and some of its implications, see J. Robinson, "The Production Function and the Theory of Capital," *Review of Economic Studies*, [XXI] No. 54, (1953–1954), 81–106; R. M. Solow, "The Production Function and the Theory of Capital," *Review of Economic Studies*, [XXIII] No. 61 (1955–1956), 101–108; J. Robinson, "Reply," *Review of Economic Studies*, [XXIII] No. 62, (1955–1956), 247; J. Robinson, "Some Problems of Definition and Measurement of Capital," *Oxford Economic Papers*, [XI] June 1959, pp. 157–166; K. J. Arrow *et al.*, "Symposium on Production Functions and Economic Growth," *Review of Economic Studies*, [XXIX] June 1962.

22 E. Malinvaud, "Capital Accumulation and Efficient Allocation of Resources," *Econometrica*, [XXI] April 1953, pp. 233–268.

23 A summary of research on the lifetimes of capital equipment as given by A. Marston, R. Winfrey, and J. C. Hempstead, *Engineering Evaluation and Depreciation* (2nd ed., New York: [McGraw-Hill,] 1953).

24 For a statement of the basic theorem, see E. Parzen, *Stochastic Processes* (San Francisco: [Holden Day,] 1962), pp. 180–181.

25 Meyer and Kuh, *Investment Decision, op. cit.*, pp. 91–94.

26 Haavelmo, *Theory of Investment, op. cit.*, pp. 162–165. Arrow, "Optimal Capital Adjustment," in *Studies in Applied Probability, op. cit.*, p. 2.

27 *Ibid.*, p. 6, fn. 1.

28 Keynes, *General Theory, op. cit.*, Chap. 11, see especially p. 136.

29 A. A. Alchian, "The Rate of Interest, Fisher's Rate of Return over Costs and Keynes' Internal Rate of Return," in *Management of Corporate Capital, op. cit.*, p. 70; and J. Hirshleifer, in *ibid.*, pp. 222–227. This conclusion of Alchian and Hirshleifer contradicts the position taken by Klein in *The Keynesian Revolution, op. cit.*

30 J. S. Duesenberry, *Business Cycles and Economic Growth* (New York: [McGraw-Hill,] 1958), pp. 49–85. Duesenberry asserts that Keynes' derivation is based on "profit maximization" (p. 85). L. Tarshis, "The Marginal Efficiency Function," *American Economic Review*, [LI] Dec. 1961, pp. 958–985. Tarshis asserts that the Keynesian theory is based on that of the "profit-maximizing firm" (pp. 958–959).

31 Fisher, *Theory of Interest, op. cit.*, pp. 159–176.

32 Alchian, in *Management of Corporate Capital, op. cit.*, p. 67; Klein (*Keynesian Revolution, op. cit.*, p. 62) follows Keynes

in identifying these two distinct approaches to the construction of the marginal efficiency schedule.

33 Alchian, *Management of Coporate Capital, op. cit., p.* 71.

34 Klein, *Keynesian Revolution, op. cit.*, esp. pp. 196–199.

35 Klein, in *Kyklos*, II, fasc. 2 (1948), 97–117; and his *Economic Fluctuations, op. cit.*

36 *Ibid.* The price of investment goods (p. 21 and p. 85) is identified with the price of capital services (p. 15).

37 A. P. Lerner, *The Economics of Control, op. cit.*, esp. pp. 330–338.

38 James G. Witte, Jr., "The Microfoundations of the Social Investment Function," *Journal of Political Economy*, [LXXI] Oct. 1963, pp. 441–456.

39 Haavelmo, *Theory of Investment, op. cit.*, pp. 194–197. See also: B. Thalberg, "An Analysis of a Market for Investment Goods," in Lutz and Hague, *Theory of Capital, op. cit.*, pp. 161–176, and "A Keynesian Model Extended by Explicit Demand and Supply Functions for Investment Goods," in *Stockholm Economic Studies*, Pamphlet Series No. 3, 1964. Lerner, *Economics of Control, op. cit.*, pp. 333–334. Witte, *op. cit.*, pp. 445–447.

40 A second difficulty with this view is that an increase in the price of investment goods may result in a rise or a fall in the supply of investment goods, depending on the relative capital intensity of the investment goods and consumption goods industries. Lerner, for example, assumes implicitly that investment goods are produced with no capital services. This difficulty was pointed out to me by James Tobin.

41 *Op. cit.*, p. 448.

42 Haavelmo, *Theory of Investment, op. cit.*, p. 196.

43 R. W. Clower, "An Investigation into the Dynamics of Investment," *American Economic Review*, [XLIV] March 1954, pp. 64–81.

44 Haavelmo, *Theory of Investment, op. cit.*, p. 196. Lerner, *Economics of Control, op. cit.*, diagram, p. 336.

Summaries

M. J. Farrell, "The New Theories of the Consumption Function," *The Economic Journal*, 69 (December 1959), pp. 678–696.

In this classic article, Farrell maintains that the acceptance of the "new" theories of the consumption function (developed by such eminent economists as Friedman, Modigliani, and Brumberg) was "prejudiced, primarily by the conjunction of valuable and highly controversial hypotheses, and secondarily by certain flaws in exposition." To avoid these prejudices, Farrell attempts an exposition of the essentials of these theories. However, in so doing, he does not discuss the utility theory which, in his opinion, is not very illuminating. Also, he avoids Friedman's concept of permanent income which, although very valuable, involves considerable uncertainties and difficulties. Instead, Farrell distinguishes between the several hypotheses advanced by the above writers, and considers the evidence for, and implications of, each hypothesis.

The author examines in detail the normal income hypothesis, the proportionality hypothesis, the short-and-long period MPC, and the Friedman effect. He then skillfully classifies the "new" theories of the consumption function on the basis of three independent hypotheses. He finds the proportionality hypothesis unnecessary and the rate-of-growth hypothesis to be substantially valid. In the case of the normal income hypothesis, he finds this to be well substantiated by farmers and businessmen in the United States, thereby proving the accuracy of this hypothesis.

The author expresses the hope that more empirical research will be conducted to test the three hypotheses developed by him. In his words, "For future surveys, one hopes that, at the very least, income for several previous years and expected future income will be recorded; it is perhaps too much to hope that cross section surveys will be replaced by the much more informative continuous budget studies."

D. Hamberg and Charles L. Schultze, "Autonomous vs. Induced Investment: The Inter-Relatedness of Parameters in Growth Models," *The Economic Journal*, 61 (March 1961), pp. 53–65.

In this article, Hamberg and Schultze undertake the task of rescuing "autonomous investment" from the "questionable" treatment it has received in the hands of Hicks and Kaldor, and also from the way Hamberg has treated it on earlier occasions. They point out that in the past many economic model builders (including Hicks and Harrod) have assumed that, in business cycle and growth models, autonomous investment does not generate productive capacity, while an increase in productive activity is imputed to induced investment. Hamberg, on the other hand, had argued that "autonomous investment, even when capacity-generating, does not require growth to render it economically justifiable. Hence, its capacity-creating effects could be ignored in a growth model (and *a fortiori* a cycle model as well)." The authors say that in economic literature two alternative views exist: (1) autonomous investment does not generate productive capacity, and (2) the capacity-creating effects of autonomous investment can be ignored in a growth model. In this article, Hamberg and Schultze attempt to show that neither view is wholly tenable and that a compromise between the two positions is a more rational way of treating autonomous investment in growth models.

Bibliography

Hans Brems, "What Induces Induced Investment?" *Kyklos*, 16 (1963), Fasc. 4, pp. 569–582.

H. P. Brown, "The Present Theory of Investment Appraisal: A Critical Analysis," *Bulletin of Oxford University Institute of Economics and Statistics*, 31 (May 1969), pp. 105–131.

H. Neisser, "The Static Theory of Aggregate Investment," *Weltwirtschaftliches Archiv*, 98 (March 1967), pp. 1–28.

Robert M. Solow, *Capital Theory and the Rate of Return* (Chicago: Rand McNally & Company, 1965), 98 pp.

6
MACRO DISTRIBUTION AND EXPECTATION

One of the many aspects of macro theory which have received little attention from economists over the years is the problem of distribution. Also, most economists seem to have neglected the theory of expectations, which is fundamental to the understanding of macroeconomics. The first two selections in this part deal with macro distribution; the third presents a summary of the way in which Keynes used expectations in developing his theory.

In the first article, Riach develops a framework for macro distribution analysis. He combines various influences which are usually included in contemporary distribution theories. Weintraub takes an altogether different approach to the same problem in the second selection. He first discusses in detail the marginal productivity and macro distribution theories and then suggests possible ways of bringing about a reconciliation between the two. In the third article, Dillard examines the effect of the application of the theory of short- and long-term expectations on investment behavior.

A Framework For Macro-Distribution Analysis[1]
P. A. Riach

I

Keynes' penetrating criticism of the neo-classical theory of employment in chapters 2 and 19 of the *General Theory* was necessarily also a criticism of the neo-classical economists' explanation of the determination of wages and income distribution at the aggregate level, for this followed as the essential complement of their employment theory. His realisation that a movement in the general level of money wages must inevitably be accompanied by a movement in

P. A. Riach, "A Framework for Macro-Distribution Analysis," *Kyklos*, 22 (1969), pp. 542–563.

money aggregate demand and thus in labour's marginal value product function shattered the simple determinacy of the neo-classical analysis.[2] It was recognised that changes in the distribution of income, via their impact upon the aggregate propensity to consume, could influence the level of output, and thus the *level* of income and the *distribution* become interdependent.[3] "For aggregate demand determines factor employment and incomes and the distribution of these incomes in turn influences the level and structure of aggregate demand."[4]

Keynes thus established the need for a drastic reappraisal of distribution theory, but seventeen years later Fellner had to write "... it (contemporary distribution theory) is a theory which calls attention to the fact that for the economy as a whole the demand side of factor markets is not independent of their supply side, although there exists at present *no formal apparatus* for a satisfactory general analysis of the nature of this interdependence."[5] But it so happened that at about the time Fellner was writing models were beginning to appear which formalized this interdependence between the level of income and the distribution of income, and over the past fifteen years we have been presented with a virtual torrent of them.[6] In general the approach has been to abandon completely the neo-classical analysis, rather than to attempt repair measures by providing it with a "formal apparatus" capable of analysing the interdependence.[7]

Kaldor in particular has specifically rejected the neo-classical approach—"The burden of Mr. Atsumi's criticism is that the 'Keynesian' theory of distribution is incompatible with the marginal productivity theory. Of course it is. As should be evident from the context of my article, I put it forward as an *alternative* to the marginal productivity principle, and not as a complement."[8]

As Kaldor's model highlights, if we postulate different saving propensities for wage-earners and capitalists we automatically obtain a tautological relationship between the distribution of income and the aggregate propensity to save (and, it follows, the ratio of investment to income).[9] The crucial step then becomes one of postulating the direction of any causal relationship. Kaldor chooses to interpret the tautology such that the distribution of income becomes the dependent variable—dependent upon the level of aggregate demand and upon investment demand in particular. Full employment is assumed, so that an increase in investment demand means an increase in the desired ratio of investment to income, which means that

for equilibrium we must have an increase in the aggregate savings propensity—this being obtained by a redistribution of income to the more thrifty capitalists. On the other hand some economists have placed the opposite interpretation upon the tautology and argued that the distribution of income is a factor influencing the level of aggregate demand and thus income; i.e., the distribution of income now becomes the independent variable and aggregate demand the dependent variable. Dunlop interpreted the direction of causation in this manner in 1950,[10] and shortly after Kaldor's model appeared Cartter published a formalised model in which the level of aggregate demand is shown to depend upon the distribution of income.[11]

Like Kaldor he operates with a two factor model—laborers and capitalists receiving wages and profits respectively, but he differs from Kaldor in allowing the income level to vary. The marginal propensity to save (equal to the average propensity to save) of capitalists is assumed to be higher than that of labour and thus the level of savings depends upon the distribution as well as the level of income.

$$S = Y[s_w \sigma + s_p(1 - \sigma)] \qquad (1)$$

where S is savings, Y income, s_w the marginal (= average) propensity to save of labor, s_p the marginal (= average) propensity to save of capitalists, and σ is the wage share.[12] It follows that aggregate demand and hence equilibrium income depend upon the distribution of income.[13]

Cartter assumes I is a linear function of the level of profits

$$I = \pi P \qquad (2)$$

where I is investment, P profits, and π is the investment/profit coefficient, which is assumed to $> 0 < 1$.

Equation (2) is rewritten as

$$I = \pi(1 - \sigma)Y \qquad (3)$$

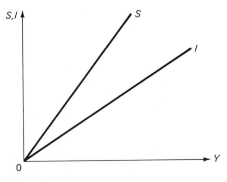

Figure 1

Thus we now have investment as well as savings as a function of the wage share and the Keynesian income equilibrium is rewritten as

$$Y[s_w\sigma + s_p(1 - \sigma)] = \pi(1 - \sigma)Y \qquad (4)$$

Cartter points out if s_w, s_p, π, and σ are all constant and the left hand side is greater than the right hand side, then the economy will contract in continuous disequilibrium towards zero, whilst in the opposite situation output will expand in continuous disequilibrium until the full employment ceiling is reached.

If *L.H.S.* > *R.H.S.* i.e., planned S > planned I [we get the result shown in Figure 1]. As Y falls towards zero with the wage share constant we have proportionate reductions in wages and profits and, with s_w, s_p, and π constant, we likewise have proportionate reductions in S and I: there are no forces operating to equilibrate savings and investment.—But if it happens that *L.H.S.* = *R.H.S.* the saving and investment functions become coincident and we have a situation of multiple equilibrium: whatever the level of output, planned savings will be identical with planned investment.

Cartter's model does not analyse the determination of factor shares, rather it shows what distribution of income would be *necessary*, given s_p, s_w, and π, to provide equilibrium income.[14] The impact of an increase in the wage share upon income

is considered,[15] but there is no discussion of the factors which may operate to change the wage share.

The common feature of these models is their explicit recognition of the income level–income distribution relationship. Kaldor has produced a model with the objective of showing the effect of the level of aggregate demand on the distribution of income, but his model only operates if there is full employment and can tell us nothing about the determination of the income level or its distribution if we have a situation of less than full employment. Cartter's model shows how the distribution of income could affect the level of income but nevertheless, in the form presented, it cannot show how a determinate level of income is achieved, and it contains no analysis as to how the income distribution itself is determined. On the other hand, the marginal productivity theory which they are intending to replace suffers from its inability to handle the interdependence between the level and the distribution of income. The principal purpose of this paper is to outline, in section three, a framework of analysis which allows for a two way relationship between the level of income and the distribution of income; thus incorporating elements of both Kaldor's and Cartter's analysis, and in addition showing how the influences of marginal productivity theory can play a part. It is deliberately called a framework of analysis in that it does not say so much which is new but rather that it puts the pieces together in a way which is different and I hope useful. It shows that by incorporating certain quite traditional hypotheses about the firm's pricing behaviour into a contemporary-style macro-distribution model the deficiencies in the Kaldor and Cartter models, which have just been noted above, can be overcome. Before putting forward this framework however it is necessary to pay close attention to the step which is involved in moving from recognising the *tautological* relationship between the investment–income ratio and the profit share to postulating a *behavioural* relationship between these two ratios. It is this aspect of the macro-distribution problem that we will consider in section two.

II

This step which is necessary in deriving a behavioural relationship involves a model of the firm's behaviour. Kaldor claims he has put forward "... a macro-economic price and distribution theory...,"[16] but it is one with crucial micro foundations. If entrepreneurs behave like Kaldorian men the direction of causation is as he postulates, but if they act as Marshallian men (or Kaleckian, or any other kind of men for that matter) the relationship is reversed and the distribution of income becomes the independent variable. In Kaldor's original article in 1956 the firm only enters the analysis implicitly and as Preiser puts it "... the very essence of the distribution process moves out of sight. The relative shares of profits and wages are solely derived from investment demand and savings propensities and are, therefore, only a by-product of decisions which have no direct connection with the distribution problem."[17]

In Kaldor's world of full employment "... the level of prices in relation to the level of money wages is determined by demand: a rise in investment, and thus in total demand, will raise prices and profit margins...."[18] The implication of this is that entrepreneurial pricing policy is to sensitively attune profit margins to the *level* of demand, and it is important to realize that Kaldor does not suggest that there is any relationship between the *level* of demand and the elasticity of demand; as there is for instance in the "Harrod effect."[19] We have in other words a world of nonmaximizing entrepreneurs whose profit margins are "thermostatically" tied

to the level of aggregate demand. In support of his interpretation of the identity Kaldor argues—"The interpretative value of the model (as distinct from the formal validity of the equations or identities) depends on the Keynesian hypothesis that investment, or rather the ratio of investment to output, can be treated as an independent variable, invariant with respect to changes in the two savings propensities s_p and s_w."[20] Certainly *investment* is the independent variable in the Keynesian system which, given the aggregate propensity to save, determines the level of income, but it is *not* "the 'Keynesian' hypothesis" that the *ratio of investment to output* is an independent variable: it is a dependent variable in the Keynesian system—dependent on the aggregate propensity to save. Only if we accept the Kaldorian hypothesis that demand-level-determined prices ensure a steady level of full employment output does the investment-output ratio become the independent variable, and this only follows on the basis of Kaldor's micro foundations!

Kaldor's model of the firm became explicit in the paper he presented at the Corfu conference in 1958.[21] There he marries Kalecki's horizontal average variable cost curve to a "Keynesian" demand function and the honeymoon takes place in the representative firm.

The representative firm is fully integrated vertically so that marginal cost *M.C.* and average variable cost *A.V.C* consist solely of labour cost, and the upper limit to output is set by the full employment *F.E.* level [see Figure 2]. There is assumed to be a minimum margin for profits over variable costs determined by the "degree of monopoly" which sets a minimum level to prices (money wage rates are assumed to be constant) and thus we obtain the reverse L-shaped supply curve. The "Keynesian" demand function "... shows for any particular output (and employment) that excess of price over prime cost which makes the effective de-

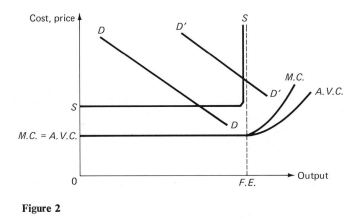

Figure 2

mand in real terms equal to that output."[22] It is in effect a function directly analogous to Hicks' *I.S.* function, but, whereas Hicks' *I.S.* function shows various combinations of income and the rate of interest giving commodity market equilibrium, Kaldor's function shows various combinations of income and the profit share which ensure equilibrium between saving and investment. Assuming a constant level of investment he obtains a negatively sloped demand function, which ensures full employment if it cuts on the vertical section of the supply curve. If instead it cuts on the horizontal section it means that the "degree of monopoly" has determined a minimum profit share and in turn an aggregate propensity to save which, with the given volume of investment, cannot establish a level of full employment; in this case the profit share becomes the independent variable and the investment–output ratio becomes the dependent variable. But provided the demand function confines its fluctuations to the vertical section of the supply curve entrepreneurial pricing behaviour, *of the type outlined above*, will ensure the maintenance of full employment equilibrium. Kaldor recognizes that in the short run profit margins are unlikely to exhibit such flexibility, so that any variation in investment from a

level consistent with full employment will lead to either unemployment or inflation in accordance with the strictly Keynesian multiplier theory.[23]

The pertinent question is whether Kaldor's long run ever comes—whether the basic underlying nature of entrepreneurial pricing behaviour is of the "thermostat" variety he outlines, and only being temporarily impeded by inflexibilities in the short run; or whether pricing behaviour is of a *fundamentally* different nature with the direction of causation in the Kaldorian identity reversed. The prediction that full employment equilibrium is automatically generated in the long run by a *laissez-faire* economy is a crucial implication of Kaldor's analysis but it has puzzled some of his readers; notably Samuelson—"As an American I find it a little ironic that just in the decade when our problems of unemployment have seemingly become chronic, Nicholas Kaldor has been reverting to a theory of full employment."[24] "Indeed our unemployment rates at persistent six per cent levels over half a dozen years suggest that to whatever economic system it (Kaldor's equation) may apply, it does not apply to American capitalism."[25] The question which must be posed is whether Kaldor's mechanism is any more effective as an automatic regulator on the consumption function than the "Pigou effect," which Kaldor himself claims is irrelevant.[26]

Kaldor has paraphrased both the marginal productivity theory and Kalecki's theory thus—"Just as the positive content of the marginal productivity theory can be summed up by the statement that the rate of profit on capital (and the margin of profit in output) is governed by the need to prevent the capital–output ratio from being either too large or too small, the positive content of 'the degree of monopoly' theory can be summed up in the sentence that 'profit margins are what they are because the forces of competition prevent them from being higher than they are and are not powerful enough to make them lower than they are.' Unfortunately neither of these statements gets us very far."[27] We could likewise paraphrase Kaldor "profit margins are what they are because if they were higher we would have unemployment and if they were lower we would have inflation"—and this does not get us any further!

What seems to have been overlooked (disregarded?) in the so-called "Keynesian" distribution theories is the position Keynes himself took with respect to macro-wage (and hence distribution) determination in *The General Theory*. Whilst he rejected the neo-classical theory of employment and thus the precise formulation of the wage theory which complemented it, he was most emphatic in his retention of a vital element in the neo-classical theory—the equality between the real wage and labour's marginal physical product.

"In emphasising our point of departure from the classical system, we must not overlook an important point of agreement. For we shall maintain the first postulate (the equality between the wage and labour's marginal product) as heretofore... It means that, with a given organisation, equipment and technique, real wages and the volume of output (and

hence of employment) are uniquely correlated..."[28] This relationship flows from what Mrs. Robinson has now christened a short-period utilization function.[29]

In essence Keynes accepted that whilst the equilibrium level of employment is determined by the forces of aggregate demand, the corresponding real wage (and hence wage share) is determined by the forces of marginal productivity. Admittedly there may be some interdependence between the level of income and the distribution of income, as we noted at the outset of this paper, but once this interaction has worked itself out and income and employment have settled in short-run equilibrium it is not inconsistent to argue that the corresponding wage reflects marginal product. Keynes' analysis of the interdependence within the neo-classical system has led to some confusion on this point— for instance Rothschild has claimed that Keynes "... has undermined the *foundations* of the old micro-economic distribution theory."[30] But in the short-run there is no reason whatever for expecting instability in *this* key foundation, the marginal physical product function, which simply reflects the physical conditions of production, and Keynes himself puts it that there is nothing in the world less prone to short-run instability than this function.[31] Thus although Keynes rejected the neo-classical formulation in which the real wage determined the level of employment he retained the marginal productivity principle and instead reversed the direction of determination.

The existence of persistently high levels of unemployment in *laissez-faire* economies, as we argued above, is *prima facie* evidence for rejecting Kaldor's model of pricing behaviour and the attempt to interpret his identity in a behavioural sense as indicating how the economy actually does operate, rather than in Pasinetti's sense as a logical framework which indicates what *ought* to happen if we are to maintain full employment equilibrium.[32] The other major branch of contemporary distributive thought, marginal productivity theory, has been subjected to a considerable barrage of criticism during its checkered life, but there is always lurking in the background the fundamental point that it does flow as an important corollary of the profit-maximizing assumption; and we do not as yet have a satisfactory general alternative assumption about entrepreneurial motivation. Thus what I now propose to put forward in section three is a model which postulates that entrepreneurs set out to maximize short-run profits and which can therefore incorporate marginal productivity as a major influence, but it is a model which allows for the interdependence between the distribution and the level of income that arises when we assume a short-run production function of the normal type, as specified below, and that the savings propensity of capitalists differs from that of wage-earners. We will see investment behaviour and the savings propensities playing a role, and also that Kalecki's basic variable, the "degree of monopoly," can be incorporated within the model.[33]

III

In line with Kaldor and Cartter we will split income between two factors labour and capital, and following Kaldor we will assume that the representative firm is fully integrated vertically, so that variable cost consists solely of wages, with the excess of output over variable cost accruing to capitalists as profit. The model only sets out to analyse a short-run situation in the traditional sense of one having a given productive capacity in existence. Net investment is being undertaken during the period but it is assumed that it does not add to effective productive capacity during this initial period of construction, and thus any change in output involves a variation in the application of labour to the given stock of capital. We assume that current production techniques permit such a variation in the capital/labour ratio, and for the moment we will assume that there is a pool of unemployed labour so that any increase in aggregate demand can be met by increasing labour input. So given our assumption of short-run profit maximization, and in addition postulating initially perfect competition in all product and factor markets, this means that real wages (equal to marginal product) will be inversely related to the level of output and employment. It also means, as Davidson has shown,[34] that if the short-run total product function is a normal, "... continuous, monotonic function which reaches, or at least approaches, a maximum as the proportion of variable to fixed factor increases,"[35] then the share of wages will fall as output increases, except in one case where it remains constant, which is when the production function is of the form:

$$Q = aL^k \text{ }^{[36]}$$

So with the exception of this latter possibility we will assume that both the real wage rate *and* the wage share are inverse functions of the level of output and employment, which is equivalent to the Keynesian position outlined above.

We will assume that the average propensity to save (equal to marginal propensity to save) of capitalists is higher than that of wage-earners and thus we obtain Kaldor's tautological relationship between the aggregate propensity to save and the profit share. But given the assumptions in the preceding paragraph we have the distribution of any given level of income being determined by the conditions of production technique (by the relationship of marginal product to average product) and thus the profit share becomes the independent variable when we move to interpreting the Kaldorian identity in a behavioural sense. We obtain the same direction of causation as in Cartter's model with the aggregate propensity to save and thus the level of aggregate demand and income dependent upon the distribution of income.

So it follows that with our assumptions about entrepreneurial motivation, production conditions and the savings behaviour of the two factors we obtain a situation of interdependence between the distribution of income and the level of income. Our assumption of short-run profit maximization along with our assumptions about production and market conditions means that the wage share is a negative function of output, and when we add our assumption about the savings propensities to this it follows that aggregate demand and output are positive functions of the wage share. What I hope to show in the context of a simple model is how the equilibrium income level and income distribution are simultaneously determined. In approach it is similar to Hicks' famous analysis in "Mr. Keynes and the 'Classics': A Suggested Interpretation," in which he analyses the interdependence between the rate of interest and the level of income.[37]

The Income Distribution Function

The income distribution YD function shows the equilibrium wage share corresponding to each level of output, which is determined by the relationship of marginal product to average product. For simplicity of analysis we will assume that it is a linear function of the form:

$$\sigma = p - rY \qquad (1)$$

(where σ is the wage share, Y is income, and p and r are constants). This function obviously cannot be linear for all values of Y as σ can only vary from zero to one; therefore we will impose the following restrictions on the function: (1) p and r are both < 1; (2) the function is only operative over a specified range of income.

The Income Level Function

The income level IS function shows the equilibrium level of income corresponding to any given wage share. Assuming initially that investment is constant, and given our assumption that $s_p > s_w$ it follows that the IS function will have a positive slope. The level of savings is a negative function of σ and a positive function of Y; thus given an increase in σ we must have an increase in Y to maintain equality with the given investment. In this form the IS function is directly comparable with Kaldor's "Keynesian" demand function discussed above [N. Kaldor, *Essays on Economic Stability and Growth*, p. 8].

The IS function can also incorporate the possibility that investment, as well as savings, may be sensitive to changes in the distribution of income. As we are operating in the short-run with a fixed capital stock a shift in the distribution of income from profits to wages will mean a decrease in the rate of profit on capital; therefore if expectations about the future rate of profit are to some extent based upon the current rate of profit there will be a fall in investment, and thus we obtain a negative relationship between σ and investment.[38] This is not to argue that current profits are the sole, or even major, determinant of investment, but simply to show that the model can accommodate a dependence of investment as well as savings on the distribution of income. A variation in investment resulting from any other force will simply mean a shift in the IS function.

Given our assumptions about savings behaviour we obtain a function of the following form:

$$S = sY - t\sigma \qquad (2)$$

(where S is savings and s and t are constants).

Likewise we obtain an investment function as follows:

$$I = b - d\sigma \qquad (3)$$

(where I is investment and b and d are

constants). Therefore our savings–investment equilibrium becomes:

$$sY - t\sigma = b - d\sigma \qquad (4)$$

and our IS function can be expressed:

$$Y = [b + \sigma(t - d)]\frac{1}{s} \qquad (5)$$

As with the YD function it has been assumed for simplicity that the IS function is linear, but because of the limits of variation of σ the IS function must also be restricted to a specified range of income.

Once we allow for the possibility that investment is also a negative function of σ we are no longer necessarily assured of an IS function with a positive slope; this will only follow if the savings–σ coefficient t is greater than the investment–σ coefficient d and here there is an obvious affinity with Pasinetti's stability conditions.[39]

In Figure 3 it is assumed that t > d and thus the IS function has a positive slope. We obtain mutually compatible values for the level of income and the distribution of income when σ is equal to OM and Y is equal to ON; at this point savings and investment are in equilibrium and simultaneously the wage share is equal to the ratio of marginal product to average product which production conditions determine at output ON. But if we were at income OP we would have a wage share of OR (determined in the Keynesian manner discussed above [N. Kaldor, *Essays on Economic Stability and Growth*, p. 10], whilst a wage share of OT would be necessary to equate savings and investment. So with S > I businessmen cut back production in an endeavour to reduce the unplanned buildup in their stocks, and equilibrium will only be restored when output settles again at ON.

We can summarize the forces determining the equilibrium wage share which is consistent with savings-investment equilibrium as follows:

From equation (1) we obtain:

$$Y = \frac{p - \sigma}{r} \qquad (6)$$

From equation (5) we obtain:

$$Y = \frac{b + \sigma(t - d)}{s} \qquad (7)$$

$$\therefore \frac{p - \sigma}{r} = \frac{b + \sigma(t - d)}{s} \qquad (8)$$

$$\therefore ps - \sigma s = rb + r\sigma(t - d) \qquad (9)$$

$$\therefore ps - rb = \sigma[s + r(t - d)] \qquad (10)$$

$$\therefore \sigma = \frac{ps - rb}{s + r(t - d)} \qquad (11)$$

which shows our equilibrium wage share as being the outcome of three interacting sets of forces:

1. Production conditions reflected in p and r;
2. The savings behaviour of the two income groups reflected in s and t;
3. Investment behaviour reflected in b and d.

The forces of marginal productivity are reflected in 1 and the Kaldor–Cartter stress on savings and investment behaviour as key distributive forces is reflected in 2 and 3. Thus the model combines elements of the three theories and attempts to provide the apparatus Fellner found lacking in 1953,[40] without abandoning the influence of marginal productivity. Although there are obvious similarities with the models of

Figure 3

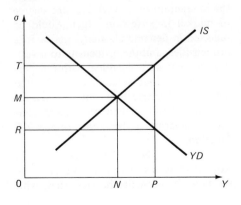

Kaldor and Cartter there are very significant differences from them both. The similarity of the *IS* function to Kaldor's "Keynesian" demand function was mentioned above but Kaldor would certainly object to its use in conjunction with marginal productivity.[41] Also, whilst our model operates quite happily in conditions of unemployment, Kaldor's model only operates at full employment and in direct contrast to our analysis he argues that: "If the share of wages at full employment were uniquely determined by the marginal productivity of labour in relation to its average productivity, it could not, at the same time be determined by the propensities to invest and to save."[42] In our model the share of wages at any given output *is* determined by the ratio of marginal product to average product; but whether or not we obtain full employment output depends on the savings and investment propensities. I would therefore suggest that this model is more Keynesian than Kaldor's "Keynesian" model. The level of investment *does* affect the distribution of income; not directly as in Kaldor's model, but via its influence in determining the equilibrium income level and thus exactly where we settle on our *YD* function.

In that it shows the dependence of savings and investment, and thus income equilibrium, on the distribution of income the *IS* function closely resembles Cartter's model, and in fact our equation (4) above closely corresponds to equation (4) in the version of Cartter's model outlined above [A. M. Cartter, *Theory of Wages and Employment*, 1959, p. 3]. But Cartter has no analysis of factor share determination (i.e., he has nothing equivalent to our *YD* funcion), the distribution of income is independent of the level of income, and there is no process by which his model can produce a determinate equilibrium income level in the way that our model does via the interaction of *YD* and *IS*.[43]

Up to now we have been assuming the existence of perfect competition and thus productivity phenomena alone have governed the behaviour of the *YD* function; but our analytical framework is equally applicable to the type of cost and demand conditions Kalecki postulates in his distribution model, which predicts that the distribution of income (and thus the behaviour of our *YD* function) depends upon "the degree of monopoly."[44] If we retain our assumption of profit maximization this variable represents the reciprocal of demand elasticity as was the interpretation in Kalecki's original formulation. It follows therefore that if elasticity of demand is independent of the level of output our *YD* function becomes horizontal and the degree of monopoly alone determines the distribution of income, which in turn, with the propensities to save and invest, determines the level of aggregate demand and income. This is the reverse of the Kaldorian hypothesis and corresponds exactly to the situation in his representative firm, noted above [N. Kaldor, *Essays on Economic Stability and Growth*, p. 8], where his "Keynesian" demand function cuts the supply function on its horizontal section: as I have said before, it basically depends upon the nature of our assumption about entrepreneurial pricing behaviour.

Alternatively demand elasticity may be inversely related to the level of economic activity in the way Harrod has postulated, in which case we would obtain a negatively sloped *YD* function as in Figure 3. The equilibrium wage share would now reflect the interaction of three forces; the degree of market imperfection which would be reflected in demand elasticity, the savings propensities, and the propensity to invest. The latter two are identical with our perfectly competitive version, but now "the degree of imperfection" or "degree of monopoly" rather than production conditions determines the nature of the *YD* function.

In this form the model is very similar to Mrs. Robinson's analysis: "We can now see how to reconcile the view that, with given propensities to consume of each class, the share of wages in national income is determined by the ratio of investment to income, with the view that (when there is surplus capacity) it is determined by the degree of monopoly. The share of profit in income is determined by the *ratio* of investment to income, but the amount of income associated with a given *rate* of investment is influenced by the amount of capacity in existence and the degree of monopoly." [45] Our model also attempts to reconcile the distributive impact of investment behaviour with "the degree of monopoly" force, but I would put it rather that—"the share of profit in income is determined by the *degree of monopoly*, but the amount of income associated with any given degree of monopoly is influenced by the rate of investment."

Given our *IS* function the level of equilibrium income, and therefore the possibility of full employment, depends on the *YD* function (and thus the degree of monopoly), and this corresponds closely with her statement: "Given the propensities to consume and the rate of investment there is a certain level of profit margins that is compatible with full employment in any short period situation." [46]

If the *YD* and *IS* functions intersect at an output level which exceeds the economy's short-run capacity we have a situation of excess demand; a possibility which we have ignored to date. In Figure 4 it is assumed that *OZ* represents the output level corresponding to full employment and thus the capacity output of our short-run model. At *OZ* the production and/or market conditions underlying the *YD* function determine a wage share of *OW*, which would only be compatible with commodity market equilibrium if output of *OX* were attainable. At *OZ* therefore investment exceeds savings and we can only achieve a situation in which the income distribution is compatible with commodity market equilibrium if the resulting inflationary process involves a

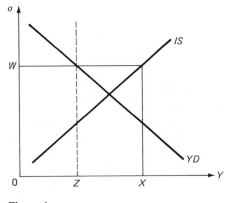

Figure 4

shift in one or other function; otherwise we will be faced with a situation of perpetual inflation. A shift to the left of the *YD* function requires a change in the production and/or market conditions which are determining the wage share of full employment output, whilst a leftward movement in the *IS* function would follow a downward revision of investment plans and/or an increase in the overall savings-income relationship.

Whether or not the inflationary process does achieve a shift in the *YD* function is the outcome of many interacting forces within the economy, which we would expect to be pushing up both the demand and cost curves of our representative firm as the pressures of excess demand bear upon both the factor and product market. Kaldor, as we noted above, assumes constant money wages [47] so that the cost curve of his representative firm remains stable and consequently he has the profit margin rising with an increase in demand. What is, of course, far more likely in such a situation is an upward movement in both the cost and demand curves, with the final outcome for the profit margin dependent on a wide range of institutional factors within the economy. The impact of excess demand on money wages and their ability to keep up with or get ahead of price increases depends on many factors: such as the extent of union organization and bargaining strength, plus the institutional arrangements for wage fixation—whether government agencies are involved directly or indirectly and the level at which wages are negotiated, firm, industry, or economy. The behaviour of prices, on the other hand, and the prospect of a higher profit margin is influenced by the extent of oligopolised market structures and how they react to the pressure of excess demand. Therefore it does not necessarily follow that an inflationary situation will automatically produce a larger profit share in the way Kaldor's model does; for instance trade unions are unlikely to be as passive as he implies, and as Rothschild has pointed out[48] they may resist not only a cut in real wages but also a decrease in the rate of real wage growth. The YD function may well shift during the inflationary process but the extent and direction of the movement is dependent on many institutional aspects of the economy.

The inflationary situation is also likely to shift the IS function as the process of rising prices bears on investment plans and savings propensities. Kaldor does not consider such possibilities in his model and he has been subjected to considerable criticism on this score, particularly from Rothschild and Sen—"The chief difficulties with the neo-Keynesian model seem to be its assumptions of (a) fixed propensities to save independent of price changes, (b) fixed *real* investment irrespective of price changes, and (c) lack of any feedback mechanism when entrepreneurial expectations are unfilled."[49] Rising prices may provoke a revision of investment plans either upward or downward depending upon a variety of factors; for instance the expectation created about the direction of future price movements, which may induce either a postponement or an advancement of investment plans, and the reaction of the monetary authority to the inflationary situation and the pressure it creates on the money supply. Likewise the propensity to

save may not be independent of rising prices as is the case in the "Pigou effect," and more recently Rothschild has argued that the propensity to save out of profits may well be a positive function of the degree of wage pressure.[50]

So the final outcome of the excess demand, the extent of the price increase and the new equilibrium wage share, is dependent on a wide range of factors which underlie the behaviour of the two functions; their movements are the more likely to be stabilizing if rising prices produce (a) a higher profit share, (b) a reduction in investment, or (c) higher savings propensities.

My objective in putting forward this framework has been to combine various influences which are commonly included in contemporary distribution theories. In particular I have attempted to show how Kaldor's investment and savings propensities can play a key distributive role within the context of a profit-maximizing model. It therefore follows that the additional influences of productivity and/or "the degree of monopoly" enter the picture, and it is only if we postulate Kaldor's "thermostat" pricing behaviour and assume a steady level of full employment that saving and investment behaviour *alone* determine the distribution of income.

An important final reminder is that the model only pretends to be able to analyse short-run movements; a long-run theory of income distribution I am afraid is another tale.

NOTES

1 I am very grateful to K. Frearson, L. McGregor, E. H. Phelps Brown, and Joan Robinson for their comments on an earlier draft of this paper, but of course sole responsibility for the contents rests with me.
2 J. M. Keynes, *The General Theory of Employment, Interest and Money* (Macmillan, 1936), pp. 257–260 in particular. P. Davidson, *Theories of Aggregate Income*

Distribution (Rutgers, 1959), p. 35. Makes this point very succinctly—"Interdependence between supply and demand is the rule rather than the exception in factor markets on any aggregate level."

3 J. M. Keynes, *op. cit.*, p. 262.

4 K. W. Rothschild, "Some Recent Contributions to a Macro-economic Theory of Income Distribution," *Scottish Journal of Political Economy* (October 1961), pp. 173–174.

5 W. J. Fellner, "Significance and Limitations of Contemporary Distribution Theory," *American Economic Review*, Papers and Proceedings (May 1953) (my emphasis).

6 I refer here, of course, to the "widow's cruse" type models which have been propounded by Kaldor, Joan Robinson, Schneider, etc.

7 One noteworthy attempt to take account of this interdependence within the context of marginal productivity theory is S. Weintraub, *An Approach to the Theory of Income Distribution* (Chilton, 1958).

8 N. Kaldor, "A Rejoinder to Mr. Atsumi and Professor Tobin," *Review of Economic Studies* (1959–1960), p. 121.

9 N. Kaldor, "Alternative Theories of Distribution," *Review of Economic Studies* (1955–1956), p. 95. The discussion of "widow's cruse" theories which follows will be basically in terms of Kaldor's theory for, whilst many other similar models have been put forward, it is Kaldor's model which has received most discussion and notoriety.

10 "This consumption function for the whole community must be affected by the relative distribution of income between wage and salary earners and other groups in the community. It might be thought that since wages and salaries on balance go to individuals with lower incomes and presumably with higher marginal propensities to consume, an increase in labor's share in the depression would be a factor tending to increase the level of income." J. T. Dunlop, *Wage Determination under Trade Unions* (Basil Blackwell, 1950), pp. 189–190.

11 A. M. Cartter, *Theory of Wages and Employment* (Irwin, 1959), pp. 155–161. The model he presents here, whilst being indeterminate, is a stimulating contribution to the analysis of the income level-income distribution interdependence, and I find it curious that it has been so overlooked in the critical literature.

12 Cartter defines savings, investment, and

profits as gross concepts—in all cases— including depreciation. He also splits profits into retained and distributed portions but we shall ignore this distinction as it is not fundamental to the analysis.

13 See Cartter, *op. cit.*, p. 159.

14 *Ibid.*, p. 157, particularly Table 11–1.

15 *Ibid.*, pp. 158–160.

16 N. Kaldor, *Essays on Economic Stability and Growth*, p. 8, fn.

17 N. Preiser, *Wachstum und Einkommensverteilung*, p. 49, quoted in K. Rothschild, "Theme and Variations—Remarks on the Kaldorian Distribution Formula," *Kyklos*, 1965, p. 655.

18 N. Kaldor, "Alternative Theories of Distribution," *Review of Economic Studies* (1955–1956), p. 95.

19 By the "Harrod Effect" I refer to Harrod's suggestion in *The Trade Cycle* (1936), pp. 20–22, that there is an inverse relationship between the level of economic activity and the elasticity of the firm's demand curve. If this was Kaldor's argument then his theory could be construed as being consistent with profit-maximizing behaviour.

20 N. Kaldor, *op. cit.*, p. 95.

21 N. Kaldor, "Capital Accumulation and Economic Growth," in F. Lutz and D. Hague (eds.), *The Theory of Capital* (1963).

22 *Ibid.*, pp. 198–199.

23 Kaldor is most explicit on this point in "A Model of Economic Growth," *The Economic Journal* (December 1957), p. 622.

24 P. A. Samuelson, "A Brief Survey of Post-Keynesian Developments," in R. Lekachman, *Keynes' General Theory. Reports of Three Decades* (St. Martins), p. 343.

25 *Ibid.*, p. 345. Australian experience supports Samuelson's position. Between 1920/1921 and 1939/1940 unemployment amongst registered trade-unionists (the only data available for the period) fell below eight per cent for only two years, and in ten of these twenty years it was in excess of ten per cent. The comparatively low unemployment rates experienced during the post-war period would appear to be the outcome of successful government intervention rather than any inherent adjustment mechanism within the system.

26 N. Kaldor, "Economic Growth and the Problem of Inflation," *Economica* (August 1959), p. 215 fn.

27 N. Kaldor, *Review of Economic Studies* (1955–1956), p. 93.

28 J. M. Keynes, *op. cit.*, p. 17.

29 J. Robinson, *Collected Economic Papers*,

Volume III (Blackwell, 1965), particularly pp. 42 and 56.

30 K. W. Rothschild, *op. cit.*, p. 173 (my emphasis).

31 J. M. Keynes, *op. cit.*, p. 279.

32 L. Pasinetti, "Rate of Profit and Income Distribution in Relation to the Rate of Economic Growth," *Review of Economic Studies* (1962), p. 279.

33 The model outlined below bears some resemblance to each of the following: Joan Robinson, "The Theory of Distribution," *Collected Economic Papers* (Volume II), pp. 145–158; E. Schneider, "Income and Income Distribution in Macro-Economic Theory," *International Economic Papers*, No. 8, pp. 111–121; S. Weintraub, *An Approach to the Theory of Income Distribution* (Chilton, 1958); Cartter, *op. cit.*, pp. 155–161.

34 P. Davidson, *op. cit.*, p. 111.

35 P. Davidson, *op. cit.*, p. 123.

36 P. Davidson, *op. cit.*, p. 110.

37 J. R. Hicks, *Econometrica* (1937).

38 Cf. Cartters' investment function, above [A. M. Cartter, *op. cit.*, p.3].

39 L. Pasinetti, *op. cit.*, pp. 275–277.

40 Cf. above [W. J. Fellner, "Significance and Limitation of Contemporary Distribution Theory," *op. cit.*, p. 1].

41 Cf. above [N. Kaldon, *Essays on Economic Stability, op. cit.*, p. 2].

42 N. Kaldor, "A Rejoinder to Mr. Atsumi and Professor Tobin," *Review of Economic Studies* (1959–1960), p. 121.

43 Cf. above [A. M. Cartter, *op. cit.*, pp. 4–5].

44 Kalecki's model first appeared in *Econometrica* (1938), pp. 97–112, and received its most recent refurbishing in *Theory of Economic Dynamics* (1954). We will abstract from two less important variables —the material costs/wages costs ratio and the industrial structure.

45 Mrs. Robinson, "The Theory of Distribution," *Collected Essays* (Volume II), p. 149. See also pp. 152–153.

46 *Ibid.*, p. 151–152.

47 N. Kaldor, "Capital Accumulation and Economic Growth," in Lutz and Hague (eds.), *The Theory of Capital* (1963), p. 197.

48 K. W. Rothschild, "The Limitation of Economic Growth Models," *Kyklos* (Volume XII, No. 4), p. 582.

49 A. K. Sen, "Neo-classical and Neo-Keynesian Theories of Distribution," *The Economic Record* (March 1963).

50 K. W. Rothschild, "Theme and Variations —Remarks on the Kaldorian Distribution Formula," *Kyklos* (Volume XVIII, No. 4).

A Macro-Theory of Pricing, Income Distribution, and Employment
Sidney Weintraub

I. INTRODUCTION

Investment largely governs profits, and profits largely comprise the savings magnitude. The low savings propensities of

Sidney Weintraub, "A Macro-Theory of Pricing, Income Distribution, and Employment," *Weltwirtschaftliches Archiv*, Band 102 (1969), pp. 11–25.

Remark: I am indebted to E. S. Phelps for some comments on an early version of this paper. L. R. Klein and Paul Davidson were also helpful on several points. Needless to say, responsibility for any failures in the argument is mine alone.

wage earners, and the high savings ratios associated with profit incomes, enter in a crucial way in determining employment, income, and income growth.

These seem to be the main inferences to be drawn from the important recent writings of Professors Joan Robinson and Nicholas Kaldor, and supplemented by Luigi Pasinetti.[1] Once exploited, these insights promise to alter our understanding of the macroeconomic process and the enterprise system itself.[2]

It may be that their work accords too little attention to the price mechanism through which income shares are determined. In any event, the dependence of distributive shares on pricing will be the theme of this paper. With income shares resolved through pricing decisions, the income and employment levels rest upon: (1) investment, (2) income shares, and (3) the respective savings ratios.

This is a turn-about in Keynesian analysis where pricing has generally been suppressed while the argument has been conducted in real terms.[3] The importance of income distribution for macroeconomics, moreover, had practically dropped from view until the seminal Kaldor–Robinson writings opened up the subject.[4]

Undoubtedly, the mainstream of macrotheory will be revised by the new views on distribution. New attention will be accorded monopoly and competition once it is perceived that pricing practices dominate income division and thereby, the income and employment level, and the growth process itself.

II. THE PRICE LEVEL AND INCOME DISTRIBUTION

An easy way of showing the connection of prices to income distribution is through a general formula for the price level, involving the wage-cost-mark-up (WCM) equation. Thus:

$$P = kw/A = w/A\Theta \qquad (1)$$

In (1), P denotes the general price level (or the level of prices in the "representative" firm), w is the average money wage per time period, A symbolizes the output per employee over the same time interval, and k stands for the average mark-up of prices over unit labor costs or the reciprocal of the wage share, Θ.[5]

One can argue, of course, that k is a structural constant so that with given unit labor costs, w/A, the structural or institutional facts control the price level. Or it might be averred that k is an endogenous

outcome of the market facts of competition and monopoly, so that income shares are moulded in the market processes. In any event, so long as k is subject to minor variations in the normal circumstances, the price level is a consequence of money wage and productivity forces.[6]

III. THE "ALL AND NOTHING" HYPOTHESIS

For a good part of the way we can adopt the ingenious simplifying assumption, often invoked by Mrs Robinson and Mr. Kaldor, that wage earners spend all their income and save nothing, while capitalists save all and consume nothing. That is, $c_w = 1$ and $s_w = 0$ and $c_r = 0$ and $s_r = 1$, where the c-terms and the s-terms refer to the respective average propensities to consume and to save.

Obviously, the "realism" of this assumption can be derided but few would doubt that it is close to the mark in economies with low living standards, with a small very wealthy class as in even England and the United States in the not too distant past. After all, a modified "All and Nothing" hypothesis has a long ancestry in economics, from Cantillon and Hume, through Malthus, not to omit Marx and, in a latter day, Kalecki.

For analytic convenience the unqualified hypothesis will be employed initially. Even after it is watered down, it provides powerful illumination.

Income Definitions

Familiar income terms and definitions will be required: C = consumption output, I = investment output, $W = wN$ = the wage bill, R = *gross* profits, or more accurately, the nonwage share in *Gross Business Product*, involving *all* distributive allocations other than wages. Government outlays and taxes will. be temporarily excluded. Subscripts identify the C and I

outputs in the two sector model that we shall diagnose.

$$C \equiv P_cQ_c \equiv W_c + R_c \qquad (2)$$

$$I \equiv P_iQ_i \equiv W_i + R_i \qquad (3)$$

$$Z \equiv C + I \equiv W + R$$
$$\equiv (W_c + W_i) + (R_c + R_i) \qquad (4)$$

Further, $\Pi + \Theta = 1$, where Π and Θ represent the "profit" (or nonwage) and wage shares, respectively, in *Gross Business Product*.

A two sector system entails at least two separate "commodities," Q_c and Q_i. Throughout, as a simplification, it will be supposed that $w_c = w_i$, or that average wage levels are equal in each of the sectors.

Profit and Consumption Relations

From the Keynesian identity of $I \equiv S$, where S denotes the savings magnitude, the "All and Nothing" hypothesis entails:

$$I = S = R \qquad (5)$$

$$C = W = W_c + W_i \qquad (6)$$

$$R_c = W_i \qquad (7)$$

Relations (5)–(7) are the "obvious" outcomes of the "All and Nothing" hypothesis. They contain a residue of explanatory insight even when the hypothesis is modified. Their content was not so "obvious" until the Kaldor–Robinson work appeared.

The Income Split in the *I*-Sector

Examining (5), once we are given any I-value, then R is immediately settled. But in relation (3), what determines W_i and thus R_i? And thereafter, W_c? It is at this stage, that is, in determining the income split in the *I*-sector consequent upon any level of *I*-outlay, that a theory of pricing, or a separate theory of income shares, is imperative. Let us pursue this.

From (3), given the money *I*-outlay, how is the *I*-sum split between the two claimants? As in (1) we can write[7]:

$$P_i = (wN_i/Q_i) + (R_i/Q_i)$$
$$= (w/A_i) + (R_i/Q_i) \qquad (1a)$$

$$= (k_iw/A_i) = w/\Theta_iA_i \qquad (1b)$$

Given a price mark-up ratio $k_i(= 1/\Theta_i)$, the system is closed. The income split in the *I*-sector is fixed up, the profit magnitude in the *C*-sector is decided, and thus, with a pricing mechanism in the *C*-sector deciding the income split there, relative income shares and absolute income magnitudes are determined.[8]

C-Sector Activity

In an economy where income is saved—the actual economy—investment is the indispensable ingredient for the maintenance of consumption activity, for otherwise sales receipts in the *C*-sector would always fall below income payments. Investment activity thus performs the vital task of shoaling up the economy, in carrying it to high levels of employment and, through enlarging capacity, to growth.[9]

The Kahn–Keynes "multiplier" described how a "dollar" of investment could lead to a multiple increase of income, in both consumption *and* investment volume. It is superfluous to repeat this familiar tool of macro-theory here. Instead, what will be done, on the "All or Nothing" premise, is to show how the income magnitude in the consumption sector is uniquely tied to the investment magnitude, *and to the distributive phenomena in I and C*, and thus implicitly, to the underlying pricing mechanism. Thus:

$$C \equiv P_cQ_c = R_c + W_c$$
$$= W_i + W_c$$
$$= \Theta_iI + \Theta_c(\Theta_iI) + \cdots$$
$$+ \Theta_c^\infty(\Theta_iI) \qquad (8a)$$

$$= \Theta_iI/(1 - \Theta_c) = I(\Theta_i/\Pi_c) \qquad (8)$$

Equation (8) is of major interest.[10] It reveals that in the "All or Nothing" world the C-volume depends wholly on distributive phenomena and the investment magnitude. If $\Theta_i = \Pi_c$, then $C = I$: both sectors are of equal size. If $\Theta_i > \Pi_c$, the C-sector will be the larger.

Employment and Resource Allocation

Some simple derivations throw added light on the "All and Nothing" economy. The results retain some interest even on more realistic assumptions.

Wage bill: $W = P_c Q_c = I(\Theta_i/\Pi_c)$ (9)

Income: $Z = P_c Q_c + P_i Q_i$
$$= I(1 + \Theta_i/\Pi_c) \qquad (10)$$

Employment: $N = (I/w)(\Theta_i/\Pi_c)$ (11)

Relative sector size: $N_c/N_i = \Theta_c/\Pi_c$ (12)

Resource use: $N_c/N = \Theta_c$ (13)

On the proviso that $\Theta = \Pi$, or that shares are equal in each sector, with each amounting to $\frac{1}{2}$, the wage bill would equal investment, income would be twice I, employment would equal I/w, and sector size $C = I$.

IV. THE "ALL AND SOMETHING" HYPOTHESIS

Greater realism follows from an "All and Something" hypothesis, involving the view that wage earners save nothing while capitalists devote a small part of their income to consumption. Manifestly, with high per capita profit income, per capita capitalist consumption may be high, despite the low c_r ratios. If the capitalist class is small it may be that $c_w W > c_r R$, where $c_r R/C \approx 0$, and $c_w W/C \approx 1$. This situation may describe some underdeveloped regions of the world with huge populations, such as India, where the ordinary standard of living is low but where there exists substantial conspicuous per capita consumption of a small group of wealthy individuals which is dwarfed, in the aggregate, by the sum of the meager consumption intakes of ordinary wage earners.

Profit and Consumption Relations

In this model the definitional relationships are as follows:

$$I = S = s_r R \qquad (14)$$

$$C = W + c_r R \qquad (15)$$

$$R_c = W_i + c_r R \qquad (16)$$

Further, if $W = R$, so that the income split is equal, then $C = W(1 + c_r)$, which approaches W as c_r approaches zero.

C-Sector Activity

Given the investment magnitude, let us consider the elements governing the size of C-activity. Thus:

$$P_c Q_c = W_i + c_{ri} R_i + W_c + c_{rc} R_c \qquad (17a)$$

$$= (\Theta_i + c_{ri}\Pi_i)I + (\Theta_c + c_{rc}\Pi_c)$$
$$\times (\Theta_i + c_{ri}\Pi_i)I + \cdots$$
$$+ (\Theta_c + c_{rc}\Pi_c)^\infty(\Theta_i + c_{ri}\Pi_i)I$$
$$(17b)$$

$$= I(\Theta_i + c_{ri}\Pi_i)/[1 - (\Theta_c + c_{rc}\Pi_c)]$$
$$= I(1 - s_{ri}\Pi_i)/(s_{rc}\Pi_c) \qquad (17)$$

From (17) it follows that high profit shares in the separate sectors, and high savings propensities of the capitalist group, will restrain the volume of C-sector activity.[11] With $s_{rc} = s_{ri} = 1$, we revert back to (8). As an extreme result, with unity savings ratios and unity profit shares, C-activity would grind to a halt.

Employment and Resource Allocation

Writing $\mu = (1 - s_{ir}\Pi_i)/s_{cr}\Pi_c$, the other major characteristics of the "All and Something" economy can be developed.

Wage bill: $W = (\Theta_c\mu + \Theta_i)I$ (18)

Employment: $N = [(\Theta_c\mu + \Theta_i)I]/w$
$$(19)$$

Relative sector size: $N_c/N_i = \Theta_c\mu/\Theta_i$
$$(20)$$

Relative resource use: N_c/N
$$= \Theta_c\mu/(\Theta_c\mu + \Theta_i) \qquad (21)$$

Thus income distribution, the investment level, and the capitalist savings ratio determine the wage bill; the wage rate must be introduced for the employment level. The relative size of the C- and I-sectors is entirely a resultant of the savings ratio and the facts on relative shares.

Implicit, therefore, is the pricing mechanism through which income distribution in the separate sectors is determined. Hence Keynesian employment and income analysis must be supplemented by a theory of price-making and thereupon, income distribution.[12]

Some Simplifications

In the "All and Something" analysis some of the important relations can be approximated by assuming $\Theta_c = \Theta_i$, and $\Pi_i = \Pi_c$, and $s_{rc} = s_{ri}$. That is, the income split in each sector is the same, and that savings out of nonwage income is unrelated to the sector in which profits are earned. Both assumptions are plausible.

On this basis $C = I[(1 - s_r \Pi)/s_r \Pi] = \mu' I$. Thereafter, we could write as approximations:

Wage bill: $W = I(\Theta/_s \Pi)$ (18a)

Relative sector size: $N_c/N_i = \mu'$ (20a)

Relative resource use: $N_c/N = \mu'/(\mu' + 1)$ (21a)

Thus the wage bill depends wholly on distributive phenomena, the savings ratio, and the investment volume; the employment level entails, in addition, the wage rate. Sector size depends entirely upon distributive phenomena and the savings ratio. A high nonwage share will enlarge I-sector relative to C, especially if the consumption propensity of the nonwage group is low.

V. THE "LARGELY AND SOMETHING" HYPOTHESIS

A giant step toward reality follows a "Largely and Something" hypothesis.

That is, wage earners are conceived to save something but still, to spend *most* of their income, perhaps 90 per cent of it, on consumption goods and services. While they save 10 per cent of their income, their chief use of income is in consumption outlays. Nonwage earners display opposite income-allocation propensities, saving most of their income, spending a smaller part. The full step to reality would involve exact specification of the c- and s-ratios and, of course, the size of income shares.

Profit and Consumption Relations

In the "Largely and Something" universe we find the following relations:

$$I = S = s_w W + s_r R \qquad \text{with } s_r > s_w \tag{22}$$

$$C = c_w W + c_r R \qquad \text{with } c_w > c_r \tag{23}$$

$$\begin{aligned} R_c &= c_r R + c_w W_i - s_w W_c \\ &= c_r R + W_i - s_w (W_i + W_c) \end{aligned} \tag{24}$$

Thus capitalist consumption augments C-profits, and wage earner savings reduce C-profits.[13]

C-Sector Activity

Expanding (25) as was done earlier in (8) and (17), we find:

$$P_c Q_c = \frac{c_{wi} + \Pi_i (c_{ri} - c_{wi})}{s_{rc} + \Theta_c (c_{rc} - c_{wc})}$$

$$I = \frac{c_{wi} (1 - m\Pi_i)}{s_{rc} (1 - n\Theta_c)}$$

$$I = vI \tag{25}$$

In (25), $m < 1 > n$.

From (25) it follows that a high profit share in the I-sector, with a low consumption proclivity for profit recipients, will curtail C-sector activity. A high savings propensity for capitalists in the C-sector, and a high profit share, spells the same outcome. A high wage share in the consumption sector would lift C-activity.

Assuming $m\Pi_i = n\Theta_c$, or that they are *nearly* equal, we have the interesting result that $C = I(c_{wi}/s_{rc})$. That is, that the consumption ratio of workers in capital goods, and the nonwage consumption ratio in the C-sector, along with the I-magnitude, fixes the extent of C-activity. This seems to be the major conclusion for the more realistic "Largely and Something" case.

Employment and Resource Allocation

On the "Largely and Something" hypothesis:

Wage bill: $W = I(\Theta_c v + \Theta_i)$
$$\approx \Theta I(v + 1) \qquad (26)$$

Relative sector size: $N_c/N_i = \Theta_c v/\Theta_i \approx v$
$$\qquad (27)$$

Relative resource use: N_c/N
$$= \Theta_c v/(\Theta_c v + \Theta_i) \approx v/(v + 1) \qquad (28)$$

The approximations here are based on the supposition of $\Theta_c = \Theta_i$. Adopting the $m\Pi_i = n\Theta_c$ hypothesis, the decisive importance of the c_w/s_r relation emerges.

In sum, savings propensities and relative shares, and the investment volume and the money wage, determine the basic economic phenomena. The price mechanism, through which shares are decided, looms in the background as an arbiter of activity and of the relative size of the C-

and I-sectors: pricing decisions cannot be ignored in determining the macroeconomic variables in view of their impact on distributive shares.

VI. A RECAPITULATION

The several results can be combined for ready reference. The tabular presentation indicates the major relations that have been deduced.[14] If we assume $\Theta_c = \Theta_i$ and thus $\Pi_c = \Pi_i$, the Keynesian multipliers yielding $Z \equiv C + I$ emerge simply as:

(1) All and Nothing: $Z = I/\Pi$
(2) All and Something: $Z = I/s_r\Pi$
(3) Largely and Something:
$$Z = I/(s_w\Theta + s_r\Pi)$$

VII. MONOPOLY, MONETARY POLICY, THE MONEY WAGE, AND GOVERNMENT

We now consider some further aspects of the economy omitted until now, specifically the influence of : (1) monopoly

Table—A Recapitulation of Relationships

VARIABLE OR RATIO	ASSUMPTION ALL AND NOTHING	ALL AND SOMETHING	LARGELY AND SOMETHING
(1) Investment and profits: $I = S =$	R	$s_r R$	$s_w W + s_r R$
(2) C-sector profits: $R_c =$	W_i	$W_i + c_r R$	$W_i + c_r R - s_w(W_i + W_c)$
(3) Value of C-output: $C =$	$W = I(\theta_i/\Pi_c)$	$W + c_r R = \mu I$	$c_w W + c_r R = vI$
(4) Wage bill:	$I(\theta_i/\Pi_c)$	$I(\theta_c\mu + \theta_i)$	$I(\theta_c v + \theta_i)$
(5) Employment structure: $N_c/N_i =$	(θ_c/Π_c)	$\theta_c\mu/(\theta_c\mu + \theta_i)$	$\theta_c v/(\theta_c v + \theta_i)$
(6) Relative size of C-sector: $N_c/N =$	θ_c	$\theta_c\mu/\theta_i$	$\theta_c v/\theta_i$

Note: In (3)–(6), $\mu = (1 - s_{ri}\Pi_i)/s_{rc}\Pi_c$ and $v = c_{wi}(1 - m\Pi_i)/s_{rc}(1 - n\theta_c)$. Also, $mc_{wi} = c_{wi} - c_{ri}$, and $ns_{rc} = s_{rc} - s_{wc}$

pricing, (2) monetary policy, (3) money wage changes, and (4) government tax and expenditure policy.

Monopoly Power

Consider, first, the effect of a rise in prices through monopoly pricing and, to begin with, assume that it occurs in the I-sector. It will simplify matters to consider this solely in the "Largely and Something" model.

We are faced with two alternatives here. We can assume that the money-I level is constant, or that the "real"-I is constant; in the latter event the money-I rises with a rise in monopoly power in the I-sector. To analyze the latter case involves study of two forces, a price force and an incremental money-I force. Hence it is easier, with no loss in generality, to hold money-I constant.

A rise in monopoly power will involve an increase in k_i and thus, a fall in the wage share Θ_i. Examining (25), this must portend a fall in C-sector activity, as well as a fall in N_i. Thus total employment will be lower, but the fall in money income will be confined to the C-sector by virtue of the hypothesis of money-I unchanged. According to (27), however, the size of the I-sector should shrink by more than C. In the "All and Nothing" model the relative sector size would not alter while in the "All and Something" circumstances the C-sector would grow relatively.

A heightened degree of monopoly power in the C-sector, involving a lower wage share there would, in the "All and Nothing" world, lower income and employment, and reduce the relative size of C. With "All and Something," the wage bill would be reduced in C, employment would fall, and the relative C-size would diminish. In the "Largely and Something" situation, more or less the same effects follow: employment, wage bill, and the relative C-size would be cut.

A rise in monopoly power always moves us closer to the "All and Nothing" world

in that it shifts income in favor of profit recipients with high savings propensities, and away from workers whose spending ratios are larger. Monopoly power, therefore, whether emanating in the C- or I-industries, requires a higher investment volume to offset its damaging employment consequences. The size of the money-I increment required will be mitigated to the extent that the propensity to consume of nonwage recipients approaches that of wage earners. Insofar as $c_r \to 0$, and $c_w \to 1$, the necessary investment load increases.[15]

Examining the case most vulnerable to unemployment under monopoly pricing tactics, the "All and Nothing" situation, if initially $\Theta_i = \Pi_c = .5$, and if monopoly pricing shifts the shares to $\Theta_i = .48$ and $\Pi_c = .52$, the effect would be to reduce employment by 1.5 million if $I = \$100$ billions and $w = \$5,000$. Small distributive changes can thus inflict substantial unemployment damage. (See formula (11).)

Monetary Mischief

Suppose that either C-sector or I-sector prices go up as a consequence of monopoly power, exemplified by an increase in the k mark-up. In these circumstances, with money wages constant at $\bar{w}$, unless the monetary authority can somehow accomplish a rise in A—the average productivity of labor—any effort on its part to "fight" inflation will entail sorry consequences for the economy. Tight money to combat inflation—and central banks seem always to be on a nontriumphal crusade against inflation—must operate to cut the I-volume. Yet unemployment engendered by monopoly pricing requires a *greater* investment volume, not a smaller volume of investment. Thus in an economy where monopoly power is increasing, inflation can scarcely be countered by monetary policy.[16] Tighter money can only compound the mischief, and may be disastrous in the final outcome.

Insofar as tight money *cuts* investment, and delays the introduction of 'cost-saving equipment, it must over time tend to *raise* prices. The only circumstance in which money policy can thus be effective in restraining the price trend—for it is doubtful if in the modern world of rigid wages it is likely to accomplish a price downturn—is by creating enough unemployment to institute some restraint on the money wage upsweep. The consequences on employment may be frightful, especially compared to a policy which has a more direct impact on money wages.[17]

Money Wages Changes

A rigid money wage level has been premised thus far. Assuming that the money wage rises, either exogenously or through Phillips curve relationships as unemployment narrows, the general macroeconomic effects can be traced. First, the price level will be affected, other things unchanged. If the *I*-sum is unchanged, the only effect is on employment, for the wage level also enters into this relationship. On the other hand, if the *I*-magnitude changes to reflect the higher prices, and to maintain real investment constant, then *C*, *W*, and *R* will also alter. Total money income, comprised of *C* + *I*, will of course be higher.

Given an increase in the average money wage level *w*, if prices rise proportionately with wages, and the real output level is unchanged, then the relative increase in profits will equal the relative wage increase.

Higher money wages and a higher sum of money profits, in an economy in which continuing *I*-outlays are contingent upon realized profits, can have important effects over time on money *I*, *and on real I*. For in a more realistic setting the higher prices shift income from rentiers to profit recipients, thereby lightening the debt burden. Further, the Stock Market need not be free of money illusion; higher money profits can affect equity prices disproportion-

ately, thereby influencing the course of real-*I* in subsequent time intervals.[18]

One further observation on the treatment of money wages as largely an exogenous variable. In the modern economy it is not uncommon for money wages to be fixed up ahead by collective bargaining agreements, for one to three year periods. Under these circumstances it is not unreasonable to treat *w* as settled for the unfolding months according to "outside" forces, namely, the prevailing contractual agreements.

Government

Government outlays and tax policies have been overlooked. We can indicate briefly how they may be incorporated into the argument.

1. Government, in implementing its programs, buys some goods from the *I*-sector. Insofar as it does so, these purchases belong under the *I*-category as "honorary investment," as D. H. Robertson once termed these outlays.[19]

2. Government hires civil servants and pays them wages (W_g). These aggregate amounts can also be regarded as a form of "honorary investment," but *on which profits are not earned*. The effects of W_g are thus transmitted to the *C*-sector through civil servant consumption intake.

3. Government buys ordinary *C*-goods for its own "household" needs (G_c). It also undertakes transfer payments to an assorted group of income recipients. These sums, too, have a "*C*-multiplier" effect on the *C*-output level analogous to wages in the *I*-sector.

4. Government levies income taxes on wage and profit incomes. Interpreting *W* and *R* as *before tax* magnitudes, the effect of income taxes is to reduce the *c*- and *s*-ratios in our formulae for the wage and profit recipients involved.

5. Insofar as Government levies sales and excise taxes, the simplest way to deal

with these is to utilize an income concept *net* of such taxes, so that we can still write $\Theta + \Pi = 1$. Otherwise, we have a new income share to contend with, namely that accruing to Government as a sort of "monopoly" income with proceeds redounding to the Treasury in a 3-way income split.[20]

VII. WAGE EARNERS AND CAPITALISTS?

The personification of income recipients as either wage earners [or] capitalists has not been evaluated in the foregoing pages.

Undoubtedly, many will feel uncomfortable with the characterization of income recipients as "workers," or wage earners, and "capitalists," or profit recipients. Perhaps the designation was fairly apt not so long ago in England and in the United States; it is not accurate now (though it may fit some lesser developed economies).

Largely, the argument could be maintained if the behavior of those receiving both wage *and* profit income was of the nature outlined: that is, if each individual compartmentalized his income into one or the other, and followed one or the other of the behavior patterns outlined.[21] Needless to say, many would reject this as an artificial description of income behavior. Especially serious would be its omission of the corporation as a source of income retention or saving.[22]

On the other hand, it is not implausible to characterize income recipients as belonging to a "low" income group, or as belonging to a "high" income group, with the former being substituted for "wage earners" in the foregoing analysis, and the latter displacing the profit group. "High" incomes and "low" incomes do conform to modern versions of capitalists and wage earners. Further, in recognition that in our economic world a good part of *Gross Business Product* (netted for excise and sales taxes) adheres to corporate entities

and institutions, the latter bodies would have to be counted in the "high" income group. For through undistributed profits and depreciation allowances, most of the gross savings in our economy—and these are linked to the investment volume—are performed by corporate entities rather than by individuals.[23]

What is the cut-off? How high is a "high" income? A "low" income? Undoubtedly, we are faced with an arbitrary classification, though not necessarily more arbitrary than characterizing individuals as "workers" or "capitalists." For the United States at the present time, a figure of $10,000 of income might serve as the bench-mark for classifying individuals and institutions up or down. Whatever the exact height of the income cut-off selected, the analytic apparatus outlined can then be brought into play for macroeconomics.[24]

IX. A RECONCILIATION OF MARGINAL PRODUCTIVITY AND MACRO-DISTRIBUTION THEORIES?

Possibly, the foregoing pages offer some means of reconciling the older marginal productivity theories of distribution, and the new macrotheories promulgated by Mrs. Robinson and Mr. Kaldor. For insofar as the distribution of shares has its origin in the pricing mechanism the door is opened to the older theories. For the k-magnitudes in either the C- or I-sectors will be determined by the forces of competition and monopoly, and the facts on profit maximization. If pure competition and profit maximization hold true for commodity markets, then k will reflect this set of facts as firms equate, at each market price, the marginal value product of labor to the money wage. If monopoly profit maximization occurs, it will be the marginal revenue product relations that will prevail in the firms as they adjust labor's marginal revenue contribution to the money wage. If profit maximization is rejected, this, too, will be reflected in the ruling k-magnitudes.

Simultaneously, the analysis stresses the crucial role of investment, income distribution, and the savings propensities in deciding the magnitude of total activity, the C- and I- profit levels, the wage bill, employment, and the relative sector size.

If this reconciliation is rejected by those who hold fast to one view or the other, what could be insisted on is that the theory of price-making, and the theory of income distribution, cannot be excluded from macroeconomic models of income determination and employment.

NOTES

1 Nicholas Kaldor, "Alternative Theories of Distribution," *The Review of Economic Studies*, Vol. XXIII, Cambridge, 1955–1956, pp. 83 sqq.—*Idem*, "Economic Growth and the Problem of Inflation," *Economica*, N. S., Vol. XXVI, London, 1959, pp. 212 sqq., 287 sqq.—*Idem*, "A Rejoinder to Mr. Findlay," *The Review of Economic Studies*, Vol. XXVII, 1959–1960, pp. 179 sqq.—*Idem*, "Marginal Productivity and the Macro-Economic Theories of Distribution, Comment on Samuelson and Modigliani," *ibid.*, Vol. XXXIII, 1966, pp. 309 sqq.—*Idem*, and James A. Mirrlees, "A New Model of Economic Growth," *ibid.*, Vol. XXIX, 1961–1962, pp. 174 sqq. —Luigi L. Pasinetti, "Rate of Profit and Income Distribution in Relation to the Rate of Economic Growth," *ibid.*, pp. 267 sqq.— *Idem*, "New Results in an Old Framework, Comment on Samuelson and Modigliani," *ibid.*, Vol. XXXIII, 1966, pp. 303 sqq.— Joan Robinson, *The Accumulation of Capital*, London, 1956.—*Idem*, "Comment on Samuelson and Modigliani," *The Review of Economic Studies*, Vol. XXXIII, 1966, pp. 307 sq.—*Idem*, *Collected Economic Papers*, Oxford, 1960, Vol. 2.

2 Their arguments are very general. They dispense with assumptions of linear and homogeneous production functions, or of factor divisibility or homogeneity, long the bane of capital theory. The analysis is independent of the assumption of profit maximization, the supposition of pure competition, or of the need for identifica- tion of the elusive entrepreneur for the attribution of profits. See Kaldor, "Marginal Productivity," *op. cit.*, p. 309.

3 Cf. Lawrence Klein's remarks on "the need to close the system by extending it in such a way that the price level is explained." Lawrence R. Klein, *The Keynesian Revolution*, 2nd ed., New York, 1966, pp. 194, 217 sqq.

4 In my own experience, when I came to write on this subject over ten years ago, I was unable to find any significant guidance in the macroeconomic literature. See Sidney Weintraub, *An Approach to the Theory of Income Distribution*, Philadelphia, 1958.—For some recognition of the problem see K. R. Boulding, *A Reconstruction of Economics*, New York, 1950, Chap. 14.

5 From the truism $PQ = kwN$, so that $(PQ/wN) = k$, or $\Theta = (wN/PQ)$, where $N =$ employment and $Q =$ real output. See Sidney Weintraub, *A General Theory of the Price Level, Output, Income Distribution, and Economic Growth*, Philadelphia and New York, 1959, Chap. 2.

6 I find no evidence of any serious change in k in recent years. See John Hotson, *International Comparisons of the Wage Mark-Up and Money Velocity*, New York, 1968, for some international estimates, and comparisons to money velocity.

7 The mark-up $k_i = 1 + R/wN = 1/\Theta_i$.

8 Kaldor avoided this in his earlier article by *assuming* full employment or thus, a predetermined income level. Considering the income and employment variability of Keynesian analysis, this is too restrictive a hypothesis. See Kaldor, "Alternative Theories of Distribution," *op. cit.*, p. 95.— As Mrs. Robinson remarked (*Collected Economic Papers, op. cit.*, Vol. 2, p. 149): "The proposition that the share of profits in income is a function of the ratio of investment to income is perfectly correct, but capacity and the degree of monopoly have to be brought in to determine what income it is that profits are a share of, and investment is a ratio to."

9 As Kaldor remarks, the Keynesian revolution was substantially one of recognizing the dominating position of investment. Thus he writes: "Keynes's theory of income generation—which can be summed up by saying... that it is investment which determines savings, and not savings which determine investment—was the really novel feature of his *General Theory*." Kaldor, "Economic Growth," *op. cit.*,

p. 214.—Also: *idem* and Mirrlees, *op. cit.*, p. 175.—Kaldor, "Marginal Productivity," *op. cit.*, p. 312, note.

10 The derivation of (8) should be obvious: the expenditure of W_i leads to a "multiplier" chain of additional income and wage-earner consumption outlay in the C-sector.

11 The terms in (8) and (17), exclusive of I, might be called a "truncated" multiplier for, unlike the Kahn–Keynes multiplier, it includes only the income chain in the C-sector, rather than the entire income chain in C *and* I.

12 Cf. Klein, *op. cit.*, pp. 217 sqq.

13 It is from relation (22) that Kaldor derives his well-known formula for the profit share, namely, that:

$$R/Y = [1/(s_r - s_w)](I/Y) - [s_w/(s_r - s_w)]$$

where Y, in Kaldor's formulation, denotes full employment income. Thus Kaldor is assuming that not only is I given but that C is predetermined, independently of pricing and the income split in the C-sector. Treating Y as a variable requires the theory of the "truncated" C-sector multiplier as in (8), (17), or (25). Cf. Kaldor, "Alternative Theories of Distribution," *op. cit.*, p. 95.

14 Profit share $\Pi\ (\equiv R/Z)$ can be formed from $I = R$, $I = s_r R$, and $I = s_w W + s_r R$ on line (1) by dividing through by z and transposing the W- and s-terms. For the rate of profit (R/K), where K denotes the value of capital, the same equations can be used. These are the important results emphasized by Professors Kaldor and Robinson.

15 Analytically, with $I = \bar{I}$ so the money-I level is maintained, monopoly power in the I-sector will lower W_i, and thus the numerator of our "truncated"-C multipliers by an amount $\Delta R_i\ (c_{wi} - c_{ri})$, where $\Delta R_i = w\Delta N_i$. Monopoly in the consumer sector will lower Θ_c to $\lambda\Theta_c$, where $\lambda < 1$, and raise Π_c to $\varepsilon\Pi_c$, where $\varepsilon > 1$. All the formulae can be modified in this way.

16 On all this, see the valuable recent analysis of Professor Abba P. Lerner, "Employment Theory and Employment Policy," *The American Economic Review*, Vol. LVII, Menasha, Wisc., 1967, Papers and Proceedings, pp. 1 sqq.

17 Thus if an Incomes Policy could command a fair degree of assent, keeping government intervention to a minimum, it would be far more instrumental for inflation control than the clumsy manœuvres in monetary policy which always tend to have a negative output-employment incidence.

18 Cf. Sidney Weintraub, *Employment Growth and Income Distribution*, Philadelphia and New York, 1966, Chap. 9.—Kaldor observes ("Economic Growth," *op. cit.*, p. 290) that "a slow and steady rate of inflation provides a most powerful aid to the attainment of a steady rate of economic progress."—On "inflation breeding inflation" through shifting Phillips curves as a price level rise is anticipated, see Edmund S. Phelps, "Phillips Curves, Expectations of Inflation and Optimal Unemployment Over Time," *Economica*, N. S., Vol. XXXIV, 1967, pp. 254 sqq.

19 D. H. Robertson, "Mr. Clark and the Foreign Trade Multiplier," *The Economic Journal*, Vol. XLIX, London, 1939, p. 354, note 3.

20 On excise taxes likened to "monopoly" prices, with the Treasury the beneficiary of the higher price, see Joan Robinson, *The Economics of Imperfect Competition*, London, 1933, p. 164.—Writing C_{net} to refer to C-output net of excise taxes, and I_{p+g} to denote private and government I-outlays, with c' and s' to represent the ratios after income taxes, for the "Largely and Something" case we have:

$$C_{\text{net}} = \frac{(c'_{wi}\Theta_i + c'_{ri}\Pi_i)I_{p+g} + c'_g W_g + G_c}{s'_{wc}\Theta_c + s'_{rc}\Pi_c} \tag{29}$$

21 Pasinetti ("Rate of Profit and Income Distribution," *op. cit.*, p. 273) comes near to saying this in the remark that "savings out of wages always turn out to be equal to workers' extra consumption out of profits."

22 Working wholly in terms of *personal* income, by wage or non-wage types, Burmeister and Taubman find "that s_r is twice the size of s_w," in the 10–17 per cent and 23–30 per cent range respectively. See Edwin Burmeister and Paul Taubman, *Labor and Non-Labor Income-Saving Propensities*, University of Pennsylvania Economics Department, Discussion Paper No. 65 (mimeogr.), p. 13 (forthcoming, *The Canadian Journal of Economics*, Toronto). For the "low-high" income classification suggested, these figures would probably be too high for the "low-income" group and too low for the "high-income" part of the total.

23 For example, in the United States in 1967, Personal Savings amounted to $40.2

billions, Capital Consumption Allowances were $69.2 billions, and Undistributed Profits were $25.2 billions. Thus even if all personal savings were performed by wage earners, 70 per cent of the total gross savings would have been contributed by corporate entities. The latter are the modern "capitalists." See *Survey of Current Business*, Vol. XLVIII, Washington, D.C., August 1968.

24 This approach would have the further advantage of aligning macroeconomics with the theory of personal (rather than functional) distribution where good data are available. The *c*- and *s*-ratios would have to be computed as averages for the aggregate of total income by each "group." For the corporate gross income consisting entirely of undistributed profits before taxes and depreciation allowances, the savings ratio would be unity. This would apply to a share (in *Gross Business Product* in 1967) as large as 19 per cent of total business sector income.

Role of Expectations in Economic Theory
Dudley Dillard

The volume of employment is determined by the propensity to consume and the inducement to invest. Since the propensity to consume is relatively stable, fluctuations in employment depend primarily upon the inducement to invest. The two determinants of the inducement to invest are the rate of interest and the marginal efficiency of capital. Since the rate of interest is relatively "sticky," fluctuations in the inducement to invest depend primarily upon changes in the marginal efficiency of capital. The two determinants of the marginal efficiency of capital are the supply price or cost and the prospective yield or return. It is the prospective yield which gives the marginal efficiency of capital its most important characteristic, its instability. Hence, a great part of the instability of economic life under capitalism is attributable to the unstable character of prospective yields from capital assets. Since it is important to account for instability of employment, and because of the role played by prospective yields in this connection, it becomes important to

Dudley Dillard, "Expectations," in *The Economics of John Maynard Keynes* (Englewood Cliffs, N.J.: Prentice-Hall, Inc., 1948), pp. 142–153.

explore the nature of the forces which determine prospective yields.

These yields which figure so prominently in determining the volume of employment are *prospective* yields because at the time an investment is made they are nothing but expectations on the part of the investor. The expectations may never be realized at all, and an entrepreneur does not really believe that everything will turn out just as he predicts when the investment is made. In other words, the investor expects to be "surprised," either favorably or unfavorably, because he cannot honestly hope that events will actually unfold in exactly the way he foresees as most probable. Thus investment decisions are governed by expectations of yield and not by actual yields. Because of the nature of capital assets, especially those of a durable type, large immediate outlays are required before any actual returns can begin to flow back to the investor. Capital assets are a link between the present and the uncertain future.

A prospective yield is what an entrepreneur expects to obtain from selling the output of his capital assets. There are two types of expectations regarding the yields of assets: (1) short-term expectations and

(2) long-term expectations. Short-term expectations concern the sales proceeds from the output of existing plant. Long-term expectations concern the sales proceeds which an entrepreneur can hope to earn with variations in the size of his plant or from the building of entirely new plant. In short-term expectations, the plant is assumed to be of a fixed size; only the output from that given sized plant is variable. In long-term expectations, the size of the plant as well as the amount of output from plant is variable.

Short-Term Expectations

Short-term expectations are more stable than long-term expectations because the *realized* results of the recent past are a relatively safe guide to what will happen in the near future, whereas there exists no past experience which will serve as a comparably safe guide to what will happen in the distant future. Realized results of past activity are important only in so far as they influence current expectations about the future. It is always the current expectations concerning prospective future yields that are relevant to current investment and therefore to current employment. In the case of short-term expectations, most of the circumstances which influence current output remain substantially the same from day to day or from week to week or month to month. In economic life, as in other areas of experience, there is a high degree of continuity over short periods. In the absence of definite evidence for expecting a change, the most recent events may be expected to continue in the near future. By their very nature, short-term expectations are subject to frequent check in the light of realized results. Since realized results are a satisfactory guide to the near future, it is relatively safe to substitute these realized results for expectations relating to the near future. Short-term expectations are relatively stable. Hence, it may be concluded that short-term expectations are less important than they would be if realized results of the recent past were not a relatively safe guide to what to expect in the near future. It is not necessary to try to predict the future when only short-term plans are in question. It is safe to rely upon past results.

Long-Term Expectations

In contrast with short-term expectations, long-term expectations regarding the probable yields of new investments in durable plant and equipment are highly unstable and therefore more important in explaining the fluctuations in aggregate investment and aggregate employment in the economic system. While we may safely assume that economic activity next week will be approximately what it was during the past week, experience tells us that we cannot safely assume the next five years will be approximately like the past five years as concerns events which will determine the yields to be received from current investments. Realized results of past years are not a trustworthy guide to future years. It is not possible in the case of durable assets to check expectations against realized results at short intervals as can be done in the case of short-term expectations.

There are some considerations affecting long-term expectations which do not rest upon the shifting sands of a precarious future. Decisions to invest are partly based upon facts regarding the existing stock of capital assets. Especially relevant are the types of assets which will be available to compete with the projected new investment. For example, a decision to build a new steel plant depends partly upon the amount of existing steel capacity. Steel capacity is a fact that can be ascertained with more or less certainty. Likewise, the ability of the existing capacity to meet the existing demand at the prices being paid for current output are data of a more or less definite nature.

But as we begin to look ahead, the horizon becomes more clouded. The probable life and maintenance of the plant the construction of which is being contemplated cannot be accurately predicted. Still less predictable are such considerations as possible changes in technology in the steel industry which would influence the rate of obsolescence of the projected plant. In the precarious zone are considerations of the general level of effective demand 10 or 20 years hence, the amount of new competition, the prices which can be realized from year to year, the prospect of war, the size of the export market, changes in tax burdens, conditions in the labor market including the level of wages and freedom from strikes, and finally, the political climate of future decades which will influence the extent of social control over industry. Concerning these latter events, there is no probability calculus upon which to base scientific judgments.

Our general ignorance of the future and the precariousness of the basis of what we think we do know about the future stand out above all other aspects of long-term expectations in an unplanned economy. The distant future is never clearly foreseen and this is especially true when entrepreneurial decisions are made by a large number of private entrepreneurs whose decisions are uncoordinated. Nevertheless, mere social survival, not to speak of economic progress, requires that decisions be made no matter how precarious the basis upon which they rest. The upshot of the extreme precariousness of the circumstances in which long-term expectations are formed is the great instability which characterizes these expectations and the consequent instability of economic life in general. Long-term expectations are subject to sudden revisions. Periods of feverish investment activity tend to be followed by periods of extreme pessimism and depression in which investment in durable capital assets falls to an extremely low level.

In making a most probable forecast as to what will happen to a long-term investment, not much weight is or can be attached to matters which are very uncertain. We cannot act in any positive fashion upon what we do not know. Hence, there is a tendency for long-term expectations to be influenced to a disproportionate degree by the ascertainable facts of the current situation and to assume that the existing summing up of the future is correct and that things will continue as they are in the absence of specific reasons for changing our expectations. Nevertheless, the things we do not know exert a powerful influence upon investment activity. For the degree of confidence with which most probable forecasts are made is affected by what we do not know. It is lack of confidence in the most probable forecasts which renders investment decisions so subject to sudden shifts. Furthermore, when there is great uncertainty about which of several alternative investment opportunities offers the highest return, there is a tendency to postpone a positive decision in the hope that the view of the future will become clearer at a later date. Thus, even when there is confidence that profitable investment opportunities do exist, the lack of confidence in ability to determine which is most profitable will tend to depress the marginal efficiency of capital and reduce the volume of investment and employment. Investors with limited resources cannot exploit all investment opportunities they believe will turn out to be profitable, and therefore they will try to make certain that their limited resources are placed where the returns are maximized. The belief that knowledge will improve is a cause of apathy in the investment market. If for some reason the vista seems to become clearer to a significant degree, apathy will give way to a wave of new investment. This bunching of positive decisions to invest following a period of apathy is one of the causes of fluctuations in employment.[1]

Influence of the Stock Market upon Prospective Yields

The prevailing state of long-term expectations in modern capitalistic societies is reflected in the activities of the stock exchange. When prospective yields are viewed favorably, stock prices tend to be high; and when prospective yields are viewed unfavorably, stock prices tend to be depressed. A purchase of securities does not, of course, represent real investment. It is purely a financial transaction involving the transfer of titles to existing wealth and does not involve the production of new wealth or of social income. Securities traded on the stock exchange are "old stocks" already outstanding in the hands of the public. When one party purchases such stocks, representing claims to existing capital assets, he increases his individual investment. But at the same time someone else disinvests to the same extent when he sells the securities. The sale is equal to the purchase and the disinvestment is equal to the investment. Aggregate social investment, as well as aggregate financial investment, remains unchanged as a result of stock exchange transactions. What matters for employment is the use of men and materials to build new factories and other forms of capital assets. When real investments of this type are made, new securities may be floated through investment banking channels and thereafter the securities may be traded on the stock exchange.

How then does stock market activity affect real investment and employment? The prices of "old" securities traded on the stock exchange influences the prices at which "new" securities can be floated in the new investment market. When the price of old securities is high, the price of new securities will tend to be high also. Ability to float new securities at high prices will encourage investment in new projects on a scale which might seem extravagant in other circumstances. High quotations for existing stocks mean that the marginal efficiency of capital for this type of enterprise is high in relation to the rate of interest and consequently the inducement to invest is strong. It is cheaper to build new capital assets of a given variety than to buy the claims to existing capital assets of the same variety. On the other hand, when the prices of securities on the stock exchange are low, it will be cheaper to buy claims to existing enterprises than to build new capital assets; the supply price (cost of building new capital assets) exceeds the demand price (present value of existing capital assets discounted at the current rate of interest); or, to express the same idea in still another way, the marginal efficiency of capital is below the rate of interest. This condition is unfavorable to the inducement to invest. In general, new investment in many types of capital assets is governed by quotations in the stock market.

In highly organized markets like the stock exchange, existing investments are revalued daily, even hourly. The chief basis for changes in valuations are changes in current expectations concerning future events which will influence future yields. Such markets are links between the present and the future. Any event that is expected to happen in the future is taken into account ("discounted") in the present prices of securities. When an event actually occurs, it will influence the prices of securities only in so far as it is "unexpected" in the sense that it has not been foreseen, or has been "uncertain" in the sense that the event confirms views previously held with less than complete confidence. For example, several commerical airplane crashes occurring over a weekend are likely to depress the prices of commercial airline stocks when the exchange opens on Monday morning because these crashes will not have been foreseen. Presidential veto of a bill to reduce business taxes, which veto has been generally expected but concerning which there has been some doubt, may tend to depress the prices of securities because what was previously uncertain becomes certain. However, in the latter case the effect will probably not be great since the veto will have been largely discounted in advance.

Speculative activity in the stock exchange contributes to the instability of the marginal efficiency of capital. If "speculation" is defined as the attempt to forecast the psychology of the market, and "enterprise" as the attempt to forecast the yield of assets over their entire life, Keynes concludes that the state of long-term expectations which governs the quotations of securities in the stock exchange is more the result of speculation than of enterprise. The tendency for speculation to outrun enterprise arises from various psychological and institutional factors connected with the precarious basis of knowledge regarding the future. Investors are aware that their individual judgments about the long-term future are practically worthless and they tend to rely upon the judgment of others who may be better informed. This is especially true of the mass of amateur investors who do not possess even the technical and business knowledge which is utilized by professionals. The main concern is what other people think. It is assumed that existing quotations accurately reflect the future, so that in the absence of specific reasons for expecting a change it is further assumed that there will be no major shifts in the market in the near future. Therefore, the only major risk lies in a change of news and views in the near future. Even the amateur may feel capable of judging the significance of new knowledge in relation to changes in stock prices. Since the market is "liquid," i.e., since anyone can sell out on a moment's notice if something drastic should happen, the investor need not worry about the long-term prospects of the enterprise in which he invests because there is no need to continue to hold these securities for a long time. Thus, in practice, long-term expectations rest upon the acceptance of a conventional judgment, i.e., the acceptance of the unique correctness of the existing estimate of the future and the assumption that only genuine new knowledge will cause a significant change. The widespread acceptance of this convention gives a certain stability to the market *so long as the convention is maintained.*

The separation of ownership from management in modern corporate business enterprise has fostered reliance upon conventional judgments. The ignorance of most shareholders in regard to the organization and functioning of the business enterprise of which they are part owners diminishes the profitability of professional attempts to judge long-term prospective yields. Instead of trying to estimate the probable yields of capital assets over their entire life, investors are guided under modern institutional arrangements by forecasts of the psychology of the market over the relatively short run. The quotations which will exist at any time reflect the dominant opinion of the mass of participants. If the dominant opinion three months hence is optimistic, the market will be good; and if dominant opinion three months hence is pessimistic, the market will be bad. One who wishes to make money in the stock market should then try to forecast what the predominant opinion will be three months hence. Since the dominant opinion is largely a conventional matter, those who make the most money in the stock market will be those who are most successful in forecasting what average opinion thinks average opinion will be three months from now. Investment becomes a psychological game which can be played by amateur and professional alike.

The investor who wishes to base his behavior upon more genuine and scientific forecasts of long-term yields is confronted with at least two major obstacles. First, the intrinsic difficulty of accurately judging the long-term future makes all such forecasts extremely precarious. There exists hardly any basis for being "scientific" in judging the prospects of a transoceanic steamship line 20 years hence. Think of the great French liner, *Normandie*, in the year 1935. Within less than ten years she had been the victim of war, fire, and scrapping. Second, the long-term yield is largely irrelevant in relation to what the price of an asset will be next week or next month. If a security now selling at 100 is expected to be down to 50 ten years hence but up to 120 next month, it is more profitable to buy the security now and sell it next month than to sell now merely because the long-term future is gloomy. The most profitable occupation for even the skilled forecaster is to anticipate market psychology, to rationalize the irrational activities of the mob of less skilled participants in the market. Hence "speculation" tends to dominate "enterprise" in the stock market.

A conventional judgment which rests on the mass psychology of a group of investors who are without knowledge or conviction about real market forces affecting long-term yields is a highly unstable basis upon which to build the capital development of a country. Resting as it does upon the assumption that things will continue as they now are unless there is reason to expect a change, the conventional judgment is stable only as long as the convention holds, i.e., as long as there is no reason to expect things to change. Ignorant investors are in no position to judge what kind of factors will make a real difference and so they may be provoked into a chain reaction of pessimism or optimism by superficial events which bear no relation to the actual long-term yield of an enterprise. Doubt as to the significance of some new event may lead to further doubt as to whether the present state of the market does sum up accurately the future. In the event of a consensus that present security prices do not accurately

reflect the future, stability, based on a convention that no longer holds, gives way to erratic fluctuations. Like all speculation based on ignorance, the market is subject to unreasonable spurts and irrational collapses. "Speculators may do no harm as bubbles on a steady stream of enterprise. But the position is serious when enterprise becomes the bubble on a whirlpool of speculation. When the capital development of a country becomes a by-product of the activities of a casino, the job is likely to be ill-done."[2]

New investment is facilitated on the one hand and impeded on the other by markets organized with a view to individual liquidity. In highly organized markets like the stock exchange, the individual wealth-owner holds his assets in a form which can readily be converted into cash. Investment is facilitated because the stock exchange enables the investor, as an individual, to liquidate his holdings at any time. This encourages individual investors to contribute to the risk-taking involved in new enterprises. On the other hand, the separation of ownership from control, the general ignorance of the majority of investors, the mass psychology which dominates the market, and the undue weight given to superficial occurrences, render the market supersensitive to slight disturbances and make the individual prone to convert his holdings into money upon relatively slight provocation, leading to easy breakdown and to a dampening of prospective yields which weaken the inducement to invest. Liquidity exists for the individual investor but not for the community as a whole. Individuals may dispose of their holdings in enterprises with specialized plant and equipment, but there is no way by which the community as a whole can liquidate these fixed assets. But in their desire to liquidate, individuals who make up the community depress the marginal efficiency of capital, weakening the inducement to invest and increasing unemployment for the community as a whole. Prior to the separation of ownership from management and the emergence of organized stock exchanges, decisions to invest in enterprise were irrevocable for the individual as well as for the community as a whole. A major contribution of the stock market is the ease with which capital can be mobilized for the development of new productive wealth, but a great disadvantage is the associated instability arising from a speculative liquidity which can lead to a paralyzing collapse of the existing productive capacity of society.

It would be misleading to suppose that instability of investment decisions is entirely the outcome of rational calculations and speculative conventions within the framework of an irrational institutional setting. The non-rational aspect of human behavior finds an outlet in the investment market. In fact, much long-term investment would never occur if investors depended upon mathematical calculation or even psychological convention. In a practical sense, the basis for scientific calculation often does not exist. The propensity of human nature toward spontaneous optimism, the human urge to action rather than inaction, the tendency for positive activity to depend upon a sort of animal spirit or *élan vital*—all these are nurtured by and at the same time contribute to the extreme uncertainty of long-term expectations. Even in the market place,

human behavior is not always guided by an "irrational passion for dispassionate rationality." Even in the money market, "the heart knows reasons that reason cannot know."

The foregoing discussion indicates clearly that instability is the outstanding short-run characteristic of the marginal efficiency of capital. Over historical time, there are upward and downward movements in the expected rates of return from new investment. Since the rate of interest does not fluctuate in a comparable manner, the rate of investment, which is determined by these two forces, must also fluctuate and in turn cause the total volume of employment and output to fluctuate. These variations in over-all economic activity follow a cyclical pattern familiarly known as the business cycle. In a later discussion we shall see that the essence of the business cycle is to be found in the more or less rhythmic fluctuations in the marginal efficiency of capital.

NOTES

1 G. L. S. Shackle, "Expectations and Employment," *The Economic Journal*, September, 1939, Vol. XLIX, No. 195, pages 442–452.
2 Keynes, *The General Theory of Employment, Interest and Money*. New York: Harcourt, Brace and Co., Inc., 1936, page 159.

Summaries

Nicholas Kaldor, "Alternative Theories of Distribution," *Review of Economic Studies*, 23 (1955–1956), pp. 83–100.

In this article, Kaldor addresses himself to an analysis of the four alternative theories of distribution: the Ricardian, or classical, theory, the Marxian theory, the neoclassical, or marginalist, theory, and the Keynesian theory.

Kaldor begins with a discussion of the Ricardian theory. He states that this theory is based on two separate principles, the marginal and the surplus principle. "The 'marginal principle,'" says Kaldor, "serves to explain the share of rent and the 'surplus principle' the division of the residue between wages and profits."

Next, Kaldor analyzes the Marxian theory, which is an extension of Ricardo's surplus principle. There are two important differences between the Ricardo principle and the Marxian theory. First, like Ricardo, Marx did not recognize the law of diminishing returns, and, therefore, did not make any distinction between rent and profits. Second, Marx regarded the supply price of labor as fixed, not in terms of "corn" but of commodities in general. "Hence he [Marx] regarded," says Kaldor, "the share of profits (including rent) in output as determined simply by the surplus of the product per unit of labour over the supply price (or cost) of labour—or the surplus of production to the consumption necessary for production."

Coming to the neoclassical, or marginalist, theory, Kaldor points out that this theory was developed from a part of the Ricardian model. He states, "The 'marginal principle' [was] introduced for the explanation of rent (which explains why both Marx and Marshall are able to claim Ricardo as their precursor)." According to Kaldor, there are two differences between the Ricardian and the neoclassical theories. First, unlike Ricardo, who employed the "principle of substitution" only when dealing with labor relative to land, the neoclassicists assumed that this relationship would hold true for one factor of production in relation to any other. Second, Ricardo proved that a "fixed" factor will earn a "surplus"; in contrast, the neoclassicists claimed that any factor variable in supply would obtain a remuneration equal to its marginal product.

Finally, Kaldor begins his discussion of the Keynesian theory by showing that, although Keynes was never interested in the problem of distribution, he nevertheless came near to formulating such a theory. Thus, the author concludes, "The principle of the Multiplier...could be alternatively applied to a determination of the relation between prices and wages, if the level of output and employment is taken as given, or the determination of the level of employment, if distribution...is taken as given."

Sidney Weintraub, "A Macroeconomic Approach to the Theory of Wages," *American Economic Review*, 46 (December 1956), pp. 835–856.

Weintraub believed that, prior to the publication of Keynes' *General Theory*, economists maintained that the neoclassical theory was adequate to cope with the theory of money wages. However, according to the author, "after Keynes' work the tide seemed to run the other way with an almost universal skepticism of the prospect of a determinate money-wage theory."

In this article, the author concerns himself with one aspect of the distribution problem; namely, the derivation of the determinate labor-demand and labor-supply functions free of the constant income postulate. To make his task manageable, he assumes that the labor force is homogeneous and that it does not consist of heterogeneous groups, which are found in real life.

Weintraub begins his analysis by outlining the Keynesian version of the theory of income and employment determination, and then proceeds to analyze the nature of the labor-demand and labor-supply functions. Thereafter, the author treats the two functions simultaneously, pointing out that "under conditions of competition it is to the intersection of the ... [labor-demand and labor-supply] curves that we must look for the equilibrium wage and volume of labor hire."

Bibliography

John Conlisk, "An Approach to the Theory of Inequality in the Size Distribution of Income," *Western Economic Journal*, 7 (June 1969), pp. 180–186.

Kurt Klappholz, "What Redistribution May Economists Discuss?" *Economica* (May 1968), pp. 194–197.

7

MONEY, INTEREST, AND MONETARY THEORY

In a broad sense, monetary theory is concerned with establishing cause-and-effect relationships between money and economic activities relating to production, distribution, consumption, economic growth, foreign trade, and so on. In a narrow sense, monetary theory concerns itself with the ways in which variations in the money supply affect the levels of aggregate spending, employment, and prices.

In the first selection in this part, Horwich constructs a model for analyzing the impact of interest on prices. The second article is a comprehensive survey by Luttrell of the ways in which changes in interest rates affect the economy and the problems which arise when interest rates are used as a monetary tool. In the third article, Samuelson explains by constructing several economic models the nature and important characteristics of classical and neoclassical monetary theories.

Monetary Theory and the Price Level*
George Horwich

I. INTRODUCTION

In recent years a substantial body of public opinion has opposed monetary restraint on the ground that higher interest rates, designed to curb inflation, raise prices by raising business costs. The net effect of

George Horwich, "Tight Money, Monetary Restraint, and the Price Level," *Journal of Finance*, 21 (March 1966), pp. 19–33.

* The author has benefited from comments and suggestions by M. June Flanders, A. P. Lerner, and the editorial reader, none of whom is responsible for any remaining flaws in the analysis.

monetary policy in controlling inflation would thus be negligible, if not actually perverse. This point of view has been particularly prevalent in official policy statements and public pronouncements by members of the Democratic party.[1] However, it is not limited to the latter group, for even Republicans, as well as nonpartisan monetary officials, have accepted the argument in principle.

The stock reply of the proponents of monetary policy is simply that interest is a small and unimportant element in total business costs.[2] But this is a fatal concession. For the rate of interest, narrowly defined (as it usually is) as the return on borrowings, is only one of many varieties of rent paid on the existing stock of capital. The relevant economic variable is in fact all property income, which constitutes as much as a third of the national income. As a first approximation, the various components of the property return, including bond interest, stock dividends, and building rentals, would be expected to rise and fall together over time.

The belief that higher interest as a cost might contribute to inflation has not been seriously discussed by contemporary economists, in spite of the widespread popularity of the argument. The failure to offer an analysis is due, I think, to our own incomplete integration of the theoretical role of interest as a production cost, as a return to the claimants of capital, and as a variable in monetary policy.

This paper outlines a framework within which the impact of interest on prices may be analyzed. There are two main building blocks in the approach, both Keynesian. One is a concept of monetary restraint, which derives from the *Treatise*. It is essentially Wicksellian: interest rates are fundamentally determined by internal forces, rather than by the monetary authority. The other building block is the assumed nature of the return to capital, which is advanced in the *General Theory*. This is the marginal efficiency relationship, which links interest movements closely to changes in the productivity of real capital. The Keynesian monetary and capital structure is set forth in Sections II and III, respectively. They are combined in Section IV, which examines the impact of tight money on the price level. Section V considers an alternative concept of monetary restraint, in which the monetary authority assumes a more independent role in setting interest rates. Section VI is a summary and conclusion. An Appendix offers a theoretical foundation for the determination of the price and output of capital and consumption goods.

II. MONETARY RESTRAINT: THE KEYNES–WICKSELL FRAMEWORK

"Tight money" is the appellation generally applied to an economy experiencing rising interest rates and rising income.[3] In the Wicksellian–Keynesian view, interest rates rise because of an excess demand for loanable funds caused by an increase in desired investment or a decrease in desired saving. This constitutes an increase in the natural rate of interest, which the market rate follows with a lag. Simultaneously money income rises, according to Wicksell, because the quantity of money supplied rises with the rate of interest (the money supply is "elastic"); or, according to Keynes, the quantity of money demanded falls with the rise of the rate of interest. In either case, there is a higher equilibrium interest rate, which is associated with a higher equilibrium level of prices and income.

In this context monetary restraint, which raises interest rates, accelerates an adjustment that would occur in any case. In the language of Wicksell, the monetary authority raises the market rate to the level of the higher natural rate.[4] The nature of the disturbance and the role of monetary policy is shown with the aid of Figure 1.

In the left diagram are the real flow functions, saving (S), which is the complement of consumption, and investment demand (I). Desired investment increases with lower interest rates, while saving decreases. Unlike the investment-interest relation, the dependency of saving on the rate of interest is not essential to our argument. In the right diagram are the stock or existing-asset functions, the demand (L) and the supply of real balances (M/P), which are the complements of the demand and supply, respectively, of all nonmonetary assets (typically financial claims or securities). The demand for real balances (liquidity preference) is a downward function of the rate of interest. The supply of real

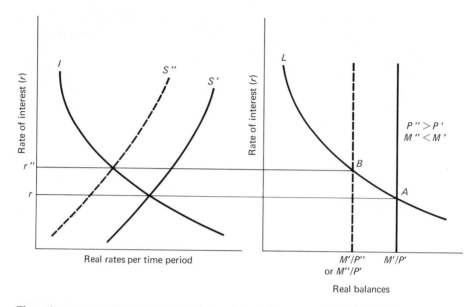

Figure 1

balances is assumed, for simplicity, to be insensitive to the interest rate. Both saving and the demand for money also depend on the level of real income, which we assume, for the present, is constant at the full employment level. Each pair of schedules in the diagram is in equilibrium at a common rate of interest r', the natural rate. The equilibrium quantity of real balances (at point A) is the ratio of M', which is the nominal stock of money, to P', the index of all prices.

Now suppose that a higher natural (i.e., equilibrium) rate of interest r'' is created by a decrease in the saving schedule from S' to S''. At r'' asset-holders want a lower quantity of real balances and, by implication, a greater quantity of nonmonetary assets or securities. These desires are measured by the movement from A to B along the liquidity preference schedule. In the absence of outside interference, the reduction in real balances will be obtained through an internally generated inflationary process.[5] Immediately following the decrease of saving, we have at r', the initial

—and, momentarily, still prevailing—rate of interest, $I > S''$, an excess of ex ante investment over desired saving. This is the spur to both higher prices and the higher market rate of interest. Given the level of real income and stock of money M', $I > S''$ persists until the market rate is r'' and prices are P''. The higher price level establishes the quantity of real balances desired at B, M'/P''.[6]

However, from the viewpoint of asset-holders, the new equilibrium at B could also be reached by reducing the quantity of money, the price level remaining constant. More precisely, there is a quantity $M'' < M'$ such that $M''/P' = M'/P''$. Restrictive monetary policy accordingly takes the form of an open-market sale conducted by the central bank, which reduces the quantity of money to M'' and raises the market rate of interest to r''. This establishes swiftly and directly the new equilibrium interest rate and real balances, both of which are otherwise achieved internally through a prolonged inflationary adjustment.

The goal of a tight monetary policy is thus the avoidance of inflation, accomplished by "raising" interest rates along a course they would naturally follow. The criticism of this policy, referred to in Section I, is that the higher interest rate nevertheless contributes to inflation by raising the interest costs of production. We are now ready to analyze this argument by considering in more detail the real forces that give rise to an increase in the equilibrium (natural) rate of interest. We assume that the monetary authority is completely successful in offsetting inflationary pressures due to a reduction in the quantity of real balances demanded. The only disturbances to the system are thus in the rate of interest, the rate of saving and investment, and any other variables that are necessary concomitants of these three.

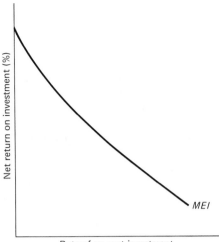

Figure 2

III. THE MARGINAL EFFICIENCY OF INVESTMENT

The role of interest as a cost of production depends upon the nature of the investment demand function. The most widely accepted investment theory is the Keynesian marginal efficiency concept, as elaborated by Lerner and Robertson.[7] In this view investment demand (ex ante investment), a downward function of interest, is derived from a short-run inverse relation between the return to (the marginal efficiency of) investment and the rate of ex post investment. This latter relationship is represented by the *MEI* line in Figure 2. The entire line is based upon a given gross marginal product of capital, which is effectively a constant in any one- or two-year period.[8] Thus the downward slope of the line is due not to changes in the gross product, but rather to variations in the net product remaining after subtraction of variable depreciation charges. The latter in turn depend upon the marginal cost and supply price of new capital goods, which in the short run vary directly with their rate of output. The greater the rate of ex post investment, the greater therefore are the output and supply price of capital. Given that the capital stock is valued at replacement, rather than historical cost, the greater are the depreciation allowances and the smaller is the net available return to the claimants of the capital stock. The rate of return, defined as the ratio of net earnings to the supply price of capital, thus falls both because of the decrease in the numerator and the increase in the denominator.[9]

Assuming that firms are rational and competitive, they will equate the percentage return on investment to the market rate of interest. That is, at any rate of interest, investment expenditures will be an amount, which, if realized ex post, will result in a return to investment just equal to the interest rate. Given accurate knowledge of the return corresponding to each rate of ex post investment, ex ante investment (*I*)—a function of interest—thus coincides exactly with the *MEI* schedule.[10]

In utilizing the Keynesian investment theory, we assume, for simplicity, that there exists only one variety of capital, the return on which is equated to "the" rate of interest. We assume also that the price of the capital stock and the direction of investment is such that the return on all existing capital units and all new investment projects is the same. Finally, we assume that all claims to capital held in the form of fixed-value financial instruments are renegotiated continuously in order to equate the coupon rate to the market rate of interest. This assumption maximizes the possible impact of higher interest rates on current business costs and the general price level.

IV. TWO DISTURBANCES

Within the framework of Sections II and III let us analyze a rise in the equilibrium rate of interest due to an autonomous (i) decrease in saving, and (ii) increase in investment.

A. Saving

A decrease in saving entails a leftward shift in the saving schedule and an upward movement along the I function. The monetary authority immediately carries out an open-market sale, which reduces the nominal supply of money and raises the market rate to the higher natural level (see Figure 1). Resources flow into consumption industries, ex ante saving and investment are maintained in constant equality, and the price level, up to this point, is unchanged.

The movement along the investment demand schedule coincides with an upward real movement along the MEI line. This implies that the increase in the rate of interest is accompanied by an increase in the net return to capital. The return rises as ex post investment and the marginal cost and supply price of capital-goods output all decline to lower equilibrium levels. All firms employing capital find that they may reduce their current depreciation charges, thereby financing

the higher coupon rates created by the higher rate of interest. Thus, while interest costs are higher, there is for every firm an added revenue available to meet this cost. Under these circumstances, there are no forces on the side of cost and production tending to alter the average price of commodities. (Any change in the price level due to the lower price of capital goods is offset by a correspondingly higher price of consumption goods, which results when consumption demand increases at the expense of saving.[11])

Given the Keynesian "interest-equalization" monetary policy and the capital-investment decision process, there are thus neither monetary nor nonmonetary sources of inflation. The only qualification to this hinges on the possibility that the transfer of resources from investment to consumption industries might be facilitated by a given increase or rate of increase in the price level. If this were true, the Keynesian monetary action would contribute to a degree of immobility, unemployment, and temporary reduction of aggregate output. Prices, as a result, would rise. One can only speculate how this would compare quantitatively, or—from a public policy viewpoint—how it should be evaluated, relative to the *permanent* inflation due to an internally stimulated movement along the liquidity preference schedule. Notice, moreover, that inflation attributable to resource immobility in this case cannot be characterized as resulting from higher interest "costs." Rather, the inflation is due to immobility originating in a decrease in demand and *revenues* in investment-goods industries.

B. Investment

An independent increase in investment results from an increase in the gross marginal product of capital. This implies that aggregate output y has also increased. The monetary disturbance is now somewhat more complex and is described with reference to Figure 3.

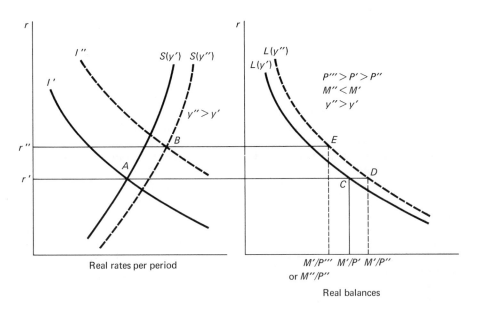

Figure 3

The initial schedules, drawn with solid lines, all meet at r', the natural rate. In the left diagram the predisturbance functions are I' and $S(y')$, which is saving based on output y'. The equilibrium is at point A. In the right diagram the beginning equilibrium is at point C, at which real balances are M'/P', the quantity determined by r' along the initial schedule $L(y')$. The investment curve increases to I'' and is accompanied by a simultaneous increase in output to y''.[12] This causes three simultaneous shifts: (i) real saving moves to the right to $S(y'')$, establishing a new saving-investment equilibrium at point B; (ii) the demand for real balances increases to $L(y'')$; (iii) given price flexibility, the increase in L lowers the general price level from P' to P'', raising the supply of real balances to M'/P''. Assuming that the demand and supply of real balances increase synchronously, the equilibrium in this market moves horizontally to point D. Now, if left to its own devices, the economy will establish a new money-market equilibrium at point E, at which

the interest rate, determined by $S(y'')$ and I'', is $r'' > r'$; real balances are M'/P''; and, since the money stock is constant throughout, the price level is higher at $P''' > P'$.[13]

The monetary authority can again perform its catalytic role of raising the market rate to the natural rate. If it assumes full responsibility for doing so, it will conduct an instantaneous open-market sale, moving the equilibrium from D to E by reducing the money supply to $M'' < M'$ and real balances to $M''/P'' = M'/P'''$. However, at point D prices are $P'' < P'$, and at E the economy is thus left with a net reduction in the price level due to the increase in output. Since we are only interested in evaluating the role of monetary policy in raising interest rates, we shall assume for analytical purposes that the lower price level is allowed to remain. We assume that prices are perfectly flexible downward in response to the rise of output, which, for the moment, is constant at y''. Under these "pure" circumstances, does the higher interest rate, viewed as a *cost* phenomenon, promise to raise prices?

Let the productivity increase, which gave rise to the increase in investment, be distributed uniformly among all firms. There are thus throughout the economy greater revenues with which to meet higher interest payments. The increased interest rate has no independent influence on costs, output, or prices, which remain at the levels described in the preceding paragraphs. Now suppose, more realistically, that some firms fail to share in the greater productivity of capital. The latter typically stems from an increase in the labor force or an innovation, neither of which will be experienced by every producer. Nevertheless, the greater interest charges on existing capital must be met by all firms, and those not sharing in the productivity rise will undergo an increase in costs unmatched by greater revenues. These firms must retrench, releasing resources. If the resources are mobile and find employment elsewhere, then aggregate output is constant and the price level again is not directly affected by the higher interest rate. However, if in the short run the necessary reallocation creates unemployment and a net reduction of output, prices will tend to rise. In the actual context of an increase in capital productivity, unemployment may simply prevent output from rising and prices from falling by their maximum amounts. It is in this sense than an increase in investment and the rate of interest—"tight money"—is a force tending to raise costs and also prices.[14]

A further possible source of inflation is again the required transfer of resources between consumption and investment industries. In the present disturbance the movement along $S(y'')$ from r' to r'' is an increase in the proportion of income saved; resources must accordingly move from consumption to investment-goods output.[15] If this transfer is in any way dependent upon inflation, then the Keynesian monetary policy will delay it. Output will

fall below y'' and prices will rise above P''.

V. MONETARY RESTRAINT: AN ALTERNATIVE VIEW

Let us now modify the analysis by assuming that monetary restriction does not coincide with an increase in the natural rate of interest. The monetary authority reduces money and raises interest in order to offset inflationary disturbances which do not themselves operate through, or entail a change in, the rate of interest. An example of such a disturbance is a direct movement from cash balances into goods—i.e., a leftward shift in the demand schedule for money—or money creation via a fiscal deficit which does not raise bank reserves.[16] The impact of tight money against such a background is discussed with reference to Figure 4. For simplicity, we describe the disturbance and the monetary response separately, though in fact they may coincide.

The system initially is in stock-flow equilibrium at interest rate r' and real balances M'/P'. The existing-asset equilibrium is at point A. Suppose that the inflationary disturbance to which the monetary authority reacts is a once-for-all decrease in the demand-for-money schedule relative to goods. In the diagram L shifts leftward from L' to L''. Assuming a fixed level of output, commodity prices rise directly to, say, P''.[17] The supply of real balances falls to M'/P'' and the existing-asset equilibrium moves horizontally from A to B.

The central bank now strives, through open-market action, to offset the higher price level. It conducts an instantaneous open-market sale, which reduces M to M'' and raises r to r''. This entails an instantaneous movement in the stock equilibrium from B to C along L''. The price level remains, for the moment, unchanged at P''. But at the higher market rate r'', ex

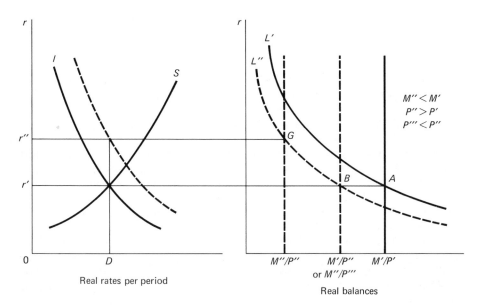

Figure 4

ante saving exceeds investment. This causes both prices and interest to fall over time via a stock-flow dynamic adjustment (output is still constant).[18] The final equilibrium is at point B, at which the market rate is again r', prices are $P''' < P''$, and real balances are $M''/P''' = M'/P''$. If the bank's objective were to stabilize the price level, then M'' would be a quantity such that $P''' = P'$.

Tight money is thus now characterized by a market rate of interest whose average level is temporarily raised. The rate rises first in response to an open-market sale, and then falls through the internal adaptive mechanism. This is in contrast to the Keynesian–Wicksellian framework in which tight money entailed an interest rate rising monotonically from one equilibrium level to another. The role of the central bank was to facilitate and accelerate that movement. In both cases the monetary policy serves to curtail simultaneously occurring inflationary pressures. In the Keynesian case the inflation was a built-in response to the move-

ment of the rate of interest. In the present action the inflation is an autonomous disturbance which the bank-induced change in money and interest endeavors to offset.

Once again, in order to evaluate any impact on the price level of the higher interest rate as a cost phenomenon, we must turn to the underlying real variables. We have seen that the capacity of firms to absorb higher interest costs depends on the net return to capital, which is a function of the level of ex post investment. In Section IV monetary tightness, as imposed by the central bank, was accompanied by constant equality between desired saving and investment, to which ex post investment corresponded. But now desired saving and investment are unequal throughout the period of higher interest rates. Neither the disturbances nor the adjustment process indicate in themselves what the level of ex post investment will be. However, we will consider several possibilities lying between the blades of the ex ante saving-investment scissors and generalize from there. We continue to assume, for the present, that total output and employment are constant.

Perhaps the simplest assumption is that ex ante and ex post investment are equal. Beginning at the initial equilibrium yield r', ex post investment moves up along the ex ante investment demand schedule I to the height of the tight money rate r'', and then down again to the unchanged equilibrium yield r'. On our assumptions, this coincides with an identical movement along the schedule of the marginal efficiency of investment. The return to investment thus moves exactly, and finances the production costs associated, with changes in the market rate of interest. The return first rises as resources move out of capital production, lowering the relative price of investment goods and the necessary depreciation allowances held against capital. Then the return falls to its original level as the sequence is reversed. This analysis parallels that of the decrease in saving (Section IV-A). In both cases the variable interest costs are accompanied by equal variations in net revenues for all firms. Profits, output, and prices are unaffected by the adjustment process.[19]

Perhaps a more realistic assumption is that resources are completely immobile. This would tend to be true the briefer is the time interval of the tight money period. Ex post investment would then remain at the predisturbance level, OD in Figure 4, which is above the ex ante levels indicated by the I schedule. It appears thus that the return to investment will remain equal to r', below the prevailing interest rates. But the only way in which unwanted capital goods can be sold to firms is by lowering their price. In the face of falling demand, this implies that the entire investment-goods supply schedule drops, reflecting a reduction in the compensation paid to resources in that industry. The supply price of capital output falls—both absolutely and relatively—and the MEI schedule (based on a given investment-goods supply function) rises initially to the location of the dashed (unlabeled) curve in Figure 4. In brief, resources stay on in the investment industry by accepting lower real returns, thereby raising the profitability of each investment-output level; the ex ante I schedule follows the movement of the MEI line.[20] As the market rate of interest falls (owing to the continuing excess of ex ante S over ex ante I), investment demand rises along the dashed curve. This permits resource payments and the supply price of capital to increase by whatever amount is required to maintain OD as the profitable investment. Thus the movement to equilibrium is one in which the I and MEI schedules gradually shift downward to their original positions. The return to investment is always as least as great as the market rate of interest. Hence, there is no independent upward pressure on costs and prices originating in the higher rate of interest.[21]

Any tendency for ex post investment to exceed the ex ante amount would be analyzed in the manner of the preceding paragraph. The marginal efficiency schedule would shift along the locus of marginal efficiency-ex post investment points, financing the higher interest rates of the adjustment period. As shown in the Appendix, the precise location of the ex post points, and thus the MEI schedule, depends on the relative shifts of the marginal cost schedules of investment and consumption industries. These shifts determine the ex post levels of output and the relative prices of the two commodities, which together determine the return to real capital.

The assumption of fixed total output and employment in a deflationary process is apt to be quite unrealistic, owing to cost and price rigidities. However, the present monetary policy is designed to offset an inflationary disturbance, and the *net* movement of the price level over time may not actually be great. The total demand for output would thereby be relatively stable, even though interest rises and stimulates an excess of saving over investment, as described.[22] But even with a stable price level, the adjustment will require a temporary reallocation of resources, except in the limiting case of constant output in each sector, noted above. Given less-than-perfect mobility between sectors, unemployment and a decline in aggregate output would thus generally occur. This would reduce aggregate saving and raise the natural rate of interest, terminating the deflationary adjustment at a higher price level and market rate of interest.

The development of unemployment and reduced output does not itself alter the basic analysis regarding the ability of firms to finance interest on capital. Whatever the degree of employment or unemployment, this ability depends on the location of the marginal efficiency schedule, which the ex ante I function will tend to follow. This is equivalent to saying that firms will not commit themselves to the payment of interest on new (and old) capital above what the return on investment promises to be.[23] And this has nothing to do, per se, with the degree of unemployment or the constancy of output. Conceivably, even though resources are idled, the movement of output and prices in the two sectors might be consistent with a movement along the predisturbance *MEI* schedule and with equality between ex ante and ex post investment, as previously described· But unemployment ought certainly to increase the range of possibilities with respect to the shift of *MEI*. To the cases already considered, we might wish to add the possibility that the movement of variables will drive *MEI* and *I below* their predisturbance location.

VI. SUMMARY AND CONCLUSION

Sections II–IV advanced a model of money and capital in which (i) policy increases in market interest rates are merely a response to prior independent increases in the natural rate of interest, and (ii) higher interest cost—or, more generally, higher rent on the existing capital stock—is financed by an increase in the net productivity of capital. If tight money (defined as simultaneous rising interest rates and inflationary pressures) is due to a decrease of saving, the greater capital productivity is provided by an allowable reduction in depreciation charges. All firms share in this productivity rise, which finances the higher interest costs. Restrictive monetary policy, aimed at raising interest rates to the natural level, tends to stabilize the price level, unless the movement of resources from investment consumption is delayed by price stability. For then unemployment and a reduction of aggregate output might furnish a nonmonetary source of inflation.

If tight money is caused by an independent increase in investment, the gross product of capital and the level of output rise directly. Interest-equalizing monetary policy is thus consistent with a decline in prices. However, the more bountiful capital stock is not likely to be distributed evenly throughout the economy. Resource reallocation within the given industrial structure (and also, possibly, between consumption and investment industries) is required. Unemployment may again result, reducing output and raising prices. Since capital productivity has increased, output may simply rise, and prices fall, less than otherwise. But just as in the decrease of saving, the monetary authority in this case is not responsible for the necessary movements of the interest rate or of resources. These would occur in any event. Only if, in curtailing the monetary inflation, the authority removes what happens to be a stimulus to resource mobility, is it guilty in any degree of causing unemployment and nonmonetary inflation.

In Section V tight money is caused by monetary contraction designed to offset inflationary disturbances which do not involve a movement in the market or natural rate of interest. The monetary authority is thus solely responsible for the higher interest rate. However, the rise in interest is only temporary, since the forces which counteract the rise in prices tend at the same time to return the interest rate to its original level. During the deflationary —or better, anti-inflationary—adjustment, ex ante saving exceeds ex ante investment. Ex post investment is thereby indeterminate and may take on a wide range of values. It is shown that any particular level of ex post investment, entailing the purchase of new capital goods, can only be effected by raising the return on investment to the level of the higher interest rate. This is accomplished by appropriate shifts in the marginal cost and supply price of both investment and consumption output. The interest costs are thus always covered by productivity changes. But the adjustment very likely will require some reallocation of resources; imperfect mobility will again cause unemployment, reduced output, and a nonmonetary source of inflation.

The tendency of tight money (defined most generally as a tendency to rising income and rising, or higher average, interest rates), in the face of monetary restraint, to raise the price level thus depends on the ease with which associated resource movements are accomplished. Only in one case can the necessary reallocation be said in some sense to result from an increase in interest "costs." That is the case of an independent increase in the investment demand schedule. The increased costs are those of a limited number of firms whose share in the greater productivity of capital is below average, and who will, accordingly, lose resources. In all other cases of tight money the resource movements, while induced by the interest rise, are not directly attributable to an increase in interest costs as such, but rather to a decline of revenues in affected industries.

The claim that higher interest rates raise prices by raising costs is thus, within our analytical framework, without much substance. Whether the natural rate is constant or increasing, greater interest payments tend to be financed by greater net productivity of real capital. The single case in which higher interest rates raise costs—that of an increase in investment demand—is one in which the overall cost structure and price level are falling because of a more productive capital stock. The real thrust of the interest rate in this case is thus only to limit a deflationary movement, not literally to create inflation.

APPENDIX

This appendix presents the theoretical underpinnings for the relationship between the stock and flow capital-goods markets, the marginal efficiency schedule, and the market for consumption goods. The model, which is an extension of the analysis of Witte,[24] is presented in Section A. Following this, successive sections apply the framework to the analysis of a decrease in saving; an increase in investment; the equality of ex ante and ex post investment, and the excess of ex post over ex ante investment in deflationary processes.

A. The Model

The capital-goods sector is described by means of three connected diagrams in Figure 5(a–c). The upper left drawing, Figure 5(a), is that of the existing or "stock" capital-goods market. On the vertical axis is P_K, the dollar price of capital goods. Also indicated on the vertical axis is $1/\rho$, the ratio of P_K to the net earnings on a unit of capital. P_K and $1/\rho$ move in the same direction, both because of the direct presence of P_K in the numerator, and the influence of P_K in determining the denominator, of $1/\rho$ [J. G. Witte, "The Microfoundations of the Social Investment Function (cf. page 7)]. The vertical line in the diagram represents the existing stock of capital, K'. The stock

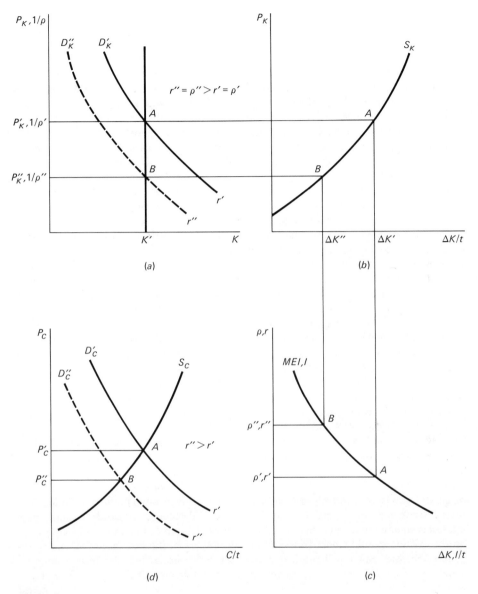

Figure 5

demand schedule is D_K, an inverse function of both P_K and the interest rate, r. The latter variable is entered as a parameter of the schedule. Given r, the resulting D_K schedule will determine a price (and net earnings) at which the rate of return is $\rho = r$.

In the upper right diagram, Figure 5(b), is the flow or production market for new capital. S_K is the marginal cost supply schedule. ΔK on the horizontal axis represents the quantity of capital or investment goods produced per period t.

Finally, in the lower right diagram, Figure 5(c), ρ and ΔK and r and I are linked up to form the marginal efficiency and investment demand schedules, respectively. Plotting ΔK (ex post investment), as indicated in the upper right diagram, against the corresponding values of ρ, as taken from the upper left diagram, we obtain the MEI schedule. Plotting I, the flow *demand* (ex ante investment) for the same quantities, ΔK, and associating it with the values of $r = \rho$, we obtain the coinciding I schedule.

Consider the impact of a change in the rate of interest, the gross marginal product of capital remaining constant. The system is initially in equilibrium at point A in all three diagrams. The interest rate is increased from r' to r''. In Figure 5(a) the D_K schedule falls from D_K' to D_K'', reducing P_K from P_K' to P_K'' and $1/\rho$ from $1/\rho'$ to $1/\rho'' = 1/r''$. Moving to the right to Figure 5(b), the desired output at P_K'' is $\Delta K'' < \Delta K'$ (at point B). Combining $\Delta K''$ with ρ'' and r'' in Figure 5(c) gives us a higher point, B, on the marginal efficiency-investment demand schedules.

What the three-way diagram makes clear is that (i) the MEI and I schedules are "market equilibrium" curves, derived from the stock and flow capital-goods markets, and are not demand schedules in the Marshallian sense[25]; and (ii) the price of capital goods is effectively determined in the stock market, where the rate of interest is equated to the percentage return on the existing capital stock. In the latter connection, the reader will recall our assumption of equality in the return on all new and existing investments. Thus the action that equates ρ and r in the upper left diagram has the same effect in the lower right diagram.

The analysis ignores the role of new capital goods in the determination of price; i.e., the stock is held constant at K', ignoring the increments forthcoming from points along S_K. For our short-run purposes, I think this is a realistic assumption. However, it can easily be relaxed. Adding the increments to K' would lower both the price and the gross marginal product of capital over time. Thus the value of ρ corresponding to a given P_K would be lowered, and the entire MEI and I schedules would drop.[26] I would argue that shifting the I schedule in this way (i) overstates the short-run influence of the growth of the capital stock on its gross product, and (ii) is one-sided, in that it ignores constantly occurring technological and population changes that simultaneously tend to raise MEI and I.

Figure 5(d), a diagram of the consumption-goods market, completes our sectoral representation of the system. D_C and S_C are, respectively, the demand and supply of new consumption goods, C, per unit time. P_C is the money price of C. Since saving is a rising function of r, D_C, based on a given real income, varies inversely with r. Thus the increase in r referred to a moment ago shifts D_C downward and lowers the equilibrium from A to B, as indicated.

B. Saving

The decrease in saving, analyzed in Section IV-A, can be illustrated by the A-B movements in Figures 5(a–c) and 6. The initial saving schedule, a rising curve, would pass through point A in Figure 5(c). The subsequent schedule would pass through point B. In Figure 6, the consumption market, the decrease of saving is offset by an initial increase in consumption demand from D_C' to D_C''. The latter schedule is based upon the initial interest rate r'. However, the increase in interest reduces demand to D_C''', which determines the final equilibrium at point B.[27]

We assume that on net the average price of commodities and total output, measured by appropriate indexes, are unchanged. However, the relative decline in P_K enables the marginal efficiency of investment to rise.

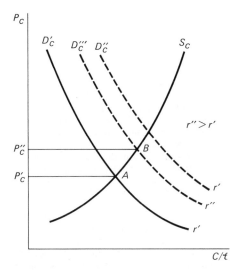

Figure 6

C. Investment

The increase in investment, described in Section IV-B, is a simultaneous increase in the gross marginal product of capital and real output of the economy. *All schedules in the investment-consumption complex shift to the right. S_K and S_C shift because of the greater productivity, and hence lower supply price, in the output of both capital and consumption goods. The shifts in S and D_C are a response to the greater real income available to both savers and consumers. MEI and thus I shift because of the reduction in S_K. The shift of I is assumed to exceed that of S, creating a higher equilibrium interest rate r''. S_C is assumed to shift more than D_C, lowering P_C.*

At the predisturbance interest rate r', D_K increases because of the spontaneous increase in the numerator of ρ, and hence ρ itself, due to the rise of capital's gross (and net) marginal product. In order to maintain equality between r' and ρ, D_K and thus P_K rise until a sufficiently higher price restores ρ to $\rho' = r'$. (In a word, the relationship between the $1/\rho$ and P_K scales is altered: at each P_K the corresponding $1/\rho$ is less.)

When r rises to its new equilibrium r'', D_C, D_K, and P_K fall somewhat below their initially higher levels. It is neither inconceivable nor inconsistent for P_K to fall below its predisturbance value. But whether it does so or not, the downward movement of P_C is assumed to dominate the general price index.

D. Ex Ante and Ex Post Investment Equal

The sequence described on page 225 entails an upward movement along a given marginal efficiency schedule from interest rate r' to r'', followed by a reverse movement back to r'. r'' is imposed from outside the system by a monetary contraction. The restoration to r' is accompanied by a fall in the general price level.

Holding the interest rate momentarily at r'' and investment at $I(r'')$, the increase in interest reduces D_K and D_C. The general deflation in prices and costs lowers D_K and D_C further, while also reducing S_K and S_C. This is because these schedules are functions of money prices. On net, D_K and S_K fall so as to determine jointly a price P_K and investment level consistent with the new point $I(r'')$ on the unchanged *MEI-I* schedule. By assumption, S_C drops more than D_C, raising consumption output and absorbing labor released from the investment sector. In order to raise ρ to the level of r'', P_K must drop relative to P_C. If this was not true in the first instance, D_K and S_K can be lowered further to accomplish it. Since D_K and S_K are lowered *equally*, they remain consistent with the given investment point $I(r'')$.

As r returns to r' and prices continue to fall, the relative price and resource shifts of the above paragraph are reversed. Ex post investment rises, consumption falls, P_K/P_C rises and hence ρ falls with r.

E. Ex Post Investment Exceeds Ex Ante Investment

In this case the initial disturbance is again an independent monetary contraction which raises r to r''. In the ensuing adjustment the general price level again falls and r returns to r'. But as this occurs, ex post investment exceeds ex ante investment, as indicated by the predisturbance I schedule, owing to complete resource immobility (see pages 225–226). Thus, while r'' lowers D_K and D_C, and general deflation lowers D_K, D_C, S_K, and S_C, the combined shifts are such as to maintain investment and consumption output at their predisturbance levels. In order to raise ρ to r'', P_K/P_C must decline, and once again there will always be a combination of shifts to accomplish this. Since $I(r'')$ now corresponds to the predisturbance investment level, while both r and ρ have increased, investment lies on a higher marginal efficiency and investment demand schedule, as drawn in Figure 4.

The relative shifts are gradually reversed as r return to r' and the price level falls.

NOTES

1 As might be expected, these pronouncements were more in evidence before the party came to power in 1961. See, for example, the statements of Democratic senators in Hearings before the Committee on Finance, United States Senate (85th Cong., 1st Sess.), *Investigation of the Financial Condition of the United States*, June–August 1957, pp. 68, 323, 342, 345, 390–391, 733, 739, 785, 952, 1093, 1402–1403. In the summer of 1959, Senator William Proxmire, of the Senate Banking and Currency Committee, circulated a questionnaire to a large number of economists in which the opening question was:

> What evidence is there to support or refute a conclusion that "tight money" serves to limit inflation enough to off-set the rising costs of borrowing and the higher total cost of everything that is paid for "on time?" (I am seeking evidence to determine the extent to which credit restraint counteracts over-all inflationary pressure, on the one hand, and the extent to which it channels the price increases into the time payment segment of the economy on the other.)

A more recent statement of Senator Proxmire's views is contained in Hearings before the Joint Economic Committee (87th Cong., 1st Sess.), *Review of Report of the Commission on Money and Credit*, August 1961, p. 256. Representatives of organized labor take a similar position. See Hearings before the Joint Economic Committee (85th Cong., 2nd Sess.), *The Relationship of Prices to Economic Stability and Growth: Commentaries*, October 1958, pp. 33 and 248.

The opinion among Democratic senators (and presidents) that higher interest rates are inflationary has an historical precedent in the writings of Thomas Tooke and the "Banking School." See, for example, Albert Feavearyear, *The Pound Sterling*, Oxford: The Clarendon Press, 1962, 2nd edition (edited and revised by Victor Morgan), p. 266, who quotes Tooke: "A high rate of interest had no effect upon prices, except perhaps to raise them, in the long period, by raising the cost of production." This "heretical" view was supported by William Newmarch's investigation into the circulation of bills of exchange for the period 1830–1853. He found no evidence that commercial credit was limited at all by rising interest rates. See Tooke and Newmarch, *History of Prices*, New York: Adelphi Co., 1857, Vol. VI. For a survey of this whole controversy, see J. R. T. Hughes, *Fluctuations in Trade, Industry and Finance*, Oxford: The Clarendon Press, 1960, pp. 228–236.

2 See the remarks by Treasury Secretary Humphrey, Hearings before the Committee on Finance, *op. cit.*, pp. 390–391; Under Secretary of the Treasury Burgess, *ibid.*, p. 733; and Chairman Martin of the Board of Governors, *ibid.*, pp. 1268–1269, 1402.

3 Rising interest rates are rarely accompanied by falling income. Hendershott and Murphy ("The Monetary Cycle and the Business Cycle: The Flow of Funds Re-Examined," *National Banking Review*, I, June 1964, p. 535) were able to find only one quarter in the entire period 1952–1962 during which interest rose while economic activity declined.

4 This view of monetary policy is advanced by Keynes in a *Treatise on Money*, London: Macmillan and Co., Ltd., 1950, Vol. I, p. 273, and Vol. II, pp. 351–352 and 362. See also D. H. Robertson, who bases similar policy prescriptions on a more purely Wicksellian model, in which the inflation is due to elasticity of the

money supply: "Industrial Fluctuation and the Natural Rate of Interest," *Economic Journal*, XLIV, December 1934, pp. 650–656 (reprinted as Ch. V in *Essays in Monetary Theory*, Staples Press, Ltd., 1940). For recent treatments, see M. J. Bailey, *National Income and the Price Level*, New York: McGraw-Hill Book Co., Inc., 1962, pp. 156–157; and G. Horwich, *Money, Capital, and Prices*, Homewood: Richard D. Irwin, Inc., 1964, pp. 450–451.

5 Cf. Horwich, *op. cit.*, Ch. IV and pp. 277–279.

6 If there are any unemployed resources or excess capacity in the economy, the adjustment will raise output along with prices. The real saving schedule and the demand for real balances both shift to the right. This will lower the natural rate somewhat below r'' and raise the equilibrium level of real balances above M'/P''. The adjustment thus terminates earlier and prices rise less than if output were constant.

7 See Keynes, *The General Theory of Employment, Interest and Money*, New York: Harcourt, Brace and Co., 1936, Ch. 11; A. P. Lerner, *The Economics of Control*, New York: The Macmillan Co., 1944, Chs. 21 and 25, and "On Some Recent Developments in Capital Theory," *American Economic Review*, LV, May 1965, pp. 284–295; D. H. Robertson, *Lectures on Economic Principles*, Vol. II, London: Staples Press, Ltd., 1958, pp. 61–68; and Horwich, *op. cit.*, pp. 40–43.

8 In any individual firm, changes in capital may, of course, create substantial changes in its marginal product in any period of time. But the marginal product of capital *averaged* over all firms in the economy, is not likely to move very much in the short run.

9 A detailed two-sector account of the derivation of the marginal efficiency and investment demand schedules is presented in the Appendix, Section A.

10 The assumption of competitive behavior among firms is not essential to the analysis. In the absence of perfect competition, the ex post marginal efficiency schedule will lie above the ex ante investment demand function. The vertical distance between the schedules will be monopoly profit. This can be handled by the subsequent analysis (Sections IV and V) by simply requiring that the two schedules shift together simultaneously in the same direction.

11 See the Appendix, Section B, for a fuller description of the impact of a shift in saving on both the investment-goods and consumption-goods sectors.

12 The increase in the marginal efficiency schedule may reflect an anticipated future increase, rather than a de facto current increase in output and the productivity of capital. In this event firms may have to resort to additional finance, including new money and the dishoarding of existing balances, in order to service new borrowings or security issues. However, as a source of inflation, this can only be a temporary, reversible phenomenon.

13 It is possible (though unlikely) for point E to lie directly above or to the right of point C, implying that the final price level is equal to or less than the beginning one. This could be the result of a greater income coefficient in saving or in the demand for money, shifting either schedule farther to the right.

14 See Appendix, Section C, for the two-sector account of an increase in investment.

15 The increase in saving at r' due to the shift of the schedule from $S(y')$ to $S(y'')$ will also require a movement of resources from consumption to investment industries, provided that (i) the spontaneous increase in output from y' to y'' is distributed between consumption and investment goods in the predisturbance ratio; (ii) the marginal rate of saving is greater than the average rate. If, for example, the marginal saving rate were less than the average, the de facto increase in investment goods due to the more productive capital stock would exceed the increase desired by savers, and resources would have to leave investment industries. However, (ii) is in fact widely accepted on both theoretical and empirical grounds. (i) is difficult to justify. I know of no commonly accepted production functions or types of technological change that guarantee this result.

16 This is the kind of disturbance (though generally it is the opposite case of hoarding) that Robertson typically is concerned with. See, e.g., *Banking Policy and the Price Level*, London: Staples Press, Ltd., 1949, pp. 53–54; and "Saving and Hoarding," *Economic Journal*, XLIII, September 1933, pp. 401–402 (reprinted as Ch. IV in *Essays in Monetary Theory*, *op. cit.*).

17 The increase in the demand for goods is assumed to be across the board, with no

effect on relative prices or the rate of interest. Thus real saving and investment remain unchanged at their initial level of equality.

18 See Horwich, *op. cit.*, pp. 179–187.

19 See the description in the Appendix, Section D.

20 The upward shift in the *I* schedule reduces the magnitude of the saving-investment gap and consequently the fall over time of the rate of interest and the speed of the deflationary adjustment. For a similar point in his criticism of Keynes' *Treatise*, see D. H. Robertson, "Mr. Keynes' Theory of Money," *Economic Journal*, XLI, September 1931, p. 401.

21 Cf. also Appendix, Section E.

22 The inflationary disturbance was assumed in n.17 to have no effect on interest or real saving and investment. Hence these variables are influenced only by the monetary contraction. Given more or less stability of the general price level, the relevant aspects of the sectoral price changes described in the Appendix, Sections D and E, are thus the relative, rather than the absolute movements.

23 We have been assuming that firms know what the marginal efficiency of various investment levels is, and that the ex ante *I* schedule invariably coincides with the *MEI* function (see p. 217). In Section IV, where the schedules undergo a once-for-all shift, and monetary policy contributes an element of stability to the adjustment process, this is not an unreasonable assumption. However, in the present context, where *MEI* may shift constantly, entrepreneurial error as to the return on investment is a more serious possibility. (Keynes himself stressed the underlying role of expectations in the marginal efficiency concept; cf. *The General Theory, op. cit.*, pp. 138–144.) Thus, if firms in the aggregate overestimate the return, offering to pay more interest than the de facto marginal efficiency on the investment justifies, *I* is above *MEI*. Costs, including interest, will exceed revenues, and output will be reduced, provoking unemployment and nonmonetary inflation.

24 J. G. Witte, Jr., "The Microfoundations of the Social Investment Function," *Journal of Political Economy*, LXXI, October 1963, pp. 441–456. Witte draws on the work of R. W. Clower, "An Investigation into the Dynamics of Investment," *American Economic Review*, XLIV, March 1954, pp. 64–81. Cf. also W. T. Newlyn, *Theory of Money*, Oxford: Oxford University Press, 1962, pp. 93–95. I have been influenced in the treatment of the consumption-goods sector by the work of S. B. Chase, Jr., *Asset Prices in Economic Analysis*, Berkeley: University of California Press, 1963, Ch. III.

25 Witte, *op. cit.*, p. 447.

26 Lerner, *The Economics of Control, op. cit.*, p. 335.

27 Strictly speaking, P_C should be entered as a parameter of the saving schedule, paralleling the use of r in determining D_C. However, taking account of this additional relationship would complicate the model considerably, requiring a full treatment of stability conditions. We avoid doing so, since the basic analysis and conclusions can, on further plausible simplifying assumptions, be retained intact.

Interest Rate Controls—Perspective, Purpose, and Problems
Clifton B. Luttrell

Throughout most of this nation's history, usury laws and other interest rate restrictions have had little impact on credit flows.

Clifton B. Luttrell, "Interest Rate Controls—Perspective, Purpose, and Problems," Federal Reserve Bank of St. Louis, *Review* (September 1968), pp. 6–14.

In recent years, however, such restrictions have interfered increasingly with credit markets. The restrictiveness of legal limits is being felt over wide areas, as a result of a rapid rise in market rates of interest to levels that are above ceilings set by usury laws and other government controls. These restrictions have been ameliorated, however, as maximum permissible rates payable by banks on deposits have been increased a number of times during the past decade when market rates exceeded their ceilings.[1]

In 1957 the Federal Reserve Board, for the first time since being granted the authority in 1933, increased the maximum permissible rates paid by member banks on time and savings deposits. Since 1957, the Board has increased maximum permissible rates seven times as market rates have risen.

Interest rate restrictions on funds flowing into financial agencies, which for many years were applied exclusively to banks, have recently been extended to include maximum rates payable by some nonbank financial intermediaries. The 1966 Interest Rate Act directed the Federal Reserve Board, the Secretary of the Treasury, the Federal Home Loan Bank Board, and the Federal Deposit Insurance Corporation to take action to reduce interest rates to the extent feasible, given the prevailing money market and economic conditions. The Federal Reserve Board was given the power to set different ceiling rates for different classes of bank deposits. Exercising this broadened authority, the Board reduced the maximum rate on consumer-type certificates of deposit to 5 per cent. In 1966 the FDIC for the first time set maximum interest rates for mutual savings banks, and the Home Loan Bank Board applied dividend restrictions to the savings and loan associations.

Despite this broadening of restrictions, a large percentage of funds has continued to flow through financial intermediaries in response to supply and demand forces. Many financial agencies, such as the farm credit banks, sales finance companies, and nonfinancial corporation lenders, remain outside Federal controls on rates payable, though subject to state usury laws on rates charged.

Lending rates of banks, savings and loan associations, and individuals are also subject to state usury laws, which impose limits which recently have been below market rates in many states. Although some areas of free market rates remain, controls are creating diversions in credit flows. The 6 per cent limit imposed on commercial bank loans in several states tends to reduce the flow of commerical bank credit to customers. Limits at the national level on rates paid by banks and savings and loan associations for funds slow the growth rate of these intermediaries.

This article accepts the basic economic premise that free markets lead to an optimum allocation of resources. It concludes that interferences with normal credit flows create inefficiencies in the financial markets that have an adverse impact on the distribution of capital and consumer goods.

Such inefficiencies in resource use can be explained within the framework of a free market. The market determines the returns to savers and allocates loanable funds among borrowers. These returns and allocations are made on the basis of supply and demand conditions. Supplies of loanable funds are determined by savings and the increments of credit created by monetary action. Many savers have the alternative of lending to intermediary savings-type financial agencies such as banks and savings and loan firms, or investing directly through equities, loans, bonds, etc. Expected marginal return is the major factor determining the volume of savings flows into the various channels. If interest rates payable by financial agencies are restricted to levels below the yields of alternative assets, flows of funds through them tend to decline. On the other hand, if such rates are determined by market demand, the flows supplied will expand with the rising demand for credit.

Demand for loan funds is a function of the marginal returns to capital plus the demand by individuals and government for current consumption in excess of current income. Each demand sector is willing to purchase funds as long as marginal returns exceed costs. Efficiency in the financial market is maximized when the marginal return on funds is equal for all sectors. The price of funds (interest rate) is thus the allocator of funds both among the various sectors—business, government, and consumer—and among the various demanding units in each sector. When this allocator is inhibited, an inefficient allocation of funds occurs.

This article is a survey of interest rate restrictions in their historical setting, first outlining their rationalization as given by contemporaries of ancient, medieval, and modern times, and concluding with a statement of current reasons for controls, control problems, and the impact of controls on various sectors of the economy.

Historical Perspective

Restrictions on interest charges were begun in ancient times. Interest payments were observed to increase the wealth of the rich and were believed to deprive the poor. Controls consisted of both religious proscriptions and legislation which limited or forbade interest.[2] Theories explaining why interest payments should be restricted were not well developed, although such payments were criticized by most philosophers.

Despite these legal and religious considerations and the strong antagonism of the philosophers, economic forces continuously fostered interest charges and payments. Economic relations had already become too complicated for gratuitous credit in much of the ancient world, and legal interest limits generally prevailed in ancient Greece. In the 4th century B.C., the Romans condoned and later fully sanctioned interest by the institution of legal rates.[3]

Following the collapse of the Roman Empire, a reaction occurred with respect to interest payments. The Christian Middle Ages treated the subject of interest charges on borrowed money more thoroughly, but with the same hostility as the earlier pagans. The exploitation of poor debtors by rich creditors appeared particularly hateful to the Christian, whose religion taught him to look upon gentleness and charity as among the greatest virtues and to think little of earthly goods. The Church, step by step, managed to introduce legislation prohibiting interest payments. Secular legislation finally fell almost entirely under the Church's influence, and severe interest rate statutes emerged, thus abrogating the more liberal Roman law.[4]

Despite the charitable instincts of the Church, businessmen were generally able to prevent the enactment of laws which carried the interest limitation principle to its ultimate conclusion. Exceptions included the privilege of public pawnbrokers, transactions by other types of banks, the indulgence in usury practices by the Jews, and the payment of interest without its being written into the contract. Lending practices which involve hidden interest and which circumvent legal restrictions are thus not peculiar to the present generation.

By the early 14th century, economic activity had quickened and personal freedom was on the upswing. Although beliefs about interest had not changed, practical compromises were beginning to appear. Luther, Zwingli, and other reformers, while believing that interest was a parasitic gain, consented to its payment within limits. This practical compromise was justified by the argument that interest could not be conveniently eradicated because man was considered so imperfect.[5]

About the middle of the 16th century, students began to examine the theoretical foundations of severe interest restrictions. Calvin rejected the scriptural basis for interest prohibition on the ground that some passages of Scripture are interpreted differently, while others are invalid because of changed circumstances. He further pointed out the similarity of interest payments to lenders and the use of money to purchase land on which a return is anticipated. Nevertheless, he believed in interest rate controls and adherence to terms established by law. Molinaeus, a French jurist, went further, refuting point by point both the pagan and scholastic doctrines of interest prohibition.[6] He maintained that the use of money yields a service, that this service is the "fruit" of money, and that the lender is injured because of use foregone.

In the 1700's, theories related to interest developed rapidly. Turgot, a French economist, made perhaps the greatest contribution.[7] He carried Calvin's interest analogy a step further, pointing out that money is the equivalent of a piece of land yielding a certain percentage of the capital sum. The owner will therefore not be inclined to invest his capital in other enterprises unless he can expect a net return as great as he would obtain through the purchase of land.[8] Turgot also noted that an increase in the quantity of money which raises commodity prices might increase the rate of interest.[9] He thereby pointed to the possibility of a positive real return on money, and that price inflation might become imbedded in the nominal rate of interest.

Following the breakdown of the hard tenets of scholastic doctrine as a result of economic analysis and the rising commercial demands for credit in the 1700's, legal restrictions on the payment of interest were generally relaxed. Most nations, however, established legal maximum usury rates. In 1545 England repealed the prohibition of interest and replaced it with a legal rate. The prohibition was later reimposed, but in 1571 it was again repealed and has never again been reinstated. The Netherlands yielded to repeal before 1600, and is an example of a sophisticated economy that developed without the shackles on interest rates required by the scholastic doctrine. Germany, with a somewhat slower commercial development, repealed the interest prohibition about the mid-1600's. Repeal came later in Italy and France, where canonistic influence was more persistent in both theory and practice.

With the exception of England, laws imposing a maximum on chargeable interest rates have persisted in most European countries. In England these laws, along with other restrictions on commerce and trade, came under intense pressure in the 1800's. Usury laws were suspended entirely in 1830 for bills under three months' maturity and were repealed for all forms of credit in 1854.[10]

Early Practices in the United States

Under the influence of the European powers, the American colonies adopted the traditions of their homeland with respect to usury. Reasons were apparently unnecessary for the continuance of this vestige of medieval and ancient views. For those who failed to recognize the limits possible under competitive conditions, restrictions were a compromise between the necessities of commerce and industry and earlier custom and belief. Protection of the "poor" borrower against exploitation by the "wealthy" lender remained a central core of most usury legislation. Legal maximums were viewed as a means of restraining the natural appetite of the lender, and the interest received was considered a gratuity resulting from the magnanimous nature of the state. The services performed by capital continued to go unrecognized by the public.

Most of the early colonies followed the English custom of establishing a legal maximum of 6 per cent, a rate that still survives in a number of states. In most states, however, usury rates have been increased, and in a few states limits on commercial bank loans have been completely eliminated (Table 1). Four of the five states which currently have no maximum limits, namely Connecticut, Maine, Massachusetts, and New Hampshire, were settled early and established the low 6 per cent maximum as colonies. Furthermore, none of the states which developed later west of the Mississippi River established maximum interest rates at the relatively low 6 per cent level.

Later United States Restrictions

In addition to the usury laws, which were a carryover from previous ages, many states in the 20th century set ceilings on the interest rates that banks could pay on deposits. These ceilings were usually imposed in connection with deposit in-

Table 1. Number of States with Specified Maximum Rates of Interest on Commercial Bank Deposits and Loans

ANNUAL INTEREST RATE	DEPOSITS[1]		LOANS[2]
	SAVINGS	TIME	
$3\frac{1}{2}$	3	—	—
4	9	8	—
$4\frac{1}{2}$	—	3	—
$5\frac{1}{2}$	—	1	—
6	—	—	11
7	—	—	5
8	—	—	12
9	—	—	1
10	—	—	11
12	—	—	4
21	—	—	1
No Maximum Rate	37	37	5

[1] In some states rates are set by the state banking authority within prescribed limits. This table excludes the state of Louisiana, which requires that banks paying 5 per cent or more must classify funds as borrowed.

[2] Maximum rate that may be set by contract. These rates are subject to legal exceptions in most states, such as rates on installment loans, investigation fees, etc. Since August 1967 some states have raised their limits.

Source: National Association of Supervisors of State Banks, "A Profile of State-Chartered Banking" (Washington, D.C., August 1967).

surance programs. Maximum interest rates permissible for state banks were, in some states, set at a lower level than those paid by national banks. To remedy this situation, the Federal Reserve Act was amended in 1927, limiting the rates paid by national banks on time, savings, and other deposits to the maximum permitted state banks in the same state.[11] Following the ensuing depression of the early 1930's, the Banking Act of 1933, with little discussion, prohibited member bank payment of interest on demand deposits and gave the Federal Reserve Board authority to set maximum rates on time and savings deposits for all member banks. These limitations were extended to nonmember insured banks by the Banking Act of 1935.

Reasons for interest rate restrictions given during the hearings related to the Banking Acts of 1933 and 1935 fell into three general categories. First, a reduction of interest rates payable by banks would tend to reduce the rates charged to bank customers. Second, interest restrictions, especially the prohibition of interest on demand deposits, would prevent the movement of funds from smaller to larger communities, and more funds would remain in the small rural communities to meet local demands. Third, restrictions on rates payable would prevent the excessive bidding up of rates which in turn leads to high-return, high-risk assets and bank failures.

Dr. Oliver M. W. Sprague, Professor of Banking and Finance, Harvard University, presented the first view. Concerning the "need" for lower interest rates, he said: ". . . I should look for it to be brought about, more, through the moderate rate of interest that banks may pay on deposits. . . ."[12] Marriner Eccles, Chairman of the Federal Reserve Board, testified: "Fixing the maximum rate of interest on deposits tends to bring down the rate on loans. That is the effect."[13] Similar views were expressed by Senator Smith W. Brookhart of Iowa, a member of the Committee on Banking and Currency, and Harry J. Haas, President of the American Bankers Association.[14]

The second view, that the prohibition of interest on demand deposits prevents the movement of funds to financial centers, was presented by Senator Carter Glass of Virginia, Chairman of the Subcommittee on Monetary Policy, Banking, and Deposit Insurance. Speaking on the floor of the Senate in 1933, Senator Glass said: ". . . this payment of interest, particularly on demand deposits, has resulted in drawing the funds from country banks to the money centers for speculative purposes."[15] Similar views were expressed by Congressman Patman of the Committee on Banking and Currency,[16] and by Ronald Ransom, Vice Chairman, Board of Governors of the Federal Reserve System.[17]

A third thread extending throughout the hearings prior to the Banking Acts of 1933 and 1935 was that interest rate restrictions were essential to prevent the excessive bidding up of rates. Benjamin M. Andersen, Jr., economist with the Chase National Bank, said: "The only place where a definite abuse existed that needed public regulation was time deposits." Senator McAdoo stated: "The bidding by banks against each other for the deposits of customers who had large deposits . . . led to unwholesome competition between banks and an unwholesome condition so far as demand deposits were concerned."[18] Leo T. Crowley, Chairman of the Federal Deposit Insurance Corporation, said: ". . . in years gone by, banks paid as high as 4, 5, and 6 per cent for what we would term 'time deposits.' They offered all kinds of premiums, like blankets and clocks . . . and the banks which perhaps should not have paid those high interest rates were the ones that were the most apt to offer the depositor an interest rate that was not sound."[19]

In 1966 a fourth reason for the control of rates payable on time and savings deposits was developed—the elimination of unsound competition between banks and other financial intermediaries. In hearings on the Interest Rate Act of 1966, excessive competition was the principal subject of discussion. Norman Strunk, Executive Vice President of the United States Savings and Loan League, reported: "The adverse effect on the flow of savings into savings and loan associations and savings banks has been severe and the situation is worsening monthly. Those commercial banks unable or unwilling to compete at the new rates are equally affected.

"The commercial banks, as short-term lenders with their funds invested in short-term business loans and high-interest-rate consumer loans, are able to charge more in periods of high interest rates, and commercial bank loans can be adjusted to higher interest rates more readily. Bank earnings, thus, can increase very rapidly in periods of rising short-term interest rates, and banks can pay higher rates on savings."[20] Similar views were expressed by John E. Horne, Chairman of the Federal Home Loan Bank Board.[21]

In addition to the need for restraining competition between banks and other financial agencies, Larry Blackmon, President of the National Association of Home Builders, emphasized the merit of giving first preference for savings to homeowners.[22] The need for at least temporary restraint on competition for funds was expressed by the Council of Economic Advisers.[23]

The Interest Rate Regulation Act of 1966, which was passed following these hearings, directed the supervisory authorities to take action to bring about a reduction of interest rates to the maximum extent feasible in the light of current money market and economic conditions. It authorized the Board of Governors of the Federal Reserve System and the Federal Deposit Insurance Corporation to prescribe different rate limitations for different classes of bank deposits, and also provided for regulating rates paid by mutual savings banks and dividends on savings and loan association shares.

THE EFFECTS OF USURY LAWS

An analysis of reasons for interest restrictions by ancient, medieval, and modern societies reveals the heavy influence of ethical and moral considerations. These considerations were heavily weighed in favor of low interest rates which were generally believed obtainable through legislation. The actual impact of usury legislation, however, probably has been contrary to the intended impact. Instead of providing lower cost credit, such laws have often retarded credit flows. The result has been a scarcity of credit available for many vital activities.

Usury Restrictions Retard Home Construction

Attempts by states to restrict interest payments have been frustrated by the interconnection of credit markets. Low ceiling rates, instead of fostering credit to the poor and for local economic development, have fostered the export of capital to other areas, despite the great demand for credit locally. Harry L. Johnson, in an article on conditions in Tennessee where low limits are placed on both usury rates and rates payable by banks, reports: "Among the more immediate and discernible economic ills which have occurred in the past and which will be aggravated by unrealistic limitations on interest rates are: (1) a decline in residential building, (2) an increase in the level of unemployment in construction, (3) a decline in the sales of building supplies, (4) an outflow of savings, (5) an increase in the rate of interest and yields on bonds issued by the State of Tennessee and its political subdivisions, and (6) increased competition for Tennessee's financial resources by out-of-state individuals and businesses."[24] The maintenance of low legal maximum rates on commercial loans might be expected to foster industrial development and economic growth. Most of the 11 states with the lowest legal limit (6 per cent), however, are not noted for wealth and vigor, or for the ease of credit conditions for the poor. About half of them are located in the Appalachian Area.[25]

Credit for home mortgages is affected adversely in states with low usury ceilings. In a speech before the Pennsylvania Bankers Association, Andrew F. Brimmer, Member of the Board of Governors of the Federal Reserve System, pointed out the adverse effects of low ceiling rates on credit flows into the home mortgage market. He stated that the reduction in the supply of funds tends to reduce activity in home building and the transfer of existing dwellings.[26]

The total volume of funds for lending is curtailed in states with low usury rate ceilings. Loanable funds search for areas of highest returns. Funds in low rate ceiling states tend to move to other states and to noncredit demands. Financial intermediaries in such states cannot effectively compete for savings, as the limited returns on loans do not transmit the free market signals to savers. The limited volume of funds flowing into such agencies results in a reduced level of loans.

Credit to Low Income Groups Reduced

Credit is more difficult for low income groups to obtain in states with low usury ceilings. Loanable funds, when restricted to low interest rates, do not seek out poor borrowers whose security is less adequate and whose repayment capacity is limited. Such credit flows more readily to borrowers with adequate assets for pledging. These borrowers can demand larger low-risk loans with handling costs at a minimum. Consequently, instead of protecting high-risk borrowers from high rates, usury laws actually prevent those borrowers from acquiring funds, or force them to seek illegal or less efficient sources.

Venture Credit Impeded

Venture or development credit, which is also risky, is retarded in states with severe usury laws. Such credit can only be extended at a higher rate of interest to offset the higher risk. In states with low maximum rates, no means to offset high risks are available. Usury laws are relatively harmless when market rates are low relative to the legal maximums, i.e., when the usury rates are not effective. They are harmful to all concerned when doing the job for which they were designed— limiting the rates chargeable.

The volume of credit flowing to low-risk individuals and well-established businesses may be almost as great under severe usury restrictions as under free market conditions. Low usury ceilings prevent other individuals and firms from effectively bidding for funds. With the higher risk users in effect excluded from the market, most funds will probably flow to low-risk individuals and firms.

LIMITS ON RATES PAYABLE TO SAVERS RESTRICT CREDIT FLOWS

Like usury laws, many restrictions on rates payable have their roots imbedded in ancient and medieval thought. For example, the belief that a reduction in interest rates payable by banks on deposits tends to reduce rates charged bank customers (and that this is a worthy objective) implies that low charges to debtors are preferable to high returns to savers. A look at the credit market indicates that the rich-creditor, poor-debtor implications carried over from the Middle Ages may not hold in modern economies.

The Rich-Creditor, Poor-Debtor Fallacy

Instead of the rich leaving funds in the banks' custody to loan out to poor bor-

rowers, the reverse may be closer to the facts. In 1957 more than half of all member bank business credit was extended to firms with net worths of $50,000 and over.[27]

Investment of savings through banks and savings and loan associations has not led to the accumulation of great wealth during the period of national controls on rates payable. For example, an investment of $10,000 in 1934 in savings deposits at ceiling rates, with 75 per cent of earnings reinvested annually, would have been worth $20,239 in 1967. Similar investments in Standard and Poor's composite list of common stocks and farm land would have been worth $232,530 and $271,476, respectively. At constant prices based on the Gross National Product price deflator, the savings deposit yield was negative, whereas the investments in common stocks and farm land rose 8 and 9 fold, respectively. These data indicate that great wealth has not been accumulated from savings-type investments in recent years. On the other hand, a large proportion of such depositors was in the middle and lower economic classes and had few alternative opportunities for investment.

Low Rates to Savers May Cause Higher Rates to Borrowers

In addition to the rich-poor fallacy, the causation assumed in the "low rates paid to savers lowers rates to borrowers" argument is questionable. Legal maximum rates, which are effective in holding rates below levels that banks and other financial agencies can afford to pay under competitive conditions, tend to reduce the flow of funds through normal channels and to divert savings into noncredit uses such as bonds, equities, real estate, etc. The smaller supply of funds moving into the credit market will meet an equal amount demanded at higher rates. Borrowers must pay the higher rates to obtain funds. Attempts to lower the rates to borrowers by limiting their opportunity to compete for funds is comparable to efforts to lower food prices by limiting the amount that farmers can spend on production. Total costs could be lowered, but output and consumption would decline, and prices of farm products and food would be increased.

A reduction in the flow of funds through efficient financial agencies and the consequent higher prices retard economic growth. Credit's contribution to growth is maximized when scarce credit resources flow most efficiently to areas where returns are greatest. Rates offered savers then transmit consumer and business demands for credit. When market rates exceed the legal maximum permitted, the appropriate signal is not transmitted to savers, and flows of funds are diverted from normal channels. Flows through the credit market decline and a greater portion of savings moves into equities, real estate, bonds, and direct loans. Credit-using activities which comprise a major part of economic growth are thus retarded. This diversion of credit flows and the consequent growth retardation are especially severe in the case of state restrictions, since funds are not only diverted to non-credit uses, but to credit uses in surrounding states.

Market Rates Distribute Credit to All Areas

The second reason for restricting interest rates payable—that uncontrolled rates paid tend to dry up loanable funds in rural areas and cause excessive concentrations of funds in the largest cities—is likewise questionable. It was contended that the speculators who borrowed funds in the largest cities could outbid borrowers in the smaller communities. Farmers, rural merchants, and other citizens would thus be without available credit, whereas bountiful supplies could be found in the large cities available to the speculators. This conception of the financial market is not consistent with the facts. The large financial agencies which gather funds are often located in the large centers, but they gather savings from both rural and urban areas, and under free market conditions distribute funds to areas where marginal returns are greatest. Rural areas have demonstrated their ability to compete for funds in national markets when provided with access to such markets. The farm credit banks are good examples of the ability of rural communities to compete for funds in the money market centers. Commercial banks likewise gather funds from savers in all areas and distribute them to areas of greatest marginal returns insofar as the banking structure permits. In some instances these distributions are in the form of direct loans, while in other cases funds are distributed to ultimate users through other financial agencies such as the farm credit banks.

Danger of Institutions Failing Overstated

The third argument for restricting rates payable—that high rates paid on savings force financial institutions into high-risk investments and ultimate failure—dates back to the early thirties. Its proponents see nothing that will serve to break the rise in rates paid on deposits when banks begin to bid against one another for funds. It is argued that the banks are compelled to take one imprudent investment step after another until asset risks reach intolerable levels and depositors' funds are ultimately lost. However, little evidence to confirm this view has been forthcoming.

George Benston found no relationship between interest rates paid on deposits and gross rate of return on investments.[28] He also found no relationship between average rates paid by banks and average risks of their portfolios, as measured by ultimate write-offs of investments. Contrary to the expectations of the high-rate, high-risk thesis, he found that interest rates paid were substituted at the margin for other operating expenses such as salaries, facilities, automated machinery, advertising, etc.

Profit maximization by banks, as in other firms, provides a more rational explanation of bank behavior. Banks are likely to use the same criterion in deciding what rate of interest to offer as they use in making other decisions relative to expense. In making decisions on hiring additional workers, they base their decisions on the expected value of services performed. They are likely to continue to hire additional help as long as the gain in value of services exceeds all costs associated with the additional labor. Marginal costs and returns, with due allowance for risks, also determine the level of interest rates that a bank decides to pay. Otherwise, the bank is not maximizing. Haywood and Linke conclude in a recent publication that "when stripped of the folklore that has grown up around it, the relevant rationale of deposit interest regulation in 1933 was price fixing, which was somewhat in vogue at the time as an anti-depression measure." [29]

A Costly Method of Protecting Financial Intermediaries

A more recent argument given for controlling interest rates payable on deposits at financial intermediaries is that sizable increases in rates paid may cause substantial hardship to savings and loan associations. In addition to destructive internal competition, destructive external competition has become a reason for restricting rates payable. It is contended that hardships would be especially severe on savings and loan associations because of the long-term nature of their assets and the short-run contracts on funds purchased. The average interest rate paid on all deposits rises immediately as rates offered increase, whereas returns increase only on new mortgage additions to the portfolio. Average earnings thus rise much more slowly than expenses.

The need for rate controls for this purpose may be questioned. The book value of aggregate reserves and undivided profits of savings and loan institutions is currently nearly twice the size of their yearly dividend payments. They also have cash and government security holdings from which payments could be made totaling over double their yearly dividend payments. These ratios prevailed even at the end of 1966, after the associations had endured their most adverse year. This means that the average association could remain solvent in an accounting sense and pay its dividends for nearly two years, even though it had no net profits. [30]

Investing on a long-term basis with short-term funds apparently calls for a substantial amount of liquidity. Such liquidity can be either in the form of short term loans or other short-term assets, such as government bonds, etc. If changes in savings and loan restrictions are necessary to provide greater liquidity, such changes are preferable to rate rigidities which deprive the community of the benefits of rate competition. Furthermore, other opportunities, such as maximum assistance from the Federal home loan banks during periods of stress, have apparently not been fully exploited. With 12 to 15 per cent of the portfolios of savings and loan associations turning over each year, assistance from the Home Loan Bank, coupled with a permissible reduction in reserves, should take care of most periods of interest rate rises for the major portion of savings and loan associations. These associations have considerable ability to withstand these periods when terms of trade are adverse. Furthermore, on the downside of interest rates, rapid accumulations of reserves can be made, offsetting losses on the upside of rate movements, and the Home Loan Bank can be repaid and reserves recouped.

Rate controls may have been the most important factor contributing to the slowdown in the housing industry during the recent periods of sharply rising general interest rates. Rising rates make yields on savings accounts at controlled levels less attractive than rates paid in the free market. There have been several setbacks in the rate of increase of savings capital of these institutions during periods of relatively high or rising interest rates. In only one quarter, however (third quarter, 1966, during which rate controls were put into effect), was there a moderate net decline. To the extent that rate controls reduced credit flows into the savings and loan industry, they affected housing adversely.

Appropriate monetary and fiscal policies are also important factors in maintaining the stability of savings and loan associations. Sharp increases in interest rates during recent years have been associated with rising prices. The real rate of return on loans and investments has been relatively stable. The rising prices can be associated with expansive fiscal and monetary actions. Thus, an important factor in maintaining relatively stable interest rates is the maintenance of fiscal and monetary policies that are conducive to stable prices.

If, as a final resort, other means are necessary to prevent widespread failures in savings and loan associations, direct Government loans through the Federal Home Loan Bank System are preferable to interest rate controls. Such assistance could be given only to the weak associations which had not adequately prepared for adverse economic conditions. In contrast to helping only the weak, rate controls widen the spread for all associations, and prevent rate competition within the banking community, and between savings and loan associations and banks. Thus, the public loses the benefit of rate competition and at the same time loses the benefit of the potential growth of both associations and banks during periods of sharply rising rates.

A major effect of rate controls is the limitation of the size of controlled firms, which in turn causes a more rapid growth in flows of funds which are not controlled.

Rate restrictions thus may not be profitable to the agencies restricted. With the slower growth rate, bank earnings are likely to be less over the longer run, and savings and loan associations will perform a declining function in the economy. The rapid growth of farm credit at the farm credit banks relative to commercial banks in the past two years may illustrate this situation. Farm credit outstanding at production credit associations and Federal land banks rose at almost double the rate of farm credit expansion at commercial banks from 1965 to 1967.

SUMMARY

Restrictions on interest rates charged and paid by competitive financial institutions are vestiges of medieval and ancient thought, and are inapplicable to modern commercial economies. They are based on false premises, operate perversely, and are economically inefficient.

The ancients banned interest for ethical reasons, the medievals for religious and moral considerations; modern restrictions are a carry-over of such ideas plus a lack of confidence in market forces. Supply and demand for loan funds rather than rate controls historically have kept interest rates at moderate levels in the United States.

Ancient and medieval desires to improve the position of poor debtors relative to rich creditors may have had some basis. There is no evidence today, however, that borrowers from financial institutions are less wealthy than their saving depositors. A floor under rates paid might be more helpful to the poor than a ceiling. Usury ceilings eliminate the poor higher-risk borrowers from the credit market and thereby channel a higher percentage of loanable funds to lower-risk customers. Consequently, any alteration of rich-poor relationships made by low usury ceilings is likely to be in favor of the wealthy.

All ceilings which alter normal flows of funds retard economic growth. Low usury ceilings prohibit the higher rates necessary to offset the higher risks of business and individual innovators. Credit tends to be channeled into well-established, low-risk functions. Low ceilings on rates payable by financial agencies tend to restrict the flow of funds through usual credit channels. Loan fund supplies are thereby reduced, affecting borrowers adversely. Such restrictions are especially harmful to long-term credit users, such as the housing industry, where credit is the major source of purchase money and interest an important part of the total costs.

The thesis that high rates paid cause institutions to invest in high-risk assets has little validity. Instead of contributing to imprudent banking practices, high rates may indicate flexibility and competitiveness in meeting the sound credit demands of the community. Bank failures result from numerous factors, both internal and external. External factors such as monetary and fiscal policies and regional economic conditions may result in deposit drains and loan losses. These factors were probably the major cause of the failures in the 1930's which led to rate ceilings. In any event, evidence indicates that when low legal limits are set on rates payable, banks substitute other expenses at the margin, such as advertising, attractive buildings, and gifts, where such substitutions are profitable.

The more recent reason for controls—that rate competition creates excessive hardships for savings and loan associations—is likewise difficult to uphold. It implies that a wider profit margin for banks is necessary to keep funds flowing through the savings and loan associations into the home building industry. This wider margin for banks was established despite the fact that bank failures were almost at the zero level. This type of assistance protects both the strong and the weak, inhibits price competition between the two types of firms and among firms within each group, and diverts funds to less desirable uses.

Greater liquidity in the form of more short-term assets is apparently necessary for a number of savings and loan associations. Some increase in such assets will permit the associations to weather most sharp increases in rates without excessive strain.

If some assistance is necessary for savings and loan associations, a reduction in price competition appears to be an extremely expensive type of aid. Greater assistance to the weaker associations through the Federal Home Loan Bank System would appear more appropriate.

Monetary and fiscal policies which contribute to greater price stability should alleviate most requests for assistance by savings and loan associations. Such policies will reduce the rate of inflation, which in turn is incorporated into interest rates, thus moderating rate increases.

Finally, controls on rates payable by financial agencies ignore the welfare of savers who invest through these agencies. Such savers perform a vital function in the economy. Rate controls deny many low income savers the right to a competitive loanable funds market. High income savers can bypass the controlled market by investing in equities, etc., but if rate controls cause them to divert funds or to lose interest income, their contribution to economic product is reduced.

NOTES

1 *Federal Reserve Bulletin*, July 1968, p. A-11. Since February 1936, maximum rates that may be paid by insured non-member banks have been the same as those for member banks.

2 Eugen von Bohm-Bawerk, *Capital and Interest*, Volume I, 4th edition, 1921, translated (South Holland, Illinois: Libertarian Press, 1959), p. 10.

3 Sidney Homer, *A History of Interest Rates* (New Brunswick, New Jersey: Rutgers University Press, 1963), p. 52.

4 Bohm-Bawerk, p. 12.

5 R. H. Tawney, *Religion and the Rise of Capitalism* (New York: The New American Library of World Literature, Inc., 1950), p. 18.

6 *Ibid.*, p. 20.

7 Joseph A. Schumpeter, *History of Economic Analysis* (New York: Oxford University Press, 1954), p. 332.

8 Bohm-Bawerk, p. 41.

9 Schumpeter, p. 332.

10 Homer, p. 187.

11 Amendment to the Federal Reserve Act, section 24, dated February 25, 1927 (44 Stat. 1224, ch. 191).

12 *Hearings Before a Subcommittee of the Committee on Banking and Currency*, United States Senate, Seventy-fourth Congress, First Session on S-1715, Part I, April 19 to May 13, 1935, p. 217.

13 *Hearings Before the Committee on Banking and Currency*, House of Representatives, Seventy-fourth Congress, First Session on H. R. 5357, February 21 to April 8, 1935, p. 330.

14 *Hearings Before the Committee on Banking and Currency*, Seventy-second Congress, First Session on S-4115, Part I, March 23–25, 1932.

15 Quoted in *Hearings Before the Committee on Banking and Currency*, House of Representatives, Seventy-eighth Congress, Second Session on H. R. 3956, December 10, 1943 to February 9, 1944, p. 2.

16 *Ibid.*, p. 679.

17 *Ibid.*, p. 16.

18 *Hearings Before a Subcommittee of the Committee on Banking and Currency*, United States Senate, Seventy-fourth Congress, First Session on S-1715, Part II, May 14–22, 1935, pp. 490–491.

19 *Hearings Before the Committee on Banking and Currency*, House of Representatives.

Seventy-fourth Congress, First Session on H. R. 5357, February 21 to April 8, 1935, p. 86.

20 *Hearings Before the Committee on Banking and Currency*, Eighty-ninth Congress, Second Session on H. R. 14026, May 9 to June 23, 1966, pp. 7–8.

21 *Ibid.*, p. 72.

22 *Ibid.*, p. 263.

23 *Ibid.*, p. 429.

24 See Harry L. Johnson, "An Island Unto Itself," *Tennessee Survey of Business*, the University of Tennessee, Volume III, No. 7, March 1968.

25 States with the 6 per cent limit as of August 1967 were: Delaware, Kentucky, Maryland, New Jersey, New York, North Carolina, Pennsylvania, Tennessee, Vermont, Virginia, and West Virginia. Since then some of the above states have raised their limits.

26 Andrew F. Brimmer, "Statutory Interest Rate Ceilings and the Availability of Mortgage Funds," Federal Reserve Bank of Philadelphia, Supplement to *Business Review*, June 1968.

27 "Memeber Bank Lending to Small Business," *Federal Reserve Bulletin*, April 1958, p. 396.

28 George J. Benston, "Interest Payments on Demand Deposits and Bank Investment Behavior," *Journal of Political Economy*, October 1964, pp. 431–449.

29 Charles F. Haywood and Charles M. Linke, *The Regulation of Deposit Interest Rates*, a study prepared for the Trustees of the Banking Research Fund, Association of Reserve City Bankers, (Chicago, Illinois: June 15, 1968), p. 3.

30 See "Does Slower Monetary Expansion Discriminate Against Housing" by Norman N. Bowsher and Lionel Kalish in the June 1968 issue of this *Review*.

What Classical and Neoclassical Monetary Theory Really Was*
Paul A. Samuelson

To know your own country you must have travelled abroad. To understand modern economics it is good to have lived long enough to have escaped competent instruction in its mysteries. When Archibald and Lipsey try to draw for Patinkin a picture of what a "classical" monetary theorist believed in, they are pretty much in the position of a man who, looking for a jackass, must say to himself, "If I were a jackass, where would I go?"

Mine is the great advantage of having once been a jackass. From 2 January 1932 until an indeterminate date in 1937, I was a classical monetary theorist. I do not have to look for the tracks of the jackass embalmed in old journals and monographs. I merely have to lie down on the couch and recall in tranquillity, upon that inward eye which is the bliss of solitude, what it was that I believed between the ages of 17 and 22. This puts me in the same advantageous position that Pio Nono enjoyed at the time when the infallibility of the Pope was being enunciated. He could say, incontrovertibly, "Before I was Pope, I believed he was infallible. Now that I am Pope, I can *feel* it."

Essentially, we believed that in the longest run and in ideal models the amount of money did not matter. Money could be "neutral" and in many conditions the hypothesis that it was could provide a good first or last approximation to the facts. To be sure, Hume, Fisher, and Hawtrey had taught us that, under

Paul A. Samuelson, "What Classical and Neoclassical Monetary Theory Really Was," *Canadian Journal of Economics*, I (February 1968), pp. 1–15.

* I owe thanks to the National Science Foundation.

dynamic conditions, an increase in money might lead to "money illusion" and might cause substantive changes—e.g., a shift to debtor-entrepreneurs and away from creditor-rentiers, a forced-saving shift to investment and away from consumption, a lessening of unemployment, a rise in wholesale prices relative to sticky retail prices and wage rates, *et cetera*.

But all this was at a second level of approximation, representing relatively transient aberrations. Moreover, this tended to be taught in applied courses on business cycles, money and finance, and economic history rather than in courses on pure theory. In a real sense there *was* a dichotomy in our minds; we were schizophrenics. From 9 to 9:50 A.M. we presented a simple quantity theory of neutral money. There were then barely ten minutes to clear our palates for the 10 to 10:50 discussion of how an engineered increase in M would help the economy. In mid-America in the mid-1930's, we neoclassical economists tended to be mild inflationists, jackasses crying in the wilderness and resting our case essentially on sticky prices and costs, and on expectations.

Returning to the 9 o'clock hour, we thought that *real* outputs and inputs and price ratios depended essentially in the longest run on real factors, such as tastes, technology, and endowments. The stock of money we called M (or, to take account of chequable bank deposits, we worked in effect with a velocity-weighted average of M and M'; however, a banking system with fixed reserve and other ratios would yield M' proportional to M, so M alone would usually suffice). An increase in M—usually we called it a doubling on the ground that after God created unity he created the second integer—would cause a proportional increase in *all* prices (tea, salt, female labour, land rent, share or bond prices) and values (expenditure on tea or land, share dividends, interest income, taxes). You will hardly believe it, but few economists in those days tried to write down formal equations for what they were thinking. Had we been asked to choose which kinds of equation system epitomized our thinking, I believe at first blush we would have specified:

A. Write down a system of real equations involving *real* outputs and inputs, and *ratios* of prices (values), and depending essentially on real tastes, technologies, market structures, and endowments. Its properties are invariant to change in the stock of money M.

B. Then append a fixed-supply-of-M equation that pins down (or up) the absolute price level, determining the scale factor that was essentially indeterminate in set A. This could be a quantity equation of exchange—$MV = PQ$—or some other non-homogeneous equation. More accurately, while A involves homogeneity of degree zero in *all* Ps, B involves homogeneity of degree 1 of Ps in terms of M.

I have purposely left the above paragraphs vague. For I doubt that the typical good classical monetary theorist had more definite notions about the *mathematics* of his system.

Moreover, I must leave room for an essential strand in our thinking. Our expositions always began with barter and worked our fundamental pricing in barter models. But then we, sensibly, pointed out the *real* inconvenience of barter and the real convenience of an abstract unit of money. Here we made explicit and tacit reference to the real facts of brokerage or transaction charges, of uncertainties of income and outgo, and so on. In short, we did have a primitive inventory theory of money holding, but we were careful to note that true money—unlike pearls, paintings, wine, and coffee—is held only for the

ultimate exchange work it can do, which depends upon the scale of *all* Ps in a special homogeneous way.

So there was another dichotomy in our minds, a very legitimate one. We had, so to speak, *qualitative* and *quantitative* theories of money. According to our qualitative theory, money was not neutral; it made a big difference. Pity the country that was still dependent upon barter, for it would have an inefficient economic system. But once this qualitative advantage had been realized by the adoption of market structures using M, the *quantitative* level of M was of no particular significance (except for indicated transient states and uninteresting resource problems involved in gold mining or mint printing). We liked the image of John Stuart Mill that money is the *lubricant* of industry and commerce. As even women drivers know, lubrication is important. But M is quantitatively a special lubricant: a drop will do as well as a poolful. So an even better image was the post-Mill one: money is like a catalyst in a chemical reaction, which makes the reaction go faster and better, but which, like the oil in the widow's cruse, is never used up. To push the analogy beyond endurance, only an iota of catalyst is needed for the process.

What I have just said makes it unmistakably clear that a classical monetary theorist would not go the stake for the belief that the real set of equations A are independent of M, depending essentially only on price ratios as in barter. If time were short on a quiz, I might carelessly write down such an approximation. But if asked specifically the question "Is Set A really independent of M?" I and my classmates would certainly answer "No" and we would cite the qualitative aspects mentioned earlier.

In a moment we shall see that this considered qualitative view requires that *M enter quantitatively in Set A in certain specified homogeneous ways.* But first let us investigate how those of us who were mathematically inclined would have handled the Set A and Set B problem. The economists interested in mathematics tended to be specialists in value theory. They had a big job just to describe the real relations of A, whether under barter or otherwise. They wanted to simplify their expositions, to sidestep extraneous complication. Hence, many would have followed the practice (which I seem to connect with Cassel's name, at least) of writing Set A purely in barter terms, and essentially giving enough equations to determine real quantities and price ratios —as follows:

$$f_i(Q_1, \ldots, Q_n, P_1, \ldots, P_n) = 0$$
$$(i = 1, 2, \ldots, 2n) \quad \text{(A')}$$

where there are n inputs or outputs, with n prices. However, the f_i functions are made to be homogeneous of degree zero in all the Ps, and, luckily, the $2n$ functions f_i are required to involve one of them as being dependent on the other, thus avoiding an overdetermination of the $2n$ functions. This homogeneity and dependence postulate enables us to write (A') in the equivalent form:

$$f_i(Q_1, \ldots, Q_n, \lambda P_1, \ldots, \lambda P_n)_\lambda \equiv 0$$
$$(i = 1, 2, \ldots, 2n) \quad \text{(A')}$$

This formulation does not contain price ratios explicitly. But since λ is arbitrary, it can be set equal to $1/P_1$ to give us price ratios, $P_i/1$. Or if you have an interest in some kind of average of prices, say $\pi(P_1, \ldots, P_n) = \pi(P)$, where π is a homogeneous function of degree one, you can rewrite A' in terms of ratios $P_i/\pi(P)$ alone, by suitable choice of λ. Hence, Set A' involves $2n - 1$ independent functions which hopefully determine a unique (or multiple) solution to the $2n - 1$ real variables $(Q_1, \ldots, Q_n, P_2/P_1, \ldots, P_n/P_1)$. With the special structure of (A'), we are now free to add any non-homogeneous

(B') we like, of the following types:

$P_1 = 1$, good 1 being taken as numéraire, or
$P_1 + P_2 = 3.1416$, or
$P_1 + P_2 + \cdots + P_n = 1$, or
$P_1[(Q_1^* + (P_2^*/P_1)Q_2^* + \cdots$
$\quad + (P_n^*/P_1)Q_n] = \bar{M}$, Fisher's Constant, where Q_i^*, $(P_i/P_1)^*$ are solutions of (A'). (B')

Of course, the last of these looks like the Fisher–Marshall formulation of the "quantity equation of exchange." But, since some Q_i are inputs, my way of writing it recognizes the realistic fact that money is needed to pay factors as well as to move goods.[1]

I do not defend this special (A', B') formulation. I am sure it was often used. And even today, if I am behind in my lectures, I resort to it in courses on pure theory. But we should admit that it is imperfect. And we should insist that the classical writers, when they did full justice to their own views, did not believe that this formulation was more than a provisional simplification.

What is a minimal formulation of (A, B) that does do full justice? I am sure that I personally, from 1937 on at least, had a correct vision of the proper version. It is as if to understand Gary, Indiana, I had to travel to Paris. I began to understand neoclassical economics only after Keynes' *General Theory* shook me up. But I am sure that I was only learning to articulate what was intuitively felt by such ancients as Ricardo, Mill, Marshall, Wicksell, and Cannan. I regret that I did not then write down a formal set of equations. I did discuss the present issue at the Econometric Society meetings of 1940, of which only an incomplete abstract appeared, and also at its 1949 meetings, where W. B. Hickman, Leontief, and others spoke; and there are fragmentary similar remarks in half a dozen of my writings of twenty years ago. The nub of the matter is contained in my 1947 specification[2] that the utility function contain in it, along with physical quantities of good consumed, the stock of M and all money Ps, being homogeneous of degree zero in $(M, P_1, \ldots, P_n)$ in recognition of money's peculiar "neutral" quantitative properties.

Frankly, I was repelled by the abstract level at which Oskar Lange, Hicks, and others carried on their discussion of Say's Law, staying at the level of equation counting and homogeneity reckoning, without entering into the concrete character of the models. And this was one of the few continuing controversies of economics from which I steadfastly abstained.

For the rest of this discussion, what I propose to do is to get off the couch and go to the blackboard and write down an organized picture of what we jackasses implicitly believed back in the bad old days.

THE WAY THINGS ARE

I abstract heroically. We are all exactly alike. We live forever, We are perfect competitors and all-but-perfect soothsayers. Our inelastic labour supply is fully employed, working with inelastically supplied Ricardian land and (possibly heterogeneous) capital goods. We have built-in Pigou–Böhm rates of subjective time preference, discounting each next-year's independent utility by the constant factor $1/(l + \rho)$, $\rho > 0$. We are in long-run equilibrium without technical change or population growth: the stock of capital goods has been depressed to the point where all own-interest-rates yielded by production are equal to r, the market rate of interest; in turn, r is equal to the subjective interest rate ρ, this being the condition for our propensity to consume being 100 per cent of income, with zero net capital formation.

We equally own land, and such capital goods as machinery and material stocks. We own, but legally cannot sell, our future stream of labour earnings. We hold cash balances, because we are *not* perfect soothsayers when it comes to the uncertainty of the timing of our in-and-out-payments, which can be assumed to follow certain probability laws in the background; this lack of synchronization of payments plus the indivisible costs of transactions (brokerage charges, need for journal entries, spread between bid and ask when earning assets are converted into or out of cash, etc.) requires us to hold money. To keep down inessential complications, while not omitting Hamlet from the scenario, I am neglecting the need for cash balances for corporations; it is as if consumer families alone need cash balances for their final consumption purchases, whereas in real life cash is needed at every vertical stage of the production process. Later we can allow our holdings of earning assets— titles to land and machines—to economize on our need for M balances, just as does the prospect of getting wage increases.

Our system is assumed to come into long-run equilibrium. This equilibrium can be deduced to be unique if we add to our extreme symmetry assumptions the conventional strong convexity assumptions of neoclassical theorizing—constant returns to scale with smooth diminishing returns to proportions, quasi-concave ordinal utility functions that guarantee diminishing marginal rates of substitution, and so on.

We should be able to *prove rigorously* what is probably intuitively obvious— doubling all M will exactly double *all* long-run prices and values, and this change in the absolute price level will have absolutely no effect on real output-inputs, on price ratios or terms of trade, on interest rate and factor shares generally.

For this system, it is not merely the case that tautological quantity equations of exchange can be written down. Less trivially, a simple "quantity theory of prices and money" holds exactly for the long-run equilibrium model. Although

Patinkin has doubts about the propriety of the concept, I think our meaning was unambiguous—and unobjectionable—when we used to say that the "demand curve for money" (traced out by shifts in the vertical supply curve of M) plotted in a diagram containing, on the x axis, M and, on the Y axis, the "value of money" (as measured by the reciprocal of *any* absolute money price $1/P_i$ or any average price level) would be a rectangular hyperbola with a geometrical Marshallian elasticity of exactly minus one.

To prove this I write down the simplest possible set of equations. These do split up into two parts, showing that there is a legitimate "dichotomy" between "real elements" and "monetary elements which determine only the absolute level of prices." Call these two parts A and B. Now this legitimate dichotomy will not be identical with the over-simple dichotomy of A' and B' mentioned earlier. If Patinkin insists upon the difference, I am in complete agreement with him. If he should prefer not to call the (A, B) split a dichotomy, that semantic issue is not worth arguing about so long as enough words are used to describe exactly what the (A, B) split is, and how it differs from the (A', B') split. If Patinkin insists on saying that my A equations do have in them a "real balance effect," I see no harm in that—even though, as will be seen, my formulation of A need involve no use of an average price index, and hence no need to work with a "deflated M" that might be called a real balance. Peculiarly in the abstract neoclassical model with its long-run strong homogeneity properties, all Ps move together in strict proportion when M alone changes and hence no index-number approximations are needed. By the same token, they do absolutely no harm: Patinkin is entitled to use any number of average price concepts and real-balance concepts he wishes. If Patinkin wishes to say that the principal neoclassical writers (other than Walras) had failed to *publish*

a clear and unambiguous account of the (A, B) equation such as I am doing here, I would agree, and would adduce the worth and novelty of Patinkin's own book and contributions. On the other hand, the present report on my recollections claims that the best neoclassical writers did *perceive* at the intuitive level the intrinsic content of the (A, B) dichotomy which I am about to present. All the more we should regret that no one fully set down these intuitions thirty years ago!

Now what about Archibald and Lipsey?[3] I want to avoid semantic questions as to what is meant by real-balance effects being operative. If they claim that the (A', B') dichotomy does justice to the tacit neoclassical models of 1930, I think they are wrong. If they think an (A', B') dichotomy does justice to a reasonably realistic long-run model of a monetary economy, I think they are also wrong. Whether, as a *tour de force*, some special, flukey (A', B') model might be found to give a representation of some monetary economy is a possibility that I should hate to deny in the abstract; but I should be surprised if this issue turned out to be an interesting one to linger on or to debate. For what a casual opinion is worth, it is my impression that Patinkin's general position—which I interpret to be essentially identical to my (A, B) dichotomy *and* to the tacit neoclassical theory of my youth—is left impregnable to recent attacks on it. There is one, and only one, legitimate dichotomy in neoclassical monetary theory.

Abjuring further doctrinal discussion, I proceed now to the equations of my simplest system.

STRUCTURE OF THE MODEL
1 Production Relations

To keep down inessentials, let land, T, real capital, K (assumed homogeneous merely as a preliminary to letting K stand for a vector of heterogeneous capital goods), and labour, L, produce real output which, because of similarity of production factors in all sectors, can be split up into the linear sum of different physical consumption goods $\pi_1 q_1 + \cdots + \pi_n q_n$ and net capital formation $\dot{K}(= dK/dt)$, namely: $K + \pi_1 q_1 + \pi_2 q_2 + \cdots + \pi_m q_m = f(K, L, T)$ where F is a production function of the Ramsey–Solow type, homogeneous of first degree, and where the π_i are constants, representing marginal costs of the ith goods relative to machines. From this function, we can deduce all factor prices and commodity prices relative to the price of the capital good P_K, namely:

$$\frac{P_i}{P_K} = \pi_i \qquad (i = 1, 2, \ldots, n) \qquad (A_{I,1})$$

$$\frac{W}{P_K} = \frac{\partial F(K, \bar{L}, \bar{T})}{\partial L}$$

the marginal productivity wage

$$\frac{R}{P_K} = \frac{\partial F(K, \bar{L}, \bar{T})}{\partial T} \qquad (A_{I,2})$$

the marginal productivity rent

$$r = \frac{\partial F(K, \bar{L}, \bar{T})}{\partial K}$$

the marginal productivity interest rate

Bars are put over L and T because their supplies are assumed to be fixed. To determine the unknown stock of capital K we need:

$r = \rho$, the subjective time preference parameter[4]

$\dot{K} = 0$, the implied steady-state long-run equilibrium condition

$r = R/P_T$, the implicit capitalization equation for the price of land $\qquad (A_{II})$

Hence, $\rho = \partial F(\bar{K}, \bar{L}, T)/\partial K$ henceforth gives us our fixed $\bar{K}$.

The above relationships determine for the representative man the wage and interest income (inclusive of land rentals expressed as interest on land values) which he can spend on the $(q_1, q_2, \ldots, q_n)$ goods and on holding of M cash balances

which bear no interest and thus cost their opportunity costs in terms of interest forgone (or, to a net borrower, the interest on borrowings). What motive is there for holding any M? As I point out in *Foundations*, one can put M into the utility function, along with other things, as a real convenience in a world of stochastic uncertainty and indivisible transaction charges.[5]

If, however, one does put M directly into U, one must remember the crucial fact that M differs from every other good (such as tea) in that it is not really wanted for its own sake but only for the ultimate exchanges it will make possible. So along with M, we must always put all Ps into U, so that U is homogeneous of degree zero in the set of monetary variables (M, $P_1, \ldots, P_m$), with the result that (λM, $\lambda P_1, \ldots, \lambda P_m$) leads to the same U for all λ.

In *Foundations*, I wrote such a U function:

$$U(q_1, q_2, \ldots, q_n; M, P_1, P_2, \ldots, P_n)_\lambda \equiv$$
$$U(q_1, \ldots, q_m; \lambda M, \lambda P_1, \ldots, \lambda P_n)$$

where Ps are prices in terms of money. Here I want merely to add a little further cheap generality. The convenience of a given M depends not only on Ps, but also upon the earning assets you hold and on your wage prospects. It is not that we will add to M the earning-asset total EA, which equals $P_T \bar{T} + P_K \bar{K}$. Nor shall we add EA after giving the latter some fractional weight to take account of brokerage and other costs of liquidating assets into cash in an uncertain world. Rather, we include such new variables in U to the right of the semicolon to get:

$$U(q_1, \ldots, q_n; M, EA, W\bar{L}, P_1, \ldots, P_n) =$$
$$U(q; x) = U(q; \lambda x)$$

That is, increasing all Ps, including those of each acre of land and machine and of hourly work along with M, will not make one better off. Thus U ends up homogeneous of degree zero in M and *all* prices $(M, P_K, P_T, W, P_1, \ldots, P_n)$ by postulate.

Now, subject to the long-run budget equation indicated below, the representative man maximizes his utility:

$$U(q_1, \ldots, q_n; M, P_K \bar{K} + P_T \bar{T}, W \bar{L}, P_1, \cdots, P_n)$$

subject to

$$\max_{[q_1, \ldots, q_n, M]} P_1 q_1 + \cdots + P_n q_n$$
$$= W\bar{L} + r(\text{Total Wealth} - M)$$

or

$$P_1 q_1 + \cdots + P_n q_n + rM$$
$$= W\bar{L} + r(TW)$$
$$= W\bar{L} + r(P_K \bar{K} + P_T \bar{T} + M^*)$$

where each representative man has Total Wealth defined as:

Total Wealth (in money value)
$$= EA + \text{Money Endowment}$$
$$= P_K \bar{K} + P_T \bar{T} + M^*$$

where M^* is the money created in the past by gold mining or by government.

The maximizing optimality conditions give the demand for all q_1 and for M in terms of the variables prescribed for the individual, namely:

$$(P_1, \ldots, P_n, W, P_K, P_T; r, \bar{K}, \bar{L}, \bar{T})$$

The optimality equations can be cast in the form:

$$\frac{\partial U / \partial q_1}{P_1} = \cdots = \frac{\partial U / \partial q_n}{P_n} = \frac{\partial U / \partial M}{r}$$

or

$$\frac{\partial U / \partial M}{\sum_1^n q_j \dfrac{\partial U}{\partial q_i} + M \dfrac{\partial U}{\partial M}}$$
$$= \frac{r}{W\bar{L} + r(P_K \bar{K} + P_T \bar{T} + M^*)}$$
$$(A_{\mathrm{III},1})$$
$$(i = 1, 2, \ldots, n)$$

$$\frac{\partial U / \partial q_i}{\sum_1^n q_j \dfrac{\partial U}{\partial q_j} + M \dfrac{\partial U}{\partial M}}$$
$$= \frac{P_i}{W\bar{L} + r(P_K \bar{K} + P_T \bar{T} + M^*)}$$
$$(A_{\mathrm{III},2})$$

But for society as a whole (and hence for the representative man who, even if he does not know it, represents $1/N$th of the total in our symmetrical situation) total money demanded, M, must end up equalling total money endowment, M^*:

$$M = M^* \qquad (A_{\mathrm{III},3})$$

An important comment is in order.[6] Although $(A_{\mathrm{III},3})$ holds for society as a whole, being essentially a definition of demand-for-money equilibrium, each representative man (one of thousands of such men) can*not* act in the belief that his budget equation has the form:

$$P_1 q_1 + \cdots + P_n q_n + rM$$
$$= W\bar{L} + r(P_K \bar{K} + P_T \bar{T} + M)$$

even though substituting $(A_{\mathrm{III},3})$ into the earlier budget equation would yield this result. What is true for all is not true for each. Each man thinks of his cash balance as costing him forgone interest and as buying himself convenience. But for the community as a whole, the total M^* is there and is quite costless to use. Forgetting gold mining and the historical expenditure of resources for the creating of M^*, the existing M^* is, so to speak, a free good from society's viewpoint. Moreover, its *effective* amount can, from the community's viewpoint, be indefinitely augmented by the simple device of having a lower absolute level of *all* money prices. To see this in still another way, with fixed labour L and land T and capital K big enough to give the interest rates equal to the psychological rate ρ, the community can consume on the production possibility equation:

$$P_1 q_1 + \cdots P_n q_n = F(\bar{K}, \bar{L}, T)$$
$$= W\bar{L} + r(P_K K + P_T \bar{T})$$

and to *each* side of this could be added rM of any size without affecting this true physical menu.

Evidently we have here an instance of a lack of optimality of laissez-faire: there is a kind of fictitious internal diseconomy from holding more cash balances, as things look to the individual. Yet if all were made to hold larger cash balances, which they turned over more slowly, the resulting lowering of absolute price would end up making everybody better off. Better off in what sense? In the sense of having a higher U, which comes from having to make fewer trips to the bank, fewer trips to the brokers, smaller printing and other costs of transactions whose only purpose is to provide cash when you have been holding too little cash.

From society's viewpoint, the optimum occurs when people are satiated with cash and have:

$\partial U/\partial M$

$= 0$ instead of $r \times$ (positive

constant) > 0

But this will not come about under laissez-faire, with stable prices.[7]

Now let us return from this digression on social cost to our equations of equilibrium. Set A consists of the (A_1) equations relating to production and implied pricing relations, and of the (A_{II}) equations relating to long-run equilibrium of zero saving and investment, where technological and subjective interest rates are equal and provide capitalized values for land and other assets. Finally, (A_{III}) are the demand conditions for the consumer, but generalized beyond the barter world to include explicitly the qualitative convenience of money *and to take into account the peculiar homogeneity properties of money resulting from the fact that its usefulness is in proportion to the scale of prices.* Though the exact form of (A_{III}) is novel, its logic is that implied by intuitive classical theories of money.

All of equations A have been cast in the form of involving ratios of prices, values, and M^* only (to put (A_{III}) in this form, multiply M into the numerators on each side). That means they are homogeneous functions of degree zero in all Ps, and M^* or M, being capable of being written in

the general form:

$$G_i\left(q_1, \ldots, q_n, K, \bar{L}, \bar{T}, r; \frac{P_K}{M}, \frac{W}{M}, \frac{R}{M}, \frac{P_1}{M}, \ldots, \frac{P_n}{M}, \frac{TW}{M}\right) = 0$$

(A)

where all the magnitudes to the left of the semicolon are "real" and all those to the right are *ratios* of a price or a value to the quantity of money. If a price ratio like P_i/P_j appears in an equation and no M, we can rewrite the ratio as $(P_i/M)/(P_j/M)$.

To the set A, we now append a decomposable single equation to fix the supply of money:

M or $M^* = \bar{M}$, an exogenous supply

(B)

This single equation is not homogeneous of degree zero in Ps and M and therefore it does pin down the absolute scale of all Ps and values in direct proportion to the quantity of M. Why? Because Set A consists of as many independent equations as there are unknown real quantities and ratios. Let us check this. Omitting fixed $(\bar{L}, \bar{T})$, we count $n + 2 + n + 5$ unknowns in G_i when we ignore both $\dot{K}$ and the $\dot{K} = 0$ equation. We count $n + 3$ equations in (A_1), 2 equations in (A_{II}), and $n + 2$ *equations* in (A_{III}). Thus $2n + 7 = 2n + 7$. Another way of looking at the matter is this: (A_I) and (A_{II}) determine all Ps as proportional to P_K. Then for fixed P_K and M^*, (A_{III}) determines all qs and M, the latter doubling when P_K and M^* double.

Summarizing, Set A determines all real quantities and all prices and values in ratio to the stock of M^*. Then equation B determines $M^* = M$ and hence the absolute level of all prices in proportion to $\bar{M}$.

Where in A or B is the quantity theory's "equation of exchange" to be found? Certainly not in B. If anywhere, an $MV = PQ$ equation must be found in A. Where? Certainly not in (A_I) or (A_{II}). In

(A_{III}) equation ($A_{III,1}$) deals with the relative marginal utility of the cash balance. By itself, it is not an $M = PQ/V$ equation. Only after all the (A_{III}) equations are solved, can we express M in a function that is proportional to any (and all) P_i:

$$M = P_i\Psi_i(\cdots)$$

where the Ψ functions depend on a great variety of real magnitudes.

This suggests to me that the late Arthur Marget was wrong in considering it a fault of Walras that, after the second edition of his *Elements*, he dropped a simple $MV = PQ$ equation. Classical and neoclassical monetary theory is much better than a crude quantity theory, although it can report similar results from special ideal experiments. In particular, correct neoclassical theory does not lead to the narrow anti-Keynesian view of those Chicago economists who allege that velocity of circulation is not a function of interest rates.

HOW *M* GETS ALLOCATED

Symmetry plays an important role in the model given here. With every man exactly alike, it does not matter where or how we introduce new money into the system; for it gets divided among people in exactly the same proportions as previous M. We classical writers were aware that the strict (A, B) dichotomy held only when every unit's M (say M^1, M^2, ...) stayed proportional to total $\overline{M} = \sum M^k$. But being careless fellows, we often forgot to warn that this was only a first approximation to more complicated incidents of gold inflations and business cycle expansions.

Can this rock-bottom simplicity be retained if we relax this extreme symmetry assumption (which renders the problem almost a Robinson Crusoe one)? Providing all income elasticities, including that for M, are (near) unity, it never matters (much) how things are divided among

people. Collective indifference curves of the Robinson Crusoe type then work for all society. The simple structure of (A_{III}) is preserved and the uniqueness of equilibrium is assured. Again, it matters not how the new M is introduced into the system.

Finally, there was an even more interesting third assumption implicit and explicit in the classical mind. It was a belief in unique long-run equilibrium independent of initial conditions. I shall call it the "ergodic hypothesis" by analogy to the use of this term in statistical mechanics. Remember that the classical economists were fatalists (a synonym for "believers in equilibrium"!). Harriet Martineau, who made fairy tales out of economics (unlike modern economists who make economics out of fairy tales), believed that if the state redivided income each morning, by night the rich would again be sleeping in their comfortable beds and the poor under the bridges. (I think she thought this a cogent argument against egalitarian taxes.)

Now, Paul Samuelson, aged 20 a hundred years later, was not Harriet Martineau or even David Ricardo; but as an equilibrium theorist he naturally tended to think of models in which things settle down to a unique position independently of initial conditions. Technically speaking, we theorists hoped not to introduce *hysteresis* phenomena into our model, as the Bible does when it says "We pass this way only once" and, in so saying, takes the subject out of the realm of science into the realm of genuine history. Specifically, we did not build into the Walrasian system the Christian names of particular individuals, because we thought that the general distribution of income between social classes, not being critically sensitive to initial conditions, would emerge in a determinate way from our equilibrium analysis.

Like Martineau, we envisaged an oversimplified model with the following ergodic property: no matter how we start the distribution of money among persons —M^1, M^2, . . .—after a sufficiently long time it will become distributed among them in a unique ergodic state (rich men presumably having more and poor men less). I shall not spell out here a realistic dynamic model but content myself with a simple example.

Half the people are men, half women. Each has a probability propensity to spend three-quarters of its today's money on its own products and one-quarter on the other sex's. We thus have a Markov transitional probability matrix of the form

$$A = \begin{bmatrix} \dfrac{3}{4} & \dfrac{1}{4} \\ \dfrac{1}{4} & \dfrac{3}{4} \end{bmatrix} = \begin{bmatrix} \dfrac{1}{2} + \dfrac{a}{2} & \dfrac{1}{2} - \dfrac{a}{2} \\ \dfrac{1}{2} - \dfrac{a}{2} & \dfrac{1}{2} + \dfrac{a}{2} \end{bmatrix}$$

with $a = \frac{1}{2}$ and

$$A^t = \begin{bmatrix} \dfrac{1}{2} + \dfrac{a^t}{2} & \dfrac{1}{2} - \dfrac{a^t}{2} \\ \dfrac{1}{2} - \dfrac{a^t}{2} & \dfrac{1}{2} + \dfrac{a^t}{2} \end{bmatrix}$$

$$\lim_{t \to \infty} A^t = \begin{bmatrix} \dfrac{1}{2} & \dfrac{1}{2} \\ \dfrac{1}{2} & \dfrac{1}{2} \end{bmatrix}, \text{ the ergodic state}$$

Suppose we start out with men and women each having M of ($100, $100). Now introduce a new $100 to women only. Our transitional sequent in dollars will then be ($200, $100), ($175, $125), ($162$\frac{1}{2}$, 137\frac{1}{2}$), ($156$\frac{1}{4}$, 143\frac{3}{4}$), ($151$\frac{9}{16}$, 148\frac{7}{16}$), . . . with the obvious limiting ergodic state ($150, $150) since the divergence from this state is being halved at each step. Such an ergodic system will have the special homogeneity properties needed for the (A, B) dichotomy.[8]

None of this denies the fact that the leading neoclassical economists often recognized cases and models in which it does make a difference, both in the short and the long run, how the new money is introduced and distributed throughout the system. One of the weaknesses of a crude quantity theory is that it treats M created by open-market purchases by the central bank as if this were the same as M left over from last century's (or last minute's) mining. A change in M, accompanied by an opposite change in a near-M substitute like government short-term bonds, is *not* shown in my Set A.

Indeed, when all men are alike and live for ever, we have too simple a model to take account of the interesting effect upon the system of permanent interest-bearing public debt which we as taxpayers know we will not have to pay off or service beyond our lifetimes.[9]

EPILOGUE

With the positive content of traditional monetary theory now written down concretely for us to see, kick, and kick at, a few comments on some controversies of the last twenty years may be in order.

Oskar Lange began one line of reasoning on price flexibility in 1939 which culminated in his 1944 Cowles book, *Price Flexibility and Employment*.[10] Hicks' *Value and Capital*,[11] with its attempt to treat bonds and money just as some extra $n + 1$ and $n + 2$ goods along with n goods like tea and salt, had, I fear, a bad influence on Lange. It led to his suppressing possible differences between stocks and flows, to attempts to identify or contrast Say's Law with various formalisms of Walrasian analysis (such as the budget equation), and to discussion in the abstract of functions of many variables possessing or not possessing certain abstract homogeneity properties. There are many interesting points raised in Lange's book, and several analytical contributions to nonmonetary economic theory. But only about a dozen pages grapple with the key problem of money (e.g., pp. 5–19), and these stay at a formalistic level that never deals with the peculiar properties and problems of cash balances. I do not say that this approach of Lange's cannot be used to arrive at valid results, but in fact it remained rather sterile for twenty years.

I had thought that Don Patinkin's work from 1947 on, culminating in his classic *Money, Interest, and Prices*, was much influenced by the Lange approach, and I thought this a pity. But, on rereading the book, I am not sure. What Patinkin and Lange have in common is a considerable dependence upon the *Value and Capital* device of lumping money in as an extra good. This approach has not kept Patinkin from arriving at a synthesis consistent with what I believe was the best of neoclassical theory, or from going beyond anything previously appearing in the literature. But it may help to account for his attributing error to earlier thinkers when a more sympathetic reading might absolve them from error. When we become accustomed to approaching a problem in a certain way and using a certain nomenclature, we must not confuse the failure to use this same language and approach with substantive error. Still, beyond that, Patinkin scores many legitimate points: monetary economists had better intuitions than they were able to articulate. Thus I suspect that my (A, B) dichotomy is really very similar to what Cassel had in mind, but the only form in which he could render it mathematically was (A′, B′), which is inadequate (as Patinkin insists, though perhaps not for all the reasons he insists on). In what sense can one say that a man believes one thing when he says something else? In this nonoperational sense: if one could subpoena Cassel, show him the two systems and the defects in one, and then ask him which fits in best with his over-all intuitions, I believe he would pick (A, B) and not his own (A′, B′).[12] I might add that Cassel is not Walras; and it seems to me that Walras comes off better on Patinkin's own account than he is given credit for.

Some will interpret Archibald and Lipsey as defending an (A′, B′) dichotomy against Patinkin's rejection of that dichotomy. If that is their primary intention —and I am not sure that it is—I fear I must side with Patinkin. Logically, one can set up (A′, B′), as I did here and as Cassel did. But I think it is bad economics to believe in such a model. *All* its good features are in the (A, B) dichotomy and none of its bad ones.

On the other hand, there is certainly much more in Archibald and Lipsey than a defence of (A′, B′) and this important part of their paper seems to me to be quite within the spirit of Patinkin's analysis and my own. Here, however, I shall comment on the two different dichotomies.

I begin with (A′, B′).

$$F_i(q, P)_\lambda \equiv F_i(q, \lambda P) \qquad (i = 2, \ldots, 2n)$$
$$\text{(A′)}$$

$$P_1 = 1 \quad \text{or}$$
$$\sum_{j=1}^{n} q_j^k P_j = \overline{V}M \qquad M = \overline{M} \qquad \text{(B′)}$$

Suppose that we can solve n of the (A′) equation to eliminate the qs, ending up with the independent homogeneous functions

$$f_i(P)_\lambda \equiv f_i(\lambda P) \equiv f_i(1, P_2/P_1, \ldots, P_n/P_1)$$
$$(i = 2, \ldots, n - 1) \quad \text{(A′)}$$
$$\sum q_j^*(P_j/M) = \overline{V} \qquad M = \overline{M} \qquad \text{(B′)}$$

Although f_i involve actually money Ps, it is not logically or empirically mandatory to interpret them as "excess-demand" functions which drive up (or down) the *money* Ps. Some students of Hicks, Lange, and Patinkin fall into this presupposition. Logically, there *could* be dynamic adjustments of price ratios—as e.g. P_i/P_1 or P_i/P_j, either of which could be written as $(P_i/M)/(P_j/M)$—of the type

$$[d(P_i/P_1)]/dt = k_i f_i(1, P_2/P_1, \ldots, P_n/P_1)$$
$$(i = 2, \ldots, n) \quad \text{(a′)}$$
$$[d(P_1/M)]/dt$$
$$= k_M[\overline{M} - \sum (P_j/P_1)(P_1/M)Q_j^*(1/V)]$$
$$\times k_j, k_m > 0 \qquad \text{(b′)}$$

where the ks are positive speed constants of adjustment and where the q^* and V may be functions of relative Ms. Such a system could dynamically determine *relative* prices within a decomposable real set (A') and then determine the absolute price level in Set B. Note that no version of Walras' Law relates (B') to (A') or (b') to (a'). Walras' Law in the form that merely reflects the Budget Equation of each consumer is expressed in the functional dependence of the $f_1(1, P_2/P_1, \ldots)$ function (which we can ignore) on the rest—namely

$$f_1(1, P_2/P_1, \ldots)$$
$$\equiv - \sum_2^n (P_j/P_1)f_j(1, P_2/P_1, \ldots)$$

If (a', b') is dynamically stable, $P_i/M \to$ constant is in agreement with the long-run quantity theory.[13]

NOTES

1 An equation like the last one could be split into two equations without altering the meaning:

$$1/FC \sum_{j=1}^n (P_j/M)Q_j^* = 1 \qquad (B'_1)$$
$$M = M, \text{ a prescribed total} \qquad (B'_2)$$

The important thing to note is that (B'$_1$), even if it looks a little like some (A') equations, is completely decomposable from the set A'.

2 P. A. Samuelson, *Foundations of Economic Analysis* (Cambridge, Mass., 1947), 119.

3 Don Patinkin, in his *Money, Interest, and Prices* (New York, 1966), summarizes his path-breaking writings on money over the last twenty years. For a critique of aspects of its first (1954) edition, see Archibald and Lipsey (*Review of Economic Studies*, XX) and articles in subsequent numbers of that journal.

4 In unpublished memos and lectures, using a Ramsey maximum analysis I have shown how the long-run steady-state condition where $r = \rho$ is approached so that K (or $K^{t+1} - K^t$) is zero. The steady-state analysis of $U (q : M, \ldots)$ here is shorthand for the perpetual stream $\sum_0^\infty U \ (q^t; M^{t+1}, \ldots)/(1 + p)^t$, etc. My colleague, Professor Miguel Sidrouski, has independently arrived at such dynamic formulations.

5 This is not the only way of introducing the real convenience of cash balances. An even better way would be to let U depend only on the time stream of qs, and then to show that holding an inventory of M does contribute to a more stable and greatly preferable stream of consumptions. The present oversimplified version suffices to give the correct general picture.

6 The next few paragraphs can be skipped without harm.

7 See P. Samuelson, "D. H. Robertson," *Quarterly Journal of Economics*, LXXVII, 4 (Nov. 1963), 517–536, esp. 535 where reference is made to earlier discussions by E. Phelps, H. G. Johnson, and R. A. Mundell. This article is reproduced in Joseph E. Stiglitz, ed., *The Collected Scientific Papers of Paul A. Samuelson* (Cambridge, Mass., 1966).

8 Let me warn that this discussion in terms of a Markov probability matrix is meant to be only indicative. The temporal sequence of decisions to exchange money for goods and services and goods for money, with all that is implied for the distribution among units of the stock of M at any time, is more complicated than this. In our most idealized models, we assumed that, whatever the complexity of the process, after enough time had elapsed the M would get distributed in a unique ergodic way. This does not beg the question, since there are models in which this is a theorem. In our more realistic moods, we tacitly used models involving *hysteresis*: Spain would never be the same after Columbus; Scarlett O'Hara would be permanently affected by the Confederate inflation, just as Hugo Stinnes was by the 1920–1923 German inflation. Obviously, in such models all real variables do not end up unchanged as a result of certain unbalanced introductions of new M into the system. In that sense realistic equations do not seem to have the homogeneity properties in $(M, P, \ldots)$ of my Set A; but if we were to write in A the variables $(M^1, M^2, \ldots)$ and not merely their sum ΣM^k, it is still possible that homogeneity properties would hold—so that doubling *all* M^k together would be consistent with doubling all Ps. But this is too delicate a question to attempt in brief compass here.

9 My *Economics* (6th ed., New York, 1964), 342, shows that $(M$, public debt) and $(\lambda M, \lambda$ public debt) play the role in more complicated systems that (M) and (λM) play in the simple classical system given

here. Crude quantity theorists should take note of this distinction, which Franco Modigliani has also insisted on.

10 (New York, 1944).

11 (Oxford, 1939).

12 Needless to say, the test is not whether Aristotle, apprised of Newton's improvements over Aristotle, would afterwards acquiesce in them; the test is whether in Aristotle's writings there are non-integrated Newtonian elements. If so, we credit him only with non-integrated intuitions.

13 A short-run quantity theory need not hold. Doubling M this minute or this week need not double this week's prices. But there is a sense in which homogeneity holds in *every* run. Suppose as a *fait accompli* we are all made to wake up with every dollar of M *exactly* doubled and every P (present *and* future) exactly doubled. If nought else has changed, we recognize this to be indeed a new equilibrium. And if the time-profile of equilibrium is unique, how can we have any other time-profile of prices? At the root of this paradox is the assumption of perfectly balanced changes in M, perfect foresight, and the postulate of uniqueness of equilibrium. All this a far cry from interpreting the stream of contemporary history.

Summaries

James Tobin, "A General Equilibrium Approach to Monetary Theory," *Journal of Money, Credit, and Banking*, 1 (February 1969), pp. 15–30.

Professor James Tobin, a "pro" in econometric model building, has developed a general equilibrium approach to monetary theory. Although Tobin modestly claims in this article that his purpose is exposition and recapitulation, he develops a very flexible model which can be extended to encompass more sectors and more assets than treated by him. In this model, the author incorporates several new features, three of which deserve special mention. He claims the following: (1) that the hypothesis that physical capital is homogeneous can now be dropped; (2) that a number of variables relating to different markets, prices, and rates of return for stock of goods can now be introduced, and houses, plants, equipment, and consumer durables can be distinguished; and (3) that categories of government and private debts can be analyzed separately.

Tobin provides the reader with an accounting framework for a theory of the capital account and goes on to establish an analytical framework for dealing with money. He skillfully deals with a money–capital economy and constructs a money–securities–capital model.

In conclusion, the author states that, according to his model: "The principal way in which financial policies and events affect aggregate demand is by changing the valuations of physical assets relative to their replacement costs. Monetary policies can accomplish such changes, but other exogenous events can too. In addition to the exogenous variables explicitly listed in the illustrative models, changes can occur, and undoubtedly do, in the portfolio preferences—asset demand functions—of the public, the banks, and other sectors. These preferences are based on expectations, estimates of risk, attitudes toward risk, and a host of other factors."

Don Patinkin, "Money and Wealth: A Review Article," *Journal of Economic Literature*, 7 (December 1969), pp. 1140–1160.

This article, although basically a critique of Pesek and Saving's book, *Money, Wealth and Economic Theory*, makes a valuable contribution to the existing theories relating to wealth and money. Patinkin begins by stating that his major objection to the conclusions reached by the authors in this book is they do not define "money" correctly.

As a basis for his objection, Patinkin points out that "central to the discussion of the 'Pigou' or 'real-balance' effect is the assumption that the stock of money is a component of the wealth of the economy, and that accordingly a change in the absolute price level changes the real value of this component, hence total wealth, and hence the level of consumption as well as other economic variables." This view, however, has not been accepted by all monetary theorists. As a matter of fact, as early as 1944, Kalecki pointed out—and Gurley and Shaw in 1960 formally stated—that the stock of money relevant for the "real-balance effect was not the usually defined concept of hand-to-hand currency plus demand deposits, but the monetary base alone."

Recently (in 1967), Pesek and Saving declared that the distinction (formalized by Gurley and Shaw) between "outside money" and "inside money" is invalid. Outside money is defined as money that is backed by foreign or government securities or gold, or fiat money issued by the government, whereas inside money is defined as money based on private domestic primary securities. The authors asserted that the total money supply should be included in the measurement of the wealth of a community. Patinkin takes issue with the authors on this subject. He clearly lays down the basic hypotheses and the logic of Pesek and Saving, and then engages in a long, arduous, and theoretical battle to "prove" that the authors' conclusions are not not fully tenable.

W. Leontief, "The Fundamental Assumption of Mr. Keynes' Monetary Theory of Unemployment," in *Essays in Economics* (New York: Oxford University Press, 1966), pp. 87–93.

This article, published in 1936 shortly after Keynes' *General Theory* made its appearance, is a classic one. On the subject of the determination of economic equilibrium, Leontief maintains that the difference between Keynes' "new" theory of economic equilibrium and the "orthodox" classical scheme is fundamentally one of assumptions. To substantiate his stand, Leontief first redefines the contested principle in precise terms, he next interprets its relevant theoretical implications, and then examines the arguments which Keynes raised against the "orthodox" solution of the problem of achieving general equilibrium. He confines himself to the strictly theoretical aspect of the maintenance of general equilibrium and, in this tightly written, short article, proves his point.

In this article, Leontief makes a valuable remark about the eclectic nature of one aspect of Keynes' theory. According to the author, the novel contribution of Keynes to the monetary "theory of total output" was that he modified one of the basic static assumptions of orthodox economists. "The static character of the proposed innovation," says Leontief, "is somewhat obscured by the fact that in his endeavor to give a realistic analysis of economic forces and interrelations, Mr. Keynes has introduced into his theory a number of dynamic considerations, most of them in one form or another already incorporated in the apparatus of the modern monetary and business cycle theory."

Bibliography

Karl Brunner and Allan H. Meltzer, "The Meaning of Monetary Indicators," in G. Horwich (ed.), *Monetary Process and Policy* (Homewood, Ill.: Richard D. Irwin, 1967), pp. 187–217.

Controlling Monetary Aggregates (Boston: Federal Reserve Bank of Boston, 1969), 174 pp.

G. Delsupehe, "The Structure of Interest Rates and Monetary Policy," *Overdruk uit Tijdschrift voor Economie*, No. 2 (1968), pp. 269–310.

David Fand, "Keynesian Monetary Theories, Stabilization Policy, and the Recent Inflation," *Journal of Money, Credit, and Banking* (August 1969), pp. 556–587.

F. H. Hahn, "The Rate of Interest and General Equilibrium Analysis," *The Economic Journal*, 65 (March 1955), pp. 52–66.

J. Hicks, "Monetary Theory and History—An Attempt at Perspective," in *Critical Essays in Monetary Theory* (New York: Oxford University Press, 1967), pp. 155–173.

Harry G. Johnson, "Monetary Theory and Policy," *American Economic Review*, 52 (June 1962), pp. 335–384.

8
PRICES, INFLATION, AND MONETARY POLICY

Monetary policy embraces all the means by which monetary authorities attempt to bring about desirable changes in the functioning of a financial system. It is generally agreed by economists that the effect of monetary policy is only indirect, because the application of such a policy can affect aggregate demand and employment through a change in the composition of liquid assets. Any change in this composition affects not only the interest rates charged for investment funds but also the aggregate demand, and both of these, of course, have an effect on the economy.

In the first selection, Brunner examines the role of monetary policy vis-à-vis national goals. In the second selection, Mundell shows that the money rate of interest rises by less than the rate of inflation and that, therefore, the real rate of interest declines during inflation. Hendershott and Horwich point out in the third article that an ideal monetary policy is one in which the market rate of interest is equated with the natural rate. In the fourth article, Johnson discusses some of the problems that a central banker faces in formulating an effective monetary policy.

The Role of Monetary Policy
Karl Brunner[*]

The development of monetary analysis in the past decade has intensified the debate concerning the role of money and monetary policy. Extensive research fostered critical examinations of the Federal Reserve's traditional descriptions of policy

Karl Brunner, "The Role of Money and Monetary Policy," Federal Reserve Bank of St. Louis, *Review* (July 1968), pp. 9–24.

[*] This paper owes a heavy debt to my long and stimulating association with Allan H. Meltzer. I also wish to acknowledge the editorial assistance of Leonall C. Andersen, Keith M. Carlson, and Jerry L. Jordan of the Federal Reserve Bank of St. Louis.

and of the arrangements governing policy-making. Some academic economists and others attribute the cyclical fluctuations of monetary growth and the persistent problem concerning the proper interpretation of monetary policy to the established procedures of monetary policy and the conceptions traditionally guiding policy-makers.

The critique of established policy procedures, which evolved from this research into questions concerning the monetary mechanism, is derived from a body of monetary theory referred to in this paper

258

as the Monetarist position. Three major conclusions have emerged from the hypotheses put forth. First, monetary impulses are a major factor accounting for variations in output, employment and prices. Second, movements in the money stock are the most reliable measure of the thrust of monetary impulses. Third, the behavior of the monetary authorities dominates movements in the money stock over business cycles.

A response to the criticisms of existing monetary policy methods was naturally to be expected and is welcomed. Four articles which defend present policy procedures have appeared during the past few years in various Federal Reserve publications.[1] These articles comprise a countercritique which argues that monetary impulses are neither properly measured nor actually transmitted by the money stock. The authors reject the Monetarist thesis that monetary impulses are a chief factor determining variations in economic activity, and they contend that cyclical fluctuations of monetary growth cannot be attributed to the behavior of the Federal Reserve authorities. These fluctuations are claimed to result primarily from the behavior of commercial banks and the public.

The ideas and arguments put forth in these articles deserve close attention. The controversy defined by the critique of policy in professional studies and the countercritique appearing in Federal Reserve publications bears on issues of fundamental importance to public policy. Underlying all the fashionable words and phrases is the fundamental question: What is the role of monetary policy and what are the requirements of rational policymaking?

The following sections discuss the major aspects of the countercritique. These rejoinders may contribute to a better understanding of the issues, and the resulting clarification may remove some unnecessary disputes. Even though the

central contentions of the controversy will remain, the continuous articulation of opposing points of view plays a vital role in the search for greater understanding of the monetary process.

A SUMMARY OF THE COUNTERCRITIQUE

The four articles relied on two radically different groups of arguments. Gramley–Chase, Kareken, and Cacy exploit the juxtaposition "New View versus Traditional View" as the central idea guiding their countercritique. The analytical framework developed by the critique is naturally subsumed for this purpose under the "Traditional View" label. On the other hand, Davis uses the analytical framework developed by the critique in order to organize his arguments.

Gramley–Chase describe their general argument in the following words:

(New) developments have reaffirmed the bankers' point of view that deposits are attracted, not created, as textbooks suggest. In this new environment, growth rates of deposits have become more suspect than ever as indicators of the conduct of monetary policy ... A framework of analysis [is required] from which the significance of time deposits and of changing time deposits can be deduced. Traditional methods of monetary analysis are not well suited to this task. The "New View" in monetary economics provides a more useful analytical framework. In the new view, banks—like other financial institutions—are considered as suppliers of financial claims for the public to hold, and the public is given a significant role in determining the total amount of bank liabilities ... Traditional analysis ... fails to recognize that substitution between time deposits and securities may be an important source of pro-cyclical variations in the stock of money even in the face of countercyclical central bank policy.[2]

This general argument guided the construction of an explicit model designed to emphasize the role of the public's and the banks' behavior in the determination of the money stock, bank credit, and interest rates.

Kareken's paper supplements the Gramley–Chase arguments. He finds "the received money supply theory" quite inadequate. His paper is designed to improve monetary analysis by constructing a theory of an individual bank as a firm. This theory is offered as an explanation of a bank's desired balance sheet position. It also appears to form the basis of a model describing the interaction of the public's and the banks' behavior in the joint determination of the money stock, bank credit, and interest rates. The whole development emphasizes somewhat suggestively the importance of the public's and banks' behavior in explanations of monetary growth. It is also designed to undermine the empirical hypotheses advanced by the Monetarist position. This is achieved by means of explicit references to specific and "obviously desirable" features of the model presented.

Cacy's article develops neither an explicit framework nor a direct critique of the basic propositions advanced by the Monetarist thesis. However, he provides a useful summary of the general position of the countercritique. The Monetarist analysis is conveniently subsumed by Cacy under a "Traditional View" which is juxtaposed to a "New View" of monetary mechanisms: "The new approach argues ... that there is no essential difference between the manner in which the liabilities of banks and nonbank financial institutions are determined. Both types of institutions are subject in the same way to the portfolio decisions of the public." [3] The new approach is contrasted with the Traditional View, which "obscures the important role played by the public and overstates the role played by the central bank in the determination of the volume of money balances." [4] The general comparison developed by Cacy suggests quite clearly to the reader that the Traditional View allegedly espoused by the Mone-tarist position cannot match the "realistic sense" of the New View advocated by the countercritique.

In the context of the framework developed by the critique, Davis questions some basic propositions of the Monetarist position:

In the past five to ten years, however, there has come into increasing prominence a group of economists who would like to go considerably beyond the simple assertion that the behavior of money is a significant factor influencing the behavior of the economy ... In order to bring a few of the issues into sharper focus, this article will take a look at some evidence for the "money supply" view ...

It confines itself to examining the historical relationship between monetary cycles and cycles in general business. The article concludes that the relationship between these two kinds of cycles does not, in fact, provide any real support for the view that the behavior of money is the predominant determinant of fluctuations in business activity. Moreover, the historical relationship between cycles in money and in business cannot be used to demonstrate that monetary policy is, in its effects, so long delayed and so uncertain as to be an unsatisfactory countercyclical weapon. [5]

AN EXAMINATION OF THE ISSUES

A careful survey of the countercritique yielded the following results. The Gramley–Chase, Kareken, and Cacy papers parade the New View in order to question the status of empirical theories used by the Monetarist critique in its examination of monetary policy. The Davis paper questions quite directly, on the other hand, the existence and relevance of the evidence in support of the Monetarist position, and constitutes a direct assault on the Monetarist critique. The others constitute an indirect assault which attempts to devalue the critique's analysis, and thus to destroy its central propositions concerning the role of money and monetary policy.

The indirect assault on the Monetarist

position by Gramley–Chase, Kareken, and Cacy requires a clarification concerning the nature of the New View. A program of analysis must be clearly distinguished from a research strategy and an array of specific conjectures.[6] All three aspects are usually mixed together in a general description. It is important to understand, however, that neither research strategy nor specific empirical conjectures are logical implications of the general program. The explicit separation of the three aspects is crucial for a proper assessment of the New View.

Section A examines some general characteristics of the countercritique's reliance on the New View. It shows the New View to consist of a program acceptable to all economists, a research strategy rejected by the Monetarist position, and an array of specific conjectures advanced without analytical or empirical substantiation. Also, not a single paper of the countercritique developed a relevant assessment of the Monetarist's empirical theories or central propositions.

In sections B and C detailed examinations of specific conjectures centered on rival explanations of cyclical fluctuations of monetary growth are presented. The direct assault on the Monetarist position by Davis is discussed in some detail in Section D. This section also states the crucial propositions of the Monetarist thesis in order to clarify some aspects of this position. This reformulation reveals that the reservations assembled by Davis are quite innocuous. They provide no analytical or empirical case against the Monetarist thesis. Conjectures associated with the interpretation of monetary policy (the "indicator problem") are presented in Section E.

A. The New View

The countercritique has apparently been decisively influenced by programmatic elaborations originally published by Gurley–Shaw and James Tobin.[7] The program is most faithfully reproduced by Cacy, and it also shaped the arguments guiding the model construction by Kareken and Gramley–Chase. The New View, as a program, is a sensible response to a highly unsatisfactory state of monetary analysis inherited in the late 1950's. A money and banking syndrome perpetuated by textbooks obstructed the application of economic analysis to the financial sector. At most, this inherited literature contained only suggestive pieces of analysis. It lacked a meaningful theory capable of explaining the responses of the monetary system to policy actions or to influences emanating from the real sector. The New View proposed a systematic application of economic analysis, in particular an application of relative price theory, to the array of financial intermediaries, their assets and liabilities.

This program is most admirable and incontestable, but it cannot explain the conflict revealed by critique and countercritique. The Monetarist approach accepted the general principle of applying relative price theory to the analysis of monetary processes. In addition, this approach used the suggestions and analytical pieces inherited from past efforts in order to develop some specific hypotheses which do explain portions of our observable environment. The New Viewers' obvious failure to recognize the limited content of their programmatic statements only contributes to maintenance of the conflict.

A subtle difference appears, however, in the research strategy. The New View was introduced essentially as a generalized approach, including a quite formal exposition, but with little attempt at specific structuring and empirical content. The most impressive statements propagated by the New View were crucially influenced by the sheer formalism of its exposition. In the context of the New View's almost empty form, little remains to differentiate one object from another. For instance, in case one only admits the *occurrence* of marginal costs and marginal yields associated with the actions of every household, firm, and financial intermediary, one will necessarily conclude that banks and non-bank financial intermediaries are restricted in size by the same economic forces and circumstances. In such a context there is truly no essential difference between the determination of bank and non-bank intermediary liabilities, or between banks and non-bank intermediaries, or between money and other financial assets.

The strong impressions conveyed by the New View thus result from the relative emptiness of the formulation which has been used to elaborate their position. In the context of the formal world of the New View, "almost everything is almost like everything else." This undifferentiated state of affairs is not, however, a property of our observable world. It is only a property of the highly formal discussion designed by the New View to overcome the unsatisfactory state of monetary analysis still prevailing in the late 1950's or early 1960's.[8]

Two sources of the conflict have been recognized thus far. The Monetarists' research strategy was concerned quite directly with the construction of empirical theories about the monetary system, whereas the New View indulged, for a lengthy interval, in very general programmatic excursions. Moreover, the New Viewers apparently misconstrued their program as being a meaningful theory about out observable environment. This logical error contributed to a third source of the persistent conflict.

The latter source arises from the criticism addressed by the New Viewers to the Monetarists' theories of money supply processes. Three of the papers exploit the logically dubious but psychologically effective juxtaposition between a "New View" and a "Traditional View." In doing this they fail to distinguish between the inherited state of monetary system analysis typically reflected by the money and banking textbook syndrome and the research output of economists advocating the Monetarist thesis. This distinction is quite fundamental. Some formal analogies misled the New Viewers and they did not recognize the logical difference between detailed formulations of empirical theories on the one side and haphazard pieces of unfinished analysis on the other side.[9]

A related failure accompanies this logical error. There is not the slightest attempt to assess alternative hypotheses or theories by systematic exposure to observations from the real world. It follows, therefore, that the countercritique scarcely analyzed the empirical theories advanced by the Monetarist critique and consequently failed to understand the major implications of these theories.

For instance, they failed to recognize the role assigned by the Monetarist view to banks' behavior and the public's preferences in the monetary process. The objection raised by the New View that "the formula [expressing a basic framework used to formulate the hypothesis] obscures the important role played by the public" has neither analytical basis nor meaning. In fact, the place of the public's behavior was discussed in the Monetarist hypotheses in some detail. Moreover, the same analysis discussed the conditions under which the public's behavior dominates movements of the money stock and bank credit.[10] It also yielded information about the response of bank credit, money stock, and time deposits to changes in ceiling rates, or to changes in the speed with which banks adjust their deposit-supply conditions to evolving market situations. Every single aspect of the banks' or the public's behavior emphasized by the countercritique has been analyzed by the Monetarist's hypotheses in terms which render the results empirically assessable. Little remains, consequently, of the suggestive countercritique assembled in the papers by Gramley–Chase, Kareken, and Cacy.[11]

B. A Monetarist Examination of the New View's Money Supply Theory

Three sources of the conflict have been discussed thus far. Two sources were revealed as logical misconstruals, involving inadequate construction and assessment of empirical theories. A third source pertains to legitimate differences in research strategy. These three sources do not explain all major aspects of the conflict. Beyond the differences in research strategy and logical misconceptions, genuinely substantive issues remain. Some comments of protagonists advocating the New View should probably be interpreted as conjectures about hypotheses to be expected from their research strategy. It should be clearly understood that such conjectures are not logical implications of the guiding framework. Instead, they are pragmatic responses to the general emphasis associated with this approach.

A first conjecture suggests that the money stock and bank credit are dominated by the public's and the banks' behavior. It is suggested, therefore, that cyclical fluctuations of monetary growth result primarily from the responses of banks and the public to changing business conditions. A second conjecture naturally supplements the above assertions. It is contended that the money stock is a thoroughly "untrustworthy" guide to monetary policy."

Articles by Gramley–Chase and Kareken attempt to support these conjectures with the aid of more explicit analytical formulations allegedly expressing the general program of the New View. The paper contributed by Gramley–Chase has been critically examined in detail on another occasion,[12] and only some crucial aspects relevant for our present purposes will be considered at this point. Various aspects of the first conjecture are examined in this and the next section. The second conjecture is examined in sections D and E.

A detailed analysis of the Gramley–Chase model demonstrates that it implies the reduced form equations

$$M = g(B^e, Y, c) \qquad g_1 > 0 < g_2$$
$$E = h(B^e, Y, c) \qquad h_1 > 0 > h_2$$
$$\text{and } h_1 > g_1 {}^{13}$$

explaining the money stock (M) and bank credit (E) in terms of the extended monetary base (B^e), the level of economic activity expressed by national income at current prices (Y), and the ceiling rate on time deposits (c).[14]

The Gramley–Chase model implies that monetary policy does affect the money stock and bank credit. It also implies that the money stock responds *positively* and bank credit *negatively* to economic activity. This model thus differs from the Monetarist hypotheses which imply that both bank credit and the money stock respond *positively* to economic activity. The Gramley–Chase model also implies that the responses of both the money stock and bank credit to monetary actions are independent of the general scale of the public's and the banks' interest elasticities. Uniformly large or small interest elasticities yield the same response in the money stock or bank credit to a change in the monetary base.

A detailed discussion of the implications derivable from a meaningfully supplemented Gramley–Chase model is not necessary at this point. We are foremost interested in the relation between this model and the propositions mentioned in the previous paragraph. The first proposition can be interpreted in two different ways. According to one interpretation, it could mean that the marginal multipliers g_i and h_i ($i = 1, 2$) are functions of the banks' and the public's response patterns expressing various types of substitution relations between different assets. This interpretation is, however, quite innocuous and yields no differentiation relative to the questioned hypotheses of the Monetarist position.

A second interpretation suggests that the growth rate of the money stock is dominated by the second component (changes in income) of the differential expression:

$$\Delta M = g_1 \Delta B^e + g_2 \Delta Y$$

This result is not actually implied by the Gramley–Chase model, but it is certainly consistent with the model. However, in order to derive the desired result, their model must be supplemented with special assumptions about the relative magnitude of g_1 and g_2, and also about the comparative cyclical variability of ΔB^e and ΔY. This information has not been provided by the authors.

Most interesting is another aspect of the model which was not clarified by the authors. Their model implies that policymakers could easily avoid procyclical movements in ΔM. This model exemplifying the New View thus yields little justification for the conjectures of its proponents.

A central property of the Gramley–Chase model must be considered in the light of the programmatic statements characterizing the New View. Gramley–Chase do not differentiate between the public's asset supply to banks and the public's demand for money. This procedure violates the basic program of the New View, namely, to apply economic analysis to an array of financial assets and financial institutions. Economic analysis implies that the public's asset supply and money demand are distinct, and not identical behavior patterns. This difference in behavior patterns is clearly revealed by different responses of desired money balances and desired asset supply to specific stimuli in the environment. For instance, an increase in the expected real yield on real capital *raises* the public's asset supply but *lowers* the public's money demand. It follows thus that a

central analytical feature of the Gramley–Chase model violates the basic and quite relevant program of the New View.

Kareken's construction shares this fundamental analytical flaw with the Gramley–Chase model, but this is not the only problem faced by his analysis. The Kareken analysis proceeds on two levels. First, he derives a representative bank's desired balance sheet position. For this purpose he postulates wealth maximization subject to the bank's balance sheet relation between assets and liabilities, and subject to reserve requirements on deposits. On closer examination, this analysis is only applicable to a monopoly bank with no conversion of deposits into currency or reserve flows to other banks. In order to render the analysis relevant for a representative bank in the world of reality, additional constraints would have to be introduced which modify the results quite substantially. It is also noteworthy that the structural properties assigned by Kareken to the system of market relations are logically inconsistent with the implications one can derive from the author's analysis of firm behavior developed on the first level of his investigation.

This disregard for the construction of an economic theory relevant for the real world is carried into the second level of analysis where the author formulates a system of relations describing the joint determination of interest rates, bank credit, and money stock. A remarkable feature of the Kareken model is that it yields no implications whatsoever about the response of the monetary system to actions of the Federal Reserve. It can say nothing, as it stands, about either open market operations or about discount rate and reserve requirement actions. This model literally implies, for instance, that the money stock and the banking system's deposit liabilities do not change as a result of any change in reserve requirement ratios.

None of the conjectures advanced by the countercritique concerning the behavior of the money stock and the role of monetary policy find analytical support in Kareken's analysis. To the extent that anything is implied, it would imply that monetary policy operating directly on bank reserves or a mysterious rate of return on reserves dominates the volume of deposits—a practically subversive position for a follower of the New View.[15]

C. Alternative Explanations of Cyclical Fluctuations in Monetary Growth

The examination thus far in this article has shown that even the most explicit formulation (Gramley–Chase) of the countercritique, allegedly representing the New View with respect to monetary system analysis, does assign a significant role to monetary policy. This examination also argued that the general emphasis given by the New View to the public's and the banks' behavior in determination of the money stock and bank credit does not differentiate its product from analytical developments arising from the Monetarist approach. It was also shown that the only explicit formulation advanced by the New Viewers does not provide a sufficient basis for their central conjectures. It is impossible to derive the proposition from the Gramley–Chase model that the behavior of the public and banks, rather than Federal Reserve actions, dominated movements in the money supply. But the declaration of innocence by the countercritique on behalf of the monetary authorities with respect to cyclical fluctuations of monetary growth still requires further assessment.

The detailed arguments advanced to explain the observed cyclical fluctuations of monetary growth differ substantially among the contributors to the countercritique. Gramley–Chase maintain that changing business conditions modify relative interest rates, and thus induce countercyclical movements in the time deposit ratio. These movements in demand and time deposits generate cyclical

fluctuations in monetary growth. On the other hand, Cacy develops an argument used many years ago by Wicksell and Keynes, but attributes it to the New View. He recognizes a pronounced sensitivity of the money stock to variations in the public's money demand or asset supply. These variations induce changes in credit market conditions. Banks, in turn, respond with suitable adjustments in the reserve and borrowing ratios. The money stock and bank credit consequently change in response to this mechanism.

Davis actually advances two radically different conjectures about causes of cyclical fluctuations of monetary growth. The first conjecture attributes fluctuations of monetary growth to the public's and banks' responses. Changing business conditions modify the currency ratio, the banks' borrowing ratio, and the reserve ratio. The resulting changes generate the observed movements in money. His other conjecture attributes fluctuations in monetary growth to Federal Reserve actions: "the state of business influences decisions by the monetary authorities to supply reserves and to take other actions likely to affect the money supply."[16]

The various conjectures advanced by Gramley–Chase, Cacy, and Davis in regard to causes of movements in money and bank credit can be classified into two groups. One set of conjectures traces the mechanism generating cyclical fluctuations of monetary growth to the responses of banks and the public; the behavior of monetary authorities is assigned a comparatively minor role. The other group of conjectures recognizes the predominant role of the behavior of monetary authorities.

In the following analysis the framework provided by the Monetarist view will be used to assess these conflicting conjectures. The emphasis concerning the nature of the causal mechanisms may differ between the various conjectures regarding sources of variations in money, but the following examination will be applied to an aspect common to all conjectures emphasizing the role of public and bank behavior.

In the context of the Monetarist framework, the money stock (M) is exhibited as a product of a multiplier (m) and the monetary base (B) (such that $M = mB$). This framework, without the supplementary set of hypotheses and theories bearing on the proximate determinants of money summarized by the multiplier and the base, is completely neutral with respect to the rival conjectures; it is compatible with any set of observations. This neutrality assures us that its use does not prejudge the issue under consideration. The Monetarist framework operates in the manner of a language system, able to express the implications of the competing conjectures in a uniform manner.

The first group of conjectures advanced by the countercritique (behavior of the public and banks dominates movements in money) implies that variations in monetary growth between upswings and downswings in business activity are dominated by the variations in the monetary multiplier. The second group (behavior of monetary authorities dominates movements in money) implies that, in periods with unchanged reserve requirement ratios and ceiling rates on time deposits, variations in the monetary base dominate cyclical changes in monetary growth. The movements of the monetary multiplier which are strictly attributable to the changing of requirement ratios can be separated from the total contribution of the multiplier and combined with the monetary base. With this adjustment, the second group of conjectures implies that the monetary base, supplemented by the contribution of reserve requirement changes to the multiplier, dominates variations in the money stock.

In this examination of constrasting explanations of monetary fluctuations, values of the money stock (M), the multiplier (m), and the monetary base adjusted for member bank borrowing (B) are measured at the initial and terminal month of each half business cycle (i.e., expansions and contractions) located by the National Bureau of Economic Research. We form the ratios of these values and write:

$$\frac{M_1}{M_0} = \frac{m_1}{m_0}\frac{B_1}{B_0} \qquad \text{or} \qquad \mu = \alpha\beta$$

The subscript 1 refers to values of the terminal month and the subscript 0 to values of the initial month. These ratios were measured for each half-cycle in the period March 1919 to December 1966. They were computed for two definitions of the money stock, inclusive and exclusive of time deposits, with corresponding monetary multipliers.

Kendall's rank correlation coefficients between the money stock ratios (μ) and the multiplier ratios (α), and between (μ) and the monetary base ratio (β) were computed. We denote these correlation coefficients with $\rho(\mu, \alpha)$ and $\rho(\mu, \beta)$. The implications of the two rival conjectures can now be restated in terms of the two coefficients. The first group of conjectures implies that $\rho(\mu, \alpha) > \rho(\mu, \beta)$; while the second group implies that in periods of unchanged reserve requirement ratios and ceiling rates on time deposits, the coefficient $\rho(\mu, \beta)$ exceeds the coefficient $\rho(\mu, \alpha)$. The second group implies nothing about the relation of the two coefficients in periods of changing reserve requirements and ceiling rates on time deposits. It follows, therefore, that observations yielding the inequality $\rho(\mu, \beta) > \rho(\mu, \alpha)$ disconfirm the first group and confirm the second group.

The correlations obtained are quite unambiguous. The value of $\rho(\mu, \beta)$ is .537 for the whole sample period, whereas $\rho(\mu, \alpha)$ is only .084. The half-cycle from 1929 to 1933 was omitted in the computations, because movements in the money stock and the multiplier were dominated by forces which do not discriminate between the rival conjectures under consideration.

The sample period, including 1929 to 1933, still yields a substantially larger value for $\rho(\mu, \beta)$. The same pattern also holds for other subperiods. In particular, computations based on observations for 1949 to 1966 confirm the pattern observed for the whole sample period. The results thus support the second group of conjectures but not the first group. These results also suggest, however, that forces operating through the multiplier are not quite negligible. The surprisingly small correlation $\rho(\mu, \alpha)$ does not adequately reveal the operation of these forces. Their effective operation is revealed by the correlation $\rho(\mu, \beta)$, which is far from perfect, even in subperiods with constant reserve requirement ratios. This circumstance suggests that the behavior of the public and banks contributes to the cyclical movements of monetary growth. The main result at this stage is, however, the clear discrimination between the two groups of conjectures. The results are quite unambiguous on this score.

Additional information is supplied by Table I. For each postwar cycle beginning with the downswing of 1948–1949, the average annual growth rate of the money stock was computed. The expression $M = mB$ was then used to compute the contribution to the average growth rate of money from three distinct sources: (i) the behavior of monetary authorities (i.e.,

the monetary base and reserve requirement ratios), and the public's currency behavior, (ii) the time deposit substitution process, and, (iii) the variations in the excess reserve and borrowing ratios of commercial banks (Wicksell–Keynes mechanism).

The rank correlations between each contribution, and the average growth rate of the money stock over all postwar halfcycles, clearly support the conclusion of the previous analysis that cyclical movements in the money stock are dominated by Federal Reserve actions.

Table I also presents the results of a similar examination bearing on causes of movements in bank credit. The reader should note the radical difference in the observed patterns of correlation coefficients. The behavior of monetary authorities, supplemented by the public's currency behavior, does not appear to dominate the behavior of bank credit. The three sources contributing to the growth rate of money all exerted influences of similar order on bank credit. It appears that bank credit is comparatively less exposed to the push of Federal Reserve actions than was the money stock. On the other hand, the money stock is less sensitive than bank credit to the timedeposit substitution mechanism emphasized by Gramley–Chase, and the Wicksell–Keynes mechanism suggested by

Table I. A Comparison of Alternative Contributions to the Average Annual Growth Rate of the Money Stock and Bank Credit

	RANK CORRELATIONS	
CONTRIBUTION MADE BY:	MONEY	BANK CREDIT
Public's currency and authorities' behavior	.905	.333
Time deposit substitution mechanism	.048	.381
Wicksell–Keynes mechanism	.143	−.333

Remarks: The figures listed state the rank correlation between the average growth rate of the money stock and bank credit with three different contributing sources.

Table II. Regressions of the Money Supply on the Monetary Base and Gross National Product*

| | REGRESSION COEFFICIENTS FOR: | | | |
| | MONETARY BASE | | GROSS NATIONAL PRODUCT | |
CYCLE	FIRST DIFFERENCES	LOG FIRST DIFFERENCES	FIRST DIFFERENCES	LOG FIRST DIFFERENCES
IV/48	2.03	.77	.04	.11
to	(9.80)	(10.02)	(3.12)	(3.39)
II/53	.92	.93	.62	.65
II/53	1.75	.63	.02	.07
to	(1.89)	(1.96)	(1.02)	(1.23)
III/57	.44	.45	.26	.30
III/57	4.59	1.66	.06	.19
to	(11.76)	(11.81)	(5.10)	(5.34)
II/60	.97	.97	.86	.67
II/60	2.76	1.08	−.01	−.03
to	(7.56)	(8.54)	(−.33)	(−.27)
III/65	.87	.89	−.08	−.07

* The monetary base was adjusted for reserve requirement changes and shifts in deposits. All data are quarterly averages of seasonally adjusted figures. The first entry in a column for each cycle is the regression coefficient, t-statistics are in parentheses, and partial correlation coefficients are below the t-statistics.

Cacy. Most astonishing, however, is the *negative* association between the average growth rate of bank credit and the Wicksell–Keynes mechanism emphasized by Cacy.

It should also be noted that the average growth rate of money conforms very clearly to the business cycle. Such conformity does not hold for bank credit over the postwar half-cycles. This blurring occurred particularly in periods when the ceiling rate on time deposits was increased. These periods exhibit relatively large contributions to the growth rate of bank credit emanating from the time deposit substitution mechanism.

A regression analysis (Table II) of the reduced form equations derived from the Gramley–Chase model confirms the central role of the monetary base in the money supply process. Estimates of the regression coefficient relating money to income are highly unstable among different sample periods, relative to the coefficient relating money to the monetary base. Furthermore, estimates of regression coefficients relating money to income occur in some periods with signs which contradict the proposition of Gramley–Chase and Cacy, or exhibit a very small statistical significance. These diverse patterns of coefficients do not occur for the estimates of coefficients relating money and the monetary base. It is also noteworthy that the average growth rate of the monetary base (adjusted for changes in reserve requirement ratios), over the upswings, exceeds without exception the average growth rate of adjacent downswings. This observation is not compatible with the contention made by Gramley–Chase that policy is countercyclical.

Additional information is supplied by Table III, which presents some results of a spectral analysis bearing on the monetary base and its sources. Spectral analysis is a statistical procedure for decomposing a time series into seasonal, cyclical, and trend movements. After such an analysis was conducted on the monetary base and its sources, a form of correlation analysis was run between movements in the monetary base and movements in its various sources. The results of this procedure (Table III) indicate that movements in Federal Reserve credit dominate seasonal and cyclical movements in the monetary base.

In summary, preliminary investigations yield no support for the contention that the behavior of banks and the public dominates cyclical movements in the money stock. The conjectures advanced by Gramley–Chase or Cacy are thus disconfirmed, whereas Davis' second conjecture that fluctuations in monetary growth may be attributed to Federal

Reserve actions seems substantially more appropriate. However, further investigations are certainly useful.

D. Relevance of Money and Monetary Actions With Respect to Economic Activity

At present, a broad consensus accepts the relevance of money and monetary policy with respect to economic activity. But this consensus concerning the relevance of money emerges from two substantially different views about the nature of the transmission mechanism. One view is the Keynesian conception (not to be confused with Keynes' view), enshrined in standard formulations of the income-expenditure framework. In this view, the interest rate is the main link between money and economic activity. The other view rejects the traditional separation of

Table III. Spectral Correlation Between the Monetary Base, Federal Reserve Credit, and Other Sources of the Base

	SPECIAL CORRELATION BETWEEN	
PERIOD IN MONTHS	MONETARY BASE AND FEDERAL RESERVE CREDIT	MONETARY BASE AND OTHER SOURCES OF THE BASE
∞	.65	.24
120	.69	.61
60	.74	.71
40	.74	.45
30	.73	.25
24	.71	.18
20	.60	.11
17.14	.43	.11
15	.51	.07
13.33	.82	.48
12	.94	.71
6	.91	.21
4	.92	—
3	.90	—

Remarks: The monetary base equals Federal Reserve Credit plus other sources of the base. The spectral analysis is based on first differences between adjacent months. The data used were not seasonally adjusted.

economic theory into parts: national income analysis (macroeconomics) and price theory (microeconomics). According to this other view, output and employment are explained by a suitable application of relative price theory. With regard to discussions of the impact of money and monetary actions on economic activity, this latter view has been termed the Monetarist position. This position may be divided into the weak Monetarist thesis and the strong Monetarist thesis. In a sense, both the New View and the Monetarist extension of the "traditional view" are represented in the weak Monetarist position.

The following discussions develop the weak and the strong Monetarist thesis. The weak thesis is compared with some aspects of the income-expenditure approach to the determination of national economic activity. The strong thesis supplements the weak thesis with special assumptions about our environment, in order to establish the role of monetary forces in the business cycle.

1. THE WEAK MONETARIST THESIS. According to the weak Monetarist thesis, monetary impulses are transmitted to the economy by a relative price process which operates on money, financial assets (and liabilities), real assets, yields on assets, and the production of new assets, liabilities and consumables. The general nature of this process has been described on numerous occasions and may be interpreted as evolving from ideas developed by Knut Wicksell, Irving Fisher, and John Maynard Keynes.[17]

The operation of relative prices between money, financial assets, and real assets may be equivalently interpreted as the working of an interest rate mechanism (prices and yields of assets are inversely related). Monetary impulses are thus transmitted by the play of interest rates over a vast array of assets. Variations in interest rates change relative prices of existing assets, relative to both yields and the supply prices of new production. Acceleration or deceleration of monetary impulses are thus converted by the variation of relative prices, or interest rates, into increased or reduced production, and subsequent revisions in the supply prices of current output.

This general conception of the transmission mechanism has important implications which conflict sharply with the Keynesian interpretation of monetary mechanisms expressed by standard income-expenditure formulations.[18] In the context of standard income-expenditure analysis, fiscal actions are considered to have a "direct effect" on economic activity, whereas monetary actions are considered to have only an "indirect effect." Furthermore, a constant budget deficit has no effect on interest rates in a Keynesian framework, in spite of substantial accumulation of outstanding government debt when a budget deficit continually occurs. And lastly, the operation of interest rates on investment decisions has usually been rationalized with the aid of considerations based on the effects of borrowing costs.

These aspects of the income-expenditure approach may be evaluated within the framework of the weak Monetarist thesis. The effects of fiscal actions are also transmitted by the relative price mechanism. Fiscal impulses, i.e., Government spending, taxing, and borrowing, operate just as "indirectly" as monetary impulses, and there is no *a priori* reason for believing that their speed of transmission is substantially greater than that of monetary impulses. The relative price conception of the transmission mechanism also implies that a constant budget deficit exerts a continuous influence on economic activity through persistent modifications in relative prices of financial and real assets. Lastly, the transmission of monetary impulses is not dominated by the relative importance of borrowing costs.

In the process, marginal costs of liability extension interact with marginal returns from acquisitions of financial and real assets. But interest rates on financial assets not only affect the marginal cost of liability extension, but also influence the substitution between financial and real assets. This substitution modifies prices of real assets relative to their supply prices and forms a crucial linkage of the monetary mechanisms; this linkage is usually omitted in standard income-expenditure analysis.

The description of monetary mechanisms in Davis' article approaches quite closely the notion developed by the weak Monetarist thesis. This approximation permits a useful clarification of pending issues. However, the criticisms and objections advanced by Davis do not apply to the weak Monetarist position. They are addressed to another thesis, which might be usefully labeled the *strong Monetarist thesis*.

2. THE STRONG MONETARIST THESIS. If the theoretical framework of the weak Monetarist thesis is supplemented with additional and special hypotheses, the *strong Monetarist thesis* is obtained. An outline of the strong thesis may be formulated in terms of three sets of forces operating simultaneously on the pace of economic activity. For convenience, they may be grouped into monetary forces, fiscal forces, and other forces. The latter include technological and organizational innovation, revisions in supply prices induced by accruing information and expectation adjustments, capital accumulation, population changes, and other related factors or processes.

All three sets of forces are acknowledged by the strong thesis to affect the pace of economic activity via the relative price process previously outlined. Moreover, the strong Monetarist point of view advances the crucial thesis that the variability of monetary forces (properly weighted with respect to their effect on economic activity) exceeds the variability of fiscal forces and other forces (properly weighted). It is argued further that major variabilities occurring in a subset of the other forces (e.g., expectations and revisions of supply prices induced by information arrival) are conditioned by the observed variability of monetary forces. The conjecture thus involves a comparison of monetary variability with the variability of fiscal forces and independent "other forces." According to the thesis under consideration, the variability of monetary impulses is also large relative to the speed at which the economy absorbs the impact of environmental changes. This predominance of variability in monetary impulses implies that pronounced accelerations in monetary forces are followed subsequently by accelerations in the pace of economic activity, and that pronounced decelerations in monetary forces are followed later by retardations in economic activity.

The analysis of the monetary dynamics, using the relative price process, is accepted by both the weak and the strong Monetarist theses. This analysis implies that the regularity of the observed association between accelerations and decelerations of monetary forces and economic activity depends on the relative magnitude of monetary accelerations (or decelerations). The same analysis also reveals the crucial role of changes in the rate of change (second differences) of the money stock in explanations of fluctuations in output and employment. It implies that any pronounced deceleration, occurring at any rate of monetary growth, retards total spending. It is thus impossible to state whether any particular monetary growth, say a 10 per cent annual rate, is expansionary with respect to economic activity, until one knows the previous growth rate. The monetary dynamics of the Monetarist thesis also explains the simultaneous occurrence of permanent price-inflation and fluctuations in output and employment observable in some countries.

The nature and the variability of the "Friedman lag" may also be analyzed within the framework of the Monetarist thesis. This lag measures the interval between a change in sign of the *second* difference in the money stock and the subsequent turning point located by the National Bureau. In general, the lag at an upper turning point will be shorter, the greater the absorption speed of the economy, and the sharper the deceleration of monetary impulses relative to the movement of fiscal forces and other forces. Variability in the *relative* acceleration or deceleration of monetary forces necessarily generates the variability observed in the Friedman lag.

What evidence may be cited on behalf of the strong Monetarist thesis? Every major inflation provides support for the thesis, particularly in cases of substantial variations of monetary growth. The attempt at stabilization in the Confederacy during the Civil War forms an impressive piece of evidence in this respect. The association between monetary and economic accelerations or decelerations has also been observed by the Federal Reserve Bank of St. Louis.[19] Observations from periods with divergent movements of monetary and fiscal forces provide further evidence. For instance, such periods occurred immediately after termination of World War II, from the end of 1947 to the fall of 1948, and again in the second half of 1966. In all three cases, monetary forces prevailed over fiscal forces. The evidence adduced here and on other occasions does not "prove" the strong Monetarist thesis, but does establish its merit for serious consideration.

Davis' examination is therefore welcomed. His objections are summarized by the following points: (a) observations of the persistent association between money and income do not permit an inference of causal direction from money to income;

(b) the timing relation between money and economic activity expressed by the Friedman lag yields no evidence in support of the contention that variations in monetary growth cause fluctuations in economic activity; (c) the correlation found in cycles of moderate amplitude between magnitudes of monetary and economic changes was quite unimpressive; (d) the length of the Friedman lag does not measure the interval between emission of monetary impulse and its ultimate impact on economic activity. Furthermore, the variability of this lag is due to the simultaneous operation and interaction of monetary and non-monetary forces.

Davis' first comment (a) is of course quite true and well known in the logic of science. It is impossible to derive (logically) causal statements or any general hypotheses from observations. But we can use such observations to confirm or disconfirm such statements and hypotheses. Davis particularly emphasizes that the persistent association between money and income could be attributed to a causal influence running from economic activity to money.

Indeed it could, but our present state of knowledge rejects the notion that the observed association is essentially due to a causal influence from income on money. Evidence refuting such a notion was presented in Section C. The existence of a mutual interaction over the shorter-run between money and economic activity, however, must be fully acknowledged. Yet, this interaction results from the conception guiding policymakers which induces them to accelerate the monetary base whenever pressures on interest rates mount, and to decelerate the monetary base when these pressures wane. Admission of a mutual interaction does not dispose of the strong Monetarist thesis. This interaction, inherent in the weak thesis, is quite consistent with the strong position and has no disconfirming value. To the contrary, it offers an explanation for the occurrence of the predominant variability of monetary forces.

The same logical property applies to Davis' second argument (b). The timing relation expressed by the Friedman lag, in particular the chronological precedence of turning points in monetary growth over turning points in economic activity, can probably be explained by the influence of business conditions on the money supply. Studies in money supply theory strongly suggest this thesis and yield evidence on its behalf. The cyclical pattern of the currency ratio, and the strategy typically pursued by monetary policymakers, explain this lead of monetary growth. And again, such explanation of the timing relation does not bear negatively on the strong conjecture.

The objection noted under Davis' point (c) is similarly irrelevant. His observations actually confirm the strong thesis. The latter implies that the correlation between amplitudes of monetary and income changes is itself correlated with the magnitude of monetary accelerations or decelerations. A poor correlation in cycles of moderate amplitude, therefore, yields no discriminating evidence on the validity of the strong thesis. Moreover, observations describing occurrences are more appropriate relative to the formulated thesis than correlation measures. For instance, observations tending to disconfirm the strong Monetarist thesis would consist of occurrences of pronounced monetary accelerations or decelerations which are *not followed* by accelerated or retarded movements of economic activity.

Point (d) still remains to be considered. Once again, his observation does not bear on the strong Monetarist thesis. Davis properly cautions readers about the interpretation of the Friedman lag. The variability of this lag is probably due to the interaction of monetary and non-monetary forces, or to changes from cycle to cycle in the relative variability of monetary growth. But again, this does not affect the strong thesis. The proper interpretation of the Friedman lag, as the interval between reversals in the rate of monetary impulses and their prevalence over all other factors simultaneously operating on economic activity, usefully clarifies a concept introduced into our discussions. This clarification provides, however, no relevant evidence bearing on the questioned hypotheses.

In summary, the arguments developed by Davis do not yield any substantive evidence against the strong Monetarist thesis. Moreover, the discussion omits major portions of the evidence assembled in support of this position.[20]

E. Countercyclical Policy and the Interpretation of Monetary Policy

The usual assertion of the New View, attributing fluctuations of monetary growth to the public's and the banks' behavior, assumed a strategic role in the countercritique. The countercritique denied, furthermore, that monetary actions have a major impact on economic activity. With the crumbling of these two bastions, the monetary policymakers' interpretation of their own behavior becomes quite vulnerable. In a previous section, the substantial contribution of the monetary base to the fluctuations of monetary growth has been demonstrated. These facts, combined with repeated assertions that monetary policy has been largely countercyclical, suggest the existence of a pronounced discrepancy between actual behavior of the monetary authorities and their interpretation of this behavior.

A crucial question bearing on this issue pertains to the proper measure summarizing actual behavior of the monetary authorities. Two major facts should be clearly recognized. First, the monetary base consists of "money" directly issued by the authorities, and every issue of base money involves an action of the monetary authorities. This holds irrespective of their knowledge about it, or their motivation and aims. Second, variations in the base, extended by suitable adjustments to incorporate changing reserve requirement ratios, are the single most important factor influencing the behavior of the money stock. And this second point applies irrespective of whether Federal Reserve authorities are aware of it or wish it to be, or whatever their motivations or aims are. Their actual behavior, and not their motivations or aims, influences the monetary system and the pace of economic activity. Thus, actual changes in the monetary base are quite meaningful and appropriate measures of actual behavior of monetary authorities.[21]

The information presented in Table IV supports the conjecture that monetary policymakers' interpretation of their own behavior has no systematic positive association with their actual behavior. Table IV was constructed on the basis of the scores assigned to changes in policies, according to the interpretation of the Federal Open Market Committee.[22] Positive scores were associated with each session of the FOMC which decided to make policy easier, more expansionary,

less restrictive, less tight, etc., and negative scores indicate decisions to follow a tighter, less expansionary, more restrictive course. The scores varied between plus and minus one, and expressed some broad ordering of the revealed magnitude of the changes.

An examination of the sequence of scores easily shows that the period covered can be naturally partitioned into subperiods exhibiting an overwhelming occurrence of scores with a uniform sign. These subperiods are listed in the first column of Table IV. The second column cumulated the scores over the subperiods listed in order to yield a very rough ranking of the policymakers' posture according to their own interpretation.

Table IV reveals that the FOMC interpreted the subperiods from August 1957 to July 1958, and from July 1959 to December 1960, as among the most expansionary policy periods. The period from November 1949 to May 1953 appears in this account as a phase of persistently tight or restrictive policy. The next two columns list the changes of two important variables during each subperiod. The third column describes changes in free reserves, and the fourth column notes changes in the monetary base. A cursory examination of the

Table IV. The Association Between Policymakers' Interpretation of Policy, Changes in the Monetary Base, and Changes in Free Reserves

PERIODS	CUMULATIVE SCORES OF POLICYMAKERS' INTERPRETATION OVER THE PERIOD	CHANGES IN FREE RESERVES OVER THE PERIOD IN $ MILLION	CHANGES IN THE MONETARY BASE OVER THE PERIOD IN $ MILLION
11/49– 5/53	−4.75	−1030	+5216
6/53–11/54	+2.63	+ 286	+1321
12/54–10/55	−3.37	− 818	+ 345
11/55– 7/56	+1.12	+ 352	+ 399
8/56– 7/57	−1.00	− 44	+ 657
8/57– 7/58	+3.50	+1017	+1203
7/58– 6/59	−2.12	−1059	+ 531
7/59–12/60	+2.62	+1239	− 53
1/61–12/62	− .63	− 428	+3288

columns immediately shows substantial differences in their broad association. The rank correlation between the various columns is most informative for our purposes.

These rank correlations are listed in Table V. The results expose the absence of any positive association between the policymakers' own interpretation or judgment of their stance and their actual behavior, as indicated by movements in the monetary base. The correlation coefficient between the monetary base and cumulated scores has a *negative* value, suggesting that a systematic divergence between stated and actual policy (as measured by the monetary base) is probable. On the other hand, the correlation between the policymakers' descriptions of their posture, and the movement of free reserves, is impressively close. This correlation confirms once again that the Federal Reserve authorities have traditionally used the volume of free reserves as an indicator to gauge and interpret prevailing monetary policies. Yet little evidence has been developed which establishes a causal chain leading from changes in free reserves to the pace of economic activity.

Another observation contained in Table IV bears on the issue of policymakers' interpretation of their own behavior. Changes in the cumulated scores and free reserves between the periods listed always move together and are perfect in terms of direction. By comparison, the co-movement between cumulated scores and changes in the monetary base is quite haphazard; only three out of eight changes between periods move together. This degree of co-movement between cumulated scores and the monetary base could have occurred by pure chance with a probability greater than .2, whereas the probability of the perfect co-movement between cumulated scores and free reserves occurring as a matter of pure chance is less than .004. The traditional

Table V. Rank Correlation Between Changes in the Monetary Base, Changes in Free Reserves, and the Cumulated Scores of Policymakers' Interpretations

Cumulated scores and base	−.09
Cumulated scores and free reserves	+.70
Free reserves and base	−.26

selection of free reserves or money market conditions, as an indicator to interpret prevailing monetary policy and to gauge the relative thrust applied by policy, forms the major reason for the negative association (or at least random association) between stated and actual policy.

Attempts at rebuttal to the above analysis often emphasize that policymakers are neither interested in the monetary base, nor do they attach any significance to it. This argument is advanced to support the claim that the behavior of the monetary base is irrelevant for a proper examination of policymakers' intended behavior. This argument disregards, however, the facts stated earlier, namely, movements in the monetary base are under the direct control and are the sole responsibility of the monetary authorities. It also disregards the fact that actions may yield consequences which are independent of motivations shaping the actions.

These considerations are sufficient to acknowledge the relevance of the monetary base as a measure summarizing the actual behavior of monetary authorities. However, they alone are not sufficient to determine whether the base is the most reliable indicator of monetary policy. Other magnitudes such as interest rates, bank credit, and free reserves have been advanced with plausible arguments to serve as indicators. A rational procedure must be designed to determine which of the possible entities frequently used for scaling policy yields the most reliable results.

This indicator problem is still very poorly understood, mainly because of ambiguous use of economic language in most discussions of monetary policy. The term "indicator" occurs with a variety of meanings in discussions, and so do the terms "target" and "guide." The indicator problem, understood in its technical sense, is the determination of an optimal scale justifying interpretations of the authorities' actual behavior by means of comparative statements. A typical statement is that policy X is more expansionary than policy Y, or that current policy has become more (or less) expansionary. Whenever we use a comparative concept, we implicitly rely on an ordering scale.

The indicator problem has not been given adequate treatment in the literature, and the recognition of its logical structure is often obstructed by inadequate analysis. It is, for instance, not sufficient to emphasize the proposition that the money supply can be a "misleading guide to the proper interpretation of monetary policy." This proposition can be easily demonstrated for a wide variety of models and hypotheses. However, it establishes very little. The same theories usually demonstrate that the rate of interest, free reserves, or bank credit can also be very misleading guides to monetary policy. Thus, we can obtain a series of propositions about a vast array of entities, asserting that each one can be a very misleading guide to the interpretation of policy. We only reach a useless stalemate in this situation.

The usual solution to the indicator problem at the present time is a decision based on mystical insight supplemented by some impressionistic arguments. The most frequently advanced arguments emphasize that central banks operate directly on credit markets where interest rates are formed, or that the interest mechanism forms the centerpiece of the transmission process. Accordingly, in both cases market interest rates should "obviously" emerge as the relevant indicator of monetary policy.

These arguments on behalf of market interest rates are mostly supplied by economists. The monetary authorities' choice of money market conditions as an indicator evolved from a different background. But in recent years a subtle change has occurred. One frequently encounters arguments which essentially deny either the existence of the indicator problem or its rational solution. A favorite line asserts that "the world is very complex" and consequently it is impossible or inadmissible to use a single scale to interpret policy. According to this view, one has to consider and weigh many things in order to obtain a "realistic" assessment in a complicated world.

This position has little merit. The objection to a "single scale" misconstrues the very nature of the problem. Once we decide to discuss monetary policy in terms of comparative statements, an ordinal scale is required in order to provide a logical basis for such statements. A multiplicity of scales effectively eliminates the use of comparative statements. Of course, a single scale may be a function of multiple arguments, but such multiplicity of arguments should not be confused with a multiplicity of scales. Policymakers and economists should therefore realize that one either provides a rational procedure which justifies interpretations of monetary policy by means of comparative statements, or that one abandons any pretense of meaningful or intellectually honest discussion of such policy.

Solution of the indicator problem in the technical sense appears obstructed on occasion by a prevalent confusion with an entirely different problem confronting the central banker—the target problem. This problem results from the prevailing uncertainty concerning the nature of the transmission mechanism and the substantial lags in the dynamics of monetary processes.

In the context of perfect information,

the indicator problem becomes trivial and the target problem vanishes. But perfect information is the privilege of economists' discourse on policy; central bankers cannot afford this luxury. The impact of their actions is both delayed and uncertain. Moreover, the ultimate goals of monetary policy (targets in the Tinbergen–Theil sense) appear remote to the manager executing general policy directives. Policymakers will be inclined under these circumstances to insert a more immediate target between their ultimate goals and their actions. These targets should be reliably observable with a minimal lag.

It is quite understandable that central bankers traditionally use various measures of money market conditions, with somewhat shifting weights, as a target guiding the continuous adjustment of their policy variables. This response to the uncertainties and lags in the dynamics of the monetary mechanism is very rational indeed. However, once we recognize the rationality of such behavior, we should also consider the rationality of using a particular target. The choice of a target still remains a problem, and the very nature of this problem is inadequately understood at this state.

This is not the place to examine the indicator and target problem in detail. A possible solution to both problems has been developed on another occasion.[23] The solutions apply decision theoretic procedures and concepts from control theory to the determination of an optimal choice of both indicator and target. Both problems are in principle solvable, in spite of the "complexity of the world." Consequently, there is little excuse for failing to develop rational monetary policy procedures.

CONCLUSION

A program for applying economic analysis to financial markets and financial institutions is certainly acceptable and worth pursuing. This program suggests that the public and banks interact in the determination of bank credit, interest rates, and the money stock, in response to the behavior of monetary authorities. But the recognition of such interaction implies nothing with respect to the relative importance of the causal forces generating cyclical fluctuations of monetary growth. Neither does it bear on the quality of alternative empirical hypotheses, or the relative usefulness of various magnitudes or conditions which might be proposed as an indicator to judge the actual thrust applied by monetary policy to the pace of economic activity.

The Monetarist thesis has been put forth in the form of well structured hypotheses which are supported by empirical evidence. This extensive research in the area of monetary policy has established that: (i) Federal Reserve actions dominate the movement of the monetary base over time; (ii) movements of the monetary base dominate movements of the money supply over the business cycle; and, (iii) accelerations or decelerations of the money supply are closely followed by accelerations or decelerations in economic activity. Therefore, the Monetarist thesis puts forth the proposition that actions of the Federal Reserve are transmitted to economic activity via the resulting movements in the monetary base and money supply, which initiate the adjustments in relative prices of assets, liabilities, and the production of new assets.

The New View, as put forth by the countercritique, has offered thus far neither analysis nor evidence pertaining relevantly to an explanation of variations in monetary growth. Moreover, the countercritique has not developed, on acceptable logical grounds, a systematic justification for the abundant supply of statements characterizing policy in terms of its effects on the economy. Nor has it developed a systematic justification for the choice of money market conditions as an optimal target guiding the execution of open market operations.

But rational policy procedures require both a reliable interpretation and an adequate determination of the course of policy. The necessary conditions for rational policy are certainly not satisfied if policies actually retarding economic activity are viewed to be expansionary, as in the case of the 1960–1961 recession, or if inflationary actions are viewed as being restrictive, as in the first half of 1966.

The major questions addressed to our monetary policymakers, their advisors, and consultants remain: How do you justify your interpretation of policy, and how do you actually explain the fluctuations of monetary growth? The major contentions of the academic critics of the past performance of monetary authorities could possibly be quite false, but this should be demonstrated by appropriate analysis and relevant evidence.

NOTES

1 Lyle Gramley and Samuel Chase, "Time Deposits in Monetary Analysis," Federal Reserve *Bulletin*, October 1965. John H. Kareken, "Commercial Banks and the Supply of Money: A Market Determined Demand Deposit Rate," Federal Reserve *Bulletin*, October 1967. J. A. Cacy, "Alternative Approaches to the Analysis of the Financial Structure, *Monthly Review*, Federal Reserve Bank of Kansas City, March 1968. Richard G. Davis, "The Role of the Money Supply in Business Cycles," *Monthly Review*, Federal Reserve Bank of New York, April 1968.
2 Gramley–Chase, pp. 1380, 1381, 1393.
3 Cacy, pp. 5, 7.
4 *Ibid.*, p. 7.
5 Davis, pp. 63–64.
6 These three aspects of the New View will subsequently be elaborated more fully. Their program of analysis refers to the application of relative price theory to analysis of financial markets and financial institutions. Their research strategy refers to a decision to initiate analysis in the

context of a most general framework. Their specific conjectures refer to propositions concerning the causes of fluctuation of monetary growth and propositions about proper interpretation of policy.
7 John G. Gurley and Edward F. Shaw, *Money in a Theory of Finance* (Washington: Brookings Institute, 1960). James Tobin, "Commercial Banks as Creators of Money," *Banking and Monetary Studies*, ed. Deane Carson (R. D. Irwin, 1963).
8 Adequate analysis of the medium of exchange function of money, or of the conditions under which inside money becomes a component of wealth, was obstructed by the programmatic state of the New View. The useful analysis of the medium-of-exchange function depends on a decisive rejection of the assertion that "everything is almost like everything else." This analysis requires proper recognition that the marginal cost of information concerning qualities and properties of assets differs substantially between assets, and that the marginal cost of readjusting asset positions depends on the assets involved. The analysis of the wealth position of inside money requires recognition of the marginal productivity of inside money to the holder. Adequate attention to the relevant differences between various cost or yield functions associated with different assets or positions is required by both problems. The blandness of the New View's standard program cannot cope with these issues. The reader may consult a preliminary approach to the analysis of the medium of exchange function in the paper by Karl Brunner and Allan H. Meltzer, in the *Journal of Finance*, 1964, listed in footnote 9. He should also consult for both issues the important book by Boris Pesek and Thomas Saving, *Money, Wealth and Economic Theory*, The Macmillan Company, New York, 1967, or the paper by Harry Johnson, "Inside Money, Outside Money, Income, Wealth and Welfare in Monetary Theory," to be published in *The Journal of Money, Credit and Banking*, December 1968.
9 As examples of the empirical work performed by the Monetarists, the reader should consult the following works: Milton Friedman and Anna Jacobson Schwartz, *A Monetary History of the United States, 1867–1960* (Princeton: Princeton University Press, 1963). Philip Cagan, *Deter-*

minants and Effects of Changes in the Stock of Money (New York: Columbia University Press, 1965). Karl Brunner and Allan H. Meltzer, "Some Further Investigations of Demand and Supply Functions for Money," *Journal of Finance*, Volume XIX, May 1964. Karl Brunner and Allan H. Meltzer, "A Credit-Market Theory of the Money Supply and an Explanation of Two Puzzles in U.S. Monetary Policy," *Essays in Honor of Marco Fanno*, 1966, Padova, Italy. Karl Brunner and Robert Crouch, "Money Supply Theory and British Monetary Experience, *Methods of Operations Research III—Essays in Honor of Wilhelm Krelle*, ed. Rudolf Henn (published in Meisenheim, Germany, by Anton Hain, 1966). Karl Brunner, "A Schema for the Supply Theory of Money," *International Economic Review*, 1961. Karl Brunner and Allan H. Meltzer, "An Alternative Approach to the Monetary Mechanism," *Subcommittee on Domestic Finance, Committee on Banking and Currency, House of Representatives*, August 17, 1964.

10 The reader will find this analysis in the following papers: Karl Brunner and Allan H. Meltzer, "Liquidity Traps for Money, Bank Credit, and Interest Rates," *Journal of Political Economy*, April 1968. Karl Brunner and Allan H. Meltzer, "A Credit-Market Theory of the Money Supply and an Explanation of Two Puzzles in U.S. Monetary Policy," *Essays in Honor of Marco Fanno*, Padova, Italy, 1966.

11 The reader is, of course, aware that these assertions require analytic substantiation. Such substantiation cannot be supplied within the confines of this article. But the reader could check for himself. If he finds, in the context of the countercritique, an analysis of the Monetarists' major hypotheses, an examination of implication, and exposure to observations, I would have to withdraw my statements. A detailed analysis of the banks' and the public's role in the money supply, based on two different hypotheses previously reported in our papers will be developed in our forthcoming books. This analysis, by its very existence, falsifies some major objections made by Cacy or Gramley–Chase. Much of their criticism is either innocuous or fatuous. Gramley–Chase indulge, for instance, in modality statements, i.e., statements obtained from other statements by prefixing a modality

qualifier like "maybe" or "possibly." The result of qualifying an empirical statement always yields a statement which is necessarily true, but also quite uninformative. The modality game thus yields logically pointless but psychologically effective sentences. Cacy manages, on the other hand, some astonishing assertions. The New View is credited with the discovery that excess reserves vary over time. He totally disregards the major contributions to the analysis of excess reserves emanating from the Monetarists' research. A detailed analysis of excess reserves was developed by Milton Friedman and Anna Schwartz in the book mentioned in footnote 9. The reader should also note the work by George Morrison, *Liquidity Preferences of Commercial Banks* (Chicago: University of Chicago Press, 1966), and the study by Peter Frost, "Banks' Demand for Excess Reserves," an unpublished dissertation submitted to the University of California at Los Angeles, 1966. The classic example of an innocuous achievement was supplied by Cacy with the assertion: "...the actual volume of money balances determined by competitive market forces may or may not be equal to the upper limit established by the central bank" (p. 8). Indeed, we knew this before the New View or Any View, just as we always knew that "it may or may not rain tomorrow." The reader should note that similar statements were produced by other authors with all the appearances of meaningful elaborations.

12 The reader may consult my chapter "Federal Reserve Policy and Monetary Analysis" in *Indicators and Targets of Monetary Policy*, ed. by Karl Brunner, to be published by Chandler House Publishing Co., San Francisco. This book also contains the original article by Gramley–Chase. Further contributions by Patric H. Hendershott and Robert Weintraub survey critically the issues raised by the Gramley–Chase paper.

13 In the Gramley–Chase model, g_3 and h_3 are indeterminant.

14 This implication was demonstrated in my paper listed in footnote 12. The monetary base is adjusted for the accumulated sum of reserves liberated from or impounded into required reserves by changes in requirement ratios.

15 Two direct objections made to the Brunner–Meltzer analysis by Kareken should be noted. He finds that the questioned

hypotheses do not contain "a genuine supply function" of deposits. Accepting Kareken's terminology, this is true, but neither does the Gramley–Chase model contain such a supply function. But the objection has no evidential value anyway. If a hypothesis were judged unsatisfactory because some aspects are omitted, all hypotheses are "unsatisfactory." Moreover, the cognitive status of an empirical hypothesis does not improve simply because an "analytical underpinning" has been provided. Kareken also finds fault with our use of the term "money supply function." Whether or not one agrees with his terminological preferences surely does not affect the relation between observations and statements supplied by the hypothesis. And it should be clear that the status of a hypothesis depends only on this relation, and not on names attached to statements.

16 Davis, p. 66. One argument about monetary policy in the same paper requires clarification. Davis asserts on p. 68 that the money supply need not be the objective of policy, and "given this fact, the behavior of the rate of growth of the money supply during the period cannot be assumed to be simply and directly the result of monetary policy decisions alone." This quote asserts that the money supply is "simply and directly the result of policy alone" whenever policy uses the money supply as a target. This is in a sense correct. But the quote could easily be misinterpreted due to the ambiguity of the term "policy." This term is frequently used to designate a strategy guiding the adjustment of policy variables. It is also frequently used to refer to the behavior of the policy variables or directly to the variables as such. The quote is quite acceptable in the first sense of "policy," but thoroughly unacceptable in the second sense.

17 The reader may consult the following studies on this aspect: Milton Friedman and David Meiselman, "The Relative Stability of Monetary Velocity and the Investment Multiplier in the United States, 1897–1958," in *Stabilization Policies*, prepared by the Commission on Money and Credit, Englewood Cliffs, 1963. The paper listed in footnote 21 by James Tobin should also be consulted. Harry Johnson, "Monetary Theory and Policy," *American Economic Review*, June 1962. Karl Brunner, "The Report of the Commission on Money and Credit," *The Journal of Political Economy*, December 1961. Karl Brunner, "Some Major Problems of Monetary Theory," *Proceedings of the American Economic Association*, May 1961. Karl Brunner and Allan H. Meltzer, "The Role of Financial Institutions in the Transmission Mechanism," *Proceedings of the American Economic Association*, May 1963. Karl Brunner, "The Relative Price Theory of Money, Output, and Employment," unpublished manuscript based on a paper presented at the Midwestern Economic Association Meetings, April 1967.

18 The paper on "The Effect of Monetary Policy on Expenditures in Specific Sectors of the Economy," presented by Dr. Sherman Maisel at the meetings organized by the American Bankers Association in September 1967, exemplifies very clearly the inherited Keynesian position. The paper will be published in a special issue of the *Journal of Political Economy*.

19 *U.S. Financial Data*, Federal Reserve Bank of St. Louis, week ending February 14, 1968. Also see "Money Supply and Time Deposits, 1914–1964" in the September 1964 issue of this *Review*.

20 Milton Friedman's summary of the evidence in the *Forty-fourth Annual Report of the National Bureau of Economic Research* is important in this respect. Davis overlooks in particular the evidence accumulated in studies of the money supply mechanism which bears on the issue raised by point (a) in the text. A persistent and uniform association between money and economic activity, in spite of large changes in the structure of money supply processes, yields evidence in support of the Monetarist theses.

The reader should also consult Chapter 13 of the book by Milton Friedman and Anna Schwartz listed in footnote 9; *Studies in the Quantity Theory of Money*, edited by Milton Friedman, University of Chicago Press, 1956; and a doctoral dissertation by Michael W. Keran, "Monetary Policy and the Business Cycle in Postwar Japan," Ph.D. thesis at the University of Minnesota, March 1966, to be published as a chapter of a book edited by David Meiselman.

21 The reader may also be assured by the following statement: "... monetary policy refers particularly to determination of the supply of (the government's) demand debt...." This demand debt coincides

with the monetary base. The quote is by James Tobin, a leading architect of the New View, on p. 148 of his contribution to the Commission on Money and Credit, "An Essay on Principles of Debt Management," in *Fiscal and Debt Management Policies*, Prentice-Hall, Englewood Cliffs, 1963.

22 The scores were published as Appendix II

to "An Alternative Approach to the Monetary Mechanism." See footnote 9.

23 The reader may consult the chapter by Karl Brunner and Allan H. Meltzer on "Targets and Indicators of Monetary Policy," in the book of the same title, edited by Karl Brunner. The book will be published by Chandler House Publishing Co., Belmont, California.

Inflation and Real Interest
Robert A. Mundell

I. INADEQUACIES OF FISHER'S THEORY

The theory of interest under inflation needs further investigation. Irving Fisher's analysis, which concluded that the money rate of interest rises by the anticipated rate of inflation or falls by the anticipated rate of deflation, was subjected to attack by Keynes: "The mistake lies in supposing that it is the rate of interest on which prospective changes in the value of money will directly react, instead of the marginal efficiency of a given stock of capital."[1] Fisher himself seems to have had misgivings about the *empirical* reliability of his explanation and presented evidence suggesting that the adjustment of money interest was only partial, concluding:

When the cost of living is not stable, the rate of interest takes the appreciation and depreciation into account to some extent, but only slightly, and, in general, indirectly. That is, when prices are rising, the rate of interest tends to be high but not so high as it should

Robert A. Mundell, "Inflation and Real Interest," *Journal of Political Economy*, 71 (June 1963), pp. 280–283. The *Journal of Political Economy* is published by the University of Chicago Press. This article will be reprinted in Robert A. Mundell, *Monetary Theory*, Goodyear Publishing Company, Inc., 1971.

be to compensate for the rise; and when prices are falling, the rate of interest tends to be low, but not so low as it should be to compensate for the fall.[2]

Later he showed that the real rate of interest was much more variable than the money rate and conjectured that:

Men are unable or unwilling to adjust at all accurately and promptly the money interest rates to changed price levels ... The erratic behavior of real interest is evidently a trick played on the money market by the "money illusion" when contracts are made in unstable money.[3]

Thus Fisher found verification for a theory of *partial* adjustment of money interest to inflation and deflation but none for his own theory of *complete* adjustment under foresight. And to attribute the discrepancy between theory and reality solely to lack of foresight is to raise doubts about the nature of the evidence that would be required to reject the theory.

The theory presented in this paper is more consistent with Fisher's empirical observations than his own theory, for it shows that anticipated inflation or deflation is likely to raise (lower) the money rate of interest by less than the rate of inflation (deflation) itself. It is also consistent with Keynes' theoretical criticism of Fisher, yet paradoxically retains the concept of an equilibrium interest rate uninfluenced by unanticipated once-for-all changes in the quantity of money.

II. INFLATION AND THE DISCREPANCY BETWEEN REAL AND MONEY INTEREST RATES

To analyze the problem I shall utilize the apparatus invented by Lloyd Metzler in his celebrated article, "Wealth, Saving, and the Rate of Interest."[4] It is assumed that wages and prices are flexible, that full employment is continuously maintained, and that the share of profits in full employment income is constant. Wealth is assumed to be held in money and shares, the real value of the latter being real profits capitalized at the going real interest rate. It is further assumed that real investment depends on the real interest rate and real saving on real balances and that wealth-holders divide their assets between money and securities in a propor-

tion which depends on the money rate of interest.

Under these conditions the equilibrium interest rate is determined by the intersection of two schedules, in some respect analogous to the Hicksian LM and IS curves (see Fig. 1). The IS schedule plots the locus of pairs of values of real interest rates and real money balances along which saving is equal to investment. Its slope is positive because an increase in the real interest rate lowers investment, causing a deflationary gap, while an increase in real balances lowers saving, causing a compensating inflationary gap. Thus, an increase in the real interest rate would have to be associated with an increase in real balances[5] in order to maintain equality between real saving and real investment. Points above and to the left of IS would be points of deflationary pressure and points below and to the right of IS would be points of inflationary pressure.

The LM schedule gives the locus of pairs of money interest rates and real money balances that is consistent with

Figure 1

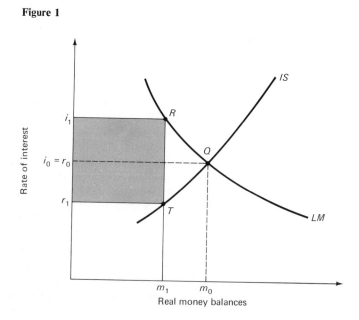

equilibrium in the money market. This schedule has a negative slope because asset-holders divide their wealth between money and securities in a proportion that depends on the opportunity cost of holding money, which is the *money* rate of interest. Thus at high money rates of interest the demand for real balances is low, and at low money interest rates the demand for real balances is high. Only along *LM* are people content to hold the existing stock of real money balances. Above *LM* there is excess liquidity and below *LM* there is deficient liquidity.

The *IS* and *LM* schedules intersect at Q, which determines the equilibrium interest rate, $r_0 = i_0$, and the equilibrium stock of real money balances, m_0. Only at Q is the desire to save equal to the incentive to invest, the demand for shares equal to the supply of shares, and the desire for real money balances equal to the existing stock of real money balances. Q is the equilibrium at which the price level is constant and, therefore, the equilibrium at which real and money interest rates are the same.

III. THE FALL IN REAL INTEREST UNDER INFLATION

Let us now consider the effects of anticipated inflation on the equilibrium. Inflation creates a discrepancy between money interest rates and real interest rates equal to the rate of inflation. This discrepancy widens the difference between the nominal earnings of shares and the return on money because the rate of depreciation of money (the inflation rate) must be added to the real return on shares to get the total cost of holding money.[6] Since the *LM* schedule is derived on the basis of a *money* rate of interest (as that measures the true cost of holding money), it follows that the *LM* schedule, as a function of the *real* rate of interest, shifts downward, at any given level of real balances, by the rate of the inflation. In

the figure, for example, at the inflation rate RT the community would wish to hold the stock of real money balances m_1 only if the real interest rate were r_1 and the nominal interest rate were i_1, the difference being the rate of inflation RT. Thus, the entire schedule *LM*, which is fixed as a function of the *money* rate of interest, shifts downward, as a function of the *real* interest rate, by the rate of inflation.

Consider now the *IS* schedule. From any given point on the schedule an expected inflation, at a given nominal rate of interest, will create a divergence between the productivity of investment and the return on saving equal to the inflation rate, for a dollar borrowed at a given money rate of interest will yield a normal real return plus the rate of appreciation in value of goods, which corresponds to the rate of inflation itself. To maintain equality between saving and investment at any given rate of inflation, the nominal interest rate must therefore rise by the rate of inflation. In the figure, for example, the point T on the *IS* schedule gives a pair of values of real interest rates and real money balances at which saving is equal to investment at a zero rate of inflation. But if the expected inflation rate were RT, a *money* interest rate of only r_1 would create a discrepancy between investment and saving. Only if the nominal interest rate were increased to i_1 would investment and saving be equal at the level of real balances, m_1. The *IS* schedule therefore remains fixed, as a function of the *real* rate of interest, but is raised by the amount RT, as a function of the *money* rate of interest.

The ingredients of the solution are now established. If we interpret the ordinate of the figure as the *real* rate of interest it becomes necessary to shift the *LM* schedule downward by the anticipated rate of the inflation, while the *IS* curve is unaltered. If, on the other hand, the ordinate is taken to refer to the *money* rate of interest, the *IS* schedule must be shifted upward by the rate of the inflation, while the *LM* curve remains fixed. More simply, it is sufficient to take account of the discrepancy between the real rate of interest (for which the existing *IS* curve applies) and the money rate of interest (for which the existing *LM* schedule is appropriate), the discrepancy being the rate of the inflation.

The inflation itself is generated by monetary expansion in excess of growth. The rate of excess monetary expansion is equal to the rate of inflation, RT. The real rate of interest falls[7] from r_0 to r_1, while the money rate of interest rises from i_0 to i_1. Real money balances are reduced from m_0 to m_1 as a consequence of the shift in expectations, and real investment and real saving are both higher than in the inflationless equilibrium. The shaded area measures the depreciation of existing money balances.[8]

IV. CONCLUSION

I have argued that the money rate of interest rises by less than the rate of inflation and therefore that the real rate of interest falls during inflation.[9] The conclusion is based on the fact that inflation reduces real money balances and that the resulting decline in wealth stimulates increased saving.[10] Real conditions in the economy are altered by the purely monetary phenomenon. The evils or benefits of inflation cannot be attributed solely to the failure of the community to anticipate it.[11]

Foreseeable fluctuations in the rate of inflation can thus have very real effects on economic activity. When prices are expected to rise, the money rate of interest rises by less than the rate of inflation giving impetus to an investment boom and an acceleration of growth. Conversely, when a rise in prices is expected to end, there occurs a stock market slump, a rise in the real rate of interest, and a deceleration of growth.

NOTES

1 *General Theory*, p. 143.
2 *The Theory of Interest* (New York, 1930), p. 43.
3 *Ibid.*, p. 415.
4 *Journal of Political Economy*, LIX (April, 1951), 93–116.
5 Wealth changes along *IS* by less than the change in real money balances since the real value of equities moves in inverse proportion to the real rate of interest; the *wealth* effect along *IS* is therefore less than the *real balance* effect, though it is still in the same direction.
6 The following discussion of the demand for money under inflationary conditions has been helped by the works of Philip Cagan, "Monetary Dynamics of Hyperinflation," in *Studies in the Quantity Theory of Money*, ed. M. Friedman (Chicago, 1956), pp. 25–117; and Martin Bailey, "Welfare Cost of Inflationary Finance," *Journal of Political Economy*, LXVI (1956).
7 The change in the rate of interest that results from the anticipation of inflation is a "permanent" change in the sense defined in my "Public Debt, Corporate Income Taxes and the Rate of Interest," *Journal of Political Economy*, LXVIII (December, 1960), 625 n. Recently Metzler's model has been subjected to further investigation, extension, and criticism (see George Horwich, "Real Assets and the Theory of Interest," *Journal of Political Economy*, LXX [April, 1962], 157–170; for references and a criticism of the monetary dynamics inherent in the system), but despite objections it seems to me that Metzler's system retains its essential utility, especially for "comparative statistics" purposes.
8 If the new money issued were spent by the government on goods, the *IS* schedule would shift upward, whereas if it were spent on securities the *LM* schedule would shift downward: the rise in money interest will be greater than that shown in the diagram in the former case and smaller in the latter instance. The textual treatment has avoided these complications by postulating (implicitly) changes in the money supply unaccompanied by any physical *quid pro quo* to the government, a procedure that is probably justifiable for purposes of isolating the theoretical effects of pure inflation, even though it be lacking in institutional foundation.
9 Charles Kennedy, in his "Inflation and the

Bond Rate," *Oxford Economic Papers* (October, 1960), pp. 269–274, interprets the "Keynesian" solution as an unchanged bond price, an interpretation that does not seem to me to take account of the word "directly" in the passage I have quoted in the introduction. I have tried to show that the change in money interest can be interpreted as being due to a shift in the marginal efficiency schedule as a function of *money* interest, or as a shift in liquidity preference as a function of *real* interest, the former being the solution Keynes presumably had in mind.

10 Although the analysis has concentrated on the division of wealth between money and equities, it can also be expected to apply to an economy in which wealth is held in other forms. Arbitrage will bring relative earnings of bonds in line with the money rate of interest (under the conditions of certainty implied in the theoretical analysis) and "cost-of-living" bonds (an instrument used in many countries accustomed to inflation) will yield a nominal return equal to the real rate of interest plus the rate of inflation. Similarly, foreign exchange will yield a return equal to the rate of inflation, as the domestic exchange rate depreciates, though the initial stock adjustment is complicated by the highly liquid attributes of foreign exchange, which imply that the flight from domestic money will be partly into foreign exchange.

11 Cf. A. P. Lerner, "The Inflationary Process—Some Theoretical Aspects," *Review of Economics and Statistics*, August, 1949; reprinted in *Essays in Economic Analysis* (London, 1953): "What is harmful about inflation is not the rise in prices but the failure to anticipate and offset them" (*Essays*, p. 330).

The Appropriate Indicators of Monetary Policy
Patric H. Hendershott and George Horwich

As late as the early 1950's the prevailing sentiment among monetary and financial economists, inherited from Keynes and the depression, was emphatically that money and monetary policy mattered very little. By the early 1960's the majority view was that money mattered significantly, but so did interest rates and real expenditure functions. Today, in the late 1960's—and doubtless into the 1970's—the overwhelming sentiment among monetary economists is that money is virtually all that matters; changes in interest rates are more apparent than real; and even that Keynesian bulwark, fiscal policy unaccompanied by changes in the stock of money, is on the defensive.

Nothing so polarizes the views of the

Patric H. Hendershott and George Horwich, "Money, Interest, and Policy," *The Proceedings of the 1969 Conference on Savings and Residential Financing*, Reprint No. 297, 1969, pp. 33–52.

opposing camps today as the majority belief that the observed stock of money can and should be the indicator of monetary policy actions. For if one can accept this proposition, and we cannot, then all the rest of the supporting doctrine follows quite automatically. This includes the following assertions: Money income is determined directly by observed changes in the stock of money, which are wholly attributable to Federal Reserve actions. All the other behavioral paraphernalia that might affect money and income—the government's propensity to spend and private propensities to save and invest and to hold and supply financial assets—are impotent; either their interest elasticities are equal to zero or infinity (depending on what it takes to deprive them of their punch) or, best of all, they are relatively stable functions that do not shift. While the inevitable wide swings in the government deficit seem inconsistent with this simplistic quantity theory world, the monetarists believe that the deficit, if privately financed, will in fact have little impact on the economy. The deficit will not alter money income because of the almost zero interest elasticity of the demand for money; it will not alter interest rates because of the virtual infinite interest elasticity of both private saving and investment. Of course, if the Federal Reserve finances an increase in the government deficit, the quantity theorists readily affirm that the resulting rise in money will raise prices. Then even interest rates will rise, for they respond mainly to inflationary expectations generated by the monetary increase.

By contrast, our framework holds that both the stock and the demand for money are interest sensitive, positive and negative, respectively. Investment, and perhaps saving, respond to interest rates in the expected direction, but rather weakly in the short run owing to long lags of adjustment. Both functions and, of course, government spending undergo frequent shifts. The short-run interest elasticities of the supply and demand for money are not high in absolute value (i.e., not over one-half), but they are high enough to give the economy a firm Keynesian tone. The eivdence for the interest sensitivity of investment and the demand for money is well established.[1] We shall describe the interest response of the observed stock of money and argue that this response renders money useless as an indicator of policy. Instead, money is an indicator of all the forces, internal and external, that determine interest rates. Within our generalized framework, we shall derive an adjusted monetary series that can serve as the indicator of monetary policy and we shall define the sense in which interest rates can be the target of policy, in spite of—or, more accurately, because of—the tendency in the economy to recurring shifts in real expenditure functions.

RELEVANT CONCEPTS: EASE, RESTRAINT, INDICATORS, TARGETS

We begin our analysis by defining the terms and concepts relevant to this discussion. These include financial ease or restraint, monetary ease or restraint, restrictive or easy monetary policy, indicators of monetary policy, and targets of monetary policy.

As the financial adjective suggests, financial restraint and ease refer to conditions in the financial markets, to the cost and availability of credit. If interest rates are rising and/or credit is being rationed, there is an excess demand for funds and financial restraint is said to exist. If interest rates are falling and credit is not being rationed, there is an excess supply of funds and financial ease exists. Similarly, as the monetary adjective suggests, monetary restraint and ease generally refer to what is happening to a monetary aggregate such as the quantity of money. If money is growing slowly or declining, monetary restraint is said to exist; if money is growing rapidly, monetary ease exists. Finally, restrictive and easy monetary policy refer to the direction of monetary policy actions. Defined appropriately, when one's indicator of monetary policy is growing slowly or declining, policy is said to be restrictive; when the indicator is growing rapidly, policy is easy.

Most monetary and financial economists would agree with these definitions. Disagreement arises when one selects a specific indicator of policy actions. Some define the indicator so that restrictive and easy monetary policy are synonymous with financial restraint and ease—i.e., with the rise and fall of interest rates or the presence and absence of credit rationing. Others define the indicator so that restrictive and easy monetary policy are synonymous with monetary restraint and ease. These views are equally incorrect.

Since both interest rates and monetary aggregates are endogenous variables that are influenced significantly by forces other than monetary policy actions, neither can be an accurate indicator of monetary policy. By definition, if an indicator of monetary policy actions alone is desired, the indicator must be independent of economic activity and fiscal policy actions. An example of such an indicator is the neutralized money stock.

Another controversial concept that often arises in discussions of monetary policy is the target of policy. Ultimate policy targets are, of course, such things as full employment, stable prices, and so on. In the present context, however, targets refer to intermediate financial targets, which, if achieved, should lead, or at least contribute, to the attainment of the ultimate goals of policy. Examples of intermediate policy targets are a constant growth rate of the quantity of money or a market rate of interest equal to the natural rate of interest.

The determination of interest rates and money is described in the next section. The endogenous nature of these variables, including their simultaneous determination in a general-equilibrium framework, is emphasized. The following section details the general inadequacies of observed interest and money as indicators, describes an appropriate indicator of monetary policy, and documents the specific errors that would have resulted from using the observed money stock or interest rates as the indicator during the 1950's. Alternative policy targets (or rules) are discussed in the last section.

INTEREST RATES, STOCK OF MONEY DETERMINED SIMULTANEOUSLY

The essential point of this section is that interest rates and the stock of money are determined simultaneously along with everything else in a general equilibrium system. Unlike the ruling majority in money and finance who pay lip service to the proposition, we believe it and make use of it. Nevertheless, we shall begin by isolating proximate or more immediate determinants of interest and money. After doing so, we shall take the broader view and describe the interaction of money and interest rates as they mesh to form the "money supply process." Finally, we shall consider an alternative to our analysis.

As is customary at this level of aggregation, a single rate of interest is taken to be a representative or average of the rates on all nonmonetary financial claims—both short and long term, government and private, equity and debt. The rate of interest varies inversely with the price of claims—or securities, to use a more precise term—and, like any price, is determined by total supply and demand. The approach to interest rate determination is thus very direct, in glorious contrast to the common obsession with *IS* and *LM* curves and other weary devices designed to conceal the underlying forces at work in the securities market. The general framework is more Wicksellian than Keynesian or Fisherian, and the guiding principle is the fact that nothing can affect the rate of interest except as it creates excess security supply or demand.

We—or at least one of us—are currently engaged in a major econometric effort in which the price and quantity of five broad, all-inclusive security categories will be explained by demand and supply schedules of each security. The study uses flow-of-funds data and, if successful, will enable decisive determination of the impact of such factors as preferred habitats, interest rate expectations, and price level expectations on the general level and structure of interest rates. We are not ready to report on the outcome of this research but can indicate something

Table I. Funds Raised by and Advanced to Domestic Nonfinancial Sectors

	1965	1966	1967	1968
Funds Raised	67.1	62.6	74.6	91.4
Private Domestic Nonfinance	66.0	62.0	66.4	79.7
Short-term Debt				
Households	11.3	8.3	7.1	15.5
Businesses	14.6	13.6	9.0	13.0
State and Local Government	1.3	0.4	1.3	0.3
Long-term Obligations				
State and Local Government	6.5	6.4	9.1	10.9
Households	16.2	11.0	11.5	15.4
Businesses	15.9	22.5	28.4	24.6
Federal Government (net)	1.1	0.6	8.2	11.8
Funds Advanced	67.1	62.6	74.6	91.4
Private Domestic Nonfinance	8.6	20.1	2.0	17.0
Households	1.8	10.7	−6.2	1.7
Businesses	1.0	3.2	0.4	7.7
State and Local Government	5.8	6.2	7.8	7.7
Financial Institutions (net)	56.0	40.7	66.1	69.2
Banks	28.3	17.3	36.1	38.6
Nonbank Saving Institutions	14.2	8.7	15.0	15.1
Other	13.5	14.6	14.9	15.5
Rest of the World (net)	−1.2	−1.6	1.7	1.6
Federal Reserve	3.8	3.5	4.8	3.7
Memorandum:				
Federal Government Funds Raised as % of Total	1.6	1.0	11.0	12.8
Federal Reserve Funds Supplied as % of Total	5.7	5.6	6.4	4.0
Long-term Business Funds Raised Plus Change in Profit Tax Liability	17.8	22.7	24.6	27.1

Data Sources for Table I: Most of the data are from the financial summary table in the flow-of-funds accounts. However, the component breakdown of private-domestic-nonfinance funds raised differs from that of the flow-of-funds, the Rest-of-the-World funds raised (from sources other than the Federal Government) have been netted against its funds advanced. Federal Government mortgages and loans to private domestic nonfinance have been netted against its funds raised, and Federal Government loans to sectors other than private domestic nonfinance (i.e., Saving and Loan Associations and the Rest of the World) have been excluded from the table.

The component breakdown is the following:
Household short-term debt: consumer credit plus banks loans n.e.c. plus other loans other than those from the Federal Government.
Business short-term debt: banks loans n.e.c. plus other loans other than those from the Federal Government.
State and local short-term debt: same as that given in the flow-of-funds.
Households long-term: 1–4 family mortgages of both household and business sectors.
Business long-term: security issues and other mortgages and Federal Government loans of both the business and household (nonprofit) sectors.
State and local long-term: bond issues and loans from the Federal Government.

of the scope of the approach to interest rate determination by considering the interaction of specific participants in the securities markets.

The upper half of Table I presents the quantities of funds raised by the private domestic nonfinancial sectors and the federal government during the last four years. The lower half of Table I contains the quantities of funds advanced by private domestic nonfinancial sectors, financial institutions, the rest of the world, and the Federal Reserve. Funds raised have been divided according to their basic investment use. Households supply short-term debt (largely consumer credit) to finance consumer durables and they supply residential mortgages to finance housing expenditures; nonfinancial businesses supply short-term debt (largely to banks) to finance inventories and they supply long-term issues to finance plant and equipment investment; and state and local governments issue their obligations, at least in part, to finance construction expenditures.

The financial flows say a great deal about the underlying real expenditures, even though there is significant substitutability of funds between uses, including expenditures on consumption and financial assets. For example, the decline in 1967 in short-term debt issued by households and businesses and its rise in 1968 follows the simultaneous slowdown and the acceleration in consumer durable and inventory expenditures.[2] Likewise, the deceleration in the growth of residential mortgages in 1966 and the subsequent acceleration in 1968 is associated with a similar movement in expenditures.[3] At first glance, business long-term issues do not appear to have moved in accord with plant and equipment expenditures. The rate of growth of the latter slowed markedly in 1967 and accelerated in 1968, while business issues continued their rapid rise in 1967 and then declined in 1968.[4] However, when account is taken of the per-

manent acceleration of corporate tax payments in 1967—businesses apparently issued long-term debt to raise the needed funds—the discrepancy between movements in issues and expenditures is eliminated. The sum of long-term business issues and the change in corporate profit tax liabilities grew slightly in 1967 and accelerated in 1968 (see the memorandum at the bottom of the table).

In the advancing of funds, the most obvious phenomenon is the substitutability between direct financing by the nonfinancial sectors, particularly households and businesses, and indirect financing by financial institutions. State and local governments advanced relatively constant amounts during these years, but households and businesses shifted in 1966 toward advancing funds directly, and in 1967, back to the normal indirect channeling of funds through financial intermediaries. Also, there was a substantial decline in funds advanced by commercial banks and nonbank savings institutions in 1966 with an increase in 1967. Other financial institutions were not affected by this relative disintermediation.

Other participants in the securities markets include the federal government (a net demander of funds), the Federal Reserve (a net supplier of funds), and the rest of the world. The latter demanded funds (on net) in 1965–1966 and supplied them in 1967–1968.

Two interesting phenomena regarding the influence of the fiscal and monetary authorities on interest rates emerge from Table I. First, in terms of their average contribution (see the memorandum at the bottom of the table), the authorities do not appear to dominate the securities market. Over this four-year period, the federal government accounted for only 6.6 per cent of the total funds raised and the Federal Reserve supplied only 5.4 per cent.[5] Second, while the Federal Reserve has supplied a relatively constant proportion of the total funds[6]—its contribution varied between 4.0 per cent and 6.4 per cent—the federal government's proportion fluctuated widely. After having been largely out of the market in 1965 and 1966, the Treasury raised $8 billion in 1967 and $12 billion in 1968, accounting for over 10 per cent of the funds raised in these two years. This is, of course, just another example of a financial phenomenon reflecting real events—in this case the substantial fiscal deficits in 1967 and 1968.[7]

QUANTITY OF MONEY AFFECTED BY RATE OF INTEREST

The determination of the quantity of money is at least as involved as the determination of the rate of interest, because the latter plays a role in determining the former. The quantity of money is equal to the amount that the public wishes to hold. This, in turn, depends importantly on the rate of interest and the level of national income. Since one of us has previously investigated the proximate determinants of the stock of money in detail,[8] we can present a simplified description of the movement of money over the course of a typical postwar business cycle. We abstract for the moment from actions of the Federal Reserve.

Consider a business upswing, characterized by an investment schedule shifting to the right. As a consequence, both interest rates and income rise. Since the rise in interest rates generates the bank reserves needed to support an increased demand for money, the money stock rises. The increase in available reserves results from an increase in member bank borrowing, a decrease in member bank excess reserves, a relative decrease in time deposits, and a *ceteris paribus* inflow of gold via the capital account of the balance of payments. Income effects on reserves work in the opposite direction, but the interest rate effects dominate.[9] Since interest and income move together, money tends to rise in the upswing. The reverse occurs in the downswing. Thus the quantity of money moves procyclically.

Of course, the Federal Reserve influences the money stock. By taking expansionary actions it initially lowers interest rates, inducing the public to hold more bank deposits, while simultaneously supplying the reserves to support them. In the longer run the actions tend to be translated into money income increases, rather than interest rate decreases. Early in the upswing the Federal Reserve is generally feeding the rising demand for money, later in the upswing it usually acts to restrain the rising demand by raising interest rates, and in the downswing it is generally attempting to offset the falling demand for money. These responses are documented in the following section.

The formal mechanism by which a rise in the rate of interest raises the quantity of money is not well understood. In order to see precisely how interest and money interact, it is necessary to extend the security market determination of interest rates in a Wicksellian direction. In that noteworthy framework, there are two kinds of interest rate, the natural or equilibrium rate and the market rate. Only the market rate is observable and it is taken to be the average of the prevailing rates on all securities. The natural rate is more abstract but is an essential part of the apparatus by which changing market rates alter the stock of money.

On a first approximation, the natural rate is defined as that market rate of interest at which desired saving and investment *would* be equal. In general, this is not the same as the prevailing market rate, since desired saving and investment are undergoing constant change and cannot be equal, except after a rather prolonged period of adjustment.

From the viewpoint of observable financial phenomena, it is necessary both to narrow and broaden the saving and investment totals relevant to the natural rate. Only those components of saving and investment channeled directly or indirectly through the money and capital—the securities—markets can have any bearing on the rate of interest, which is, as we noted, an inverse function of the price of claims. Moreover, since saving and investment are continuing or flow variables, characteristic of a growing economy, they generate a flow demand and flow supply, respectively, of nonmonetary financial claims. The natural rate is thus the rate of interest at which the flow supply and flow demand for securities would be equal.

Securities are defined in the broadest possible sense to include all nonmonetary claims. The security supply side is thus extended beyond Wicksell to include the very considerable quantity of government debt in this country. Its relevance to the rate of interest as a source of continuing flow supply is substantial, and on at least one occasion in recent years, overwhelming.[10]

There is no unique natural rate. There is only one at any instant of time, but there will be a different one for every combination of all the variables that determine saving, investment, the government deficit, and, thereby, flow security demand and supply. Since saving depends significantly on disposable income, which in turn is a function of government tax receipts, the balanced portion of the government budget is also relevant to the level of the natural rate.

The market rate, once again, is the observed rate and is determined by all security supplies and demands—new flows and pre-existing stocks of claims combined. In a brief interval, the flows are negligible and market rate is determined solely in the existing-securities market.

When the market rate and the flow equilibrium or natural rate are the same, the market rate is constant over time and, for a given growth rate of the economy, so is the endogenously determined money stock. When, because of rising investment prospects or increasing government borrowing, an increased rate of security supply raises the natural rate, there is at the still unchanged market rate an excess flow supply of securities. The excess securities cause the price of securities to fall and the yield to rise, whereupon they are purchased by bankers, expanding total bank credit and the money stock.[11] This process continues, with the yield on securities (the market rate) gradually rising toward the natural rate, carrying the money stock with it. The increase in expenditures financed by the additional quantity of money will raise the general price level and possibly output as well.

In the opposite case when the natural rate falls below the market rate, there is at the higher market rate an excess flow demand for securities. The excess security demand lowers the market rate and induces bankers to sell off earning assets, contracting bank credit and money. In response, the price level and probably output fall. The greater the gap there is between the market rate and the natural rate, the greater, of course, is the force altering market rates and the stock of money.

WICKSELLIAN FRAMEWORK EXPLAINS MONEY AND RATE MOVES

It is important to stress that the movements of the market rate in the Wicksellian system are intended to be "real" in the sense that they do not merely reflect changes in the expected rate of price level movement. Suppose a rise in the nominal (quoted) market rate on fixed money-value claims is in fact caused by widely held inflationary expectations. The rise would apply equally to the nominal natural rate, which is simply that interest rate at which saving and investment happen to be equal. As a consequence, the difference between the market and natural rates, whether in real or nominal units, would be unchanged and could have no impact on the quantity of money.

The use of the Wicksellian framework to explain observed movements in interest rates and the money stock is thus qualified by the requirement that the nominal and real rates shift only gradually relative to each other. What is the empirical evidence that expectations of price level change have in fact influenced the trends and cycles of interest rates in the postwar period?

Recently there have been two serious studies of the influence of price expectations on interest rates. A dissertation using Fisherian methodology by William E. Gibson, formerly of the University of Chicago, concluded that a 1 per cent rise in the price level raises the short-term rate .33 per cent and the long-term rate .06 per cent—both after a lapse of 10 years.[12] Using his price index (the GNP deflator), interest rates, and weighting system, annual real series of the prime commercial paper rate and the Moody Aaa bond

yield were computed. Each year's price change was carried forward four years in both nominal interest series, applying the sum of the fourth-to-tenth-year weights to the fourth year. The patterns of the resulting real series, plotted in Figure 1, are scarcely distinguishable from the nominal ones.

A study by Thomas Sargent reports results that are consistent with Gibson's.[13] Sargent is not explicit about the long-run effect of expected price changes on nominal rates, but arrives at the longest expectational lag that has yet been claimed; only 2 per cent of the long-run response occurs in the first year and the full response does not occur for 40 years. Unless the long-run effect is unbelievably large, Sargent's results imply an even smaller impact of price expectations on interest rates than do Gibson's.

Thus the evidence supporting the price-expectations hypothesis as a major determinant of postwar interest rates is not yet available. Moreover, in evaluating the 1960's with reference to wholesale prices, the index of which is the most sensitive

Figure 1. Selected Short- and Long-Term Interest Rates (1950–1968)

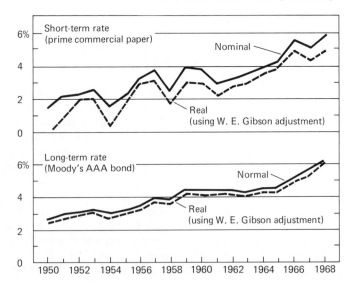

and least biased by quality changes, 1964 concludes a seven-year period of unbroken price stability. It is not evident how a very strong case can be made for the impact of price expectations on interest rates in the succeeding two or three years. When one considers that the ratio of total funds raised to GNP rose by one-fourth between 1966 and 1968, even with rising interest rates, an alternative explanation involving price expectations is hardly needed.[14]

Nevertheless, it is entirely possible that the more rapid inflation of 1967 and 1968 may have generated inflationary expectations in the credit markets, particularly since last fall. Even this is a speculative assertion, without rigorous econometric documentation. There were, after all, a thousand occasions on which Gibson and Sargent were unable to find more than a modicum of impact of much larger price level changes on interest rates. Their experience contradicts the monetary voices in government, industry, and the academy that proclaim, but do not demonstrate, that price level expectations, rather than real forces, are largely responsible for interest rate movements in this decade.[15]

In this section we shall illustrate, first logically and later empirically, the pitfalls of using either observed money or interest rates as indicators of monetary policy. In between we describe an appropriate indicator and examine its behavior in the postwar period.

IS OBSERVED MONEY EVIDENCE OF EXPANSIONARY POLICY?

The hazards of attributing observed interest rate movements to policy actions (exogenous forces), while ignoring the influence of endogenous forces, are well known and frequently cited.[16] The pitfalls of evaluating observed monetary changes as the consequence of Federal Reserve policies, while neglecting endogenous sources of fluctuation, are seldom appreciated.[17] As a purely hypothetical, but relevant illustration of the inadequacies of the money stock as an indicator of policy, consider the following example. Suppose that extraordinary demands for funds drive the natural rate to extremely high levels—perhaps 12 per cent. Assume that in the absence of monetary policy actions, the market rate is 5 per cent and rising, and the endogenously determined money stock is advancing at an annual rate of 9 per cent. The Federal Reserve reduces the growth rate of money from 9 per cent to 6 per cent as it raises market rates from 5 per cent to 7 per cent. The market rate is still below the natural rate, but the discrepancy has been reduced from 7 per cent to 5 per cent and monetary growth cut by 33 per cent. Whether the continued growth rate of the observed money stock is the proper rate depends on the current rate of inflation, the extent of unemployment, the balance of payments, and the allocative and political effects of still higher market rates of interest. The main question here is, whether, in these circumstances, observed monetary behavior can be taken as prima facie evidence of expansionary monetary policy actions. Is it accurate to say, as many would, that in this example the central bank is pursuing an easy money policy, even while it has reduced the growth rate of money by one-third of what it otherwise would have been? We think not.

Just as we have illustrated the inappropriateness of the observed money stock as an indicator of the central bank's influence on money, so we may contrive an example in which interest rate movements are a deceptive measure of policy impact. In the preceding example, suppose that the natural rate of 12 per cent would, in the absence of policy, itself raise the market rate from 5 per cent to 7 per cent within a year's time. The Federal Reserve considers this an unacceptable annual increase and limits the interest rate rise to

1 per cent by raising the growth rate of money from the endogenous 9 per cent to 10 per cent. Obviously, the fact that interest rates continue to rise is no evidence of restrictive policy actions.

Neither example is intended to question the ability of the Federal Reserve to fix the growth rate of money or the interest rate at any desired level. Nor is stability of either the monetary growth rate or interest rates defended as a goal of policy. The purpose is merely to emphasize that endogenous responses should not be confused with Federal Reserve actions.

MUST DISTINGUISH BETWEEN ENDOGENOUS, EXOGENOUS COMPONENTS

An accurate indicator of Federal Reserve policy actions must distinguish between the endogenous and exogenous components of either interest or money. Which series is analyzed is probably inconsequential, because their exogenous components should have similar cyclical patterns; the only systematic cyclical movement in them would be due to Federal Reserve actions. For example, since a Federal Reserve open-market purchase simultaneously lowers interest rates and increases the money stock, a measure of the impact of current Federal Reserve actions on interest rates is likely to exhibit the same cyclical turning points as would a measure of the impact of such actions on the money stock.

The neutralized money stock represents an empirical effort to derive an exogenous monetary series. It is calculated in the following way.[18] First, a money-stock identity is derived by substituting for the member-bank demand deposit component of the narrowly defined money stock. The money-stock identity includes exogenous components (the Federal Reserve's portfolio of government securities, Treasury cash holdings, and so on) and endogenous

components, and the coefficient of most components is the reciprocal of the reserve requirement against demand deposits. The endogenous components are: borrowings from the Federal Reserve, the U.S. gold stock, currency outside banks, Federal Reserve float, member bank time deposits, and excess reserves. Second, regression equations explaining these endogenous components are estimated. The principal regressors are such patently endogenous variables as national income and interest rates. Third, neutralized or "exogenized" components are calculated by applying the computed regression coefficients to cycle-free or trend values of income and interest rates. Finally, the neutralized money stock is calculated by applying the coefficients in the money-stock identity to the neutralized components. The resulting series, from which the impact of the business cycle has effectively been removed, reflects the influence of only Federal Reserve policy actions and other exogenous forces.[19] Thus it is a measure of monetary policy that is analogous to the full-employment budget surplus measure of fiscal policy. Just as the latter reflects the influence of fiscal policy, not the business cycle, on the budget surplus, the neutralized money stock reflects the influence of monetary policy, not the business cycle, on the money stock.

NEUTRALIZED MONEY STOCK: INTERESTING CHRONICLE

The neutralized money stock offers an interesting chronicle of Federal Reserve policies during the 1952–1964 period (see Figure 2).[20] During those years, there were three recessions: 1953–1954, 1957–1958, and 1960–1961. In the year prior to the 1953 recession, the neutralized money stock was rising, but it accelerated in August 1953, the first month of that recession. It continued to rise strongly

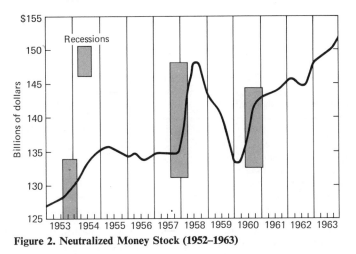

Figure 2. Neutralized Money Stock (1952–1963)

past the end of the recession in August 1954 into the subsequent upswing. Monetary restraint, signaled by the turnaround in neutralized money, occurred in April 1955, the eighth month of the boom, and continued, with a brief respite during the second half of 1956, through all the rest of the upswing and beyond, until November 1957, the fourth month of the 1957–1958 recession. The sharpest increase in neutralized money over the entire period began at this point and continued through the first half of 1958. A very pronounced decline in neutralized money began in August 1958, the fourth month of the upswing, and ended in March 1960, anticipating the 1960–1961 recession by three months. The ensuing monetary expansion continued, with 1962 as an exception, at least through 1964.[21]

A brief summary of the timing of antirecession monetary policies is probably of interest, particularly in light of the severe criticisms that have been made of these policies.[22] Analysis of the neutralized money stock suggests that policy switched to ease in the first month of the 1953–1954 recession, the fourth month of the 1957–1958 recession, and actually anticipated the 1960–1961 recession by three months. Thus, on the average, policy switched to ease in the first month of postaccord

recessions. This analysis of policy contrasts markedly with the earlier studies of Brunner and Meltzer, and Kareken and Solow. The former, for example, contend that policymakers did not switch to ease, on the average, until the ninth month of these recessions. The extreme differences between the conclusions of these studies and those based on the neutralized money stock are due to differences in the indicator of monetary policy actions selected and to errors in the analysis of earlier investigators.[23] Regarding the choice of indicator, both Brunner and Meltzer and Kareken and Solow chose money-stock related indicators, whose turning points, as we show below, tend to lag those of policy. The principal error was Brunner and Meltzer's analysis of annual changes, rather than monthly or quarterly changes, in their indicator. Since turning points in an annual-change series tend to lag those in the observed series, this procedure reinforced the bias toward an unfavorable interpretation of policy already introduced by the selection of a money-stock related variable as the indicator of policy.

Popular indicators of monetary policy fall into two general categories: money-market variables and money-stock related variables. The former, which include such variables as free reserves and the

Table II. Comparison of Turning Points of Observed Money (Mo), the Bill Rate (R), and Neutralized Money (Mn)

NEW POLICY	DATE SUGGESTED BY ANALYSIS OF Mn	MONTHS TURNING POINT OF Mo FOLLOWED THAT OF Mn	MONTHS TURNING POINT OF R PRECEDED THAT of Mn
Ease	August 1953	9 later	2 earlier
Restraint	April 1955	21 later	10 earlier
Ease	November 1957	3 later	1 earlier
Restraint	August 1958	11 later	2 earlier
Ease	March 1960	5 later	3 earlier

three-month Treasury bill rate, are biased toward a favorable assessment of policy; the latter, which include such variables as the money stock, however defined, and the monetary base, however extended or adjusted, are biased toward an unfavorable assessment of policy. That is, turning points in money-market variables tend to precede policy reversals, while those of money-stock related variables tend to follow policy reversals.

Table II illustrates the bias in the selection of policy turning points that is introduced by analyzing observed movements in money-market or money-stock related variables. The dates of policy reversals, as denoted by turning points in neutralized money, and the turning points in the observed money stock and the three-month bill rate, relative to these reversals, are recorded. Notice that the turning points in observed money *always* follow those in neutral money and that those in the bill rate *always* precede those of neutral money. For example, a policy switch from ease to restraint, as revealed by the downturn of neutral money, will be preceded by the rise in the bill rate and followed by the fall in the observed stock of money. The average lag in turning points of observed money behind those of neutral money is 9.8 months; the average lead in turning points of the bill rate relative to neutral money is 3.6 months. The average timing discrepancies for policy reversals to

ease are a 5.7 month lag for the observed money stock and a 2.0 month lead for the bill rate.[24]

The short lead in peaks in the bill rate relative to policy reversals to ease suggests that during this period policy makers might have been responding to the bill rate or the money market, rather than to economic activity or the goods market. This implication is reinforced by the fact that in the one recession where the bill rate fell after the peak in economic activity—1957–1958—the Federal Reserve was very late in taking action, while in the single recession where the bill rate declined substantially before the peak in economic activity—1960–1961—the Federal Reserve anticipated the recession.[25]

If a vote were taken today among monetary and financial economists, to say nothing of Congressmen, economic advisers to the President, journalists, and the general public, there is little doubt that a rule requiring the Federal Reserve each year to raise the stock of money within relatively narrow bounds would win hands down. Viewed as a delayed reaction to the catastrophe of 1929–1933 and other major monetary miscalculations, the advocacy of a monetary growth rule is understandable. However, in general, such a rule is a crude policy that does not represent the best the central bank can and should aspire to in the 1970's. It is only a minimum risk policy aimed at preventing severe monetary errors. It provides no offsets against the more frequent real disturbances to the economy and assigns no stabilization role to fiscal policy.

A constant growth rate of money of, say 3 or 4 per cent a year, is designed to counter the deflationary tendency of a growing economy. Under ideal circumstances, rising output would be met by equal demand at more or less constant prices. The economy would achieve the growth equivalent of the stable equilibrium of *IS* and *LM*—the schedules we disparaged earlier in this paper. In particular, the growth rule would stabilize the *LM* schedule by neutralizing the tendency of falling prices to shift it downward.

NATURAL RATE WILL FLUCTUATE

Of course, the equilibrium will not last. Inventory and fixed investment cycles will continue to occur, and future government deficits to finance wars in Southeast Asia or on urban poverty would not be too surprising. In terms of the *IS-LM* framework, the *IS* curve, where *I* includes the government deficit, will continue to undergo substantial fluctuations. In Wicksellian terms, the natural rate will fluctuate. With monetary policy unable to respond selectively to disturbances, the movement of the natural rate will be translated into an equal movement of the market rate. The *LM* schedule, once again, will shift gradually to the changing equilibrium defined by the intersection of *IS* and the supply function of output. This time, however, *LM* will be moved not by the exogenous money stock, but by the price level, fed by endogenous monetary responses.

If policy were free from the shackles of a monetary growth rule, it could, if it wished, carry *LM* immediately to its new equilibrium by altering the growth rate of money. This would equate the market rate to the natural rate instantly, prevent-

ing the endogenous stock of money, the demand for money, and thereby the price level from responding to a discrepancy between the rates as part of an internal adjustment process. Or, if the bank were so disposed, it could maintain some degree of difference between the market and natural rates in exchange for some amount of price level or output movement. This might be done at the trough of the business cycle when the natural rate, having risen above the market rate, is allowed to pull money, velocity, prices, employment, and output up along with it. Some inflation might also be tolerated at high employment if, as was considered earlier, an extremely high natural rate might draw the market rate above politically acceptable levels.

IDEAL MONETARY POLICY: EQUATION OF MARKET TO NATURAL RATE

The ideal monetary policy is one in which the central bank, starting at a position of full employment, acts immediately to equate the market rate to the natural rate. At the same time the fiscal authority manipulates the natural rate by tax and expenditure policies so as to keep it within a politically acceptable range. The fiscal authority is also responsible for taking action against disturbances that do not involve changes in market or natural rates—destabilizing direct movements between money and commodities. This leaves both the Treasury and the central bank with a clean and clear understanding of what each must do. The central bank has a mandate to take interest rates as the immediate target of policy. But it is the relation between the market and the natural rate, conditioned by ultimate goals such as full employment and stable prices, that shapes policy, never the observed market rate alone.[26]

This approach has many advantages. It enables the central bank to do what it does naturally—to operate in the financial markets and set a proper interest rate. It defines the proper interest rate.[27] It limits the lags in the effect of policy to the very little time required for a change in market rates to spread from one security to another. For policy tries only to prevent unwanted movements of the price level and output, not to reduce prices or raise GNP through an inevitable time consuming process.

The natural rate has not yet been measured. Its measurement, however, is not far off. As part of the econometric study of financial markets referred to earlier, three natural rates—a residential mortgage, a combined bond-equity, and an aggregate short-term—will be measured. With these rates in hand, the consequences of a policy of equating the market and natural rates will be relatively easy to evaluate. We are confident that these consequences will support such a policy.

NOTES

1 On the demand for money see F. Modigliani and R. Rasche, "Central Bank Policy and the Money Supply," *The Journal of Money, Banking, and Credit*, I, February 1969 (forthcoming); and F. deLeeuw, "The Demand for Money: Speed of Adjustment, Interest Rates, and Wealth," in G. Horwich, ed., *Monetary Process and Policy: A Symposium* (Homewood, Ill.: Richard D. Irwin, Inc., 1967), pp. 167–186. On the investment response, see the investment studies produced by the Federal Reserve–MIT research project (summarized in F. deLeeuw and E. M. Gramlich, "The Channels of Monetary Policy," *Journal of Finance*, XXIV, May 1969).

2 Consumer durable expenditures fell from $14.9 billion in 1966 to $12.1 billion in 1967 and rose to $16.9 billion in 1968; inventory expenditures fell from $14.7 billion to $6.1 billion and rose back to $7.6 billion in 1968.

3 Residential construction expenditures on 1–4 family units fell from $20.0 billion in 1965 to $18.0 billion in 1966, rose slightly to $18.6 billion in 1967, and accelerated to $21.9 billion in 1968.

4 Plant and equipment expenditures (including net direct investment abroad) rose from $81.6 billion in 1965 to $91.4 billion in 1966, $92.3 billion in 1967, and $99.0 billion in 1968.

5 The Federal Reserve percentage is not purported to be an accurate measure of its impact on the securities markets. For one thing, changes in reserve requirements (and the discount rate and Regulation Q) do not show up in this series, but they have significant impacts on the banking sytem's ability to supply funds. For another, if the Federal Reserve is simply offsetting the impact of an external event on bank reserves, say a gold drain caused by the Vietnam war, one might not wish to view the Federal Reserve as making a positive contribution to the supply of funds.

6 Annual data conceal some interesting quarterly variations. For example, the Federal Reserve was a substantial seller of securities in the fourth quarter of 1968.

7 The average surplus for 1965 and 1966 was $1 billion; the average deficit for 1967 and 1968 was $9 billion.

8 P. H. Hendershott, *The Neutralized Money Stock: An Unbiased Measure of Federal Reserve Policy Actions* (Homewood, Ill.: Richard D. Irwin, Inc., 1968).

9 The resulting increase in income causes a drain of bank reserves into currency, but it also increases Federal Reserve float and member bank borrowing (by increasing the demand for bank loans), and these somewhat more than offset the impact of the currency drain on reserves. In addition, the increase in income raises imports of foreign goods, which contracts the money stock by inducing a gold outflow. On net, the increase of income in the upswing reduces bank reserves.

10 The federal government accounted for nearly two-thirds of the 20 per cent increase in total funds raised in 1967.

11 The bank purchase reflects more than the interest rate sensitivity in the banking system's demand for securities (or equivalently, free reserves) at a given reserve level. Other interest rate responses raise total bank reserves. Foreigners buy some of the securities with funds other than U.S. bank demand deposits and households purchase some of their securities by first converting time deposits into demand deposits. This leads to a direct increase in demand deposits; firm demand deposit

balances rise more than household and foreign demand balances fall on net. At the same time, these transactions increase excess bank reserves above desired levels and thus lead to additional purchases of securities by the banks themselves.

12 William E. Gibson, *Effects of Money on Interest Rates* (University of Chicago doctoral dissertation, 1967).

13 Thomas J. Sargent, "Commodity Price Expectations and the Interest Rate," *Quarterly Journal of Economics*, LXXXIII, February 1969, pp. 127–140.

14 The causes of the rise in interest rates throughout most of 1966 are somewhat less obvious. The total funds series, relative to 1965, fell from 9.8 to 8.4 per cent of the GNP. One important factor raising interest rates was the actual decline in observed money, reflecting the restrictive action of the Federal Reserve as measured by the decline in effective unborrowed reserves (see below, note 21). This was the "crunch" of that year. However, it occurred in the second half of the year, while market rates rose from the very beginning of 1966.

The cause of the earlier rise in interest rates might be due to fluctuations in desired saving. The only evidence we can provide on the movement in desired saving is indirect, and involves a comparison of total personal income to disposable personal income. If the two income aggregates rise by equal relative amounts, then personal taxes are exercising a constant impact on disposable income, and on that account, desired saving should remain a constant fraction of GNP. In 1966 personal taxes rose 15 per cent, while personal income increased only 9 per cent. Disposable income thus increased only 8 per cent. Most of this effect, due to a sharp rise in federal government receipts and expenditures, was felt in the first half of the year. The evidence would seem to indicate that the decline of the total funds series is, at least in part, cause by a movement along the total *I* plus *G* schedule due to a leftward shift of saving and a later reduction of money. Thus, in the first half of the year, the natural rate was driven above the market rate, tending to draw the market rate toward it, while in the second half, the market rate rose directly through monetary action.

Evidence that the rise in interest rates might also be due to an outward shift of the private investment schedule, even though total funds raised in 1966 fell, can be gleaned from Table I. Long-term business issues actually rose in 1966, while mortgages fell. The latter is the most interest-responsive borrowing component. The evidence would seem to indicate that in the face of rising business issues, the other investment components were merely re-acting to the rising interest rate (the *G* component fell marginally during the year).

15 There is thus no documented justification for the publication of the "real" rate of interest by the St. Louis Federal Reserve Bank in the 1968–1969 winter issues of its *Review* (see the December 1968 issue, p. 5, and January 1969, p. 6). The St. Louis "real" rate is the long-term corporate Aaa yield reduced by the preceding twenty-four months' average annual percentage movement of the implicit GNP deflator. The Fisherian zeal of that institution would shock no one more than Irving Fisher, who himself stressed the fantastically long lags in the formation of price level expectations and their impact on interest rates in this country. In particular, for the long-term rate of interest, he found that price changes influenced interest rates for over a 20-year period; half the total effect of an increase in the price level is not felt until 7.3 years later. See Irving Fisher, *The Theory of Interest* (New York: Kelley and Millman, Inc., 1954), p. 423.

16 The first (and perhaps best) discussion of these hazards appeared a full decade ago. See Milton Friedman, *A Program for Monetary Stability* (New York: Fordham University Press, 1959), pp. 39–45.

17 One of the rare statements in which the pitfalls are appreciated is K. Brunner and A. H. Meltzer, "The Meaning of Monetary Indicators," in G. Horwich, ed., *Monetary Process and Policy: A Symposium* (Richard D. Irwin, Inc., 1967), pp. 187–217. Brunner and Meltzer carefully point out the inadequacies of the money stock as the ideal indicator, noting that "It misstates the magnitude of changes in the policy variables ... and incorporates the influence of ... feedback effects" (p. 197). Recently Meltzer seems to have lost this appreciation; see "Controlling Money," Federal Reserve Bank of St. Louis *Review*, May 1969, pp. 16–24.

18 See *The Neutralized Money Stock, op. cit.*, Chap. 9, esp. p. 103.

19 An important underlying assumption in the neutralization procedure is that the

explanatory variables whose cyclical fluctuations are removed are not themselves influenced by current Federal Reserve actions. This is certainly true of income in any quarter, which may reflect past, but hardly current, monetary policy actions. However, interest rates are, as we have been arguing, jointly determined by internal forces and monetary and fiscal policies. The fact that interest rates are not entirely endogenous causes the neutralized money stock to rise and fall more precipitously than it otherwise would, but failing to take account of the Federal Reserve's influence on interest rates does not alter the turning points of neutralized money. On this, see *The Neutralized Money Stock, op. cit.*, p. 105.

20 The original neutralization of the money stock contained a computational error that was kindly pointed out by Michael Hamburger and has been corrected. In equation (6.6) on page 70 of *The Neutralized Money Stock, op. cit.*, the U.S. bill-Eurodollar deposit rate differential should have been expressed as a linear combination of recent changes in, not levels of, the U.S. bill rate. Thus the bill rate terms in equation (6.10) on page 72 should also be increments, not levels. (This error did not affect the "modified" neutralized money stock.)

21 For the years since 1964, preliminary evidence supports the use of effective unborrowed reserves (unborrowed reserves adjusted for changes in legal reserve requirements) as a proxy for neutralized money. Analysis of this series implies that the monetary expansion continued until mid-1966, the beginning of the "crunch." (Effective unborrowed reserves combines three of the variables generally taken to be exogenous Federal Reserve policy instruments in econometric models: unborrowed reserves, the legal reserve requirement against member bank demand deposits, and that against time deposits. The series is regularly published in the Federal Reserve *Bulletin* in the table "Aggregate Reserves and Member Bank Deposits" on page A17.)

22 See K. Brunner and A. H. Meltzer, "An Alternative Approach to the Monetary Mechanism," Subcommittee on Domestic Finance, Committee on Banking and Currency, 88th Cong., 2nd Sess. (Washington, D.C.: U.S. Government Printing Office, 1964), and J. Kareken and R. M. Solow, "Lags in Monetary Policy," *Stabilization Policies* (Englewood Cliffs,

N.J.: Prentice-Hall, Inc., 1963), pp. 1–96.

23 For documentation of these errors, see P. H. Hendershott, "The Inside Lag in Monetary Policy: A Comment," *Journal of Political Economy*, LXXIV, October 1966, pp. 519–523.

24 Given the apparently smaller bias in turning points of the bill rate relative to that of the observed money stock, it is difficult to understand the basis for the frequent assertion that interest rates are a more misleading policy indicator than is the observed money stock (see, e.g., Brunner and Meltzer, "The Meaning of Monetary Indicators," *op. cit.*, p. 204).

25 This could be interpreted as striking evidence that the Federal Reserve in fact pursues a policy of equating the market rate of interest to the natural rate (see the following section). If the Federal Reserve believes that movements in the market rate are caused primarily by movements in the same direction in the natural rate [see p. 291 above], then changes in the bill rate (a key market rate) would in the Wicksellian framework call for central-bank-induced opposite changes in the stock of money (as reflected in the neutralized series). For example, a fall in the bill rate due to a fall in the natural rate tends to reduce the stock of money, spending, and ultimately economic activity. The Wicksellian central bank response, aimed at heading off these endogenous consequences, is to lower the market rate immediately by engaging in open-market purchases.

26 For a detailed discussion of the stabilization program described in this paragraph, see G. Horwich, "A Framework for Monetary Policy" in K. Brunner, ed., *Targets and Indicators of Monetary Policy* (San Francisco: Chandler Publishing Co., 1969). This volume contains the proceedings of a conference held at the University of California, Los Angeles, in April 1966.

27 In a paper presented to the Savings and Residential Financing Conference three years ago, Warren Smith also advanced interest-rate policy as the proper target of central banking stabilization efforts. See Warren L. Smith, "Some Reflections on Interest Rates and Their Economic Implications," *Conference on Savings and Residential Financing* (Chicago: U.S. Savings and Loan League, 1966), pp. 44–57. However, Smith did not provide a criterion for the appropriate interest rate in terms of an immediate target level, as we have suggested here in the form of the natural rate.

Problems of Efficiency in Monetary Management
Harry G. Johnson

I. INTRODUCTION

Monetary management as generally understood means the management of the money supply and monetary and credit-market conditions by the monetary authority (the central bank) in the pursuit of certain general social objectives. These objectives may either be assigned to the central bank by the national government or be left to the central bank to establish for itself, depending on whether the central bank is a subordinate instrumentality of national economic policy or is allowed a substantial measure of independence. In the past, economists specializing in the study of monetary management have been predominantly either institutionalists concerned with the detailed structure of the financial system and the precise institutional ways in which the central bank operates on that system in pursuit of its objectives, or economic historians concerned with the evolution of the financial organization of a particular country or countries, the theories of monetary management advocated by historically influential personages, and the influence of these theories on legislation affecting the structure of the financial system and the central bank's concept of its role and functions. (There have, of course, always been nonspecialist critics of financial organization and monetary management, some of whom have in due course achieved the status of historically influential personages.) With the profes-

Harry G. Johnson, "Problems of Efficiency in Monetary Management," *Journal of Political Economy*, 76 (September–October 1968), pp. 971–990. The *Journal of Political Economy* is published by the University of Chicago Press.

sionalization of economics, the accompanying increase in confidence in the scientific approach to economic problems, and the resulting tendency to apply the scientific approach increasingly to problems of economic policy—problems in normative rather than positive economic science—that has occurred since the 1930's and especially since the Second World War, economists concerned with monetary management have become decreasingly concerned with institutional and historical questions per se and increasingly concerned with normative problems—that is, with problems of efficiency in monetary management. This approach requires the application of economic theory—and in some cases of econometrics—more intensively to the processes and practices of monetary management than has generally been the case in the past.

The purpose of this paper is to survey some of the problems of efficiency in monetary management, as they have emerged from recent theorizing and research. For this purpose, three aspects of the problem of efficiency are distinguished: (1) structural efficiency, by which is meant efficiency in the ordinary economic sense of the banking system considered as an industry whose primary function from the monetary point of view is to provide the means of payment (currency and deposits subject to check) for the economy, though from a broader point of view it also plays an important part in the capital market as a medium for saving and an allocator of capital among competing borrowers; (2) efficiency in stabilization policy, that is, policy directed at keeping the economy on a desired course and correcting deviations from that course;

and (3) efficiency in secular economic policy, that is, efficiency with respect to the choice of the desired level and trend over time of the major macroeconomic variables that reflect the economy's performance. It should be emphasized that these last two problems are, generally speaking, not problems of monetary management alone, if monetary management is identified with central bank policy, but are rather problems in the joint use of monetary, fiscal, and possibly exchange rate policy for the purpose of economic stabilization and the fulfilment of the general objectives of full employment, price stability, economic growth, and balance-of-payments equilibrium. In some cases, it is possible to indicate theoretical solutions to the problems of efficiency; in other cases, it is only possible to indicate the considerations that must enter into an efficient solution. Where the analysis depends upon assumptions about institutional practices, it should be understood that the reference is to the monetary and banking institutions of the United States, United Kingdom, and other countries in the British tradition of banking, so that the conclusions may not be directly applicable to other countries, particularly those of Continental Europe.

II. PROBLEMS OF STRUCTURAL EFFICIENCY

As already mentioned, the banking system can be regarded as an industry that, on the one hand, provides a payments mechanism for the economy and, on the other hand, through its payments-mechanism operations and the acceptance of interest-bearing noncheckable deposits, assembles capital for investment in various forms of assets, thereby playing an important part in the capital market.

There is at the foundation of normative (welfare) economics a presumption that free competition will promote the effi-cient performance of economic activities; and this presumption would seem to apply to the banking industry, with important qualifications deriving from the special characteristics of money to be noted below. Free competition in the banking industry would lead banks to compete for checkable deposits by offering interest and charging competitive rates related to costs for the provision of the services of the payments mechanism, in order to obtain funds for investment. It would also lead banks in their lending operations to provide those loan facilities and invest in those marketable assets that the banks could manage with an efficiency superior to that of other financial institutions. The result, assuming that the banking system remained competitive, would be to maximize efficiency in the provision of a payments mechanism and in the allocation of capital, with one potentially important qualification.

Efficiency in the allocation of capital would follow from the usual arguments for free competition among rival business firms; the achievement of efficiency in the provision of the payments mechanism, however, requires some explanation since it involves an application of monetary theory. Briefly, the payment of competitive interest rates on checkable deposits means that holding assets in monetary form would entail no alternative opportunity cost for wealth-owners other than the real social costs—operating expenses and a normal rate of return on the capital employed—of maintaining the system of checking accounts, so that the public would be encouraged to satiate its desire for liquidity. At the abstract level of pure theory, the costs of maintaining a system of bank accounts—as distinct from the costs of using these accounts to make payments—can be regarded as negligible: In theoretical terms, money can be provided at zero social cost. Maximization of welfare requires that a good that can be provided at zero marginal social cost should be provided in the quantity that yields zero marginal utility, that is, that satiates demand, and this result would be insured by the payment of competitive interest rates on checkable deposits. Similarly, the charging of competitive costs for the use of the services of the payments mechanism would induce the deposit-holding public to make optimal use of that mechanism: in other words, to arrange its monetary transactions so as to use the bank account payments mechanism only for transactions that are privately worth their social cost. In short, a competitive banking system would encourage the public to hold the socially optimum quantity of money and make socially optimum use of the payments mechanism.

This conclusion, however, is subject to a qualification that arises from the availability of currency—coin, but especially notes—as an alternative means of making payments. This alternative medium of exchange is non-interest-bearing, and it would be extremely difficult, though not necessarily impossible, to arrange for the issue of an interest-bearing currency. On the other hand, the issuing authority (the treasury or the central bank) bears the real resource costs of providing currency. In the case of the coinage, the direct costs are the capital cost of the metal and the running costs of coining and recoining and the loss of metal through abrasion. In the case of paper money, there is the cost of the special paper and of design, printing, and reprinting. In addition, in both cases there is the additional direct cost of security precautions and the indirect cost of policing against forgery. The coinage is known to be directly profitable, as a general rule: When it ceases to be so because of a rise in the value of the metal used, steps are taken fairly quickly to restore its profitability by substitution of cheaper metals. The issue of paper money also is generally assumed to be directly profitable, in the sense that

the interest earned by the issuing authority on assets bought with paper money exceeds the running cost of providing the paper money; though there are limits to the validity of this assumption, as evidenced by the fact that the Bank of England some years ago found it necessary to curb a vogue for making payments in newly printed money by requesting the customers of banks to make do with already-used Bank of England notes. Whether coinage and the issue of paper money are socially profitable when the indirect costs of policing against forgery are taken into account is an unresolved question. But on the assumption that the issue of notes and coin is socially profitable, in the sense of yielding a surplus above the cost of production and policing, it follows that the private cost of holding currency exceeds the social cost, or that the private return from holding currency falls short of the social return. On the other hand, the private cost of using currency for making payments falls short of the social cost, insofar as the circulation of currency leads to its deterioration; but this aspect of the use of currency can probably be safely disregarded as of trivial importance, since the social cost of individual exchanges of currency, in the form of physical depreciation of the medium of exchange, must be negligible. The substantive point therefore is that, because the private cost of holding currency (the interest foregone) substantially exceeds the social cost (raw material, value added, and policing), free competition in banking, by making the private and social cost of deposit-holding coincide, would tend to produce a socially nonoptimum overallocation of resources to the provision of deposit money and underallocation of resources to the provision of currency for holding. The charging of full cost for the use of the deposit payments mechanism would similarly promote overuse of currency and underuse of deposits in making payments, though this source of inefficiency can be regarded as negligible for the reasons already given. The social loss resulting from the stimulus to excessive deposit-holding relative to currency-holding would depend on the elasticity of substitution between the two forms of money in the demand of users of money. On the assumption that currency cannot be issued other than as a non-interest-bearing asset, achievement of the "second-best" welfare optimum would require a tax on the holding of deposit money at a rate somewhere between zero and the competitive interest rate on deposits, the precise tax rate depending on the relative strength of the effects of the tax in discouraging the holding of checkable bank deposits as compared with untaxed nonmonetary assets and encouraging the holding of currency as compared with checkable bank deposits. This qualification of the argument for free competition in banking is disregarded in the remainder of the analysis.

The case just presented for free competition in commercial banking depends crucially on the assumption that a banking system in which competition among banks was unregulated by legislation or central bank supervision would remain competitive. Historical experience strongly suggests, however, that unrestricted competition among banks tends to lead to concentration of the industry through expansion of the larger units and through mergers. The reason presumably is that there are significant economies of scale—both in the operation of the deposit payments mechanism and in the operation of the lending and investment side of the banking business—which give a profit incentive to concentration and, on the payments side at least, may indicate the social desirability of operating the banking business as a public utility. In the United States, the tendency to concentration has been held in check at a relatively early stage of concentration by public fears of a banking monopoly given expression through banking legislation, which falls to the responsibility of the individual states in the federal system of American government; but the trend to concentration has nevertheless been persistent. The U.S. banking system therefore can probably be fairly described as competitive and efficient within the framework of legislation governing it, but possibly socially inefficient in providing a payments mechanism in the sense that a national "giro" system of some sort might reduce substantially the cost of making payments. In the United Kingdom, control over bank mergers of an "informal" but nevertheless effective sort, designed to prevent bank mergers in restraint of competition, was introduced after the wave of mergers that occurred toward the end of the First World War. The result has been to consolidate and perpetuate a situation of oligopolistic competition in British banking, which appears socially inefficient from a variety of points of view, but which has been tolerated and even encouraged by the monetary authorities since it lends itself readily to control by persuasion and directive in subservience to the objectives of economic policy. Britain, incidentally, to improve the efficiency of her payments mechanism, is in the process of introducing a "giro" system with which the banks will have to compete.

In general, the presence of economies of scale in the banking business forces social policy concerned with efficiency to contemplate the familiar choice between (a) designing a regulatory system that will enable private competitive organizations to obtain the economies of scale while preventing them from exercising monopoly power, and (b) replacing private enterprise by a public utility that will obtain the efficiency of a monopoly while operating in the public interest. With the rapid development of the electronic computer as an instrument of efficient large-scale bookkeeping, the feasibility of a single national, or even international, credit payments system that would be less expensive than traditional commercial bank payments operations is more likely; and it is possible that in the long run such systems will replace the checking facilities provided at present by the commercial banks, which would presumably revert to institutions primarily occupied in lending out savings deposits intrusted to them. In the meantime, however, to the extent that society values the preservation of a private enterprise, nonmonopolized commercial banking system, the case for free competition remains relevant.

The analysis thus far has been concerned with the efficiency of the banking system, considered as an industry like any other industry. The banking system cannot, however, in strict logic, be so treated, because of the special characteristics that distinguish its product—money, the means of payment—from the products of other private enterprises—real goods and services. The crucial difference between the banking industry and other industries is that whereas other industries provide real goods and services that the public demands, so that a stable equilibrium of demand and supply will be attained under competition, the banking industry provides nominal money—money denominated in marks, pounds, dollars, or other monetary units of account—while the public demands real balances—stocks of purchasing power. The public can adjust the real value of any given quantity of nominal money balances supplied by the banking system to that quantity of real balances it desires to hold by changing the price level through its efforts to substitute goods for real balances when real balances are excessive at the current price level, and to substitute real balances for goods when real balances are insufficient at the current price level. In the alternative Keynesian framework of analysis, excess real balances lower the rate of interest, increase investment and possibly con-

sumption demand, and so raise prices—and conversely for deficient real balances. Thus, in terms of static theory, the quantity of nominal balances supplied will be in neutral equilibrium; any other quantity could be made the equilibrium quantity through appropriate changes in the price level. Less abstractly, a competitive banking system would be under constant incentive to expand the nominal money supply and thereby initiate price inflation. With random economic variations, uncertainty, and "money illusion" on the part of the banks (defined as confidence in the stability of the value of money), the price level would be inherently unstable; variations in it would produce changes in bank lending and the quantity of money that would reinforce the initial change.

Stability in the trend of prices (a special case of which is price stability) and in the trend of expectations about the future course of prices—which are generally agreed to be important to the social welfare—requires social control over the total quantity of money supplied by the banking system. By tradition, this control is exercised by the central bank. According to the general equilibrium theory of a monetary economy, central bank control presupposes the power to determine one nominal monetary magnitude in the system and one interest rate. In traditional central banking practice, this requirement is fulfilled by the central bank's control over the quantity of cash reserves available to the commercial banking system, its reserves being its own note and deposit liabilities (less currency in circulation among the public), and by the convention that its notes and deposits bear zero interest for the holder.

For the same reasons that economic efficiency requires the payment of interest on deposit money held by the public, optimal resource allocation requires the payment of interest by the central bank on its liabilities held as reserves by the commercial banks, at a rate determined by the yield on its assets less operating costs. This principle by itself is somewhat ambiguous, since as a government-sponsored monopoly the central bank is under no pressure to practice efficiency in its staffing and other management policies and is under considerable pressure to use its resources to lend to government at subsidized rates; and it should be extended by a stipulation of central bank efficiency in both office and portfolio management. The principle also raises the practical problem of implementation with respect to commercial bank holdings of reserves of currency, which as already mentioned conventionally bears no interest. Payment of interest on commercial bank holdings of central bank deposits but not on their holdings of currency would create an incentive for the banks to hold an excessive ratio of deposits to currency in their reserves. This incentive could possibly be removed by the central bank paying interest on the reported average currency holdings of the commercial banks. The convention of nonpayment of interest by the central bank on commercial bank reserves constitutes in effect a tax on the creation and use of deposit money, which militates against the efficient provision of a payments mechanism. The incidence of this tax falls entirely on the deposit-holding public if the banking system is competitive and banking services can be provided at constant cost; it is shared between the public and the banks if the banking industry is subject to rising costs as scale increases or if the banking industry is monopolized or oligopolistic.

As just mentioned, the central bank can control the price level if it fixes the yield on its liabilities and controls the quantity thereof through open-market operations, quite consistently with free competition in the banking industry. It will, of course, have to acquire from experience an accurate knowledge of the factors determining the ratios of reserves to deposits the commercial banks will choose in their own self-interest to hold under varying circumstances; but this is a legitimate part of the task of central bank management. In the actual practice of central banking, however, reliance is placed on additional instruments and techniques of control over the commercial banks. From the point of view of the theory of monetary control, these additional controls are unnecessary, if not positively mischievous; and their effect for the most part is to impose taxation on the commercial banks and ultimately on the users of deposit money, additional to what is imposed by the nonpayment of interest on bank reserves, to the detriment of efficiency in the long-run allocation of the economy's resources between the provision of the payments mechanism and other uses.

In the grand tradition of central banking, and especially in the practice of the Bank of England, great emphasis is placed on the use of rediscount policy, especially changes in the rediscount rate, as an instrument of monetary policy—in British practice, the primary instrument. The availability of the rediscount facility in fact, however, constitutes a breach in the central bank's control of the volume of its liabilities, permitting the commercial banks to offset the central bank's open-market operations by temporary or renewed borrowing; and this breach has to be plugged by the establishment of conventions against continued or "excessive" use of the facility, supported ultimately by the threat of central bank denial of the facility to a transgressor, a situation undesirable because it intrusts the central bank with the exercise of arbitrary and ill-defined authority. At least in the presence of a well-developed capital market, and on the assumption of intelligent and responsible monetary management by the central bank, the commercial banks should be able to manage their reserve positions without the need for the central bank to function as "lender of last resort." Apart from this consideration, it is questionable whether changes in the rediscount rate perform very efficiently as signals of the central bank's intentions with respect to monetary policy—if communication of this kind is desirable, there are other ways of providing it. And at a deeper level of analysis it is questionable whether the central bank is well advised to aim at exercising monetary control through the fixing of the level of short-term interest rates rather than through the determination of the reserve base of the monetary system. Finally, the fact that in British practice changes in bank rate derive much of their leverage from the conventional fixing of interest rates on clearing bank deposits, advances, and other accounts by a percentage margin below or above bank rate raises the question whether a cartelized pricing policy of this type serves the interests of economic efficiency.

As already mentioned, the conventional nonpayment of interest on commercial bank reserve holdings of central bank liabilities constitutes an implicit tax on the provision of deposit money through the commercial banking system. The burden of this tax is increased by the stipulation of minimum or average cash reserve ratios, to the extent that such stipulation obliges the banks to hold a larger volume of non-interest-earning reserves than they would voluntarily choose to hold for the efficient conduct of their business. By comparison with conventional average reserve ratio requirements, legal minimum requirements impose an additional burden, since the banks must guard against violation of the requirement by holding excess cash reserves or by keeping their noncash assets sufficiently liquid to be able to meet unexpected reserve drains. In addition to this implicit tax imposed through the central bank's monopoly of the provision of cash reserves and the government's power to impose reserve requirements, the commercial banks, and ultimately the deposit-holding public, are taxed indirectly in a variety of other ways through regulations adopted either to control the banks' commercial operations, to facilitate central bank control, or to cushion the market for government debt against the impact of monetary policy. Thus, prohibiting the banks from undertaking certain kinds of lending or restricting the amount of such lending they can undertake, either permanently or in times of restrictive monetary policy, reduces the commercial profitability of banking; so does the fixing of liquid asset ratios, which obliges the banks to hold a larger proportion of lower-yielding assets than they would voluntarily choose and may also reduce the yield on these assets below what it would otherwise be. In similar fashion, the fixing of maximum interest rates on certain kinds of bank lending, such as consumer loans and mortgage lending, acts as an implicit tax by confining banks to those loans in these categories for which the credit risk is low enough to justify lending at the permitted rate.

The rule or convention against the payment of interest on checking accounts which exists in some countries is a special kind of tax, since it is levied on the depositors for the benefit of the banks rather than the government. The main argument for not paying interest on checking accounts, that it prevents reckless competition for deposits among banks, has been shown to be unsupported by the empirical evidence in the country where the argument is most fashionable (the United States) and is inconsistent also with the broad range of historical evidence. In any case the rule is impossible to enforce, since banks can get around it in part by crediting notional interest earnings against charges for deposit operation until charges are reduced to zero (as in England), or by offering free checking and other services proportioned to the size of the customer's account, and by competing via other attractions, such as gifts of merchandise (in the United States) or a plethora of conveniently located branches (as in England). To the extent that the ban on paying interest is effective, the result is a socially inefficient restriction on the holding of checking deposits; to the extent that interest can only be received by making free use of the payments mechanism, the result is the encouragement of socially excessive use of that mechanism; and to the extent that implicit interest earnings are returned to the customer in banking services and convenience that he would not freely choose if offered the alternative of cash payments, the result is a partial waste of resources.

From the point of view of the monetary authority, the various interferences with the commercial banks' freedom to choose the composition of their asset portfolios to maximize profits, discussed above, have the advantages (apparent or real) of increasing the predictability of commercial bank response to monetary policy action and of improving the short-run effectiveness of monetary control of economic activity. The latter is particularly the case where directives can strike at borrowers who have no other source of credit than the commercial banks (such as many consumers and small businesses), or where maximum lending rates imposed on certain types of bank-lending lead the banks to discontinue such lending when interest rates rise. Even from the point of view of effectiveness of control, however, such selectivity has corresponding disadvantages: Credit discrimination against particular classes of borrower or of loan-financed activity may involve short-run disruption of established financial relations and in the longer run distort the growth of the economy and reduce its efficiency. From the point of view of structural efficiency considered here, the most relevant consideration is that by imposing an implicit tax on commercial

banking, these techniques of control restrict the scale of the check-payment system provided by the commercial banks to something below the social optimum. They also encourage the growth, in competition with the commercial banks, of rival financial institutions which offer money substitutes to asset holders and conduct lending operations similar to those of the banks, more or less free of the burden of implicit taxation imposed by monetary management proximately on the banks and ultimately on their depositors.

Furthermore, in this connection it is important to note that the burden of implicit taxation on the commercial banking system and its depositors is in general an increasing function of the level of interest rates. This is obviously so with respect to the taxation implicit in the compulsory holding of non-interest-bearing reserves, and also with respect to interest ceilings on particular categories of bank lending. As regards depositors, the burden of the ban on interest payments for checking deposits obviously increases as the general level of interest rates increases—with a consequent tendency for depositors to shift out of such deposits into substitutes bearing a more flexible rate of interest. The banks, by contrast, derive from this ban in the short run additional earnings which may compensate or more than compensate them for the greater loss of interest on their reserve holdings; but in the longer run, the effect must be to reduce the relative scale of the banking industry by reducing the relative attractiveness of its product.

The general effect of these various implicit taxes on commercial banking, in the context of the general trend toward rising interest rates since the Second World War, has undoubtedly been to contribute to the development of competing financial intermediaries and a relative loss of business to them by the banks. The spokesmen for the banking community have generally reacted to this development by arguing for the application to their competitors of the same sort of reserve requirements and control by directives as those to which the banks are subjected. This is an argument, however, for what is technically known as a "second-best" solution, which might or might not produce an improvement from the social point of view. That is, while the equalization of conditions of competition between banks and rival financial intermediaries would improve the allocation of a given amount of resources between the two types of institutions, the imposition of comparable taxation on all intermediaries would involve a socially nonoptimal restriction of all financial intermediation as compared with alternative economic activities, and the social loss on this account might outweigh the gain from improved allocation of resources among financial intermediaries. Improvement from the social point of view is far more likely to be attained by mitigation of the special implicit tax burden which existing techniques of monetary control impose on the commercial banking system.

III. PROBLEMS OF EFFICIENCY IN STABILIZATION POLICY

Stabilization policy, as defined above, comprises the use of the government's instruments of economic control—monetary policy, fiscal policy, and possibly exchange rate policy as well as more direct and selective controls—to keep the economy on a desired path of evolution in the face of spontaneous destabilizing developments in the economic system. The general nature of the corrective actions that may need to be taken is familiar from the Keynesian theory of income determination and the associated theories of fiscal and monetary policy. These theories are, however, couched in terms of static equilibrium analysis,

whereas the stabilization problem in practice requires the use of policy instruments which operate with a varying ("distributed") lag on an economic system that responds to both spontaneous and policy-induced changes according to its own distributed lag pattern. This fact creates a problem of efficiency in the design and operation of stabilization policy, quite apart from the problem of efficiency in the selection of the desired path of evolution of the economy, to be considered in the next section.

Ideally, those responsible for stabilization policy should be armed both with full knowledge of the distributed lag structures according to which the economy reacts to spontaneous and policy-induced changes, and with the means of forecasting accurately the spontaneous changes that it is the responsibility of stabilization policy to offset. Near-perfect or perfect stabilization would then be possible. In practice, however, forecasting ability is limited, and the authorities have to rely to a large extent on responding in their policy actions to deviations of the current or immediately past performance of the economy from the desired path of evolution. Moreover, knowledge of the pattern and time distribution of lags in the response of the economy to spontaneous and policy-induced changes is also limited. This situation raises problems of efficiency in the design of policy responses to deviations in actual from desired performance; questions about the efficiency of stabilization policies as traditionally practiced, especially by central banks, in achieving a significant improvement in the stability of the economy; and the general problem of improving the stabilization operations of the central banks by founding them more securely on economic analysis of and empirical research on the stabilization problem.

The problem of efficient policy-response design in a system in which policy responds to deviations of actual from desired performance ("errors") is very similar to the engineering problem of designing efficient automatic control mechanisms and has been explored most thoroughly by electrical engineers interested in economic policy problems, notably by A. W. Phillips. An obvious point that emerges from this exploration is the importance of rapid reaction of policy to the observation of errors: The longer the lag in policy response, the lower the degree of improvement in stability that can be achieved, and the more likely is a policy response of a given magnitude to destabilize rather than stabilize the system. Less obvious, but in some respects more important, is the fact that an efficient system of economic control (stabilization) requires some mixture of three types of control reaction—the mixture and magnitudes of the control reactions depending on the general characteristics of the economic system being controlled, the lengths of the time lags in the reaction of the system to change, and the structures or time profiles of the various lags.

The three types of control reaction can be characterized as different ways of formulating the error in the performance of the system for the purposes of taking corrective policy action. Control may be based on three mathematical expressions of the error—its current level (*proportional control*), its cumulative value (*integral control*), and its rate of change (*derivative control*). Each has its advantages and disadvantages from the viewpoint of efficient stabilization. Proportional control has the advantage of pulling the economy in the right direction so long as it is off-target, but for that very reason it must fall short of the goal of stabilization; in addition, a sufficiently strong control response operating with a sufficiently long lag will introduce fluctuations. Integral control will keep the economy on target if it is already there and will tend to return it to the desired path in case of

errors, but it involves a strong tendency toward overshooting especially if it operates with a long lag. Derivative control tends to stabilize the economy at its current level of operation—whatever that level may be—and may also induce fluctuations about that level if applied forcefully but with a long lag. Thus, for efficient stabilization, the three must be used in combination, both the relative and the absolute dependence on each having to be determined from the characteristics of the economy mentioned above.

The engineering approach to the requirements of an efficient stabilization policy leaves something to be desired from the economic point of view, since it formulates the problem in mechanical terms of achieving approximation to a desired stable path without reference either to the social costs of deviating from that path, or to the economy's reactions to the control operation itself. Further, this approach assumes somewhat inconsistently that disturbances cannot be forecast and that lags in policy response to errors cannot be altered, but that the requisite information on the lag structures of the economy's response to changes can be obtained. Nevertheless, the analysis does raise questions about the likely efficiency in stabilization policy of traditional central bank policy formation procedures, and it points to the need for scientific study of lag structures in the economy and in policy responses to change and for the use of the results of such study in the design of appropriate policy responses.

The prevalence of lags in the response of the policy-makers to changes in the economy, and in the response of the economy to changes in economic policy, together with the variability of these lags, has led a number of monetary experts to question whether traditional central banking operations can contribute much to the stabilization of the economy. Some—

notably Milton Friedman—have become convinced by theoretical and empirical analysis that efforts at short-run stabilization given the present state of knowledge and with present institutional practices are likely to do more harm than good, and they have consequently argued that such efforts should be abandoned in favor of a "monetary rule" according to which the monetary authority would be obliged to expand the money supply at a steady rate proportional to the normal rate of growth of the demand for money as the economy expands with stable prices. The argument for this proposal is partly that while a rule of this kind would not do as well as an ideal stabilization policy, it would produce better results than stabilization policy as actually practiced. More fundamentally, the proposal rests on the belief that arbitrary changes in monetary policy have been a more important source of economic disturbance than spontaneous changes arising in the private sector of the economy and that the primary problem of stabilization policy is to create a stable monetary environment within which the private sector can calculate rationally.

A number of economists have been concerned recently with the alternative possibility of improving the central bank's methods of management of stabilization policy to make it more effective in achieving its objectives. Formally, the central bank (and, more generally, the economic policy authorities) can be conceived of as making policy decisions on the basis of certain "indicator" variables, which are taken to reflect the current state and direction of the economy and adjusting the "instrument" variables of policy to alter the levels of "target" variables which are assumed to govern the operations of the economy. (The same variable may serve in more than one capacity.) The problem of maximizing effectiveness then becomes a series of subproblems in the choice of the most reliable indicator variable or variables, and the choice of

target variables at once amenable to control by the central bank by use of its policy instruments and potent in governing the economy, these choices requiring an empirically validated knowledge of the structure of the economy and the time lags of its responses. One of the chief issues in this area is whether the central bank should seek to control the economy by controlling the level of interest rates, or the level of some monetary magnitude such as total money supply, bank cash reserves, the "free" reserves of the banking system, or the cash base of the entire monetary system. There is a theoretical presumption in favor of control of a monetary magnitude rather than interest rates (and, among the monetary magnitudes, in favor of the cash base) on the grounds of directness of control and clarity of theoretical significance of what is being controlled, but the issue can only be resolved by empirical exploration.

Like the application of control-system engineering to the design of monetary policy responses, work on these lines has tended to suffer somewhat from taking stabilization per se as the objective of policy and the measure of success. Even on this mechanical basis, a generally acceptable measure of performance with respect to stabilization of the economy is not easy to devise. In the broader context of economic theory, however, the purpose of short-run stabilization is to increase the economic welfare of the community, and an economic measure of the success of stabilization policy would have to specify what welfare is presumed to be in this context and how it is affected by stabilization policy operations. A major implication of the concept of "stability" as an objective of policy is that stability will improve the accuracy of the calculations and predictions on the basis of which resources are allocated among current uses and between current consumption and investment for the satisfaction of future needs. This suggests that both the formulation of policy and the evaluation of its success require a formal definition of the economic costs of instability more sophisticated than some mechanical measure of the deviations of indicator variables from a trend or norm. It also suggests that there may arise internal contradictions between the objective of stabilization policy and the means employed to implement it, in the sense that stabilization operations, by disturbing public expectations derived from previous experience, may cause more distortions of private economic calculations than they prevent. The proponents of a "monetary rule" believe that stability would be improved by removing the possibility of arbitrary discretionary policy changes by the central bank. Whether that belief is justified or not, it is clear that knowledge of the mechanisms by which the expectations of the public are formed, and the influence on these expectations of policy actions, is of great importance to the design of short-run stabilization policy, and these mechanisms cannot be fully satisfactorily dealt with by compressing them into the distributed lag structure of the economy.

IV. PROBLEMS OF EFFICIENCY IN SECULAR ECONOMIC POLICY

Short-run stabilization policy is concerned with minimizing deviations of the economy from its desired trend path of evolution. Secular economic policy is concerned with the selection of the desired trend path of evolution itself. While the objectives relevant to this social choice comprise at least the standard four of full employment, price stability, economic growth at a satisfactory rate, and balance-of-payments equilibrium, with possibly the addition of a fifth in the form of an equitable distribution of income, the analysis of the choice as it affects the use of the macroeconomic instruments of

stabilization policy (monetary and fiscal policy) has concentrated on the first two, and specifically on the conflict or possible trade-off between full employment and price stability.

The possibility of a conflict between the objectives of full employment and price stability was discerned by writers on economic policy very soon after Keynes' *General Theory* had demonstrated that full employment was legitimately an objective of economic policy. (Previously, when the concern of policy was limited to the achievement of price stability, a similar conflict had been discerned between internal and external stability in a fixed exchange rate system, a conflict which is still urgent but lies outside the scope of this paper.) Analysis of this conflict and the social choice it made necessary was, however, confined to elaboration of the problem and exploration of the possibility of mitigating it by institutional reforms designed to increase the perfection of competition in the goods and labor markets of the economy, until the nature of the choice involved was formalized in the concept of the "Phillips curve."

The Phillips curve in its simplest form hypothesizes a relation between the percentage of unemployment in the economy and the rate of increase in wages or prices (the rate of price increase being lower than the rate of wage increase by the rate of increase of productivity), such that the rate of inflation increases more than proportionately as the percentage of unemployment falls and decreases less than proportionately as the percentage of unemployment increases. (In idealized geometrical textbook representations, the rate of inflation asymptotically approaches infinity as the unemployment percentage approaches zero; as the percentage of unemployment increases, inflation turns into deflation, and the rate of deflation asymptotically approaches a constant as unemployment increases.) This hypothesis derived great appeal from the fact that early empirical work, based on British data, appeared to confirm the presence of a surprisingly stable econometric relationship of this type; subsequent research, however, has called into question both the theoretical foundations and the statistical reliability of the curve.

Assuming the reality of the Phillips curve, society can be envisaged as choosing the socially optimum combination of unemployment and inflation available to it on its Phillips curve as the target which fiscal and monetary policy should be directed toward achieving. Additionally, society would seek to use its control over the institutions of competition to shift the Phillips curve as far as possible in the favorable direction of less inflation with a given rate of unemployment and vice versa. The choice of position on a given Phillips curve can be formalized in the notion of a social preference system, attributing greater social welfare to less unemployment and less inflation, the optimal choice being represented by the tangency of an indifference curve of the preference system with the Phillips curve.

This formalization, while popular, is unfortunately rather empty of economic content, since it simply postulates that society is able to weigh more unemployment against more inflation in some unspecified manner to arrive at a preferred position. Yet the rate of inflation and the rate of unemployment, unlike the nuts and apples of conventional individual preference theory, are not strictly comparable objects of choice which can be rationally evaluated according to this theoretical schema. From one important point of view, indeed, the avoidance of inflation and the maintenance of full employment can be most usefully regarded as conflicting class interests of the bourgeoisie and the proletariat, respectively, the conflict being resolvable only by the test of relative political power in the society and

its resolution involving no reference to an overriding concept of the social welfare.

If some concept of the general welfare is to be applied, it would seem necessary to go beyond the mere postulation of a social preference function comprising inflation and unemployment rates as arguments, into an analysis of the relative social costs of inflation and unemployment. The formulation of these costs turns out to be more difficult than may appear at first sight.

With respect to unemployment, it would seem natural to measure the social cost by the loss of potential output it causes; and this method has in fact been followed by the U.S. Council of Economic Advisers, among others. But this measure tends to overstate the social cost, for several reasons. One of the most important is that an expansion of employment is secured partly by a reduction in unemployment and partly by an expansion of the labor force through increased participation in it by housewives, older people, and youths, and by the working of more hours by the existing labor force. To the extent that the people or hours added to the labor supply are drawn from activities that contribute to economic welfare but are not included in the conventional measures of national income or output—such as the services of housewives in the home, or merely the enjoyment of leisure—the apparent expansion of output associated with increased employment is largely fictitious. Conversely, the reduction of output associated with an increased unemployment rate will be largely fictitious, to the extent that those who retire from the active labor force, or cut down their working hours, have been in the margin of indifference between paid employment and other, unpaid activities. The problem becomes even more serious when the activities which are close substitutes for paid employment are of the nature of an investment in increasing future earning power, as when the state of demand for labor influences the choices of youth between taking immediate employment or remaining in school for a longer period, or when overtime hours compete with self-education. Another relevant consideration is that, where workers become unemployed, the idle time is usually of some value to the unemployed individual, either as leisure time, or as time for self-employment in the improvement of the individual's housing facilities, or as time to be used for searching the labor market for better employment opportunities. The value of these uses of "idle" time should be subtracted from the value of the output lost by unemployment to arrive at the true social cost of the latter.

With respect to inflation, the appropriate formulation of the social cost depends on the assumption made about whether the inflation is expected by the public or not. If inflation is assumed not to be expected, in the sense that in spite of actual inflation people continue to make their economic decisions on the basis of an assumed stability in the value of money, inflation entails no true social cost (waste of real resources) but only a redistribution of resources from the holders of assets whose value is fixed in terms of money to those whose liabilities are fixed in terms of money. It might, however, be possible to assign a social cost—or possibly a social benefit—to such redistributions according to whether the redistribution were judged to be undesirable or desirable. If on the other hand inflation is assumed to be expected, in the sense that the calculations underlying people's decisions incorporate the rate of increase in prices that is actually occurring, market rates of interest on securities and loans fixed in monetary terms will rise to include compensation for the rate of fall in the value of money, and there will be no redistribution of resources from creditors to debtors in the market for debt instruments contracted in monetary

terms. There will, however, be a redistribution of real resources from creditors to debtors on monetary assets the rate of return on which is not fixed in a competitive market; specifically, if by convention or law, currency (and possibly bank deposits subject to check) bears no interest, holders of money will suffer a loss of real resources to the issuers of money (the monetary authority, and possibly the commercial banks). Since this loss will by assumption be expected, it will create a tendency for the holders of money to economize on their holdings of it by using real resources in various ways to substitute for it (for example, by increasing the frequency of income receipts or planning a closer matching of current receipts and payments); and this substitution will involve a waste of resources which, together with whatever social cost or value is attached to the redistribution of resources from holders to issuers of money, will constitute the social cost of inflation in this case.

The formulation of the costs and benefits of different combinations of inflation and unemployment in this way, and the determination of the optimum position on the Phillips curve by a cost-minimization criterion of social choice, rests however on the crucial assumption that the position of the Phillips curve is given independently of the expected rate of inflation, so that society can choose to move along the Phillips curve by an appropriate choice of fiscal and monetary policy. It has recently been argued by Friedman and Phelps that this assumption does not make economic sense and, consequently, that the Phillips curve cannot be used as a basis for secular policy-making. Their contention is that the statistical Phillips curve is derived from historical experience characterized by considerable variability of price movements and by consequent uncertainty about what rate of inflation or deflation to expect, and so incorporates the average expectation about prospective price movements during the period (which may be assumed to be an average expectation of price stability). If the monetary authority, instead of allowing variability of unemployment and inflation rates, attempted to pin the economy down to a particular position on the Phillips curve which involved a nonzero rate of price change, the public would come to expect this rate of price change and attempt to incorporate it in wage bargains and price-determination decisions. Consequently, in diagrammatic terms, the Phillips curve would shift upward. The unemployment rate initially associated with price stability would gradually come to require the rate of inflation the authorities had selected as their target, so that the benefit of lower unemployment would gradually disappear leaving no offset to the costs of inflation; or, conversely, unemployment could only be held at a level lower than that consistent with price stability by ever accelerating inflation and the associated rising social cost.

On this analysis, society does not in fact face a choice between alternative combinations of rates of inflation and rates of unemployment. Instead, the choices facing it involve securing transitional benefits from less unemployment currently and in the near future, at the expense of greater costs of inflation in the more remote future. The socially optimal choice will depend on the time lag in the adjustment of the economy's expectations to experience, and on the social rate of time preference used to discount the present benefits from increased employment and the future cost of more rapid inflation.

If the social rate of time preference is assumed to be zero, or attention is focused on the long-run equilibrium growth path of the economy, the problem of efficient economic policy becomes that of choosing the optimal rate of price inflation or deflation. This problem raises some extremely complex theoretical issues if the influence of monetary policy on

growth, as mediated by the target rate of price change, is assumed to be the only instrument for affecting economic growth available to the policy makers, and if (as is customary in contemporary models of growth in a monetary economy) the rate of saving is assumed to be influenced by the rate of inflation. If, on the other hand, the policy makers are assumed to have sufficient other policy instruments at their disposal for the analyst to be able to isolate the influence of the chosen price trend on monetary behavior from its influence on the "real" side of the economic system, the solution becomes much simpler. If the distinguishing characteristic of money, as contrasted with other assets, is taken to be the nonpayment of explicit interest on it, it follows from welfare-maximizing principles of the type analyzed in the second section of this paper that the optimal monetary policy entails deflation of prices at a rate equal to the rate of return on nonmonetary assets. This would provide an implicit rate of return on money sufficient to encourage optimal holdings of it, that is, to reduce the marginal private cost of money-holding to equality with its (approximately zero) marginal social cost. If, on the other hand, the system of provision of money were made to conform to the requirements of the social optimum, on the lines suggested in that section, the public's holdings of money would be optimal regardless of the rate of inflation or deflation chosen by the authorities, since the real rate of return on money holdings would be the same as the real rate of return on alternative assets, and the chosen rate of price change would be neutral with respect to the social welfare achieved. That being the case, it could be argued that the authorities should aim at the achievement of price stability rather than at any nonzero rate of price change, inflationary or deflationary, on the consideration not so far introduced into the analysis that the costs of rational economic calculations will be less with price stability than when prices are expected to change at some rate, even though those expectations are held with certainty.

SELECTED BIBLIOGRAPHY

Part I

Friedman, Milton. *A Program for Monetary Stability.* New York: Fordham Univ. Press, 1959.

Johnson, Harry G. "Monetary Theory and Policy," *A.E.R.*, LII, No. 3 (June, 1962), 335–384. Reprinted in *Essays in Monetary Economics.* London: Allen & Unwin, 1967.

———. *Alternative Guiding Principles for the Use of Monetary Policy in Canada* (Princeton Internat. Finance Series No. 44), November, 1963. Reprinted in *Essays in Monetary Economics.* London: Allen & Unwin, 1967.

Part II

Johnson, Harry G. "The Report on Bank Charges," *Banker's Magazine*, CCIV (August, 1967), 64–68.

Meltzer, Allan. "Major Issues in the Regulation of Financial Institutions," *J.P.E.* (Suppl.), LXXV, No. 4, Pt. II (August, 1967), 482–501; and comments by M. A. Adelman, A. L. Marty, James Tobin, and Charls E. Walker.

Part III

Phillips, A. W. "Stabilization Policy in a Closed Economy," *Econ. J.*, LIX, No. 254 (June, 1954), 290–323.

Saving, T. R. "Monetary-Policy Targets and Indicators," *J.P.E.* (Suppl.), LXXV, No. 4, Pt. II (August, 1967), 446–456; and comments by George Horwich and William C. Hood.

Part IV

Johnson, Harry G. "Money in a Neo-Classical One-Sector Growth Model," in *Essays in Monetary Economics.* London: Allen & Unwin, 1967.

Phelps, E. S. "Phillips Curves, Expectations of Inflation and Optimal Unemployment over Time," *Economica*, XXXIV, No. 135 (August, 1967), 254–281.

Phillips, A. W. "The Relation between Unemployment and the Rate of Change of Money Wages in the United Kingdom, 1862–1957," *Economica*, XXV, No. 100 (November, 1958), 283–299.

Reuber, G. L. "The Objectives of Canadian Monetary Policy, 1949–61: Empirical 'Trade-Offs' and the Reaction Function of the Authorities," *J.P.E.*, LXXII, No. 2 (August, 1964), 109–132.

Summaries

Milton Friedman, "The Role of Monetary Policy," *American Economic Review,* 63 (March 1968), pp. 1–17.

Milton Friedman, as president of the American Economic Association, concerns himself in this address with the role that monetary policy can and should play in a nation's efforts to achieve several of its economic goals.

The author begins his address by outlining the tasks he believes monetary policy cannot perform: (1) it cannot peg interest rates for more than very limited periods; and (2) it cannot peg the rate of unemployment for more than very limited periods. He then raises a logical question: What can monetary policy do? He claims it can prevent money from becoming a major source of economic disturbance and that it does provide a stable background for the economy. He further states that it can be a factor in countering major disturbances arising in the economic system created by nonmonetary factors.

Friedman goes on in his address to lay down the rules by which monetary policy should be formulated. In his words, "The first requirement is that the monetary authority should guide itself by magnitudes that it can control, not by ones that it cannot control ... A second requirement for monetary policy is that the monetary authority avoid sharp swings in policy."

At the end of his address, Friedman makes a strong case for steady monetary growth at a predetermined rate so as to create "a monetary climate favorable to the effective operation of those basic forces of enterprise, ingenuity, invention, hard work, and thrift that are the true springs of economic growth." Friedman goes on to say, "That is the most we can ask from monetary policy at our present state of knowledge. But that much—and it is a great deal—is clearly within our reach."

Paul A. Samuelson and Robert M. Solow, "Analytical Aspects of Anti-Inflation Policy," *American Economic Review*, 50 (May 1960), pp. 177–194.

In this article, Samuelson and Solow make an attempt to apply the Phillips curve concept to the problem of inflation in the United States. The Phillips curve—named after A. W. Phillips, a British economist who first applied this curve to the British economy—proves that the rate of change of money wages (or prices) is inversely related to the rate of unemployment, with prices stabilizing at some moderately high level of employment and rising rapidly as employment declines. Samuelson and Solow explain in their article that their objective is to determine whether or not the Phillips curve concept applies equally well to the U.S. scene.

Samuelson and Solow begin by examining many of the pitfalls encountered in attempting to distinguish between cost and demand inflation. They then undertake an empirical examination of U.S. unemployment data to determine the relationship between prices and unemployment. Finally, in an attempt to develop some policy guidelines, they compare the American position with Phillips' findings for the United Kingdom. The authors conclude that, given recent productivity trends, price stability in the United States can be maintained only if 5 to 6 per cent of the labor force remains unemployed. If, however, an unemployment rate of no more than 3 per cent is sought, then the economy more than likely would be expected to experience a 4 or 5 per cent rate of price inflation.

At the end of the article, the authors warn that one should use his findings in this regard very cautiously, as any discussion of the relationship between the unemployment rate and the rate of inflation is at best an inexact science.

Bibliography

Karl R. Bopp, "Introduction to the Federal Reserve System," Federal Reserve Bank of Philadelphia, *Business Review*, January 1970, pp. 3–29.

James S. Duesenberry, "Tactics and Targets of Monetary Policy," *Morgan Guaranty Survey* (September 1969), pp. 7–14.

Abba P. Lerner, "The Economist's Can Opener," *Western Economic Journal*, 6 (March 1968), pp. 94–96.

9
FISCAL THEORY AND POLICY

In recent years, much has been written about the various ways in which the instruments of fiscal policy may be used to regulate a country's aggregate demand and influence its overall economic trend. Unfortunately, however, economists have not given adequate attention to either relating each of the fiscal policy instruments to a set of national targets or developing an empirically supported and effective theory of the budgetary process.

In the first selection in this part, Johansen discusses in detail the ways in which a country's several fiscal policy instruments may be used to achieve its national economic goals. In the second article, Davis, Dempster, and Wildavsky develop a theory of the budgetary process by making an empirical study of the government's use of its funds. The final selection is a classic study by Somers, in which he establishes the relation between expenditure and tax effects in the formulation of a national fiscal policy.

Targets and Instruments of Fiscal Policy
Leif Johansen

2.1 TARGETS AND INSTRUMENTS IN GENERAL

The following general discussion of targets and instruments properly belongs under what one might call general theory of economic policy. It is, however, of such great importance for the understanding of public economics that I find it useful to include the main features here.

The presentation will appear rather abstract; so if it seems difficult to associate economic realities with this discussion during the first reading, it is better to continue without spending too much time on this section. It is then recommended to

Leif Johansen, "Targets and Instruments," in *Public Economics* (Chicago: Rand McNally and Company, 1968), pp. 10–25.

return to it again after reading the next chapter, which deals with the macroeconomic effects of fiscal policy.

2.1.1. General Description of the Economic System

Let us assume that the mechanism of the economic system under observation can be described by the following set of conditions:

$$f_1(x_1 \cdots x_I; t_1 \cdots t_J) = 0$$
$$\vdots \qquad \vdots \qquad (2.1)$$
$$f_I(x_1 \cdots x_I; t_1 \cdots t_J) = 0$$

$$\begin{matrix} t_1 \\ \vdots \\ t_J \end{matrix} \text{ are determined directly by the government} \quad (2.2)$$

The variables included in this system are divided into two groups. The variables

$t_1 \cdots t_J$ are variables which the government controls directly. They can be tax-rates, public expenditure of different kinds, etc. These can be utilized by the government in economic policy, and we can call them the government's means of policy or instrument variables. The variables $x_1 \cdots x_I$ are all the other economic variables which it is found necessary or useful to include in the analysis.

When the government has decided which values it will give its instrument variables $t_1 \cdots t_J$ the equations (2.1) will generally determine the values of the variables $x_1 \cdots x_I$. The x's are thus not directly determined by the government, but it is obvious that the values the x's will assume generally must depend on which values the government has given the t's. We can thus consider the t's as instruments by which the government can indirectly influence the values of the x's. This further explains the term "instrument variables" for the t's.

The system (2.1) can generally be solved in such a way that we get the x's expressed in terms of the t's. This can be written in the following way:

$$x_1 = g_1(t_1 \cdots t_J)$$
$$\vdots \qquad\qquad (2.3)$$
$$x_I = g_I(t_1 \cdots t_J)$$

The above system is so general that it prompts the question whether it can convey any information at all. It does, however, make clear an important connection between the number of instruments the government has at its disposal and the number of targets which it can set up without the set of targets and instruments becoming contradictory. This connection is of importance in clarifying almost any problem in economic policy.

2.1.2. The Number of Targets and the Number of Instruments

Let us assume that the government has certain targets which can be formulated by demanding that K of the variables $x_1 \cdots x_I$ shall take on certain values. This

is marked thus:

$$x_1 = \bar{x}_1$$
$$\vdots \qquad\qquad (2.4)$$
$$x_K = \bar{x}_K$$

assuming that the variables are numbered in such a way that it is the K first variables for which the government has targets.[1]

The question is now whether the goal expressed by (2.4) can be achieved within the system described by (2.1) and (2.2). To examine this we insert the values from (2.4) in the equations in (2.1), now regarding $t_1 \cdots t_J$ as variables which can be adjusted so that the equations are satisfied with the desired values of $x_1 \cdots x_K$. This way of regarding $t_1 \cdots t_J$ does not conflict with what has been expressed in (2.2). It only means that we wish to calculate which values the government must determine for $t_1 \cdots t_J$ in order to achieve the targets (2.4). While doing this calculation one must, of course, consider $t_1 \cdots t_J$ as unknown variables.

The insertion mentioned can be expressed by (2.5):

$$f_1(\bar{x}_1 \cdots \bar{x}_K, x_{K+1} \cdots x_I; t_1 \cdots t_J) = 0$$
$$\vdots \qquad\qquad\qquad \vdots \qquad\qquad (2.5)$$
$$f_I(\bar{x}_1 \cdots \bar{x}_K, x_{K+1} \cdots x_I; t_1 \cdots t_J) = 0$$

In this system there are now in all $I - K + J$ unknown quantities, viz., $x_{K+1} \cdots x_I$ and $t_1 \cdots t_J$. The number of equations is I. If we assume that the equations are independent and—in those cases where we have fewer, or as many, equations as unknowns—that they are not contradictory, we can have the following different cases:

(a) $I - K + J > I$, i.e., $J > K$:
    more unknown quantities than
    equations

(b) $I - K + J = I$, i.e., $J = K$:
    as many unknown quantities
    as equations   (2.6)

(c) $I - K + J < I$, i.e., $J < K$:
    more equations than unknown
    quantities

In the case of (a) we have more unknown quantities than equations and there will usually be several ways in which to satisfy (2.5) with the given values of $x_1 \cdots x_K$. In the case of (b) we have as many equations as unknown quantities, and there will usually be one and only one set of values for the unknown quantities which satisfy the equations. This means that there is only one set of values for the instrument variables $t_1 \cdots t_J$, enabling the targets concerning the variables $x_1 \cdots x_K$ to be achieved. In the case of (c) we have more equations than there are unknown variables, and the system cannot be fulfilled. This means that there does not exist any set of values for the instrument variables $t_1 \cdots t_J$ such that they will lead to all the targets in (2.4) being achieved simultaneously.

We see from the arrangement (2.6) that what determines which of the three cases we shall have is whether the number of instruments J is greater than, equal to, or smaller than the number of targets K.

We can formulate the above conclusions almost like a catchphrase, in the following way: to achieve a given number of targets the government must have at least the same number of instruments. Or: the government cannot set more targets than the number of instruments available to it.

With special forms of the equations describing the system it may happen that one target is automatically achieved with the fulfilment of another target. Or it may happen that two proposed targets are incompatible, even if one has the sufficient number of instruments according to the rules given above. These special cases will not be further treated here. A discussion of such cases is provided by Bent Hansen.[2]

2.1.3. The Efficiency of an Instrument with Regard to a Target

Consideration of the relationships between the number of targets and the number of instruments must be supplemented by consideration of the efficiency of the instruments. It will be of little use to have a great number of means of policy at one's disposal if they are not efficient.

Assume that we are in a situation where $x_k = x_k^0$ and that we wish to get into a situation where $x_k = \bar{x}_k = x_k^0 + \varDelta x_k$. It is then natural to turn to an instrument which is such that only a small change in the value of the quantity expressing this instrument is sufficient to produce the wanted change in the value of x_k. Here, of course, it is not clear what is to be understood by a "small" change in t_j. We can suppose that there exists, for institutional reasons, only a certain finite range of variation for t_j; and when we say that a change in t_j is "small" we see the change in relation to this range of possible variations.

From such a way of thinking we could say that the instrument t_j is more efficient with respect to the target variable x_k the bigger the derivative

$$\frac{\partial g_k(t_1 \cdots t_J)}{\partial t_j} \qquad (2.7)$$

where g_k is one of the functions introduced by (2.3). If this derivative is great a certain change in t_j will, of course, produce a great change in the value of x_k; or differently expressed: a certain change in the value of x_k can be produced by a small change in the value of t_j.

In (2.7) we observe a change in t_j while all other t's are kept constant. But here an important question is raised. If we change one t_j while others are kept constant, then not only will x_k change its value, but usually *all* the x's will be changed. If we then have many targets which we wish to keep while we change the value of x_k from x_k^0 into the new, desired value, then the x's expressing these other targets will also be changed.

In this situation we could then proceed in such a way that we not only change the one t_j, but also the values of a series of the other instruments, so as to arrive at a new situation where the one x_k is changed as desired, while the other x's for which we have targets are kept constant. The other t's which we now have changed do, however, also affect the one x_k whose value we were interested in changing. The result of this is that we must now also change the value of the instrument t_j—the one we first thought of using—by more or by less than we intended when we did not worry about the values of the other x's. From this point of view we could define the efficiency of an instrument with respect to a variable in a new way, viz., the efficiency of an instrument with respect to a variable is expressed by that change in the value of this instrument which is necessary to produce a certain change in the value of a target variable, when other instruments are used in such a way that the values of other target variables are kept constant.[3]

The line of thought here indicated does, however, also lead to certain difficulties. The measure of efficiency which we get by this way of thinking will, for instance, depend on which other set of instruments we have at our disposal. Moreover, it is somewhat arbitrary to attach the effect on x_k to a certain instrument t_j, when we actually change a whole set of instruments.

This discussion shows that generally it is necessary to consider all instruments in connection with all targets. It is as a rule hardly possible to define in a satisfactory way a concept such as we have tried to find, viz., a concept expressing the efficiency of *one* instrument with respect to *one* target variable.

It can, however, be the case with certain instruments and certain target variables that a given instrument affects a given target variable considerably, but only has small effects for other target variables. Formally this will be reflected in the following way:

$$\frac{\partial g_k(t_1 \cdots t_j)}{\partial t_j} \quad \text{is ``great''}$$

$$\frac{\partial g_h(t_1 \cdots t_j)}{\partial t_j} \quad \text{is ``small'' for } h \neq k \qquad (2.8)$$

In such a case we can say that t_j is a *selective* instrument with respect to x_k, and then the measure (2.7) will be a suitable measure of the efficiency of this instrument.

A more thorough formal discussion of the concept of efficiency of an instrument has been carried out by Jan Tinbergen.[4]

2.1.4. Can the Use of the Instruments Be Decentralized?

Within the formal framework outlined above we shall consider the question of delegating to different institutions the power to take decisions as to actions involving the various instruments.

Let us assume that we have $J = K$, i.e., that we have as many instruments as we have targets. Can we then "share out" these instruments to various institutions and instruct the institutions to see to the achievement of their particular target? In the case now under consideration we shall have

$$x_1 = g_1(t_1 \cdots t_K)$$
$$\vdots \qquad\qquad (2.9)$$
$$x_K = g_K(t_1 \cdots t_K)$$

which can be solved with respect to $t_1 \cdots t_K$:

$$t_1 = h_1(x_1 \cdots x_K)$$
$$\vdots \qquad\qquad (2.10)$$
$$t_K = h_K(x_1 \cdots x_K)$$

In the form (2.9) the equations indicate which values we shall get for the x's with which we associate targets if $t_1 \cdots t_K$ are given certain values. In the form (2.10) the equations indicate which values we must give $t_1 \cdots t_K$ if we want certain values for $x_1 \cdots x_K$. Generally the value of every single target variable will depend on the values of all the instruments $t_1 \cdots t_K$. And conversely, the necessary value for an instrument variable will generally depend on all the targets. This complicates a decentralization of targets and instruments. The value of the target variable given to a certain institution to "look after" will depend on what all the other institutions do; and to determine the necessary value of the instrument assigned to that particular institution does in principle require knowledge also of the targets which come under other institutions.

In certain cases, however, it can happen that a target variable is virtually independent of all save one, or one definite group of instruments, and simultaneously that this instrument (or these instruments) has (have) only a small influence on other target variables. Expressed differently, it could be said that we then have one selective instrument, or a group of these, with respect to one target variable, while at the same time other instruments are neutral with respect to this target variable. In such a case we can delegate this target and the appurtenant instruments to a separate institution without disturbing other targets. This institution may then only be notified of the target, but does not need information from any central authority about how the instruments are to be used.

In practice a complete neutrality and selectivity will hardly occur. On the other hand, it seems unthinkable that all instruments at the government's disposal should be centrally determined and co-ordinated. As a rough principle we could say, then, that instruments affecting many targets ought to be employed centrally, while instruments affecting only one or a small number of targets can to a larger extent be decentralized.[5]

In connection with the question of centralization and decentralization so many other considerations also, of course, assert themselves that this rule will not always hold. We return to some of these considerations in Chapter 8.

2.1.5. Maximization of a Preference Function

To determine targets as in (2.4) one must combine two different things. Firstly, the targets expressed by (2.4) must reflect what we *want*. But next they must also reflect what we judge it *possible* to obtain. The latter condition involves considerations as to how the economic system actually works and the limitations to which it is subjected, and to this extent it is a question of matters that in principle are objectively recognizable. It would be more satisfactory were it possible to separate these two matters. On the one side could then be set out one's preferences, in some form or other, while on the other side could be set out a model containing all available information about the workings of the economic system and its limitations.

This can be obtained in principle by operating with a preference function, which we could write as

$$W = W(x_1, \ldots, x_l) \qquad (2.11)$$

This function should then be maximized within the range of existing possibilities, that is, under the conditions, in the form of equations and inequalities, to which the system is exposed. In such an analysis there would be no rules of the type we have had before, as to the number of targets and of instruments. With this last formulation there is one target, viz., to maximize W, and for that target all the instruments present are used.

A realistic preference function will have to be a function of very many variables, and with a complicated structure. One can choose a somewhat simpler way, by letting W express the most essential aspects of the preferences, while letting other aspects be expressed in the form of equations and inequalities of different kinds. Such questions, together with the question of how the establishment of a preference function could be imagined, are thoroughly treated in connection with the work on decision models carried out by Professor Ragnar Frisch at the Institute of Economics at the University of Oslo.

2.2. THE MOST IMPORTANT TARGETS CONSIDERED IN PUBLIC ECONOMICS

Many of the targets considered in public economics are quite obvious. For the sake of order it can, however, be useful to set up a list of the most important of these targets.

2.2.1. High Current Private Consumption

In itself, this target is obvious. Some people may perhaps say that it is important to keep a relatively low current consumption, thereby being able to save and invest and thus securing a higher consumption in future. This is, however, a thought that only asserts itself when we look at the question of co-ordinating a series of different targets which partly oppose each other. Otherwise it is clear enough that *in itself* high consumption now is a desirable thing.

2.2.2. The Satisfaction of Collective Wants

The concern here is with satisfaction of the need for goods which are of such a nature that they cannot be split up and sold to some individual buyers, while other people are excluded from consuming these goods. The production and distribution of these goods can therefore not be regulated through the usual markets. The clearest examples of such goods are those that have to do with the maintenance of law and order, but there are also such things as, for instance, the regulation of watercourses to protect against flooding, expansion of communications, etc. Purely collective goods in this sense hardly exist, as many of those things that usually come under the heading collective goods *could be imagined* split up and sold to individual buyers. This is the case, for instance, with education, and one might also imagine police

protection being individualized and sold in a market. But although there are thus many border-line cases, it is yet convenient to operate with the expression "collective wants" as a term for certain types of requirements. Accounts often give the impression that the satisfaction of such wants has been the original task of the state. Historically this may perhaps be somewhat dubious, but there is no doubt that for a long time it has been, and still is, one of the government's most important tasks.

2.2.3. The Ensuring of Economic Growth

Since economic growth demands net investments, this target may to a certain degree conflict or compete with the target of high current consumption. The question might then be asked whether it is the business of the government to set up targets in these two fields. Could not the government leave it to separate individuals to strike a balance between present consumption and economic growth, through their choice between saving and consumption? The answer to this (without treating it in greater detail here) is that existing market mechanisms are hardly suited to ensure a result which is in any precise accordance with the inhabitants' own preferences about present consumption versus economic growth. There is also the observed fact that the citizens often vote for a policy giving a higher investment rate than the same citizens would produce were all investment to be decided by voluntary private saving, without any actions on the part of the government with a view to maintaining high investment. Finally, as already mentioned, the government now constitutes such a large part of the entire economy that its actions must have consequences for almost all economic units or circumstances whether this is intended or not. This makes it difficult to imagine a policy purporting to be neutral with regard to the question of present consumption and economic growth. And this, then, also means that the government cannot avoid giving a certain consideration to this issue.

2.2.4. Influence on the Distribution of Income

Here, too, it might be asked whether it is a "natural" objective for the government to influence the distribution of income. There is no need, here, to discuss this question, only to bear in mind the fact that there are very few countries where the citizens accept the income distribution that comes into existence of itself in the markets. They usually wish to interfere in various ways, through the government, to adjust this distribution. The question of distribution of income does, however, have different aspects. One could look at (a) the distribution of individual earnings, (b) distribution according to family type, (c) distribution among industries, and (d) distribution over geographical areas. Even though instruments of fiscal policy can be used, and are used, in connection with the last two aspects here mentioned, only the first two are traditionally considered as belonging to the field of public economics.

2.2.5. High Employment

The target of high or full employment can be based on two different considerations. Firstly, high employment can be set up as a target because high production is desirable. If so, it is really unnecessary to set it up beside the targets we already have set out above. Secondly, however, the target of high employment can be set up from social and political considerations which count *in addition* to the importance of employment for the sake of production. In this case there is reason to note it as a target on a par with those noted above.

The employment target is often formulated as a demand for *full* employment.

This is not yet a completely unambiguous formulation because different definitions have been put forward as to what is to be understood by full employment. How, for instance, should one regard purely "frictional unemployment" which is caused by the fact that it takes time for the labour force to move between sectors, and how should one regard seasonal unemployment? Also, there is reason to take note of the circumstance that it is quite possible to have full employment on different levels of employment. Depending on wage- and tax-conditions, etc., a greater or lesser number of people may choose to offer their services. Furthermore, there may be full employment with either long or short working hours, and consequently full employment with different levels of production.

2.2.6. Satisfactory External Trade Balance

This target will not be precisely formulated here. In certain situations a country may want to import capital, while during other periods it may wish to manage without, etc. The point here is only that the government must give attention to external trade and set up certain objectives in this field.

Actually, a target concerning the balance of external trade is a reflex of the other targets already mentioned. When a country wishes to avoid an unfavourable payments situation, this may, for instance, be because such a situation might lead to difficulties with respect to the import of raw materials necessary for the country's production; or it may be because such a situation might limit freedom of manoeuvre in economic policy. This will then reflect back on the targets already mentioned. To this extent it should be unnecessary to set up this as an independent objective. But one might also wish for a particular development in external trade on the more political grounds that one does not want to develop a relationship of dependence vis-à-vis foreign countries. In such a case, this is a factor on a par with those mentioned above.

2.2.7. A Stable Price Level

This, too, is not a fundamental objective such as the targets of high consumption, the satisfaction of collective wants, etc. If the targets previously mentioned could be achieved at any time, regardless of how the price level developed, then there would be small reason to concern oneself about the latter. When a stable price level is, nevertheless, set up as a target, this may be because it is considered that a rising price level, *due to effects which are not allowed for by the model in use*, may complicate the achievement of the above-mentioned targets. The following factors are probably the most important: (a) A rising price level may undermine the possibilities for rational calculation. (b) A shifting price level will lead to a transference of wealth between persons and groups who have net monetary claims, and persons or groups having net debts. This may be considered unjust. (c) A rising price level can lead to export difficulties.

If we have a model which allows for the effects mentioned under (a)–(c) it is unnecessary to introduce a stable price level as a target in the model. Conversely, if we have a model not allowing for these effects, we can "correct" this imperfection in the model by introducing a stable price level as a separate target. A similar argument applies under 2.2.6.

The target of a stable price level can be understood in several ways. It can apply to the price level for the entire national product, or it can apply to the price level for consumer goods; it can apply to the price level inclusive of sales tax and net excises or the so-called factor price level, i.e., prices exclusive of sales tax and excises. It can be of some importance in these matters which particular price level is referred to in wage negotiations, for instance, or is involved in wage agreements.

2.2.8. Efficient Use of National Resources

In various situations state interference or direct governmental management may effect a more efficient use of a country's resources than would result from leaving things "to themselves." Such situations may occur, for instance, when the real social costs of a production are not fully expressed in the private cost-accounting, or when a certain production or activity affords a utility which cannot in its entirety be sold to buyers in the ordinary way. This is what in the theory of welfare economics is called "indirect effects," or is characterized as deviations between private and social marginal costs or marginal utilities. (If the divergence between private and social utilities makes itself strongly felt, we may approach the field of what were earlier called collective goods.) As another example, there may be cases where a certain production activity, under unregulated market conditions, leads to monopoly and thus to less efficient use of resources. This can, *inter alia*, apply in cases with strongly declining average cost curves. In such cases optimal output will be impossible under private production without state subsidies, or interference of some other kind, because a price in accordance with the marginal costs would create a deficit.

The target of efficient use of a country's resources is also derived from the more primary objectives mentioned earlier. But if we are working within the framework of a model which is not sufficiently detailed to consider various kinds of factors bearing on efficiency, there are grounds for setting this up as an independent target in the same way as in the previous instance.

In sections 2.2.1 to 2.2.8. the various targets have been quite loosely described.

It is unnecessary at this point to enter into more precise definitions, neither shall we adopt any particular attitude to these different targets. The purpose of the list is only to point out the most important factors usually included in the setting up of economic targets in a country like Norway. We shall return later to more careful discussions of most of the issues raised in the above survey of targets.

It is not certain that all the targets mentioned can be simultaneously a-chieved if they are set up as absolute demands. In principle, the most satis-factory thing would be, as mentioned before, to establish a preference function depending upon magnitudes which ex-press the factors in this list. Failing that, one must set up targets concerning these magnitudes, taking into account what one thinks can actually be obtained. Through a process of trial-and-error, experimenting with different targets, one might then perhaps approach a solution in the vicinity of what one would have obtained by setting up a preference function and maximizing it.

One main concern of the following chapters will be to discuss the extent to which the targets mentioned here might be combined, and to what extent they might conflict with each other under various conditions. These questions can-not, of course, be answered without stating, for every situation, precisely which instruments are available. Targets conflicting with each other when *one* set of instruments is available, might be con-sistent if one has *another* set of instruments at one's disposal.

2.3. INSTRUMENTS IN PUBLIC ECONOMICS

The instruments at the government's disposal can be said to come under the following main headings:

1. instruments of fiscal policy,

2. instruments of monetary policy,
3. direct interference through orders and prohibitions,
4. the government's own business activity.

The difference between monetary policy and fiscal policy is not clear and un-ambiguous. The distinction can, for instance, be drawn according to the following criteria:

a. According to the institutions making the decisions. One might, for instance, say that the political decisions made by the central bank belong to monetary policy, while those made by particular state institutions belong to fiscal policy (*other* state institutions than the central bank if, as in Norway, this is owned by the state). Such a distinction may, however, be somewhat arbitrary. When these state institutions and the central bank are closely co-ordinated, it will often be quite practical matters which decide who is to make the various kinds of decision.

b. One might imagine drawing the dis-tinction according to the objectives being pursued. One might, for instance, say that that which aims at influencing the value of money, currency condi-tions, etc., is monetary policy, while fiscal policy is that which seeks to meet the collective wants and influence employment. It is, however, apparent from the previous general discussion of targets and instruments that it is hardly possible to draw any rational distinction along these lines.

c. One can draw the distinctions accord-ing to which markets the various measures have a *direct* bearing on. Consequently, one might say that monetary policy is that which pri-marily influences the markets for financial claims, while fiscal policy comprises all other state receipts and payments. This is more or less equiva-lent to another definition sometimes applied: fiscal policy determines the development of the government's net debt (inclusive of central bank money in private hands), while monetary policy determines its composition.

We shall here largely keep to the criterion given under (c). Fiscal policy will then be a principal part of public economics. In addition, we shall deal with parts of what comes under point 4 in the list above. Similarly, we shall concern ourselves with that which lies on the borderline between fiscal policy and monetary policy. This applies, *inter alia*, to some problems concerning the public debt. Instruments coming under the head of direct interference, will only be dealt with in so far as they relate to fiscal policy.

Considering the division of the instruments of the state given above, one might ask where is the place of industrial policy, social policy, and so on. The reply might often be that matters concerning various *total* sums are matters of fiscal policy, while the question of the use of these total sums in various fields can be a question of industrial policy, social policy, etc. For the rest, it is hardly fruitful to speculate further on the subdivisions of the political sphere.

Should one wish to subdivide the instruments of fiscal policy into categories, it may be done by the following arrangement:

Fiscal policy
- Payments to the government.
  - Taxes.
  - Excises. } Taxes in a broad sense.
  - Duties.
  - Sale of goods and services.
- Payments from the government.
  - Purchase of goods and services.
  - Payment of subsidies and social benefits (transfers).

How are we to envisage the number of instruments in such a context? Can we, for instance, say that *one* tax constitutes *one* instrument? Not necessarily. If we have an income tax where the tax makes up a certain percentage of the taxpayer's income beyond a certain tax-free minimum, we can say that we are dealing with two instruments, viz., the size of the exemption and the tax rate. These can then be used to meet two groups of considerations, viz., considerations concerning the over-all demand level, and considerations concerning the distribution of disposable income.

From this point of view, one might imagine acquiring just as many instruments as one could wish for, by framing complicated forms of taxation including many kinds of allowances, tax percentages, brackets of progression, etc. This is schematically correct, but there remains the question whether the instruments provided in this way are efficient with respect to the targets.

In principle, we ought to count as an instrument only that over which the government has direct control. Accordingly, the *amount* brought in by a particular tax, for instance, should not be regarded as a public instrument, as this will, of course, depend on the dispositions of the private sector. What the government directly controls, are tax rates, allowances, etc., and it is these which are really the government's instruments. For the sake of convenience, we shall, however, often treat the incoming tax yields themselves as instruments. If the government possessed complete information as to the reactions of the private sector to various kinds of interference, it would always be able to work out a definite correspondence between tax rates and tax yields,[6] and the simplification we make in considering the tax yield as the instrument would then not be of a serious kind. In certain situations this issue can, however, be of great importance. This applies especially in dealing with situations which involve great uncertainty of some kind or other.

It may seem somewhat difficult to fit the municipalities into the formula of targets and instruments which has been discussed. One way to regard this, might be to say that the state here chooses to undertake a decentralization based on the kind of considerations we made in section 2.1.4, as the municipalities have the responsibility for achieving targets of a local character, and have been given instruments which, when used within the limits drawn up by the state, through its legislation on local government and taxation, do not complicate the government's policy in other respects. Other ways of regarding this, however, also present themselves. We shall return to some problems concerning municipal economy in the final chapter.

NOTES

1 The above formulation includes the case where the government might have targets which are expressed by the variables $x_1 \cdots x_I$ being subjected to certain requirements in the form of equations, for instance that certain variables shall assume certain proportions to each other, or that there shall be a given difference between certain variables, etc. Such constraints can generally be expressed in this way: $F(x_1 \cdots x_I) = 0$. If, however, we have such a constraint we can only introduce a new variable x_{I+1} defined by $x_{I+1} = F(x_1 \cdots x_I)$ and introduce this equation of definition in addition to those already included in (2.1) while simultaneously introducing $x_{I+1} = \bar{x}_{I+1} = 0$ among the targets in (2.4).

2 See Chapter I in: *The economic theory of fiscal policy* (London, 1958).

3 The greater the efficiency of the instrument, the smaller this number will be. It would therefore, perhaps, be more natural to use the inverse of this number.

4 See especially Chapter VII in: *On the theory of economic policy* (Amsterdam, 1952).

5 Problems of the type here touched upon are thoroughly treated by Jan Tinbergen in: *Centralization and decentralization in economic policy* (Amsterdam, 1954).

6 This correspondence would involve also the other instruments.

A Theory of the Budgetary Process[*]
Otto A. Davis, M. A. H. Dempster, and Aaron Wildavsky

There are striking regularities in the budgetary process. The evidence from over half of the nondefense agencies indicates that the behavior of the budgetary

Otto A. Davis, M. A. H. Dempster, and A. Wildavsky, "A Theory of the Budgetary Process," *American Political Science Review*, 60 (September 1966), pp. 529–547.

* The research was sponsored by Resources for the Future. We received valuable criticism from Rufus Browning, Sam Cohn, W. W. Cooper, Richard Cyert, Nelson Polsby, Herbert Simon, and Oliver Williamson, research assistance from Rose Kelly, and editorial assistance from Jean Zorn. Mrs. E.

process of the United States government results in aggregate decisions similar to those produced by a set of simple decision rules that are linear and temporally stable. For the agencies considered, certain equations are specified and compared with data composed of agency requests (through the Bureau of the Budget) and

Belton undertook the laborious task of compiling the raw data. We are grateful to Resources for the Future and to our colleagues, but the sole responsibility for what is said here is our own.

Congressional appropriations from 1947 through 1963. The comparison indicates that these equations summarize accurately aggregate outcomes of the budgetary process for each agency.

In the first section of the paper we present an analytic summary of the federal budgetary process, and we explain why basic features of the process lead us to believe that it can be represented by simple models which are stable over periods of time, linear, and stochastic.[1] In the second section we propose and discuss the alternative specifications for the agency-Budget Bureau and Congressional decision equations. The empirical results are presented in section three. In section four we provide evidence on deviant cases, discuss predictions, and future work to explore some of the problems indicated by this kind of analysis. An appendix contains informal definitions and a discussion of the statistical terminology used in the paper.

I. THE BUDGETARY PROCESS

Decisions depend upon calculation of which alternatives to consider and to choose.[2] A major clue toward understanding budgeting is the extraordinary complexity of the calculations involved. There are a huge number of items to be considered, many of which are of considerable technical difficulty. There is, however, little or no theory in most areas of policy which would enable practitioners to predict the consequences of alternative moves and the probability of their occurring. Nor has anyone solved the imposing problem of the interpersonal comparison of utilities. Outside of the political process, there is no agreed upon way of comparing and evaluating the merits of different programs for different people whose preferences vary in kind and in intensity.

Participants in budgeting deal with their overwhelming burdens by adopting aids to calculation. By far the most important aid to calculation is the incremental method. Budgets are almost never actively reviewed as a whole in the sense of considering at once the value of all existing programs as compared to all possible alternatives. Instead, this year's budget is based on last year's budget, with special attention given to a narrow range of increases or decreases.

Incremental calculations proceed from an existing base. (By "base" we refer to commonly held expectations among participants in budgeting that programs will be carried out at close to the going level of expenditures.) The widespread sharing of deeply held expectations concerning the organization's base provides a powerful (although informal) means of securing stability.

The most effective coordinating mechanisms in budgeting undoubtedly stem from the roles adopted by the major participants. Roles (the expectations of behavior attached to institutional positions) are parts of the division of labor. They are calculating mechanisms. In American national government, the administrative agencies act as advocates of increased expenditure, the Bureau of the Budget acts as Presidential servant with a cutting bias, the House Appropriations Committee functions as a guardian of the Treasury, and the Senate Appropriations Committee as an appeals court to which agencies carry their disagreements with House action. The roles fit in with one another and set up patterns of mutual expectations which markedly reduce the burden of calculation for the participants. Since the agencies can be depended upon to advance all the programs for which there is prospect of support, the Budget Bureau and the Appropriations Committees respectively can concentrate on fitting them into the President's program or paring them down.

Possessing the greatest expertise and the

largest numbers, working in the closest proximity to their policy problems and clientele groups, and desiring to expand their horizons, administrative agencies generate action through advocacy. But if they ask for amounts much larger than the appropriating bodies believe reasonable, the agencies' credibility will suffer a drastic decline. In such circumstances, the reviewing organs are likely to cut deeply, with the result that the agency gets much less than it might have with a more moderate request. So the first guide for decision is: do not come in *too* high. Yet the agencies must also not come in too low, for the reviewing bodies assume that if agency advocates do not ask for funds they do not need them. Thus, the agency decision rule might read: come in a little too high (padding), but not too high (loss of confidence).

Agencies engage in strategic planning to secure these budgetary goals. Strategies are the links between the goals of the agencies and their perceptions of the kinds of actions which will be effective in their political environment. Budget officers in American national government uniformly believe that being a good politician—cultivation of an active clientele, development of confidence by other officials (particularly the appropriations subcommittees), and skill in following strategies which exploit opportunities—is more important in obtaining funds than demonstration of agency efficiency.

In deciding how much money to recommend for specific purposes, the House Appropriations Committee breaks down into largely autonomous subcommittees in which the norm of reciprocity is carefully followed. Specialization is carried further as subcommittee members develop limited areas of competence and jurisdiction. Budgeting is both incremental and fragmented as the subcommittees deal with adjustments to the historical base of each agency. Fragmentation and specialization are increased through the

appeals functions of the Senate Appropriations Committee, which deals with what has become (through House action) a fragment of a fragment. With so many participants continually engaged in taking others into account, a great many adjustments are made in the light of what others are likely to do.

This qualitative account of the budgetary process contains clear indications of the kind of quantitative models we wish to develop. It is evident, for example, that decision-makers in the budgetary process think in terms of percentages. Agencies talk of expanding their base by a certain percentage. The Bureau of the Budget is concerned about the growth rates for certain agencies and programs. The House Appropriations Committee deals with percentage cuts, and the Senate Appropriations Committee with the question of whether or not to restore percentage cuts. These considerations suggest that the quantitative relationships among the decisions of the participants in the budget process are linear in form.

The attitudes and calculations of participants in budgeting seem stable over time. The prominence of the agency's "base" is a sign of stability. The roles of the major participants are powerful, persistent, and strongly grounded in the expectations of others as well as in the internal requirements of the positions. Stability is also suggested by the specialization that occurs among the participants, the long service of committee members, the adoption of incremental practices such as comparisons with the previous year, the fragmentation of appropriations by program and item, the treatments of appropriations as continuously variable sums of money rather than as perpetual reconsiderations of the worth of programs, and the practice of allowing past decisions to stand while coordinating decision-making only if difficulties arise. Since the budgetary process appears to be stable over periods of time, it is reasonable to estimate the relationships in budgeting on the basis of time series data.

Special events that upset the apparent stability of the budgetary process can and do occur. Occasionally, world events take an unexpected turn, a new President occupies the White House, some agencies act with exceptional zeal, others suffer drastic losses of confidence on the part of the appropriations subcommittees, and so on. It seems plausible to represent such transient events as random shocks to an otherwise deterministic system. Therefore, our model is stochastic rather than deterministic.

The Politics of the Budgetary Process contains a description of strategies which various participants in budgeting use to further their aims. Some of these strategies are quite complicated. However, a large part of the process can be explained by some of the simpler strategies which are based on the relationship between agency requests for funds (through the Budget Bureau) and Congressional appropriations. Because these figures are made public and are known to all participants, because they are directly perceived and communicated without fear of information loss or bias, and because the participants react to these figures, they are ideal for feedback purposes. It is true that there are other indicators—special events, crises, technological developments, actions of clientele groups—which are attended to by participants in the budgetary process. But if these indicators have impact, they must quickly be reflected in the formal feedback mechanisms—the actions of departments, the Bureau of the Budget, and Congress—to which they are directed. Some of these indicators (see section IV) are represented by the stochastic disturbances. Furthermore, the formal indicators are more precise, more simple, more available, more easily interpreted than the others. They are, therefore, likely to be used by participants in the budgetary process year in and year out. Present decisions are based largely on past experience, and this lore is encapsulated in the amounts which the agencies receive as they go through the steps in the budgetary cycle.

For all the reasons discussed in this section, our models of the budgetary process are linear, stable over periods of time, stochastic, and strategic in character. They are "as if" models: an excellent fit for a given model means only that the actual behavior of the participants has an effect equivalent to the equations of the model. The models, taken as a whole, represent a set of decision rules for Congress and the agencies.

II. THE MODELS

In our models we aggregate elements of the decision-making structure. The Budget Bureau submissions for the agency are used instead of separate figures for the two kinds of organizations. Similarly, at this stage in our analysis, we use final Congressional appropriations instead of separating out committee action, floor action, conference committee recommendations, and so on. We wish to emphasize that although there may be some aggregation bias in the estimation of the postulated structure of decision, this does not affect the linearity of the aggregate relationships. If the decisions of an agency and the Bureau of the Budget with regard to that agency depend linearly upon the same variable (as we hypothesize), then the aggregated decision rule of the two, treated as a single entity, will depend linearly upon that variable. By a similar argument, the various Congressional participants can be grouped together so that Congress can be regarded as a single decision-making entity. While the aggregating procedure may result in grouping positive and negative influences together, this manifestly does not affect the legitimacy of the procedure; linearity is maintained.[3]

Our models concern only the requests presented in the President's budget for an individual agency and the behavior of Congress as a whole with regard to the agency's appropriation. The models do not attempt to estimate the complete decision-making structure for each agency from bureau requests to departments to submission through the Budget Bureau to possible final action in the Senate and House. There are several reasons for remaining content with the aggregated figures we use. First, the number of possible decision rules which must be considered grows rapidly as each new participant is added. We would soon be overwhelmed by the sheer number of rules invoked. Second, there are genuine restrictions placed on the number of structural parameters we can estimate because (a) some data, such as bureau requests to departments, are unavailable, and (b) only short time series are meaningful for most agencies. It would make no sense, for example, to go back in time beyond the end of World War II, when most domestic activity was disrupted.[4]

Since the agencies use various strategies and Congress may respond to them in various ways, we propose several alternative systems of equations. These equations represent alternative decision rules which may be followed by Congressional and agency-Budget Bureau participants in the budgetary process. One important piece of data for agency-Budget Bureau personnel who are formulating appropriations requests is the most recent Congressional appropriation. Thus, we make considerable use of the concept "base," operationally defined as the previous Congressional appropriation for an agency, in formulating our decision rules. Since the immediate past exercises such a heavy influence on budgetary outcomes, Markov (simultaneous, difference) equations are particularly useful. In these Markov processes, the value of certain variables at one point in time is dependent on their value at one or more immediately previous periods as well as on the particular circumstances of the time.

We postulate several decision rules for both the agency-Budget Bureau requests and for Congressional action on these requests. For each series of requests or appropriations, we select from the postulated decision rules that rule which most closely represents the behavior of the aggregated entities. We use the variables

y_t the appropriation passed by Congress for any given agency in the year t. Supplemental appropriations are not included in the y_t.

x_t the appropriation requested by the Bureau of the Budget for any given agency for the year t. The x_t constitutes the President's budget request for an agency.

We will also introduce certain symbols representing random disturbances of each of the postulated relationships. These symbols are explained as they are introduced.

A. Equations for Agency-Budget Bureau Decision Rules

The possibility that different agencies use different strategies makes it necessary to construct alternative equations representing these various strategies. Then, for each agency in our sample, we use time series data to select that equation which seems to describe best the budgetary decisions of that agency. In this section we present three simple models of agency requests. The first states agency requests as a function of the previous year's appropriation. The second states requests as a function of the previous appropriation as well as a function of the differences between the agency request and appropriation in the previous year. The third states requests as a function of the previous year's request. In all three linear models provision is made for a random variable to take into account the special circumstances of the time.

An agency, while convinced of the worth of its programs, tends to be aware that extraordinarily large or small requests are likely to be viewed with suspicion by Congress; an agency does not consider it desirable to make extraordinary requests, which might precipitate unfavorable Congressional reaction. Therefore, the agency usually requests a percentage (generally greater than one hundred per cent) of its previous year's appropriation. This percentage is not fixed: in the event of favorable circumstances, the request is a larger percentage of the previous year's appropriation than would otherwise be the case; similarly, the percentage might be reduced in the event of unfavorable circumstances.

Decisions made in the manner described above may be represented by a simple equation. If we take the average of the percentages that are implicitly or explicitly used by budget officers, then any request can be represented by the sum of this average percentage of the previous year's appropriation plus the increment or decrement due to the favorable or unfavorable circumstances. Thus

$$x_t = \beta_0 y_{t-1} + \xi_t \qquad (1)$$

The agency request (through the Budget Bureau) for a certain year is a fixed mean percentage of the Congressional appropriation for that agency in the previous year plus a random variable (normally distributed with mean zero and unknown but finite variance) for that year.

is an equation representing this type of behavior. The average or mean percentage is represented by β_0. The increment or decrement due to circumstances is represented by ξ_t, a variable which requires some special explanation. It is difficult to predict what circumstances will occur at what time to put an agency in a favorable or unfavorable position. Numerous events could influence Congress' (and the public's) perception of an agency and its programs—the occurrence of a destructive hurricane in the case of the Weather Bureau, the death by cancer of a friend of an influential congressman, in the case of the National Institutes of Health, the hiring (or losing) of an especially effective lobbyist by some interest group, the President's becoming especially interested in a program of some agency as Kennedy was in mental health, and so on. (Of course, some of them may be more or less "predictable" at certain times to an experienced observer, but this fact causes no difficulty here.) Following common statistical practice we may represent the sum of the effects of all such events by a random variable that is an increment or decrement to the usual percentage of the previous year's appropriation. In equation (1), then, ξ_t represents the value which this random variable assumes in year t.

We have chosen to view the special events of each year for each agency as random phenomena that are capable of being described by a probability density or distribution. We assume here that the random variable is normally distributed with mean zero and an unknown but finite variance. Given this specification of the random variable, the agency makes its budgeting decisions as if it were operating by the postulated decision rule given by equation (1).

An agency, although operating somewhat like the organizations described by equation (1), may wish to take into account an additional strategic consideration: while this agency makes a request which is roughly a fixed percentage of the previous year's appropriation, it also desires to smooth out its stream of appropriations by taking into account the difference between its request and appropriation for the previous year. If there were an unusually large cut in the previous year's request, the agency submits a "padded" estimate to make up for the loss in expected funds; an unusual increase is followed by a reduced estimate to avoid unspent appropriations. This behavior may be represented by equation or decision rule

$$x_t = \beta_1 y_{t-1} + \beta_2(y_{t-1} - x_{t-1}) + \chi_t \quad (2)$$

The agency request (through the Budget Bureau) for a certain year is a fixed mean percentage of the Congressional appropriation for that agency in the previous year plus a fixed mean percentage of the difference between the Congressional appropriation and the agency request for the previous year plus a stochastic disturbance.

where χ_t is a stochastic disturbance, which plays the role described for the random variable in equation (1), the β's are variables reflecting the aspects of the previous year's request and appropriation that an agency takes into account: β_1 represents the mean percentage of the previous year's request which is taken into account, and β_2 represents the mean percentage of the difference between the previous year's appropriation and request $(y_{t-1} - x_{t-1})$ which is taken into account. Note that $\beta_2 < 0$ is anticipated so that a large cut will (in the absence of the events represented by the stochastic disturbance) be followed by a padded estimate and vice versa.[5]

Finally, an agency (or the President through the Bureau of the Budget), convinced of the worth of its programs, may decide to make requests without regard to previous Congressional action. This strategy appeals especially when Congress has so much confidence in the agency that it tends to give an appropriation which is almost identical to the request. Aside from special circumstances represented by stochastic disturbances, the agency's request in any given year tends to be approximately a fixed percentage of its request for the previous year. This behavior may

be represented by

$$x_t = \beta_3 x_{t-1} + \rho_t \quad (3)$$

The agency request (through the Budget Bureau) for a certain year is a fixed mean percentage of the agency's request for the previous year plus a random variable (stochastic disturbance).

where ρ_t is a stochastic disturbance and β_3 is the average percentage. Note that if the agency believes its programs to be worthy, $\beta_3 > 1$ is expected.[6]

These three equations are not the only ones which may be capable of representing the actual behavior of the combined budgeting decisions of the agencies and the Bureau of the Budget. However, they represent the agency-Budget Bureau budgeting behavior better than all other decision rules we tried.[7]

B. Equations for Congressional Decision Rules

In considering Congressional behavior, we again postulate three decision equations from which a selection must be made that best represents the behavior of Congress in regard to an agency's appropriations. Since Congress may use various strategies in determining appropriations for different agencies, different Congressional decision equations may be selected as best representing Congressional appropriations for each agency in our sample. Our first model states Congressional appropriations as a function of the agency's request (through the Budget Bureau) to Congress. The second states appropriations as a function of the agency's request as well as a function of the deviation from the usual relationship between Congress and the agency in the previous year. The third model states appropriations as a function of that segment of the agency's request that is not part of its appropriation or request for the previous year. Random variables are included to take account of special circumstances.

If Congress believes that an agency's request, after passing through the hands of the Budget Bureau, is a relatively stable index of the funds needed by the agency to carry out its programs, Congress responds by appropriating a relatively fixed percentage of the agency's request. The term "relatively fixed" is used because Congress is likely to alter this percentage somewhat from year to year because of special events and circumstances relevant to particular years. As in the case of agency requests, these special circumstances may be viewed as random phenomena. One can view this behavior as if it were the result of Congress' appropriating a fixed mean percentage of the agency requests; adding to the amount so derived a sum represented by a random variable. One may represent this behavior as if Congress were following the decision rule

$$y_t = a_0 x_t + \eta_t \qquad (4)$$

The Congressional appropriation for an agency in a certain year is a fixed mean percentage of the agency's request in that year plus a stochastic disturbance.

where a_0 represents the fixed average percentage and η_t represents the stochastic disturbance.

Although Congress usually grants an agency a fixed percentage of its request, this request sometimes represents an extension of the agency's programs above (or below) the size desired by Congress. This can occur when the agency and the Bureau of the Budget follow Presidential aims differing from those of Congress, or when Congress suspects that the agency is padding the current year's request. In such a situation Congress usually appropriates a sum different from the usual percentage. If a_1 represents the mean of the usual percentages, this behavior can be represented by equation or decision rule

$$y_t = a_1 x_t + v_t \qquad (5)$$

where v_t is a stochastic disturbance representing that part of the appropriations attributable to the special circumstances that cause Congress to deviate from a relatively fixed percentage. Therefore, when agency aims and Congressional desires markedly differ from usual (so that Congress may be said to depart from its usual rule) the stochastic disturbance takes on an unusually large positive or negative value. In order to distinguish this case from the previous one, more must be specified about the stochastic disturbance v_t. In a year following one in which agency aims and Congressional desires markedly differed, the agency makes a request closer to Congressional desires, and/or Congress shifts its desires closer to those of the agency (or the President). In the year after a deviation, then, assume that Congress will tend to make allowances to normalize the situation. Such behavior can be represented by having the stochastic disturbance v_t generated in accordance with a first order Markov scheme. The stochastic component in v_t is itself determined by a relation

$$v_t = a_2 v_{t-1} + \varepsilon_t \qquad (6)$$

where ε_t is a random variable. The symbol v_t therefore stands for the stochastic disturbance in the previous year (v_{t-1}) as well as the new stochastic disturbance for the year involved (ε_t). Substituting (6) into (5) gives

$$y_t = a_1 x_t + a_2 v_{t-1} + \varepsilon_t \qquad (7)$$

The Congressional appropriation for an agency is a fixed mean percentage of the agency's request for that year plus a stochastic disturbance representing a deviation from the usual relationship between Congress and the agency in the previous year plus a random variable for the current year.

as a complete description of a second Congressional decision rule. If Congress never makes complete allowance for an initial "deviation," then $-1 < a_2 < 1$ is to be expected.

To complete the description of this second Congressional decision rule, we will suppose $0 < a_2 < 1$. Then, granted a deviation from its usual percentage, Congress tends to decrease subsequent deviations by moving steadily back toward its usual percentage (except for the unforeseeable events or special circumstances whose effects are represented by the random variable ε_t). For example, if in a particular year $v_{t-1} > 0$, and if in the following year there are no special circumstances so that $\xi_t = 0$, then $v_t = a_2 v_{t-1} < v_{t-1}$. The deviation in year t is smaller than the deviation in year $t - 1$. However, if $-1 < a_2 < 0$ after an initial deviation, Congress tends to move back to its usual rule (apart from the disturbances represented by the random variable ε_t) by making successively smaller deviations which differ in sign. For example, if $v_{t-1} > 0$, then apart from the disturbance ε_t it is clear that $v_t = a_2 v_{t-1} < 0$, since $a_2 < 0$. Finally, if $a_2 = 0$, decision rule (7) is the same as the previous rule (4).

The specialization inherent in the appropriations process allows some members of Congress to have an intimate knowledge of the budgetary processes of the agencies and the Budget Bureau. Thus, Congress might consider that part of the agency's request (x_t) which is not based on the previous year's appropriation or request. This occurs when Congress believes that this positive or negative remainder represents padding or when it desires to smooth out the agency's rate of growth. If Congress knows the decision rule that an agency uses to formulate its budgetary request, we can let λ_t represent a dummy variable defined as $\lambda_t = \xi_t$ if the agency uses decision rule (1); $\lambda_t = \beta_2(y_{t-1} - x_{t-1}) + \chi_t$ if the agency uses decision rule (2); and, $\lambda_t = \rho_t$ if the agency uses decision rule (2). Suppose that Congress appropriates, on the average, an amount which is a relatively fixed per-

centage of the agency's request plus a percentage of this (positive or negative) remainder λ_t. This behavior can be represented by the "as if" decision rule

$$y_t = a_3 x_t + a_4 \lambda_t + v_t \qquad (8)$$

The Congressional appropriation for an agency is a fixed mean percentage of the agency's request for a certain year plus a fixed mean percentage of a dummy variable which represents that part of the agency's request for the year at issue which is not part of the appropriation or request of the previous year plus a random variable representing the part of the appropriation attributable to the special circumstances of the year.

where v_t is a stochastic disturbance whose value in any particular year represents the part of the appropriation attributable to the agency's special circumstances of the year. One might expect that Congress takes only "partial" account of the remainder represented by λ_t, so $0 < a_4 < 1$.

III. EMPIRICAL RESULTS

Times series data for the period 1947–1963 were studied for fifty-six non defense agencies of the United States Government. The requests (x_t) of these agencies were taken to be the amounts presented to Congress in the President's budget. For eight sub-agencies from the National Institutes of Health, data for a shorter period of time were considered, and the requests (x_t) of these eight sub-agencies were taken to be their proposals to the Bureau of the Budget.[8] In all instances the Congressional decision variable (y_t) was taken to be the final appropriation before any supplemental additions. The total appropriations (without supplements) of the agencies studied amounted to approximately twenty-seven per cent of the nondefense budget in 1963. Over one-half of all nondefense agencies were investigated; the major omissions being the

Post Office and many independent agencies. A minimum of three agencies was examined from each of the Treasury, Justice, Interior, Agriculture, Commerce, Labor, and Health, Education and Welfare Departments.[9]

If the agency-Budget Bureau disturbance is independent of Congressional disturbance,[10] the use of ordinary least squares (OLS) to estimate most of the possible combinations of the proposed decision equations is justified. OLS is identical to the simultaneous full information maximum likelihood (FIML) technique for most of the present systems. This is not so, however, for some systems of equations because of the presence of an autocorrelated disturbance in one equation of the two and the consequent nonlinearity of the estimating equations. In equation (6) the stochastic disturbance for year t is a function of the value of the disturbance in the previous year. In a system of equations in which autocorrelation occurs in the first equation, an appropriate procedure is to use OLS to estimate the alternative proposals for the other equation, decide by the selection criteria which best specifies the data, use the knowledge of this structure to estimate the first equation, and then decide, through use of appropriate criteria, which version of the first equation best specifies the data.

The principal selection criterion we used is that of maximum (adjusted) correlation coefficient (R). For a given dependent variable this criterion leads one to select from alternative specifications of the explanatory variables, that specification which leads to the highest sample correlation coefficient. The estimations of the alternative specifications must, of course, be made from the same data.[11] The second criterion involves the use of the d-statistic test for serial correlation of the estimated residuals of a single equation.[12] This statistic tests the null hypothesis of residual independence against the alterna-

tive of serial correlation. We used the significance points for the d-statistic of Theil and Nagar.[13] When the d-statistic was found to be significant in fitting the Congressional decision equation (4) to an agency's data, it was always found that equation (7) best specified Congressional behavior with respect to the appropriations of that agency in the sense of yielding the maximum correlation coefficient. A third criterion is based on a test of the significance of the sample correlation between the residuals of (4) and the estimated λ_t of the equation selected previously for a given agency. David's significance points for this statistic were used to make a two-tailed test at the five per cent level of the null hypothesis that the residuals are uncorrelated.[14] When significant correlation occurred, it was always found that Congressional decision equation (8), in which a function of the deviation from the usual relationship between request and the previous year's appropriation enters explicitly, best specified appropriation behavior with respect to the agency in question.

The statistical procedures were programmed for the Carnegie Institute of Technology's Control Data G-21 electronic computer in the 20-Gate algebraic compiling language. The selection among alternate specifications according to the criteria established was not done automatically; otherwise all computations were performed by machine. Since the results for each agency are described in detail elsewhere,[15] and a full rendition would double the length of the paper, we must restrict ourselves to summary statements.

The empirical results support the hypothesis that, up to a random error of reasonable magnitude, the budgetary process of the United States government is equivalent to a set of temporally stable linear decision rules. Estimated correlation coefficients for the best specifications of each agency are generally high. Although the calculated values of the

Table 1. Best Specifications for Each Agency Are High

| | FREQUENCIES OF CORRELATION COEFFICIENTS | | | | | | | | | |
	$1 - .995$	$- .99$	$- .98$	$- .97$	$- .96$	$- .95$	$- .94$	$- .93$	$- .90$	$- .85 - 0$
Congressional	21	8	15	4	5	2	2	1	5	2	2
Agency-Bureau	9	2	2	8	5	2	4	3	5	11	10

multiple correlation coefficients (R's) tend to run higher in time series than in cross-sectional analysis, the results are good. We leave little of the variance statistically unexplained. Moreover the estimated standard deviations of the coefficients are usually much smaller than one-half of the size of the estimated coefficients, a related indication of good results. Table 1 presents the frequencies of the correlation coefficients.

The fits between the decision rules and the time series data for the Congressional decision equations are, in general, better than those for the agency-Bureau of the Budget equations. Of the 64 agencies and sub-agencies studied, there are only 14 instances in which the correlation coefficient for the agency (or sub-agency) equation was higher than the one for the corresponding Congressional equation. We speculate that the estimated variances of the disturbances of the agency-Budget Bureau decision rules are usually larger because the agencies are closer than Congress to the actual sources that seek

to add new programs or expand old ones.

Table 2 presents a summary of the combinations of the Agency-Bureau of the Budget and Congressional decision equations. For those agencies studied, the most popular combinations of behavior are the simple ones represented by equations (4) and (1) respectively. When Congress uses a sophisticated "gaming" strategy such as (7) or (8), the corresponding agency-Bureau of the Budget decision equation is the relatively simple (1). And, when Congress grants exactly or almost exactly the amount requested by an agency, the agency tends to use decision equation (3).

Our discussion thus far has assumed fixed values for the coefficients (parameters) of the equations we are using to explain the behavior underlying the budgetary process. In the light of the many important events occurring in the period from 1946 to 1963, however, it seems reasonable to suppose that the appropriations structure of many government agencies was altered. If this is

Table 2. Budgetary Behavior Is Simple

SUMMARY OF DECISION EQUATIONS				
Agency-Budget Bureau		1	2	3
	4	44*	1	8
Congress	7	1	0	0
	8	12	0	0

* Includes eight sub-agencies from the National Institutes of Health.

correct, the coefficients of the equations—literally, in this context, the values represented by the on-the-average percentages requested by the agencies and granted by Congress—should change from one period of time to the next. The equations would then be temporally stable for a period, but not forever. The year when the coefficient of an equation changes from one value to another is termed the "shift point." The time series we are using are so short that it is possible to find only one meaningful shift point in each of the two equations that describe the budget request and appropriation best fitting an agency. We, therefore, broke each time series into two parts and used Chow's F-statistic[16] to determine temporal stability by testing the null hypothesis that the underlying coefficients did not shift (against all alternatives) for the individual equations. We used four categories for the coefficients of a decision equation defined as follows:

Temporally very stable: The F-statistic is small and the coefficients estimated from the first and last parts of the series are virtually the same.

Temporally stable: The F-statistic is small, but the coefficients estimated from the first and last parts of the series appear to be different.

Not temporally stable: The F-statistic is large but not significant at the ten per cent level and the coefficients estimated from the first and last parts of series appear to be different.

Temporally unstable: The F-statistic is significant at the ten per cent level.

Of the Congressional decision equations, six were temporally very stable, 12 were temporally stable, 12 were not temporally stable, and 28 were temporally unstable. Of the agency-Bureau of the Budget decision equations, four were temporally very stable, 18 were temporally stable, 18 were not temporally stable, and 18 were temporally unstable.[17] Since a substantial

Table 3. Congressional Behavior Tends to Become More Sophisticated

FIRST PERIOD DECISION EQUATIONS

	1	2	3
4	45	0	10
7	1	0	0
8	2	0	0

SECOND PERIOD DECISION EQUATIONS

	1	2	3
4	35	1	9
7	1	0	0
8	12	0	0

majority of cases fall into the not temporally stable and temporally unstable categories, it is evident that while the process is temporally stable for short periods, it may not be stable for the whole period.

Table 3 presents a summary of the combinations of the agency-Bureau of the Budget and Congressional decision equations when each series is broken into two parts. These specifications are referred to as "first period" and "second period" for all agencies even though the years at which the time series were broken vary. While the most frequent combinations of behavior are the simple ones represented by equations (4) and (1) respectively, there is a marked tendency for Congressional behavior to become more sophisticated: the incidence of the gaming behavior represented by equation (8) increases over time.[18]

The budgetary process seems to become more linear over time in the sense that the importance of the "special circumstances" appears to diminish. Table 4 presents frequencies of the correlation coefficients for the first and second periods. Although

Table 4. The Budgetary Process Is Becoming More Linear

	FREQUENCIES OF CORRELATION COEFFICIENTS										
	$1 - .995$	$- .99$	$- .98$	$- .97$	$- .96$	$- .94$	$- .92$	$- .90$	$- .80$	$- .60$	$- 0$
First Period	9	5	8	5	3	6	8	4	18	24	21
Second Period	27	5	13	8	8	15	7	5	12	8	6

there is a different number of correlation coefficients in each period (111 in the first period and 114 in the second)[19] Table 4 shows clearly that fits are better for the second period, which is sufficient evidence of increasing linear tendencies. To us it seems reasonable to expect an increasing use of simplifying rules of thumb as the budget grows in size and the pressure of time on key decision makers increases. Yet this is only one of a number of possible explanations. For example, the data are not deflated for changes in the price level during the early years. Since there were larger increases in the price level during the early years, this might help explain why the fits are better during the second period.

When only one shift point is presumed, most shifts are discovered during the first two budgets of the Eisenhower Administration (1954–1955). Table 5 presents, for both Congressional and agency-Budget Bureau decision equations, frequencies of the shift points for (a) those equations whose coefficients are in the not temporally stable or temporally unstable categories and (b) those agencies for which the decision rules of the participants appeared to change. While it is certainly

possible that shift points do not occur as dramatically and as sharply as shown here, and that it may take several years for actual behavior to change noticeably, Table 5 nevertheless makes it clear that likely shifts are concentrated in the first period of the Eisenhower administration.

We said, in Section II, that we expected β_0, β_1, and β_3, to be greater than one, and β_2 to be negative. In 56 instances this expectation is satisfied, but eight exceptions were noted. In the two cases where the estimated $\beta_3 < 1$, explanations are immediately available. First, the fit for the Bureau of Employment Security is not good. Second, the Office of Territories evidences most un-Parkinsonian behavior: its activities decline with a decrease in the number of territories. In the six other exceptions, the estimated coefficient is $\beta_0 < 1$. For three of these, Congress tends to appropriate an amount greater than the request, and two of the three represent an interesting phenomenon. When those parts of requests and appropriations directly related to loans are omitted from the data for both the Rural Electrification Administration and the Federal Housing Administration, the estimated coefficients are of the magnitudes expected with

Table 5. Likely Shift Points Are Concentrated in the First Years of the Eisenhower Administration

	FREQUENCIES OF SHIFT POINTS															
Year	48	49	50	51	52	53	54	55	56	57	58	59	60	61	62	T
Congressional	0	2	3	1	0	1	17	16	1	1	3	0	0	1	0	46 (40)
Agency-Bureau	0	2	4	0	2	3	15	13	3	0	2	1	0	2	1	37 (36)

$\beta_0 > 1$ and $a_0 < 1$. However, when the data relating to loans are include, then $\beta_0 < 1$ and $a_0 > 1$. Apparently, Congress favors the loan programs more than do the agencies or the Budget Bureau.

As a rule, the d-statistics resulting from fitting the best specifications were not significant. It would thus appear that all major underlying trended variables (with the possible exception of variables with the same trend) have been accounted for by these specifications. When an exception to this rule did exist, the authors made a careful examination of the residuals in an effort to determine the reason for such a situation. It appeared that in most of these instances the cause was either (a) that the coefficients shifted slowly over several years and not abruptly at one point in time, or (b) that restricting the search to only one shift point left undetected an additional shift either very early or very late in the series.

In an attempt to unmask the trended variable most likely (in our opinion) to have been ignored, and to cast some light upon the notion of "fair share," final appropriations y_t for each agency were regressed on total nondefense appropriations z_t. This time series was taken from the *Statistical Abstract of the United States*. The results were poor. Indeed, the sample correlations between y_t and z_t are usually worse than those between y_t and x_t. Moreover, the d-statistics are usually highly significant and the residual patterns for the regression show the agency's proportion of the nondefense budget to be either increasing or decreasing over time. However, it should be noted that even those exceptional cases where the agency trend is close to that of the total nondefense appropriation do not invalidate the explicit decision structure fitted here. A similar study, with similar results, was conducted at the departmental level by regressing y_t for the eight National Institutes of Health on y_t for the Public Health Service, the agency of which they are a part. Finally, the y_t for selected pairs of agencies with "similar" interests were regressed on each other with uniformly poor results.

Although empirical evidence indicates that our models describe the budgetary process of the United States government, we are well aware of certain deficiencies in our work. One deficiency, omission of certain agencies from the study, is not serious because over one-half of all nondefense agencies were investigated. Nevertheless, the omission of certain agencies may have left undiscovered examples of additional decision rules. We will shortly study all agencies whose organizational structure can be traced. We will also include supplemental appropriations.

A more serious deficiency may lie in the fact that the sample sizes, of necessity, are small. The selection criterion of maximum sample correlation, therefore, lacks proper justification, and is only acceptable because of the lack of a better criterion. Further, full-information maximum likelihood estimators, and especially biased ones, even when they are known to be consistent, are not fully satisfactory in such a situation, although they may be the best available. However, the remedy for these deficiencies must await the results of future theoretical research on explosive or evolutionary processes.

IV. THE DEVIANT CASES AND PREDICTION: INTERPRETATION OF THE STOCHASTIC DISTURBANCES

The intention of this section is to clarify further the interpretation of the stochastic disturbances as special or unusual circumstances represented by random variables. While those influences present at a constant level during the period serve only to affect the magnitude of the coefficients, the special circumstances have an important, if subsidiary, place in these models. We have indicated that although outside observers can view the effects of special circumstances as a random variable, anyone familiar with all the facts available to the decision-makers at the time would be able to explain the special circumstances. It seems reasonable therefore to examine instances where, in estimating the coefficients, we find that the estimated values of the stochastic disturbances assume a large positive or negative value. Such instances appear as deviant cases in the sense that Congress or the agency-Budget Bureau actors affected by special circumstances (large positive or negative values of the random variable) do not appear to be closely following their usual decision rule at that time but base their decisions mostly on these circumstances. The use of case studies for the analyses of deviant phenomena, of course, presupposes our ability to explain most budgeting decisions by our original formulations. Deviant cases, then, are those instances in which particular decisions do not follow our equations. It is possible to determine these deviant instances simply by examining the residuals of the fitted equations: one observes a plot of the residuals, selects those which appear as extreme positive or negative values, determines the year to which these extreme residuals refer, and then examines evidence in the form of testimony at the Appropriations Committees, newspaper accounts, and other sources. In this way it is possible to determine at least some of the circumstances of a budgetary decision and to investigate whether or not the use of the random variables is appropriate.[20]

Finally, it should be pointed out that in our model the occurrence of extreme disturbances represents deviant cases, or the temporary setting aside of their usual decision rules by the decision-makers in the process, while coefficient shifts represent a change (not necessarily in form) of these rules.

From the residuals of one-half of the estimated Congressional decision equations, a selection of 55 instances (approximately 14 per cent of the 395 Congressional decisions under consideration) were identified as deviant.[21] Table 6 shows the yearly frequency of the occurrence of deviant cases. It is apparent that deviancy grows in years of political change: in 1948 the Republican 80th Congress made a determined effort to reduce appropriations submitted by the Democratic President; the years 1953 through 1955 mark the beginning of Eisenhower's Presidency; the large number of deviant cases in 1962 and 1963 are related to the accession to office of Kennedy and Johnson. The latter category of deviant cases, we will explain later, may be mis-classifications in the sense that the passage of time and the corresponding accumulation of additional evidence may reveal shift points, i.e., changes in the "average percentages" of the decision processes, rather than "exceptional circumstances." Nevertheless, this fact causes no particular problem in light of our purposes here, and the cases may be viewed as if they are appropriately classified.

Table 7 categorizes the cases according to estimates of why deviance occurred. It should be noted that the largest category, significant policy change, involves the

Table 6. Deviant Cases Cluster in Years of Political Change

YEAR	'48	'49	'50	'51	'52	'53	'54	'55	'56	'57	'58	'59	'60	'61	'62	'63
Number of Cases	8	2	1	1	1	4	6	4	1	1	2	3	4	2	8	7

Table 7. Deviant Cases May Be Viewed as Random Events

CATEGORIES OF DEVIANCE	NUMBER OF CASES
Significant policy change	20
Fiscal policy change	8
Felt need of Congressional supervision	6
Amended estimate due to a time factor	6
Single event	5
Large new legislative program	4
Reorganization of agency	1
Nonidentifiable	5
Total $N =$	55

lack of a budgetary base for the agency in question. In order to highlight the meaning we give to random phenomena, an illustration of each category follows. This analysis explains why, although the deviant cases are understandable to an experienced observer or participant, an outsider would have to regard them as essentially random disturbances to an otherwise deterministic system. Indeed, not two events in the categories of Table 7 are likely, *a priori*, either to be the same or to occur in any particular year.

Significant Policy Change

The Southwestern Power Administration is typical of agencies whose appropriations fluctuate unduly because basic policy is being negotiated. Deviance was evident in 1948, 1949, 1954, and 1955. The SPA continually requested funds for the building of transmission lines, and Congress repeatedly eliminated the request from their appropriations, insisting that private enterprise would supply the necessary facilities. In 1948 the Bureau of the Budget recommended $7,600,000 of which only $125,000 was appropriated, with stringent and explicit instructions that printing and mailing of materials calculated to increase clientele among rural and municipal electrical cooperatives cease.

The Korean War increased demands for electric power. Deviance occurred in 1955 not because of appropriations cuts but because of House floor amendments and Senate Appropriations Committee increases. Public policy then became stabilized as Congress established a budgetary base. The following years fit our equations.

Fiscal Policy Changes

The Foreign Agricultural Service's 1963 appropriation is deviant in appropriation figures, but, because $3,117,000 was provided by transferring funds from Sec. 32, the total budget for FAS is close to the Budget Bureau's initial request.

Felt Need of Congressional Supervision

The House Committee reports on Office of Territories for 1953 show a lack of confidence in the agency. The tenor can be judged by House Report 1622: "The Department was advised last year that the Committee did not intend to provide appropriations for an endless chain of capital investment in the Alaska Railroads. Army testimony was conflicting as to the need for a road and railways. There is need for a coordinated plan before the Committee can act intelligently with regard to the railroad."

Amended Estimate Due to Time Factor

Typical of this type of deviance is the Commodity Stabilization Service's appropriation for 1958. On the basis of figures from County Agricultural Agents, Secretary Ezra Taft Benson scaled down his request from $465 million to $298 million. A more accurate estimate was made possible because of added time.

Large New Legislative Program

This is especially apt to affect an agency if it is required to implement several new programs simultaneously The Commissioner of Education said in reference to the student loan program, "We have no way of knowing because we never had such a program, and many of the institutions never had them." The NDEA Act alone had ten new entitlements.

Reorganization of an Agency

The only example is the Agricultural Marketing Service's appropriation for 1962. Funds were reduced because of a consolidation of diverse activities by the Secretary of Agriculture and not through reorganization as a result of Congressional demands.

Non-Identifiable

This applies, for example, to the Public Health Service where a combination of lesser factors converge to make the agency extremely deviant for 1959, 1960, 1961, and 1962. Among the apparent causes of deviance are publicity factors, the roles of committee chairmen in both House and Senate, a high percentage of professionals in the agency, and the excellent press coverage of health research programs. No one factor appears primarily responsible for the deviance.

Our models are not predictive but explanatory. The alternative decision equations can be tried and the most appropriate one used when data on requests and appropriations are available. The appropriate equation explains the data in that, given a good fit, the process behaves "as if" the data were generated according to the equation. Thus, our explanatory models are backward looking: given a history of requests and appropriations, the data appear as if they were produced by the proposed and appropriately selected scheme.

The models are not predictive because the budget process is only temporally stable for short periods. We have found cases in which the coefficients of the equations change, i.e., cases in which there are alterations in the realized behavior of the processes. We have no *a priori* theory to predict the occurrence of these changes, but merely our *ad hoc* observation that most occurred during Eisenhower's first term. Predictions are necessarily based upon the estimated values of the coefficients and on the statistical properties of the stochastic disturbance (sometimes called the error term). Without a scientific method of predicting the shift points in our model, we cannot scientifically say that a request or an appropriation for some future year will fall within a prescribed range with a given level of confidence. We can predict only when the process remains stable in time. If the decision rules of the participants have changed, our predictions may be worthless: in our models, either the coefficients have shifted or, more seriously, the scheme has changed. Moreover, it is extremely difficult to determine whether or not the observation latest in time represents a shift point. A sudden change may be the result either of a change in the underlying process or a temporary setting aside of the usual decision rules in light of special circumstances. The data for several subsequent years are necessary to determine with any accuracy whether a change in decision rules indeed occurred.

It is possible, of course, to make conditional predictions by taking the estimated coefficients from the last shift point and assuming that no shift will occur. Limited predictions as to the next year's requests and appropriations could be made and might turn out to be reasonably accurate. However, scholarly efforts would be better directed toward knowledge of why, where, and when changes in the process occur so that accurate predictions might be made.

The usual interpretation of stochastic (in lieu of deterministic) models may, of course, be made for the models of this paper, i.e., not all factors influencing the budgetary process have been included in the equations. Indeed, many factors often deemed most important such as pressure from interest groups, are ignored. Part of the reason for this lies in the nature of the models: they describe the decision process in skeleton form. Further, since the estimations are made, of necessity, on the basis of time series data, it is apparent that any influences that were present at a constant level during the period are not susceptible to discovery by these methods. However, these influences do affect the budgetary process by determining the size of the estimated coefficients. Thus, this paper, in making a comparative study of the estimated coefficients for the various agencies, suggests a new way of approaching constant influences.

No theory can take every possible unexpected circumstance into account, but our theory can be enlarged to include several classes of events. The concentration of shift points in the first years of the Eisenhower administration implies that an empirical theory should take account of changes in the political party controlling the White House and Congress.

We also intend to determine indices of clientele and confidence so that their effects, when stable over time, can be gauged.[22] Presidents sometimes attempt to gear their budgetary requests to fit their desired notion of the rate of expenditures appropriate for the economic level they wish the country to achieve. By checking the Budget Message, contemporary accounts, and memoirs, we hope to include a term (as a dummy variable) which would enable us to predict high and low appropriations rates depending on the President's intentions.

V. SIGNIFICANCE OF THE FINDINGS

We wish to consider the significance of (a) the fact that it is possible to find equations which explain major facets of the federal budgetary process and (b) the particular equations fitted to the time series. We will take up each point in order.

A. It Is Possible to Find Equations for the Budgetary Process

There has been controversy for some time over whether it is possible to find laws, even of a probabilistic character, which explain important aspects of the political process. The greatest skepticism is reserved for laws which would explain how policy is made or account for the outcomes of the political process. Without engaging in further abstract speculation, it is apparent that the best kind of proof would be a demonstration of the existence of some such laws. This, we believe, we have done.

Everyone agrees that the federal budget is terribly complex. Yet, as we have shown, the budgetary process can be described by very simple decision rules. Work done by Simon, Newell, Reitman, Clarkson, Cyert and March, and others, on simulating the solution of complex problems, has demonstrated that in complicated situations human beings are likely to use heuristic rules or rules of thumb to enable them to find satisfactory solutions.[23] Braybrooke and Lindblom have provided convincing arguments on this score for the political process.[24] Wildavsky's interviews with budget officers indicate that they, too, rely extensively on aids to calculation.[25] It is not surprising, therefore, as our work clearly shows, that a set of simple decision rules can explain or represent the behavior of participants in the federal budgetary process in their efforts to reach decisions in complex situations.

The most striking fact about the equations is their simplicity. This is perhaps partly because of the possibility that more complicated decision procedures are reserved for special circumstances represented by extreme values of the random variable. However, the fact that the decision rules generally fit the data very well is an indication that these simple equations have considerable explanatory power. Little of the variance is left unexplained.

What is the significance of the fact that the budgetary process follows rather simple laws for the general study of public policy? Perhaps the significance is limited; perhaps other policy processes are far more complex and cannot be reduced to simple laws. However, there is no reason to believe that this is the case. On the contrary, when one considers the central importance of budgeting in the political process—few activities can be carried on without funds—and the extraordinary problems of calculation which budgeting presents, a case might better be made for its comparative complexity than for its simplicity. At present it is undoubtedly easier to demonstrate that laws, whether simple or complex, do underlie the budgetary process than to account for other classes of policy outcomes, because budgeting provides units of analysis (appropriations requests and grants) that are readily amenable to formulating and testing propositions statistically. The dollar figures are uniform, precise, numerous, comparable with others, and, most important, represent an important class of policy outcomes. Outside of matters involving voting or attitudes, however, it is difficult to think of general statements about public policy that can be said to have been verified. The problem is not that political science lacks propositions which might be tested. Works of genuine distinction like Herring's *The Politics of Democracy*, Truman's *The Governmental Process*, Hyneman's *Bureaucracy in a Democracy*, Neustadt's *Presidential Power*, Buchanan and Tullock's *The Calculus of Consent*, contain implicit or explicit propositions which appear to be at least as interesting as (and potentially more interesting than) the ones tested in this paper. The real difficulty is that political scientists have been unable to develop a unit of analysis (there is little agreement on what constitutes a decision) that would permit them to test the many propositions they have at their command. By taking one step toward demonstrating what can be done when a useful unit of analysis has been developed, we hope to highlight the tremendous importance that the development of units of analysis would have for the study of public policy.

B. The Significance of the Particular Equations

Let us examine the concepts that have been built into the particular equations. First, the importance of the previous year's appropriation is an indication that the notion of the base is a very significant explanatory concept for the behavior of the agencies and the Budget Bureau. Similarly, the agency-Budget Bureau requests are important variables in the decisions of Congress. Second, some of the equations, notably (7) and (8) for Congress, and (2) for the agency-Budget Bureau, incorporate strategic concepts. On some occasions, then, budgeting on the federal level does involve an element of gaming. Neither the Congress nor the agencies can be depended upon to "take it lying down." Both attempt to achieve their own aims and goals. Finally, the budgetary process is only temporally stable. The occurrence of most changes of decision rules at a change in administration indicates that alterations in political party and personnel occupying high offices can exert some (but not total) influence upon the budgetary process.

Our decision rules may serve to cast some light on the problem of "power" in political analysis. The political scientist's dilemma is that it is hardly possible to think about politics without some concept of power, but that it is extremely difficult to create and then to use an operational definition in empirical work. Hence,

James March makes the pessimistic conclusion that "The Power of Power" as a political variable may be rather low.[26] The problem is particularly acute when dealing with processes in which there is a high degree of mutual dependence among the participants. In budgeting, for example, the agency-Budget Bureau and Congressional relationships hardly permit a strict differentiation of the relative influence of the participants. Indeed, our equations are built on the observation of mutual dependence; and the empirical results show that how the agency-Budget Bureau participants behave depends on what Congress does (or has done) and that how Congress behaves depends on what the agency-Budget Bureau side is doing (or has done). Yet the concept of power does enter the analysis in calculations of the importance that each participant has for the other; it appears in the relative magnitude of the estimated coefficients. "Power" is saved because it is not required to carry too great a burden. It may be that theories which take power into account as part of the participants' calculations will prove of more use to social science research than attempts to measure the direct exercise of influence. At least we can say that theories of calculation, which animate the analysis of *The Politics of the Budgetary Process* and of this paper, do permit us to state and test propositions about the outcomes of a political process. Theories of power do not yet appear to have gone this far.

In the field of economics, work has long been done on organizational units called industrial firms. In political science, however, despite the flurry of excitement over organization theory, there has been no empirical demonstration of the value of dealing with various public organizations as comparable entities. By viewing governmental bodies not as distinctly different agencies but as having certain common properties (here, in budgetary calculations and strategies), we hope to have shown the utility to empirical theory of treating organizations *qua* organizations. Despite the differences among the organizations studied—some follow different decision rules and are affected by different random disturbances—it is analytically significant to explain their behavior by virtue of features they share as organizations.

It should be clear that we are dealing with general models of organizations and not with individual policies. One cannot say anything directly about water, land, health, or other transportation policies, from inspection of our models of a given agency. But this limit is not inherent in our approach. It is possible, for example, to calculate from our data present and future estimated rates of growth for virtually all domestic agencies since World War II. Agencies with similar growth rates may be segregated and examined for common features. The growth rates of agencies in similar areas of policy, such as public health and natural resources, may be compared, and the fortunes of policies in those areas deduced. Individual agencies may be broken down into sub-units or the courses of certain policy programs charted to explain the differential treatment they receive. While pursuing this type of analysis, we hope to have one advantage. We shall be working from a general model of the budgetary process. It will, therefore, be possible for us to locate our efforts within this larger scheme. To know whether one is dealing with a normal or deviant case, to know one's position in this larger universe, is to be able to give more general meaning to the individual and particular circumstances with which one must be involved in handling small parts of the total process.

The general mode of analysis we have developed here may be pursued in many different contexts. Similar studies could be undertaken in state and local governments as well as foreign countries.[27] Private firms and public agencies may be conceptualized in parallel terms through their budgetary mechanisms.[28] By comparing the processes underlying budgeting in a variety of political and economic systems, it may be possible to state more elegantly and precisely the conditions under which different forms of behavior would prevail.

APPENDIX

On the Definition of Terms

Certain of the technical terms required in the paper are here given informal definitions.

COEFFICIENT: A coefficient of an equation is a parameter or number that is said to have some given but usually unknown value. The α's and β's used in the models are the coefficients of the equations in which they appear. Since the values of the coefficients are usually unknown, they must be estimated statistically from available data. In this paper, the coefficients (α's and β's) are average representations of the real percentages of requests made by agencies and appropriations granted by Congress.

LINEAR: An equation is linear if it has no square or higher order terms. Thus $y = \alpha x$ is linear whereas $y = \alpha x^2$ is not linear. (Remember that for two variables linear means "in a straight line.")

STOCHASTIC: A variable is stochastic, a term meaning random, if the particular value that it assumes is a matter of chance and the set of values that it can assume is capable of being described by a probability distribution or density. The distribution gives the probability of the random variable assuming the various allowable values.

VARIANCE: The variance is defined as $E(x - \mu)^2$, where x is a random variable, μ is its mean, and E stands for "the expected value of." One can think of variance as a measure of the dispersion or spread of the probability distribution governing the random variable.

LINEAR REGRESSION EQUATION: A linear regression equation is a particular model of the relationship between two or more variables. The model has the form

$$y_i = \beta_0 + \beta_1 x_{1i} + \beta_2 x_{2i} + \cdots + \beta_k x_{ki} + \varepsilon_i$$

where β_0 is the unknown constant term, the other β's are unknown coefficients, and ε_i is a random variable. In this notation, y_i represents the value of the dependent variable on the ith observation and $x_{1i}, x_{2i}, \ldots, x_{ki}$ represents in a similar manner the values of the independent variables for the same observation. From a set of n observations, each of which consists of particular values for the dependent and independent variables, the regression operation estimates values for the unknown coefficients and the constant term; the regression operation also estimates n values of the random variable, which are called residuals. When the sets of observations on the dependent and independent variables refer to successive periods, the observations are called time series and we say that the values of y_i are generated by a stochastic process.

STOCHASTIC DISTURBANCE: This is a name for the random variable in a regression equation. It is also called the error term. Thus, in the equation $y_t = \alpha x_t + \varepsilon_t$, the term ε_t represents a stochastic disturbance (or random variable), which is usually assumed to be normally distributed with mean zero and finite but unknown variance.

DIFFERENCE EQUATION: An equation which describes the value of a variable in one period in terms of the value of either that variable or another variable in some previous period is a difference equation. For example, $x_t = \beta y_{t-1}$ is a difference equation. If a random variable is present, the equation is called a stochastic difference equation. Thus, if ε is a random variable, $x_t = \beta y_{t-1} + \varepsilon_t$ is a stochastic difference equation and the successive values of x may be thought of as a stochastic process.

UNSTABLE, EVOLUTIONARY, OR EXPLOSIVE PROCESS: A process is said to be unstable, evolutionary, or explosive if the expected values of the successive values taken by the process are increasing. For example, the stochastic difference equation $y_t = \gamma y_{t-1} + \varepsilon_i$, where $\gamma > 1$, generates an evolutionary process.

SERIALLY INDEPENDENT: If successive realizations of a random variable are serially independent, the value it assumes in one period is independent of the value it assumed in a previous period. This can be described mathematically as $E(x_t | x_{t-1}) = E(x_t)$, meaning that the expected value of random variable x at period t does not depend upon the value that the random variable x assumed at period $t - 1$. It follows that the expected simple correlation between x_t and x_{t-1} will be zero, if the random variable x is serially independent. For example, in our models, the assumption of serial independence of the disturbances reflects the belief that special circumstances in one year either do not affect special circumstances in succeeding years or that their influence enters explicitly into our model (as in equation (8) and the equations of footnote 4).

The Meaning of a Markov Process

For our purposes, a Markov process generating some random variable x is a process for which the value of x at time t depends upon the values assumed by that random variable at one or more earlier periods plus the value assumed by some stochastic disturbance at time t. A Markov process is "first order" if the variable x_t takes on a value that depends only upon the value of the variable x_{t-1} in the pre-

vious period plus the value of a stochastic disturbance at time t. Thus

$$x_t = \alpha x_{t-1} + \varepsilon_t$$

is a first order Markov process, where ε_t is a random variable with a given distribution and α is a nonzero constant. A second order Markov process can be described by

$$x_t = \alpha_1 x_{t-1} + \alpha_2 x_{t-2} + \varepsilon_t$$

where both α_1 and α_2 are nonzero constants. The value of the variable x_t now depends upon its values in two previous periods.

On the Meaning of Goodness of Fit

An intuitive notion of good fit for a linear regression equation is that in a scatter diagram the observations should cluster about the fitted line. Probably the most popular measure of good fit is the square of the multiple correlation coefficient (R^2), which may often be interpreted as the percentage of the variance of the dependent variable that is explained by the postulated linear relationship (regression). For our models, however, this interpretation is not valid, although the adjusted R gives a rough measure of the goodness of fit. The closer to 1 that the adjusted R is, the better the fit.

On Standard Deviations of Coefficient Estimates

Speaking roughly, these standard deviations measure the reliability of the estimates of the coefficients. The smaller the estimated standard deviation, the more accurate the estimated coefficient is likely to be. If we had another series of data generated from the same process, the smaller the standard deviation of the coefficient (estimated from the first data) in relation to the size of this coefficient, the more likely it is that a new estimate made on the basis of the hypothetical new series of data would be close to the estimate made from the original data. Generally, one hopes the estimated standard deviation of the coefficient is at least as small as one-half the size of the estimated coefficient.

On Biased and Unbiased Estimators

Think of the problem of trying to determine the average IQ of students at a large university. Suppose the administration would not allow access to records and one did not wish to give IQ tests to all students. One might select a certain number of students at random (a sample) and given them the tests. The test scores of these students are sample observations. One might compute the average of these test scores and claim that he has an estimate of the mean IQ of all students at the University. The estimator is the formula for the average of the sample observations. If he repeated the process, taking a new sample, it is possible that the estimator would produce a slightly different estimate of the mean. However, the estimator would still have a certain expected value. If the expected value of the estimator can be proven to equal the population parameter (the mean IQ of all the students example) then the estimator is said to be unbiased. Otherwise, it is said to be biased.

On Consistent Estimators

An estimator is consistent if it approaches nearer and nearer to the true value of a parameter (in our case, a coefficient) as the size of the sample is increased. A consistent estimator may be biased (it may approach closer to but never actually equal the parameter), but if the sample from which it is estimated is large enough this bias will be small.

On Least-Squares Estimators and the Meaning of Temporally Stable Processes

This discussion specifically refers to process (4) although it is equally applicable to all processes. Consider

$$y_t = \alpha_0 x_t + \eta_t$$

where α represents the coefficient of the equation or the "on the average" percentage of the request that is granted by Congress and η_t is a stochastic disturbance (random variable) that represents the variation in the request over time that may be assigned to special circumstances. We assume that η_t is normally distributed with mean zero and finite but unknown variance. The coefficient is unknown and must be estimated on the basis of available data. The data are the requests x_t and the corresponding appropriations y_t. We do not know the values assumed by the stochastic disturbance. Our estimates of the values assumed by the stochastic disturbance are the residuals of the fitted regression equation. If, for a given agency, we observe the requests and appropriations over a specified period of time, we could plot the data in a scatter diagram (Figure 1). The line drawn in Figure 1 would be our estimated line (the line resulting from our estimate of α).

The vertical positive and negative distances of the points from the fitted line are the values of the residuals, our estimates of the values assumed by the stochastic disturbance. The least-squares estimates of the coefficients are those values of the coefficients which make the sum of the squares of these distances a minimum. In Figure 1 there is no discernible pattern of departure of the points from the line.

Thus, we can say that the process is temporally stable (i.e., fixed over time)

Figure 1

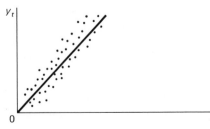

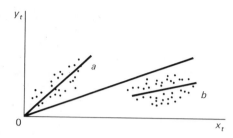

Figure 2

and presume that the true value of the coefficient (we know only its estimated value) remained constant during the period under consideration. A temporally stable process is one in which the value of the true coefficient does not change during the period under consideration. This should not be confused with a stable or nonevolutionary process, i.e., one whose values do not tend to grow, but fluctuate about some level.

If we again plotted the requests and appropriations data for an agency and found the results to be as in Figure 2, the longest line would represent our first fitted equation (or the equation resulting from our first estimate of the value of the coefficient). The points (alternately the residuals) form a pattern of departure from the fitted line. In the early years (a) they fall mostly above the line and in the later years (b) they fall mostly below the line. The process must have been temporally unstable for the period as a whole, i.e., the coefficient had one true value during the first years of the period and a different true value during the last years.

A temporally unstable process is one in which the true coefficient assumes two or more values during the period under consideration. Since we only know the estimated coefficient, we must examine the residuals to determine whether such a pattern is present. Then, we select what appears to be the probable year of change, and fit two lines such as those drawn in above. We then compute the F-statistic to

make our statistical test to determine, at a given level of significance, whether or not the true value of the coefficient shifted. If it was found to shift, the process was temporally stable for some period of time but not necessarily for the entire series of time periods examined.

The Meaning of a Shift Point and a Break Point

The two second lines fitted to Figure 2 represent the true process. The year during which the coefficient changes (the year when the pattern shifts from clustering about line (a) to clustering about line (b)) is referred to as a shift point. If what appears at first to be a shift in the true value of the coefficient is actually an alteration in behavior so that one equation fits the first sub-period and another equation must be used for the second sub-period, we still refer to the year of the change in realized behavior as a shift point. Break point is the term used to describe a suspected shift point but for which the F-test indicates that the true coefficient value did not shift.

NOTES

1 See the Appendix for explanations of terms and concepts.
2 The description which follows is taken from Aaron Wildavsky, *The Politics of the Budgetary Process* (Boston, 1964). Portions of the comments on the House Appropriations Committee are from Richard Fenno, "The House Appropriations Committee as a Political System: The Problem of Integration," this *Review*, 56 (1962), 310–324.
3 See H. Thiel, *Linear Aggregation of Economic Relations* (Amsterdam, 1954).
4 Our subsequent discussion of "shift" or "break" points should also make clear that it is not realistic to expect meaningful time series of great length to be accumulated for most agencies in the United States government.
5 Since some readers may not be familiar with the notation we are using, a brief explanation may be in order. As a co-

efficient of the equation, β_2 is an unknown number that must be estimated from the data, and this coefficient multiplies another number $(y_{t-1} - x_{t-1})$ that may be computed by subtracting last year's request from last year's appropriation. We want the equation to say that the agency will try to counteract large changes in their appropriations by changing their normal requests in the next year. If the agency asks for much more than it thinks it will get and its request is cut, for example, the expression $(y_{t-1} - x_{t-1})$ will be a negative number written in symbolic form as $(y_{t-1} - x_{t-1}) < 0$. A rule of multiplication says that a negative number multiplied by another negative number gives a positive number. If an agency pads its request, however, it presumably follows a cut with a new request which incorporates an additional amount to make allowance for future cuts. In order to represent this behavior, that is to come out with a positive result incorporating the concept of padding, the unknown coefficient β_2 must be negative ($\beta_2 < 0$).

6 The agency that favors its own programs should increase its requests over time. In the absence of the stochastic disturbance (when the random variable is 0), the request in a given year should be larger than the request in the previous year so that $x_t > x_{t-1}$. Therefore, the unknown coefficient β_3 must be larger than one ($\beta_3 > 1$) since it multiplies last year's request.

7 Other gaming strategies are easily proposed. Suppose, for example, that a given agency believes that it knows the decision rule that Congress uses in dealing with it, and that this decision rule can be represented by one of (4), (7), or (8) above. Presume, for reasons analogous to those outlined for (8), that this agency desires to take into account that positive or negative portion of the previous year's appropriation y_{t-1} that was not based on the previous year's request x_{t-1}. This consideration suggests

$$x_t = \beta_4 y_{t-1} + \beta_5 \Delta_{t-1} + \delta_t$$

as an agency decision rule where Δ_{t-1} is a dummy variable representing in year $t-1$ the term not involving x_{t-1} in one of (4), (7), or (8) above. If one believes that agency and Bureau of the Budget personnel are sufficiently well acquainted with the senators and congressmen to be able to predict the value of the current stochastic disturbance, then it becomes reasonable to examine a decision rule of the form

$$x_t = \beta_6 y_{t-1} + \beta_7 \Delta_t + \sigma_t$$

where Δ_t is defined as above. No evidence of either form of behavior was found, however, among the agencies that were investigated. We also estimated the parameters of the third order autoregressive scheme for the requests of an individual agency,

$$x_t = \beta_8 x_{t-1} + \beta_9 x_{t-2} + \beta_{10} x_{t-3} + \tau_t$$

in an attempt to discover if naive models would fit as well as those above. In no case did this occur and generally the fits for this model were very poor. A similar scheme was estimated for the appropriations y_t of an individual agency with similar results with respect to equations (4), (7), and (8) above. Since the "d" statistic suggests that no higher order Markov process would be successful, no other rules for agency behavior were tried.

8 Agency proposals to the Bureau of the Budget are not reported to the public and could be obtained only for these eight sub-agencies.

9 Three interrelated difficulties arise in the analysis of the time series data x_t, y_t for an agency. The first problem is the choice of a technique for estimating the parameters of the alternate schemes in some optimal fashion. Given these estimates and their associated statistics, the second problem is the choice of criteria for selecting the model best specifying the system underlying the data. Finally, one is faced with the problem of examining the variability of the underlying parameters of the best specification. We believe that our solution to these problems, while far from optimal, is satisfactory given the present state of econometric knowledge. See our presentation in "On the Process of Budgeting: An Empirical Study of Congressional Appropriations," by Otto Davis, M. A. H. Dempster, and Aaron Wildavsky, to appear in Gordon Tullock (ed.), *Papers on Non-Market Decision Making*, Thomas Jefferson Center, University of Virginia. See especially section 4 and the appendix by Dempster, which contains discussions and derivations of estimation procedures, selection criteria and test statistics for the processes in Section II of this paper.

10 We make the assumption that these two disturbances are independent throughout

the paper. Notice, however, that dependence between the disturbances explicitly enters decision equation (8) of section II and those of footnote 7. For these equations, the assumption refers to the disturbance of the current year. That is, we allow the possibility that special circumstances may affect a single participant (Bureau of the Budget or Congress) as well as both. When the latter case occurred, our selection criteria resulted in the choice of equation (8) as best specifying Congressional behavior.

11 We are estimating the unknown values of the coefficients (or parameters) of regression equations for each agency. All of our estimators are biased. We use biased estimators for the simple reason that no unbiased estimators are known. The property of consistency is at least a small comfort. All of our estimators are consistent. It might be noted that all unbiased estimators are consistent, but not all consistent estimators are unbiased.

12 This statistic is known as the Durbin–Watson ratio. A description of the test may be found in J. Johnston, *Econometric Methods* (New York, 1963), p. 92.

13 H. Theil and A. L. Nagar, "Testing the Independence of Regressional Disturbances," *Journal of the American Statistical Association*, 56 (1961), 793–806. These significance points were used to construct further significance points when necessary. See Davis, Dempster, and Wildavsky, *op. cit.*

14 The test is described in T. W. Anderson, *An Introduction to Multivariate Analysis* (New York, 1958), pp. 69–71. See Dempster's appendix to Davis, Dempster, and Wildavsky, *op. cit.*, for some justification of the use of the test.

15 See Davis, Dempster, and Wildavsky, *op. cit.*

16 G. C. Chow, "Tests of Equality between Sets of Coefficients in Two Linear Regressions," *Econometrica*, 28 (1960), 591–605, and the appendix to Davis, Dempster, and Wildavsky, *op. cit.*

17 In a few instances an inspection of the residuals indicated that a shift point occurred so early or so late in the series that it was not possible to compute a meaningful stationarity F-statistic. In these few cases the deviant observations were dropped and the usual analysis performed on the shortened time series. Thus we "forced" a break in every case in order to perform subsequent operations.

18 The apparent discrepancy between the latter part of Table 3 and Table 1 is caused by the fact that for two agencies, the Bureau of the Census and the Office of Education, although the agency-Bureau of the Budget decision equations are temporally stable and best specified as (1), when a shift point is forced, the criteria indicate (3) for the latter period

19 Some of the ,shift points appeared to occur so early in the series that it was not possible to calculate a correlation coefficient.

20 The importance of analyzing deviant cases is suggested in: Milton M. Gordon, "Sociological Law and the Deviant Case," *Sociometry*, 10 (1947); Patricia Kendall and Katharine Wolf, "The Two Purposes of Deviant Case Analysis," in Paul F. Lazarsfeld and Morris Rosenberg (eds.), *The Language of Social Research* (Glencoe, 1962), pp. 103–137; Paul Horst, *The Prediction of Personal Adjustment: A Survey of the Logical Problems and Research Techniques* (New York, 1941); and Seymour Lipset, Martin Trow, and James Coleman, *Union Democracy* (New York, 1960).

21 We are indebted to Rose M. Kelly, a graduate student in the Department of Political Science, University of California, Berkeley, who did the research on the deviant cases and provided the data for Tables 6 and 7.

22 See Wildavsky, *op. cit.*, pp. 64–68, for a discussion of clientele and confidence. In his forthcoming book, *The Power of the Purse* (Boston, 1966), Richard Fenno provides further evidence of the usefulness of these categories.

23 Geoffrey P. E. Clarkson, *Portfolio Selection: A Simulation of Trust Investment* (Englewood Cliffs, N.J., 1962); G. P. E. Clarkson and H. A. Simon, "Simulation of Individual and Group Behavior," *American Economic Review*, 50 (1960), 920–932; Richard Cyert and James March (eds.) *A Behavioral Theory of the Firm* (Englewood Cliffs, N.J., 1963); Allen Newell, "The Chess Machine: An Example of Dealing with a Complex Task by Adaptation," *Proceedings of the Western Joint Computer Conference* (1955), pp. 101–108; Allen Newell, J. C. Shaw, and H. A. Simon, "Elements of a Theory of Human Problem Solving," *Psychological Review*, 65 (1958), 151–166; Allen Newell and H. A. Simon, "The Logic Theory Machine: A Complex Information Proc-

essing System," *Transactions on Information Theory* (1956), 61–79; W. R. Reitman, "Programming Intelligent Problem Solvers," *Transactions on Human Factors in Electronics*, HFE-2 (1961), pp. 26–33; H. A. Simon, "A Behavioral Model of Rational Choice," *Quarterly Journal of Economics*, 60 (1955), 99–118; and H. A. Simon, "Theories of Decision Making in Economics and Behavioral Science," *American Economic Review*, 49 (1959), 253–283.

24 David Braybrooke and Charles Lindblom, *A Strategy of Decision* (New York, 1964).

25 Wildavsky, *op. cit.*, pp. 8–63.

26 James March, "The Power of Power," in David Easton (ed.), *Varieties of Political Theory* (Englewood Cliffs, N.J., 1966), pp. 39–70.

27 See the forthcoming studies by John P. Crecine on budgeting in Pittsburgh, Detroit, and Cleveland, and by Donald Gerwin on the Pittsburgh School District. Aaron Wildavsky will attempt to apply variations of the models in this paper to Oakland, California.

28 Aaron Wildavsky, "Private Markets and Public Arenas," *The American Behavioral Scientist*, 9, no. 7 (Sept.1965), 33–39.

The Impact of Fiscal Policy on National Income
Harold M. Somers

The past decade has witnessed a growing recognition of the *economic* effects of government finance. Government expenditures and revenues, government borrowing and debt repayment are studied, not for their impact on the Treasury, but for their impact on the economy. It is recognized now more than ever before that each aspect of government finance may be used as an instrument of economic policy to influence the size of the nation's income or alter the character of the nation's output. At first the problems of the depression and now the necessities of the war have converted "government finance" into "fiscal policy." The theory of fiscal policy, reborn in the depression, nurtured during the recovery and matured in the war, has become the handmaiden of the government official and the political economist.

In spite of the great amount of attention it has received, the theory of fiscal policy still lacks complete co-ordination of its various faculties and still suffers from frequent reversion to its childhood days. During the time of deep depression when the multiplier theory was developed it was taken for granted by many economists that deficits were the appropriate instrument for raising the level of national income. Since widespread unemployment and underemployment existed there was little need for differentiating real from money income, since a general rise in prices was not very likely and, in any case, was desirable. During the war, however, we wish to raise only the *real* income or the physical output, and then only the output of war materials, and keep down as much as possible the money national income and the price level. How must the theory of fiscal policy be changed as a result of these new objectives and altered conditions? And when the war is over will we have to resort to deficit-spending to prevent a depression? Are deficits, which were required to *raise* the level of national income, appropriate

Harold M. Somers, "The Impact of Fiscal Policy on National Income," *Canadian Journal of Economics and Political Science*, 8 (August 1942), pp. 364–385.

for *maintaining* a high level of national income? We must exercise the greatest care in answering these questions and we must guard against glibly applying some ready formula which we ourselves have carried over from the pre-war days of business depression. It is necessary first of all to examine the structure of fiscal policy (Part I) and trace through the interrelations among expenditures, taxation, borrowing, debt repayment, and national income (Part II). Then we can see how fiscal policy may be used to achieve desired ends and avoid dangerous pitfalls during the war (Part III) and in the post-war period (Part IV).

I. THE STRUCTURE OF FISCAL POLICY

The individual instruments of fiscal policy—expenditures, taxation, borrowing and debt repayment—have already been subjected to meticulous examination by economists. The multiplier theorist has explored the effects of expenditures, and the tax theorist has built up an enormous literature dealing with every nook and cranny of tax incidence and effects. Borrowing and debt repayment, in themselves, have not been studied so widely but there is a substantial literature even on these subjects. Although the individual instruments of fiscal policy have been studied carefully the theory of fiscal policy as a whole lacks integration. The terminology and interests of the tax theorist have not been the same as those of the multiplier theorist while the borrowing and debt repayment expert has busied himself with matters monetary and capital to which the others have, in the main, paid only passing attention. As a result, in the present state of fiscal theory, it is difficult to make adequate allowance for the effects of taxation, borrowing, and debt repayment in trying to determine the consequences of any particular volume of government expenditures. Instead of being an integral part of the analysis these effects usually take the unsatisfactory form of "modifications" or "qualifications."

The immediate task is to study each instrument of fiscal policy on some comparable basis and then construct a comprehensive picture of fiscal policy as a whole. In undertaking this analysis it is necessary, in the first instance, to study the effects of taxation by itself, without regard to the consequences of spending the funds received; and to study the effects of expenditures by themselves, without regard to the results of the various methods employed to obtain the funds required. A similar procedure is followed in studying the effects of borrowing and debt retirement. In every case the same broad types of effects are considered. Printing of new money has economic effects only in so far as the money is spent, hence printing of new money is not considered separately. Credit creation for government expenditures forms part of borrowing, in this case from the banking system. Since we wish ultimately to see how fiscal policy influences consumption, investment, and national income as a whole, we must consider the extent to which each instrument of fiscal policy involves some impact on the nation's supply of purchasing power and the extent to which it involves some impact on the nation's supply of loanable funds. The impact on purchasing power serves as a starting point for the study of subsequent effects on consumer spending and the impact on loanable funds serves as a starting point for the study of subsequent effects on investment.

Expenditures

Through the medium of expenditures the government *releases* both purchasing power and loanable funds. For the most part, a release of purchasing power is involved, as in the case of administrative expenses, relief, public works and most national defence items. By purchasing goods or services the government directly transfers purchasing power to the firms and individuals concerned. But there has recently grown up another type of government disbursement of funds whereby the government merely lends its money (nominally, at least) and does not give it away or purchase outright any goods or services. This has been true of a number of credit corporations set up by the government. The extension of credit tends to have the same sort of ultimate effects on national income as the outright purchase of goods and services by the government but the path taken by these effects is different. Government expenditures resulting from lending activities augment the supply of loanable funds and thus tend to increase the availability of capital and ease the terms of private borrowing. The effects of this depend on the nature of the inducement to invest and on the possibility of obtaining funds from other sources, for instance, the banks. On the other hand, the direct purchase of goods and services by the government means, in and of itself, that the community's supply of purchasing power is augmented. Thus we may carry over into our later discussion the two categories of government disbursement of funds—those which involve a *release of purchasing power* and those which involve a *release of loanable funds*.

Taxation

In the case of tax revenues we have an *absorption* of funds by the government; and here again we may consider the funds involved to be of two types. To some extent, taxation transfers to the Treasury funds which would have been spent on consumers' goods. This is true in some degree of sales taxes and of income taxes on low-income groups. But some taxes impinge on savings, which may have augmented the supply of loanable funds. These two parts of taxation have different effects on the national income. The first

part directly reduces consumers' expenditures and national income while the second has only an indirect effect operating through the availability of capital supplied by individual income recipients. As a result of this type of taxation the terms of borrowing for private investment may be less favorable than they would otherwise have been. Where bank credit is freely available there may possibly be no restrictive effects whatever arising from the absorption of loanable funds through taxation. Taxation, then, involves both an *absorption of purchasing power* and an *absorption of loanable funds*.

Borrowing

When we turn to borrowing we again find an instance of government *absorption* of funds. It might seem that since the money is borrowed the funds involved must necessarily be loanable funds. But if we are concerned with the use to which the funds would have been put if they had not been lent to the government then we can see, paradoxically perhaps, that not all funds lent to the government need be loanable funds. In the case of some bonds issued during the war and more clearly in the case of compulsory savings, the money lent to the government would, to some extent at least, have been spent on consumption goods. If the borrowed money comes from a restriction of consumption as a result of public pressure accompanying the borrowing campaign, the effects are different from those which result when the borrowed money comes from credit expansion or from savings which would have taken place anyway. The ordinary multiplier analysis takes it for granted that the borrowing of the money in itself is completely innocent of any effects as far as expansion and contraction are concerned. But government borrowing might reduce private consumption and, depending on the state of the banking system, might discourage private investment. Hence, in the case of borrowing as in the case of taxation we should consider separately the *absorption of purchasing power* and the *absorption of loanable funds*.

Debt Repayment

We should not leave out of account the *release* of funds through debt payment, which goes on even when a net increase in the debt is taking place. The repayment of the debt (interest payments being considered part of expenditures) might seem to involve solely a release of loanable funds. For the most part, this is true, since the funds paid out by the government in retiring debt will probably be put on the capital market for the purchase of securities. But in some cases, the government bonds represent a definite savings programme on the part of the individual, with the retirement of the bonds marking the culmination of the programme and the spending of the money involved. The repayment of bonds sold in war time through the use of public pressure or compulsion will also have the effect of stimulating consumer spending. On the whole, the repayment of debt tends to stimulate consumption to the same extent that the borrowing of the money tended to curtail it. Debt repayment may then be considered to involve a *release of purchasing power* as well as a *release of loanable funds*.

Net Government Release of Purchasing Power

With this breakdown of each instrument of fiscal policy we can obtain an estimate of the extent to which the government adds directly to the community's purchasing power. It is generally considered a mistake to regard the whole of government expenditures as a net addition to purchasing power because there are offsetting effects in the form of taxation. Hence the magnitude of the deficit, sometimes modified to take account of a few capital items within expenditures and taxation,[1] is generally regarded as the appropriate indicator of the government's net contribution to the community's purchasing power. The deficit (or some variant of the deficit) is almost universally used as the appropriate multiplicand of the multiplier principle. But if the foregoing dissection of fiscal policy has any validity, the deficit, that is the extent to which expenditures are financed out of borrowing, gives a misleading picture of the government's contribution to the community's purchasing power. Moreover, the borrowed money may represent some reduction in the community's purchasing power. Nor should we regard the whole of taxation as being an item to offset expenditures; some taxes are completely innocent of any detrimental effects operating directly on purchasing power. Finally, we should take account of the debt repayment activities of the government. In short, we should add together those parts of expenditures and debt repayment which involve a *release* of purchasing power; and deduct those parts of taxation and borrowing which involve an *absorption* of purchasing power. In this way we can take account of the purchasing power effects of each instrument of fiscal policy and obtain a measure of the *net government release of purchasing power*. This, not the expenditures nor the deficit, is the appropriate measure of the government's direct contribution to the nation's purchasing power and is the appropriate multiplicand of the multiplier principle. It may conceivably be negative in some circumstances, that is, there may be a net government absorption of purchasing power.

Net Government Absorption of Loanable Funds

The other effects of each instrument of fiscal policy must not be ignored. Government borrowing involves mainly (and, in ordinary times, entirely) an absorption of loanable funds. Likewise taxation almost invariably absorbs some loanable funds.

These elements which involve an *absorption* of loanable funds should be added together; and from them should be deducted those parts of expenditures and debt retirement which constitute a *release* of loanable funds. In this way we obtain a measure of the *net government absorption of loanable funds*. In other words, we obtain a measure of the net amount of funds the government withdraws from the money and capital markets. To take only the amount of government borrowing, as is usually done, is incorrect because taxes also involve a withdrawal of capital to some extent; and at the same time the government puts some of these funds back into the capital market through its expenditures and repayment of debt. There may be a net release rather than absorption of loanable funds on the part of the government in some circumstances. In deriving the overall measure representing the net absorption or release of loanable funds we should not lose sight of the individual segments making up this overall measure. The overall measure must be treated with the care required wherever we deal with broad concepts and ignore qualitative considerations. In the case of loanable funds, in particular, quality is a vital consideration: a plenitude of funds in the call money market is of no use to a family desiring to build a house; nor need a scarcity of funds in the long-term capital market have a detrimental effect on a business seeking to renew a thirty-day note.

Conversion of Loanable Funds Into Purchasing Power

Each instrument of fiscal policy may then be considered to have a purchasing-power element and a loanable-funds element. Borrowing and taxation *absorb* both purchasing power and loanable funds while expenditures and debt repayment *release* both purchasing power and loanable funds. To use Professor Plumptre's terms,[2] we may say that expenditures and

debt repayment have *expansive* effects while borrowing and taxation have *restrictive* effects. We have broken up each of the expansive and restrictive effects into two parts: the effect on purchasing power and the effect on loanable funds. There is usually a net absorption of loanable funds and a net release of purchasing power. Where there is no change in the government's cash balance and no government printing of money to finance expenditures, the net government absorption of loanable funds is identically *equal to* the net government release of purchasing power. The fisc is essentially a mechanism which converts loanable funds into purchasing power. In determining the extent of this conversion we must not confine our attention to deficit spending as is so often done. Each instrument of fiscal policy—expenditures, taxation, borrowing and debt repayment—combines elements of loanable funds with elements of purchasing power and plays a part in the government's conversion of loanable funds into purchasing power.

II. EXPANSIVE EFFECTS OF A BALANCED BUDGET

We have suggested above that the *net government release of purchasing power* rather than the *deficit* is the appropriate indicator of the direct expansive impact of fiscal policy, and is thus the appropriate multiplicand of the multiplier principle. This emphasis on the net government release of purchasing power directs attention to the expansive effects of expenditures financed through certain types of taxes. Since it is possible to have a net government release of purchasing power when the budget is balanced it is possible to have an expansive effect on national income when the budget is balanced. For instance, if expenditures are $100 billion, made up of $95 billion release of purchasing power and $5 billion release of loanable funds, and if tax revenues are also $100 billion (thus balancing the budget), made up of $80 billion absorption of purchasing power and $20 billion absorption of loanable funds, the net government release of purchasing power is $15 billion ($95 billion release through expenditures minus $80 billion absorption through taxation). At the same time, the indirect restrictive impact is potentially $15 billion in the form of a net absorption of loanable funds ($20 billion absorption through taxation minus $5 billion release through expenditures). Whether this indirect restrictive influence is actually felt depends on the state of the banking system and the general availability of capital. In any case there is a direct expansive impact of $15 billion even though the budget is balanced.

The direct expansive impact of fiscal policy may be greater than that indicated by the size of the deficit. For instance, if tax revenues are only $20 billion in the above example, and borrowing is $80 billion, both involving solely an absorption of loanable funds, the net government release of purchasing power is $95 billion ($95 billion release through expenditures with no absorption through taxes and borrowing). Thus there is a direct expansive impact of $95 billion with a deficit of $80 billion. There may be a direct expansive effect even with a budget surplus. For instance, if expenditures are only $50 billion, constituting solely a release of purchasing power, and tax revenues are $80 billion (making a budget surplus of $30 billion), constituting $40 billion absorption of loanable funds and $40 billion absorption of purchasing power, the net government release of purchasing power is $10 billion ($50 billion release through expenditures minus $40 billion absorption through taxation). In this case there is a direct expansive effect of $10 billion even though there is a budget surplus of $30 billion.

On the other hand, the direct expansive

effect may be less than that indicated by the size of the deficit and there may even be a direct restrictive effect when there is a balanced budget or when there is a deficit. If expenditures are $100 billion, releasing $80 billion purchasing power and $20 billion loanable funds, if tax revenues are $90 billion, absorbing $75 billion purchasing power and $15 billion loanable funds, and if borrowing is $10 billion, absorbing loanable funds of the same amount, the net government release of purchasing power is only $5 billion ($80 billion release through expenditures minus $75 billion absorption through taxation). Thus we have a direct expansive impact of only $5 billion when there is a deficit of $10 billion. If expenditures are the same as above and tax revenues are also $100 billion, absorbing $90 billion purchasing power and $10 billion loanable funds, there is a net absorption of $10 billion purchasing power ($90 billion absorption through taxation minus $80 billion release through expenditures). Thus there is a direct restrictive effect of $10 billion even though there is a balanced budget. If expenditures are again the same but tax revenues are $90 billion, absorbing $85 billion purchasing power and $5 billion loanable funds, and borrowing is $10 billion, absorbing only loanable funds, then the net absorption of purchasing power is $5 billion ($85 billion absorption through taxation minus $80 billion release through expenditures). Thus we have a restrictive effect of $5 billion even though there is a deficit of $10 billion.

The situation where the expansive impact is greater than that indicated by the deficit, including the limiting case where there is an expansive impact with no deficit at all, is of particular interest for our later discussion of war and post-war finance. The multiplier principle operates on the net release of purchasing power in the usual way so that we can have the multiplier principle operating with a balanced budget. Where there is a multiplier effect, the total expansion of national income is even greater than that indicated by the net government release of purchasing power. For instance, where the budget is balanced and the net government release of purchasing power is $10 billion, the total increase in national income is $50 billion if the marginal propensity to consume is $\frac{4}{5}$ and we assume induced investment to be nil. Since we are interested in all aspects of fiscal policy we must also consider the possibility that the increased income resulting from the operation of the multiplier will increase tax revenues. In case we begin with a deficit, the increased tax revenues will reduce the deficit. To what extent does this, in turn, reduce the multiplier effect? And is there any possibility of increasing tax revenues sufficiently to balance the budget without reducing the multiplier effect? If the latter question can be answered in the affirmative the likelihood of having an expansive effect on national income with a balanced budget is greatly increased. As a result of our earlier analysis we can say that we may have an expansive impact even when we begin with a balanced budget. Can we also say that if we begin with a deficit the increased national income resulting from the operation of the multiplier will increase tax revenues sufficiently to remove the initial deficit and balance the budget? In other words, can the multiplier pay for itself? If so, we can have an expansive effect with a balanced budget even if we begin with expenditures financed through borrowing, for the increased income will yield tax revenues sufficient to pay off the debt initially incurred to finance the expenditures. Although it has always been recognized that the operation of the multiplier will automatically result in some increase in tax revenues[3] it has been denied most emphatically that the budget can be balanced in this way.[4]

Three types of taxes are considered here: taxes coming out of income as a whole, such that both consumption and savings are affected; taxes affecting consumption alone; and taxes involving a transfer of savings and not affecting consumption at all. The terms "taxes on income," "taxes on consumption," and "taxes on savings" are used below in these respective senses. The actual form of the tax is not intended to be specified by the descriptive terms employed. An income tax, for instance, may be so devised as to have any one of these three effects, depending on exemptions, progressiveness, etc. Each type of tax will be studied under conditions where there is only induced consumption and no induced investment. Consideration will also be given to the situation where there is a positive or a negative amount of induced investment. A closed system is assumed.

Taxes on Income

We may first consider the case where the tax structure is such that taxes come out of income as a whole, affecting consumption and savings proportionally. Where the marginal propensity to consume is $\frac{4}{5}$ then this fraction of income net of taxation will be consumed. If the tax structure is such that 50 per cent of any *increased* income is collected by the Treasury, it can be shown that expenditures of $10 billion will result in tax revenues of more than $8.3 billion and an increased national income of more than $16.6 billion. Thus with a deficit of less than $1.7 billion we have an increase of $16.6 billion in income, a multiplication of 10.[5] Without taxation, and with the same marginal propensity to consume, there would be a multiplication of only 5. We can obtain an increase in income of $50 billion by incurring a deficit of only $5 billion, provided we are willing to spend $30 billion to begin with and remove 50 per cent of all increased income through taxation.[6] Otherwise, we would require a deficit of $10 billion in order to obtain an increase in income of $50 billion. It is evident that taxation results in a considerable efficiency in terms of the deficit required to achieve any ,given increase in income.

The results obtained when the tax structure affects income as a whole can be generalized for any percentage of increased income diverted to the Treasury through taxation, for any marginal propensity to consume and for any desired increase in income. Formulae can be derived to represent the interrelationship involved.[7] Where the marginal propensity to consume out of income net of income taxes is $\frac{4}{5}$ and the desired increase in income is $5 billion, the effect of various percentages of increased income diverted to the Treasury through taxation is shown in Figure 1.[8] Here we can see that the initial expenditures required to achieve the desired increase in income are greater the higher the rate of taxation. Tax revenues increase more than the required expenditures, however, with the result that the deficit falls as the tax rate rises. Where none of the increased income is taxed away $1 billion of expenditures and deficit are required to increase income the desired amount. Where the whole of increased income is taxed away $5 billion of expenditures are required but since there are

tax revenues of an equal amount there is no deficit. The budget can be balanced in this way but the multiplier process itself is nipped in the bud since the income initially created by the government is drawn back into the Treasury. Between these two extremes there is an evident efficiency in terms of the deficit required to yield the desired increase in income. The effective multiplier is greater the higher the percentage of increased income diverted to the Treasury.

Taxes on Consumption

In the foregoing discussion we dealt with taxes which are paid out of income as a whole. The reduced income, at each turnover, resulted in both reduced consumption and reduced saving, since the same marginal propensity to consume was applied to the reduced income. We may now consider the case of taxes (however imposed) which have the effect solely of reducing consumption. After the government spends its funds, income of an equivalent amount is created. Part of this is spent on consumption, and it is that part to which the tax rate is applied. In the previous case the tax rate was first applied to the income created by the government spending. As a result of this difference in

Figure 1. Expenditures and Deficit Required to Increase Income $5 Billion with Taxes on Income. Marginal Propensity to Consume = 4/5

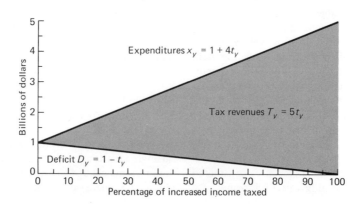

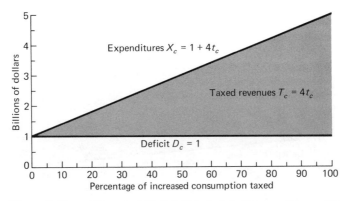

Figure 2. Expenditures and Deficit Required to Increase Income $5 Billion with Taxes on Consumption. Marginal Propensity to Consume = 4/5

the nature of the taxation involved there are some important differences in the results.[9] As we can see from Figure 2,[10] the deficit required to obtain any desired increase in income is the same no matter what the percentage of increased consumer outlay diverted to the Treasury. The higher the tax rate the higher the required initial expenditures; but the deficit remains unchanged because the tax revenues increase by exactly the same amount as the expenditures. The sole determinant of the deficit required is the marginal propensity to consume. There is no point whatever in resorting to this type of taxation in trying to balance the budget. Not only is it impossible to balance the budget but no reduction whatever can be achieved in the deficit required to obtain any desired increase in income.

Taxes on Savings

It is when we come to taxes which fall only on savings and do not reduce the amount of consumption that the most striking results are obtained. The specific form of the tax may vary—it may be an ordinary income tax on increased income or a tax on the nonconsumed portion of increased income—so long as there is no detrimental effect on consumption. Here we may expect that the multiplier would

not be affected; that is true, but what is more important is that the amount of taxable savings is precisely equal to the initial expenditures.[11] Hence it is possible to balance the budget in this way. In other words, we can have a balanced budget and a multiplier effect at the same time, the extent of the multiplier effect being determined solely by the marginal propensity to consume and not being diminished at all by the fact that we are balancing the budget.[12] Here, above all, it becomes evident that the emphasis placed on deficits by the multiplier theory has obscured an important characteristic of fiscal policy.

The expenditures and deficit required to obtain an increase of $5 billion in income are shown in Figure 3, where the marginal propensity to consume is $\frac{4}{5}$ and the taxes imposed do not have any detrimental effects on consumption.[13]

The total effect on income is the same without and with the tax and the expenditures required to achieve any increase in income are independent of the tax. The deficit required to achieve any increase in income is, however, affected by the tax, the deficit falling as the tax rate rises. If a tax rate of 100 per cent is levied on the increased saving then the multiplier can operate as usual with no net deficit whatever. The government begins with some

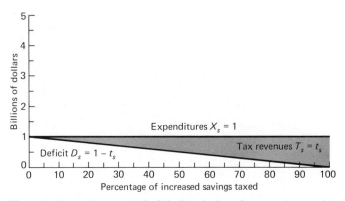

Figure 3. Expenditures and Deficit Required to Increase Income $5 Billion with Taxes on Savings. Marginal Propensity to Consume = 4/5

deficit spending, income is increased, and the nonconsumed portion of the income is taxed away. The tax revenue derived in this way is exactly equal to the initial expenditures, hence the deficit is nil. This result superficially resembles but is actually radically different from that obtained in the case of income taxes. There it was possible to have income formation with a balanced budget only if the whole income initially created by the government is taxed away. Here we are taxing away only the nonconsumed portions of the increased income as it is created. No new leakage results; we are merely piping the existing leak to the Treasury while in the case of consumption taxes the whole tax constitutes an additional leakage, hence the multiplier effect is reduced with the increase in taxation.

In balancing the budget in this manner at no time do we tax all or even the major portion of the increase in income. We tax only savings and then only the *increased* savings resulting from the operation of the multiplier. Thus we tax only a part of the increased income and only a part of the saved portion of the whole of income (using the term "saved" here in the sense of money income not spent on consumption). In other words, as income is created, only part of it is spent and goes to create more income. The unspent

portion leaks out; and it is necessary only to pipe the leak into the Treasury in order to have a balanced budget and an active multiplier at the same time. Hence, we would expect no detrimental effects on the income rate which existed before the government spending programme was instituted. In short, the government can have a multiplier programme of any magnitude with a balanced budget. The greater the initial expenditures the greater the effect on income; and, at the same time, the greater the tax revenues. These tax revenues do not interfere at all with the operation of the multiplier. They can be made equal to the initial expenditures, thus balancing the budget, without interfering with income formation.

Induced Investment

The discussion of taxation presented above has been confined to the multiplier principle in the narrow sense, which deals with induced consumption alone. There would ordinarily be some induced investment as well, either positive or negative. Moreover, there is a strong possibility that the tax programme adopted will affect the inducement to consume and the inducement to invest.

We may consider the last point for a moment. If there is some positive induced investment as a result of the operation of the multiplier then the ease with which the budget can be balanced is increased, since the income created at each turnover of the multiplier is greater than it otherwise would be. To some extent, however, this tax involves a diversion to the Treasury of income which might otherwise have been made available to the private capital market, thus easing the terms of borrowing. The inducement to invest might therefore be less than it would have been if none of the income had been diverted to the government. But this must not be interpreted to mean that investment is reduced below the level it would have attained without the government spending programme. The tax applies only to the income created by the government spending programme. If a fraction of the saved part of that increased income is diverted to the Treasury, the supply of loanable funds which had previously existed would not be impaired at all—at least not by the tax programme. The government's borrowing programme might conceivably tighten the capital market, but the monetary policy pursued by many countries during the past decade makes it evident that such a problem need not arise. The monetary policy adopted may be such as to increase the supply of loanable funds and thus ease the terms of borrowing.[14] The government's borrowing programme need have no detrimental effect on investment, and the tax programme considered here can, at most, have only a detrimental effect on *increases* in the rate of investment. Increased investment might be curtailed because of a reduction in business savings through high taxes on increased income. Even here, assuming that an easy money policy is maintained, it is doubtful whether the advantages of internal over outside financing are so great that firms will resist additional investment in spite of favourable profit expectations resulting from the induced consumption. If it happens that profit expectations are unfavourable de-

spite the government's spending programme and the resulting induced consumption, so that induced investment would be nil or negligible anyway, no reduction in income results from any effects which a high income tax on increased income might have on the supply of loanable funds, the terms of additional private borrowing and the inducement to increase investment.

The complicated nature of the inducement to invest makes it difficult to formulate precisely the magnitude of induced investment. The simple functional relation between induced investment and induced consumption, as expressed in the acceleration principle, is open to question. Whatever the relation is, however, the existence of any positive induced investment reduces the deficit required to achieve any given increase in income.

Conclusions

The formulae developed above can by no means be employed as quantitative guides to practical policy. The analysis is designed merely to suggest the nature of the effects which various types of taxes may have on national income and on the budget. Although the amounts of induced consumption (marginal propensity to consume) and induced investment cannot be forecast accurately, we need not refrain from making estimates (perhaps "guesses") regarding at least the order of magnitude of these items. Then the foregoing analysis may be employed to give a rough idea of the consequences to be expected from various tax policies. There is unquestionably the possibility of obtaining a relatively large multiplier effect with a relatively small deficit; or even of eliminating the deficit entirely. Where we consider the multiplier effect operating through induced consumption alone, then, clearly, tax revenues involving merely a diversion of savings to the Treasury, that is, tax revenues which do not involve a reduction of consumption, do not hamper the operation of the multiplier principle. To the extent that the tax is of this sort the multiplier effect can be obtained with a balanced budget. Ordinarily a tax will involve a reduction in consumption as well as a diversion to the Treasury of funds which would not, in any case, have been spent on consumption. The reduction in consumption reduces the multiplier effect; and in order to obtain any given multiplier effect the consumption taxes must be offset by greater expenditures, with the result that, to obtain any multiplier effect, a given deficit is necessary regardless of the magnitude of the consumption taxes. Thus a tax which has the effect of reducing consumption as well as diverting to the Treasury that part of income which would not have been consumed in any case, is worth while from the point of view of reducing the deficit required to obtain the given multiplier effect and perhaps even of making that multiplier effect possible without any deficit at all. The reduction in consumption can be offset by increased expenditures equal to those tax revenues derived from the reduced consumption; hence the Treasury comes out even on this score. The diversion to the Treasury of savings which would have taken place in any case does not interfere with the multiplier and thus makes possible a reduction in the deficit. Thus it is that a tax of this sort involves some efficiency for the Treasury. No harm in the form of a reduced multiplier effect can befall the economy. The Treasury might have to increase its expenditures a little because the taxes may have some effect in the direction of reducing consumption, but the deficit does not rise because the increased expenditures will at least be offset by increased tax revenues. In short, the initial expansive impact of fiscal policy and the subsequent multiplier effects may be, and ordinarily are, radically different from those suggested by the size of the deficit.

We may now consider the implications of this analysis for war and post-war fiscal policy. In time of war the main task of fiscal policy is to maximize the production of war materials without bringing about an *inflationary* rise in income and prices. In the post-war period the main task of fiscal policy will be to keep up the level of national income and prevent a *deflationary* fall in income and prices. We shall consider briefly, first, war finance and the inflationary gap—and, second, post-war finance and the deflationary gap.

III. WAR FINANCE AND THE INFLATIONARY GAP

The inflationary gap in war time is the excess of prospective consumer spending over the aggregate dollar value of the goods and services available for consumption at their current market prices. If that excess is not removed, prices of the goods and services will tend to rise, the excess of purchasing power acting with increases in costs to promote price rises. What brings about the inflationary gap in the first place? The excess of purchasing power making up the inflationary gap is a result of the release of purchasing power through government expenditures, not offset by an equivalent absorption of purchasing power through taxation and borrowing. Once the amount of consumer goods and services becomes fixed, any *net* government release of purchasing power contributes to an inflationary rise in prices. The inflationary gap, in fact, arises from the net government release of purchasing power. The inflationary gap and the net government release of purchasing power are indicators of the extent to which it will be difficult to enforce price ceilings and rationing. The net government release of purchasing power might be considered the origin of the inducement to violate the price ceilings and to engage in "black market" operations.

In order to reduce the inflationary gap the government should reduce its net release of purchasing power. This does not mean that the government should finance all expenditures through taxation and thus balance the budget. Whether the budget is balanced is a minor question as far as the elimination of the inflationary gap is concerned. As shown above, even if the budget is balanced, fiscal policy may have an expansive, and thus in war time, an inflationary, effect. The foregoing discussion of the expansive effects of a balanced budget should direct attention away from the deficit and towards the true expansive element in fiscal policy, namely the net government release of purchasing power. In considering the extent to which fiscal policy contributes to the inflationary gap, and the extent to which it can be used to reduce the inflationary gap, we would be misled completely if we concentrated attention on the size of the deficit. The important thing is to devise a taxation and borrowing programme which absorbs purchasing power (rather than just loanable funds) of an amount equal to the release of purchasing power through government expenditures. If there is a net release of purchasing power by the government there is an inflationary gap and a strong pressure in the direction of price increases. Given the level of expenditures dictated by military necessity and the availability of resources, fiscal policy should try to reduce the resulting inflationary gap as much as possible. This means that the restrictive instruments of fiscal policy—taxation and borrowing—should be so designed as to reduce the gap, i.e., reduce the net government release of purchasing power. In other words, taxation and borrowing should absorb purchasing power rather than just loanable funds.

The restrictive and, in war time, anti-inflationary effect of such taxation and borrowing is not confined to the initial absorption of purchasing power. Just as the release of purchasing power has an upward multiplier effect in addition to the initial expansive impact, so the ab-sorption of purchasing power has a downward multiplier effect in addition to the initial restrictive impact. The money which is diverted to the Treasury and is not spent on consumption does not create income and is, therefore, not spent on consumption again. Since the level of expenditures and thus the potential inflationary impact is usually given in war time, fiscal policy under such conditions is really concerned more with the downward multiplier, by way of taxation and borrowing which can be modified at will, than with the upward multiplier, which results from the given expenditures. The problem is one of creating as great a downard multiplier as possible through the use of taxation and borrowing to offset as far as possible the upward multiplier effect of the expenditures. Since the inflationary gap arises from the net government release of purchasing power the aim of fiscal policy in war time should be to reduce the net government release of purchasing power to zero. The conclusion is inescapable that a policy of heavy consumption taxes and compulsory purchase of bonds must be adopted.

IV. POST-WAR FINANCE AND THE DEFLATIONARY GAP

In the post-war period there will be the problem of maintaining national income at a level high enough to provide full employment. If the whole national income were respent by private individuals and firms, the income would automatically keep itself up. There is a possibility, however, that not all income will be respent by private individuals and firms, and that there will be a deflationary gap to be filled by fiscal policy. Whether or not this gap develops will depend on the magnitude of consumer expenditures and on the opportunities for private investment. The former will probably be substantial but some difficulties may arise respecting the latter. Conversion of capital goods from war to peace production may require very little net investment; and major new industries involving heavy capital equipment may not make their appearance. Hence, it is at least possible that the volume of private investment will fall short of the amount of income not spent on consumption. National income will necessarily fall unless the government makes up the difference through a substantial release of purchasing power. The repayment of public debt incurred during the war will have this effect to some extent, and the rest will have to come out of continued government expenditures. In short, it is likely that considerable government expenditures will have to be continued in the period of post-war reconstruction if national income is to be maintained at a high level. Does this mean that the already great public debt must continue to rise?

Our earlier study of tax revenues points to the possibility of obtaining a relatively large multiplier effect with a relatively small deficit; or even of eliminating the deficit entirely. The fear, however unfounded, of the consequences of an ever-growing public debt might discourage government expenditures sufficient to maintain national income at a high level. But a recognition of the fact that the expansive effect on national income might be obtained with a balanced budget or, at least, with a relatively small deficit, might make it easier for the government to undertake whatever level of expenditures may be necessary. If a deflationary gap develops it is more important to keep up the level of expenditures than it is to balance the budget, and if a choice must be made between the two, the former policy must be selected. But we do not necessarily have to choose between the two. We can have a high level of expenditures and a balanced budget, and yet have a substantial expansive impact of fiscal policy sufficient to fill the deflationary gap.

It cannot be emphasized too strongly that a policy of balancing the budget when there is a deflationary gap to be filled is appropriate only if certain very special conditions are satisfied: (1) national income must be high when the policy is adopted: (2) government expenditures must be maintained at a high level; and (3) the tax structure must be such as to impinge as little as possible on private consumption and investment. On the first condition, if the national income is allowed to fall when the war is over then a deficit-spending programme should be adopted to raise the level of national income. Any attempt to raise the national income from a low level by means of a balanced budget might needlessly retard recovery since heavy taxation combined with unfavourable expectations might have a considerably unfavourable effect on private consumption and investment. On the second condition, a balanced budget with a level of expenditures insufficient to fill the deflationary gap would only result in a decline in income. On the third condition, it should be remembered that fiscal policy must be such as to result in a net release of purchasing power if any expansive effect is to be felt and the gap is to be filled.

The precise nature of the tax structure required to cope with a deflationary gap will depend on the size of the gap and on the state of the inducement to consume and invest. Contrary to tax policy in war-time, the tax structure in the post-war period should interfere as little as possible with private consumption and investment. The deflationary gap, and thus the required expenditures and tax revenues, will almost certainly be much smaller in magnitude than present government expenditures since there will be some increase in private consumption, if not in private investment, after the war is over and present restrictions are removed. Such being the case, sufficient tax revenues could probably be obtained merely by modifying the war-time tax structure so as to eliminate those taxes which impinge most severely on consumer expenditures. This suggests the raising of income-tax exemptions and the reduction of tax rates on lower and lower-middle income groups. It is not likely that the deflationary gap will be so great that what remains of the tax structure after the above modifications will be unable to produce enough revenue to pay for the expenditures required to fill the gap. The taxes will absorb mainly loanable funds while the expenditures will release mainly purchasing power, so that there will be a net release of purchasing power to fill the gap. The absorption of loanable funds might conceivably interfere with the inducement to invest and thus make the gap greater than it otherwise would be. But, beginning with the high level of national income made possible by the war effort, the government need fear less than ever the unfavourable effects which taxation may have on investment in producers' and consumers' capital goods. Provided the government acts soon enough in its post-war expenditure policy, that is, before income is given a chance to fall, expectations of both consumers and investors will be high and taxation will have little tendency to reduce the amount of consumption or investment which takes place. If the banking system is able, and present indications are that it will be, the financing of both consumption and investment will be facilitated by instalment financing, the purchase of industrial securities, and the extension of short-term loans by the banks.

A policy of avoiding a further increase in public debt after the war will have the effect of preventing a cumulative increase in the deflationary gap. The higher the propensity to consume the smaller the gap. The propensity to consume is partly a function of the distribution of income, the more even the distribution, the higher the propensity to consume and the smaller the gap. If deficits continue after the war there will be a continued

strengthening of the *rentier* element and a barrier to the more even distribution of income. Hence, a policy of balancing the budget will avoid the necessity of a continued increase in government expenditures. At the same time, the high progressive taxes required to balance the budget at the level of expenditures required to maintain full employment will tend to even out the distribution of income and thus reduce the deflationary gap. Hence, a policy of large government expenditures and balanced budgets will result in a cumulative reduction in the deflationary gap and thus will ultimately result in a reduction in government expenditures and taxation.

In one way or another the deflationary gap must be filled if a fall in national income is to be prevented. To help fill the gap the government must see to it that its release of purchasing power through expenditures and repayment of debt is greater than its absorption of purchasing power through taxation and borrowing. To prevent any fall in national income in the post-war period fiscal policy must aim to make the net government release of purchasing power *equal to* the deflationary gap. This will require government spending, but since the post-war period will begin with a high level of national income it is likely that the government can fill the deflationary gap without resorting to *deficit* spending.

NOTES

1 As in the measures known as "the net contribution of the Federal Government to national buying power" or "the net income-increasing expenditure of the Federal Government." For a description of the measures see H. H. Villard, *Deficit Spending and the National Income* (New York, 1941), Part III. For a criticism of the treatment of taxation see A. H. Hansen, *Fiscal Policy and Business Cycles* (New York, 1941), p. 190 n.; and for a further discussion of this question see C. O. Hardy, "Fiscal Policy and the National Income" (*American Economic Review*, vol. XXXII, March 1942, pp.

103–110) and J. W. Angell, *Investment and Business Cycles* (New York and London, 1941), chap. XII and p. 325 n.

2 See A. F. W. Plumptre, "An Approach to War Finance" (*Canadian Journal of Economics and Political Science*, vol. VII, Feb. 1941, pp. 1–12).

3 See, for instance, R. F. Kahn, "The Relation of Home Investment to Unemployment" (*Economic Journal*, vol. XLI, June 1931, pp. 173–198); M. Mitnitzky, "The Effects of a Public Works Policy on Business Activity and Employment" (*International Labour Review*, vol. XXX, Oct. 1934, pp. 435–456); and J. M. Clark, *Economics of Planning Public Works* (Washington, 1935), chap. IX.

4 See Paul A. Samuelson, "Theory of Pump-Priming Re-examined" (*American Economic Review*, vol. XXX, Sept. 1940, pp. 492–506).

5 With expenditures of 10, a marginal propensity to consume equal to $\frac{4}{5}$ and a tax structure such that 50 per cent of increased income is diverted to the Treasury we have the following:

Increased income

$$= 10\left\{1 + \left(\frac{4}{5}\cdot\frac{1}{2}\right) + \left(\frac{4}{5}\cdot\frac{1}{2}\right)^2 + \cdots \infty\right\}$$

$$= 10\cdot\frac{5}{3} = 16.666^+$$

Tax revenues

$$= 10\left\{\frac{1}{2} + \frac{1}{2}\left(\frac{4}{5}\cdot\frac{1}{2}\right) + \frac{1}{2}\left(\frac{4}{5}\cdot\frac{1}{2}\right)^2 + \cdots \infty\right\}$$

$$= 10\cdot\frac{5}{3}\cdot\frac{1}{2} = 8.333^+$$

Deficit
$$= 10 - 8.333^+ = 1.666^+$$

Effective multiplier
$$= \frac{16.666^+}{1.666^+} = 10$$

6 Replacing expenditures of 10 with expenditures of 30 in the above, we have:

Increased income $= 30\cdot\frac{5}{3} = 50$
Tax revenues $= 30\cdot\frac{5}{3}\cdot\frac{1}{2} = 25$
Deficit $= 30 - 25 = 5$
Effective multiplier $= \frac{50}{5} = 10$

7 Let $\alpha =$ the marginal propensity to consume
$t_y =$ the proportion of increased income diverted to the Treasury in the form of taxation
$T_y =$ the tax revenues
$X_y =$ the initial government expenditures
$Y_y =$ the total increase in income
$D_y =$ the deficit $= X_y - T_y$

The we have the following sets of values:
Taxes on Income

PERIOD	INCOME	TAX
I	X_y	$X_y t_y$
II	$X_y(1 - t_y)\alpha$	$X_y t_y(1 - t_y)\alpha$
III	$X_y(1 - t_y)^2\alpha^2$	$X_y t_y(1 - t_y)^2\alpha^2$

PERIOD	INCOME NET OF TAX	CONSUMPTION
I	$X_y(1 - t_y)$	$X_y(1 - t_y)\alpha$
II	$X_y(1 - t_y)^2\alpha$	$X_y(1 - t_y)^2\alpha^2$
III	$X_y(1 - t_y)^2\alpha^2$	$X_y(1 - t_y)^3\alpha^3$

From these we derive the following formulae:

$$Y_y = X_y\{1 + (1 - t_y)\alpha + (1 - t_y^2\alpha^2 + \cdots \infty\}$$

$$= \frac{X_y}{1 - (1 - t_y)\alpha}$$

$$X_y = Y_y\{1 - (1 - t_y)\alpha\}$$

$$T_y = X_y t_y\{1 + (1 - t_y)\alpha + (1 - t_y)^2\alpha^2 + \cdots \infty\}$$

$$= Y_y t_y$$

$$D_y = X_y - T_y = Y_y(1 - t_y)(1 - \alpha)$$

$$t_y = 1 - \frac{D_y}{Y_y(1 - \alpha)}$$

8 These results are obtained by substituting $Y_y = 5$ and $\alpha = \frac{4}{5}$ in the formulae for X_y, T_y, and D_y.

9 Let $t_c =$ the proportion of increased consumer outlay diverted to the Treasury in the form of taxation
$T_c =$ the tax revenues
$X_c =$ the initial government expenditures
$Y_c =$ the total increase in income
$D_c =$ the deficit $= X_c - T_c$

Then we have the following sets of values:
Taxes on Consumption

PERIOD	INCOME	CONSUMER OUTLAY
I	X_c	$X_c\alpha$
II	$X_c\alpha(1 - t_c)$	$X_c\alpha^2(1 - t_c)$
III	$X_c\alpha^2(1 - t_c)^2$	$X_c\alpha^3(1 - t_c)^2$

PERIOD	TAX	CONSUMPTION
I	$X_c\alpha t_c$	$X_c\alpha(1 - t_c)$
II	$X_c\alpha^2(1 - t_c)t_c$	$X_c\alpha^2(1 - t_c)^2$
III	$X_c\alpha^3(1 - t_c)^2 t_c$	$X_c\alpha^3(1 - t_c)^3$

From these we derive the following formulae:

$$Y_c = X_c\{1 + \alpha(1 - t_c) + \alpha^2(1 - t_c)^2 + \cdots \infty\}$$

$$= \frac{X_c}{1 - \alpha(1 - t_c)}$$

$$X_c = Y_c\{1 - \alpha(1 - t_c)\}$$

$$T_c = X_c\alpha t_c\{1 + \alpha(1 - t_c) + \alpha^2(1 - t_c)^2 + \cdots \infty\}$$

$$= Y_c\alpha t_c$$

$$D_c = X_c - T_c = Y_c(1 - \alpha)$$

10 These results are obtained by substituting $Y_c = 5$ and $\alpha = \frac{4}{5}$ in the formulae for X_c, T_c, and D_c.

11 This may be seen by reference to the tables contained in Fritz Machlup, "Period Analysis and Multiplier Theory" (*Quarterly Journal of Economics*, vol. LIV, Nov. 1939, 1–27). If the initial expenditure is unity and the marginal propensity to consume is $\frac{4}{5}$ then the total increase in income will be 5. During the process of increasing the income, $\frac{1}{5}$ of this amount, i.e., unity, will have "leaked out." Just as the total increase in income is the sum of the infinite series, $1 + \frac{4}{5} + (\frac{4}{5})^2 \cdots$, so the total leakage is the sum of the infinite series, $\frac{1}{5} + \frac{1}{5}(\frac{4}{5}) + \frac{1}{5}(\frac{4}{5})^2 + \cdots$, or, $\frac{1}{5}\{1 + \frac{4}{5} + (\frac{4}{5})^2 + \cdots\}$. This has a value of unity.

12 Let t_s = the proportion of increased savings diverted to the Treasury in the form of taxation

T_s = the tax revenues

X_s = the initial government expenditures

Y_s = the total increase in income

D_s = the deficit = $X_s - T_s$

Then we have the following sets of values:

Taxes on Savings

PERIOD	INCOME	CONSUMPTION
I	X_s	$X_s\alpha$
II	$X_s\alpha$	$X_s\alpha^2$
III	$X_s\alpha^2$	$X_s\alpha^3$

PERIOD	SAVINGS	TAX
I	$X_s(1 - \alpha)$	$X_s(1 - \alpha)t_s$
II	$X_s\alpha(1 - \alpha)$	$X_s\alpha(1 - \alpha)t_s$
III	$X_s\alpha^2(1 - \alpha)$	$X_s\alpha^2(1 - \alpha)t_s$

From these we derive the following formulae:

$$Y_s = X_s(1 + \alpha + \alpha^2 + \cdots \infty)$$

$$= \frac{X_s}{1 - \alpha}$$

$$X_s = Y_s(1 - \alpha)$$

$$T_s = X_s(1 - \alpha)t_s\{1 + \alpha + \alpha^2 + \cdots \infty\}$$

$$= \frac{X_s(1 - \alpha)t_s}{1 - \alpha} = Y_s(1 - \alpha)t_s$$

$$D_s = X_s - T_s = Y_s(1 - \alpha)(1 - t_s)$$

$$t_s = 1 - \frac{D_s}{Y_s(1 - \alpha)}$$

13 These results are obtained by substituting $Y_s = 5$ and $\alpha = \frac{4}{5}$ in the formulae for X_s, T_s, and D_s.

14 See Harold M. Somers, "Monetary Policy and the Theory of Interest" (*Quarterly Journal of Economics*, vol. LV, May 1941, pp. 488–507).

Summaries

Earl R. Rolph, "Debt-Management: Some Theoretical Aspects," *Public Finance*, 16 (1961), pp. 105–120.

"In recent years," says Earl Rolph, "debt-management has become a lively subject of discussion in the United States. The large size of the federal debt has made it a perennial political topic ... Academic economists, once reluctant to delve into the intricacies of debt-management, have overcome any lingering modesty about suggesting reforms." In this article, the author discusses some theoretical issues connected with debt management, and draws some valuable conclusions for the benefit of fiscal policy makers.

Rolph first defines the term "debt management," and then discusses two of the theoretical problems in debt management: (1) the effects of changing the *size* of the net debt, or, in other words, the effects of increasing or decreasing the outstanding debt, and (2) the effects of changing the *composition* of the net debt. Next, the author explores the distributional aspects of debt management, and concludes by outlining some rational debt-management and fiscal policies.

Arthur Smithies, "The Planning-Programming-Budgeting System," *American Economist* (Spring 1968), pp. 7–12.

In this John R. Commons lecture, Arthur Smithies, an outstanding economist and an expert in the field of public finance, makes a strong case for the planning-programming-budgeting system (PPBS). Since the PPBS is not a popular term among economists and public policy makers, Smithies points out that the "PPBS is essentially an application and extension of the economics of choice to public decision-making." Proponents of the PPBS claim that, insofar as a sound and an efficient budgeting system is concerned, it is far superior to the current budgetary process and, therefore, should replace the existing system. However, they concede that there are certain obstacles to a smooth changeover from the present to the PPBS. For one thing, the present system functions remarkably smoothly; for another, the PPBS is likely to be costly. In spite of these obstacles, however, the author recommends an early adoption of the PPBS.

Bibliography

David M. Kennedy *et al.*, "Purposes of the Budget of the United States," in *Report of the President's Commission on Budget Concepts.* Washington, D.C.: U.S. Government Printing Office, October 1967, pp. 11–23.

John F. Kennedy, "Fiscal Myths," Commencement Address at Yale University, June 11, 1962, pp. 1–9.

A. T. Peacock, "The Public Sector and the Theory of Economic Growth," *Scottish Journal of Political Economy*, 6 (February 1959), pp. 1–12.

Raymond J. Saulnier, "The Limitations on Fiscal Policy—Some Problems in the 'New Economics,'" *Proceedings of a Conference on The New Economics: Implications for Business* (New York: Tax Foundation, Inc., 1966), pp. 18–24.

Joseph Scherer, "A Primer on Federal Budgets," Federal Reserve Bank of New York, *Monthly Review* (April 1965), pp. 79–88.

L. C. Thurow, "A Fiscal Policy Model of the United States," *Survey of Current Business*, 49 (June 1969), pp. 45–57.

James Tobin, *An Essay on the Principles of Debt Management.* Yale University, Cowles Foundation Paper, No. 195, 1963, pp. 143–218.

10
MONETARY AND FISCAL POLICY

Since the beginning of the postwar era, most countries have been faced with economic problems substantially different in character from those of earlier years. These problems have led to the development of at least three new approaches to the formulation of monetary and fiscal policies. Proponents claim that money plays the most important role in influencing aggregate output and employment; therefore, primary reliance should be placed on monetary policy. Economists favoring the second approach maintain that while monetary policy is effective in combating inflation, it cannot prevent a recession. The third approach, which is supported by the largest number of professional economists, is one which is based upon the premise that monetary and fiscal tools are complementary as well as competitive instruments for reaching a set of national goals. Consequently, concerned economists attempt to study and explain the whole range of questions associated with the "mix" of monetary and fiscal policies.

Monetary Versus Fiscal Actions*
Leonall C. Andersen and Jerry L. Jordan

High employment, rising output of goods and services, and relatively stable prices are three widely accepted national economic goals. Responsibility for economic

Leonall C. Andersen and Jerry L. Jordan, "Monetary and Fiscal Actions: A Test of Their Relative Importance in Economic Stabilization," Federal Reserve Bank of St. Louis, *Review*, 50 (November 1968), pp. 11–23.

* The authors give special thanks for helpful comments on earlier drafts to: Robert Basmann, Karl Brunner, James Buchanan, Albert Burger, Keith Carlson, David Fand, Milton Friedman, Gary Fromm, Michael Levy, Thomas Mayer, A. James Meigs, David Meiselman, Allan Meltzer, Richard Puckett, David Rowan, James Tobin, Robert Weintraub, and William Yohe. The authors are, of course, solely responsible for the analyses and results presented in this article.

stabilization actions to meet these goals has been assigned to monetary and fiscal authorities. The Federal Reserve System has the major responsibility for monetary management. Fiscal actions involve Federal Government spending plans and taxing provisions. Governmental units involved in fiscal actions are the Congress and the Administration, including the Treasury, the Bureau of the Budget, and the Council of Economic Advisers.

This article reports the results of recent research which tested three commonly held propositions concerning the relative importance of monetary and fiscal actions in implementing economic stabilization policy. These propositions are: The response of economic activity to fiscal actions relative to that of monetary

373

actions is (I) greater, (II) more predictable, and (III) faster. Specific meanings, for the purposes of this article, of the broad terms used in these propositions are presented later.

This article does not attempt to test rival economic theories of the mechanism by which monetary and fiscal actions influence economic activity. Neither is it intended to develop evidence bearing directly on any causal relationships implied by such theories. More elaborate procedures than those used here would be required in order to test any theories underlying the familiar statements regarding results expected from monetary and fiscal actions. However, empirical relationships are developed between frequently used measures of stabilization actions and economic activity. These relationships are consistent with the implications of some theories of stabilization policy and are inconsistent with others, as will be pointed out.

A brief discussion of the forces influencing economic activity is presented first. Next, with this theory as a background, specific measures of economic activity, fiscal actions, and monetary actions are selected. The results of testing the three propositions noted above, together with other statements concerning the response of economic activity to monetary and fiscal forces, are then presented. Finally, some implications for the conduct of stabilization policy are drawn from the results of these tests.

A THEORETICAL VIEW OF ECONOMIC ACTIVITY

Our economic system consists of many markets. Every commodity, service, and financial asset is viewed as constituting an individual market in which a particular item is traded and a price is determined. All of these markets are linked together in varying degrees, since prices in one market influence decisions made in other markets.

About a century ago, Leon Walras outline a framework for analyzing a complex market economy. Such an analysis includes a demand and a supply relationship for every commodity and for each factor of production. Trading in the markets results in prices being established which clear all markets, i.e., the amount offered in a market equals the amount taken from the market. According to this analysis, outside occurrences reflected in shifts in demand and supply relationships cause changes in market prices and in quantities traded. These outside events include changes in preferences of market participants, in resource endowments, and in technology. Financial assets were not viewed as providing utility or satisfaction to their holders and were therefore excluded from the analysis.

Later developments in economic theory have viewed financial assets as providing flows of services which also provide utility or satisfaction to holders. For example, a holder of a commercial bank time deposit receives liquidity service (ease of conversion into the medium of exchange), store of value service (ability to make a future purchase), risk avoidance service (little risk of loss), and a financial yield. According to this later view, economic entities incorporate choices among goods, services, *and* financial assets into their decision-making processes.

The fact that economic entities make choices in both markets for goods and services and markets for financial assets requires the addition of demand and supply relationships for every financial asset. Market interest rates (prices of financial assets) and changes in the stocks outstanding of most financial assets are determined by the market process along with prices and quantities of goods and services.

These theoretical developments have enlarged the number of independent forces which are regarded as influencing market-determined prices, interest rates, quantities produced of commodities, and stocks outstanding of financial assets. Government and monetary authorities are viewed as exerting independent influences in the market system. These influences are called fiscal and monetary policies or actions. Random events, such as the outbreak of war, strikes in key industries, and prolonged drought, exert other market influences. Growth in world trade and changes in foreign prices and interest rates, relative to our own, influence exports and therefore are largely an outside influence on domestic markets.

Market expectations have also been assigned a significant factor in markets, but these are not viewed as a distinctly independent force. Expectations result

from market participants basing their decisions on movements in market-determined variables, or they are derived from market responses to the expected results of random events, such as the outbreak of a war or the anticipation of changes in fiscal or monetary policy.

These dependent and independent market variables are summarized in Exhibit I. The dependent variables are determined by the interplay of market forces which results from changes in the independent variables. Market-determined variables include prices and quantities of goods and services, prices and quantities of factors of production, prices (interest rates) and quantities of financial assets, and expectations. Independent variables consist of slowly changing factors, forces from outside our economy, random events, and forces subject to control by fiscal and monetary authorities. A change in an independent variable (for example, a fiscal or a monetary action) causes changes in many of the market-determined (dependent) variables.

EXHIBIT I. Classification of Market Variables

DEPENDENT VARIABLES

Prices and quantities of goods and services

Prices and quantities of factors of production.

Prices (interest rates) and quantities of financial assets.

Expectations based on:
 a. movements in dependent variables.
 b. expected results of random events.
 c. expected changes in fiscal and monetary policy.

INDEPENDENT VARIABLES

Slowly changing factors:
 a. preferences.
 b. technology.
 c. resources.
 d. institutional and legal framework

Events outside the domestic economy:
 a. change in total world trade.
 b. movements in foreign prices and interest rates.

Random events:
 a. outbreak of war.
 b. major strikes.
 c. weather.

Forces subject to control by:
 a. fiscal actions.
 b. monetary actions.

MEASURES OF ECONOMIC ACTIVITY AND OF MONETARY AND FISCAL ACTIONS

Three theoretical approaches have been advanced by economists for analyzing the influence of monetary and fiscal actions on economic activity. These approaches are the textbook Keynesian analysis derived from economic thought of the late 1930's to the early 1950's, the portfolio approach developed over the last two decades, and the modern quantity theory of money. Each of these theories has led to popular and familiar statements regarding the direction, amount, and timing of fiscal and monetary influences on economic activity. As noted earlier, these theories and their linkages will not be tested directly, but the validity of some of the statements which purport to represent the implications of these theories will be examined. For this purpose, frequently used measures of economic activity, monetary actions and fiscal actions, are selected.

Economic Activity

Total spending for goods and services (gross national product at current prices) is used in this article as the measure of economic activity. It consists of total spending on final goods and services by households, businesses, and governments plus net foreign investment. Real output of goods and services is limited by resource endowments and technology, with the actual level of output, within this constraint, determined by the level of total spending and other factors.

Monetary Actions

Monetary actions involve primarily decisions of the Treasury and the Federal Reserve System. Treasury monetary actions consist of variations in its cash holdings, deposits at Federal Reserve banks and at commercial banks, and issuance of Treasury currency. Federal Reserve monetary actions include changes in its portfolio of Government securities, variations in member bank reserve requirements, and changes in the Federal Reserve discount rate. Banks and the public also engage in a form of monetary actions. Commercial bank decisions to hold excess reserves constitute a monetary action. Also, because of differential reserve requirements, the public's decisions to hold varying amounts of time deposits at commercial banks or currency relative to demand deposits are a form of monetary action, but are not viewed as stabilization actions. However, they are taken into consideration by stabilization authorities in forming their own actions. Exhibit II summarizes the various sources

EXHIBIT II. Stabilization Actions and Their Measurement

STABILIZATION ACTIONS	FREQUENTLY USED MEASUREMENTS OF ACTIONS

1. Monetary Actions
Federal Reserve System
  a. open market transactions.
  b. discount rate changes.
  c. reserve requirement changes.
 	
Treasury
  a. changes in cash holdings.
  b. changes in deposits at Reserve banks.
  c. changes in deposits at commercial banks.
  d. changes in Treasury currency outstanding.
 	
2. Fiscal Actions
Government spending programs.
Government taxing provisions.
	1. Monetary Actions
	  Monetary base.*
	  Money stock, narrowly defined.*
	  Money plus time deposits.
	  Commercial bank credit.
	  Private demand deposits.
	2. Fiscal Actions
	  High-employment expenditures.*
	  High-employment receipts.*
	  High-employment surplus.*
	  Weighted high-employment expenditures.
	  Weighted high-employment receipts.
	  Weighted high-employment surplus.
	  National income account expenditures.
	  National income account receipts.
	  Autonomous changes in Government tax rates.
	  Net Government debt outside of agencies and trust funds.

* Tests based on these measures are reported in this article. The remaining measures were used in additional tests. These results are available on request.

of monetary actions related to economic stabilization.

The monetary base[1] is considered by both the portfolio and the modern quantity theory schools to be a strategic monetary variable. The monetary base is under direct control of the monetary authorities, with major control exerted by the Federal Reserve System. Both of these schools consider an increase in the monetary base, other forces constant, to be an expansionary influence on economic activity and a decrease to be a restrictive influence.

The portfolio school holds that a change in the monetary base affects investment spending, and thereby aggregate spending, through changes in market interest rates relative to the supply price of capital (real rate of return on capital). The modern quantity theory holds that the influence of the monetary base works through changes in the money stock which in turn affect prices, interest rates, and spending on goods and services. Increases in the base are reflected in increases in the money stock which in turn result directly and indirectly in increased expenditures on a whole spectrum of capital and consumer goods. Both prices of goods and interest rates form the transmission mechanism in the modern quantity theory.

The money stock is also used as a strategic monetary variable in each of the approaches to stabilization policies, as the above discussion has implied. The simple Keynesian approach postulates that a change in the stock of money relative to its demand results in a change in interest rates. It also postulates that investment spending decisions depend on interest rates, and that growth in aggregate spending depends in turn on these investment decisions. Similarly, in the portfolio school of thought changes in the money stock lead to changes in interest rates, which are followed by substitutions in asset portfolios; then finally, total spending is affected. Interest rates, ac-

cording to this latter school, are the key part of the transmission mechanism, influencing decisions to hold money versus alternative financial assets as well as decisions to invest in real assets. The influence of changes in the money stock on economic activity, within the modern quantity theory framework, has already been discussed in the previous paragraph.[2]

The monetary base, as noted, plays an important role in both the portfolio and the modern quantity theory approaches to monetary theory. However, there remains considerable controversy regarding the role of money in determining economic activity, ranging from "money does not matter" to "money is the dominant factor." In recent years there has been a general acceptance that money, among many other influences, is important. Thomas Mayer, in a recent book, summarizes this controversy. He concludes:

All in all, much recent evidence supports the view that the stock of money and, therefore, monetary policy, has a substantial effect. Note, however, that this reading of the evidence is by no means acceptable to all economists. Some, Professor Friedman and Dr. Warburton for example, argue that changes in the stock of money do have a dominant effect on income, at least in the long run, while others such as Professor Hansen believe that changes in the stock of money are largely offset by opposite changes in velocity.[3]

The theories aside, changes in the monetary base and changes in the money stock are frequently used as measures of monetary actions. This article, in part, tests the use of these variables for this purpose. Money is narrowly defined as the nonbank public's holdings of demand deposits plus currency. Changes in the money stock mainly reflect movements in the monetary base; however, they also reflect decisions of commercial banks to hold excess reserves, of the nonbank public to hold currency and time deposits, and of the Treasury to hold demand deposits at commercial banks. The monetary base reflects monetary actions of the Federal Reserve, and to a lesser extent, those of the Treasury and gold flows. But changes in the base have been found to be dominated by actions of the Federal Reserve.[4]

Other aggregate measures, such as money plus time deposits, bank credit, and private demand deposits, are frequently used as monetary indicators (Exhibit II). Tests using these indicators were also made. The results of these tests did not change the conclusions reached in this article; these results are available on request. Market interest rates are not used in this article as strategic monetary variables since they reflect, to a great extent, fiscal actions, expectations and other factors which cannot properly be called monetary actions.

Fiscal Actions

The influence of fiscal actions on economic activity is frequently measured by Federal Government spending, changes in Federal tax rates, or Federal budget deficits and surpluses. The textbook Keynesian view has been reflected in many popular discussions of fiscal influence. The portfolio approach and the modern quantity theory suggest alternative analyses of fiscal influence.

The elementary textbook Keynesian view concentrates almost exclusively on the direct influence of fiscal actions on total spending. Government spending is a direct demand for goods and services. Tax rates affect disposable income, a major determinant of consumer spending, and profits of businesses, a major determinant of investment spending. Budget surpluses and deficits are used as a measure of the net direct influence of spending and taxing on economic activity. More advanced textbooks also include an indirect influence of fiscal actions on economic activity through changes in market interest rates. In either case, little con-

sideration is generally given to the method of financing expenditures.

The portfolio approach as developed by Tobin attributes to fiscal actions both a direct influence on economic activity and an indirect influence. Both influences take into consideration the financing of Government expenditures.[5] Financing of expenditures by issuance of demand debt of monetary authorities (the monetary base) results in the full Keynesian multiplier effect. Financing by either taxes or borrowing from the public has a smaller multiplier effect on spending. Tobin views this direct influence as temporary.

The indirect influence of fiscal actions, according to Tobin, results from the manner of financing the Government debt, that is, variations in the relative amounts of demand debt, short-term debt, and long-term debt. For example, an expansionary move would be a shift from long-term to short-term debt or a shift from short-term to demand debt. A restrictive action would result from a shift in the opposite direction. As in the case of monetary actions, market interest rates on financial assets and their influence on investment spending make up the transmission mechanism.

The modern quantity theory also suggests that the influence of fiscal actions depends on the method of financing Government expenditures. This approach maintains that financing expenditures by either taxing or borrowing from the public involves a transfer of command over resources from the public to the Government. However, the net influence on total spending resulting from interest rate and wealth changes is ambiguous. Only a deficit financed by the monetary system is necessarily expansionary.[6]

High-employment budget concepts have been developed as measures of the influence of fiscal actions on economic activity.[7] In these budget concepts, expenditures include both those for goods and services and those for transfer payments, adjusted for the influence of economic activity. Receipts, similarly adjusted, primarily reflect legislated changes in Federal Government tax rates, including Social Security taxes. The net of receipts and expenditures is used as a net measure of changes in expenditure provisions and in tax rates. These high-employment concepts are used in this article as measures of fiscal actions (Exhibit II). Tests were also made alternatively using national income account Government expenditures and receipts, a series measuring autonomous changes in Government tax rates, a weighted high-employment expenditure and receipt series, and a series of U.S. Government debt held by the public plus Federal Reserve holdings of U.S. Government securities. These tests did not change the conclusions reached in this article. Results of these tests are available on request.

Other Influences

Measures of other independent forces which influence economic activity are not used in this article. Yet this should not be construed to imply that these forces are not important. It is accepted by all economists that the nonmonetary and nonfiscal forces listed in Exhibit I have an important influence on economic activity. However, recognition of the existence of these "other forces" does not preclude the testing of propositions relating to the relative importance of monetary and fiscal forces. The analysis presented in this study provides indirect evidence bearing on these "other forces."

TESTING THE PROPOSITIONS

This section reports the results of testing the three propositions under consideration. First, the concept of testing a hypothesis is briefly discussed.

Next, the results of regression analyses which relate the measures of fiscal and monetary actions to total spending are reported. Finally, statistics developed from the regression analyses are used to test the specific propositions.

The Concept of Testing a Hypothesis

In scientific methodology, testing a hypothesis consists of the statement of the hypothesis, deriving by means of logic testable consequences expected from it, and then taking observations from past experience which show the presence or absence of the expected consequences. If the expected consequences do not occur, then the hypothesis is said to be "not confirmed" by the evidence. If, on the other hand, the expected consequences occur, the hypothesis is said to be "confirmed."

It is important to keep the following point in mind. In scientific testing, a hypothesis (or conjecture) may be found "not confirmed" and therefore refuted as the explanation of the relationship under examination. However, if it is found to be "confirmed," the hypothesis cannot be said to have been proven true. In the latter case, however, the hypothesis remains an acceptable proposition of a real world relationship as long as it is found to be "confirmed" in future tests.[8]

The results presented in this study all bear on what is commonly called a "reduced form" in economics. A reduced-form equation is a derivable consequence of a system of equations which may be hypothesized to represent the structure of the economy (i.e., a so-called structural model). In other words, all of the factors and causal relations which determine total spending (GNP) are "summarized" in one equation. This reduced-form equation postulates a certain relationship over time between the independent variables and the dependent variable—total spending. Using appropriate statistical procedures and selected measures of variables, it is possible to test whether or not the implications of the reduced-form equation have occurred in the past. If the implied relationships are not confirmed, then the relationship asserted by the reduced-form equation is said to have been refuted. However, not confirming the reduced form does not necessarily mean that the whole "model," and all of the factors and causal relations contained in it, are denied. It may be only that one or more of the structural linkages of the model is incorrect, or that the empirical surrogates chosen as measures of monetary or fiscal influence are not appropriate.[9]

Frequently one encounters statements or conjectures regarding factors which are asserted to influence economic activity in a specific way. These statements take the form of reduced-form equations, and are sometimes attributed to various theories of the determination of economic activity. As stated previously, this study does not attempt to test the causal linkages by which fiscal and monetary actions influence total spending, but is concerned only with the confirmation or refutation of rival conjectures regarding the strength and reliability of fiscal and monetary actions based on frequently used indicators of such actions.

Measuring the Empirical Relationships

As a step toward analyzing the three propositions put forth earlier, empirical relationships between the measures of fiscal and monetary actions and total spending are established. These relationships are developed by regressing quarter-to-quarter changes in GNP on quarter-to-quarter changes in the money stock (M) and in the various measures of fiscal actions: high-employment budget surplus ($R - E$), high-employment expenditures (E), and high-employment receipts (R). Similar equations were estimated where changes in the monetary base (B) were used in place of the money stock.

Changes in all variables were computed by two methods. Conventional first differences were calculated by subtracting the value for the preceding quarter from the value for the present quarter.[10] The other method used is an averaging procedure used by Kareken and Solow called central differences.[11] The structure of lags present in the regressions was estimated with use of the Almon lag technique.[12] The data are seasonally adjusted quarterly averages for the period from the first quarter of 1952 to the second quarter of 1968.[13]

As discussed previously, statements are frequently made from which certain relationships are expected to exist between measures of economic activity on the one hand and measures of monetary and fiscal actions on the other hand. Such relationships consist of a direct influence of an action on GNP and of an indirect influence which reflects interactions among the many markets for real and financial assets. These interactions work through the market mechanism determining the dependent variables listed in Exhibit I. The postulated relationships are the total of these direct and indirect influences. Thus, the empirical relationship embodied in each regression coefficient is the *total* response (including both direct and indirect responses) of GNP to changes in each measure of a stabilization action, assuming all other forces remain constant.

The results presented here do not provide a basis for separating the direct and indirect influences of monetary and fiscal forces on total spending, but this division is irrelevant for the purposes of this article. The interested reader is referred to the Appendix for further elaboration of these points.

Using the total response concept-changes in GNP are expected to be positively related to changes in the money stock (M) or changes in the monetary base (B). With regard to the high, employment surplus (receipts minus expenditures), a larger surplus or a smaller deficit is expected to have a negative influence on GNP, and conversely. Changes in high-employment expenditures (*E*) are expected to have a positive influence and changes in receipts (*R*) are expected to have a negative influence when these variables are included separately.

Considering that the primary purpose of this study is to measure the influence of a few major forces on changes in GNP, rather than to identify and measure the influences of all independent forces, the results obtained are quite good (Table I). The R^2 statistic, a measure of the per cent of the variance in changes in GNP explained by the regression equation, ranges from .53 to .73; these values are usually considered to be quite good when first differences are used rather than levels of the data. All of the estimated regression coefficients for changes in the money stock or the monetary base have the signs implied in the above discussion (equations 1.1 to 2.4 in Table I) and have a high statistical significance in most cases. The estimated coefficients for the high-employment measures of fiscal influence do not have the expected signs in all cases and generally are of low statistical significance. These regression results are discussed in greater detail below.

MONEY AND THE MONETARY BASE. The total response of GNP to changes in money or the monetary base distributed over four quarters is consistent with the postulated relationship (i.e. a positive relationship), and the coefficients are all statistically significant. The coefficients of each measure of monetary action may be summed to provide an indication of the overall response of GNP to changes in monetary actions. These summed coefficients are also statistically significant and consistent with the postulated relationships. The results obtained for measures of monetary actions were not affected significantly when measures of fiscal actions other than those reported here were used in the regressions.

HIGH-EMPLOYMENT BUDGET SURPLUS. As pointed out previously, the high-employment surplus or deficit is often used as a measure of the direction and strength of fiscal actions. Equation 1.1 summarizes the total response of GNP to changes in money and changes in the high-employment surplus. The coefficients of the high-employment surplus estimated for the contemporaneous and first lagged quarter have the expected sign, but the coefficients are of very low statistical significance and do not differ significantly from zero. The signs of the coefficients estimated for the second and third lagged quarters are opposite to the expected signs. The sum of the coefficients (total response distributed over four quarters) is estimated to have a positive sign (opposite the postulated sign) but it is not statistically significant. These results provide no empirical support for the view that fiscal actions measured by the high-employment surplus have a significant influence on GNP. In principle, these results may have occurred either because the high-employment surplus was not a good measure of fiscal influence, or because fiscal influence was not important during the sample period.[14]

EXPENDITURES AND RECEIPTS. Simple textbook Keynesian models of income determination usually demonstrate, theoretically, that changes in tax rates exert a negative influence on economic activity, while changes in Government expenditures exert a positive influence. Equations 1.2 and 1.3 provide tests of these propositions. The signs of the coefficients estimated for tax receipts are the same as the hypothesized signs for only the first and second lagged quarters. However, since these coefficients (individually and the sums) are of low

Table I. Regression of Changes in GNP on Changes in Monetary and Fiscal Actions

FIRST DIFFERENCES	(EQUATION 1.1)		(EQUATION 1.2)			(EQUATION 1.3)		(EQUATION 1.4)		
	ΔM	$\Delta(R-E)$	ΔM	ΔE	ΔR	ΔM	ΔE	ΔB	ΔE	ΔR
t	1.57* (2.17)	−.15 (.65)	1.51* (2.03)	.36 (1.15)	.16 (.53)	1.54* (2.47)	.40 (1.48)	1.02 (.49)	.23 (.67)	.52 (1.68)
$t-1$	1.94* (3.60)	−.20 (1.08)	1.59* (2.85)	.53* (2.15)	−.01 (.03)	1.56* (3.43)	.54* (2.68)	5.46* (3.37)	.37 (1.36)	.02 (.07)
$t-2$	1.80* (3.37)	.10 (.55)	1.47* (2.69)	−.05 (.19)	−.03 (.10)	1.44* (3.18)	−.03 (.13)	6.48* (4.10)	−.21 (.84)	−.17 (.64)
$t-3$	1.28 (1.88)	.47* (1.95)	1.27 (1.82)	−.78* (2.82)	.11 (.32)	1.29* (2.00)	−.74* (2.85)	3.05 (1.54)	−.93* (3.10)	.14 (.39)
Sum	6.59* (7.73)	.22 (.45)	5.84* (6.57)	.07 (.13)	.23 (.32)	5.83* (7.25)	.17 (.54)	16.01* (5.67)	−.54 (.89)	.51 (.67)
Constant	1.99* (2.16)		2.10 (1.88)			2.28* (2.76)		1.55 (1.22)		
R^2	.56		.58			.60		.53		
S.E.	4.24		4.11			4.01		4.35		
D-W	1.54		1.80			1.78		1.71		

CENTRAL DIFFERENCES	(EQUATION 2.1)		(EQUATION 2.2)			(EQUATION 2.3)		(EQUATION 2.4)		
	ΔM	$\Delta(R-E)$	ΔM	ΔE	ΔR	ΔM	ΔE	ΔB	ΔE	ΔR
t	1.50 (1.84)	−.24 (.91)	1.58* (2.01)	.53 (1.52)	.32 (1.05)	1.54* (2.45)	.63* (2.21)	.61 (.28)	.28 (.73)	.87* (2.55)
$t-1$	2.11* (3.61)	−.23 (1.16)	1.57* (2.78)	.60* (2.44)	−.04 (.17)	1.63* (3.57)	.59* (2.61)	5.42* (3.16)	.50 (1.87)	−.07 (.27)
$t-2$	1.89* (3.18)	.15 (.81)	1.41* (2.45)	−.15 (.60)	−.11 (.47)	1.43* (3.16)	−.16 (.71)	6.87* (3.92)	−.27 (1.04)	−.33 (1.31)
$t-3$	1.06 (1.36)	.52 (1.90)	1.26 (1.72)	−.96* (3.15)	.18 (.48)	1.13 (1.71)	−.86* (3.07)	3.51 (1.71)	−1.26* (3.65)	.35 (.87)
Sum	6.56* (8.16)	.21 (.47)	5.80* (7.57)	.02 (.04)	.34 (.54)	5.74* (8.45)	.19 (.77)	16.41* (6.95)	−.75 (1.37)	.82 (1.16)
Constant	2.02* (2.48)		2.00* (2.14)			2.30* (3.55)		1.24 (1.14)		
R^2	.66		.72			.73		.67		
S.E.	3.35		3.03			2.97		3.26		
D-W	.88		1.14			1.13		1.05		

Note: Regression coefficients are the top figures, and their "t" values appear below each coefficient enclosed by parentheses. The regression coefficients marked by an asterisk (*) are statistically significant at the 5 per cent level. R^2 are adjusted for degrees of freedom.

S.E. is the standard error of the estimate, and D-W is the Durbin–Watson statistic.

statistical significance, no importance can be attached to this variable. Inclusion of changes in receipts (ΔR) in equation 1.2 does not improve the overall results, in terms of R^2 and the standard error of estimate, compared with equation 1.3, from which receipts are excluded.

These results provide no support for theories which indicate that changes in tax receipts due to changes in tax rates exert an overall negative (or any) influence on economic activity. The results are consistent with theories which indicate that if the alternative to tax revenue is borrowing from the public in order to finance Government spending, then the influence of spending will not necessarily be greater if the funds are borrowed rather than obtained through taxation. They are also consistent with the theory that consumers will maintain consumption levels at the expense of saving when there is a temporary reduction in disposable income.

The signs of the coefficients estimated for high-employment expenditures in equations 1.2 and 1.3 indicate that an increase in Government expenditures is mildly stimulative in the quarter in which spending is increased and in the following quarter. However, in the subsequent two quarters this increase in expenditures causes offsetting negative influences. The overall effect of a change in expenditures distributed over four quarters, indicated by the sum, is relatively small and not statistically significant. These results are consistent with modern quantity theories which hold that Government spending, taxing, and borrowing policies would have, through interest rate and wealth effects, different impacts on economic activity under varying circumstances.[15]

Three Propositions Tested

The empirical relationships developed relating changes in GNP to changes in the money stock and changes in high-employment expenditures and receipts are used to test the three propositions under consideration. The results of testing the propositions using changes in the money stock are discussed in detail in this section. Similar results are reported in the accompanying tables using changes in the monetary base instead of the money stock. Conclusions drawn using either measure of monetary actions are similar.

Proposition I states that fiscal actions exert a larger influence on economic activity than do monetary actions. A test of this proposition involves an examination of the size of the regression coefficients for high-employment expenditures relative to those for money and the monetary base.[16] Proposition I implies that the coefficients for ΔE would be larger, without regard to sign, than those for ΔM and ΔB.

The coefficients presented in Table I are not appropriate for this test because the variables have different time dimensions and are a mixture of stocks and flows. An appropriate measure is developed by changing these regression coefficients to "beta coefficients" which eliminate these difficulties (Table II). These coefficients take into consideration the past variation of changes in each independent variable relative to the past variation of changes in GNP.[17] The size of beta coefficients may be, therefore, directly compared as a measure of the relative contribution of each variable to variations in GNP in the test period.

According to Table II, the beta coefficients for changes in money are greater than those for changes in high-employment expenditures for the quarter in which a change occurs and during the two following quarters. The coefficients for changes in the monetary base are greater for the two quarters immediately following a change in the base. In the lagged quarters in which the beta coefficients for ΔE are largest, a negative sign is associated with the regression

Table II. Measurements of the Relative Importance of Monetary and Fiscal Actions

FIRST DIFFERENCES (EQUATIONS 1.2 AND 1.4)

	BETA COEFFICIENTS						PARTIAL COEFFICIENTS OF DETERMINATION					
QUARTER	ΔM	ΔE	ΔR	ΔB	ΔE	ΔR	ΔM	ΔE	ΔR	ΔB	ΔE	ΔR
t	.24	.14	.05	.06	.09	.16	.07	.02	.01	*	.01	.05
$t-1$	.26	.20	*	.31	.14	.01	.14	.08	*	.18	.03	*
$t-2$	.24	-.02	-.01	.37	-.08	-.05	.12	*	*	.24	.01	.01
$t-3$	.20	-.30	.03	.17	-.36	.04	.06	.13	*	.04	.16	*
Sum	.94	.02	.07	.91	-.21	.16	.45	*	*	.38	.02	.01

CENTRAL DIFFERENCES (EQUATIONS 2.2 AND 2.4)

	BETA COEFFICIENTS						PARTIAL COEFFICIENTS OF DETERMINATION					
QUARTER	ΔM	ΔE	ΔR	ΔB	ΔE	ΔR	ΔM	ΔE	ΔR	ΔB	ΔE	ΔR
t	.26	.20	.09	.04	.11	.25	.07	.04	.02	*	.01	.11
$t-1$	.26	.23	-.01	.31	.19	-.02	.13	.10	*	.16	.06	*
$t-2$	.23	-.06	-.03	.40	-.10	-.09	.11	.01	*	.23	.02	.03
$t-3$	.20	-.36	.05	.20	-.47	.10	.05	.16	*	.05	.21	.01
Sum	.95	.01	.10	.95	-.27	.24	.53	*	.01	.49	.04	.03

* Less than .005.

Table III. Simulated Response of an Increase in Government Expenditures Financed by Monetary Expansion (Millions of Dollars)

QUARTER	INCREASE IN GOVERNMENT EXPENDITURES			REQUIRED INCREASE IN MONEY			TOTAL RESPONSE IN GNP	
	CHANGE IN EXPENDITURES	IMPACT EFFECT ON GNP	CUMULATIVE EFFECT ON GNP	CHANGE IN MONEY STOCK	IMPACT EFFECT ON GNP	CUMULATIVE EFFECT ON GNP	IMPACT EFFECT ON GNP	CUMULATIVE EFFECT ON GNP
1	$1000	$400	$400	$250	$ 385	$ 385	$ 785	$ 785
2	0	540	940	250	775	1160	1315	2100
3	0	− 30	910	250	1135	2295	1105	3205
4	0	−740	170	250	1458	3753	718	3923
5	−1000	−400	−230	0	1072	4825	672	4595
6	0	−540	−770	0	682	5507	142	4737
7	0	30	−740	0	323	5830	353	5090
8	0	740	0	0	0	5830	740	5830

coefficient, indicating a lagged contractionary effect of increased expenditures. As a measure of the total contribution over the four quarters, the sum of the beta coefficients for changes in money and the monetary base are much greater than those for changes in expenditures.

Proposition I may also be tested by the use of partial coefficients of determination. These statistics are measures of the per cent of variation of the dependent variable remaining after the variation accounted for by all other variables in the regression has been subtracted from the total variation. Proposition I implies that larger coefficients should be observed for fiscal actions than for monetary actions. Table II presents the partial coefficients of determination for the variables under consideration. For the quarter of a change and the subsequent two quarters, these coefficients for ΔM are much greater than those for ΔE. With regard to ΔB, the coefficients are about equal to those for ΔE in the first quarter and are much greater in the two subsequent quarters. The partial coefficients of determination for the total contribution of each policy variable to changes in GNP over four quarters may be developed. Table II shows that the partial coefficients of determination for the overall response of ΔGNP to ΔM and ΔB range from .38 to .53, while those for ΔE are virtually zero.

Other implications of the results presented in Table I may be used to test further the relative strength of the response of GNP to alternative government actions under conditions where "other things" are held constant. Three alternative actions are assumed taken by stabilization authorities: (1) the rate of government spending is increased by $1 billion and is financed by either borrowing from the public or increasing taxes; (2) the money stock is increased by $1 billion with no change in the budget position; and (3) the rate of government spending is increased by $1 billion for a year and is financed by increasing the money stock by an equal amount.

The impact on total spending of the first two actions may be measured by using the sums of the regression coefficients presented for equation 1.3. A billion dollar increase in the rate of government spending would, after four quarters, result in a permanent increase of $170 million in GNP. By comparison, an increase of the same magnitude in money would result in GNP being $5.8 billion permanently higher after four quarters.

The results of the last action are presented in Table III.[18] The annual rate of government spending is assumed to be increased by $1 billion in the first quarter and held at that rate for the following three quarters. This would require an increase in money of $250 million during each of the four quarters to finance the higher level of expenditures. Since we are interested only in the result of financing the original increase in expenditures by monetary expansion, expenditures must be reduced by $1 billion in the fifth quarter. If expenditures were held at the higher rate, money would have to continue to grow $250 million per quarter. According to Table III, GNP would rise to a permanent level $5.8 billion higher than at the beginning. This increase in GNP results entirely from monetary expansion.

According to these three tests, the regression results implied by Proposition I did not occur. Therefore, the proposition that the response of total demand to fiscal actions is greater than that of monetary actions is not confirmed by the evidence.

Proposition II holds that the response of economic activity to fiscal actions is more predictable than the response to monetary influence. This implies that the regression coefficients relative to their standard errors (this ratio is called the "*t*-value"), relating changes in E to changes in GNP, should be greater than the corresponding measures for changes in M and in B. The greater the t-value, the more confidence there is in the estimated regression coefficient, and hence, the greater is the reliability of the estimated change in GNP resulting from a change in the variable. These t-values are presented in Table IV.

An examination of this table indicates greater t-values for the regression coefficients of the two monetary variables than for the fiscal variable, except for the third quarter after a change. Also, the t-values for the sum of the regression coefficients for ΔM and ΔB are large, while those for ΔE are not statistically significant from zero. Since the regression results implied by Proposition II did not appear, the proposition is not confirmed.

Proposition III states that the influence of fiscal actions on economic activity occurs faster than that of monetary actions. It is tested by examining the characteristics of the lag structure in the regressions. Proposition III implies that beta coefficients for ΔE should be greater than those for ΔM in the quarter of a change and in those immediately following. It also implies that the main response of GNP to fiscal actions occurs within fewer quarters than its response to monetary actions.

The beta coefficients are plotted in the chart.[19] A change in the money stock induces a large and almost equal response in each of the four quarters. The largest response of GNP to changes in the monetary base occurs in the first and second quarters after a change. The beta coefficients for changes in M are greater than those for changes in E for the quarter of a change and the following quarter, indicating comparatively smaller response of GNP to fiscal actions in these first two quarters. Moreover, the largest coefficient for ΔE occurs for the third quarter after a change.

The expected regression results implied by Proposition III were not found. Therefore, the proposition that the major impact of fiscal influence on economic activity occurs within a shorter time

Table IV. Measurement of Reliability of the Response of GNP to Monetary and Fiscal Actions ("t-values" of Regression Coefficients[1])

	FIRST DIFFERENCES					
QUARTER	ΔM	ΔE	ΔR	ΔB	ΔE	ΔR
t	2.03	1.15	0.53	0.49	0.67	1.68
$t-1$	2.85	2.15	0.03	3.37	1.36	0.07
$t-2$	2.69	0.19	0.10	4.10	0.84	0.64
$t-3$	1.82	2.82	0.32	1.54	3.10	0.39
Sum	6.57	0.13	0.32	5.67	0.89	0.67

	CENTRAL DIFFERENCES					
QUARTER	ΔM	ΔE	ΔR	ΔB	ΔE	ΔR
t	2.01	1.52	1.05	0.28	0.73	2.55
$t-1$	2.78	2.44	0.17	3.16	1.87	0.27
$t-2$	2.45	0.60	0.46	3.92	1.04	1.31
$t-3$	1.72	3.15	0.48	1.71	3.65	0.87
Sum	7.57	0.04	0.54	6.95	1.37	1.16

[1] t-values associated with equations 1.2, 1.4, 2.2, and 2.4 in Table I.

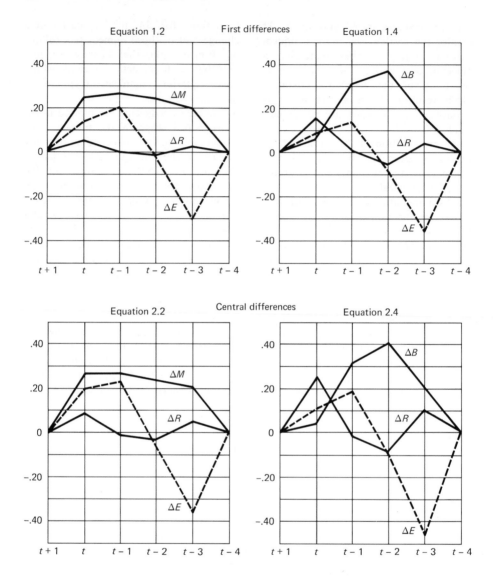

Measures of Lag Response

interval than monetary influence is not confirmed.

SUMMARY. This section tested the propositions that the response of economic activity to fiscal actions relative to monetary actions is (I) larger, (II) more predictable, and (III) faster. The results of the tests were not consistent with any of these propositions. Consequently, either the commonly used measures of fiscal influence do not correctly indicate the degree and direction of such influence, or there was no measurable net fiscal influence on total spending in the test period.

The test results are consistent with an alternative set of propositions. The response of economic activity to monetary actions compared with that of fiscal actions is (I') larger, (II') more predictable, and (III') faster. It should be remembered that these alternative propositions have not been proven true, but this is always the case in scientific testing of hypothesized relationships. Nevertheless, it is asserted here that these alternative propositions are appropriate for the conduct of stabilization policy until evidence is presented proving one or more of them false.

There is a major qualification to these statements. Since the propositions were tested using the period first quarter 1952 to second quarter 1968, it is implicitly assumed in making these statements that the general environment prevailing in the test period holds for the immediate future.

IMPLICATIONS FOR ECONOMIC STABILIZATION POLICY

Rejection of the three propositions under examination and acceptance of the alternatives offered carry important implications for the conduct of economic stabilization policy. All of these implications point to the advisability of greater reliance being placed on monetary actions than on fiscal actions. Such a reliance would represent a marked departure from most present procedures.

The finding that statements which assert that changes in tax rates have a significant influence on total spending are not supported by this empirical investigation suggests that past efforts in this regard have been overly optimistic. Furthermore, the finding that the response of total spending to changes in Government expenditures is small compared with the response of spending to monetary actions strongly suggests that it would be more appropriate to place greater reliance on the latter form of stabilization action.

Finding of a strong empirical relationship between economic activity and either of the measures of monetary actions points to the conclusion that monetary actions can and should play a more prominent role in economic stabilization than they have up to now. Furthermore, failure to recognize these relationships can lead to undesired changes in economic activity because of the relatively short lags and strong effects attributable to monetary actions.

Evidence was found which is consistent with the proposition that the influence of monetary actions on economic activity is more certain than that of fiscal actions. Since monetary influence was also found to be stronger and to operate more quickly than fiscal influence, it would appear to be inappropriate, for stabilization purposes, for monetary authorities to wait very long for a desired fiscal action to be adopted and implemented.

Evidence found in this study suggests that the money stock is an important indicator of the total thrust of stabilization actions, both monetary and fiscal. This point is argued on two grounds. First, changes in the money stock reflect mainly what may be called discretionary actions of the Federal Reserve System as it uses its major instruments of monetary management—open market transactions, discount rate changes, and reserve requirement changes. Second, the money stock reflects the joint actions of the Treasury and the Federal Reserve System in financing newly created Government debt. Such actions are based on decisions regarding the monetization of new debt by Federal Reserve actions, and Treasury decisions regarding changes in its balances at Reserve banks and commercial banks. According to this second point, changes in Government spending financed by monetary expansion are reflected in changes in the monetary base and in the money stock.

A number of economists maintain that the major influence of fiscal actions results only if expenditures are financed by monetary expansion. In practice, the Federal Reserve does not buy securities from the Government. Instead, its open market operations and other actions provide funds in the markets in which both the Government and private sectors borrow.

The relationships expressed in Table I may be used to project the expected course of GNP, given alternative assumptions about monetary and fiscal actions. Such projections necessarily assume that the environment in the period used for estimation and the average relationships of the recent past hold in the future. The projections are not able to take into consideration the influences of other independent forces; therefore, they are not suitable for exact forecasting purposes. However, they do provide a useful measure of monetary and fiscal influences on economic activity.

An example of such projections using equation 1.3 is presented in Table V. Equation 1.3 related quarter-to-quarter

changes in GNP to changes in the money stock and changes in high-employment expenditures, both distributed over four quarters.

Assumptions used in computing the projections of quarterly changes in GNP reported in Table V include: (a) high-employment expenditures were projected through the second quarter of 1969 under the assumption that Federal spending in fiscal 1969 will be about 5 per cent (or $10 billion) greater than fiscal 1968; (b) Federal spending was assumed to continue increasing at a 5 to 6 per cent rate in the first two quarters of fiscal 1970; and (c) quarter-to-quarter changes in the money stock were projected from III/68 to IV/69 for four alternative constant annual growth rates for money: 2 per cent, 4 per cent, 6 per cent, and 8 per cent.

The highest growth rate of the money stock (8 per cent) indicates continued rapid rates of expansion in GNP during the next five quarters. The slowest growth rate of money (2 per cent) indicates some slowing of GNP growth in the fourth quarter of this year and further gradual slowing throughout most of next year.

The projections indicate that if the recent decelerated growth in the money stock (less than 4 per cent from July to October) is continued, and growth of Government spending is at about the rate indicated above, the economy would probably reach a noninflationary growth rate of GNP in about the third quarter of 1969 and would then accelerate slightly. These projections, of course, make no assumptions regarding the Vietnam war, strikes, agricultural situations, civil disorders, or any of the many other non-controllable exogenous forces.

Table V. Projected Change in GNP with Alternative Rates of Change in Money Stock[1]

QUARTER	ASSUMED RATES OF CHANGE IN MONEY STOCK[2]			
	2%	4%	6%	8%
1968/III[3]	17.9	17.9	17.9	17.9
IV	14.6	16.0	17.5	19.0
1969/I	12.0	15.0	18.0	20.7
II	11.0	15.2	19.4	23.7
III	6.8	12.3	18.0	23.4
IV	8.0	13.7	19.4	25.2

[1] First differences of quarterly data. All variables are in billions of dollars. Projections are based on coefficients of equation 1.3 in Table I.
[2] Assumed alternative rates of change in the money stock from III/68 to IV/69.
[3] Preliminary estimate by the Department of Commerce.

NOTES

1 The monetary base is derived from a consolidated monetary balance sheet of the Federal Reserve and the Treasury. See

Leonall C. Andersen and Jerry L. Jordan, "The Monetary Base: Explanation and Analytical Use," in the August 1968 issue of this *Review*. Since the uses of the base are bank reserves plus currency held by the public, it is often called "demand debt of the Government." See James Tobin, "An Essay on Principles of Debt Management," in *Fiscal and Debt Management Policies*, The Commission on Money and Credit, Prentice-Hall, Inc., Englewood Cliffs, N.J., 1963. In some analyses, Tobin includes short-term Government debt outstanding in the monetary base.

2 Also see Leonall C. Andersen and Jerry L. Jordan, "Money in a Modern Quantity Theory Framework," in the December 1967 issue of this *Review*. For an excellent analysis of these three monetary views see David I. Fand, "Keynesian Monetary Theories, Stabilization Policy and the Recent Inflation," a paper presented to the Conference of University Professors, Ditchley Park, Oxfordshire, England, Sept. 13, 1968.

3 Thomas Mayer, *Monetary Policy in the United States*, Random House N.Y., 1968, pp. 148–149.

4 For a discussion of these points see: Karl Brunner, "The Role of Money and Monetary Policy," in the July 1968 issue of this *Review*.

5 Tobin, pp. 143–213.

6 The importance of not overlooking the financial aspects of fiscal policy is emphasized by Carl F. Christ in "A Simple Macroeconomic Model with a Government Budget Restraint," *Journal of Political Economy*, Vol. 76, No. 1, January/February 1968, pp. 53–67. Christ summarizes (pages 53 and 54) that "the multiplier effect of a change in government purchases cannot be defined until it is decided how to finance the purchases, and the value of the multiiplier given by the generally accepted analysis [which ignores the government budget restraint] is in general incorrect . . . (the) multiplier effect of government purchases may be greater or less than the value obtained by ignoring the budget restraint, depending on whether the method of financing is mainly by printing money or mainly by taxation."

7 See Keith M. Carlson, "Estimates of the High-Employment Budget: 1947–1967," in the June 1967 issue of this *Review*. The high-employment budget concept was used in the *Annual Report of the Council of Economic Advisors* from 1962 to 1966. For a recent analysis using the high-employment budget, see "Federal Fiscal Policy in the 1960's" *Federal Reserve Bulletin*, September 1968, pp. 701–718. According to this article, "the concept does provide a more meaningful measure of the Federal budgetary impact than the published measures of actual Federal surplus or deficit taken by themselves."

8 For a detailed discussion of testing hypotheses in reference to monetary actions, see Albert E. Burger and Leonall C. Andersen, "The Development of Testable Hypotheses for Monetary Management," a paper presented at the annual meeting of the Southern Finance Association, November 8, 1968. It will appear in a forthcoming issue of the *Southern Journal of Business*, University of Georgia, Athens, Georgia.

9 A more specific statement relating to these considerations is presented in the Appendix.

10 Changes in GNP, R, and E are quarterly changes in billions of dollars measured at annual rates, while changes in M and B are quarterly changes in billions of dollars. Changes in GNP, R, and E are changes in flows, whereas changes in M and B are changes in a stock. Since all of the time series have strong trends, first differences tend to increase in size over time. Statistical considerations indicate that per cent first differences would be more appropriate. On the other hand, regular first differences provide estimates of multipliers which are more useful for the purposes of this study. Test regressions of relative changes were run and they did not alter the conclusions of this article.

11 John Kareken and Robert M. Solow, "Lags in Monetary Policy," in *Stabilization Policies* of the research studies prepared for the Commission on Money and Credit, Prentice-Hall, Inc., 1962, pp. 18–21.

12 Shirley Almon, "The Distributed Lag Between Capital Appropriations and Expenditures," *Econometrica*, Vol. 33, No. 1, January 1965, pp. 178–196.

13 As a test for structural shifts, the test period was divided into two equal parts and the regressions reported here were run for each sub-period and for the whole period. The Chow test for structural changes accepted the hypothesis that the sets of parameters estimated for each of the sub-periods were not different from each other or from those estimated for

the whole period, at the five per cent level of significance. As a result, there is no evidence of a structural shift; consequently, the whole period was used.

14 It was suggested to the authors that a weighted high-employment budget surplus might be a better measure of fiscal influence than the usual unweighted series. For an elaboration of such a weighted series, see Edward M. Gramlich," Measures of the Aggregate Demand Impact of the Federal Budget," in *Staff Papers of the President's Commission on Budget Concepts*, U.S. Government Printing Office, Washington, D.C., October 1967. Gramlich provided weights from the FRB-MIT model of the economy for constructing a weighted series. It was further suggested that the level of the high-employment budget surplus was a more appropriate measure of fiscal actions. Coefficients of fiscal influence were estimated using both changes in the weighted series, and levels of the high-employment surplus. The results did not change any of the conclusions of this article.

15 John Culbertson points out that in a financially constrained economy (i.e., no monetary expansion to finance Government expenditure), expenditures by the Government financed in debt markets in competition with private expenditures can very possibly "crowd out of the market an equal (or conceivably even greater) volume that would have financed private expenditures." He asserts that it is possible to have a short-lived effect of Government spending on total spending if the financial offsets lag behind its positive effects. The results obtained for ΔE in this article are consistent with his analysis. See John M. Culbertson, *Macroeconomic Theory and Stabilization Policy*, McGraw-Hill Inc., New York, 1968, pp. 462–463.

16 Since little response of GNP to ΔR was found, further discussions consider only ΔE.

17 Arthur S. Goldberger, *Econometric Theory*, John Wiley & Sons, Inc., December 1966, New York, pp. 197–200.

18 The authors wish to give special thanks to Milton Friedman for suggesting this illustration and Table III. However, the formulation presented here is the sole responsibility of the authors.

19 The Almon lag structure was developed by using a fourth degree polynomial and constraining the coefficients for $t - 4$ to zero. The regressions indicate that four quarters constitute an appropriate response period for both fiscal and monetary actions. Equations using up to seven lagged quarters were also estimated, but there was little response in GNP to fiscal and monetary actions beyond the three quarter lags reported.

Monetary and Fiscal Policy—Comparisons and Alternatives
Henry C. Wallich

I shall begin with what seems to me the popular view of fiscal and monetary policy. Like academics, the average individual needs a frame of reference in which to analyze and place his ideas. The theory which, more than any other, shapes

Henry C. Wallich, "Monetary and Fiscal Policy—Comparisons and Alternatives," in *Conference on Savings and Residential Financing, 1966* (Chicago: U.S. Savings and Loan League, 1966), pp. 21–31.

popular thinking in this respect is that the world is divided into the "good guys" and the "bad guys." It is very clear who are the "good guys" and who are the "bad guys" in the arena of monetary and fiscal policy. Fiscal policy means the "good guys." They cut taxes, they are for full employment, they are for the little fellow, they increase benefits, they are for fast growth. Politically, they are identified with Democrats.

The "bad guys" very plainly are the people favoring monetary policy: Bill Martin, bankers, high interest rates, high cost of homes and cars, stagnation, unemployment—these are the images. This "good guy, bad guy" image, which comes in part out of the populist tradition, reaches into the very highest places in our hierarchy. The New Economics, in a way, has done its share to foster that image by continually stressing the virtues of expansion and criticizing the evils of restrictionism. To be sure, when one reads these statements more carefully, they usually are qualified, being written by competent economists. But the average individual does nor read fine print, hence the New Economics is largely identified, I think, with expansionism. This identification is now coming home to roost; it has created a political climate in which it is very difficult to turn the economy around.

THE PROFESSIONAL VIEW

Going from the popular to the professional level, what is the professional image of fiscal and monetary policy? There is a grain of truth in the popular image. It is true that monetary policy somehow is associated more with restrictionism than with expansionism. This is true, first, because very probably monetary policy is more powerful per restriction. As you recall, you push on a string when you want to use monetary policy for expansion. But when you pull on a string (one should more properly say, pull on a rubber band) you do get some effect.

The Federal Reserve unquestionably is more concerned with price stability than are other parts of the government. I think this would be true no matter who is in the Federal Reserve. If, 10 years from now, we should reassemble here, and if the rate of inflation at that time should be 20 per cent, and if an administration spokesman at that time should say that 20 per cent

was undesirable but tolerable, there would be someone in the Federal Reserve trying to get the rate down from 20 per cent to 10 per cent. His image would be blackened as a reactionary and restrictionist who is concerned with money and not with people. It would be the professional bias that comes from working with monetary policy that will put the Federal Reserve into the same position at 20 per cent inflation as it does at 2 per cent.

On the side of fiscal policy, the professional attitude in the recent discussion about whether to raise taxes has been, by my standards, a sound one. That is to say, there has been a widespread demand to raise taxes. It is not the prescription that Paul McCracken has given us; but, after the recent discussion in the press, being one-sidedly expansionist is not a charge that can be leveled against a majority of the academic profession.

SPEED OF ACTION

We have shown through widespread public expression that fiscal and monetary policies are indeed two-way streets. If they are to be two-way streets, they must be maneuverable. Paul McCracken has said some very illuminating things about maneuverability of the two policies. As you know, one can distinguish the recognition lag, the action lag, and the operating lag. The first two—the time it takes to recognize the need for action and the time it takes to take the action— are the inside lag, and the time it takes the action to take effect on the economy is the outside lag. For monetary policy, the inside lag is short. The Federal Reserve, in the postwar period, has been pretty quick to recognize changes in the economy. That, I think, is the preponderant finding of people like Karl Brunner and Allan Meltzer and, to a lesser extent, I think, of Robert Solow and John Kareken. By and large, the Federal

Reserve deserves a good rating on that score.

THE INSIDE LAG

Fiscal policy's inside lag is very long. The remarks that Paul McCracken made underscored this fact. I shall come to the outside lag in just a minute, but let me say what I think could be done about shortening the inside lag. This is important in the case of fiscal policy. The procedures proposed are two: one, to give the President administrative discretion over tax rates; the other, to expedite congressional procedures through advance hearings that would let the Congress carry a tax change to the point where all that is needed is a joint resolution. The Congress takes a dim view of the first of these. Its members would not dream, apparently, of giving the President enduring discretion. And the Congress does not like the second, either. As a distinguished member of the Ways and Means Committee said, "You put down your chips when you know what the game is," but you do not legislate in advance.

A member of Congress once said that there was no problem with a tax change; a tax cut, particularly, would go through the Congress as fast as a declaration of war. We have seen that that is not necessarily so. Our last tax cut took a year and a half.

One possible device that has not been explored much is standby authority for the President, under limiting conditions. This proposal to vote an increase and let the President put it into effect, thereby tying his hands in all respects except the timing, seems to arise from the general unpopularity of the idea of a tax increase. It is a political "hot potato." Perhaps in that way we may yet get some semblance of administrative discretion. It will not be what economists have dreamed of, but it would be at least better than nothing.

What is the application of all this to the present situation? We have discovered that tax increases are highly unpopular. That seems to mean that in every other year—every election year—fiscal policy is stymied and cannot be used for restraint. The experience also casts doubt on the feasibility or advisability of flexibility for tax cuts. It might just possibly mean that, if that power existed, there would be a tax cut every election year.

The present situation presents a stalemate. Business is against a tax increase, labor is against an increase, the politicians are against an increase, Paul McCracken is against an increase. Who is for it? The academic establishment is, but apparently we have not been able to put it over. So instead of a great occasion to demonstrate what fiscal policy can do—that it is a two-way street, that it is a flexible instrument that can be used quickly in succession, with first a tax cut, then a tax increase—we now appear to be giving a national demonstration that the technique does not work properly, that it cannot be used flexibly, that it is politically handcuffed. We are in great danger of discrediting the instrument. I think Paul McCracken has already drawn the conclusion that the instrument is not as good as it promised, but I am still hopeful.

THE OUTSIDE LAG

After this consideration of the inside lag, let me turn to the outside lag. Walter Heller has used an elegant formulation to show that the outside-lag fiscal policy is shorter than the outside-lag monetary policy. He said fiscal policy deals with income, while monetary policy deals with assets. Changes that have to work their way through the asset and liability structure inevitably take longer than actions that work directly on income. Every epigram is a half-truth formulated so as to annoy the fellow who believes the other half, and Walter Heller certainly irritated those who believe that monetary policy can work fast even outside.

I think a more accurate formulation is that, insofar as a policy instrument works on consumption, it is likely to work fast and, insofar as it works on investment, it is likely to work slowly. It is quite true that monetary policy works predominantly on investment and so, necessarily, effects are likely to be slow. Fiscal policy works on consumption to the extent that we are dealing with taxes that affect individual income. It works on investment to the extent that it works on the corporate income tax, on the investment tax credit, and indirectly on investment through the accelerator effects of changing consumption expenditures. On balance, therefore, Heller probably is quite right. Fiscal policy probably is the faster working of the two.

We have a good deal of empirical evidence. There are the monumental studies of the Commission on Money and Credit. Albert Ando and Cary Brown examined the effect of a tax cut or increase. They found that on consumption a tax change works quite fast; within the quarter after the tax change there is a 60 per cent response and in the second quarter a 76 per cent response, with some qualifications. As far as investment is concerned, a change in the corporate income tax leads to an 86 per cent response in new orders in the same quarter. Ultimately, the change in new orders is twice the change in corporate taxes and profits. But what is the lag between new orders and deliveries? And here we come upon another uncertainty. What is it that really matters to economic activity? Is it new orders, or is it payments and deliveries? Murray Weidenbaum has made a plausible case for arguing that it is orders and thus that the lag in the response to changes in taxes on corporations or changes in the investment tax credit would be relatively short.

Lags in monetary policy are much more debatable. We have a greater range of studies and less unanimity. Milton Friedman says that the lag is very long—12 to 18 months—because he looks at the rate of change in the money supply and the level of economic activity. Some analysts, however, find it hard to understand why these two variables should be related. If one relates money supply itself and economic activity, it turns out that there is virtually no lag at all. This leaves a question that all of us must have asked at one time: Which is the chicken and which is the egg? Is it economic activity that predominantly determines money, or is it money that predominantly determines economic activity?

Another way of studying monetary policy is to look at Federal Reserve policy actions as manifested in the movement of reserves. Then the impact of conditions in the money market and capital market upon new orders and upon deliveries may be studied. Kareken and Solow have tried this. They have found very variable and very long lags. This finding was arrived at earlier in quite a different way by Tom Mayer, who asked people how long it actually took to build a house or a big industrial complex. Distributing the lags of these expenditures, he found that monetary policy has a very long lag. But this evidence has been controverted by others, such as William White. It leaves one in a state of agnosticism.

Now let us apply these findings to today's problem. If you start with a presumption that some kind of restraint is needed, it seems clear that we ought to act on consumption rather than on investment. If we try to act on investment, the response probably will come too late. That speaks against an increase in the corporate income tax rate and against a reduction in the investment tax credit. It argues in favor of fiscal policy restraint rather than monetary policy restraint. All of this rests, of course, on the premise that the present situation requires further restraint.

THE PREDICTABILITY CONTROVERSY

The question of lags is very closely related to the question of predictability, and that issue has raised a good deal of dust lately. In the September 1965 issue of the *American Economic Review*, the first 100 pages are taken up by what one might call the controversy of Friedman and Meiselman versus the rest. "The rest" are Albert Ando and Franco Modigliani, Michael DePrano and Thomas Mayer, and, earlier, Don Hester in the *Review of Economics and Statistics*. All of them have attacked Friedman and Meiselman but, as far as I can see, the two still stand bloody but unbowed. This discussion is fundamental to governmental policy-making. Friedman and Meiselman deny the validity of the rather common assumption that the relationship of investment to income is stabler than the relationship of money to income. They argue that the quantity theory relationship is stabler than the Keynesian relationship. Of course this has infuriated good Keynesians.

Friedman and Meiselman begin very impressively with a test of what are autonomous expenditures. One of the useful contributions they make is to show that no one really knows what is meant by autonomous expenditures. The textbook says, Take autonomous expenditures, multiply them by the multiplier, and the result is income. But autonomous expenditures break down into many types of investment, public spending, and exports. Choices must be made. Friedman and Meiselman's test can be challenged. It requires certain assumptions which do not always seem justified. In some cases, it does not even give a proper answer. The test leads them to adopt some very queer autonomous variables: not total govern-

ment expenditures, but the government deficit; not exports, but net foreign investment, and, of course, investment. Taking these variables and relating them to income over a long period of time, but for many subperiods, they get, on the whole, a pretty bad fit. They then take money and relate it to income, and, except for the 1930's they get a pretty good fit. Ergo, money is better than autonomous expenditures and the quantity theory is better than Keynes.

WHAT THE CRITICS SAY

What do the critics say? They say, first, that this is a questionable issue because no one, least of all Friedman, will use a simple consumption function such as is imputed here. He simply uses current income, not assets or past income. They show that the equations that Friedman and Meiselman used are merely reduced forms of a structural model which one can only say is misspecified. The whole argument thus occurs in a kind of artificial straight jacket which does not allow the relevant questions to come up.

The critics then go through the exercise of answering Friedman and Meiselman on the latter's own grounds. What do they find? Ando and Modigliani break down autonomous expenditures in great detail. It is very interesting to see what seems to be autonomous in government expenditures and what seems to be induced; what part of taxes is induced and what part is autonomous. These, I think, are all very useful contributions. Using their definitions, Ando and Modigliani get a fine fit for the autonomous income relation. Then, claiming to have refuted Friedman and Meiselman on that side of the argument, they turn to the money relation. They throw out actual money and substitute potential money on the grounds that actual money is partly induced; banks borrow from the Federal Reserve in response to loan demand. Therefore, what one really should take as money is the amount that can be invested on the basis of the reserves the Federal Reserve wants the banks to have. This means to eliminate borrowed reserves and "use up" excess reserves. Redefining money in this way as "potential money," they get a miserable fit for the money-income relation.

De Prano and Mayer do something else. They plug in one seemingly autonomous variable after another, and each time their R^2 becomes a little better. Then they plug in some induced variables, such as tax revenues or imports, and R^2 goes down. What gives the highest R^2 is the test for what constitutes exogenous variables. For those variables they get a pretty good fit, about as good as Friedman and Meiselman get for their money relation.

Friedman and Meiselman reject all this. They say, quite rightly, that they have applied an objective test to what constitutes autonomous expenditures. The critics have simply been on a fishing expedition; they have tried out what gives a good fit, and have settled on that. This is not a proper scientific procedure. In particular, when large amounts of GNP, such as all public expenditures, are thrown into autonomous expenditures, the dependent part of GNP becomes relatively small. Friedman and Meiselman point out quite correctly that much of the charm of Keynesian theory then disappears. The charm is that from a very small variable—autonomous expenditures—it is possible to explain a very large thing—total income. But when finally a good part of the total is thrown into autonomous, it becomes fairly easy to explain the GNP. They say, not without some justification, that the critics have not found an answer to a question, but rather have discovered a question to which there is an answer.

At that point the debate stands. I am sure there will be further work. I think the particular way in which the debate has been started, in the narrow, two-variable, single-equation system, is not a very fruitful one. Undoubtedly it will be carried over into the equation systems. But the problems brought up by Friedman and Meiselman are very fruitful—such as their challenge to the concept of autonomous expenditure.

What does all this mean to our present problem of whether or not to use monetary or fiscal policy in order to cope with the present overheating? By and large, I think the discussion need not dissuade us from the use of fiscal policy. Friedman might say that it argues against the use of fiscal policy. But when arbitrary tax changes are made, such as might be enacted now, there is no question what is autonomous, except in a model which makes Congressional reactions a behavioral response to an economic situation. One can always say that a tax change is an autonomous event and treat it as such. From there on, the rest follows; one can, by means of a multiplier, compute the consequences. Hence, even if Friedman and Meiselman were right, this need not stop us from using fiscal policy in this particular situation.

RELATIVE STRENGTH OF MONETARY, FISCAL POLICY

What is important to the choice between monetary and fiscal policy is the relative strength of the two. The general feeling is that fiscal policy is a more powerful tool. Clearly, this depends on the scale on which the two tools are used. In fact, monetary policy rarely is used on a massive scale, largely because the effects are unpredictable and the Federal Reserve is afraid of overshooting. This is one reason for downgrading the strength of monetary policy.

A second question about the strength of monetary policy relates to the transmission mechanism, discussion of which I shall postpone for a moment. If one takes a hard quantity-theory line, a change in money produces a proportionate change in income. If one changes money enough, one will change income enough. The whole question of whether or not a monetary policy is powerful disappears. It becomes a question merely of scale of operation.

If one's view of the transmission mechanism is not that of pure quantity theory, but that it works through interest rates or through availability or through the volume of credit, then questions of the power of monetary policy do arise. Then all depends on the elasticity of investment with respect to interest rates and on the possible existence of a liquidity trap that may prevent interest rates from falling sufficiently. In that case, there are factors that soften the effects of monetary policy.

INTERNATIONAL OBSTACLES TO MONETARY POLICY

One further weakness of monetary policy needs to be noted. Robert Mundell has pointed out that under conditions of international capital mobility, monetary policy becomes increasingly ineffective. We experienced this in the recession of 1960–1961; we could not cut interest rates as much as we should have liked to, owing to the possible outflow of funds. Japan and Germany have experienced this in their monetary policy operations. It turns out that when a country with international capital mobility wants to tighten, money flows in from abroad. Local firms borrow abroad unless an exchange control is imposed which conflicts with the premise of capital mobility. Monetary policy then becomes more of an instrument to regulate the balance of payments than to regulate domestic activity.

The United States, in a nearly closed large economy, is still far from that point. Monetary policy in the American economy still has a good degree of independence, but the balance of payments does clip the wings of the Federal Reserve in its freedom of domestic policy making.

I have not said much about the strength of fiscal policy. It, too, seems proportional to the size of the action taken, and more clearly so than monetary policy. There is one question mark, however. We do not know what is the effect of a temporary tax cut. (I do not know why it is so much easier to say "tax cut" than "tax increase." I think the New Economics has so shaped even one's organs of speech that one can only say "tax cut.") But it we should raise taxes, let us say, for only six months, it might turn out to be a monetary policy operation like the recent prepayment of taxes by corporations and to some extent individuals. The effect might be much less than in the case of a permanent change.

After comparing the relative strength of the two tools, the question naturally arises as to the mix. Paul McCracken has covered this problem more than adequately. Just to review very briefly, we have two instruments aimed principally at one goal—the level of economic activity. The mix has side effects. It may favor the growth of the economy or disfavor it; it may favor the balance of payments or injure it.

A given level of economic activity can be achieved with a tight budget and easy money. That is the growth-oriented mix. Savings are created via the budget and can be fed back to investment in the private sector. This mix is hard on the balance of payments, because low interest rates encourage outflows.

Tight money and easy budgets are the balance-of-payments-oriented mix. It attracts funds from abroad but it is hard on growth, because deficits absorb investable funds unless the government itself makes the investments. For the balance of payments, the problem of the mix poses itself in a particular way. There are occasions when an economy faces a conflict of internal and external stability. This has been the case in the United States until recently; it was the case in the United Kingdom during the 1920s. The case may be one of unemployment and a balance-of-payments deficit. That combination calls for a particular mix. It would be wrong, then, to tighten the budget in order to restrain imports and improve the balance of payments, and to ease monetary policy in order to stimulate domestic employment. That mix, as Robert Mundell has shown very elegantly, will get the economy into a worse and worse situation. It is a disequilibrium pattern. If the mix is reversed so that monetary policy is used to improve the balance of payments by both restraining imports and attracting capital, and fiscal policy is used to stimulate domestic employment, the economy will move toward an equilibrium position. Here the mix is very important; it must be right.

What does this mean in our present situation? It is quite clear that we have ceased to have an internal-external conflict. We have a payments deficit and have long had one. But we have shifted from underemployment to overemployment. Therefore monetary policy and fiscal policy must both pull in the same direction. We have the classic situation now of a country suffering domestic inflation and a balance-of-payments deficit, and the classic answer is very simple. Both hands must be used to pull in the same direction; that is, both monetary and fiscal policy must be used to scotch both the domestic and the international imbalance.

COORDINATION VERSUS INDEPENDENCE

The mix problem implies that there should be an all-wise and all-powerful government, manned by some economist-king who delicately combines policies and shapes their influence as needed. That

kind of coordination of monetary and fiscal policy we do not have. In the recent discount rate change, the Federal Reserve stepped out of line, giving evidence that coordination is very capable of breaking down.

Should we have more coordination, or should we leave things as they are? The argument for coordination is very simple. In the old days, monetary policy was the only anticyclical tool of the government. Moreover, it was regarded as really a technical application of the rules of the game. It was not a political matter. Today, the government has many instruments and it is recognized that monetary policy, which is only one of many, is an eminently political variable. It is not merely the application of certain rules that can safely be left to competent technicians.

It is popular to say that the President should have power over monetary policy in order to coordinate the two instruments. That implies, however, something that is not at all true, namely, that the President has power over fiscal policy. He does not have such power. He proposes, Congress disposes. It is not clear where the locus of fiscal policy is; but so long as the President does not have power over short-term fiscal policy, I can see no logical reason to concentrate monetary power in his hands.

But the argument really is not a logical or an economic one. It is a pragmatic one. The people who like a softer monetary policy are for coordination; the people who prefer a harder monetary policy favor Federal Reserve independence. Why is this? When there has been a conflict between the Federal Reserve and the administration, which has been a rare event, really, the pattern has always been very clear: the Federal Reserve is for the harder, and the administration is for the softer, policy. Hence, the pragmatic answer is that to choose coordination means to choose a softer policy; to choose independence is to choose a harder policy. I have a strong suspicion that if the recent trend in appointments to the Federal Reserve Board should continue, and if some day the Federal Reserve should be more liberal than the rest of the government, some of my friends will discover the virtues of Federal Reserve independence and I shall be arguing for coordination.

NEW TOOLS

This leaves me with (a) very little time to speak and (b) several topics that I wanted to cover. On the matter of tools of policy, our problem, very briefly, is that monetary policy has been too unimaginative; the Federal Reserve has been so happy to get back to the 1920s that it has never observed that we are in a different decade. Fiscal policy has been too imaginative. We have never developed a simple device for moving taxes up and down; we always mix in some element of reform. This is understandable. But until it is agreed what is a neutral tax cut, and until the defenders of the poor stop arguing that, when taxes are raised, neutrality means equal increases in the tax burden and, when taxes are lowered, neutrality means equal changes in post-tax income, while the friends of the rich say the opposite, the problem is to decide on a neutral tax cut or increase and use it flexibly when the need arises.

There remains the grave question of the transmission mechanism. I have left this to the last because I think it is the most perplexing and humiliating issue in all the area. Concerning fiscal policy, we do seem to know more or less how the transmission mechanism works. We do have uncertainty about what constitutes autonomous expenditures. We do have the further uncertainty about whether orders or final payments exert the principal effect. But, by and large, how fiscal policy works I think we know.

How monetary policy works we do not

know. We have historical experience and we have various theoretical models, but we do not know whether it is the money supply, as Milton Friedman says; or the interest rate, as Keynes said; or the volume of credit, as the Federal Reserve says. If Milton Friedman is right, many things go by the wayside. It then does not matter whether money is created by loans to business, by a budget deficit, or by buying government bonds from investors with high liquidity preference. This seems implausible to me. Also, if Milton Friedman is right and if it is the money supply and not the manner of its creation that is important, then interest rates may go by the board.

HOW DO CHANGES IN MONEY WORK?

In that case, we have to ask ourselves: If it looks as if changes in money do not work through interest rates, how on earth do they work? If the answer is that they do work through interest rates after all, then we can dispense with the money supply. We can say that if we can set interest rates at some particular level, we will get all the effects that are needed, let the money supply be what it may. To differentiate between money and interest rates as parts of the transmission mechanism, it is necessary to postulate that money does not work through interest rates. If it does not work through interest rates, we can throw most of our models in the wastebasket and start afresh, perhaps with a simple quantity theory.

Do these perplexities, which I have stated with some exaggeration, have any application to our present situation? They have a very profound application. Interest rates have been rising; the money supply has been rising. By the interest rates standard, the Federal Reserve has conducted a tight policy or a tightening policy. By money supply standards, it has conducted a very easy policy. Recently, in a colloquy before the Joint Economic Committee, Walter Heller said that monetary policy had been permissive in this long expansion, and the tone of his voice suggested that he meant grudgingly permissive. Raymond J. Saulnier said that monetary policy had been extremely expansionary. Heller referred to interest rates; Saulnier, to money supply.

As long as we cannot answer this question, we really know very little about monetary policy. Applying that particular lesson to our present situation, we are brought back to the conclusion that it is fiscal policy to which we ought to turn. I shall rest my case on the suggestion that we need a quick, temporary tax increase now.

Monetary Versus Fiscal Actions: Comments*
Frank de Leeuw and John Kalchbrenner

A recent article by Andersen and Jordan answers many of the criticisms of earlier single-equation studies of the relation between money and income.[1] It makes use of distributed lags instead of fixed-point lags. It uses high-employment Federal receipts and expenditures instead of actual receipts and expenditures. It represents monetary policy by the monetary base as well as the money supply. These technical improvements should make their conclusion that fiscal policies have no perceptible effect on GNP movements all the more disturbing to those of us who have

been inclined to believe that fiscal policies have powerful effects on income.

The purpose of this "Comment" is to examine whether these conclusions hold up under a careful examination of the statistical requirements of single-equation models and their presence or absence in the Andersen–Jordan equations. We are led, in the course of the examination, to try some alternative equations with important differences in results. The alternative equations seem to us to cast considerable doubt on the Andersen–Jordan skepticism about fiscal policy.

Frank de Leeuw and John Kalchbrenner, "Monetary and Fiscal Actions: A Test of Their Relative Importance in Economic Stabilization—Comment," Federal Reserve Bank of St. Louis, *Review* (April 1969), pp. 6–11.

* We wish to thank the staff of the Federal Reserve Bank of St. Louis, especially Messrs. Andersen and Jordan, for supplying us with data and for making the pages of the *Review* available to us. This "Comment" was first presented at a seminar at the Federal Reserve Board on January 16, 1969, and was followed by a lively and helpful discussion by Messrs. Andersen, Jordan, and other colleagues in the Federal Reserve System. Responsibility for the statements in this "Comment" rests, of course, solely with the authors.

THE STATISTICAL REQUIREMENTS OF SINGLE-EQUATION MODELS

Two different ways of describing the St. Louis equations bring into focus the central problem that has concerned us. One way to describe the equations is to say that they are attempts at using multiple regression to measure the influence on GNP of certain exogenous government policy variables. By exogenous we here mean variables that can be heavily and directly influenced by policymakers. Variables which are not easily influenced by policymakers are not particularly useful ones to have in a regression, except as they reduce uncertainty about the coefficients of the policy variables.

A second way to describe the St. Louis equations is that they are reduced forms of some underlying more complex model of the economy. In any model of this kind the current endogenous variables—the ones the model attempts to explain—depend on past values of the endogenous variables and on the exogenous variables. By exogenous we now mean variables which do not respond to current movements in the endogenous variables.[2] By solving for the past endogenous variables, we can in principle reduce the system to a relation between each current endogenous variable and current and lagged exogenous variables. A linear relation between GNP and exogenous variables is a simple approximation to such a reduced-form relationship. Relations between the general price level and exogenous variables or some interest rate and exogenous variables would be other reduced-form relationships. From a statistical viewpoint, the assumption that the exogenous variables do not respond to movements of the endogenous variables is crucial. For if we call exogenous in a GNP equation some "X" which itself strongly responds to current economic developments, we don't know whether we are measuring the influence of "X" on the economy, the economy on "X", or some third force on both "X" and the economy.

These two descriptions of the St. Louis equations use the word exogenous in two different senses. In the first description exogenous means a variable subject to control by policymakers, while in the second, exogenous means a variable which does not respond to current endogenous forces. Clearly these two definitions do not correspond. The best known example of a conflict is the case of tax receipts. Tax receipts are exogenous in the policy sense of being subject to manipulation by policymakers, but they are clearly not exogenous in the statistical sense of not responding to current movements in the endogenous variable income.

The art of learning something from single-equation regressions of the St. Louis type consists in devising variables which can be manipulated by policymakers but which have been adjusted in such a way they are not terribly sensitive to current movements in the endogenous variables. If an explanatory variable does not meet the first requirement, it is not an effective policy instrument. If it does not meet the second requirement, then it is impossible to know what is influencing what, or how serious the problem of bias is in the equation. Failure to meet this second requirement has been a major criticism of regressions of GNP on the money supply.[3] Only if we can devise fiscal and monetary policy representations which get around this second problem will the single-equation approach be able to tell us something about the effects of macroeconomic policies.

Andersen and Jordan are already aware of this problem of devising variables that are exogenous under both definitions. That is presumably the reason for using high-employment Federal receipts and expenditures which are clearly much less affected by current endogenous movements in income than are actual receipts and expenditures. It also is the most powerful reason, it seems to us, for using the monetary base rather than the money supply. They have clearly moved in the right direction in both these respects. Our central doubt about the article, however, is whether they have gone far enough in purging their policy variables of the influence of current movements in economic activity. We feel that both the tax variable and the monetary base variable may still reflect the influence of current economic developments, and this leads us to try to represent monetary and fiscal policies by time series which are not quite the same as those of Andersen and Jordan.

The Reduced-Form Approach

Before examining the tax and monetary base variables, however, we would like to make two general remarks about the reduced-form or single-equation approach. One is that while there is much we can do in the way of adjusting policy measures for obvious and measurable endogenous influences, it is extremely difficult to devise variables which *fully* meet both definitions of exogenous. The problem is not simply that the variables policymakers influence are also influenced by current economic developments; part of the problem is that policymakers themselves are naturally influenced in their decisions by current developments. We may conjecture, however, that the endogenous responses of policymakers are much less mechanical or predictable than, say, the influence of income fluctuations on tax receipts, and are less likely to be serious sources of bias.

The second remark is that there are a host of other problems with the single-equation approach. Many exogenous variables (in the statistical sense) have to be left out while others are aggregated to crowd everything into one equation, in spite of likely dissimilarities in effects. There is no obvious reason why these problems should bias the coefficients in one direction and not in another for the included variables. If we were trying to devise the most useful single equation, however, there are other modifications we would try. We do not do so here in order to stay within the spirit of the Andersen–Jordan article.

Fiscal Variables

The tax variable is represented in the St. Louis article by high-employment receipts in current dollars. Adjusting actual receipts to a high-employment level is probably as good a job as we can do of eliminating the influence of fluctuations in real output, but this fails to eliminate the influence of inflation. That is, even full-employment tax receipts, when they are expressed in current dollars, go up faster during a period of rapidly rising prices than they do during a period of price stability. The tax variable, then, is still not exogenous in the statistical sense since it responds to current movements in the price level.

Fortunately, there is a simple way to eliminate, or largely eliminate, this source of bias. Instead of using full-employment receipts this period we can adjust last period's receipts to current prices by multiplying full-employment receipts by a ratio of this period's general price level to last period's general price level. When we subtract this inflated last-period figure from the current figure, we get the difference in full-employment receipts expressed in this period's prices. It seems to us that this is a clear improvement over the Andersen–Jordan variable.

The Monetary Base

Our next, and principal, concern is with the monetary base. The base may be expressed as the sum of three components: unborrowed reserves (including the adjustments for reserve requirement changes), borrowed reserves, and currency. For the base to be exogenous in a statistical sense, it must be assumed that the sum of these three components is largely independent of current disturbances in the endogenous variables. It appears to us that this assumption is open to debate. We would like to consider whether a variable with the properties we need could be more closely approximated by omitting borrowed reserves, or currency, or both.

BORROWED RESERVES. Few would disagree with the proposition that, at least as the discount window has been administered for the last fifteen years, member bank borrowings have responded strongly to current movements in business loan demand and interest rates. The question of interest, however, is not whether borrowings are endogenous, since presumably that would be a matter of common agreement. Rather the question is whether there is a strong tendency for movements in borrowing to be offset by movements in some other component of the base. If there is a tendency for endogenous responses in borrowing to be offset by movements in other components of the base, then the total base contains offsetting endogenous influences and we should prefer the total base for the St. Louis regressions. If there is not such a tendency, then adjusting the base to remove borrowings produces a better monetary policy variable than the total base. Inclusion of borrowings in this latter case might lead to a statistical confusion between the effects of a high monetary base on the economy with the effects of a booming economy on borrowing and, hence, on the base.

The question is, then, whether unborrowed reserves or currency tend to fall when something happens in the general economy to make borrowings rise.[4] There are circumstances in which the answer probably is yes. For example, if the central bank is watching the rate of growth of bank credit or of the stock of money as an indicator of its effect on the economy, then an increase in borrowing which supports a rate of growth greater than the target rate might provoke a reduction in unborrowed reserves to put the rate of growth of credit or money back on target. It is easy, however, to think of circumstances in which a rise in borrowing might produce a reinforcing movement in unborrowed reserves if the level of borrowing itself is one of the statistics the central bank uses as an index of its effects, as it was during much of the 1950's. For then an increase in borrowing might well lead the central bank to expand unborrowed reserves in order to get borrowing back on target. Since it is not hard to think of unborrowed reserves responding in either direction to a change

in borrowing during the sample period of the regressions, it seems to us better to represent monetary policy by a variable which excludes member bank borrowing.

CURRENCY. There is a widespread agreement that the demand for currency responds to movements in income or some measure of transactions. We can again, as a matter of algebra, express the reduced-form equation for GNP in terms of either reserves plus currency or in terms of reserves alone. The question once more is whether there is some strong tendency on the part of other components of the monetary base to offset the response of currency to current transactions or other endogenous influences. In the case of currency, there is an automatic mechanism making for an offset, since the usual procedure by which the public obtains more currency involves an initial decrease in vault cash or in bank reserves. The existence of this mechanism is one argument in favor of using the sum of reserves plus currency rather than reserves alone as a monetary policy variable.

There is more to the problem, however, than this automatic response. The reason is that over the sample period of the regressions, the central bank has tended to focus on banking and money market data in judging its current effect. It has not paid particular attention to movements in currency. If there is an increase in the rate of growth of currency—as there was 7 or 8 years ago—it is not permitted to cause a lower rate of growth of unborrowed reserves unless the central bank happens to want a lower rate of growth of reserves for other reasons. The net result is that an endogenous change in currency may well affect the monetary base, and that the base excluding currency may be a more suitable variable for the present study.

Because of these characteristics of member bank borrowing and currency, it seems to us well worth while to rerun the St. Louis equations with various alternative definitions of the monetary policy variable. We are not certain which of the definitions is preferable; therefore, we are not prepared to defend one set of regression results as superior to the others. We are, however, inclined to doubt the validity of conclusions about policy effects which are supported under one definition but contradicted under another.

ALTERNATIVE SINGLE-EQUATION RESULTS

Table I contains the results of carrying out the above-mentioned modifications to the St. Louis equations. They are based upon the same sample period as that used in the St. Louis regressions, I/1952–II/1968, and data furnished by Andersen

Table 1. Regressions of Quarterly Changes in GNP (Current Dollars) on Current and Lagged Changes in Monetary and Fiscal Policy Variables (Sample Period—I/1952 to II/1968)

	REGRESSION EQUATIONS				
	1	2		3	
	ST. LOUIS RESULTS	USING ADJUSTED BASE, ADJUSTED HIGH-EMPLOYMENT RECEIPTS		USING ADJUSTED BASE LESS CURRENCY, ADJUSTED HIGH-EMPLOYMENT RECEIPTS	
Length of Lags (quarters)	4	4	8	4	8
Monetary Policy variable	ΔB	ΔBa	ΔBa	ΔRu	ΔRu
sum of coefficients	15.8	10.4	12.3	2.4	11.6
	(5.5)	(3.4)	(2.8)	(0.6)	(1.6)
Federal Expenditures variable	ΔE	ΔE	ΔE	ΔE	ΔE
sum of coefficients	−0.5	0.4	0.6	1.7	2.5
	(−0.8)	(0.7)	(0.6)	(3.7)	(4.1)
Federal Receipts variable	ΔR	ΔRa	ΔRa	ΔRa	ΔRa
sum of coefficients	0.5	−0.3	−0.5	−1.6	−2.8
	(0.6)	(−0.3)	(−0.4)	(−1.8)	(−2.6)
Constant	1.6	3.6	3.0	6.4	5.0
	(1.2)	(2.8)	(1.9)	(5.3)	(3.6)
R^2/S.E.	.51/4.4	.46/4.5	.53/4.2	.42/4.7	.56/4.1

Note: Figures given are regression coefficients; the "t" statistics appear below each coefficient, enclosed by parentheses.

ΔB = change in monetary base (currency plus total member bank reserves adjusted for reserve requirement changes)
ΔBa = change in adjusted base (B less changes in member bank borrowings)
ΔRu = change in unborrowed reserves (Ba less changes in currency, or unborrowed reserves adjusted for reserve requirement changes)
ΔE = change in high-employment expenditures, current dollars
ΔR = change in high-employment receipts, current dollars
ΔRa = change in high employment receipts in current period prices (last period's receipts multiplied by ratio of current prices to last period's prices)

and Jordan were used to obtain the modified regressions in our equations. We used the same Almon technique for estimating the distributed lags, and we adhered to the Andersen–Jordan use of fourth degree polynomials in the estimation procedure. In short, we have remained quite close to the approach used by Andersen and Jordan, making only those changes which appear to us relevant to the question of statistical independence of the independent variables in the regressions.

The first equation presented in Table I is our replication of the St. Louis results, using the total monetary base and unadjusted high-employment expenditures and receipts. The very slight differences of these results from those of Andersen and Jordan are presumably due to program and computer differences. In Table I, we have presented the sums of the weighted

coefficients of the distributed lags of the independent variables, and the *t*-ratios of the sums. The patterns of the weighted coefficients for each regression are presented graphically in Figure 1. Solid lines portray four-quarter distributions; dashed lines portray eight-quarter distributions.

The second equation indicates the results of making two of the changes indicated above. First, member bank borrowings were deducted from the total monetary base to obtain the adjusted base, *Ba*. Second, the high-employment receipts variable was adjusted for price changes using the implicit price deflator for GNP. Two sets of results for this variant are presented, one with four-quarter distributed lags on the independent variables, and one with eight-quarter lags. In both cases the results differ from the first equation in the following manner: (i) although the monetary policy variable

Figure 1. Lag Distributions: Regressions of Changes in GNP on Changes in Policy Variables

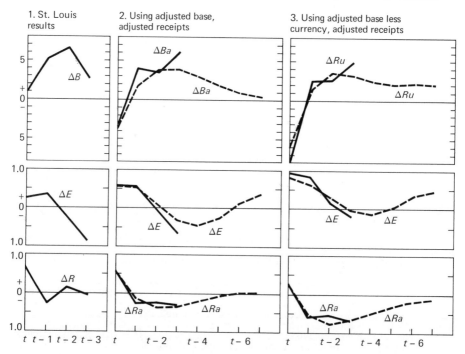

remains the predominant influence in terms of *t*-ratios, the monetary multiplier decreases in size; and (ii) although the two fiscal policy variables remain insignificant statistically, the coefficients of the expenditures and receipts variables have the expected sign. These changes are due mostly to the adjustment of the monetary base rather than to the adjustment of high-employment receipts.

The third equation makes use of the monetary base adjusted to exclude currency holdings as well as borrowed reserves, leaving unborrowed reserves, *Ru*.[5] The expenditure and receipts variables are the same as in equation (2). Results are again shown for four- and eight-quarter lags.

For the four-quarter lag distributions, the following changes are observed: (i) the monetary policy variable becomes insignificant statistically, and the size of the monetary multiplier decreases markedly compared with either equation (1) or (2); (ii) the expenditure multiplier rises to 1.7 with a *t*-ratio well above 2; and, (iii) the receipts variable has a multiplier of −1.6 with a *t*-ratio slightly below 2.

The shape of the lag distributions for the four-quarter distributions in equation (3) were such that it appeared desirable to extend the length of the lags. With eight-quarter lag distributions, the results are: (i) the monetary multiplier estimate is once again of the same order of magnitude as in equations (1) and (2), and the *t*-ratio rises to 1.6; (ii) the expenditure variable multiplier rises to 2.5 and retains a high *t*-ratio; and, (iii) the receipts multiplier rises to −2.8 with a *t*-ratio above 2.

By way of comparison, the multipliers for similar variables in the Federal Reserve/M.I.T. model are as follows:[6]

1. For unborrowed reserves, the multiplier over eight quarters varies between 10 and 15, depending upon initial conditions.
2. Although not directly comparable with high-employment expenditures, the Federal purchases multiplier in the model is approximately 2.5. For average Federal expenditures (purchases and transfers) the multiplier is between 2 and 2.5. These values, again, are for eight quarters.
3. For Federal personal taxes, the multiplier is about −1.9. A multiplier including other taxes has not been calculated. It would probably also be less than 2.0 in absolute size for eight quarters for most other taxes, but might be higher for the investment tax credit.

The lag patterns portrayed in Figure 1 suggest longer lags for monetary and tax policies than for expenditures. In fact, in most of the equations contemporaneous changes in the monetary base and tax policies have "wrong" signs. These contemporaneous coefficients are puzzling, and we have no economic explanation of them.

The weights associated with the high-employment expenditure variable fall off rapidly for all of the four-quarter lag distributions. With eight-quarter distributions they fall and rise again. Andersen and Jordan indicate that the negative values at the tail of the four-quarter distributions are consistent with the hypothesis that rising Federal outlays "crowd out" private spending through their influence on interest rates. We note that the pattern of the weights when the lag distribution is extended to eight quarters resembles the early stages of a multiplier-accelerator cycle. It is, of course, impossible to demonstrate the superiority of either conclusion from results such as these.

CONCLUSION

We feel these results cast serious doubt on the Andersen–Jordan conclusions about fiscal policy. With alternative and highly plausible measures of Federal receipts and the monetary base, fiscal policy appears to exert a significant influence on GNP in the expected direction. Monetary policy also appears to exert a powerful influence.

More headway on these problems seems to us to depend on the development of measures of policy which we can be confident meet the statistical requirements of exogeneity. Possibly a detailed examination of Open Market Committee records would be helpful in constructing a better measure of monetary policy. Perhaps different measures for different policy-making epochs are necessary. Until we succeed in settling the statistical questions, extreme caution is advisable with respect to any economic interpretations.

NOTES

1 This article, "Monetary and Fiscal Actions: A Test of Their Relative Importance in Economic Stabilization," by Leonall C. Andersen and Jerry L. Jordan, appeared in the November 1968 issue of this *Review*, pp. 11–24. [See p. 373.]

2 The statistical requirement is that exogenous variables be independent of the disturbance terms of the system. Failure to meet this requirement implies that an exogenous variable is not independent of the endogenous variables, and is what we mean by an exogenous variable "responding" to movements in endogenous variables.

3 For example, see the criticism of the Friedman–Meiselman results by Ando and Modigliani in the *American Economic Review*, September 1965, pp. 711–713.

4 Note that this is different from the question of what happens to the components of the base when the Federal Reserve exogenously changes its policy. Our interest here is in the response of the base to *endogenous* forces.

5 This variable is actually unborrowed reserves adjusted for reserves requirement changes during the period. For a discussion of the original monetary base and the reserve requirement adjustment see Leonall Anderson and Jerry Jordan, "The Monetary Base–Explanation and Analytical Use," in the August 1968 issue of this *Review*.

6 See Frank de Leeuw and Edward Gramlich, "The Channels of Monetary Policy," forthcoming in the Federal Reserve *Bulletin*.

Summaries

John F. Helliwell, "Monetary and Fiscal Policies for an Open Economy," *Oxford Economic Papers*, 21 (March 1969), pp. 35–46.

In this article, which deals with the problems of monetary and fiscal policy mix, Helliwell examines the various models that have been used in the past to illustrate the problems of and the possibilities in the choices of monetary and fiscal policies for an open economy. He suggests some qualifications and extensions of these models.

Helliwell begins his article by discussing the efficacy of employing several models that embrace various combinations of fixed- and flexible-exchange rates. He points out that the analytical difference between the fixed- and flexible-exchange-rate systems is that in a fixed system the exchange *rate* is assumed fixed, whereas in the latter system the exchange reserves are assumed fixed. The author further states that the object of this discussion is to determine whether or not an exchange-rate system affects the ease with which monetary and fiscal policies can be used to attain internal and external economic stability.

Following a discussion of the differences between fixed- and flexible-exchange-rate systems and the comparative advantage of monetary and fiscal policies under both systems, Helliwell argues "that these issues are not important if the policy-makers on a fixed rate system are not willing or able to permit substantial fluctuations in their reserves, or those on a flexible rate system not willing to see substantial fluctuations in the exchange rate."

Finally, Helliwell suggests that there are three different kinds of studies which can be undertaken: (1) studies discussing the forward exchange market, (2) the interaction between policies adopted by separate countries, and (3) the possibilities for a more general optimizing approach to policy selection. In the end, the author states that more theoretical and empirical work needs to be done before the right combinations of monetary and fiscal policies can be found in an open economy.

Roy Harrod, "Are Monetary and Fiscal Policies Enough?" *Economic Journal*, 74 (December 1964), pp. 903–916.

Sir Roy Harrod, one of the outstanding British theoretical economists, begins by reviewing his contribution to the theory of growth and certain criticisms of this contribution by some economists, such as Professor S. S. Alexander. He states that "to meet Professor Alexander's criticism, I frame the concept of a 'representative entrepreneur,'" and concerns himself with this theoretical entrepreneur in the rest of the article.

Harrod raises the basic question, Are monetary-fiscal tools sufficient to achieve a set of generally accepted national goals? His answer is a categotical "no," if the objective is to reach a goal not achievable by the use of monetary and fiscal weapons. He goes on to say that, in specific terms, if the objective of a free enterprise system is to secure optimum growth without demand inflation, given the "behavioral pattern of the entrepreneurial class," monetary and fiscal policies could not alone suffice to achieve this objective. He states further that, as a consequence, free enterprise societies must possess an additional instrument if they are to function efficiently. This would have to be over and above the extra weapons which are needed to secure a proper incomes policy and to preserve the balance-of-payments equilibrium without retarding domestic growth.

Bibliography

Leonall C. Andersen and Jerry L. Jordan, "Monetary and Fiscal Actions: A Test of Their Relative Importance in Economic Stabilization," Federal Reserve Bank of St. Louis, *Review* April (1969), pp. 12–16.

John H. Kareken, "The Mix of Monetary and Fiscal Policies," *Journal of Finance*, 22 (May 1967), pp. 241–246.

11
INCOME FLUCTUATIONS

Studying the causes and cures of wide fluctuations in income has always fascinated economists. In the first article in this part, Jorgenson establishes a causal relationship between economic fluctuations and economic growth by constructing a dynamic input–output system. In the second selection, Kurihara criticizes existing cylical growth models and builds a new model by using purely endogenous variables. He maintains that using his new model makes it unnecessary to resort to artificial exogenous constraints or superfluous autonomous growth factors when attempting to clarify the essentially self-generating nature and process of cyclical growth.

Growth and Fluctuations: A Causal Interpretation
Dale W. Jorgenson

I. INTRODUCTION

A steady growth path of outputs for the dynamic input–output system[1] with a constant rate of growth in each sector of the economy is an equilibrium of the system in a highly restricted sense. There is a set of positive output proportions and an associated constant rate of growth which satisfy the equations defining equilibrium for the system.[2] It is not as yet clear whether this equilibrium will persist once established or whether the equilibrium so established is stable. Stability as usual has two senses: first, global stability requires that for arbitrary initial output levels, the unique equi-

Dale W. Jorgenson, "Growth and Fluctuations: A Causal Interpretation," *Quarterly Journal of Economics*, 74 (August 1960), pp. 416–436.

librium output proportions will be attained after some sufficiently long period of time; secondly, local stability implies that for small shocks, whatever their origin, the system will return to its equilibrium path. In previous work on the dynamic input–output system it has been shown that the system describing output time-paths has a dual interpretation determining a time-path of relative prices for all goods in the economy.[3] Consideration of the stability of the output system and its dual reveals a dual instability theorem: If the output system is stable, the dual or price system must be unstable, both locally and globally. The converse is also true.[4] If the output system is unstable, the price system may also be unstable; this state of affairs appears to prevail in all empirical dynamic input–output systems so far derived.[5] These results suggest that as it stands the dynamic input–output system is an incomplete model of the economic system.

Two proposals have been made for completing the system: The first is to make the accumulation of stocks irreversible; stocks may be accumulated at any rate whatever; but they can be decumulated only at a rate equal to the wearing out of capital equipment.[6] No way has been found to implement this notion econometrically; the well-known switching problem offers serious obstacles to empirical work based on irreversibility.[7] A second proposal is to interpret the system as a model of optimal capital accumulation.[8] This interpretation is of interest for applications of the dynamic input–output system to the planning of economic development. There is no evidence at present that a model of capital accumulation involving explicit maximization would be useful in explaining the operation of any actual economic system.

In this paper we present a third proposal for completing the dynamic input–output system. This proposal is to imbed the system in a disequilibrium theory, that is, a theory which purports to explain the behavior of an economic system which is not in long-run equilibrium growth. The source of this theory is in a series of hypotheses about short-run reactions of entrepreneurs to disequilibrium situations, drawn mainly from the older literature on processes of cumulative expansion and contraction during business cycles.[9] It is postulated that entrepreneurs and other decision-makers react to disequilibrium by altering output and investment policies. In another paper,[10] disequilibrium reactions to excessive supply and demand, drawn from the classical adjustment mechanisms of Marshall, Walras, and Wicksell, are described and their consequences for stability of the system assessed. Reactions to excessive or deficient inventories or to excess or over-strained capacity of fixed equipment are excluded from consideration. The classical adjustment mechanisms for output levels arise out of consideration of a stationary state situation in which adjustments of stock levels are disregarded. In an economic system in which capital expansion is required for expansion of output, disequilibrium in the level of stocks held is of significance at least equal to that of excess demand or supply.

In what follows we shall discuss equilibrium reaction mechnaisms for excessive or deficient stocks. The fundamental mechanism is based on the notion of some kind of long-run normal quantity of stock of each kind—plant, equipment, and inventory—which entrepreneurs desire to hold. This notion underlies Metzler's analysis of the inventory cycle[11] and Goodwin's flexible accelerator.[12] The origin of the underlying idea can be traced back to theories of investment espoused by Kaldor and Kalecki,[13] and by many earlier writers on the acceleration principle.[14] When entrepreneurs possess an equilibrium stock level, investment is set so as to expand capacity in accord with expected increases in output levels. However, when stock levels are out of equilibrium, entrepreneurs alter their investment plans so as to bring stocks back to normal. The rate at which deficiencies and excesses are reduced is determined by a wide array of economic and technical factors. Although it would be of some interest to examine the effects of such factors individually, it is not possible to go into detail here. The disequilibrium adjustments will be assumed to be of the simplest possible form: The adjustment is proportional to the deficiency or excess. This type of adjustment mechanism is familiar from the theory of stability of the stationary state.[15] Alternative mechanisms of interest would include upper limits to the decumulation of excess stock—the irreversibility of capital accumulation discussed by many business cycle theorists[16]; upper limits to accumulation in accord with the capacity of investment goods industries[17]; and asymmetry between upward and downward movements in adjustments of capital stock.[18] The disequilibrium theory to be discussed, when combined with the original dynamic input–output system comprises a complete theory of output determination. The complete system is causal in the sense of Orcutt, Wold, and Simon.[19] Disequilibrium feeds on itself as in the cumulative process of Wicksell,[20] providing an interpretation of short-run fluctuations in economic activity as the consequence of disequilibrium. The long-run equilibrium growth path, on the other hand, is determined purely technologically, by input–output and stock-flow relationships which change only slowly over time. The complete system provides a causal interpretation of economic growth and fluctuations.

II. THE DYNAMIC INPUT–OUTPUT SYSTEM

The dynamic input–output system in its closed form is a multisector generalization of the Lundberg–Harrod–Domar growth model.[21] The system may be written as a system of simultaneous, first-order, linear, differential equations:

$$x = Ax + B\dot{x} \qquad (1)$$

where x is a vector of activity levels; x_i, the ith component of x, represents the rate of output of the ith industry or sector. A is a matrix of input–output coefficients; a_{ij}, the element of the ith row and jth column of A, is the amount of the ith output required by the jth sector for one unit of its own output. In the one sector version of the system, A is a constant marginal propensity to consume. B is a matrix of stock-flow coefficients so that b_{ij} is the amount of the ith industry's output which must be held by the jth

sector for each unit of its own rate of output. In the one sector version B is the "relation" or accelerator coefficient. All output is allocated to two uses: Current consumption in production of other goods and services (including labor services); and accumulation of capital, which is assumed to be strictly proportional to the rate of increase in the output of the accumulating sector. This is easily seen to be a rigid version of the acceleration principle described above.[22]

By noting that the matrix $B^{-1}(I - A)$ is the inverse of a non-negative matrix, it is easily shown that there is a positive characteristic solution of this system and an associated positive characteristic value.[23] The positive solution is interpreted as long-run equilibrium output proportions and the characteristic value as a positive rate at which all output levels will be expanding. Moreover, this set of output proportions is unique[24] so that the rate of growth is the only rate of growth at which all output levels remain non-negative. The condition of non-negativity of output levels is necessary in order to retain the economic interpretation of the system. The equilibrium path of the dynamic input–output system is strictly analogous to the Harrod–Domar growth model which it generalizes. There is a positive rate of growth which will persist so long as the system is in equilibrium, that is, so long as the long-run equilibrium output proportions persist. The equilibrium path for the complete dynamic input–output system may be described as follows: (1) All output levels are at capacity and there are no excessive or deficient holdings of stocks; (2) the output of each industry is equal to demands for current consumption and for investment in the expansion of capacity; there are no excess demands or excess supplies for commodities in the economy; (3) finally, the unique positive set of output proportions and the associated constant rate of growth are established.

The stability of this equilibrium path remains to be discussed. In fact there are two separate stability problems. The first is this: Among all output levels which satisfy the equations describing the equilibrium system, is the uniquely positive set of output proportions stable from arbitrary but non-negative initial conditions (global stability) and is it stable for small movements away from the equilibrium proportions such that the equilibrium conditions (1) and (2) are satisfied (local stability)? This is the problem of macroeconomic stability discussed by Hawkins, Georgescu-Roegen, and more recently by Dorfman, Samuelson, and Solow.[25] Macroeconomic instability arises when for certain capital structures the unique positive vector of sector output levels is dominated by some other solution of the system, violating the requirement that outputs be non-negative in long-run equilibrium. As we have already indicated, this condition can occur for empirically derived dynamic input–output systems.[26] If the dynamic input–output model is not macroeconomically stable, the economic interpretation of the model cannot be retained. Necessary and sufficient condition for global stability of the equilibrium system, that is, for global macroeconomic stability, is that the initial output levels lie in the subspace spanned by characteristic vectors of the system associated with characteristic values smaller in real part than the equilibrium rate of growth.[27]

Necessary and sufficient condition for local stability of the equilibrium system, that is for local macroeconomic stability, is that all perturbations lie in the subspace spanned by characteristic vectors of the system associated with characteristic values less than or equal to the equilibrium rate of growth in real part.[28]

If the dynamic input–output system is not macroeconomically stable, the economic interpretation of the model cannot be retained. Therefore, if initial conditions for the system or arbitrary perturbations fail to satisfy the conditions for macroeconomic stability, the system must be out of equilibrium. In this state its movement is no longer described by the equilibrium system alone. In what follows we propose the following resolution of the problem of macroeconomic instability: First, treat the long-run equilibrium path of outputs as a solution of the equilibrium system, determined technologically by input–output and stock-flow coefficients. Secondly, explain deviations from the conditions required for macroeconomic stability by a disequilibrium theory based not on technology but on the activity of decision-makers in a situation of disequilibrium. A further stability problem remains: If the system is not initially in equilibrium will the movement of the disequilibrium variables lead to a reestablishment of long-run equilibrium growth proportions and the associated rate of expansion of all output levels; or is disequilibrium cumulative in the sense that a departure leads farther and farther away from the long-run equilibrium growth path? This second stability problem is analogous to the stability of tatonnements in Walrasian general equilibrium or to stability of the cumulative process of Wicksell.[29] To resolve this stability problem it is necessary to examine various hypotheses concerning the mechanism by which decision-makers adjust to disequilibrium. Before this task can be undertaken it is necessary to define precisely a set of disequilibrium variables.

If the dynamic input–output system is initially in disequilibrium, output is not equal to demands for output—from current consumption and for current expansion of capacity. The difference between the actual level of output and the required rate is an excess supply of the corresponding commodity, defined as follows:

$$\xi \equiv x - Ax - Bx \qquad (2)$$

ξ is a vector of excess supplies of the commodities produced by each sector. For example, ξ_i is the excess supply of the ith commodity. If ξ_i is negative, it represents excess demand for the commodity. If the level of stocks of the ith commodity held by all sectors in the economy is represented by s_i, in equilibrium, when all inventories are at desired levels and production is at capacity,

$$s = Bx \tag{3}$$

the level of stocks held is proportional to the levels of output of each industry holding the stocks. The constant of proportionality is given by b_{ij}, the stock-flow coefficient representing the amount of stock of the ith commodity which must be held per unit of output of the jth industry. In the event that there is excess capacity or deficient holdings of stocks, this equality no longer holds. A set of disequilibrium stock variables may then be defined as follows:

$$\psi \equiv s - Bx \tag{4}$$

where ψ_i represents the excess stock of the ith commodity held throughout the economy. If this quantity is negative it represents deficient holdings of the corresponding commodity. By definition the output of any commodity is equal to current consumption plus changes in stocks, whether these changes are desired or not, so that:

$$x \equiv Ax + \dot{s} \tag{5}$$

Differentiating the relation defining ψ, the vector of excessive stock levels, we obtain:

$$\dot{\psi} \equiv \dot{s} - B\dot{x} \tag{6}$$

so that:

$$x \equiv Ax + B\dot{x} + \dot{\psi} \tag{7}$$

and the rate of change of excess inventories or excess capacity is equal to the excess supply of the corresponding commodity:

$$\dot{\psi} \equiv \xi \tag{8}$$

which is the fundamental stock-flow identity for the disequilibrium system. The problem of disequilibrium analysis is this: What governs the movements of the excessive or deficient stocks, ψ?

III. STABILITY OF THE DYNAMIC INPUT–OUTPUT SYSTEM: INVESTMENT POLICY

The first disequilibrium mechanism to be discussed is based on the reaction of investment policy to excessive or deficient holdings of stocks. The actual rate of investment is equal to the level necessary to maintain current increases in output, increased or diminished by alterations in the discrepancy between actual and desired holdings of stocks. Investment in the ith commodity, say $\dot{s}_i$, is the sum of investments made by each sector which holds commodity i as a stock, just sufficient to maintain the normal stock-flow ratio at current output levels. This induced or desired investment level for the jth sector is $b_{ij}\dot{x}_j$; the sum of desired or induced investments over all sectors is $\sum_{j=1}^{n} b_{ij}\dot{x}_j$. The second component of investment is a change in excessive or deficient holdings of stock which is proportional to present excess holdings of all commodities by all sectors. Where the constant of proportionality is k_{ij}, representing the proportion of investment in the ith commodity to excess stocks of the jth, the total adjustment of investment levels in the ith commodity throughout the economy is $\sum_{j=1}^{n} k_{ij}(s_j - \sum_{h=1}^{n} b_{jh}x_h)$, so that total investment in the ith commodity is given by:

$$\dot{s}_i = \sum_{j=1}^{n} b_{ij}\dot{x}_j + \sum_{j=1}^{n} k_{ij}\left(s_j - \sum_{h=1}^{n} b_{jh}x_h\right)$$
$$(i = 1 \cdots n) \tag{9}$$

The relation of this mechanism to Metzler's model of the inventory cycle[30] may be made more apparent by rewriting the system in matrix form:

$$\dot{s} = B\dot{x} + K(s - Bx) \qquad (10)$$

where $\dot{s}$ is a vector with components $\dot{s}_i$, B is a matrix of stock-flow coefficients, K is a matrix of reaction coefficients, s and $\dot{x}$ are stock and output vectors, and $\dot{x}$ is a vector with elements representing the rate of change of outputs.

Recalling from the previous section that total investment is output less current consumption we have:

$$x - Ax = \dot{s} = B\dot{x} + K(s - Bx) \qquad (11)$$

The mechanism may be rewritten as follows:

$$x = Ax + B\dot{x} + K(s - Bx) \qquad (12)$$

where x is a vector of output levels, representing current production; $Ax + B\dot{x}$ is expected sales or normal long-run demand for each commodity; the difference between current production and normal sales is proportional to (not necessarily equal to) the existing deficiency or excess in holdings of stocks. In Metzler's period analysis, it is postulated that entrepreneurs undertake to remove the entire deficiency or excess in stock in a single period, thereby generating further excesses and deficiencies. More recently, Mills[31] has given an interpretation of the inventory cycle in which stock adjustment in each period is proportional to but not equal to the outstanding excess or deficiency. This is the mechanism of adjustment we have attempted to describe here. The adjustment of stocks is proportional to, but not necessarily equal to, the difference between current holdings and desired holdings at the current level of output.[32]

The elements of the matrix of adjustment coefficients K represent the rate of response of investment levels in each industry to excessive or deficient holdings

of each commodity as a stock. In a highly decentralized economy, sector output levels are set with reference only to current stocks and current demands for the commodity produced by the sector in question. All off-diagonal elements of K would be zero in this case. Excess demands for any other commodity would affect the output level of a given sector only through effects on orders for that sector's output induced by investment or disinvestment in other commodities. In an economic system which is not perfectly decentralized, excess demand for a commodity might have two possible effects: First, it could lead to an increase in output by the sector, partly to satisfy demands, partly to accumulate inventories; secondly, entrepreneurs in other sectors, perceiving a disequilibrium situation in some other sector than their own would increase their orders for the commodity in short supply to insure their own supply of the commodity and also to hedge against possible changes in relative prices resulting from the disequilibrium. If the rise in speculative demand for the commodity outweighed the increase in output induced by the excess demand, the situation would be worsened. This is the mechanism underlying Harrod's discussion of the instability of the long-run equilibrium growth path.[33] A simple mechanism satisfying Harrod's requirement that excess demand result in an increase in excess demand has been treated in another paper.[34] In what follows we will consider the decentralized case; in this case deficient stocks lead to a rise in investment in the commodity, so that k_{ii} is negative for all sectors. Moreover, in the decentralized case it may be assumed that all off-diagonal elements of K are zero; disequilibrium in one sector affects output levels and investment policies in other sectors only through its effect on current consumption and desired accumulation of the commodities produced by the other sectors.

The stability of the dynamic input–output system under the type of adjustment mechanism envisoned in Metzler's inventory cycle may best be analyzed by still a third interpretation of the adjustment mechanism. First, note that the mechanism may be written:

$$\dot{s} - B\dot{x} = K(s - Bx) \qquad (13)$$

and, recalling that $\psi = s - Bx$, where ψ is the excess of actual stocks over desired stocks, this mechanism may be written:

$$\dot{\psi} = K\psi \qquad (14)$$

Then, using the definition of the disequilibrium variables:

$x = Ax + B\dot{x} + \psi$ the complete system is given by:

$$x = Ax + B\dot{x} + \psi \qquad (15)$$
$$\dot{\psi} = K\psi$$

In normalized form this system is written:

$$\dot{x} = B^{-1}(I - A)x \qquad -B^{-1}K\psi \qquad (16)$$
$$\dot{\psi} = \qquad\qquad K\psi$$

which is easily seen to be a decomposable system.[35]

The fact that the complete system is decomposable has two interesting economic implications. First, if the disequilibrium variables are initially zero, the complete system collapses into the dynamic input–output system:

$$x = Ax + B\dot{x} \qquad (17)$$

which is Leontief's original version of the closed system.[36] A second economic implication of decomposability is that the variables of the complete system may be divided into two sets which are ordered causally in the sense of Wold, Simon, and Orcutt[37]—the equilibrium variables x and disequilibrium variables ψ. The time path of the disequilibrium variables depends only on the values assumed by these variables. In this sense disequilibrium is cumulative in the manner of the classical processes of economic fluctuation in the

older literature of the business cycle. A departure from equilibrium generates a reaction which increases or reduces the departure. The equilibrium variables, in this case the levels of output of each sector, are affected by reactions to disequilibrium; excess stocks modify investment policy and thereby levels of output. Along with the familiar elements of the matrix multiplier[38] and Leontief's multisector accelerator, observed levels of output are caused by the existence of disequilibrium in holdings of stocks; however, stock levels remain in equilibrium once the system has returned from disequilibrium. In this sense they are independent of the levels of output achieved in equilibrium.

As we have pointed out earlier, macroeconomic stability is essential if the economic interpretation of the system is to be retained. In the event that initial conditions are such that the equilibrium system is not macroeconomically stable on the hypothesis that the system is initially in equilibrium, then it must be concluded that the system is out of equilibrium. Necessary and sufficient condition for macroeconomic stability in the large and in the small is that the initial conditions for the equilibrium system and all subsequent perturbations must lie in the subspace spanned by characteristic vectors of $B^{-1}(I - A)$ with characteristic value less in real part than the equilibrium rate of growth,[39] and the equilibrium output proportions associated with this rate of growth. For any set of initial output levels, the initial conditions for the equilibrium system may be represented:

$$x(0) = Xc = X_1c_1 + X_2c_2 \qquad (18)$$

where X is the fundamental matrix of $B^{-1}(I - A)$, that is, the matrix whose columns are characteristic vectors of $B^{-1}(I - A)$. Associated with the initial output levels $x(0)$, there is a unique vector of constants c. If X_1 is the matrix of characteristic vectors associated with characteristic values less than the equilibrium rate of growth, together with the uniquely non-negative characteristic vector, representing long-run equilibrium output proportions, and X_2 is the matrix of the remaining characteristic vectors, then for macroeconomic stability (global and local) it is necessary and sufficient that $c_2 = 0$. This condition enables us to calculate the initial values of the disequilibrium variables, $\psi(0)$. First, we expand the initial conditions in terms of the fundamental matrix of the complete system, say Z:

$$
\begin{bmatrix} x(0) \\ \cdots \\ \psi(0) \end{bmatrix} = Z\hat{c} = \begin{bmatrix} X & Y \\ \hline 0 & I \end{bmatrix} \begin{bmatrix} c_1 \\ c_2 \\ \cdots \\ c_3 \end{bmatrix} \quad (19)
$$

where X is as above (18), I is the identity matrix, and Y is composed of the remaining elements of the last N characteristic vectors of the total system. Now, assuming c_1 given as the constants corresponding to the "equilibrium" part of the solution, and assuming c_2 zero, as required by macroeconomic stability, we may solve for c_3 and $\psi(0)$. First, inverting Z, we have:

$$
\begin{bmatrix} c_1 \\ 0 \\ \cdots \\ c_3 \end{bmatrix} = \begin{bmatrix} X^{-1} & -X^{-1}Y \\ \hline 0 & I \end{bmatrix} \begin{bmatrix} x(0) \\ \cdots \\ \psi(0) \end{bmatrix} \quad (20)
$$

Hence:

$$
\begin{bmatrix} c_1 \\ 0 \end{bmatrix} = X^{-1}x(0) - X^{-1}Y\psi(0) \quad (21)
$$

$$
c_3 = \psi(0)
$$

The first of this pair of vector equations may be solved for $\psi(0)$ and hence c_3, as follows:

$$
\psi(0) = -Y^{-1}X\begin{bmatrix} c_1 \\ 0 \end{bmatrix} - Y^{-1}x(0) \quad (22)
$$

The fundamental problem of the stability of growth, that is, of the tendency of the system toward or away from steady growth equilibrium, must be resolved by empirical investigation. The parameters of the input–output matrix A, the stock-flow matrix B, and the matrix of reaction coefficients K must be estimated from empirical data. For this purpose it is unnecessary to observe excessive or deficient stocks directly.[40] It is sufficient to observe levels of output in each sector. Since A and B are long-run parameters, they may be estimated from cross-section data.[41] Then K may be estimated from time series, since the elements of K represent short-run reaction coefficients. Given a series of output levels in each sector, we may utilize the cross-section estimates of A and B as follows: First, we differentiate the disequilibrium relation (14) to obtain:

$$
\dot{\psi} = K\psi \quad (23)
$$

But, by definition of the disequilibrium variables we have:

$$
\psi = x - Ax - B\dot{x} \quad (24)
$$
$$
\dot{\psi} = \dot{x} - A\dot{x} - B\ddot{x}.
$$

Hence, the system may be rewritten in the form:

$$
\dot{x} - A\dot{x} - B\ddot{x} = K(x - Ax - B\dot{x}) \quad (25)
$$

From the output series x, we may calculate Δx, the vector of first differences of x, which may be used to approximate $\dot{x}$; it would also be necessary to calculate $\Delta^2 x$ as an approximation to $\ddot{x}$. Then, substituting Δx and $\Delta^2 x$ in the relation (25), we obtain the following estimating form:

$$
\Delta x - A\,\Delta x - B\,\Delta^2 x = K(x - Ax - B\,\Delta x) \quad (26)
$$

In advance of econometric implementation of the system, it may be noted that since the fundamental matrix of the complete model is decomposable, the characteristic values or intrinsic rates of growth of the characteristic solutions are those of $B^{-1}(I - A)$ and K. Since it is required that the equilibrium system be macroeconomically stable in order to retain the economic interpretation of x as a vector of output levels, the characteristic value or rate of growth associated with the long-run equilibrium output proportions is the largest rate of growth of the equilibrium system. For long-run stability of the equilibrium output proportions within the complete system it is required that the characteristic roots of K be less than the equilibrium rate of growth. This condition is sufficient for relative stability of the equilibrium output proportions.[42] In the case of a decentralized system, the characteristic values of K are simply the elements along the diagonal of K, since all other elements are zero. But these elements are negative since deficient stock of a commodity increases the rate of investment in that commodity over the normal rate of investment determined by the expansion of output levels. Hence, in the case of a decentralized system, stability of the dynamic input–output system is assured. This result is contrary to the arguments of Sargan that Harrod's mechanism for stability of growth generalizes to the dynamic input–output system.[43] A close examination of Sargan's argument reveals that he requires for instability that there be one positive characteristic root of the complete system. But if this root is the equilibrium rate and all other characteristic roots are less than this rate in real part, steady growth equilibrium is stable. A similar misunderstanding of the notion of relative stability underlies Allen's discussion[44] of the stability of the one-sector version of the dynamic input–output system, the familiar Harrod–Domar model of growth.

IV. STABILITY OF THE DYNAMIC INPUT–OUTPUT SYSTEM: OUTPUT POLICY

In the previous section, a causal interpretation of growth and fluctuations was developed on the hypothesis that excessive or deficient stocks of goods affect the level of output through their effect on investment policies. If the system for determination of output levels is not in equilibrium, then adjustment follows a causal chain: Excess stocks depress investment levels; depressed rates of investment result in a reduction in output levels. In this section the consequences of an alternative hypothesis are examined, namely, suppose that it is output policy, not investment policy, which entrepreneurs attempt to control. The effects of excess or deficient stocks will be observed not in the actual level of output, but in changes in the level of output. The specific form of the hypothesis is that the rate of change of the output of the ith commodity is equal to the rate of change of demand plus a change which is proportional to the excess stock of the jth commodity. Where the constant of proportionality is represented by h_{ij}, the change in the output level of the ith commodity as a result of excessive or deficient holdings of the jth commodity will be $h_{ij}(s_j - \sum_{k=1}^{n} b_{jk}x_k)$. The change in the output level of the ith commodity in response to all excessive and deficient stocks is given by the expression:

$$\sum_{j=1}^{n} h_{ij}\left(s_j - \sum_{k=1}^{n} b_{jk}x_k\right) \qquad (i = 1 \cdots n) \tag{27}$$

Or, in matrix notation:

$$H(s - Bx) \tag{28}$$

which is the change of output levels in each sector in response to excessive and deficient stocks, where s is a vector of stock levels, x is a vector of output levels, B is the familar stock-flow matrix, and H is the matrix of reaction coefficients h_{ij}. To derive an expression for the total change in output levels, the disequilibrium adjustment must be added to the change in demand. This is the sum of changes in current consumption:

$$\sum_{j=1}^{n} a_{ij}\dot{x}_j \qquad (i = 1 \cdots n) \tag{29}$$

plus changes in current investment for the expansion of stocks:

$$\sum_{j=1}^{n} b_{ij}\ddot{x}_j \qquad (i = 1 \cdots n) \qquad (30)$$

The rate of change of the ith output level is given by the expression:

$$\dot{x}_i = \sum_{j=1}^{n} a_{ij}\dot{x}_j + \sum_{j=1}^{n} b_{ij}\ddot{x}_j$$
$$+ \sum_{j=1}^{n} h_{ij}\left(s_j - \sum_{j=1}^{n} b_{jk}x_k\right)$$
$$(i = 1 \cdots n) \quad (31)$$

Or, in matrix notation:

$$\dot{x} = A\dot{x} + B\ddot{x} + H(s - Bx) \qquad (32)$$

where A is an input–output matrix and the remaining quantities are defined as above.

In a decentralized economy, the output level of any given sector would depend only on the excess stock of the corresponding commodity. For a centralized economy or one which is imperfectly decentralized, entrepreneurs could be expected to alter their level of output in response not only to changes in orders—current demand—but also in response to the anticipation concerning changes in orders. Such anticipations would take into account, among other things, prospective levels of output in other sectors. These prospective levels of output would depend on the current level of stocks in relation to the desired level, for each commodity in the economy. If a sector uses a commodity for which stocks are deficient, it may reduce its level of output in order to conserve its supplies; if a sector sells its output for consumption in any industry in which excessive stocks of that industry's output have arisen, the producing sector may be expected to cut back its own production in anticipation of a diminution of orders. It is not possible to assign a definite direction to the reaction of the output of a sector to excess stocks of the output of any other sector without empirical determination of the actual sign. If the system is decentralized, the output

level of each sector depends only on excess stocks of the corresponding commodity; the effects of other excess stocks is indirect: Through adjustments in other output levels, the level of excess or deficiency in stocks of a given sector is altered. In the decentralized case, the matrix of reaction coefficients, H is a diagonal matrix. If output levels increase when stocks are deficient and decrease when stocks are excessive, each of the diagonal elements of H is negative. In this case, the complete system is easily seen to be relatively stable in the sense that disequilibrium movements gradually die out in relation to the overall upward movement of the economic system.

First, recalling the definition of excess demands (2), the complete system may be written:

$$\dot{x} = A\dot{x} + B\ddot{x} + \dot{\xi} \qquad (33)$$

where $\dot{\xi}$ is the vector of changes in excess demand levels. Next, using the definition of excess demand (or supply) and the fundamental stock-flow identity (2,8), we have:

$$\dot{x} = A\dot{x} + B\ddot{x} + \ddot{\psi} \qquad (34)$$

Now, using the definition of excess stocks, $\psi = s - Bx$, the disequilibrium relation has the simple form:

$$\ddot{\psi} = H\psi \qquad (35)$$

Combining this disequilibrium relation with the definition of excess demand and supply (8) we may write the complete system as follows:

$$x = Ax + B\dot{x} + \psi \qquad (36)$$
$$\ddot{\psi} = H\psi$$

This system is easily seen to be decomposable so that it possesses a causal interpretation: The disequilibrium variables affect the set of equilibrium variables representing output levels through the changes in output levels induced by excess or deficient stocks. However, when the system is initially in equilibrium, it continues along an equilibrium path and the levels of excess stock and of excess demand remain at a zero level. In the analysis of adjustments to disequilibrium by means of investment policy, a necessary and sufficient condition for equilibrium, that is, for macroeconomic stability of the equilibrium system:

$$x = Ax + B\dot{x} \tag{37}$$

was that excess stocks are zero for all sectors initially. In this case the complete system collapses into the equilibrium system and its course is then governed by the equilibrium system alone. In the present case, where the rate of change of excess supply depends on the level of undesired stocks, this condition is necessary but not sufficient, for suppose that $\xi = \psi$, the level of excess supply is zero; then if $\psi \neq 0$, that is, if undesired stocks are not at zero level for all commodities in the economic system, $\dot{\psi}$ is not zero and hence $\xi = \psi$, the level of excess supply cannot remain at zero. The equilibrium in demand and supply for each commodity cannot persist. Necessary and sufficient condition for an equilibrium such that the complete system is governed by the equilibrium system alone is easily seen to be:

$$\psi = \dot{\psi} = 0 \tag{38}$$

In this case, $\ddot{\psi}$, the rate of change in excess demand or excess supply, is also zero and the complete system is governed by the equilibrium system alone.

To compute the initial levels of excess stock, ψ, and excess demands, $\dot{\psi} = \xi$, we expand the initial conditions in terms of the fundamental matrix of the complete system:

$$\begin{bmatrix} x(0) \\ \cdots \\ \psi(0) \\ \dot{\psi}(0) \end{bmatrix} = \begin{bmatrix} X & Y_1 & Y_2 \\ \cdots & \cdots & \cdots \\ 0 & Z_{11} & Z_{12} \\ 0 & Z_{21} & Z_{22} \end{bmatrix} \begin{bmatrix} d_1 \\ d_2 \\ \cdots \\ d_3 \\ d_4 \end{bmatrix} \tag{39}$$

where X is the fundamental matrix of $B^{-1}(I - A)$ and the remaining elements

correspond to the remaining characteristic vectors of the complete system (36). In order to calculate the initial values of the disequilibrium variables—excess stocks, $\psi(0)$, and excess demands, $\dot{\psi}(0)$, it is necessary to take into account, not only the condition which is equivalent to macroeconomic stability, $d_2 = 0$. It is also necessary to use observations on the actual stock levels in the economic system at any given period of time, the vector s, in order to compute the level of excess by the relation:

$$\psi(0) = s(0) - Bx(0) \tag{40}$$

Then we have two vector equations in the constants d_3, d_4:

$$x(0) = Xd_2 - Y_1d_3 - Y_2d_4 \tag{41}$$
$$\psi(0) = x(0) - Bx(0) = Z_{11}d_3 - Z_{12}d_4$$

Using these equations we obtain:

$$x(0) - Xd_2 = Y_1d_3 - Y_2d_4 \tag{42}$$
$$s(0) - Bx(0) = Z_{11}d_3 - Z_{12}d_4$$

Or, in matrix notation:

$$\begin{bmatrix} x(0) - Xd_2 \\ s(0) - Bx(0) \end{bmatrix} = \begin{bmatrix} Y_1 & Y_2 \\ Z_{11} & Z_{12} \end{bmatrix} \begin{bmatrix} d_3 \\ d_4 \end{bmatrix} \tag{43}$$

So that:

$$\begin{bmatrix} d_3 \\ d_4 \end{bmatrix} = \begin{bmatrix} Y_1 & Y_2 \\ Z_{11} & Z_{12} \end{bmatrix}^{-1} \begin{bmatrix} x(0) - Xd_2 \\ s(0) - Bx(0) \end{bmatrix} \tag{44}$$

These values may then be inserted in the equation for $\psi(0)$, to obtain:

$$\psi(0) = Z_{21}d_3 - Z_{22}d_4 \tag{45}$$

which completes the calculation of the initial conditions for the system.

In the case of an imperfectly decentralized economic system, the stability of the model cannot be analyzed prior to econometric implementation of the disequilibrium theory. However, for a decentralized system, the characteristic roots of the system are easily seen to be the characteristic values of the matrix $B^{-1}(I - A)$, associated with the equilibrium part of the system, together with characteristic values of the matrix:

$$\begin{bmatrix} 0 & I \\ H & 0 \end{bmatrix} \quad (46)$$

all of which are imaginary. Each root of this matrix is simply the root of one of the characteristic values of H. But in the decentralized case, these roots are imaginary numbers, since the characteristic values of H are all negative. This implies immediately that the unique positive set of output proportions of long-run equilibrium growth is stable within the complete system since the real part of all characteristic roots of the system other than those of the equilibrium system is zero. If the system is initially out of equilibrium, or if shocks drive the economy away from equilibrium growth, a system of oscillations in the adjustment of output levels is set up. Since these oscillations have constant amplitude and fixed period, they continue to be propagated through the economy by means of adjustment of output levels. However, relative to the level of output in each sector, the oscillations gradually die out; that is, the oscillations are purely transitory and will eventually be swamped in the long-run upward movement of the economy. Although the cycles retain constant amplitude measured in terms of output, the amplitude steadily diminishes in relation to the actual level of output, which is rising at the long-run equilibrium rate of growth.

For estimation of the parameters of the equilibrium system, it is possible to eliminate the disequilibrium variables altogether, obtaining an expression for the complete system in terms of the output levels alone. This is as follows:

$$x - Ax - B\dot{x} = H[\ddot{x} - A\ddot{x} - B\dddot{x}] \quad (47)$$

The estimating form is obtained by replacing $\dot{x}$ with Δx, and so on:

$$\begin{aligned} x - Ax &- B\,\Delta x \\ &= H(\Delta^2 x - A\,\Delta^2 x - B\,\Delta^2 x) \quad (48) \end{aligned}$$

where A and B are estimated from cross-section data, as in the mechanism previously considered. H may then be estimated from time series.

V. SUMMARY AND CONCLUSION

In this paper we have examined the possibility of resolving the problem of causal indeterminacy in dynamic input–output analysis by means of an explicit disequilibrium theory. We have discussed two separate disequilibrium mechanisms: The first is based on the alteration of investment policy, which in a decentralized system may be considered to be primarily an inventory adjustment by the sector for which excess or deficient stocks of output exist. The actual adjustment mechanism is assumed to follow the law of proportional effect: The adjustment of investment levels is proportional to the excess or deficiency in stocks held. A second mechanism is based on disequilibrium adjustments through output rather than investment policy. The adjustment is assumed to be proportional to the excess or deficiency in stocks held. Both mechanisms admit of a unidirectional or causal interpretation. If the system is initially in equilibrium, that is, if the system is initially macroeconomically stable, then it will continue in equilibrium until external shocks drive it from the equilibrium path. When the system is out of equilibrium, a new type of stability problem arises: Will it return to the equilibrium path? This stability problem cannot be definitely resolved until the theory of disequilibrium which we have proposed has been implemented econometrically. However, if the assumption of perfect decentralization is a good approximation to reality, it can be stated on a priori grounds that either of the two disequilibrium mechanisms we have discussed implies stable adjustment.

The problem under discussion— macro-economic instability and its consequences —is not peculiar to situations involving direct applications of input–output analysis. Such a problem will arise in any dynamic model which generalizes the Harrod–Domar growth model; in particular, such a problem of macro-economic instability arises in detailed analysis of even simple two-sector models of capital accumulation like those discussed by Marx and recently by Mrs. Robinson.[45] Theoretical models of this type are essential for investigations of such problems as balance among sectors in economic development and the relation between international trade (sectors are countries) and economic growth. Explicit disequilibrium theory provides one means of retaining the economic interpretation of multi-sector growth models based on the Harrod–Domar theory of growth.

Perhaps equal in importance to the conclusion that the fundamental notions of the Harrod–Domar theory may form the basis of a multi-sector, multi-industry, or multi-country theory of growth is the conclusion that the equilibrium theory, which has been the basis of much current theoretical work on economic dynamics, is seen to be only a part of the theory of business cycles and growth. The form taken by the disequilibrium theory, with its uni-directional or causal interpretation, provides a direct link between equilibrium theories of growth and fluctuations like those of Harrod, Hicks, and Hansen–Samuelson[46] and the older theories of the business cycle based on the cumulative process of Wicksell[47] and other mechanisms derived from the theory of self-sustaining adjustment processes. In order to retain the economic interpretation of the so-called post-Keynesian theory of growth and fluctuations, it is necessary to restore to consideration precisely those aspects of the economic dynamics which are emphasized in pre-Keynesian or classical theories of prosperity and depression.

NOTES

1 See especially: W. W. Leontief, "Dynamic Analysis," in *Studies in the Structure of the American Economy*, ed. W. W. Leontief (New York: Oxford University Press, 1953), pp.53–92. Further discussion of the system and a nearly complete bibliography may be found in: R. M. Solow, "Competitive Valuation in a Dynamic Input-output System," *Econometrica*, Vol. 27 (Jan. 1959), pp. 30–53.

2 For proof of these facts, see: R. Dorfman, P. A. Samuelson, and R. M. Solow, *Linear Programming and Economic Analysis* (New York: McGraw-Hill, 1958), p. 297, fn. 1.

3 Solow, *op. cit.*: also: M. Morishima, "Prices, Interest, and Profits in a Dynamic Leontief System," *Econometrica*, Vol. 26 (July 1958), pp. 358–380; further references are given in Solow's paper.

4 Proof is given by: D. Jorgenson, "On a Dual Stability Theorem," *Econometrica*, forthcoming.

5 Several examples, which are to be taken as illustrative, are given in: K. Iversen, *Machine Solutions of Linear Differential Equations*, unpublished Ph.D. thesis, Harvard University, 1954.

6 This proposal has been made by Leontief, *op. cit.*

7 The switching problem is discussed by Leontief, *op. cit.*, by M. McManus, "Self-contradiction in Leontief's Dynamic Model," *Yorkshire Bulletin of Economic and Social Research*, Vol. 6 (May 1957), pp. 1–21, and by H. Uzawa, "Note on Leontief's Dynamic Input–output System," *Proceedings of the Japan Academy*, Vol. 32 (Feb. 1956), pp. 79–82.

8 This proposal has been discussed from the point of view of linear programming by H. Uzawa, "On the Efficiency of Leontief's Dynamic Input–output System," *Proceedings of Japan Academy*, Vol. 32 (Mar. 1956), pp. 157–160, by H. Wagner, "A Linear Programming Solution to Dynamic Leontief Type Models," *Management Science*, Vol. 3 (April 1957), pp. 234–254, by Dorfman, Samuelson, and Solow, *op. cit.*, Chap. 11, pp. 281–300; and more recently by M. Morishima, *op. cit.*, and R. Solow, *op. cit.* Another approach, from the point of view of dynamic programming in the sense of Bellman, is discussed in detail by R. Bellman, *Dynamic Programming* (Princeton: Princeton University Press, 1957), see especially

Chap. VI, "Bottleneck Problems in Multi-Stage Production Processes," and the references listed there.

9 The main source of information on the older theories of the business cycle is, of course: G. Haberler, *Prosperity and Depression* (2d rev. ed.; Cambridge: Harvard University Press, 1958; 1st ed., 1936).

10 D. Jorgenson, "On the Stability of the Dynamic Input–output System," *Review of Economic Studies*, forthcoming.

11 The main references to the work of L. Metzler are: "The Nature and Stability of Inventory Cycles," *Review of Economics and Statistics*, XXIII (Aug. 1941), 113–129; "Business Cycles and the Modern Theory of Employment," *American Economic Review*, XXXVI (June 1946), 278–291; "Factors Governing the Length of Inventory Cycles," *Review of Economics and Statistics*, XXIX (Feb. 1947), 1–15; "Three Lags in the Circular Flow of Income," in *Income, Employment and Public Policy, Essays in Honor of Alvin H. Hansen* (New York: Norton, 1948), pp. 11–32.

12 R. M. Goodwin, "Secular and Cyclical Aspects of the Multiplier and Accelerator," in *Income, Employment and Public Policy, Essays in Honor of Alvin H. Hansen* (New York: Norton, 1948), pp. 108–132.

13 N. Kaldor, "A Model of the Trade Cycle," *Economic Journal*, L (Mar. 1940), 78–92. M. Kalecki, "A Theory of the Business Cycle," *Review of Economic Studies*, IV (Feb. 1937), 77–97.

14 A complete set of references is given by Haberler, *op. cit.*, p. 87. This theory has recently been revived by Smithies and Duesenberry: A. Smithies, "Economic Fluctuations and Growth," *Econometrica*, Vol. 25 (Jan. 1957), pp. 1–52. J. S. Duesenberry, *Business Cycles and Economic Growth* (New York: McGraw-Hill, 1958).

15 The mechanism considered in the literature is: Price changes are proportional to excess demand. For references to work on stability through 1947, see: P. A. Samuelson, *Foundations of Economic Analysis* (Cambridge: Harvard University Press, 1947), Part II; for recent references see: K. Arrow, H. Block, and L. Hurwicz, "On the Stability of Competitive Equilibrium, II," *Econometrica*, Vol. 27 (Jan. 1959), pp. 82–109.

16 Especially, J. R. Hicks, *A Contribution to the Theory of the Trade Cycle* (London: Oxford University Press, 1950); also: Leontief, *op. cit.*

17 Hicks, *op. cit.*

18 L. Koyck, *Distributed Lags and the Theory of Investment* (Amsterdam: North-Holland Press, 1954).

19 G. Orcutt, "Actions, Consequences, and Causal Relations," *Review of Economics and Statistics*, XXXIV (Nov. 1952), 305–313; H. Wold (with the assistance of L. Jureen), *Demand Analysis* (New York: Wiley, 1953); H. Simon, "Causal Ordering and Identifiability," in *Studies in Econometric Method*, ed. W. Hood and T. Koopmans (New York: Wiley, 1953), pp. 49–74.

20 K. Wicksell, *Interest and Prices* (London: Macmillan, 1936; 1st ed. (in German), 1898); *Lectures on Political Economy*, II, *Money* (London: Routledge, 1935; 1st ed. (in Swedish), 1906).

21 It is not well known that the so-called "fundamental equation" of the Harrod–Domar theory of growth was anticipated by E. Lundberg, *Studies in the Theory of Economic Expansion* (New York: Kelley and Millman, 1954; 1st ed., 1937), p. 185, fn. 1; see also: R. Harrod, *Towards a Dynamic Economics* (London: Macmillan, 1948); the original discussion is in "An Essay in Dynamic Theory," *Economic Journal*, XLIX (Mar. 1939), 14–33. E. Domar, *Essays in the Theory of Economic Growth* (New York: Oxford University Press, 1957); "Capital Expansion, Rate of Growth, and Employment," *Econometrica*, Vol. 14 (April 1946), pp. 137–147.

22 See fn. 14, and the accompanying text.

23 Provided that B^{-1} exists and $B^{-1}(I - A)$ is indecomposable. See: G. Debreu and I. Herstein, "Non-negative Square Matrices," *Econometrica*, Vol. 21 (Oct. 1953), pp. 597–607.

24 *Ibid.*

25 D. Hawkins, "Some Conditions of Macroeconomic Stability," *Econometrica*, Vol. 16 (Oct. 1948), pp. 309–322; N. Georgescu-Roegen, "Relaxation Phenomena in Linear Dynamic Models," in *Activity of Production and Allocation*, ed. T. Koopmans (New York: Wiley, 1951), pp. 116–131; Dorfman, Samuelson, and Solow, *op. cit.*

26 Iversen, *op. cit.*

27 For proof, see: D. Jorgenson, "On a Dual Stability Theorem," *Econometrica*, forthcoming.

28 For proof, see: *Ibid.*
29 For references to Walrasian stability analysis, see fn. 15. The original discussion is contained in: L. Walras, *Elements of Pure Economics* (Homewood, Ill.: Irwin, 1954; 1st ed. (in French), 1874); see also: K. Wicksell, *op. cit.*
30 See fn. 11 for references.
31 E. S. Mills, "Expectations, Uncertainty and Inventory Fluctuations," *Review of Economic Studies,* XXII (1954–1955), 15–22.
32 This mechanism is, of course, the flexible accelerator of Goodwin; see fn. 12 for reference. A similar, but not identical mechanism is discussed by H. Rose, "The Possibility of Warranted Growth," *Economic Journal,* LXIX (June 1959), 313–333.
33 Harrod, *op. cit.*
34 D. Jorgenson, "On the Stability of the Dynamic Input–output System," *Review of Economic Studies,* forthcoming.
35 Decomposability is defined by: G. Debreu and I. Herstein, *op. cit.*
36 Leontief, *op. cit.*
37 For references see fn. 19.
38 For references and discussion, see: R. Solow, "On the Structure of a Linear Model," *Econometrica,* Vol. 20 (Jan. 1952), pp. 29–46.
39 See fn. 27, and fn. 28, and the accompanying text.
40 In the same way and for essentially the same reason it is unnecessary to observe "transitory income" in Friedman's theory of consumption: See M. Friedman, *A Theory of the Consumption Function* (Princeton: Princeton University Press, 1957).
41 Cross-section data necessary for this purpose are available from the 1947 interindustry study. The basic reference

for the input–output matrix is: W. D. Evans and M. Hoffenberg, "The Interindustry Relations Study for 1947," *The Review of Economics and Statistics,* XXXIV (May 1952), 97–142. The basic reference for the stock-flow matrix is: R. N. Grosse, "Capital Requirements for the Expansion of Industrial Capacity" (Washington, D.C.: Executive Office of the President, Bureau of the Budget, Office of Statistical Standards, Vol. I, Parts 1 and 2, November 30, 1953; mimeographed).
42 For proof, apply the theorem on relative stability in: D. Jorgenson, "On a Dual Stability Theorem," *Econometrica,* forthcoming.
43 J. Sargan, "The Instability of the Leontief Dynamic Model," *Econometrica,* Vol. 26 (July 1958), pp. 381–392.
44 R. G. D. Allen, *Mathematical Economics* (London: Macmillan, 1957).
45 K. Marx, *Capital,* II (Chicago: Kerr, 1933; 1st ed. (in German), 1885). J. Robinson, *The Accumulation of Capital* (London: Macmillan, 1956). The fact that the underlying model for such two-sector models of capital accumulation is essentially a closed form of the dynamic input–output system is demonstrated by: M. Morishima, "Some Properties of a Dynamic Leontief System with a Spectrum of Techniques," *Econometrica,* forthcoming.
46 Harrod, *op. cit.*; Hicks, *op. cit.*; P. A. Samuelson, "Interactions between the Multiplier Analysis and the Principle of Acceleration," *Review of Economic Statistics,* XXI (May 1939), 75–78; and "A Synthesis of the Principle of Acceleration and the Multiplier," *Journal of Political Economy,* XLVII (Dec. 1939), 786–797.
47 Wicksell, *op. cit.*

An Endogenous Model of Cyclical Growth
Kenneth K. Kurihara

The state of "steady growth" without inflation or unemployment represents how

Kenneth K. Kurihara, "An Endogenous Model of Cyclical Growth," *Oxford Economic Papers,* 12 (October 1960), pp. 243–248. Reprinted by permission of the Clarendon Press, Oxford.

we should like to see our industrial society behave. But what we have in the real world is the mixed phenomenon of "cyclical growth."[1] Recently a number of attempts have been made to explain this phenomenon, and the most crucial question of comparative dynamics still remains largely unanswered, namely: By what mechanism, if any, are these two [the rate of growth of effective demand and the rate of growth of productive capacity] brought into alignment?[2]

For the prevailing models would have us believe as if intrinsically irregular exogenous shocks could logically account for essentially regular cycles common to all growing advanced market economies,[3] as if the structure of a growing economy were fundamentally so unstable as to require exogenous constraints (e.g. a ceiling and a floor) for recurrent oscillations,[4] or as if self-limiting cycles capable of occurring without growth could realistically be associated with growth.[5] This note implies a criticism of all these models of cyclical growth.

However, the main purpose of this note is to suggest an alternative approach to cyclical growth in terms of *purely endogenous* variables and in the belief that such an approach would be more useful in clarifying the essentially self-generating nature and process of cyclical growth without resort to artificial exogenous constraints (including noneconomic erratic shocks) or to superfluous autonomous growth factors. The main proposition of this note is that *endogenously* determined investment is the *common* maker of cycles and growth. I shall implement this proposition by building a different model and cyclical growth on appropriate assumptions.

Our comparative dynamic system has its demand side and its supply side. The latter side presents no particular difficulty, though the choice of an appropriate rate of growth to represent it is somewhat problematical. For our express purpose of explaining cyclical growth endogenously, the appropriate standard of reference on the *supply* side seems to be that which is suggested by Harrod's explicit concept of the warranted rate "proper" with full employment[6] or by Domar's implicit concept of the full-capacity rate of growth.[7] In either case we get a steady path of dynamic equilibrium with a positive constant rate of growth around which cyclical oscillations are to occur.

It is, however, on the *demand* side of a growing economy that we encounter plenty of difficulty. Joan Robinson sounded the keynote of the difficulty when she complained: "But when we are concerned with an economy which is off the steady path, the acceleration principle becomes a great impediment to clear thinking."[8] Her bone of contention has, of course, to do with the offsetting effect of capital accumulation on income-induced investment stressed so articulately by M. Kalecki[9] and so ominously implied in both Keynes' marginal efficiency of capital theory and Domar's allusion to "the dual character of investment."[10] In view of such complaints against the acceleration principle we shall work, below, with a different assumption about entrepreneurial behaviour. As for saving, we shall assign to it a rather stabilizing role in the drama of cyclical growth in order to let investment play the star role of generating cycles and growth. Since, moreover, we are interested in fundamental analysis we shall assume a pure closed economy without the government sector and the foreign-trade sector—throughout the following discussion.

The question now is: by what route is the demand side of a growing economy turbulently connected with its supply side? To answer this question in an operationally significant way, it seems useful to spell out the functional relations involved on both the demand and supply sides, as follows.

We begin with the investment-*demand* function of the *nonlinear* form

$$I_t = f(Y_{t-1}) - \eta K_{t-1}$$
$$\left(\frac{\partial I}{\partial Y} > 0, \quad \frac{\partial I}{\partial K} < 0 \right) \quad (1)$$

based on the assumption that investment-demand is an increasing function of income but a decreasing function of capital. Here I is net real investment-demand, Y net real national income demanded or simply effective demand, K existing real capital, η a positive constant, and t and $t - 1$ the present and previous periods. Equation (1) implies

$$
\begin{aligned}
I_{t+1} - I_t &= [f(Y_t) - \eta K_t] \\
&\quad - [f(Y_{t-1}) - \eta K_{t-1}] \quad (2)
\end{aligned}
$$

which shows that net investment-demand is capable of increasing from time t to time $t + 1$ as long as the positive effect of income expansion is greater than the negative effect of capital accumulation, and vice versa. It is this nonlinear investment-demand function which serves as a dynamic multiplicand in the multiplier equation of the form

$$
\begin{aligned}
Y_{t+1} - Y_t &= \frac{1}{s}\{[f(Y_t) - \eta K_t] \\
&\quad - [f(Y_{t-1}) - \eta K_{t-1}]\} \\
&\qquad\qquad (s = \text{const.}) \quad (3)
\end{aligned}
$$

where s is the marginal-average propensity to save assumed to remain constant. Putting $\{[f(Y_t) - \eta K_t] - [f(Y_{t-1}) - \eta K_{t-1}]\}/Y_t = \delta_t$ and dividing both sides of equation (3) by Y_t, we get the *cyclically variable* rate of growth of effective demand (g):

$$
g \equiv \frac{Y_{t+1} - Y_t}{Y_t} = \frac{\delta_t}{s} \quad (4)
$$

which reveals that the rate of growth of effective demand is uniquely determined by the dynamic behaviour of the ratio of additional nonlinear investment-demand to income ($\delta = \delta_t \neq \text{const.}$), when the saving ratio remains constant ($s = \bar{s}$). There is, of course, no reason to suppose that the rate of growth of effective demand given by (4) always coincides with the rate of growth of productive capacity, except by accident or by design. This is where we must turn to the supply side.

On the simplifying assumption of a special production function with output having the homogeneity of first degree as to capital-input, we can have:

$$
Y'_{t+1} - Y'_t = \frac{1}{b}(K_{t+1} - K_t)
$$
$$
(b = \text{const.}) \quad (5)
$$

where Y' is net real national income supplied or simply productive capacity obtainable by fully utilizing the existing stock of capital, b the marginal-average ratio of capital to potential full-capacity output, and $1/b$ therefore the marginal-average productivity of capital. Here we assume b to remain constant, as in the familar Harrod–Domar growth models (our b being equivalent to Harrod's C_r and our $1/b$ to Domar's σ).

Equilibrium growth without excess demand or excess capacity requires the condition

$$
Y_{t+1} - Y_t = Y'_{t+1} - Y'_t
$$
or
$$
\frac{1}{s}(I_{t+1} - I_t) = \frac{1}{b}(K_{t+1} - K_t) \quad (6)
$$

to be satisfied. From (6) we immediately derive the required increase in investment-demand for equilibrium growth:

$$
\begin{aligned}
I_{t+1} - I_t &= s\frac{1}{b}(K_{t+1} - K_t) \\
&= g'(K_{t+1} - K_t) \quad (7)
\end{aligned}
$$

where g' is the *secularly constant equilibrium* rate of growth of productive capacity. For in equilibrium we have $Y_t = Y'_t$, $Y_{t+1} - Y_t = Y'_{t+1} - Y'_t$, and $(Y'_{t+1} - Y'_t)/(1/b) = s Y_t$ (left-hand side of which being net investment, or simply $\Delta K \equiv I \equiv \Delta Y'/(1/b)$, and the right-hand side being net savings), implying

$$
\begin{aligned}
g' &\equiv \frac{Y'_{t+1} - Y'_t}{Y'_t} = \frac{1/b(K_{t+1} - K_t)}{Y'_t} \\
&= \frac{1/b s Y_t}{Y_t} = \frac{1}{b}s \quad (8)
\end{aligned}
$$

The change in nonlinear investment-demand from time t to time $t + 1$ given by

(7) is what we have been seeking as the basic endogenous mechanism to generate *self-limiting* oscillations around the steady path of dynamic equilibrium represented by g'. To see the working of this stabilizing-destabilizing endogenous mechanism, it is only necessary to contemplate what would happen if the condition specified by (7) failed to be satisfied. Writing $I_{t+1} - I_t$ and $K_{t+1} - K_t$ simply as ΔI and ΔK, we may illustrate the cyclical implications of equation (7), as follows:

If $\Delta I > g' \Delta K$, then a self-limiting *upward* divergence.

If $\Delta I < g' \Delta K$, then a self-limiting *downward* divergence.

If $\Delta I = g' \Delta K$, then *equilibrium* growth without divergences.

It is to be emphasized that the upward divergence due to the endogenous inequality of the form $\Delta I > g' \Delta K$ (excess-*demand* growth) is only temporary and eventually reversed by the nonlinearity involved in ΔI itself, that is, by the depressing impact of capital *accumulation* outstripping the stimulating effect of income *expansion*, as equations (1) and (2) clearly indicate. Conversely, the downward divergence due to $\Delta I < g' \Delta K$ (excess *capacity* growth) is to be reversed by the stimulating effect on capital *decumulation* outrunning the depressing impact of income *contraction*. Thus the nonlinear behaviour of net investment-demand over time is capable of generating "limit cycles" around the steady path of dynamic equilibrium with a positive constant rate of growth. It is also to be noticed that the capital implicit in ΔI has a demand-decreasing effect, whereas the capital explicit in $g' \Delta K$ has a capacity-increasing effect. It is this dual role of capital which makes that variable at once the common determinant of cycles and growth, as suggested at the outset.

By way of summarizing our comparative-dynamic system represented by

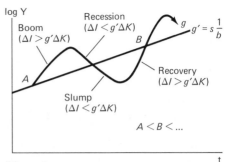

Figure 1

(1)–(8) we may make a brief diagrammatic analysis on the basis of Figure 1.

In Figure 1 the upward sloping g' curve is given by equation (8) and represents the steady path of dynamic equilibrium with a positive constant rate of growth, while the wave-like g curve is given by equation (4) and represents the variable rate of growth of effective demand. The time-path of cyclical movements around the g' line is governed by the working of the basic endogenous mechanism given by equation (7). Our economy might be thought of as starting from point A on the g' curve corresponding to, say, time t (measured along the horizontal axis); booming along the g curve according to $\Delta I > g' \Delta K$; reaching the peak at time $t + 1$; taking a downturn as the nonlinearity makes for $\Delta I < g' \Delta K$ (if above the g' curve, a recession; if below it, a slump, as the arrow indicates); slumping along the g curve to the trough at time $t + 2$; taking an upturn as the nonlinearity makes for $\Delta I < g' \Delta K$; and finally getting back on the g' curve at a higher point $(B > A)$. So one limit cycle is completed, only to give rise to another, and so on. It is to be noticed that the amplitude of fluctuations involved in Figure 1 is approximately constant, that is, neither forever increasing to require some exogenous constraints nor forever decreasing to require noneconomic shocks —in order to keep oscillations going. If the fluctuations of constant amplitude are to be narrowed as a matter of deliberate policy, policy-makers would have to work with the structural parameters s and δ on the demand side, as equation (4) implies.

Policy considerations aside, the above analysis seems to obviate resort to exogenous hypotheses of any kind (see nn. 3, 4, and 5) for explaining the mixed phenomenon of cyclical growth. That analysis may also have met some of the familiar objections to linear models, the acceleration principle, "mathematical instability" (infinite divergences), and erratic-shock theories.

NOTES

1 For original insights into cyclical growth, see J. A. Schumpeter, *Business Cycles*, 1939, and *The Theory of Economic Development*, 1934; J. M. Keynes, "Notes on the Trade Cycle" (ch. 22) and "Sundry Observations on the Nature of Capital" (ch. 16), in the *General Theory*.

2 See R. C. O. Matthews, "Duesenberry on Growth and Fluctuations," *Economic Journal*, Dec. 1959.

3 This random-shock approach is exemplified by J. S. Duesenberry, *Business Cycles and Economic Growth*, 1958.

4 This constraint-cycle approach is seen in R. F. Harrod, *Towards a Dynamic Economics*, 1948, and J. R. Hicks, *A Contribution to the Theory of the Trade Cycle*, 1958.

5 This nonlinear approach to incidental growth is seen in R. M. Goodwin, "A Model of Cyclical Growth," *The Business*

Cycle in the Post-War World (E. Lundberg, ed.), 1955, and N. Kaldor, "The Relation of Economic Growth and Cyclical Fluctuations," *Economic Journal*, Mar. 1954.

6 See R. F. Harrod, "An Essay in Dynamic Theory," *Economic Journal*, Mar. 1939, and also "Domar and Dynamic Economics," *ibid.*, Sept. 1959. It is to be noticed that his other notion of warranted growth elaborated in the *Dynamic Economics* is associated with "involuntary unemployment." His "natural" rate of growth is not, as Matthews in the already cited article seems to believe, the suitable rate with which to juxtapose the rate of growth of effective demand, since the "natural" rate is not only exogenously determined but also needlessly used as an artificial constraint to the upswing in some models.

7 As I indicated elsewhere, Domar does not work out "the supply side" of a growing economy, limiting himself to the rate of effective demand (or "income," in his terminology). But his "sigma effect," when fully worked out, would give us the rate of growth of *productive capacity* (see E. D. Domar, "Expansion and Employment," *American Economy Review*, Mar. 1947: also my *The Keynesian Theory of Economic Development*, 1959, pp. 67 ff.

8 See J. Robinson, *The Rate of Interest and Other Essays*, 1952, p. 163.

9 See M. Kalecki, "A Macrodynamic Theory of Business Cycles," *Econometrica*, Oct. 1935.

10 Domar, *op. cit.* Apparently Domar is more interested in trends than in cycles. By contrast, Harrod seems interested in both cycles and growth, judging from his stimulating discussion of the "actual" and "warranted" rates of growth in his *Dynamic Economics*.

Summaries

Gregory C. Chow, "The Acceleration Principle and the Nature of Business Cycles," *Quarterly Journal of Economics*, 77 (August 1968), pp. 403–418.

This study is the outcome of an attempt to understand the role that acceleration plays in causing or dampening business cycles. While acknowledging the important contributions of J. M. Clark (1917) and Samuelson (1939) toward the understanding of the factors which cause business cycles, the author points out that he is attempting to formulate mathematically the acceleration principle and offer some strong statistical evidence in support of this formulation. Describing the technical nature of his study, Chow states, "The present paper is partly the outcome of an analytical study of the dynamic properties of such a linear stochastic system. The tools employed are the autocovariances and the spectral densities of the time series so generated. The presentation of results on these matters . . . [is] self-contained."

Chow begins his paper by formulating the acceleration principle. He then proceeds to gather some evidence supporting the validity of this principle. Next, he shows that without an acceleration equation, a system of nonstochastic linear demand equations for the components of national output cannot produce oscillations in the variables. He goes on to derive "the autocovariance matrix and the spectral density matrix . . . in an elementary fashion." Finally, he shows that random shocks, when introduced into an otherwise nonoscillatory system, can generate cycles.

Chow concludes his paper with the following words: "In a deterministic model consisting only of demand equations which obey simple distributed lags, the acceleration equation is necessary for prolonged oscillations. However, when random shocks are introduced, prolonged oscillations in the deterministic system (complex roots) will be neither necessary nor sufficient for generating distinct cycles . . . An obvious moral is that the nature of business cycles can be understood only by an integrated view of the deterministic as well as the random elements."

Hyman P. Minsky, "The Integration of Simple Growth and Cycle Models," in Michael J. Brennan (ed.), *Patterns of Market Behavior* (Providence: Brown University Press, 1965), pp. 175–192.

At the beginning of this article, Minsky explains in the following words his reasons for having undertaken this study: "Various ceiling models of cycles or cyclical growth have appeared. In all except one, Kurihara's model, the rate of growth of the ceiling is exogenous. However, the saving and investing that takes place as income is at or below the ceiling implies that the ceiling grows. This paper investigates the conditions under which the rate of growth of ceiling income, as generated by the demand-determined division of income between investment and consumption, is sufficiently large that self-sustained growth can take place."

In the author's opinion, existing econometric income models are of two kinds: short-run forecasting models and long-run growth models. Both kinds of models, he claims, are one-sided and incomplete. For instance, economists working with growth models take into account either aggregate demand or aggregate supply, but not both demand and supply. Furthermore, monetary and financial phenomena are rarely included in these models. Also, these model-builders rarely pay attention to how the productive capacity ceiling is generated or how the interaction of the production ceiling with demand determination takes place. The author develops his cyclical growth model by focusing attention on the intermediate-term, thereby enabling him to integrate aggregate demand and supply determination in a growth model. However, for practical reasons he too ignores monetary-financial feedbacks in the growth process.

In this article, Minksy mathematically presents his integrated growth and cycle model, and graphically illustrates its function under various changes. In conclusion, he states, "Given that technological change, whether embodied or disembodied, takes place, and that the effect of technological change is to increase the rate of growth of ceiling income beyond that which would result just from accumulations, it has been shown that the ceiling income can grow fast enough so that self-sustained growth is possible. Therefore, in a technically dynamic world, we have to look beyond productive capacity constraints to explain the observed pattern of cyclical growth."

Arthur F. Burns, *The Management of Prosperity*. The Fairless Lectures, Carnegie Institute of Technology, Pittsburgh, 1965, pp. 13–29.

In this lecture delivered at the Carnegie Institute of Technology in 1965, Arthur Burns (now chairman of the Board of Governors of the Federal Reserve System), critically examines the nature of the economic expansion which the United States has enjoyed in the 1960s. A noted scholar in the field of the causes and consequences of business cycles, Burns predicted in 1965 that the expansion which began in February 1961 would be sustained for some time. He warned, however, that, unless proper steps were taken, the economy would suffer from serious bouts of inflation. In retrospect, it appears that both of Burns' predictions were accurate.

Much of Burns' analysis in this lecture of the economic expansion during the 1960s has business cycle overtones. For instance, he observes that the U.S. economy showed signs of recovery soon after Kennedy became president in 1960 and embraced an expansionist policy. However, according to Burns, this recovery was not due so much to Kennedy's expansionary policy as it was the result of business firms having voluntarily undertaken new investment projects. In another context, the author attributes the long economic expansion to what he calls "new economics." Thus, "One factor underlying the sustained expansion has undoubtedly been the willingness of the federal government to pursue a liberal fiscal policy, and to support it with as much monetary ease as the state of our balance of payments might allow. The principle of balancing the budget annually had already been abandoned ... Kennedy [pursued a policy of] deliberate adoption of budgetary deficits without regard to their duration or the stage of the business cycle, as long as a gap existed between the nation's actual production and what it theoretically could produce if unemployment did not exceed four percent."

Burns concludes his lecture with the following advice: "While a change of economic policy always involves some risk, I believe that the managers of our national prosperity will have the best chance of extending the current expansion if they will, on the one hand, deal more realistically with the structural causes of unemployment and, on the other, take steps to slow down the rate of growth of bank credit and curb for a while the increase in federal spending on civilian programs."

Bibliography

Ana M. M. Mantel, "A Model of Economic Fluctuations," *Yale Economic Essays*, 8 (Spring 1968), pp. 83–151.

R. C. O. Matthews, "Duesenberry on Growth and Fluctuations," *The Economic Journal*, 69 (December 1959), pp. 749–765.

Thomas O. Nitsch, "Toward a 'Newer' Model of the 'Business' Cycle—Part II," *Bentley Business and Economic Review*, February 1969, pp. 63–90.

Hugh Rose, "Real and Monetary Factors in the Business Cycle," *Journal of Money, Credit, and Banking*, 1 (May 1969), pp. 138–153.

12
INTERNATIONAL TRADE, FINANCE, AND ORDER

The mechanism by which a country attempts to achieve international trade and financial equilibrium is a highly complex one. The degree of this complexity varies according to the country's stage of economic development, the importance of foreign trade vis-à-vis national income, and the economic conditions prevailing in the rest of the world. Economists generally agree that an imbalance in a country's balance of payments, either a "chronic deficit" or a "chronic surplus," is undesirable and that steps should be taken by that country to improve the situation. The economist's classic remedy for this imbalance is to control capital flows by changing the interest rate differentials. In recent years, the use of flexible exchange rates has also been suggested as an important tool for solving international trade problems.

In the first selection in this part, which was published in November 1969, Bloomfield provides a general survey of recent trends in international economics. In the next article, Machlup examines alternative international monetary arrangements from one point of view—the way in which these arrangements promote, weaken, or endanger the free enterprise system. The third and concluding article is by Johnson. In it he argues in favor of a flexible exchange rate system.

Recent Trends in International Economics[*]
Arthur I. Bloomfield

This article attempts to sketch some of the main trends in international economics during the five years that have elapsed since the last such survey was published in *The Annals*.[1] In so doing, it provides a

Arthur I. Bloomfield, "Recent Trends in International Economics," American Academy of Political and Social Science, *Annals*, 386 (November 1969), pp. 148–167.

* Because of the frequent references in this

guide to some of the voluminous literature that has appeared since 1965 in the two main theoretical branches of this field: the "pure" (or "real") theory of international trade and international monetary (or balance-of-payments) theory.[2] Empirical and policy-oriented studies, which comprise so large and important a part of the literature on international economics generally, will, in the main, be by-passed.

Even with regard to purely theoretical studies, space limitations permit only a selective treatment of the literature and a bare clue as to the content of the individual publications referred to.

THEORY OF COMPARATIVE ADVANTAGE

There have been further refinements of the Heckscher–Ohlin (or "factor-proportions") version of the theory of comparative advantage, which states, on the basis of rigorous assumptions, that a country will export those goods which use a relatively large amount of its relatively abundant factor of production and import those goods which, if produced at home, use a relatively large amount of its relatively scarce factor. This contrasts with the earlier classical (Ricardian) version of the theory, which explained the commodity composition of trade in terms of international differences in comparative factor productivities.

Kenen criticizes what he regards as a *simpliste* concept of capital used in the factors-proportions analysis—the supposition that disembodied "waiting" enters into production as a separate input—and

---

article to certain economic journals, they will be abbreviated as follows:

AER	American Economic Review
CJEPS	Canadian Journal of Economics and Political Science
CJE	Canadian Journal of Economics
Ec	Economica
Ecra	Econometrica
EJ	Economic Journal
ER	Economic Record
IER	International Economic Review
JPE	Journal of Political Economy
Kyk	Kyklos
Man	The Manchester School
OEP	Oxford Economic Papers
QJE	Quarterly Journal of Economics
RES	Review of Economics and Statistics
WA	Weltwirtschaftliches Archiv

builds a model with fixed stocks of capital and labor which are inert until improved by acts of investment, generating service flows that enter into production. The two-country version of his model yields most of the conventional Heckscher–Ohlin results, but one of the important modifications is that a difference in capital scarcity, measured by relative interest rates, can affect factor-service flows, and, thus, the pattern of the commodity composition of trade.[3]

Ford analyzes the Heckscher–Ohlin model in cases where there are (1) three goods, three factors, and three countries and (2) three factors and two of each of the other variables; Vanek examines the case of more than two factors. They argue that, contrary to what is sometimes believed, it is possible in such cases to make meaningful statements regarding the relative factor-intensity of goods and factor-endowment positions, or to derive meaningful theorems regarding international specialization patterns.[4]

Bhagwati demonstrates that, contrary to what is thought, certain restrictions on demand conditions have to be specified if the two-country, two-commodity models of comparative advantage, whether the Ricardian or the Heckscher–Ohlin version (using the *price* definition of factor abundance in the latter case), are to be proved.[5] Ford indicates the conditions under which a particular pattern of trade can simultaneously conform to, or be explained by, both the factor-proportions and classical theories of comparative advantage.[6]

Bardhan analyzes the pattern of international specialization (and the effect of trade on factor prices) when the Heckscher–Ohlin assumption of identical production functions by industry in the trading countries is replaced by the assumption of neutral intercountry differences in production functions. He shows that the Heckscher–Ohlin predictions would not be borne out in a number of the resulting cases that he distinguishes.[7] A geometrical proof of his results is furnished by Mishan.[8] Bardhan further analyzes the patterns of comparative advantage and international specialization in a model of a growing international economy.[9]

INDUCTIVE TESTING OF THEORY OF COMPARATIVE ADVANTAGE

Inductive testing of the Heckscher–Ohlin theory continues, and further efforts have been made to "explain" the famous Leontief Paradox according to which the United States, in contrast to the expectations of that theory, appears, in practice, to export labor-intensive products and to import capital-intensive ones.[10]

Hodd empirically tests the Heckscher–Ohlin theory by investigating trade flows between the United States and the United Kingdom, and between the United Kingdom and the rest of the world, in selected years. He obtains results that appear to be inconsistent with the traditional form of that theory.[11] A *regional* test of the theory, applied to the South and non-South regions of the United States, is made by Moroney and Walker. Contrary to their expectations, they find some indication that industries requiring a relatively high capital-labor ratio in production are more heavily concentrated in the South than those requiring a relatively low capital-labor ratio.[12] In rebuttal, Estle argues that this is not a refutation of the Heckscher–Ohlin theory, since the South is in fact a relatively capital-abundant, not labor-abundant, region. Applying the same kind of test to New England, a relatively labor-abundant region compared with the rest of the United States, he finds that its comparative advantage lies in labor-intensive industries, as would be predicted by the theory.[13]

The labor and natural-resource requirements of United States exports and import-replacements for 1962, on the basis of the 1958 input-output table, are computed by Weiser, who finds that "the Leontief Paradox continues to exist." Accepting Vanek's earlier explanation for that paradox, which runs in terms of the scarcity of natural resources and their complementarity with the abundant factor, capital—requiring both to be conserved in United States foreign trade —he finds the pattern of changes in factor requirements between 1947 and 1962 to be consistent with a dynamic interpretation of that explanation.[14] Naya demonstrates empirically the importance of natural resources in explaining the observed capital-labor structure of the foreign trade of Japan, India, and Canada, but notes that the Vanek complementarity hypothesis does not appear to apply to Japan and India.[15]

Distinguishing material and human capital, and arguing that the United States exports are intensive in both together, Kenen makes a number of calculations that come very close to disposing of the Leontief Paradox.[16] Roskamp and McMeekin find that an earlier Leontief-Paradox-type result for West Germany for 1954 disappears when human capital is introduced as a third factor of production along with physical capital and labor.[17]

The role of labor skills in international trade is carried forward in a series of papers by Keesing,[18] who modifies the Heckscher–Ohlin model to incorporate different qualities of labor as separate factors. He demonstrates empirically that international differences in skill-endowments powerfully affect the pattern of trade in manufactured goods not closely tied to natural resources. For countries, such as the United States, that are relatively abundant in labor skills, exports tend to be skill-intensive compared with import-competing production.

A number of other recent writers, following up earlier suggestive leads by economists such as Hoffmeyer, Kindleberger, Kravis, and Linder, explore empirically influences other than factor proportions affecting trade in various manufactured goods, and especially United States trade in manufactures in general. They stress such factors as innovation, product-differentiation, research-and-development expenditures, economies of scale, transport, and marketing costs, and "technological gaps" as sources of international competitive strength and specialization in industrial products.[19] A synthesis of some of these factors in a "product cycle" model of international trade and investment is attempted by Vernon.[20] A more rigorous model, though it focuses more narrowly on the role of product-differentiation in "intra-industry" specialization in international trade, is developed by Grubel.[21] Other writers have noted that patterns of trade specialization are also influenced by the nature of tariff structures (see the later section in this article).

Earlier studies, especially by Minhas (1963), had cast doubt upon the empirical validity of the strong-factor-intensity hypothesis underlying the Heckscher–Ohlin theorem—that there is a unique ordering of industries by factor-intensity, regardless of relative factor prices—and had emphasized the importance in practice of factor-intensity reversals, a theoretical possibility that had already been widely recognized in the literature. A number of recent writers have questioned Minhas' methods and conclusions, and deny that the strong-factor-intensity hypothesis has been disproved.[22]

FACTOR-PRICE EQUALIZATION

There has been further discussion and elaboration of the factor-price equalization theorem which states that, given certain assumptions, free trade will equalize the real returns to productive factors internationally without factor movements.

Samuelson investigates the conditions under which free trade will equalize not only the *rentals* on capital goods (as postulated by the standard theorem), but also interest rates among countries. He shows that the equalization of the former will usually, though not necessarily, imply an equalization of the latter.[23] According to Komiya, the factor-price equalization theorem holds when a third, nontraded, good is introduced into the standard model.[24] Melvin contends that "there is no a priori reason for believing that there is less likelihood of factor price equalization in the three-good, two-factor case than there is in the two-good, two-factor case."[25] Johnson holds that "the larger the number of goods relative to the number of factors the more likely is free trade to lead to factor-price equalisation."[26] Ford suggests that the theorem may hold, under specified conditions, in the three-factor, two-commodity case.[27] The problem of factor-price equalization in the context of a model of capital-accumulation is analyzed by Inada.[28] That the last word on the subject has not yet been said is suggested by a lengthy debate by I. F. Pearce, L. M. McKenzie, and P. A. Samuleson.[29]

THE STOLPER–SAMUELSON THEOREM

The Stolper–Samuelson theorem relating to the effect of protection on the relative and absolute rewards of the productive factors (1942)—as qualified by Metzler (1949) and other writers—has met with less attention in the recent literature.

Minabe[30] and Batra[31] analyze the theorem under conditions of variable returns to scale, but reach differing conclusions as to its validity in such circumstances. Minabe's main finding is that if the production-possibility curve is concave to the origin, the theorem always holds. But, as Batra notes, this would be true if the theorem were concerned only with the relative, and not also as it is with the absolute, rewards of the factors. In turn, he argues that protection would always raise the relative reward of the scarce factor, but might, at the same time, lower its absolute reward if the economy undergoes overall diminishing returns. Thus, the theorem, properly stated, may not hold in the presence of nonconstant returns even when the production-possibility curve is concave to the origin. Ford demonstrates, despite some opinion to the contrary, that it is *possible* for the theorem to be upheld even (1) when there are three factors and (2) when factors are not perfectly transferable between industries.[32]

TRADE AND WELFARE

With regard to the normative or welfare aspects of trade theory, the recent literature has produced no work comparable in scope or influence to Meade's *Trade and Welfare* (1955). Nevertheless, the recent output in this field has been voluminous, notably in re-examinations of arguments for protection, in extensions of optimum-tariff theory, in analyses of the costs of protection, and (see next section of this article) in elaborations of customs-union theory.[33] Only a few samples can be cited here.

In a comprehensive article, Johnson analyzes the welfare effects of tariffs, subsidies on trade, and alternative government interventions in the presence of a wide assortment of domestic distortions—such as externalities in production and consumption, price rigidities, factor immobilities, and distortions in factor markets—that have been the basis for a whole range of arguments for protection.[34] His main points are "that welfare maximization requires a correc-tion of the relevant domestic distortion by an appropriate tax or subsidy on production, consumption, or factor use, and not a tax or subsidy on international trade; and that, given the presence of a domestic distortion, protection designed to offset it may decrease welfare rather than increase it." The primary argument for protection as a means of maximizing economic welfare, he argues, is the optimum-tariff argument.

Related ground is covered, within a somewhat broader framework, in a masterly survey of the theory of commerical policy by Bhagwati.[35] He examines a wide range of cases of justifiable departures from what he calls "unified exchange rates" (where the relative incentive to produce and consume tradable goods, as provided by their domestic relative prices, is identical with that obtaining internationally), and he indicates the optimal forms of departure in each case, whether domestic taxes-cum-subsidies on production, consumption, or factor use; tariffs; or trade subsidies. Notable is his treatment of optimal policy interventions to achieve various "noneconomic" objectives such as self-sufficiency and specific levels of production in certain lines of activity. The conclusions of his study are broadly in harmony with those of Johnson, to the extent that their treatments overlap.[36]

The factors determining the optimum-tariff *gain,* as contrasted with the optimum-tariff rate, are analyzed by Johnson on the basis of models capable of yielding quantitative results. He concludes that the potential relative welfare gain from optimal tariff policies may typically be comparatively small for less developed countries.[37] That the optimum tariff argument is applicable in a situation involving capital-accumulation over time is demonstrated by Findlay.[38] Friedlander and Vandendorpe focus on how a country can exploit a degree of monopoly power in international trade by imposing *either* a production tax or a consumption tax; they conclude that a country "can normally be expected to reach a higher level of welfare...under the optimal tariff than under either an optimal consumption or an optimal production tax."[39]

Integrating the analysis of the gains from trade with that of international investment, Kemp investigates the optimal combination of tariff and tax on earnings from foreign investment from a national standpoint. He reaches the "paradoxical" conclusion that under certain circumstances "either the optimum tariff or the optimal tax on foreign earnings, or both, may be negative."[40] A similar conclusion, among many others, is reached by Jones in an extension of Kemp's analysis.[41] A parallel literature is continuing to develop on the national gains from foreign investment, treated separately.[42]

THE THEORY OF CUSTOMS UNIONS

Customs-union theory, or the theory of discriminatory tariff changes, has expanded considerably since the pioneering contribution of Jacob Viner in 1950. Viner's model, which analyzed the welfare effects of a customs union in terms of "trade creation" and "trade diversion" (production effects), was subsequently extended by Meade, Lipsey, and others by taking account of consumption effects and by relaxing other of its assumptions. From these various studies and the technical apparatus developed, there emerged a number of useful generalizations concerning the circumstances under which a customs union is likely to increase, or not to increase, welfare.[43]

This work has been carried forward in a recent book by Vanek, the distinctive features of which are exclusive use of a general-equilibrium rather than partial-equilibrium approach and of ordinal rather than cardinal preference functions.

On this basis, he analyzes, in a large number of possible cases, the effects of a customs union on the welfare of the participating countries and of the rest of the world, depending upon such considerations as the size and degree of "economic similarity" of countries, the level of tariffs before the formation of the union, and the degree of trade-liberalization. His 107 conclusions, many of which break new ground, are neatly summarized at the end of the book.[44]

Cooper and Massell argue that some members of a proposed customs union would be at least as well off, and quite possibly better off, if they reduced their own tariffs unilaterally and nonpreferentially. They reach this conclusion by distinguishing two exhaustive components of the welfare effect of a customs union: a tariff-reduction component, which accounts for both trade-creation and the consumption effect, and a pure-trade-diversion component; the former incorporates the sole source of (static) gain that might result from a customs union.[45] This conclusion is shown by Arndt to be crucially dependent upon the assumption that the terms of trade are unchanged. If this assumption is dropped, "the terms-of-trade effect of the customs union may be of sufficient strength to produce a net improvement in welfare over any non-preferential situation."[46] In another paper, Arndt breaks up the nonunion world into a number of heterogeneous countries, in place of the customary procedure of treating it as a perfectly homogeneous entity. He shows that the usual conclusion that terms-of-trade movements will lead to a deterioration in the welfare of the "outside world" has only limited relevance to the multicountry situation. He further shows that when exclusion from the union involves more than a single country, the incentives to elect nonmembership will be increased for some countries by the final form of the union.[47] Some theoretical aspects of customs unions among developing countries are analyzed in papers by Cooper and Massell[48] and by Mead.[49]

THE THEORY OF EFFECTIVE PROTECTION

The past five years have witnessed the rapid development of a new approach to the analysis and measurement of the effects of commercial policy on the patterns of world trade and specialization: the theory of effective protection. The traditional theory of tariffs assumes that protection is given only to final consumption goods, and that these are produced entirely by the original factors of production. By contrast, the new approach as developed particularly by Johnson[50] and Corden,[51] is based on the fact that many traded commodities are raw materials and intermediate goods (themselves usually subject to tariffs) which serve as inputs at different stages of the production process. An important distinction thus emerges between the *nominal* tariff rates on traded commodities (final and intermediate) and the rates of protection accorded by the tariff structure to particular production processes. The latter are referred to as *effective* rates of protection, or rates of protection of value added. They take into account the tariffs on material inputs as well as outputs, and may differ widely from the corresponding nominal tariff rates on the output of the process or activity concerned.

Specifically, the effective rate of protection may be defined as the percentage increase in value added per unit in an economic activity made possible by the tariff structure, relative to the situation in the absence of tariffs. It depends not only on the tariff on the commodity produced by the activity, but also on the input coefficients and the tariffs on the inputs.[52] The effective rate of protection in a production process will be higher than the nominal tariff rate, given the input coefficients, if the weighted-average tariff rate on the imported inputs is lower than the tariff rate on the output of that process; and it will be lower than the tariff rate if the opposite prevails. The effective protective rate can indeed be negative, even if the nominal rate is positive. The possibility of divergence between effective and nominal rates of protection results from the fact that tariffs on outputs provide a subsidy to domestic production of the outputs in question, whereas tariffs on inputs impose a tax on the domestic production of the outputs into which they enter. The effective degree of protection is the net result of the opposite effects that tariffs on outputs and inputs have on value added in the activity concerned.

Statistical investigations of the tariff structures of major industrial countries have shown that effective rates of protection, in the wide range of industries examined, are with few exceptions higher, and often much higher, than the corresponding nominal rates.[53] This fundamentally reflects the fact that the typical tariff structure of developed countries (and, for that matter, of less developed countries) involves "escalation" of tariff rates by stage of production, such that rates are zero or low on raw materials, fuels, and partially processed materials, higher on semimanufactures, and higher still on finished goods. Escalation thus gives effective protection at rising rates— and at rates higher than the nominal tariff rates—to goods at successive stages of the production process.

Such a pattern of effective protective rates has important implications for the patterns of world trade, specialization, and development. As various writers have shown, it biases world trade toward raw materials, fuels, and semifabricates; toward consumers goods of a luxury nature; and toward producers and consumers goods featured by technological superiority, which are capable of overcoming the barriers imposed by high effective protection. In particular, it creates special difficulties for the export from the less developed countries of manufactured goods and processed materials, and biases their exports towards dependence on primary products in their unprocessed form, thereby serving, potentially, to inhibit economic development in these countries.[54]

The theory of effective protection has a number of other important empirical and theoretical applications, providing new insights into old problems. It has enabled a more precise assessment of the extent of the welfare losses imposed on less developed countries by their own trade restrictions and interventions.[55] It has permitted a reconsideration of the problem of measuring the "height" or restrictiveness of national tariff levels.[56] It has been fruitfully applied to an analysis of the effects of trade preferences.[57] It has provoked a number of statistical analyses of the relationship between effective protective rates and labor-intensiveness in manufacturing industries in various developed countries, including the United States, on the hypothesis that, if labor is the relatively scarce factor in these countries, one might expect to find a systematic relationship between the two.[58] And it has been applied in other directions.[59]

In the meantime, the theory as originally propounded is being subjected to modifications and extensions with regard to the interpretation and magnitudes of effective protective rates, and their effects on the direction of domestic-resources flows, when some of its more restrictive assumptions, such as zero elasticity of substitution between inputs, are relaxed.[60]

THE THEORY OF ECONOMIC POLICY IN AN OPEN ECONOMY

The theory of the balance of payments has shifted since 1945 from its traditional concern with automatic-adjustment mechanisms to an explicit theory of balance-of-payments policy.[61] One of the earlier policy-oriented models was developed by Meade in his *The Balance of Payments* (1952). Its basic idea was that in order to achieve two targets—internal balance (defined as full employment without inflation) and external balance (defined mainly in terms of current-account transactions)—a country needed two instruments or policy-variables: expenditures (aggregate-demand) policy and exhange-rate variation (or wage-price flexibility). If only one instrument is available, as when exchange rates are fixed, it is possible for conflicts of objectives to arise (in the so-called "dilemma cases"). Mundell in 1962, by introducing capital movements into the model and by showing that fiscal and monetary policy (the two components of expenditures policy) have differential effects on the capital account of the balance of payments, had demonstrated that, by an appropriate mix of fiscal and monetary policies, a country, even under a system of fixed exchange rates, could simultaneously attain the two goals of internal and external balance. He showed that this result required the "assignment" of each policy variable to that goal on which it exerted the relatively greater effect; under fixed exchange rates, this meant that monetary policy should be directed to maintaining external balance and fiscal policy to internal balance. The opposite pairing of instruments and targets, he argued, would lead to dynamic instability.

The Mundell model has attracted much attention in the recent literature and has been subjected to a number of modifications and extensions. By incorporating additional variables into its basic framework, various writers have widened the range of possible cases and appropriate policy-prescriptions. In particular, they have shown that it need no longer be true that monetary policy always has a comparative advantage in dealing with the balance of payments and fiscal policy, in dealing with domestic income and employment. For example, to raise income and employment without upsetting the balance of payments, the appropriate mixture of policies need no longer be fiscal expansion and monetary contraction, as Mundell suggested. It might instead be fiscal contraction and monetary expansion, or both fiscal and monetary expansion. In some cases, there might be no unique assignment of instruments to goals at all.

Some of the modifications of the Mundell model which have led to conclusions such as these might be briefly noted. Johnson, for example, makes capital movements dependent, not only on interest rates, but also on the level of income; and he distinguishes differing degrees of interest-mobility and of income-mobility of capital flows.[62] In addition to making use of this distinction, Jones makes imports dependent, not only on the aggregate level of income, but also on its composition, on the assumption that the import components of the various categories of expenditures differ; this enables monetary and fiscal policy, by acting on the composition of output, to influence the trade balance by more than one route.[63] A similar assumption concerning imports has been made independently by Ott and Ott, and plays a crucial role in their model in determining the proper pairing of instruments and targets.[64] Willett and Forte extend the Mundell model to take account of stock-adjustments, as distinct from flows of international capital, and also of the interest cost of attracting capital from abroad.[65] Patrick further expands the model to take into account, not only the distinctions between stocks and flows of capital and between the interest-mobility and the income-mobility of capital movements, but also the interactions of

national economic policies in a two-country world. With regard to the last, he emphasizes, among other things, the need for consistency of the balance-of-payments targets of the two countries if they are to achieve their internal and external goals.[66] (In his article, Mundell had disregarded automatic feedbacks through the balance of payments or the possibility of foreign-policy responses to policy changes in the "home" country.)

The problem of economic policy-making in a two-country model is studied in depth by Cooper. He explores the effects of co-ordination between policy-makers in the two countries on the path of adjustment to disturbances, as affected by different degrees of economic interdependence between them. He shows that as interdependence increases, the case for international co-ordination of policy-making—for directing all the policy instruments at all the targets—becomes more compelling.[67] The two-country case, and other problems in the theory of economic policy under fixed exchange rates, are analyzed in an article by Niehans, the main theme of which is the need to replace the Meade–Mundell "fixed-target"-type models with a more general optimizing approach, some of the implications of which he explores.[68]

In addition to the development of abstract models of the kinds just described, there has been extensive discussion in the recent literature, at a more practical level, of means of reconciling external and internal objectives of economic policy and of improving the balance-of-payments adjustment process within the framework of the present international monetary system. These studies examine, not only fiscal-monetary-policy mixes and their practical limitations, but also such matters as income policies, international co-ordination of policies, general criteria for guiding national and collective policies for restoring and maintaining balance in international payments, and control of capital movements.[69]

ALTERNATIVE EXCHANGE-RATE SYSTEMS

Macromodels of the kinds discussed in the preceding section have also been used by various writers to focus on the comparative efficiency of monetary and fiscal policy in achieving domestic income targets under systems of "fixed" and "flexible" exchange rates.[70] Krueger argues that, with capital movements responsive to interest-rate differentials, both fiscal and monetary policy are more effective under flexible rates than under fixed rates in raising the level of income.[71] Johnson shows that the interest-mobility of capital increases the advantage of fiscal policy over monetary policy under fixed rates, and vice versa under flexible rates, whereas the income-mobility of capital facilitates the task of increasing income without adverse balance-of-payments effects under the former system, but reduces the leverage of both fiscal and monetary policy over income under the latter.[72] In yet another model, Sohmen concludes that monetary policy as a countercyclical instrument is more effective under flexible than under fixed rates, but that fiscal policy may be a more powerful stabilization tool under fixed or flexible rates, depending upon the marginal propensity to import, the degree of capital-mobility, and the interest- and income-elasticities of the demand for money.[73]

With the acceptance by most economists of the desirability of greater exchange-rate flexibility than now exists, and with awareness of the political difficulties of realizing freely floating exchange rates in practice, interest has tended to shift increasingly from the issue of "fixed" versus "flexible" rates to the pros and cons of more limited forms of exchange flexibility.[74] The main proposals recently advanced, along with numerous variants thereof, are the "band" scheme for a wider spread around parities within which exchange rates would be allowed to fluctuate; the "sliding parity" (or "crawling peg") under which parities would be continuously changed by small amounts in the face of continuing payments disequilibria; and some combination of both.[75] These policy-oriented analyses have produced no major contributions to theory. On the other hand, important theoretical studies have been made, by Hause[76] and Johnson,[77] of the welfare costs of exchange-rate stabilization in the presence of fluctuations in domestic, relative to foreign, price levels, and of the welfare losses imposed by periodic, discrete changes in exchange rates.

THEORY OF EXCHANGE-DEVALUATION

Perhaps the most actively debated issue in international monetary theory during the past two decades has been concerned with the nature of the conditions under which exchange-devaluation will improve the trade balance, along with the role of terms-of-trade changes in devaluation. The past five years, in contrast, have been a period of comparative calm in this area.

Negishi examines the relations between the results of several approaches to the problem of stability of the foreign exchanges. He argues, among other things, that gross substitutability among all commodities *or* the absence of all cross-price effects *and* the Marshall–Lerner condition, is sufficient for stability of the foreign-exchange market.[78] Gray shows that, where market structure permits or enforces the maintenance of exports expressed in foreign currencies after devaluation, the Marshall–Lerner condition overstates the actual requirement for devaluation to be effective, and that the trade balance in such cases will be more responsive to devaluation than that condition would suggest.[79] Calling attention to the fact that the well-known formulas which express the trade-balance effect of a devaluation in terms of price-elasticities assume an infinitesimal variation of the exchange rate, Olivera derives formulas showing the effect of a finite devaluation.[80] Kreinen derives a formula showing the conditions under which a devaluation would improve the *income* terms of trade.[81]

THEORY OF FORWARD EXCHANGE

The theory of forward exchange continues to attract considerable attention. A veritable flood of models of the foreign-exchange market has recently made an appearance. These models extend and refine, without, for the most part, fundamentally altering, the modern theory of forward exchange developed in the 1950s and early 1960s by Spraos, Tsiang, and Sohmen; that theory had, in turn, built on and radically qualified the earlier interest-parity theory of Keynes. Like their more immediate predecessors, the recent studies analyze the interplay of interest arbitrage, commercial covering, and exchange speculation in determining the forward-exchange rate; and they explore the linkages between the forward and spot markets, with particular attention to the role of speculative behavior. The extent to which recent authors subject their models to statistical testing and analyze the implications of their findings for forward-exchange policy and monetary policy is noteworthy.

Grubel has produced a rigorous book on the forward exchanges, of which some of the more novel features include the incorporation of the Tobin–Markowitz portfolio analysis and the treatment of triangular arbitrage.[82] By analyzing the operations of a single export-import firm,

Kenen demonstrates the basic similarity of purpose in *all* forward-exchange transactions, whether "covering," "arbitrage," or "speculation."[83] An analysis of the role of uncertainty in forward-exchange speculation, within the framework of von Neumann–Morgenstern expected utility-maximization, is made by Feldstein.[84] A slim monograph by Sohmen adds to his earlier contributions, particularly by incorporating into his analysis the existence of many forward-exchange markets of differing maturities.[85] Arndt develops, and tests empirically, a theory of speculative behavior in the exchange market with a distributed-lag model of expectation formation at its core.[86] A model of the foreign-exchange market that has attracted much attention is that developed by Stein in connection with his examination of the interest-elasticity of short-term capital movements.[87] A number of other models have also recently been constructed and empirically tested.[88]

INTERNATIONAL LIQUIDITY

The problem of international liquidity has played a central role during the past decade in academic (and governmental) discussions and debates on reform of the present international monetary system. In the process, there has developed a large literature on such questions as the meaning and measure of "adequacy" of international reserves for individual countries and for the world as a whole, the determinants of the demand for reserves, and, at a more practical level, the most appropriate means of increasing the stock or rate of growth of reserves of the world economy. Although the debate has clarified many of the underlying issues, there is, as yet, no general agreement on the answers to these questions. At the governmental plane, however, international agreement has finally been reached on a plan to create new international-reserve assets, in the form of so-called Special Drawing Rights, to supplement those now existing.[89]

A feature of the recent literature in this field has been the number of attempts, on the basis of explicit models, to measure quantitatively the adequacy of, or demand for, reserves on the part of individual countries. Heller derives a formula for determining the optimal amount of reserves that a country should hold. It is based on the principle that a country should balance, at the margin, the gain from holding reserves (the avoidance of the cost of real adjustment to payments deficits, with allowance for the probability of occurrence of a deficit of a given size) and the opportunity cost of holding reserves (the real resources foregone). He applies his formula to sixty countries, comparing the optimal reserves so obtained with actual reserves.[90] Kenen and Yudin, assuming that the demand for reserves by an individual country reflects its expectations concerning future payments disturbances (based on past experience), construct a cross-sectional equation from the experience of several major countries that explains the typical country's demand for reserves. They find that reserve holdings are, in fact, related to the variance of past (expected future) disturbances.[91] Regression analyses by Courchane and Youssef for nine countries yield the result that the demand of individual countries for reserves (assuming the existence of a stable demand function over time) can be represented as a function of the money supply and of the long-term interest rate (a proxy for the opportunity cost of holding reserves).[92] Although these studies constitute an advance over the earlier *qualitative* concepts of reserve needs (measured by ratios of reserves to imports and the like), they are still subject to heroic assumptions. Fleming lays down a sophisticated conceptual framework from which one might derive a quantitative estimate of needed world reserve growth over a given period, but does not himself attempt such a derivation.[93]

In a review article, Clower and Lipsey take a dim view of the possibility of deriving dependable quantitative measures of reserve adequacy, largely because of the unpredictability of speculative attacks, the accommodation to which is among the main reasons for holding official reserves under a fixed exchange-rate system.[94] Machlup, on the other hand, questions the customary concept of reserve adequacy. He argues:

It cannot be reasonably said of any particular amount of reserves, either in a particular country or in a group of countries, that it is needed or adequate, but it can be said convincingly that an *increase* in reserves will be needed or adequate to prevent restrictions on foreign trade and payments. Emphasis on the *size* of reserves is mistaken, emphasis on *additions* to reserves is justified.[95]

Explicit theoretical analyses have recently been made of a related problem: if a new international reserve asset is to be created, at little or no cost to the issuing agency—unlike gold which absorbs real resources in its creation—how is the asset to be distributed and how are the gains accruing from its issue to be shared among the participating countries? This has come to be known as the "seignorage problem." The nature of the gain and the implications of alternative ways of distributing it are analyzed by Johnson,[96] Machlup,[97] and Grubel.[98]

THE ECONOMICS OF FOREIGN AID

The literature on what might be called the economics of foreign aid continues to accumulate. Apart from a number of general texts,[99] and studies dealing with particular aspects of foreign aid,[100] further comprehensive aid theories and formal models of the aid-and-growth process have been developed. These models work out the conditions under which external assistance can help the recipient countries to achieve targeted, self-sustaining rates of growth; and they enable projections to be made of the amounts of aid and the time periods required to achieve this goal under varying assumptions.

In a "two-gap" model of aid and development, Chenery and Strout emphasize the separate limits imposed on the growth process by shortage of skills, savings, and foreign exchange, respectively, and they analyze the role of external assistance in relieving each of these bottlenecks and in making possible an acceleration of growth. Distinguishing consecutive phases in the transition to self-sustaining growth, according to which each of these constraints predominates, they specify the kinds of internal structural changes (in terms of marginal savings and import ratios, export-growth rates, and the like) needed for foreign aid to facilitate the transition from phase to phase. They estimate the extent to which the recent development performance in a large number of aid-recipient countries meets the specified requirements for the achievement of self-sustaining growth, and they make projections to explain the range of future growth possibilities in each country and the corresponding aid requirements under alternative assumptions as to internal policies.[101]

A model by Fei and Paauw, focusing on the savings limitation to growth, analyzes the relation between external assistance and the mobilization of domestic savings in achieving a given rate of self-sustaining growth. Their model is applied to a sample group of less developed countries, yielding numerical answers to such questions as the duration of the required capital inflow, its time path and accumulated value, and the domestic savings required.[102] Sengupta, also emphasizing the savings gap, constructs a model designed to enable a calculation of the minimum number of years required to attain a given rate of self-sustaining growth, in cases where the capital comes in the forms of grants, loans, or direct investments.[103] Qayum concentrates on whether or not, and under what conditions, foreign loans are, on balance, of long-run economic advantage to the borrowing countries when allowance is made for interest charges and repayment obligations. He works out the critical set of loan terms (interest rates and repayment periods) that separate advantageous and disadvantageous loans.[104]

TRADE AND GROWTH

During the postwar period, a large and diversified literature has developed on what might be termed, for want of a more descriptive title, "trade and growth." Included under this broad rubric are theoretical, empirical, and policy-oriented studies dealing with various aspects of the interrelations between growth, on the one hand, and trade, trade policies, and aid, on the other. Some of the recent literature in this broad area has already been referred to in this article under those sections where inclusion seemed most appropriate. A few other such studies, which could not easily be fitted into the individual sections, will be noted here.

In the more abstract, formal category, for instance, are the studies of Pryor[105] and Komiya,[106] which analyze the effects of growth on the terms of trade and the balance of payments, respectively. Other recent models could be cited.[107] Another facet of the trade-growth problem is explored in a recent book by Linder: Is the traditional theory of international trade, with its general policy presumption in favor of free trade, the most suitable tool for analyzing the effects of trade on the less developed countries and for formulating their commercial policies? Linder, like many of his predecessors, answers no, and he suggests an alternative approach.[108] Closely related are studies which develop and analyze arguments for protection in the particular case of less developed countries, and which examine the impact of tariffs and trade controls on the growth and welfare of these economies. The vast postwar literature on trade, growth, and the developing countries has recently been surveyed by Meier.[109]

A policy-oriented literature has developed around the proposals advanced by the less developed nations at the first session in 1964 of the United Nations Conference on Trade and Development (UNCTAD). These proposals included increased use of international commodity agreements to stabilize and raise primary-product prices; external compensatory financing to offset periodic declines in export earnings; reduced trade barriers in the developed countries against the traditional and newer exports of the developing nations; and, most controversial, the grant of tariff preferences to the latter's exports of manufactured and semimanufactured goods. These proposals and others were again advanced at the second session of UNCTAD in 1968.[110] Underlying them were the assumptions that, if some such actions were not taken, the "foreign-exchange gap" of the developing countries would further widen, to the detriment of their growth targets,[111] and a growing awareness that their industrialization depends, not on protectionist policies, but on expanded markets abroad for their exports.

These and related proposals are analyzed by Johnson, who concedes that present world trading arrangements, institutionalized in the General Agreement on Trade and Tariffs (GATT), have tended to disfavor the less developed countries, not because of GATT's underlying principles, but because those principles have been subverted by the tariff-bargaining techniques and agricultural protectionism of industrial countries. On the other hand, he takes a dim view of international commodity agreements and raises questions about the wisdom and benefit of granting preferences to the industrial exports of the developing countries. He favors remedial action by the developed countries, within the existing GATT framework, in the form of nondiscriminatory reductions of tariffs and other trade barriers, especially those that weigh most heavily on the exports of the less developed nations, if need be, by the United States acting unilaterally. He argues also that many of the trading difficulties of the developing countries are of their own making because of their inflationary and import-substitution policies and their refusal to adjust downward their overvalued exchange rates.[112] Similar ground is covered, though in less rigorous, more controversial fashion, by Pincus.[113] Macbean questions the assumption that the developing countries suffer from violent fluctuations in their export earnings and that these constitute a serious impediment to growth.[114] Trade preferences and other forms of discrimination are examined by Patterson, including preferences for the less developed countries.[115]

NOTES

1 C. P. Kindleberger, "Trends in International Economics," *The Annals* (March 1965), pp. 170–179.

2 The literature on international economic theory has been the subject of numerous surveys and syntheses, nearly all of them appearing in 1965 or earlier. See especially J. Bhagwati, "The Pure Theory of International Trade: A Survey." *EJ* (March 1964), pp. 1–84; J. S. Chipman, "A Survey of the Theory of International Trade," *Ecra* (July 1965), pp. 477–519; *ibid.* (October 1965), pp. 685–760; and *ibid.* (January 1966), pp. 18–76; W. M. Corden, *Recent Developments in the Theory of International Trade*, Special

Papers in International Economics, no. 7 (Princeton, N.J.: Princeton University Press, 1965); R. E. Caves, *Trade and Economic Structure* (Cambridge, Mass.: Harvard University Press, 1960); and A. O. Krueger, "Balance-of-Payments Theory," *Journal of Economic Literature* (March 1969), pp. 1–26.

3 P. B. Kenen, "Nature, Capital, and Trade," *JPE* (October 1965), pp. 437–460.

4 J. L. Ford, "On the Structure of, and Gains from, International Trade," *Kyk*, 1965, no. 4, pp. 670–684; and J. Vanek, "The Factor-Proportions Theory: The *N*-Factor Case," *Kyk*, 1968, no. 4, pp. 749–756. A. Amano ("Intermediate Goods and the Theory of Comparative Advantage: A Two-Country, Three-Commodity Case," *WA*, 1966, no 2, pp. 340–345) provides an example of a two-country, three-commodity model (the third commodity being an intermediate good) where pretrade price (cost) ratios, in a classical comparative-advantage framework, do not correctly predict the final pattern of trade.

5 J. Bhagwati, "The Proofs of the Theorems on Comparative Advantage," *EJ* (March 1967), pp. 75–83.

6 J. L. Ford, "On the Equivalence of the Classical and Factor-Proportions Models in Explaining International Trade Patterns," *Man* (May 1967), pp. 185–198.

7 P. K. Bardhan, "International Differences in Production Functions, Trade, and Factor Prices," *EJ* (March 1965), pp. 81–87.

8 E. J. Mishan, "International Factor Price Determination with Neutral Technical Progress," *Ec* (August 1966), pp. 330–335.

9 P. K. Bardhan, "International Trade Theory in a Vintage-Capital Model," *Ecra* (October 1966), pp. 756–767, and "On Factor-Accumulation and the Pattern of International Specialization," *Review of Economic Studies* (January 1966), pp. 39–44. See also N. Minabe, "The Heckscher–Ohlin Theorem, the Leontief Paradox, and Patterns of Economic Growth," *AER* (December 1966), pp. 1193–1211.

10 W. W. Leontief, "Domestic Production and Foreign Trade," *Proceedings of the American Philosophical Society* (September 1953), pp. 332–349.

11 M. Hodd, "An Empirical Investigation of the Heckscher–Ohlin Theory," *Ec* (February 1967), pp. 20–29. Hodd's results have been challenged by M. Borchert, "An Empircial Investigation of the Heckscher–Ohlin Theory: A Comment," *Ec* (May 1969), pp. 193–195.

12 J. R. Moroney and J. M. Walker, "A Regional Test of the Heckscher–Ohlin Hypothesis," *JPE* (December 1966), pp. 573–586.

13 E. F. Estle, "A More Conclusive Regional Test of the Heckscher–Ohlin Hypothesis," *JPE* (December 1967), pp. 886–888.

14 L. A. Weiser, "Changing Factor Requirements of United States Foreign Trade," *RES* (August 1968), pp. 356–360.

15 S. Naya, "Natural Resources, Factor Mix, and Factor Reversal in International Trade," *Papers and Proceedings*, *AER* (May 1967), pp. 561–570.

16 Kenen, "Nature, Capital, and Trade," pp. 455–458.

17 K. W. Roskamp and G. C. McMeekin, "Factor Proportions, Human Capital, and Foreign Trade: The Case of West Germany Reconsidered." *QJE* (February 1968), pp. 152–160.

18 D. B. Keesing, "Labor Skills and International Trade," *RES* (August 1965), pp. 287–294; "Labor Skills and Comparative Advantage," *Papers and Proceedings*, *AER* (May 1966), pp. 249–258; and "Labor Skills and the Structure of Trade in Manufacturers," in P. B. Kenen and R. Lawrence, eds., *The Open Economy: Essays in International Trade and Finance* (New York: Columbia University Press, 1968), pp. 3–18. For a related paper, see H. Waehrer, "Wage Rates, Labor Skills, and United States Foreign Trade," *ibid.*, pp. 19–39.

19 W. Gruber, D. Mehta, and R. Vernon, "The R & D Factor in International Trade and International Investment of U.S. Industries," *JPE* (February 1967), pp. 20–38; D. B. Keesing, "The Impact of Research and Development on United States Trade," *JPE* (February 1967), pp. 38–48; G. C. Hufbauer, *Synthetic Materials and the Theory of International Trade* (Cambridge, Mass.: Harvard University Press, 1966); S. Hirsch, *Location of Industry and International Competitiveness* (New York: Oxford University Press, 1967); and L. T. Wells, Jr., "Test of a Product Cycle Model of International Trade: U.S. Exports of Consumer Durables," *QJE* (February 1969), pp. 152–162.

20 R. Vernon, "International Investment and International Trade in the Product Cycle," *QJE* (May 1966), pp. 190–207.

21 H. G. Grubel, "Intra-Industry Specialization and the Pattern of Trade," *CJEPS* (August 1967), pp. 374–388.

22 See, e.g., D. S. Ball, "Factor-Intensity Reversals in International Comparison of Factor Costs and Factor Use," *JPE* (February 1966), pp. 77–80; J. R. Moroney, "The Strong-Factor-Intensity Hypothesis: A Multisectoral Test," *JPE* (June 1967), pp. 241–249; and H. B. Lary, *Imports of Manufactures from Less Developed Countries* (New York: National Bureau of Economic Research, 1968).

23 P. A. Samuelson, "Equalization by Trade of the Interest Rate along with the Real Wage," in R. E. Baldwin *et al.*, *Trade, Growth, and the Balance of Payments* (Chicago: Rand McNally, 1965), pp. 35–52.

24 R. Komiya, "Nontraded Goods and the Pure Theory of International Trade," *IER* (June 1967), pp. 132–152.

25 J. R. Melvin, "Production and Trade with Two Factors and Three Goods," *AER* (December 1968), p. 1259.

26 H. G. Johnson, "The Possibility of Factor-Price Equalisation when Commodities Outnumber Factors," *Ec* (August 1967), p. 288.

27 J. L. Ford, "More on the Factor-Price Equalisation Theorem," *Kyk*, 1966, no. 2, pp. 260–266.

28 K. I. Inada, "Free Trade, Capital-Accumulation, and Factor-Price Equalization," *ER* (September 1968), pp. 322–341.

29 *IER* (October 1967), pp. 255–306.

30 N. Minabe, "The Stolpher–Samuelson Theorem under Conditions of Variable Returns to Scale," *OEP* (July 1966), pp. 204–212.

31 R. Batra, "Protection and Real Wages Under Conditions of Variable Returns to Scale," *OEP* (November 1968), pp. 353–360.

32 J. L. Ford, "Protection and the Real Return of the Scarce Factor," *Man* (May 1966), pp. 179–188. See also B. Södersten and K. Vind, "Tariffs and Trade in General Equilibrium," *AER* (June 1968), pp. 400–405, for a denial of the validity of Metzler's qualification to the theorem.

33 Some of the recent work appears to be concerned more with welfare economics than with international economics as

such. See, e.g., J. Bhagwati, "The Gains from Trade Once Again," *OEP* (July 1968), pp. 137–148; and M. C. Kemp, "Some Issues in the Analysis of Trade Gains," *OEP* (July 1968), pp. 149–161.

34 H. G. Johnson, "Optimal Trade Intervention in the Presence of Domestic Distortions," *Trade, Growth, and the Balance of Payments*, pp. 3–34.

35 J. Bhagwati, *The Theory and Practice of Commercial Policy: Departures from Unified Exchange Rates*, Special Papers in International Economics, no. 8 (Princeton, N.J.: Princeton University Press, 1968).

36 For recent related analyses, see P. M. Mieszkowski, "The Comparative Efficiency of Tariffs and Other Tax-Subsidy Schemes as a Means of Obtaining Revenue or Protecting Domestic Production," *JPE* (December 1966), pp. 587–599; and V. K. Ramaswami and T. N. Srinivasan, "Optimal Subsidies and Taxes When Some Factors Are Traded," *JPE* (July–August 1968), pp. 569–582. Infant-industry arguments are explored by H. G. Grubel, "The Anatomy of Classical and Modern Infant-Industry Arguments," *WA* (December 1966), pp. 325–342; T. Negishi, "Protection of the Infant Industry and Dynamic Internal Economies," *ER* (March 1968), pp. 56–67; and R. E. Baldwin, "The Case Against Infant-Industry Tariff Protection, *JPE* (May–June 1969), pp. 295–305.

37 H. G. Johnson, "The Gain from Exploiting Monopoly and Monopsony Power in International Trade," *Ec* (May 1968), pp. 151–156.

38 R. Findlay, "Efficient Accumulation, International Trade, and the Optimum Tariff," *OEP* (July 1968), pp. 211–220.

39 A. F. Friedlander and A. L. Vandendorpe, "Excise Taxes and the Gains from Trade," *JPE* (September–October 1968), pp. 1058–1068.

40 M. C. Kemp, "The Gain from International Trade and Investment: A Neo-Heckscher–Ohlin Approach," *AER* (September 1966), pp. 788–809.

41 R. W. Jones, "International Capital Movements and the Theory of Tariffs and Trade," *QJE* (February 1967), pp. 1–38. See the comment by K. I. Inada and M. C. Kemp in *ibid.* (August 1969), pp. 524–528.

42 See, e.g., I. F. Pearce, and D. C. Rowan. "A Framework for Research into the Real Effects of International Capital

Movements," in T. Bagiotti, ed., *Essays in Honour of Marco Fanno* (Padua, 1966), vol. 2, pp. 505–535; and M. Frankel, "Home Versus Foreign Investment: A Case against Capital Export," *Kyk*, 1965, no. 3, pp. 411–433. World welfare gains resulting from international diversification of portfolios through foreign investment are analyzed by H. G. Grubel, "Internationally Diversified Portfolios: Welfare Gains and Capital Flows," *AER* (December 1968), pp. 1299–1314.

For further recent studies in the field of trade and welfare, the interested reader is referred to: W. M. Corden, "Monopoly, Tariffs, and Subsidies," *Ec* (February 1967), pp. 50–58; D. J. Horwell, "On Export Subsidies and Import Tariffs," *Ec* (November 1966), pp. 472–474, and "Optimum Tariffs and Tariff Policy," *Review of Economic Studies* (April 1966), pp. 147–158; H. G. Johnson, "The Costs of Protection and Self-Sufficiency." *QJE* (August 1965), pp. 356–372, and "The Possibility of Income Losses from Increased Efficiency or Factor Accumulation in the Presence of Tariffs," *EJ* (March 1967), pp. 151–154; M. C. Kemp, "Notes on the Theory of Optimum Tariffs," *ER* (September 1967), pp. 395–404; M. Michaely, "A Note on Tariffs and Subsidies," *AER* (September 1967), pp. 888–891; and R. Dardis, "Intermediate Goods and Gains from Trade," *RES* (November 1967), pp. 502–509.

43 For a survey of the earlier literature, see R. G. Lipsey, "The Theory of Customs Unions: A General Survey, " *EJ* (September 1960), pp. 498–513.

44 J. Vanek, *General Equilibrium of International Discrimination: The Case of Customs Unions* (Cambridge, Mass.: Harvard University Press, 1965).

45 C. A. Cooper and B. F. Massell, "A New Look at Customs-Union Theory," *EJ* (December 1965), pp. 742–747.

46 S. W. Arndt, "On Discriminatory *vs.* Non-Preferential Tariff Policies," *EJ* (December 1968), pp. 971–979. His argument is accepted and extended by B. F. Massell, "A Reply, and Further Thoughts on Customs Unions," *EJ* (December 1968), pp. 979–982.

47 S. W. Arndt, "Customs Union and the Theory of Tariffs, " *AER* (March 1969), pp. 108–118.

48 C. A. Cooper and B. F. Massell, "To-wards a General Theory of Customs Unions for Developing Countries," *JPE* (October 1965), pp. 461–476.

49 D. C. Mead, "The Distribution of Gains in Customs Unions between Developing Countries," *Kyk*, 1968, no. 4, pp. 713–736. For further recent contributions to customs-union theory, see M. Michaely, "On Customs Unions and the Gains from Trade," *EJ* (September 1965), pp. 577–583; and E. J. Mishan, "The Welfare Gains of a Trade-Diverting Customs Union Reinterpreted," *EJ* (September 1966), pp. 669–672. At a more practical level is the article of B. Balassa, "Trade Creation and Trade Diversion in the European Common Market," *EJ* (March 1967), pp. 1–17, which also surveys other empirical studies in this field.

50 H. G. Johnson, "The Theory of Tariff Structure, with Special Reference to World Trade and Development," in H. G. Johnson and P. B. Kenen, *Trade and Development* (Geneva, 1965), pp. 9–29, and H. G. Johnson, "The Theory of Effective Protection and Preferences," *Ec* (May 1968), pp. 119–138.

51 W. M. Corden, "The Structure of a Tariff System and the Effective Protective Rate," *JPE* (June 1966), pp. 221–237.

52 In terms of an input–output system, the effective protective rate for activity j requiring several inputs $(i = 1, 2, \ldots, n)$ can be expressed as follows:

$$g_j = \frac{t_j - \sum_{i=1}^{n} a_{ij} t_i}{1 - \sum_{i=1}^{n} a_{ij}}$$

where g_j = effective protective rate for activity j; a_{ij} = share of i in cost of j in the absence of tariffs; t_j = nominal tariff rate on j; and t_i = nominal tariff rate on i.

53 G. Basevi, "The United States Tariff Structure," *RES* (May 1966), pp. 147–160; and B. Balassa, "Tariff Protection in Industrial Countries: An Evaluation," *JPE* (December 1965), pp. 573–594.

54 See Johnson, "The Theory of Tariff Structure," pp. 21 ff.; and B. Balassa, "The Impact of the Industrial Countries' Structure on Their Imports of Manufactures from Less-Developed Areas," *Ec* (November 1967), pp. 372–383, and "Tariff Protection in Industrial Nations and Its Effects on the Exports of Processed Goods from Developing Countries," *CJE* (August 1968), pp. 583–594.

55 See, e.g., R. Soligo and J. Stern, "Tariff Protection, Import Substitution, and Investment Efficiency," *Pakistan Development Review* (Summer 1965), pp. 249–270; S. R. Lewis, Jr., and S. E. Guisinger, "Measuring Protection in a Developing Country: The Case of Pakistan," *JPE* (November–December 1968), pp. 1170–1198; and B. Balassa and D. M. Schydlowsky, "Effective Tariffs, Domestic Cost of Foreign Exchange, and the Equilibrium Exchange Rate," *JPE* (May–June 1968), pp. 348–360.

56 Balassa, "Tariff Protection in Industrial Countries," pp. 587–594; and Johnson, "The Theory of Effective Protection," pp. 128–132.

57 H. G. Johnson, *Economic Policies Towards Less Developed Countries* (Washington, D.C.: Brookings, 1965), pp. 163–211; and Johnson, "The Theory of Effective Protection," pp. 132–137.

58 The findings of these studies have been conflicting. See Basevi, "The United States Tariff Structure," pp. 157–160; Balassa, "Tariff Protection in Industrial Countries," pp. 585–587; D. S. Ball, "United States Effective Rate of Protection and the Question of Labor Protection in the United States," *JPE* (May–June 1968), pp. 443–461; and G. Zandano, "The Heckscher–Ohlin Model and the Tariff Structures of Industrial Countries," *Quarterly Review*, Banca Nazionale del Lavoro (March 1969), pp. 46–65.

59 R. I. McKinnon, "Intermediate Products and Differential Tariffs: A Generalization of Lerner's Symmetry Theorem," *QJE* (November 1966), pp. 584–615; and S. E. Guisinger, "Negative Value Added and the Theory of Effective Protection," *ibid.* (August 1969), pp. 415–433.

60 See, e.g., B. F. Massell, "The Resource-Allocative Effects of a Tariff and the Effective Protection of Individual Inputs," *ER* (September 1968), pp. 369–378; and J. C. Leith, "Substitution and Supply Elasticities in Calculating the Effective Protective Rate," *QJE* (November 1968), pp. 588–601.

61 Some work on the theory of automatic payments adjustment has, of course, continued. Recent studies in this field seem to have concentrated largely on the differences between international and interregional adjustment. See T. Scitovsky, "The Theory of Balance-of-Payments Adjustment," *JPE* (August 1967), Supplement, pp. 523–531; M. von Neumann Whitman, *International and Interregional Adjustment: A Synthetic View*, Studies in International Finance, no. 19 (Princeton, N.J.: Princeton University Press, 1967); and, in a broader framework, R. I. McKinnon and W. E. Oates, *The Implications of International Economic Integration for Monetary, Fiscal, and Exchange-Rate Policy*, Studies in International Finance, no. 16 (Princeton, N.J.: Princeton University Press, 1966). For another aspect of the theory, see J. O'Connell, "An International Adjustment Mechanism with Fixed Exchange Rates," *Ec* (August 1968), pp. 274–282.

62 H. G. Johnson, "Some Aspects of the Theory of Economic Policy in a World of Capital Mobility," *Essays in Honour of Marco Fanno*, vol. 2, pp. 345–359. See the comments of R. S. Ablin, "Income, Capital Mobility, and the Theory of Economic Policy," *Kyk*, 1968, no. 1, pp. 102–119.

63 R. W. Jones, "Monetary and Fiscal Policy for an Economy with Fixed Exchange Rates," *JPE* (July–August 1968), part 2, pp. 921–943. Jones also experiments with additional instruments and targets.

64 D. J. Ott and A. F. Ott, "Monetary and Fiscal Policy: Goals and the Choice of Instruments," *QJE* (May 1968), pp. 313–325.

65 T. D. Willett and F. Forte, "Interest-Rate Policy and External Balance," *QJE* (May 1969), pp. 242–262. Focusing on the effect of monetary policy on capital movements in the United States balance of payments, they argue "that an increase in interest rates is likely to improve the U.S. balance of payments only in the short-run while portfolios are being reallocated in response to changed interest incentives and that in the longer run [with portfolio growth] the effects are likely to be quite adverse, with increased interest costs exceeding newly attracted capital flows" (p. 244).

66 J. Patrick, "The Optimum Policy Mix: Convergence and Consistency," in Kenen and Lawrence, eds., *The Open Economy*, pp. 263–288.

67 R. N. Cooper, "Macroeconomic Policy Adjustment in Interdependent Economies," *QJE* (February 1969), pp. 1–24.

68 J. Niehans, "Monetary and Fiscal Policies in Open Economies under Fixed

Exchange Rates: An Optimizing Approach," *JPE* (July–August 1968), part 2, pp. 893–920. See also J. F. Helliwell, "Monetary and Fiscal Policies for an Open Economy," *OEP* (March 1969), pp. 35–55; and H. G. Johnson, "Theoretical Problems of the International Monetary System," in R. N. Cooper, ed., *International Finance* (Baltimore, 1969), pp. 304–323. Johnson's discussion is based, in part, on papers delivered by various economists at a conference in September 1966. Those papers have since been published in R. A. Mundell and A. K. Swoboda, eds., *Monetary Problems of the International Economy* (Chicago: University of Chicago Press, 1969), which appeared too late for consideration in this article. In a two-country or multicountry world, there emerges also what has been called the "redundancy problem," in the form of a "spare" policy instrument in the system available for use. For, in an N-country world, the achievement of $N - 1$ balance-of-payments targets automatically determines the payments position of the Nth country. See Johnson, *ibid.*, pp. 318–323.

69 See, e.g., *The Balance of Payments Adjustment Process* (Paris, 1967); W. Fellner, F. Machlup, and Others, *Maintaining and Restoring Balance in International Payments* (Princeton, N.J.: Princeton University Press, 1966); O. Emminger. "Practical Aspects of the Problem of Balance-of-Payments Adjustment." *JPE* (August 1967), part 2, pp. 512–522; R. N. Cooper, *The Economics of Interdependence* (New York: McGraw-Hill, 1968); J. M. Fleming, "Guidelines for Balance-of-Payments Adjustment Under the Par-Value System," *Essays in International Finance*, no. 67 (Princeton, N.J.: Princeton University Press, 1968); and H. G. Johnson, "Problems of Balance of Payments Adjustment in the Modern World," and A. I. Bloomfield, "Rules of the Game of International Adjustment?," in C. R. Whittlesey and J. S. G. Wilson, eds., *Essays in Money and Banking in Honour of R. S. Sayers* (New York: Oxford University Press, 1968), pp. 26–46 and pp. 113–129.

70 This line of inquiry has been opened up by R. A. Mundell in three articles in *CJEPS* (November 1961, November 1963, and August 1964).

71 A. O. Krueger, "The Impact of Alternative Government Policies under Varying Exchange Systems," *QJE* (May 1965), pp. 195–208.

72 Johnson, "Some Aspects of the Theory of Economic Policy."

73 E. Sohmen, "Fiscal and Monetary Policies Under Alternative Exchange-Rate Systems," *QJE* (August 1967), pp. 515–523. See also M. C. Kemp, "Monetary and Fiscal Policy Under Alternative Assumptions about International Capital Mobility," *ER* (December 1966), pp. 598–605.

74 See, e.g., F. Machlup, G. Haberler, H. C. Wallich, P. B. Kenen, and M. Friedman, "Round Table on Exchange Rate Policy," *Papers and Proceedings*, *AER* (May 1969), pp. 357–369; and A. Lanyi, "The Case for Floating Exchange Rates Reconsidered," *Essays in International Finance*, no. 72 (Princeton, N.J.: Princeton University Press, 1969).

75 See J. E. Meade, "Exchange-Rate Flexibility," in *International Payments Problems* (Washington, D.C.: American Enterprise Institute, 1965), pp. 67–82; G. N. Halm, "Toward Limited Exchange Rate Flexibility," *Essays in International Finance*, no 73 (Princeton, N.J.: Princeton University Press, 1969); J. Williamson, "The Crawling Peg," *Essays in International Finance*, no. 50 (Princeton, N.J.: Princeton University Press, 1965); and J. Black, "A Proposal for the Reform of Exchange Rates," *EJ* (June 1966), pp. 288–295.

76. J. C. Hause, "The Welfare Costs of Disequilibrium Exchange Rates," *JPE* (August 1966), pp. 333–352.

77 H. G. Johnson, "The Welfare Costs of Exchange-Rate Stabilization," *JPE* (October 1966), pp. 512–518.

78 T. Negishi, "Approaches to the Analysis of Devaluation," *IER* (June 1968), pp. 218–227.

79 H. P. Gray, "Imperfect Markets and the Effectiveness of Devaluation," *Kyk*, 1965, no. 3, pp. 512–530.

80 J. H. G. Olivera, "A Note on Finite Devaluation," *WA*, 1966, no. 2, pp. 346–350.

81 M. E. Kreinen, "Devaluation and the Income Terms of Trade," *Kyk*, 1967, no. 2, pp. 487–491.

82 H. G. Grubel, *Forward Exchange, Speculation, and the International Flow of Capital* (Stanford, Calif.: Stanford University Press, 1966).

83 P. B. Kenen, "Trade, Speculation, and the Forward Exchange Rate," in Baldwin, *et al.*, *Trade, Growth, and the Balance of Payments*, pp. 143–169.

84 M. S. Feldstein, "Uncertainty and Forward Exchange Speculation," *RES* (May 1968), pp. 182–192.

85 E. Sohmen, *The Theory of Forward Exchange*, Studies in International Finance, no. 17 (Princeton, N.J.: Princeton University Press, 1966).

86 S. W. Arndt, "International Short-term Capital Movements: A Distributed Lag Model of Speculation in Foreign Exchange," *Ecra* (January 1968), pp. 59–70.

87 J. L. Stein, "International Short-term Capital Movements," *AER* (March 1965), pp. 40–66. See the comments on that paper by H. P. Gray, D. G. Heckerman, A. B. Laffer, P. H. Hendershott, and T. D. Willett in *AER* (June 1967), pp. 548–565, and Stein's reply, *ibid.*, pp. 565–570. For a further empirical application of the model, see J. L. Stein and E. Tower, "The Short-Run Stability of the Foreign Exchange Market," *RES* (May 1967), pp. 173–185.

88 See, e.g., S. W. Black, "Theory and Policy Analysis of Short-Term Movements in the Balance of Payments," *Yale Economic Essays* (Spring 1968), pp. 5–78; H. R. Stoll, "An Empirical Study of the Forward Exchange Market Under Fixed and Flexible Exchange Rate Systems," *CJE* (February 1968), pp. 55–78; J. Helliwell, "A Structural Model of the Foreign Exchange Market," *CJE* (February 1969), pp. 90–106; and E. R. Canterbery, "A Dynamic Theory of Foreign Exchange," *National Banking Review* (June 1967), pp. 397–413. See, further, P. A. Frevert, "A Theoretical Model of the Forward Exchange," *IER* (June 1967), pp. 153–167, and *ibid.* (October 1967), pp. 307–326.

89 For a detailed analysis of this plan and its implications, see F. Machlup, *Remaking the International Monetary System* (Baltimore: Johns Hopkins Press, 1968).

90 H. R. Heller, "Optimal International Reserves," *EJ* (June 1966), pp. 296–311. See also his paper. "The Transactions Demand for International Means of Payments," *JPE* (January–February 1968), pp. 141–145.

91 P. B. Kenen and E. B. Yudin, "The Demand for International Reserves," *RES* (August 1965), pp. 242–250.

92 T. J. Courchane and G. M. Youssef, "The Demand for International Reserves," *JPE* (August 1967), part 1, pp. 404–413.

93 M. Fleming, "Toward Assessing the Need for International Reserves," *Essays in International Finance*, no. 58 (Princeton, N.J.: Princeton University Press, 1967).

94 R. Clower and R. Lipsey, "The Present State of International Liquidity Theory," *Papers and Proceedings, AER* (May 1968), pp. 586–595. See the other articles in the same issue (pp. 596–651) by A. Kakfa, G. Plescoff, F. M. Bator, R. N. Cooper, and J. M. Letiche, for analyses of other facets of the problem.

95 F. Machlup, "The Need for Monetary Reserves," *Banca Nazionale del Lavoro Quarterly Review* (September 1966), p. 203.

96 Johnson, "Theoretical Problems of the International Monetary System, pp. 330–334.

97 F. Machlup, "The Cloakroom Rule of International Reserves," *QJE* (August 1965), pp. 337–355.

98 H. G. Grubel, "The Cloakroom Rule of International Reserves: Comment," *QJE* (August 1966), pp. 485–487. See also R. I. McKinnon, "Private and Official International Money," *Essays in International Finance*, no. 74 (Princeton, N.J.: Princeton University Press, 1969), pp. 17–23.

99 I. M. D. Little and M. J. Crawford, *International Aid* (Chicago: Aldine, 1966); G. Ohlin, *Foreign Aid Policies Reconsidered* (Paris, 1966) and R. F. Mikesell, *The Economics of Foreign Aid* (Chicago: Aldine, 1968).

100 From a large recent literature, one might cite only the following: J. Pincus, *Economic Aid and International Cost Sharing* (Baltimore: Johns Hopkins Press, 1965); H. W. Singer, "External Aid: For Plans or Projects?" *EJ* (September 1965), pp. 539–545; A. Carlin, "Project Versus Programme Aid: From the Donor's Viewpoint," *EJ* (March 1967), pp. 48–58; and R. I. Gulhati, "The 'Need' for Foreign Resources, Absorptive Capacity, and Debt Servicing Capacity," and M. ul Haq, "Tied Credits—A Quantitative Analysis," in J. H. Adler, ed., *Capital Movements and Economic Development* (London, 1967), pp. 240–260, 326–351.

101 H. B. Chenery and A. M. Strout, "Foreign Assistance and Economic Development," *AER* (September 1966), pp. 679–733. See also I. Adelman and H. B. Chenery, "Foreign Aid and Economic Development: The Case of Greece,"

RES (February 1966), pp. 1–19. A critical evaluation of the models of Chenery and his collaborators is made by J. C. H. Fei and G. Ranis, "Comment" (with "Reply" by Chenery and Strout) in *AER* (September 1968), pp. 912–916. For further discussion of various "gap" models, see H. Kitamura, "Trade and Capital Needs of Developing Countries and Foreign Assistance," *WA*, 1966, no. 2, pp. 303–324.

102 J. C. H. Fei and D. S. Paauw, "Foreign Assistance and Self-Help: A Reappraisal of Development Finance," *RES* (August 1965), pp. 251–267.

103 A. Sengupta, "Foreign Capital Requirements for Economic Development," *OEP* (March 1968), pp. 38–55.

104 A. Qayum, "Long-Term Economic Criteria for Foreign Loans," *EJ* (June 1966), pp. 358–369. For other mathematical models of capital movements and growth see K. Hamada, "Economic Growth and Long-Term International Capital Movements," *Yale Economic Essays* (Spring 1966), pp. 49–96; and K. K. Kurihara, "International Capital Movements and National Economic Growth," *Economia Internazionale* (November 1966), pp. 597–608.

105 F. L. Pryor, "Economic Growth and the Terms of Trade," *OEP* (March 1966), pp. 45–57.

106 R. Komiya, "Economic Growth and the Balance of Payments: A Monetary Approach," *JPE* (January–February 1969), pp. 35–48.

107 E.g., P. K. Bardhan, "Equilibrium Growth in the International Economy," *QJE* (August 1965), pp. 455–465; and N. Minabe, "Economic Growth and International Trade in a Simple Dynamic Leontief Model," *CJEPS* (February 1966).

108 S. B. Linder, *Trade and Trade Policy for Development* (New York: Frederick A. Praeger, 1967).

109 G. M. Meier, *The International Economics of Development* (New York: Harper & Row, 1968). See also M. De Vries, "Trade and Exchange Policy and Economic Development: Two Decades of Evolving Views," *OEP* (March 1966), pp. 19–44.

110 U.N., UNCTAD, Second Session, New Delhi, *Report and Annexes*, vol. I (New York: United Nations, 1968). Four other volumes deal with specialized problems.

111 For a critical view of the model of economic growth implicit in the UNCTAD recommendations, see D. Wall, "Import Capacity, Imports, and Economic Growth," *Ec* (May 1968), pp. 157–168.

112 Johnson, *Economic Policies Toward Less Developed Countries.*

113 J. Pincus, *Trade, Aid, and Development* (New York: McGraw-Hill, 1967).

114 A. I. Macbean, *Export Instability and Economic Development* (Cambridge, Mass.: Harvard University Press, 1966).

115 G. Patterson, *Discrimination in International Trade* (Princeton, N.J.: Princeton University Press, 1966). See also G. Curzon, *Multilateral Commercial Diplomacy* (London, 1965) for GATT and the developing countries.

International Monetary Systems and the Free Market Economy
Fritz Machlup

It would be unreasonable to expect that anyone could devise an international

Fritz Machlup, "International Monetary Systems and the Free Market Economy," in *International Payments Problem*, A Symposium sponsored by the American Enterprise Institute for Public Policy Research, Washington, D.C., 1966, pp. 153–176.

monetary system serving all purposes optimally. Since people's aims are different, and to some extent incompatible with one another, *no* system can be "objectively" called the best. Only if we could first agree on a single objective to be given absolute top priority or if we could agree on preference scales for mutual trade-offs among different objectives would it be possible for us to judge one of the plans superior to all the rest. There is, of course, no chance for such agreement ever to be obtained.

SAVING THE MARKET ECONOMY

The Free-Enterprise System

Since this conference is being held under the auspices of the American Enterprise Institute, which I understand stands for the free-enterprise system, I propose to examine alternative international monetary arrangements from chiefly one point of view: how do they promote, secure, weaken, or endanger the free-enterprise system?

I need hardly warn against possible confusion between business enterprises and the free-enterprise system. I am not interested in how any existing enterprises might be harmed or benefited—say, export industries, importers, import-competing industries, corporations with foreign subsidiaries, and so forth. My only concern will be the satisfactory working and maintenance of the economic system, that is, of a free-market economy guided by competitively determined prices.

In such a system, private initiative has the widest possible opportunities to enter whatever market, trade, or industry may look attractive, and this "attractiveness" is the result of the free supply of productive services and unrestricted demand for products. Prices reflect relative scarcities, but only real, not artificially created scarcities. Accordingly, the allocation of productive resources will be efficient and will result in the largest possible output.

Let us recognize that the maintenance of the free-enterprise system is not an ultimate value. It is an intermediate value only, that is, it is valued only because it is instrumental to the achievement of ultimate values. One of these is the high national income obtained with the efficient resource allocation guided by competitive market prices. Another is the growth of productivity obtained thanks to the opportunities afforded to private initiative. Third and fourth are the gratifications that are derived from the realization of economic freedom and from the personal independence afforded by the wide dispersion of economic power. Fifth are the blessings of political freedom, which are complementary with economic freedom and dispersion of power and are far less likely to be obtained in systems without economic freedom, private property, and free enterprise.

Degrees of Injury and Types of Injurious Policies

In a discussion of the effects which international monetary arrangements may have upon the maintenance of the free-enterprise system it is easy to fall into exaggeration and declare moderately serious injuries to be deadly and fatal. But it is also possible to underestimate certain dangers and regard as harmless what in the long run may prove crippling. It may be helpful to distinguish three degrees of "injury" and assign tentatively to each some typical measures with typical effects, with the proviso that reassessments and reassignments may be called for in special circumstances. (After all, social, political, and economic systems may have different degrees of resistance to injurious influences, just as some people may easily shake off pneumonia while others may all but die from a common cold.)

I propose to regard as injuries of the first degree those which merely reduce the effectiveness and efficiency of the system but, by reducing the productivity of resources and by discriminating in favor of special interests, make claims for the merits of the free-enterprise system less credible and may therefore undermine the people's allegiance to it. As second degree, I regard obstructions in the system which cause it to collapse or make its performance so poor that efforts to replace it become inevitable. Third degree would be measures which themselves imply the abolition of the system in effect, if not also in name.

Among the policies and effects of policies which are likely to produce injuries of the first and second degree are (a) continuous inflation, (b) continuous unemployment, (c) trade restrictions, (d) payments and exchange restrictions, and (e) other direct controls. The last two, if they are of an especially comprehensive, discretionary, and discriminatory nature, may produce third-degree injuries, in that they may involve virtual replacement of the market economy by a centrally directed one.

Frequently policies injuring the market economy are interrelated, in that any one of them is apt to lead to another. Serious unemployment may invite the pursuit of inflationary policies, adoption of trade restrictions, and imposition of direct controls. Serious inflation may invite the adoption of payments and exchange restrictions and other direct controls. Of course, we must not be arbitrary in attributing the adoption of any of these policies (and the blame for their injurious effects) to particular monetary arrangements. Such attribution presupposes that we can demonstrate the reasons why one particular monetary system would be more likely than other systems to invite or induce these policies. This will not always be easy. A "system" is a mode of reaction of certain "variables" to certain responses, usually to changes in other "variables"; the reactions may sometimes have effects which are considered undesirable and the authorities may feel called upon to prevent either the reactions or their effects; in attempting this they may resort to "dangerous" policies because they believe the dangers in question to be smaller than the ones they are trying to prevent. Thus, if we say that a certain monetary system is likely to lead to the adoption of this or that policy, we are implicitly making assumptions about the "typical" sensitivity of the authorities to the "undesirability" of certain developments and about the "typical" judgment of the authorities regarding the comparative harm inflicted either by the normal reactions of the system or by the policies adopted to prevent or offset them.

INFLATION

The 100 Percent Gold Standard

The gold standard has the reputation of being inflation-proof, or at least less inflation-prone than any other international monetary system. This reputation would be deserved only if one were to think of a gold standard without any uncovered bank notes, currency notes, and bank deposits; with the further proviso that the discovery of new gold mines, the invention of better techniques of mining and refining, and increases in the price of gold never increased the monetary gold stocks of the world at a rate faster than that at which the production of other goods and services increases. None of these conditions is realistic. Even if one is inclined to dismiss the probability of discoveries, inventions, or gold-price hikes allowing gold production to cause inflationary boosts, one has to recognize that a gold standard in which the supply of money and circulating media depends solely on the production of new gold has not existed for centuries and is not being proposed by anybody.

I, personally, would perhaps vote for such a 100-percent gold standard if it were seriously proposed. For I should like to try a system where the quantity of money is not a "policy variable" but is "given" to us in a way that nobody can do anything about (just as in the case of the weather, about which we may complain but to which we must adjust as well as we can without being able to change it). But since man has learned that he *can* increase the quantity of money, independent of gold production, he will not give up the chance of creating money if he wants to. He may outlaw money creation by private counterfeiters, but he does not wish to halt all money creation by his government or money creation by the commercial-banking system.

Gold-Reserve Requirements

A good many persons, though few economists, hold that legally fixed gold-reserve requirements are a barrier against inflation. These people have recognized that central banks and commercial banks can and do create money. But they believe that the requirement of commercial banks to hold reserves of central bank notes or deposits in a certain ratio to their own deposit liabilities, and the requirement of central banks to hold reserves of gold (or gold certificates) in a certain ratio to their note and deposit liabilities will effectively bar inflationary expansion of the money supply. It is well known, however, that central banks either reduce the reserve requirements or increase the reserves of the commercial banks whenever the authorities choose to do so—and they often do so with inflationary effects. And, likewise, the legislatures of practically all countries reduce or set aside the gold-reserve requirements of their central banks whenever they judge these requirements to become effective in preventing an expansion or in compelling a contraction of the money supply.

We should perhaps admit the possibility of some situations having occurred in history in which the existence of gold-reserve requirements did in fact keep a central bank from pursuing an expansionary policy which it would otherwise have chosen to pursue. That the legal requirements were reduced or set aside in every serious inflation as soon as they seemed to "require" a halt in the monetary expansion is not yet a proof against the existence of other cases in which central banks abstained and de-

sisted from inflations solely because there were these requirements and they wanted to obey them. If such cases existed, however, any other kind of legal limitation of money creation by the central bank might have been equally effective. A law-abiding central bank could be restrained with equal effectiveness by any kind of "formula" determining a maximum for its note and deposit liabilities. Instead of providing that these liabilities must not exceed three, four, or five times their gold reserves, the law could provide that they must not exceeed certain multiples of any other magnitudes—say, population, labor force, real national product, or what not. To be sure, any such formula could be changed at will by a legislature bound on inflation, but so can gold-reserve requirements be changed, and indeed they have been changed hundreds of times.

(In order to guard against a possible misunderstanding, I should add parenthetically that I am not arguing here against a reduction or abolition of the present legal gold-reserve requirements in the United States. These requirements reduce international confidence in the willingness of the United States to keep its promise to convert foreign, officially-held dollars into gold. They do not act as an effective limitation in the issue of Federal Reserve notes, for nobody doubts that they would be swept aside as soon as they interfered with an increase in note circulation. Hence, our gold-reserve requirements are nonsense as well as a nuisance, and ought to be abolished.)

The Adjustment Mechanism of the Gold Standard

Another feature of the gold standard may act as an effective deterrent of inflationary expansions of the money supply: what classical writers called the "specie-flow mechanism" and what now is often called the "automatic adjustment of the balance of payments." Under the gold standard, any country that has expanded its money supply at too fast a rate relative to other countries will suffer a deficit in its balance of payments; the resulting outflow of gold will automatically reduce the quantity of money in circulation by the amount paid for the gold purchased from the monetary authorities.

This adjustment mechanism may act in two ways to limit inflation: as a deterrent and as a correction. For in *fear* of a gold outflow central banks are likely to abstain from excessive expansions; but if they nevertheless have overexpanded, the *actual* outflow will reduce circulation. This corrective contraction can, however, be offset by the central bank through domestic credit extension and open-market purchases if it does not obey the old rules of the gold-standard game and is not deterred by fears of losing more gold. In any case, the gold outflow of one country is a gold inflow to another country, causing an automatic expansion with possibly inflationary consequences there. Countries engaged in expanding credit can thus impose involuntary inflations upon other countries. The same adjustment mechanism which is credited with the potentiality of causing a corrective contraction in one country must therefore be blamed for possibly unwanted expansions of the money supply in other countries. It is an open question whether on balance the adjustment mechanism under the gold standard, especially if the orthodox rules of the game are no longer observed and contractions are "politically intolerable," operates more effectively to *prevent* inflations or to *spread* inflations. A correct reading of the historical record may suggest that the second effect is the stronger one. That is to say, the "gold-standard mechanism" has been first and foremost responsible for spreading inflationary movements from countries that are leading to countries that are (willingly or unwillingly) following in the pursuit of monetary expansion.

This judgment is so seriously in contradiction to common opinion that one cannot expect to convince easily those who have from their school days always believed in the gold standard as the best preventive of inflation. All I can do here is to repeat and emphasize the proposition that, when political resistance to contraction is greater than to expansion (and this is true everywhere nowadays) and when therefore the contractionary effects of the adjustment mechanisms are largely or completely offset in deficit countries, the net effect of the adjustment mechanism on all countries taken together is necessarily inflationary.

Apart from the controversial judgment as to whether the existence of an adjustment mechanism limits or facilitates inflation in the participating countries considered as a group, there should be no controversy about the fact that the same mechanism can operate with other assets than gold used as "foreign reserve." Gold movements can be (and largely have been) replaced by movements of foreign exchange. As far as the chief reserve-currency country—the United States—is concerned, the exchange-reserve mechanism does not always work exactly as it would with gold movements; but for all other countries it does. Gold movements can also be replaced by transfers of claims against international financial organizations, without the working of the adjustment mechanism being altered thereby. Hence, if it is only the international adjustment mechanism that is wanted, this can be had without the gold standard.

International Reserve Creation

The proposals for the creation of an international reserve center with power to create additional reserves for national monetary authorities are opposed partly because of their inflationary potentialities. History has shown that many national central banks have at times abused their power to create national money; it is no doubt possible that an international central bank may abuse its power to create international money and produce world inflation. If the management is dominated by countries in need of capital and eager to get more funds to buy from other countries, the rate of reserve creation may become excessive. One should add in fairness that the opposite is also possible: if the management is dominated by countries content with their reserve position, the rate of reserve creation by the international organization may be so seriously inadequate as to impose deflationary pressures upon a majority of countries.

The question of rules and voting rights may therefore be of great importance. One may venture the proposition than an international reserve-creating organization in which developing countries and other deficit countries can obtain a majority of votes will probably operate as an instrument of world inflation; on the other hand, an organization in which unanimity of members is required for any reserve-creating action is likely to operate with excessive caution, leading to deflation and consequent restrictions and controls in several countries.

One often hears, especially from experts whose experience is confined to economies that have heavily suffered from inflation, that there is no real danger of deflation. Let them reflect the fact that a rate of reserve creation smaller than the rate of increase in world production—note that I said world production, not world trade—is likely to subject several countries to declining ratios of foreign reserves to domestic money supply. The smaller the increase in the world's total foreign reserves, the more countries will be exposed to the trauma of falling reserve ratios. This may be a trauma only because of the upbringing of central bankers (with all the myths and legends taught for centuries), but the trauma is not any less real for that matter and it induces them

not only to restrict credit but also to urge adoption of restrictions of foreign trade, payments, and capital movements, often in the form of direct controls. It is true that inflation often leads to such restrictions and controls, but losses of reserves by individual countries under a system excessively restrictive in the creation of reserves for the world as a whole are virtually certain to generate the imposition of restrictions and controls. There is no virtue in steering clear of the Scylla of inflation if this runs us into the Charybdis of restrictions and controls adopted in a general battle for larger shares of an inadequate total of reserves.

From these considerations I conclude that the unyielding opposition to plans of international reserve creation, merely because they may involve the possibility of inflationary abuse, is short-sighted. The danger of inadequate reserves is no less real and no less serious. To be sure, we must think of institutional arrangements by which both inflationary excesses and deflationary paralyses· can be prevented. If the source of reserves during the last 15 years is now drying up or being walled up, another source or other sources must be found. It is foolish to invite atrophy merely because hypertrophy is bad.

It is also quite unreasonable to hide behind the slogan of these plans being politically "premature." If they are premature in the sense that politicians are unwilling to discuss, let alone adopt, them, then those who hold that the plans are meritorious should not resign themselves to a ten-year period of inaction but, instead, should get busy teaching the politicians that they had better open their minds. That a promising arrangement is premature may mean no more than that we have allowed our politicians to lag behind in their intellectual development.

Flexible Exchange Rates

The opposition to systems of flexible exchange rates, to the extent that it presents arguments, claims that rate flexibility facilitates inflationary policies. This, if correct, would be the most serious charge leveled against the economists' pet proposal. The point has been argued in two ways, one based on economic psychology, the other on economic history. We shall examine both.

The psychological argument involves the attitudes of central bankers and of the politicians on whose approval their appointments and reappointments depend. One of the most difficult tasks of central bankers is to resist political pressures for most inflationary credit policies. This resistance can be successful only if the politicians appreciate its underlying reasons and sustain the unpopular decisions of the central bank management. In the past, losses of foreign reserves and fears of such losses have had the strongest appeal in the warnings against easier money and faster credit expansion. If flexible exchange rates mean that no official reserves are deployed in attempts to peg the rates at fixed levels, no reserves will be lost. Thus, the restraints are gone and the resistance to inflationary policies is weakened.

In answer to this argument the supporters of flexible rates submit that even stronger restraints may replace the lost ones. If the central banker can point to a decline in the foreign value of the currency and to the danger of a further decline, he will impress his critical patrons even more than he was able to do by pointing his finger at the reserve position. If the nation's currency continues to lose value in the world market, this may be presented as a more serious indictment of an inflationary policy than if the nation loses more of its foreign reserve.

The opponents of flexibility are not convinced by this reply. They can quote statements made by the supporters of flexibility to the effect that declining exchange rates may have important adjustment functions, and, in addition, may give the government more leeway in pursuing alternative policy objectives which may have priority over the maintenance of exchange stability. If variations in exchange rates are functional, they become respectable. One cannot at the same time claim that a decline in the exchange value of the currency should be approved, because it serves a good purpose, but it should also be feared, because it marks a failure in official policy.

This rejoinder may embarrass supporters of exchange-rate flexibility, for it suggests that some of their pronouncements have been infelicitously formulated, to say the least. Variations in exchange rates may serve a good purpose and indeed, in some circumstances, may be imperative. But if they give "independence" to the monetary authorities, legislatures will have to be very specific in stating the objectives for which this independence may be used. Freedom from the chains of fixed exchange rates must not mean complete discretion for the authorities to do what they feel may be "good" at the moment. They would have to be given rules to obey or targets to meet, and depreciations or appreciations of the currency in the foreign-exchange market would have to be shown to be consistent with the pursuit of these rules or targets. If central bankers were no longer to be responsible for maintaining fixed exchange rates, they would have to be held responsible for strict conformance with specific rules or for the closest attainment of a specific target. (I may note that one should guard against specifying several mutually inconsistent targets, as they may be the outcome of political compromise.)

Leaving this argument, we may say that on theoretical grounds it cannot be established that central bankers would be more inclined to inflate under flexible-rate systems that under fixed-rate systems. Let us now examine the historical evidence that has been adduced on this issue.

The monetary history of several countries includes periods of flexible exchange rates. These have usually been periods of inflation. On the other hand, when they had fixed exchange rates, the same countries avoided or contained inflation. Thus, "history teaches" that exchange-rate flexibility "goes together" with inflation.

If the historians searched a little harder, they would find that most of these inflations had begun while the countries were still on fixed exchange rates. Unable to maintain fixed rates while all other prices were rising, the countries in question adopted flexible rates until they had the political strength and courage to stop the inflation and let the exchange find its new level. It is, therefore, quite wrong to attribute these inflations to exchange-rate flexibility. If anything could be "learned" merely from reading these historical records, it would be that most inflations started under fixed exchange rates and were eventually stopped under flexible rates.

Semi-Automatic Inflation

In an examination of the responsibility of the monetary system for inflations of money supply and price levels, one must not fail to mention the systematic, built-in inflations, that is, those that are not due to policy but are due to observance of the rules of the game inherent in the system. Under the gold standard, under the gold-exchange standard, and under any other system committing the monetary authorities to purchase gold, foreign currencies, or other "reserve assets" at fixed prices, expansion of the domestic supply and, with it, of effective demand is semi-automatic in the sense that only a deliberate policy to offset the expansion, by operations violating the spirit of the system, can prevent inflation. These inflations have a function as part of the balance-of-payments adjustment of the economies concerned, but this does not change the fact that they are inflations arising directly from the monetary systems adopted.

These "imported" inflations, as they are sometimes called, are not the spectacular inflations reported by the textbooks. Often, however, they are sufficiently serious to be considered in a survey of inflationary processes attributable to monetary arrangements. Indeed, they are perhaps the only inflations that may really be blamed on a monetary system, in contradistinction to inflations that are due to the fiscal and monetary policies of the authorities.

Special mention should be made of the automatic inflation to be expected from a drastic increase in the price of gold. A doubling in the price of gold, as is demanded by those who advocate return to the full gold standard, would raise the official gold reserves of the free world from $41 to $82 billion. If $23 of the $41 billion increase were used to replace present foreign-exchange reserves—though this would hardly be possible inasmuch as many of the monetary authorities would insist on carrying working balances in foreign exchange—a net increase of $18 billion would swell the official reserves and would, no doubt, be reflected in a huge increase in the lending capacities of the national banking systems. But even if these official profits from the revaluation of the gold could be sterilized for a time, the profits made by private gold hoarders, especially by those who hold gold in expectation of an increase in its price, would surely be realized and the doubled buying power of the gold dishoarders would be exercised in the markets. In addition, it would boost the reserves of the banking systems. Private gold holdings have been estimated to be about $16 billion. (This may be wrong, but it is the only figure I have.) Assume that large amounts of gold are held by Indian and Arab princes and peasants who would not sell even after a price increase; suppose that between $5 and $8 billions of the private stocks at their present value might be offered to the monetary authorities if the price is doubled. We might then have to expect, from this source, a flood of between $10 and $16 billion to inundate the markets of the free world; and I see no way of erecting any effective dams against it. This "automatic" inflation due to a gold-price increase has not been sufficiently discussed by either advocates or opponents.

The Causes of Inflation

The distinction between these built-in and semi-automatic inflations, in which the money supply is expanded in observance of a rule prescribed by the monetary system, and discretionary inflations, in which the expansion is a matter of policy decisions, is perhaps too simple, inasmuch as it puts too many types of policy into the same category. One may choose to subdivide discretionary inflations in several ways, according to the methods in which the money supply is expanded, or to the first spenders of the created moneys, or to the objectives pursued by those who make the decisions leading to the expansion.

This distinction provides no spot for what some economists like to call "inflations caused by structural factors," a phrase and a theory serving as an excuse for the politicians responsible for inflations in certain developing countries. It is true, of course, that conditions in some countries make it difficult to finance large investments in any other way than through inflation and impossible for a political party to get elected or re-elected except on programs too ambitious to be financed without using the printing press. One cannot prevent anybody calling these or other political conditions "structural," but the monetary expansions in these countries are still the result of policy, albeit a policy that is not easy to refrain from. Inflations neither "grow" out of the soil against the will of man, nor do they fall from heaven; they are decided upon and arranged for by men in charge of fiscal and monetary policies—and can be avoided by these men if they are determined to do so and have the courage to resist pressures and temptations.

Discretionary inflations may be considered to be the outgrowth of ideology. It is illusory to hope that they can be avoided by the adoption of formal rules such as gold-reserve requirements, obligations to redeem currency into gold, or promises to sell foreign currencies at fixed rates. Where there is a will to avoid inflation, legal and institutional limitations on money creation will not be needed; and where there is a high propensity to inflate, legal and institutional limitations will be disregarded, altered, suspended, or abolished.

UNEMPLOYMENT

Causes and Cures

Before one can sensibly discuss the relationship between monetary systems and the emergence of unemployment, a few fundamental propositions about the "causes" of unemployment must be understood. We have to distinguish, before all, why unemployment *arises* and why it *persists*.

Unemployment arises

1. if the supply of labor increases, while the demand for labor and money wage rates remains unchanged;
2. if the demand for labor decreases, while the supply of labor and money wage rates remains unchanged;
3. if money wage rates are increased, while supply and demand for labor remain unchanged.

Unemployment that has arisen for any of these reasons will disappear

a. if the demand for labor is sufficiently increased;

b. if the supply of labor is sufficiently reduced;

c. if money wage rates are sufficiently lowered.

If none of these things occurs, unemployment will persist. It is poor logical practice to regard the non-occurrence of an event as a "cause" of any other event or situation. Hence, the failure of demand to increase, of supply to decrease, or of wage rates to be lowered cannot reasonably be called "causes" of unemployment. Causes are the events or changes that *generate* unemployment. If one chooses to ask why unemployment, caused by (1), (2), or (3), *persists*, one may enumerate the potential events or changes that, if they actually occurred, could reduce or remove it. It is arbitrary to select only one "non-occurrence" as an explanation of the non-disappearance of unemployment.

This arbitrariness, unfortunately, has become common practice among specialists on unemployment. Since they believe that little or nothing can be done to reduce the supply of labor and/or to lower money wage rates, they concentrate on increases in effective demand as the only practically possible "cure" for unemployment (cure, of course, only if labor supply and wage rates do not increase with the demand). Thus they insist that the failure of demand to increase or to be increased is responsible for the persistence of unemployment. But since many of these specialists are not careful in their language, they speak of "demand deficiency" as the *cause* of unemployment—even though the evidence is clear that the demand for labor has not declined at all.

Monetary Systems and the Emergence of Unemployment

We must now examine the question whether a particular international monetary system may be held "responsible" for the emergence of unemployment. This could be reasonably said, after what we have just concluded, about a monetary system that forces an *absolute reduction* in money supply and effective demand upon an economy. The only systems that do this are the fully automatic gold standards and those systems with fixed foreign-exchange rates under which offsetting operations are ruled out. Under these semi-automatic systems credit expansions to offset the contractionary effects of a sale of foreign exchange out of official reserves would be prohibited. Advocates of such systems would probably blame the unemployment that arose out of the net reduction in effective demand on a "non-occurrence," namely, on the failure of wage rates to fall. Some of the advocates, however, believe that under such a stern system the labor market would become more perfect in the sense that wages would respond to changes in demand in both directions, that is, that they would fall sufficiently to eliminate any unemployment that arose.

Monetary Systems and the Persistence of Unemployment

We sometimes hear our present gold-exchange standard being held responsible for the high rate of unemployment in the United States, although the quantity of money has never been allowed to contract, even after 15 years of deficit in the accounting balance of payments. Complainants have charged that the obligation to maintain fixed exchange rates and a fixed price of gold have prevented the monetary authorities from pursuing an effective full-employment policy. In the context, this would have meant a policy of increasing the money supply sufficiently (through a combination of fiscal and monetary policies) to raise effective demand to levels that would take care of both the increase in labor force and the increase in wage level. However, since wage rates might go up with every increase in effective demands for goods and services, the full-employment goal might have been impossible to realize. Still, one should not deny the possibility of some unemployment being absorbed, at least temporarily, by the creation of monetary demand at rates that are not compatible with balance in international accounts and, hence, not consistent with the maintenance of fixed exchange rates.

Some advocates of flexible exchange rates refer to this "independence," permitting the monetary authorities to pursue a full-employment policy, as an argument in support of their recommendations, whereas others in the same camp, not believing in the long-run effectiveness of monetary full-employment policies, reject it. There are, however, other connections between unemployment and flexible exchange rates. Whenever unemployment is caused by increases in wage rates, the currency would be apt to depreciate in the free exchange markets. Especially in small countries, this rise in the prices of foreign currencies could be almost immediate upon, if not anticipatory of, an announcement that trade unions were asking for higher wage rates. Since the unions would probably wish to avoid bearing the responsibility for the depreciation of the currency, and, in addition, would realize that prices of imported goods (and of exportable goods) would rise, and reduce real incomes, even before the wage contract was concluded, their attitudes might change radically. They would probably learn to keep their ambitions down to what could be obtained without unemployment or inflation. (On the other hand, inasmuch as this point refers chiefly to small countries, one has to admit that small countries, with high ratios of foreign trade to national income, may find fluctuating exchange rates too unsettling for their price structure, and may, therefore, prefer to maintain fixed rates in terms of the currency of the largest country among its large trading partners.)

CONTROLS

Differences in Degree and in Kind

When we distinguished three degrees of injury to the free-enterprise system, we assigned inflation and unemployment to both the first (mild) and the second (serious, possibly fatal) degree, while controls and restrictions could cause injuries of any degree. Although the degree of injury depends not only on the type of control or restriction but also on the sensitiveness and fragility of the economy concerned, it may be permissible to associate types of control or restriction with particular degrees of injury they are likely to inflict on a free-market economy.

Trade barriers (tariffs, quotas) and restrictions of capital movements of a mild and impersonal sort, not involving discretionary decisions by control authorities favoring particular firms or industries, may be regarded as measures likely to cause injuries of the first degree.

Trade restrictions of a seriously discriminatory and discretionary sort (especially in countries in which foreign trade is a large share of national income), selective payments restrictions, and foreign-exchange restrictions of a discriminatory and discretionary sort may be considered as causing injuries of the second degree.

Direct controls which, deliberately or in effect, make the allocation of productive resources in most of the largest sectors of the economy largely a matter of governmental or collective decision making, guided not by market-price relations but by discretionary administrative programmation or improvisation, cause injuries of the third degree in that they virtually abolish the market economy.

Perhaps we should explain how foreign-exchange controls may be in all three categories. Assume that particular types of capital exports, say purchases of foreign securities and bank loans to foreign borrowers, become subject to special taxes, quantitative limitations, or even complete prohibition. Such measures may reduce the efficiency and effectiveness of the economy, but there is little danger they will cause it to collapse. Assume, secondly, that imports and/or foreign payments become subject to license and that the control authorities decide to classify certain imports as "luxury," for which no licenses will be granted, others as "desirable," for which certain amounts of foreign exchange will be allocated, and the rest as "necessary," for which all required exchange will be granted. Such a system is almost certain to cause serious damage to the market economy, so serious that it may eventually collapse. If such an economy is one where the import components of most lines of production are large and where the allocation of foreign exchange determines what quantities of what products can be produced by what firms, the exchange controls imply a virtual abolition (or suspension) of the market economy.

With such subtle distinctions the borderlines cannot help being blurred. Thus, if we now undertake to examine to what extent different international monetary systems are more or less likely to lead to situations in which governments will be inclined to introduce or strengthen controls and restrictions of various types, we shall not be able to be very specific. The propensity to introduce controls is a combination of internal convictions and external pressures. Only the latter, as they are apt to develop in a certain "concatenation of circumstances," can be "deduced" from assumptions about the working of various monetary systems.

Gold Standard and Import Barriers

The gold standard has the reputation, spread by innumerable textbooks, of having been a great promoter of international trade, chiefly because it secured fixed parities of exchange and thus allowed traders to count on exchange rates re-maining unchanged. In the minds of our teachers, the gold standard was usually linked with free trade, the absence of trade barriers being the complementary instrument in obtaining for the enlightened nations the greatest possible benefit from international division of labor.

The association, however, has most of the time been only an ideal one: as a theoretical idea in international economics and as a political ideal of nineteenth-century liberalism. In actual fact, the marriage between gold standard and free trade came late and did not last long. From the earliest times of mercantilism, the desire to maintain a gold standard meant a desire to keep and attract gold, and this desire led governments to introduce import restrictions. The raising of import barriers in the name of avoiding an outflow and of securing an inflow of gold—and thus in the name of maintaining the gold standard—was the practical rule, while liberalization of imports was the rare exception, in the centuries under the gold standard.

In the twentieth century, when capital movements assumed larger dimensions, the same objective—to keep and attract gold and to maintain fixed exchange rates—led to the introduction of restrictions of capital exports, and thus inhibited the flow of capital to the uses in which it would be most productive.

Fixed Exchange Rates, Trade Barriers, Exchange Restrictions

The ideal association may be fixed exchange rates and uninhibited flows of goods and capital; the actual association, alas, is fixed exchange rate and restrictions of foreign trade and capital movements. This had been true for the gold exchange standard, as it had been for the gold standard. The record of legislative and executive actions restricting trade and payments is quite unequivocal: most of these actions were justified as necessary in order to maintain fixed exchange rates or to economize the foreign reserve needed to defend fixed exchange rates.

Apart from the clear historical record, the theoretical chain of causation is almost self-evident. Countries committed to maintaining fixed exchange rates believe they need to maintain certain ratios of foreign reserves to central bank liabilities. When these reserve ratios decline, either because central bank liabilities increase or because foreign reserves are lost, a contraction of credit is prescribed by the orthodox rules. But, since credit contraction and higher interest rates are unpopular, pressures to resort to restrictions on the import of goods and on the export of capital become too strong to be resisted.

It is no use demonstrating the illogic of maintaining fixed exchange rates by restricting trade and payments—of showing that, since fixed rates are supposed to promote trade, it is idiotic to secure fixed rates by restricting trade. Fixed rates are a means to an end, but the end is sacrificed in order to save the means. Silly, indeed, yet precisely this is done, again and again, and we must not think that reality is not reality simply because it offends against good common sense.

Plans to Create Additional Reserve Assets

The present debate about insufficient or excessive "international liquidity" cannot be understood if one thinks merely of the ratio of world reserves to world trade or of the ratios of individual countries' foreign reserves to the largest deficits these countries have sustained in the past. On these scores the verdict is clearly that "international liquidity, including borrowing facilities" has been, and will be for a long time, excessive. The trouble is that the "need" for foreign reserves has quite different sources. These reserves are not needed, as the most naïve writers believe,

to "finance international trade"; nor is there a need for foreign reserves in a particular ratio to total world trade or to the imports of individual nations; nor are additional reserves needed as a contingency for prospective payments deficits, since most of the industrial nations, with the conspicuous exceptions of Britain and the United States, now possess foreign reserves far in excess of any past or prospective deficits. What then are foreign reserves needed for?

They are not "needed" at all, strictly speaking. But monetary authorities make a fuss if they do not have all that they think they ought to have. Let me explain this by comparing the typical central banker with my wife, though this might be too flattering for most central bankers. How many dresses does my wife need? One, seven, 31, or 365? You may think that one dress is all she really needs— and even this is only because of our "culture pattern." I assure you, however, that she thinks she needs more. Whether she wants 25 or 52 depends on her upbringing and on the Joneses with whom she wishes to keep up. Perhaps she wants to maintain a fixed ratio of dresses to the family income. If that ratio declines, she will fuss and fret, and if I were to keep her from getting additional clothes, she would impose restrictions and controls affecting my home life and our external relations with friends and acquaintances. I conclude that the right amount of clothes owned by my wife is that which keeps her from fussing and fretting and spares me the danger of unpleasant restrictions. Before I leave this analogy between women and central bankers, let me point out that "rights" to borrow dresses from friends or from rental agencies would not take care of the matter in the least. Most women want to own their dresses, not to borrow them. I wish that my friends at the IMF would take full cognizance of the psychological difference between owning and borrowing.

Central bankers look not at their clothes closets but at their balance sheets, and they like to see among their assets foreign reserves far in excess of what they would need to cover their nudities; they would like to maintain certain ratios of foreign reserves to total liabilities. The ratio may be merely a matter of tradition or of fashion or, if you will, of religious doctrine. There is no point quarreling with such normative matters. The point is that most central bankers start fussing when the reserve ratio declines. Their liabilities have got to increase year after year, because notes and deposits, the domestic money supply, must increase if deflation is to be avoided. With labor force and productive facilities increasing continuously, and money wages refusing to go down, central bankers have to provide the additional money to avoid continuous deflation and increasing unemployment. Being used to certain traditional reserve ratios, they want their foreign reserves to increase roughly in proportion with their total liabilities. Not that they need it in any sense other than my wife needs more clothes. But if the central banks lose foreign reserves, and even if they find their reserve ratios declining, there will be demands for policies conducive to the inflow of reserves. I conclude that the "need" for reserves is determined by the ambitions of the monetary authorities. I submit we ought to see to it that they get foreign reserves in amounts sufficient to be happy and satisfied; in amounts, that is, that will keep them from urging or condoning policies restricting imports or capital movements.

Now let us assume that world reserves in the years to come will increase only through gold production at the present gold price, and let us ask what the probabilities are that countries will have to begin "defending" their reserve ratios.

If nine countries of a group of 10 have been accumulating enormous amounts of reserves owing to the deficit of the tenth country, the likelihood of any one of the nine suffering a deficit during that period is small. If now the tenth country stops having a deficit, and the other nine, taken together, stop having a surplus, then it becomes highly probable that some of these nine will develop deficits and will lose reserves to the others. Moreover, even if none were developing a deficit, they would all experience declining reserve ratios, inasmuch as their domestic money supplies would grow (say, between 3 and 6 percent a year). Thus the probability of declining reserve ratios of most of these countries, and of declining reserves of some, would be considerable. Given the unpopularity of fighting for reserves by means of deflationary policies, it becomes highly probable that some countries would resort to further restrictions on imports and on capital outflows. Since such restrictions are imposed or stiffened much faster than they are abolished or relaxed, it may not help much if the swings from deficit to surplus are relatively short. The countries with improved balances might hesitate to liberalize, while the countries moving into deficit positions might hasten to impose restrictive measures. To avoid such developments, recommendations have been made to create additional foreign reserves for the countries concerned.

The acceptance of plans for the provision of additional reserves would no doubt reduce the danger of a stiffening of trade restrictions and reintroduction of payments restrictions. On the other hand, more abundant reserves hold the danger of inflationary policies. A choice between these two dangers should perhaps be resolved in favor of reserve creation, for one may have more confidence in the will power of central bankers to forgo the use of their increased lending power arising from increased foreign reserves than one may have in the good sense and backbone of the legislative and executive branches of governments to abstain from restricting imports and controlling capital movements when foreign reserves decline.

Methods of Creating Additional Reserves

There are, in principle, four ways of creating additional foreign reserves: (1) in the process of financing a deficit in a country's balance of payments, (2) in exchange for "dormant" liabilities of countries participating in a distribution of gratis reserves, (3) through the upvaluation of existing gold reserves, and (4) through the sale of newly produced or dishoarded gold to monetary authorities.[1]

Several variants exist of the first two ways. For example, the deficit-financing method has actually been practiced (a) as surplus countries have accepted as official reserves the official liabilities of a reserve-currency country in deficit, and (b) as the IMF has sold to countries in deficit convertible currencies (these currencies having been issued previously by the member countries and held by the Fund) and accepted the currencies of deficit countries in payment. Several other variations have been proposed, the most famous being the financing of payments deficits by (c) a Keynesian Clearing Union issuing deposit liabilities to surplus countries and (d) a Triffinian IMF with expanded powers issuing deposit liabilities to surplus countries; and the most recent being various schemes proposed by the IMF to the Ossola Committee.

The use of some of these techniques of reserve creation may delay the stiffening of restrictions on the part of deficit countries, but at the same time induce surplus countries to impose controls against the import of foreign capital. For, unwilling to submit to the inflationary consequences of the prolonged inflows, but unwilling also (or not permitted) to fence them off either by refusing to buy foreign currencies and gold, or by paying reduced prices for foreign currencies, these countries are likely to take direct measures to keep out foreign capital. This has actually been done in recent years in several countries of Europe "suffering" from large surpluses in their balances of payments on capital account. What a spectacle to see both the remitting and the receiving countries fight private movements, and this in the name of maintaining "convertibility of the currences at fixed exchange rates"!

The second method of reserve creation, the free distribution of reserves among a group of cooperating countries, is regarded as absurd by those who believe that foreign reserves can serve only one sensible function: to finance deficits in the balance of payments. If these critics cannot see the purpose of distributing additional reserves to countries that do not need them for meeting deficits, they are overlooking the psychological "need" for holding large reserves and for maintaining traditional reserve ratios. They also overlook that this need is not satisfied by promised or assured borrowing facilities (such as those provided or proposed by the IMF) but only by owned reserves, decorating the balance sheet for everybody to see and giving people, especially the central bankers themselves, a feeling of comfort.

If additional reserve assets allocated to monetary authorities in some agreed fashion meet their desire for "reserves to hold but not to spend" (in addition to the reserves they may have to spend), the propensities to impose restrictions and controls on trade and payments can be successfully neutralized. As long as foreign reserves have to be "earned," that is, can be acquired only by surpluses in the balance of payments, there will be a tendency to restrict imports of goods and exports of capital. If owned reserves can be obtained without being earned through surpluses, a bias in favor of restrictions on trade and payments, which has plagued the world for centuries, may be effectively reduced. The only alternative to this scheme is to educate bankers, central bankers, and the common people to see that foreign-reserve ratios "ought" to be declining year after year, since a noninflationary growth rate of domestic money supplies cannot be matched by the growth rates of foreign reserves attainable under given institutions. However, such a change in traditions may have dangers for monetary policy and may, therefore, be regarded as inferior to schemes for creating additional reserves at a "normal" annual rate.

Little has to be said here concerning the creation of new gold reserves by methods (3) and (4). The increase in reserves obtained in these ways would also stop the "battle" for reserves for a good many years and neutralize propensities to restrict trade and payments—especially in the case of the third method, which represents another way of distributing gratis reserves (though only to those holding gold at the time of the gold-price increase). But serious dangers of inflation are involved, notwithstanding the naive beliefs of some gold worshippers who cannot understand that the inflationary effects of an increase in reserves by a large amount are the same whether the reserves are glittering gold or whether they are pieces of paper or entries on a balance sheet.

The Prerogatives of an International Reserve Institution

If the world—meaning the men of influence—continues to believe in systems with fixed exchange rates, the establishment of new international organizations providing additional reserve assets, or the extension of powers of existing international organizations to provide additional "international liquidity," is almost inevitable. The diehards, opposing any big change, fight a battle against progressives on two fronts: against the supranationalists and against the free-marketeers. They are not quite sure where the greater danger lies: in allowing a supranational institution to "manage" international financial affairs or in allowing national authorities to become independent of fixed exchange rates and forcing them to accept the verdict of a free market in currencies. At this point we shall discuss the implications which an international reserve center à la Triffin may have for the imposition or strengthening of controls and restrictions of trade and payments.

Most of the critics' distrust of the management of an international or supranational reserve center relates to the possibility of excessive leniency vis-à-vis countries in deficit and, hence, excessive creation of foreign reserves that would be forced upon surplus countries in exchange for their products, their productive resources, and claims on their productive facilities. The very same leniency would no doubt tend to avoid or delay the resort to restrictions and direct controls on the part of deficit countries. Lenient or stern in its lending policies, the international reserve center would surely exert its influence on the side of freeing, not on the side of restricting, international trade and payments. However wrong the international authorities might be in their judgment regarding the "right" amounts of loans to grant or securities to purchase, they would almost certainly be opposed to restrictive measures and direct controls by national authorities.

I doubt that this argument will impress those who regard the establishment of an international reserve institution with power to create reserves as politically intolerable, or at least as premature by several years. Since the opposition to the Triffin Plan and to all Triffinesque proposals is based on political convictions, economic arguments will not make much difference.

Flexible Exchange Rates and the "Propensity to Control"

The opposition to flexible exchange rates is based either on debatable economic arguments or only on the flat assertion that flexibility would be "impractical." The latter contention is nothing but an admission of the inability to formulate reasoned arguments. In order to prove that something is impractical one has to indicate just what makes it so. Discussion and analysis of the presented reasons may either confirm or disconfirm the assertion. It happens that the most intransigent opponents of exchange-rate flexibility refuse to give reasons; their apodictic claim that it is impractical may therefore be translated into the statement "I am against it, but cannot give any good reasons."

These angry comments, explainable by frequent irritation, though perhaps unduly irritating to others, may be gratuitous at this point. For on our agenda at the moment is only the relationship between exchange-rate flexibility and the inclination of governments to impose restrictions and controls. On this issue a strong position has been taken by the proponents of flexibility: since trade restrictions and exchange controls have so often been justified by the need to defend fixed exchange rates, the adoption of flexible rates would remove this justification and, therefore, would work for liberalization of trade and payments. This argument has probably been the most persuasive and convincing one in changing the allegiance of many economists from fixed to flexible rates. Many an adherent of stable foreign exchange rates has learned that fixed rates were rarely equilibrium rates, but were usually pegged at a disequilibrium level and all too often maintained with the aid of trade restrictions and payments controls. In contrast, flexible rates in a free market could be genuinely stable, provided the monetary authorities followed a policy oriented toward this target. The authorities seem to be less determined to pursue such a policy if they can rely on large foreign reserves enabling them to peg the exchange rate at a fixed disequilibrium level. If in the process they lose considerable amounts of foreign reserves, they are tempted, and perhaps driven, to safeguard the maintenance of the fixed rates with the aid of prohibition, rationing, and other restrictive measures—which economists rightly regard as much more injurious to the functioning of the free-market economy than variable, or even widely fluctuating, rates could be.

Thus, many advocates of flexible exchange rates are really in favor of stable exchange rates; they oppose fixed rates only because fixed rates are so often disaligned rates, maintained only by means of coercive and restrictive controls. If there were any reliable guaranty that fixed rates would not lead to controls, these economists might still favor fixed rates. But such guaranties are unrealistic as long as governments are committed to a policy of preventing an adjustment process that works through credit contraction and price deflation. If monetary contraction is ruled out, depreciation is the only effective alternative to restriction and control. If depreciation is also ruled out, restrictions and controls seem inevitable.

This argument is plausible. But in order to make it cogent one would have to show that the propensity to restrict trade and payments would really be effectively neutralized under flexible exchange rates. Yet, if relative stability of exchange rates remains an objective under flexible rates, governments might still resort to restrictions whenever the free market threatened to reveal that the currency had lost some of its true exchange value. Just as governments have used controls to defend fixed rates, they might use controls to defend stable rates. Indeed, it would not be very surprising if the authorities in charge of monetary and fiscal policy were seriously impressed by the pronouncements of the advocate of flexibility to the effect that any depreciation of the currency would clearly reveal their mistakes and misdeeds. They would then no doubt be tempted to apply measures that conceal the manifestations of the failures.

Why has this possibility been overlooked or disregarded? Evidently because flexible exchange rates are meant to be free-market rates, and free markets, by definition, rule out restrictions and controls. One must not, however, jump from definitions and analytical propositions to conclusions about the real world. If flexible rates are *meant* to be rates established in free markets, this does not guarantee that the markets would in fact be left free from government controls and restrictive interferences with supply and demand. If language serves a function not only in communicating but also in persuading, perhaps we ought to speak always of "free-market exchange rates" rather than of flexible rates. Still, it would be naive to trust a terminological gimmick when governments are bent on using controls.

Different Pressures Towards Controls

In certain situations the pressures and temptations to apply restrictive measures and controls may still be greater under fixed than under flexible exchange rates. The difference is probably small or nil where a country's inflationary policies are the chief factor in causing trouble; internal inflation and external stability simply do not go together and governments may try to "fight" the ultimately inevitable depreciation by applying controls—no matter whether they have "fixed" exchange rates or merely want to pretend they have "stable" rates. The difference may be significant, however, where the government is not at fault, where, for example, the disequilibrating causes lie in nonmonetary autonomous ("structural") changes or in the policies of foreign countries. In such instances the decision to let variations of exchange rates in the free markets reflect the changed situation and achieve real (allocative)

adjustment to it might find public acceptance and approval as being eminently sensible (and not an admission of guilt); a commitment to fixed rates, on the other hand, might push the government into restricting trade and controlling payments.

That there is a difference in the degree of pressure toward restrictions and controls under fixed and under flexible exchange rates may become clearer if we once more consider some of the alternative actions at the disposal of a country trying to restore balance in its payments position. A country attempting to remove a surplus can (1) expand its money supply and inflate its price level, (2) upvalue its currency or let it appreciate relative to other currencies, (3) increase taxes and/or reduce government spending (without reducing the money supply) so that interest rates become less attractive for internationally mobile loanable funds, (4) lower its import barriers to attract foreign goods, (5) encourage foreign travel and other payments to foreign nationals, (6) encourage the export of capital and discourage (by special taxes or other discriminatory treatment) the inflow of foreign capital. A country attempting to remove a deficit can (1) contract its money supply and deflate its price level, (2) devalue its currency or let it depreciate relative to other currencies, (3) reduce taxes and/or increase government spending (without increasing the money supply) so that interest rates become more attractive for internationally mobile loanable funds, (4) increase its import barriers to keep out foreign goods, (5) discourage or restrict foreign travel and other payments to foreign nationals, (6) discourage, restrict, or prohibit the export of capital and encourage the import of foreign capital.

With a commitment to fixed exchange rates, alternatives No. 2 are ruled out. Alternatives No. 1 are regarded as undesirable for a surplus country (imposed inflation) and intolerable for a deficit country (imposed deflation with increased unemployment). Alternatives No. 3 are unpopular in a surplus country and somewhat unreliable in a deficit country. This leaves alternatives Nos. 4, 5, and 6, all of which are in the domain of restrictive and discriminatory measures and controls. To be sure, some are in the direction of liberalization, for example, No. 4 for a surplus country, but though this may please economists and statesmen it would be resisted by many influential businessmen and politicians. In many countries the line of least resistance will lead to No. 6 for surplus countries and to Nos. 4, 5, and 6 for deficit countries.

If, on the other hand, the principle of exchange-rate flexibility is accepted, so that alternatives No. 2 are distinct possibilities, the drift toward dirigist measures may be reduced or avoided, at least in those instances in which the imbalance cannot be blamed on wrong policies of the government.

This argument, admittedly, is rather speculative. But where we lack experience, speculate is all we can do. And regarding issues as important as the ones under discussion, we cannot afford not to speculate. The drift toward restrictions and controls appears to be so strong and so dangerous that any possibility of attenuating it must be explored.

CONCLUSION

In lining up the dangers which alternative monetary arrangements may present for the preservation of a free-market, free-enterprise economy we started with a list of five: inflation, unemployment, trade restrictions, payments and exchange restrictions, and other direct controls. Since the spectrum between slightly restrictive measures and comprehensive direct controls defies easy compartmentalization, we decided to treat restrictions and controls under one heading.

From several points of view this merger was perhaps unwise. There is a world of difference between the increase in the import duties for some specific manufactured products (even if the proponents refer to the deficit in the balance of payments as one of the supporting arguments presented to the legislature) and the imposition of foreign exchange controls giving wide discretionary powers to some agency; and another world (or perhaps only half a world) between these controls and the introduction of central comprehensive planning taking charge of the allocation of all productive resources in the nation. To put all under one common heading, "Controls," may appear simplistic, perhaps even hysterical. It can be defended, however, in this essay because it has allowed us to avoid much repetition. The same properties of a monetary system that under certain conditions result in reactions increasing the governments' inclinations to resort to more effective import restrictions will also be the source of pressures toward more direct and more comprehensive controls. It would surely have been wasteful of time and space to devote separate sections to the examination of the different restrictive and dirigist pressures and tendencies.

Inflation and unemployment injure the economy not only directly (through inefficient use and nonuse of productive resources) but also indirectly in that they usually lead to the adoption of restrictive measures and direct controls. These restrictions and controls as a rule aggravate the direct injuries and in extreme cases cripple or abolish the free-market economy. The most agonizing problems arise when certain control measures look promising as remedies (or palliatives) for inflation or unemployment but may permanently weaken or paralyze the market mechanism. Even those who regard direct controls as the market economy's public enemy No. 1 may be in honest doubt whether they should reject or accept another "small" dose of controls in order to dampen an inflation that threatens to lead eventually to a headlong drive into comprehensive controls. Similar trade-offs may exist between other alternative dangers, between immediate and postponed dangers, between dangers judged to be smaller but more certain and others more serious but less certain. No wonder, under such circumstances, that equally reasonable people sharing the same general objectives and holding the same general theories will differ in their advice and recommendations.

NOTE

1 For a more elaborate discussion of the alternative methods of reserve creation, see Fritz Machlup, *Involuntary Foreign Lending* (Uppsala: Almquist and Wiksell, 1965).

The Case for Flexible Exchange Rates[*]
Harry G. Johnson

By "flexible exchange rates" is meant rates of foreign exchange that are determined daily in the markets for foreign exchange by the forces of demand and supply, without restrictions imposed by governmental policy on the extent to which rates can move. Flexible exchange rates are thus to be distinguished from the present system (the International Monetary Fund system) of international monetary organization, under which countries commit themselves to maintain the foreign values of their currencies within a narrow

Harry G. Johnson, "The Case for Flexible Exchange Rates, 1969," Federal Reserve Bank of St. Louis, *Review* (June 1969), pp. 12–24.

* The title acknowledges the indebtedness of all serious writers on this subject to Milton Friedman's modern classic essay, "The Case for Flexible Exchange Rates," written in 1950, and published in 1953 [M. Friedman, *Essays in Positive Economics* (Chicago: University of Chicago Press, 1953), pp. 157–203, abridged in R. E. Caves and H. G. Johnson (eds.), *Readings in International Economics* (Homewood, Ill.: Richard D. Irwin, for the American Economic Association, 1968), chapter 25, pp. 413–437].

margin of a fixed par value by acting as residual buyers or sellers of currency in the foreign exchange market, subject to the possibility of effecting a change in the par value itself in case of "fundamental disequilibrium." This system is frequently described as the "adjustable peg" system. Flexible exchange rates should also be distinguished from a spectral system frequently conjured up by opponents of rate flexibility—wildly fluctuating or "unstable" exchange rates. The freedom of rates to move in response to market forces does not imply that they will in fact move significantly or erratically; they will do so only if the underlying forces governing demand and supply are themselves erratic—and in that case any international monetary system would be in serious difficulty. Finally, flexible exchange rates do not necessarily imply that the national monetary authorities must refrain from any intervention in the exchange markets; whether they should intervene or not depends on whether the authorities are likely to be more or less intelligent and efficient speculators than the private speculators in foreign exchange—a matter on which empirical judgment is frequently inseparable from fundamental political attitudes.

The fundamental argument for flexible exchange rates is that they would allow countries autonomy with respect to their use of monetary, fiscal, and other policy instruments, consistent with the maintenance of whatever degree of freedom in international transactions they chose to allow their citizens, by automatically ensuring the preservation of external equilibrium. Since in the absence of balance-of-payments reasons for interfering in international trade and payments, and given autonomy of domestic policy, there is an overwhelmingly strong case for the maximum possible freedom of international transactions to permit exploitation of the economies of international specialization and division of labor, the argument for flexible exchange rates can be put more strongly still: flexible exchange rates are essential to the preservation of national autonomy and independence consistent with efficient organization and development of the world economy.

The case for flexible exchange rates on these grounds has been understood and propounded by economists since the work of Keynes and others on the monetary disturbances that followed the First World War. Yet that case is consistently ridiculed, if not dismissed out of hand, by "practical" men concerned with international monetary affairs, and there is a strong revealed preference for the fixed exchange rate system. For this one might suggest two reasons: First, successful men of affairs are successful because they understand and can work with the intricacies of the prevalent fixed rate system, but being "practical" find it almost impossible to conceive how a hypothetical alternative system would, or even could, work in practice; Second, the fixed exchange rate system gives considerable

prestige and, more important, political power over national governments to the central bankers entrusted with managing the system, power which they naturally credit themselves with exercising more "responsibly" than the politicians would do, and which they naturally resist surrendering. Consequently, public interest in and discussion of flexible exchange rates generally appears only when the fixed rate system is obviously under serious strain and the capacity of the central bankers and other responsible officials to avoid a crisis is losing credibility.

Pressures Towards a More Flexible Exchange Rate System

The present period has this character, from two points of view. On the one hand, from the point of view of the international economy, the long-sustained sterling crisis that culminated in the devaluation of November 1967, the speculative doubts about the dollar that culminated in the gold crisis of March 1968, and the franc-mark crisis that was left unresolved by the Bonn meeting of November 1968 and still hangs over the system, have all emphasized a serious defect of the present international monetary system.[1] This is the lack of an adequate adjustment mechanism—a mechanism for adjusting international imbalances of payments towards equilibrium sufficiently rapidly as not to put intolerable strains on the willingness of the central banks to supplement existing international reserves with additional credits, while not requiring countries to deflate or inflate their economies beyond politically tolerable limits. The obviously available mechanism is greater automatic flexibility of exchange rates (as distinct from adjustments of the "pegs"). Consequently, there has been a rapidly growing interest in techniques for achieving greater automatic flexibility while retaining the form and assumed advantages of a fixed rate system. The chief contenders in this connection are the "band" proposal, under which the permitted range of exchange rate variation around parity would be widened from the present one per cent or less to, say, five per cent each way, and the so-called "crawling peg" proposal, under which the parity for any day would be determined by an average of past rates established in the market. The actual rate each day could diverge from the parity within the present or a widened band, and the parity would thus crawl in the direction in which a fully flexible rate would move more rapidly.

Either of these proposals, if adopted, would constitute a move towards a flexible rate system for the world economy as a whole. On the other hand, from the point of view of the British economy alone, there has been growing interest in the possibility of a floating rate for the pound. This interest has been prompted by the shock of devaluation, doubts about whether the devaluation was sufficient or may need to be repeated, resentment of the increasing subordination of domestic policy to international requirements since 1964, and general discontent with the policies into which the commitment to maintain a fixed exchange rate has driven successive Governments—"stop-go policies," higher average unemployment policies, incomes policies, and a host of other domestic and international interventions.

From both the international and the purely domestic point of view, therefore, it is apposite to reexamine the case for flexible exchange rates. That is the purpose of this essay. For reasons of space, the argument will be conducted at a general level of principle, with minimum attention to technical details and complexities. It is convenient to begin with the case for fixed exchange rates; this case has to be constructed, since little reasoned defense of it has been produced beyond the fact that it exists and functions after a fashion, and the contention that any change would be for the worse. Consideration of the case for fixed rates leads into the contrary case for flexible rates. Certain common objections to flexible rates are then discussed. Finally, some comments are offered on the specific questions mentioned above, of providing for greater rate flexibility in the framework of the IMF system and of floating the pound by itself.

THE CASE FOR FIXED EXCHANGE RATES

A reasoned case for fixed international rates of exchange must run from analogy with the case for a common national currency, since the effect of fixing the rate at which one currency can be converted into another is, subject to qualifications to be discussed later, to establish the equivalent of a single currency for those countries of the world economy adhering to fixed exchange rates. The advantages of a single currency within a nation's frontiers are, broadly, that it simplifies the profit-maximizing computations of producers and traders, facilitates competition among producers located in different parts of the country, and promotes the integration of the economy into a connected series of markets for products and the markets for the factors of production (capital and labor). The argument for fixed exchange rates, by analogy, is that they will similarly encourage the integration of the national markets that compose the world economy into an international network of connected markets, with similarly beneficial effects on economic efficiency and growth. In other words, the case for fixed rates is part of a more general argument for national economic policies conducive to international economic integration.

International Immobility

The argument by analogy with the domestic economy, however, is seriously defective for several reasons. In the first place, in the domestic economy the factors of production as well as goods and services are free to move throughout the market area. In the international economy the movement of labor is certainly subject to serious barriers created by national immigration policies (and in some cases restraints on emigration as well), and the freedom of movement of capital is also restricted by barriers created by national laws. The freedom of movement of goods is also restricted by tariffs and other barriers to trade. It is true that there are certain kinds of artificial barriers to the movement of goods and factors internally to a national economy (apart from natural barriers created by distance and cultural differences) created sometimes by national policy (e.g., regional development policies) and sometimes by the existence of state or provincial governments with protective policies of their own. But these are probably negligible by comparison with the barriers to the international mobility of goods and factors of production. The existence of these barriers means that the fixed exchange rate system does not really establish the equivalent of a single international money, in the sense of a currency whose purchasing power and whose usefulness tends to equality throughout the market area. A more important point, to be discussed later, is that if the fixity of exchange rates is maintained, not by appropriate adjustments of the relative purchasing power of the various national currencies, but by variations in the national barriers to trade and payments, it is in contradiction with the basic argument for fixed rates as a means of attaining the advantages internationally that are provided domestically by a single currency.

Concern over Regional Imbalance

In the second place, as is well known from the prevalence of regional development policies in the various countries, acceptance of a single currency and its implications is not necessarily beneficial to particular regions within a nation. The pressures of competition in the product and factor markets facilitated by the common currency instead frequently result in prolonged regional distress, in spite of the apparent full freedom of labor and capital to migrate to more remunerative locations. On the national scale, the solution usually applied, rightly or wrongly, is to relieve regional distress by transfers from the rest of the country, effected through the central government. On the international scale, the probability of regional (national in this context) distress is substantially greater because of the barriers to both factors and goods mobility mentioned previously; yet there is no international government, nor any effective substitute through international co-operation, to compensate and assist nations or regions of nations suffering through the effects of economic change occurring in the environment of a single currency. (It should be noted that existing arrangements for financing balance-of-payments deficits by credit from the surplus countries in no sense fulfill this function, since deficits and surpluses do not necessarily reflect respectively distress in the relevant sense, and its absence.)

Lack of Central Control of Currencies

Thirdly, the beneficent effects of a single national currency on economic integration and growth depend on the maintenance of reasonable stability of its real value; the adjective "reasonable" is meant to allow for mild inflationary or deflationary trends of prices over time. Stability in turn is provided under contemporary institutional arrangements through centralization of control of the money supply and monetary conditions in the hands of the central bank, which is responsible for using its powers of control for this purpose. (Formerly, it was provided by the use of precious metals, the quantity of which normally changed very slowly.) The system of fixed rates of international exchange, in contrast to a single national money, provides no centralized control of the overall quantity of international money and international monetary conditions. Under the ideal old-fashioned gold standard, in theory at least, overall international monetary control was exercised automatically by the available quantity of monetary gold and its rate of growth, neither of which could be readily influenced by national governments, operating on national money supplies through the obligation incumbent on each country to maintain a gold reserve adequate to guarantee the convertibility of its currency under all circumstances at the fixed exchange rate. That system has come to be regarded as barbarous, because it required domestic employment objectives to be subordinated to the requirements of international balance; and nations have come to insist on their right to use interventions in international trade and payments, and in the last resort to devalue their currencies, rather than proceed farther than they find politically tolerable with deflationary adjustment policies.

The result is that the automatic mechanisms of overall monetary control in the international system implicit in the gold standard have been abandoned, without those mechanisms being replaced by a discretionary mechanism of international control comparable to the national central bank in the domestic economic system, to the dictates of which the national central banks, as providers of the currency of the "regions" of the international economy, are obliged to conform. Instead, what control remains is the outcome on the one hand of the jostling among surplus and deficit countries, each of which has appreciable discretion with respect to how far it will accept or evade pressures on its domestic policies mediated through pressures on its balance of payments, and

on the other hand of the ability of the system as a system to free itself from the remnants of the constraint formerly exercised by gold as the ultimate international reserve, by using national currencies and various kinds of international credit arrangements as substitutes for gold in international reserves.

In consequence, the present international monetary system of fixed exchange rates fails to conform to the analogy with a single national currency in two important respects. Regions of the system are able to resist the integrative pressures of the single currency by varying the barriers to international transactions and hence the usefulness of the local variant of that currency, and in the last resort by changing the terms of conversion of the local variant into other variants; moreover, they have reason to do so in the absence of an international mechanism for compensating excessively distressed regions and a mechanism for providing centralized and responsible control of overall monetary conditions. Second, in contrast to a national monetary system, there is no responsible centralized institutional arrangement for monetary control of the system.

This latter point can be rephrased in terms of the commonly held belief that the fixed rate system exercises "discipline" over the nations involved in it, and prevents them from pursuing "irresponsible" domestic policies. This belief might have been tenable with respect to the historical gold standard, under which nations were permanently committed to maintaining their exchange rates and had not yet developed the battery of interventions in trade and payments that are now commonly employed. But it is a myth when nations have the option of evading discipline by using interventions or devaluation. It becomes an even more pernicious myth when it is recognized that abiding by the discipline may entail hardships for the nation that the nation will not tolerate being applied to particular regions within itself, but will attempt to relieve by interregional transfer payments; and that the discipline is not discipline to conform to rational and internationally accepted principles of good behavior, but discipline to conform to the average of what other nations are seeking to get away with. Specifically, there might be something to be said for an international monetary system that disciplined individual nations into conducting their policies so as to achieve price stability and permit liberal international economic policies. But there is little to be said for a system that on the one hand obliges nations to accept whatever rate of world price inflation or deflation emerges from the policies of the other nations in the world economy, and on the other hand obliges or permits them to employ whatever policies of intervention in international trade and payments are considered by themselves and their neighbors not to infringe the letter of the rules of international liberalism.

"Harmonization" and "Surveillance"

The defenders of the present fixed rate system, if pressed, will generally accept these points but argue the need for a solution along two complementary lines: "harmonization" of national economic policies in accordance with the requirements of a single world currency system, and progressive evolution towards international control of the growth of international liquidity combined with "surveillance" of national economic policies. The problem with both is that they demand a surrender of national sovereignty in domestic economic policy which countries have shown themselves extremely reluctant to accept. The reasons for this have already been mentioned; the most important are that there is no international mechanism for compensating those who

suffer from adhering to the rules of the single currency game, and that the nations differ sharply in their views on priorities among policy objectives, most notably on the relative undesirability of unemployment on the one hand and price inflation on the other. The main argument for flexible exchange rates at the present time is that they would make this surrender of sovereignty unnecessary, while at the same time making unnecessary the progressive extension of interventions in international trade and payments that failure to resolve this issue necessarily entails.

The case for fixed exchange rates, while seriously defective as a defense of the present system of international monetary organization, does have one important implication for the case for flexible exchange rates. One is accustomed to thinking of national moneys in terms of the currencies of the major countries, which currencies derive their usefulness from the great diversity of goods, services, and assets available in the national economy, into which they can be directly converted. But in the contemporary world there are many small and relatively narrowly specialized countries, whose national currencies lack usefulness in this sense, but instead derive their usefulness from their rigid convertibility at a fixed price into the currency of some major country with which the small country trades extensively or on which it depends for capital for investment. For such countries, the advantages of rigid convertibility in giving the currency usefulness and facilitating international trade and investment outweigh the relatively small advantages that might be derived from exchange rate flexibility. (In a banana republic, for example, the currency will be more useful if it is stable in terms of command over foreign goods than if it is stable in terms of command over bananas; and exchange rate flexibility would give little scope for autonomous domestic policy.) These countries, which probably constitute a substantial numerical majority of existing countries, would therefore probably choose, if given a free choice, to keep the value of their currency pegged to that of some major country or currency bloc. In other words, the case for flexible exchange rates is a case for flexibility of rates among the currencies of countries that are large enough to have a currency whose usefulness derives primarily from its domestic purchasing power, and for which significant autonomy of domestic policy is both possible and desired.

THE CASE FOR FLEXIBLE EXCHANGE RATES

The case for flexible exchange rates derives fundamentally from the laws of demand and supply—in particular, from the principle that, left to itself, the competitive market will establish the price that equates quantity demanded with quantity supplied and hence clears the market. If the price rises temporarily above the competitive level, an excess of quantity supplied over quantity demanded will drive it back downwards to the equilibrium level; conversely, if the price falls temporarily below the competitive level, an excess of quantity demanded over quantity supplied will force the price upwards towards the equilibrium level. Application of this principle to governmental efforts to control or to support particular prices indicates that, unless the price happens to be fixed at the equilibrium level—in which case governmental intervention is superfluous—such efforts will predictably generate economic problems. If the price is fixed above the equilibrium level, the government will be faced with the necessity of absorbing a surplus of production over consumption. To solve this problem, it will eventually have to either reduce its support price, or devise ways either of limiting production (through quotas, taxes, etc.) or of increasing consumption (through propaganda, or distribution of surpluses on concessionary terms). If the price is fixed below the equilibrium level, the government will be faced with the necessity of meeting the excess of consumption over production out of its own stocks. Since these must be limited in extent, it must eventually either raise its control price, or devise ways either to limit consumption by rationing, or reduce the costs of production (e.g., by producer subsidies, or by investments in increasing productivity).

Effects of Fixed-Rate Disequilibrium

Exactly the same problems arise when the government chooses to fix the price of foreign exchange in terms of the national currency, and for one reason or another that price ceases to correspond to the equilibrium price. If that price is too high, i.e., if the domestic currency is undervalued, a balance-of-payments surplus develops and the country is obliged to accumulate foreign exchange. If this accumulation is unwelcome, the government's alternatives are to restrict exports and encourage imports either by allowing or promoting domestic inflation (which in a sense subsidizes imports and taxes exports) or by imposing increased taxes or controls on exports and reducing taxes or controls on imports; or to appreciate its currency to the equilibrium level. If the price of foreign exchange is too low, the domestic currency being overvalued, a balance-of-payments deficit develops and the country is obliged to run down its stocks of foreign exchange and borrow from other countries. Since its ability to do this is necessarily limited, it ultimately has to choose among the following alternatives: imposing restrictions on imports and/or promoting exports (including imports and exports of assets, i.e., control of international capital movements); deflating the economy to reduce the demand for imports and increase the supply of exports; deflating the economy to restrain wages and prices and/or attempting to control wages and prices directly, in order to make exports more and imports less profitable; and devaluing the currency.

In either event, a deliberate choice is necessary among alternatives which are unpleasant for various reasons. Hence the choice is likely to be deferred until the disequilibrium has reached crisis proportions; and decisions taken under crisis conditions are both unlikely to be carefully thought out, and likely to have seriously disruptive economic effects.

All of this would be unnecessary if, instead of taking a view on what the value of the currency in terms of foreign exchange should be, and being therefore obliged to defend this view by its policies or in the last resort surrender it, the government were to allow the price of foreign exchange to be determined by the interplay of demand and supply in the foreign exchange market. A freely flexible exchange rate would tend to remain constant so long as underlying economic conditions (including governmental policies) remained constant; random deviations from the equilibrium level would be limited by the activities of private speculators, who would step in to buy foreign exchange when its price fell (the currency appreciated in terms of currencies) and to sell it when its price rose (the currency depreciated in terms of foreign currencies).

On the other hand, if economic changes or policy changes occurred that under a fixed exchange rate would produce a balance-of-payments surplus or deficit, and ultimately a need for policy changes, the flexible exchange rate would gradually either appreciate or depreciate as required to preserve equilibrium. The movement of the rate would be facilitated and smoothed by the actions of private speculators, on the basis of their reading of current and prospective economic and policy developments. If the government

regarded the trend of the exchange rate as undesirable, it could take counter-active measures in the form of inflationary or deflationary policies. It would never be forced to take such measures by a balance-of-payments crisis and the pressure of foreign opinion, contrary to its own policy objectives. The balance-of-payments rationale for interventions in international trade and capital movements, and for such substitutes for exchange rate change as changes in border tax adjustments or the imposition of futile "incomes policies," would disappear.

If the government had reason to believe that private speculators were not performing efficiently their function of stabilizing the exchange market and smoothing the movement of the rate over time, or that their speculations were based on faulty information or prediction, it could establish its own agency for speculation, in the form of an exchange stabilization fund. This possibility, however, raises the questions of whether an official agency risking the public's money is likely to be a smarter speculator than private individuals risking their own money, whether if the assumed superiority of official speculation rests on access to inside information it would not be preferable to publish the information for the benefit of the public rather than use it to make profits for the agency at the expense of unnecessarily ill-informed private citizens, and whether such an agency would in fact confine itself to stabilizing speculation or would try to enforce an official view of what the exchange rate should be —that is, whether the agency would not retrogress into *de facto* restoration of the adjustable peg system.

Freeing Domestic Economic Management

The adoption of flexible exchange rates would have the great advantage of freeing governments to use their instruments of domestic policy for the pursuit of domestic objectives, while at the same time removing the pressures to intervene in international trade and payments for balance-of-payments reasons. Both of these advantages are important in contemporary circumstances. On the one hand, there exists a great rift between nations like the United Kingdom and the United States, which are anxious to maintain high levels of employment and are prepared to pay a price for it in terms of domestic inflation, and other nations, notably Western Germany, which are strongly adverse to inflation. Under the present fixed exchange rate system, these nations are pitched against each other in a battle over the rate of inflation which is to prevail in the world economy, since the fixed rate system diffuses that rate of inflation to all the countries involved in it. Flexible rates would allow each country to pursue the mixture of unemployment and price trend objectives it prefers, consistent with international equilibrium, equilibrium being secured by appreciation of the currencies of "price stability" countries relative to the currencies of "full employment" countries.

On the other hand, the maximum possible freedom of trade is not only desirable for the prosperity and growth of the major developed countries, but essential for the integration of the developing countries into the world economy and the promotion of efficient economic development of those countries. While the postwar period has been characterized by the progressive reduction of the conventional barriers to international trade and payments —tariffs and quotas, inconvertibility and exchange controls—the recurrent balance-of-payments and international monetary crises under the fixed rates system have fostered the erection of barriers to international economic integration in new forms—aid-tying, preferential governmental procurement policies, controls on direct and portfolio international investment—which are in many ways more subtly damaging to efficiency and growth than the conventional barriers.

The removal of the balance-of-payments motive for restrictions on international trade and payments is an important positive contribution that the adoption of flexible exchange rates could make to the achievement of the liberal objective of an integrated international economy, which must be set against any additional barriers to international commerce and finance, in the form of increased uncertainty, that might follow from the adoption of flexible exchange rates. That such additional uncertainty would be so great as to seriously reduce the flows of international trade and investment is one of the objections to flexible rates to be discussed in the next section.

The Mechanics of Flexible Exchange Rates

At this point, it is sufficient to make the following observations. First, as pointed out in the preceding section, under a flexible rate system most countries would probably peg their currencies to one or another major currency, so that much international trade and investment would in fact be conducted under fixed rate conditions, and uncertainty would attach only to changes in the exchange rates among a few major currencies or currency blocs (most probably, a U.S. dollar bloc, a European bloc, and sterling, though possibly sterling might be included in one of the other blocs). For the same reason— because few blocs would imply that their economic domains would be large and diversified—the exchange rates between the flexible currencies would be likely to change rather slowly and steadily. This would mean that traders and investors would be able normally to predict the domestic value of their foreign currency proceeds without much difficulty.

But, secondly, traders would be able to hedge foreign receipts or payments through the forward exchange markets, if they wished to avoid uncertainty; if there were a demand for more extensive forward market and hedging facilities than now exist, the competitive profit motive would bring them into existence.

Third, for longer-range transactions, the economics of the situation would provide a substantial amount of automatic hedging, through the fact that long-run trends towards appreciation or depreciation of a currency are likely to be dominated by divergence of the trend of prices inside the currency area from the trend of prices elsewhere. For direct foreign investments, for example, any loss of value of foreign currency earnings in terms of domestic currency due to depreciation of the foreign currency is likely to be roughly balanced by an increase in the amount of such earnings consequent on the relative inflation associated with the depreciation. Similarly, if a particular country is undergoing steady inflation and its currency is depreciating steadily in consequence, money interest rates there are likely to rise sufficiently to compensate domestic investors for the inflation, and hence sufficiently to compensate foreign portfolio investors for their losses from the depreciation.

Finally, it should be noted that the same sort of political and economic developments that would impose unexpected losses on traders and investors through depreciation under a flexible exchange rate system, would equally impose losses in the form of devaluation, or the imposition of restrictions on trade and capital movements, under the present fixed rate system.

THE CASE AGAINST FLEXIBLE EXCHANGE RATES

The case against flexible exchange rates, like the case for fixed exchange rates, is rarely if ever stated in a reasoned fashion.

Instead, it typically consists of a series of unfounded assertions and allegations, which derive their plausibility from two fundamentally irrelevant facts. The first is that, in the modern European economic history with which most people are familiar, flexible exchange rates are associated either with the acute monetary disorders that followed the First World War, or with the collapse of the international monetary system in the 1930s; instead of being credited with their capacity to function when the fixed exchange rate system could not, they are debited with the disorders of national economic policies that made the fixed exchange rate system unworkable or led to its collapse. The second, and more important at this historical distance from the disastrous experiences just mentioned, is that most people are accustomed to the fixed exchange rate system, and are prone to assume without thinking that a flexible rate system would simply display in an exaggerated fashion the worst features of the present fixed rate system, rather than remedy them.

The historical record is too large a topic to be discussed adequately in a brief essay. Suffice it to say that the interwar European experience was clouded by the strong belief, based on pre–First World War conditions, that fixed exchange rates at historical parity values constituted a natural order of things to which governments would seek eventually to return, and that scholarly interpretation of that experience leaned excessively and unjustifiably towards endorsement of the official view that any private speculation on the exchanges based on distrust of the ability of the authorities to hold an established parity under changing circumstances was necessarily "destabilizing" and anti-social. It should further be remarked that European interwar experience does not constitute the whole of the historical record, and that both previously

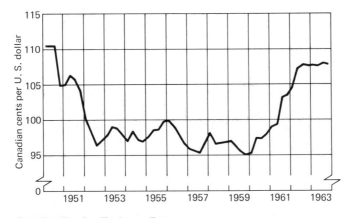

Canadian Foreign Exchange Rate
Note: Canada was on a floating exchange rate from late 1950 to
mid-1962. The sharp movements at both ends of the period represent
the transition from fixed rates to flexible rates. Once the free market
equilibrium rate was established, it moved in a relatively narrow
quarter-to-quarter range. Source: Bank of Canada

(as in the case of the United States dollar
from 1862 to 1879) and subsequently (as
in the case of the Canadian dollar from
1950 to 1962) there have been cases of
a major trading country maintaining a
flexible exchange rate without any of the
disastrous consequences commonly forecast by the opponents of flexible rates.

The *penchant* for attributing to the
flexible rate system the problems of the
fixed rate system can be illustrated by a
closer examination of some of the arguments commonly advanced against floating exchange rates, most of which allege
either that flexible rates will seriously
increase uncertainty in international transactions, or that they will foster inflation.

Flexible Rates and Uncertainty

INSTABILITY OF THE EXCHANGE
RATE. One of the common arguments
under the heading of uncertainty is that
flexible rates would be extremely unstable
rates, jumping wildly about from day to
day. This allegation ignores the crucial
point that a rate that is free to move under
the influence of changes in demand and
supply is not forced to move erratically,
but will instead move only in response to
such changes in demand and supply—
including changes induced by changes in
governmental policies—and normally will
move only slowly and fairly predictably.
Abnormally rapid and erratic movements
will occur only in response to sharp and
unexpected changes in circumstances;
and such changes in a fixed exchange rate
system would produce equally or more
uncertainty-creating policy changes in the
form of devaluation, deflation, or the imposition of new controls on trade and payments. The fallacy of this argument lies
in its assumption that exchange rate
changes occur exogenously and without
apparent economic reason; that assumption reflects the mentality of the fixed
rate system, in which the exchange rate
is held fixed by official intervention in
the face of demand and supply pressures

for change, and occasionally changed arbitrarily and at one stroke by governmental decisions whose timing and magnitude is a matter of severe uncertainty.

REDUCTION OF FOREIGN TRADE. A related argument is that uncertainty about the domestic currency equivalent of foreign receipts or payments would seriously inhibit international transactions of all kinds. As argued in the preceding section, trends in exchange rates should normally be fairly slow and predictable, and their causes such as to provide more or less automatic compensation to traders and investors. Moreover, traders averse to uncertainty would be able to hedge their transactions through forward exchange markets, which would, if necessary, develop in response to demand. It is commonly argued at present, by foreign exchange dealers and others engaged in the foreign exchange market, that hedging facilities would be completely inadequate or that the cost of forward cover would be prohibitive. Both arguments seek to deny the economic principle that a competitive system will tend to provide any good or service demanded, at a price that yields no more than a fair profit. They derive, moreover, from the experience of recent crises under the fixed rate system. When exchange rates are rigidly fixed by official intervention, businessmen normally do not consider the cost of forward cover worth their while; but when everyone expects the currency to be devalued, everyone seeks to hedge his risks by selling it forward, the normal balancing of forward demands and supplies ceases to prevail, the forward rate drops to a heavy discount, and the cost of forward cover becomes "prohibitive." Under a flexible exchange rate system, where the spot rate is also free to move, arbitrage between the spot and forward markets, as well as speculation, would ensure that the expectation of depreciation was reflected in depreciation of the spot as well as the forward rate, and hence tend to keep the cost of forward cover within reasonable bounds.

INCENTIVE TO "DESTABILIZING SPECULATION." A further argument under the heading of uncertainty is that it will encourage "destabilizing speculation." The historical record provides no convincing supporting evidence for this claim, unless "destabilizing speculation" is erroneously defined to include any speculation against an officially pegged exchange rate, regardless of how unrealistic that rate was under the prevailing circumstances. A counter-consideration is that speculators who engage in genuinely destabilizing speculation—that is, whose speculations move the exchange rate away from rather than towards its equilibrium level—will consistently lose money, because they will consistently be buying when the rate is "high" and selling when it is "low" by comparison with its equilibrium value; this consideration does not, however, exclude the possibility that clever professional speculators may be able to profit by leading amateur speculators into destabilizing speculation, buying near the trough and selling near the peak, the amateur's losses being borne out of their (or their shareholders') regular income. A further counter-consideration is that under flexible rates, speculation will itself move the spot rate, thus generating uncertainty in the minds of the speculators about the magnitude of prospective profits, which will depend on the relation between the spot rate and the expected future rate of exchange, neither of which will be fixed and independent of the magnitude of the speculators' transactions. By contrast, the adjustable peg system gives the speculator a "one-way option": in circumstances giving rise to speculation on a change in the rate, the rate can only move one way if it moves at all, and if it moves it is certain to be changed by a significant amount—and possibly by more, the stronger is the speculation on a change. The fixed exchange rate system courts "destabilizing speculation," in the economically incorrect sense of speculation against the permanence of the official parity, by providing this one-way option; in so doing it places the monetary authorities in the position of speculating on their own ability to maintain the parity. It is obviously fallacious to assume that private speculators would speculate in the same way and on the same scale under the flexible rate system, which offers them no such easy mark to speculate against.

Flexible Rates and Inflation

The argument that the flexible exchange rate system would promote inflation comes in two major versions. The first is that under the flexible rate system governments would no longer by subject to the "discipline" against inflationary policies exerted by the fixity of the exchange rate. This argument in large part reflects circular reasoning on the part of the fixed rate exponents: discipline against inflationary policies, if necessary for international reasons, is necessary only because rates are fixed, and domestic inflation both leads to balance-of-payments problems and imposes inflation on other countries. Neither consequence would follow under the flexible exchange rate system. Apart from its external repercussions, inflation may be regarded as undesirable for domestic reasons; but the fixed rate system imposes, not the need to maintain domestic price stability, but the obligation to conform to the average world trend of prices, which may be either inflationary or deflationary rather than stable.[2] Moreover, under the adjustable peg system actually existing, countries can evade the discipline against excessively rapid inflation by drawing down reserves and borrowing, by imposing restrictions on international trade and payments, and in the last resort by de-

valuing their currencies. The record since the Second World War speaks poorly for the anti-inflationary discipline of fixed exchange rates. The reason is that the signal to governments of the need for anti-inflationary discipline comes through a loss of exchange reserves, the implications of which are understood by only a few and can be disregarded or temporized with until a crisis descends—and the crisis justifies all sorts of policy expedients other than the domestic deflation which the logic of adjustment under the fixed rate system demands. Under a flexible rate system, the consequences of inflationary governmental policies would be much more readily apparent to the general population, in the form of a declining foreign value of the currency and an upward trend in domestic prices; and proper policies to correct the situation, if it were desired to correct it, could be argued about in freedom from an atmosphere of crisis.

The second argument to the effect that a flexible exchange rate would be "inflationary" asserts that any random depreciation would, by raising the cost of living, provoke wage and price increases that would make the initially temporarily lower foreign value of the currency the new equilibrium exchange rate. This argument clearly derives from confusion of a flexible with a fixed exchange rate. It is under a fixed exchange rate that wages and prices are determined in the expectation of constancy of the domestic currency cost of foreign exchange, and that abrupt devaluations occur that are substantial enough in their effects on the prices of imports and of exportable goods to require compensatory revision of wage bargains and price-determination calculations. Under a flexible rate system, exchange rate adjustments would occur gradually, and would be less likely to require drastic revisions of wage- and price-setting decisions, especially as any general trend of the exchange rate and prices would tend to be taken into account in the accompanying calculations of unions and employers. Apart from this, it is erroneous to assume that increases in the cost of living inevitably produce fully compensatory wage increases; while such increases in the cost of living will be advanced as part of the workers' case for higher wages, whether they will in fact result in compensatory or in less than compensatory actual wage increases will depend on the economic climate set by the government's fiscal and monetary policies. It is conceivable that a government pledged to maintain full employment would maintain an economic climate in which any money wage increase workers chose to press for would be sanctioned by sufficient inflation of monetary demand and the money supply to prevent it from resulting in an increase in unemployment. But in that case there would be no restraint on wage increases and hence on wage and price inflation, unless the government somehow had arrived at an understanding with the unions and employers that only wage increases compensatory of previous cost of living increases (or justified by increases in productivity) would be sanctioned by easier fiscal and monetary policy. That is an improbable situation, given the difficulties that governments have encountered with establishing and implementing an "incomes policy" under the fixed rate system; and it is under the fixed rate system, not the flexible rate system, that governments have a strong incentive to insist on relating increases in money incomes to increases in productivity and hence are led on equity grounds to make exceptions for increases in the cost of living. It should be noted in conclusion that one version of the argument under discussion, which reasons from the allegation of a persistent tendency to cost-push inflation to the prediction of a persistent tendency towards depreciation of the currency, must be fallacious: it is logically impossible for all currencies to be persistently depreciating against each other.

CONTEMPORARY PROPOSALS FOR GREATER EXCHANGE RATE FLEXIBILITY

Increased Flexibility in the IMF System

The extreme difficulties that have been encountered in recent years in achieving appropriate adjustments of the parity values of certain major currencies within the present "adjustable peg" system of fixed exchanges rates, as exemplified particularly in the prolonged agony of sterling from 1964 to 1967 and the failure of the "Bonn crisis" of November 1968 to induce the German and French governments to accept the revaluations of the franc and the mark agreed on as necessary by the officials and experts concerned with the international monetary system, have generated serious interest, especially in the United States Administration, in proposals for reforming the present IMF system so as to provide for more flexibility of exchange rates. It has been realized that under the present system, a devaluation has become a symbol of political defeat by, and a revaluation (appreciation) a symbol of political surrender to, other countries, both of which the government in power will resist to the last ditch; and that this political symbolism prevents adjustments of exchange rates that otherwise would or should be accepted as necessary to the proper functioning of the international monetary system. The aim therefore is to reduce or remove the political element in exchange rate adjustment under the present system, by changing the system so as to allow the anonymous competitive foreign exchange market to make automatic adjustments of exchange rates within a limited range.

The two major proposals to this end are

the "wider band" proposal and the "crawling peg" proposal. Under the "wider band" proposal, the present freedom of countries to allow the market value of their currencies to fluctuate within one per cent (in practice usually less) of their par values would be extended to permit variation within a much wider range (usually put at five per cent for argument's sake). Under the "crawling peg" proposal, daily fluctuations about the par value would be confined within the present or somewhat wider limits, but the parity itself would be determined by a moving average of the rates actually set in the market over some fixed period of the immediate past, and so would gradually adjust itself upwards or downwards over time to the market pressures of excess supply of or excess demand for the currency (pressures for depreciation or appreciation, rise or fall in the par value, respectively).

Both of these proposals, while welcomed by advocates of the flexible exchange rate system to the extent that they recognize the case for flexible rates and the virtues of market determination as contrasted with political determination of exchange rates, are subject to the criticism that they accept the principle of market determination of exchange rates only within politically predetermined limits, and hence abjure use of the prime virtue of the competitive market, its capacity to absorb and deal with unexpected economic developments.[3] The criticism is that *either* economic developments will not be such as to make the equilibrium exchange rate fall outside the permitted range of variation, in which case the restriction on the permitted range of variation will prove unnecessary, *or* economic change will require more change in the exchange rate than the remaining restriction on exchange rate variation will permit, in which case the problems of the present system will recur (though obviously less frequently). Specifically, sooner or later

the exchange rate of a major country will reach the limit of permitted variation, and the speculation-generating possibility will arise that the par value of that currency will have to be changed by a finite and substantial percentage, as a result of lack of sufficient international reserves for the monetary authorities of the country concerned to defend the par value of the currency.

In this respect, there is a crucial difference between the wider band proposal and the crawling peg proposal. The wider band system would provide only a once-for-all increase in the degree of freedom of exchange rates to adjust to changing circumstances. A country that followed a more inflationary policy than other nations would find its exchange rate drifting towards the ceiling on its par value, and a country that followed a less inflationary policy than its neighbors would find its exchange rate sinking towards the floor under its par value. Once one or the other fixed limit was reached, the country would to all intents and purposes be back on a rigidly fixed exchange rate. The crawling peg proposal, on the other hand, would permit a country's policy, with respect to the relative rate of inflation it preferred, to diverge permanently from that of its neighbors, but only within the limits set by the permitted range of daily variation about the daily par value and the period of averaging of past actual exchange rates specified for the determination of the par value itself. For those persuaded of the case for flexible exchange rates, the crawling peg is thus definitely to be preferred. The only question is the empirical one of whether the permitted degree of exchange rate flexibility would be adequate to eliminate the likelihood in practice of a situation in which an exchange rate was so far out of equilibrium as to make it impossible for the monetary authorities to finance the period of adjustment of the rate to equilibrium by use of their international reserves and international borrowing power. This is an extremely difficult empirical question, because it involves not only the likely magnitude of disequilibrating disturbances in relation to the permitted degree of exchange rate adjustment, but also the effects of the knowledge by government of the availability of increased possibilities of exchange rate flexibility on the speed of governmental policy response to disequilibrating developments, and the effects of the knowledge by private speculators that the effects on the exchange rate of current speculation will determine the range within which the exchange rate will be in the future, on the assumption that the crawling peg formula continues to hold.

Evaluation of how both the wider band and the crawling peg proposals should work in practice requires a great deal of empirical study, which has not yet been carried out on any adequate scale. In the meantime, those persuaded of the case for flexible exchange rates would probably be better advised to advocate experimentation with limited rate flexibility, in the hope that the results will dispel the fears of the supporters of the fixed rate system, than to emphasize the dangers inherent in the residual fixity of exchange rates under either of the contemporary popular proposals for increasing the flexibility of rates under the existing fixed rate systems.

A Floating Pound?

The argument of the preceding sections strongly suggests the advisability of a change in British exchange rate policy from a fixed exchange rate to a market-determined flexible exchange rate. The main arguments for this change are that a flexible exchange rate would free British economic policy from the apparent necessity to pursue otherwise irrational and difficult policy objectives for the sake of improving the balance of payments,

and that it would release the country from the vicious circle of "stop-go" policies of control of aggregate demand.

A flexible exchange rate is not of course a panacea; it simply provides an extra degree of freedom, by removing the balance-of-payments constraints on policy formation. In so doing, it does not and cannot remove the constraint on policy imposed by the limitation of total available national resources and the consequent necessity of choice among available alternatives; it simply brings this choice, rather than the external consequences of choices made, to the forefront of the policy debate.

The British economy is at present riddled with inefficiencies consequential on, and politically justified by, decisions based on the aim of improving the balance of payments. In this connection, one can cite as only some among many examples the heavy protection of domestic agriculture, the protection of domestic fuel resources by the taxation of imported oil, the subsidization of manufacturing as against the services trades through the Selective Employment Tax, and various other subsidies to manufacturing effected through tax credits. One can also cite the politically arduous effort to implement an incomes policy, which amounts to an effort to avoid by political pressure on individual wage- and price-setting decisions the need for an adjustment that would be effected automatically by a flexible exchange rate. A flexible exchange rate would make an incomes policy unnecessary. It would also permit policy towards industry, agriculture, and the service trades to concentrate on the achievement of greater economic efficiency, without the biases imparted by the basically economically irrelevant objectives of increasing exports or substituting for imports.

The adoption of flexible exchange rates would also make unnecessary, or at least less harmful, the disruptive cycle of "stop-go" aggregate demand policies which has characterized British economic policy for many years, British Governments are under a persistently strong incentive to try to break out of the limitations of available resources and relatively slow economic growth by policies of demand expansion. This incentive is reinforced, before elections, by the temptation to expand demand in order to win votes, in the knowledge that international reserves and international borrowing power can be drawn down to finance the purchase of votes without the electorate knowing that it is being bribed with its own money—until after the election the successful party is obliged to clean up the mess so created by introducing deflationary policies, with political safety if it is a returned government, and with political embarrassment if it is an opposition party newly come to power. If the country were on a flexible exchange rate, the generation of the "political cycle" would be inhibited by the fact that the effort to buy votes by pre-election inflationary policies would soon be reflected in a depreciation of the exchange rate and a rise in the cost of living. Even if this were avoided by use of the Government's control of the country's international reserves and borrowing powers to stabilize the exchange rate, a newly elected Government of either complexion would not be faced with the absolute necessity of introducing deflationary economic policies to restore its international reserves. It could instead allow the exchange rate to depreciate while it made up its mind what to do. Apart from the question of winning elections, Governments that believed in demand expansion as a means of promoting growth could pursue this policy *à outrance*, without being forced to reverse it by a balance-of-payments crisis, so long as they and the public were prepared to accept the consequential depreciation of the currency; Governments that believed instead in other kinds of policies would have to argue for and defend them on their merits, without being able to pass them off as imposed on the country by the need to secure equilibrium in the balance of payments.

The Feasibility of Floating

While these and other elements of the case for a floating pound have frequently been recognized and advocated, it has been much more common to argue that a flexible exchange rate for sterling is "impossible," either because the position of sterling as an international reserve currency precludes it, or because the International Monetary Fund would not permit it. But most of the arguments for the presumed international importance of a fixed international value of sterling have been rendered irrelevant by the deterioration of sterling's international position subsequent to the 1967 devaluation, and in particular by the Basle Facility and the sterling area agreements concluded in the autumn of 1968, which by giving a gold guarantee on most of the overseas sterling area holdings of sterling have freed the British authorities to change the foreign exchange value of sterling without fear of recrimination from its official holders. Moreover, the relative decline in the international role of sterling, and in the relative importance of Britain in world trade, finance, and investments that has characterized the post-war period, has made it both possible and necessary to think of Britain as a relatively small component of the international monetary system, more a country whose difficulties require special treatment than a lynch-pin of the system, the fixed value of whose currency must be supported by other countries in the interests of survival of the the system as a whole.

Under the present circumstances, adoption of a floating exchange rate for the pound would constitute, not a definitive reversal of the essential nature of the IMF system of predominantly fixed exchange rates, but recognition of and accommodation to a situation in which the chronic weakness of the pound is a major source of tension within the established system. The International Monetary Fund is commonly depicted in Britain as an ignorantly dogmatic but politically powerful opponent of sensible changes that have the drawback of conflicting with the ideology written into its Charter. But there is no reason to believe that the Fund, as the dispassionate administrator of an international monetary system established nearly a quarter of a century ago to serve the needs of the international economy, is insensitive to the tensions of the contemporary situation and blindly hostile to reforms that would permit the system as a whole to survive and function more effectively.

NOTES

1 The exchange speculation in favor of the Deutsche Mark in early May 1969 is only the latest example of instability in the present fixed exchange rate system.
2 A good example is Germany, which is suffering from balance-of-payments surpluses, because its price increases have been less than the average world trend.
3 It is quite likely that a crawling peg would not have provided an equilibrium exchange rate in France after the events of May 1968.

Summaries

Otmar Emminger, "Practical Aspects of the Problem of Balance-of-Payments Adjustment," *Journal of Political Economy*, 75 (August 1967), pp. 512–522.

The proper functioning of the international monetary system is a continuing source of concern to monetary economists. In the past few years, discussion in the area of monetary economics has turned from the problem of international liquidity to that of the balance-of-payments adjustment mechanism. In this paper, Emminger, an official of the Deutsche Bundesbank, addresses himself to the practical aspects of the problem of the balance-of-payments adjustment.

At the outset, Emminger points out that he does not wish to consider the manipulation of exchange rates as a method for solving balance-of-payments problems. Instead, he confines himself to "problems of adjustment within the framework of a system of fixed exchange rates," and puts special emphasis "on problems which we have encountered in practical attempts at some international co-ordination of economic policies and in discussions on rules of the game or a code of good behavior."

Emminger devotes a good portion of his article to the problems of diagnosis and identification. He also states the extent to which surplus and deficit countries should take the responsibility for correcting imbalances in their balance of payments. He maintains that this responsibility cannot be met adequately unless these countries develop a strategy for the "right mix of monetary and fiscal policies."

In discussing the role of the adjustment mechanism as an effective policy tool, Emminger remarks, "Has the adjustment *mechanism* 'virtually' broken down in the present international economy? Not at all. In cases where a serious attempt was made to eliminate a big external deficit by restraining domestic demand, the adjustment mechanism nearly always worked with astonishing speed and vigor... Thus, the 'mechanism' as such has not broken down. It simply has not always been used—for good and bad reasons."

Hans W. Singer, "Distribution of Gains Between Investing and Borrowing Countries," *American Economic Review*, 40 (May 1950), pp. 473–510.

In this classic article, Singer's objective is to develop a sound international policy for both the advanced and the underdeveloped countries. The author first points out that it is erroneously believed by many economists that less developed countries (LDCs) derive immense benefits from international trade and that the benefits they derive from this trade greatly affect their national incomes. This misunderstanding exists primarily because three important economic facts are rarely recognized: (1) that foreign trade tends to be proportionately most important when incomes are lowest, (2) that fluctuations in the value and volume of foreign trade tend to be proportionately more violent in the LDCs than in developed countries, and, therefore, also more important in relation to national income, and (3) that "fluctuations in foreign trade tend to be immensely more important for underdeveloped countries in relation to that small margin of income over subsistence needs which forms the source of capital formation, for which they often depend on export surpluses over consumption goods required from abroad."

In addition to the above belief, says Singer, the importance of foreign trade in the LDCs is obscured by another factor—the discrepancy in the productivity of labor between export and domestic industries. The former industry is capital-intensive, while the latter is labor-intensive. Hence, statistics relating to the use of labor in export versus domestic industries in the LDCs do not adequately reflect the importance of foreign trade.

Having established a sound basis for his conclusions, Singer proceeds to build a theoretical model and "proves" with the help of this model that the LDCs benefit immensely from international trade. On the basis of this proof, he asserts that "we should encourage a greater amount of reinvestment of the income from existing foreign investment as directed to changing comparative advantage of LDCs from the production of primary goods to the production of manufactures.... The opportunity to invest abroad and to receive the related future income may thus permit a greater rate of growth for advanced countries. In general, there is likely to be a powerful mutuality of interest between investor countries and borrowing countries."

Robert Solomon, *Observations on the International Monetary System*. Paper presented before the Joint International Trade and Fiscal Policy Seminars at Harvard University, March 24, 1969.

In the foreign sector, both the international liquidity problem and the balance-of-payments adjustment problem plague theoretical economists and policy makers. However, in recent years, more attention has been paid to the latter problem because it has been felt that the responsibilities of those countries that suffer from either chronic balance-of-payments deficits or surpluses are not properly understood.

In this paper, Solomon, who is an adviser to the Board of Governors of the Federal Reserve System, addresses himself to both of the problems mentioned above. First, he explains the important connection between liquidity and the balance-of-payments adjustment. He then asks—and subsequently answers—the question: Why is it that economists are concerned about the balance-of-payments adjustment? Further, he contends that an assurance of adequate reserve liquidity is necessary before a country's balance-of-payments adjustment problem can be solved. Finally, the author states he is unenthusiastic about experimenting with exchange-rate flexibility on the grounds that this might interfere with the process that generates adequate international liquidity.

Bibliography

Henry G. Aubrey, *Behind the Veil of International Money*, Essays in International Finance, No. 71, International Finance Section, Department of Economics, Princeton University, Princeton, N.J., January 1969.

W. M. Corden, "The Pure Theory of International Trade," in *Recent Developments in the Theory of International Trade* (Princeton, N.J.: Princeton University, International Finance Section, 1965), pp. 24–41.

James L. Ford, "On the Structure of, and Gains from, International Trade," *Kyklos* (1965), pp. 670–683.

Isaiah Frank, "New Perspective on Trade and Development," *Foreign Affairs* (April 1967), pp. 520–540.

Milton Friedman, "The Euro-Dollar Market: Some First Principles," *Morgan Guaranty Survey* (October 1969), pp. 4–14.

Robert A. Mundell, "Theory of Optimum Currency Areas," *American Economic Review*, 51 (September 1961), pp. 657–665.

Rudolf R. Rhomberg, "A Model of the Canadian Economy Under Fixed and Fluctuating Exchange Rates," *Journal of Political Economy*, 72 (February 1964), pp. 1–31.

Akria Takayama, "The Effects of Fiscal and Monetary Policies Under Flexible and Fixed Exchange Rates,'" *Canadian Journal of Economics*, 2 (May 1969), pp. 190–209.

Gordon L. Williams, "When a World Money System Is Out of Date," *Business Week*, March 22, 1969, pp. 70–94.

Ralph A. Young, "Making Peace With Gold," *Morgan Guaranty Survey*, June 1968, pp. 3–14.

13
PLANNING, DEVELOPMENT, AND GROWTH

One of the major economic goals of every nation is the attainment of an accelerating economic growth rate with full employment of resources. According to established growth theory, economic growth cannot be accelerated without an attendant increase in the rate of capital formation. Increasing the rate of capital formation requires greater savings and this could, of course, mean a reduction in consumption expenditure. Sound economic planning facilitates the formulation of a coordinated and consistent economic policy and helps to achieve both a high rate of economic growth and a higher standard of living.

In the first selection in this part, Hagen examines the tools that are available to economists for achieving the objectives of economic planning. The second article is a survey by Hicks of the contributions economists have made over the years to the theory of economic growth.

In the concluding article, Myint argues that orthodox economic theory has a greater significance for any developing nation wishing to increase its rate of economic growth.

The Aims and Tools of Economic Development Planning
Everett E. Hagen

NATIONAL GOALS AND GOVERNMENTAL DECISIONS

No nation has as its only goal a maximum rate of economic growth. Even though this goal may be in the forefront of public discussion, when decisions are taken it is balanced against other national purposes. One of these other purposes is a maximum

Everett E. Hagen, "The Aims and Tools of Economic Development Planning," in Everett E. Hagen, ed., *Planning Economic Development* (Homewood: Richard D. Irwin, Inc., 1963), pp. 7–19.

current living standard; there is a limit below which the government will not reduce its current services and a limit above which it will not increase its taxation of private incomes in order to increase the rate of development expenditures.

A third goal is reduction in the inequality of income distribution. This too may conflict with economic growth. Government services to lower income groups may use resources that might otherwise have gone into government investment, and tax measures designed to reduce inequality in income distribution

491

may reduce private investment by lessening the incentive of higher income individuals to invest.

Still another goal is employment for all who wish to work. This goal will usually not conflict with those already mentioned. If there are unemployment of laborers and some idle capacity in the nation's factories and shops, both current living standards and the rate of growth can usually be increased and the distribution of income made less unequal by measures which increase aggregate demand and thereby put idle workers and capacity to work. However, if workers are unemployed or underemployed but there is no idle productive capacity, then additional equipment must be provided if the idle laborers are to be given work. If capital is scarce, it is possible that providing simple equipment for all of the idle or partly idle workers will result in less production and a lower rate of economic growth than providing more elaborate equipment for some of the workers and leaving the others without work. Also, beyond a certain point measures to increase employment may worsen the distribution of income by causing inflation, which injures low-income groups.

Attainment of various other national goals may also reduce the rate of economic development. Many nations have reduced their rate of economic growth in order to increase their military strength. Others have diverted resources from economic growth in order to satisfy regional demands or the demands of various politically influential groups, erect national monuments, or increase national unity by improving interregional communication even though the expenditure was not economically justified. In still other cases a nation has erected a steel mill even though its operation is a heavy continuing drain on the economy, and a nation which has no scientific base on which to conduct nuclear research and will have no use for nuclear power in the foreseeable future

has used some of its material resources and human talent to establish a nuclear research laboratory, the purpose, or at least the effect, being to give the nation or its leaders a sense of being modern.

This is by no means a complete list of national goals but it suggests some of the main ones which impinge on economic development. The purpose of economic development planning is not to supplant planning toward these other objectives. Rather it is to aid the nation's leaders in framing and executing a program which will balance these goals against each other and achieve the degree of each that will yield the greatest satisfaction to the people of the country. Planning should make clear to the nation's leaders the cost in reduced attainment of one of these goals which may result from measures aimed at attainment of another, so that to the maximum extent possible all the consequences of each measure will be taken into account in making decisions.

THE IMPACT OF GOVERNMENT ON THE ECONOMIC SYSTEM

Neither is economic planning intended necessarily to increase the degree of government control over the economic system; rather it is intended to make government officials aware of the effects of governmental actions to avoid an inadvertent impact. Almost any governmental activity affects the private as well as the public sector of the economic system whether or not an effect is intended. In the non-Communist industrial countries, in most of which government employment plus government purchases from private enterprises absorb 18 to 20 per cent of the nation's total productive capacity and government expenditures including interest on the public debt and so-called transfer payments constitute a still higher percentage of total expenditures, this impact is conspicuous. It is equally certain in underdeveloped countries even though the government may use less than one half as large a share of the nation's production.

Any change in the rate of government expenditures will affect private consumption or investment. Suppose, for example, that the government expands its road-building program at a time when there is some slack in the economy and plants making cement, steel reinforcing rods, and other construction materials are operating below capacity. Then the increased production of road materials can be carried out without causing a reduction in other production. Indeed, if the government finances the road construction not by an increase in tax rates but by borrowing from the banks, the increased consumer income resulting from the increased governmental activity will result in increased consumer spending (the well-known "multiplier effect"), and production of consumer goods as well as of road-construction materials will increase. The increase in sales may also stimulate an increase in private investment.

On the other hand, if all workers are fully employed and there is no idle productive capacity, the government will be able to obtain labor and materials for road construction only by attracting them from other production, and other production will fall. (The unusually high demand for labor may cause additional individuals to enter the labor force, so that other production does not decline by as much as road-construction activity increases, but there will be some decline.) Even if the government finances the road construction by increasing tax rates, private income and spending will normally remain as high as before since the expenditures on the road projects will provide added income equal to the reduction in incomes caused by the tax increase. The decrease in the supply of goods on the private market without any decrease in demand will cause some degree of inflation. If at such a time of full employment the government finances the road construction by borrowing the needed

funds, the degree of inflation will of course be greater.

In any of these cases, if the roads are needed and well planned, in addition to the other effects their construction will increase the convenience of transport and facilitate economic growth.

Thus a change in government expenditures, without any other governmental action, may greatly affect private economic activity.

Apart from the changes in the rate of governmental expenditures, fiscal or monetary measures also affect the level and nature of private consumption or investment. Banking policies may permit the commercial banks to extend credit liberally; or the government may establish a government-owned development bank, development corporation, mortgage bank, or agricultural credit system; or it may foster the development of private or joint public-private institutions for the same purpose. If individuals with entrepreneurial spirit exist in the country, such measures will increase the rate of private investment.

The government may induce increased private consumption by measures to foster the extension of consumer credit if the necessary banking institutions have evolved in the country. Its major tool, however, apart from expenditure increases, is likely to be tax reduction, which will leave consumers more spendable income. By the tax reduction it chooses the government will influence the type of increase in consumption and private production which follows.

A property tax reduction may take any of various forms and have any of various effects. Generally speaking, a reduction in the corporation profits tax will favor investment as against consumption more than a reduction in other taxes, and it will favor high-income consumers, since (especially in low-income countries) corporations are likely to be owned mainly by high-income individuals. Reduction in sales and excise taxes and customs duties on widely used consumer goods will favor lower-income groups; reductions of such taxes on luxuries will tend to favor higher-income groups; and reductions on capital goods will somewhat stimulate investment. One or another income class will be favored by a reduction in personal income tax rates, and certain types of consumption expenditures will therefore be increased more than others, depending on the nature of the reduction. A reduction in income tax rates, especially one which decreases the rate of graduation of the tax, may also induce increased private investment. Contrasting considerations apply if the government wishes to reduce the rate of private consumption or investment. Deliberately or inadvertently, therefore, government fiscal and monetary policies will affect relative incomes, the nature of consumer expenditures, and also the level and nature of private investment.

Private consumption or investment cannot ordinarily be increased simply by government regulations aimed at doing so, but they can be reduced in this way, if the regulations can be enforced. Moreover, regulations not directly aimed at the level of investment or production may nevertheless greatly affect them. The impact of regulating prices or wages, regulations imposing obligations on the employer concerning unemployment or retirement compensation, or regulations concerning the right to discharge employees have obvious impacts; the impact of all other government regulations which limit freedom of individual or corporate action is equally certain though not necessarily equally great.

A type of regulation that often has especially great impact on private production is regulation of the purchases and use of foreign exchange. If the foreign exchange earnings of a country are not sufficient to finance the purchases abroad which the government and private buyers desire, instead of devaluing the currency the government may directly regulate the use of foreign exchange. This may be done by selective customs duties, import rationing, or various other methods. By whatever method, the government's choice of the types of imports to restrict most sharply will determine what types of private consumption and investment, as well as public expenditures abroad, are penalized.

In short, then, whether or not a government intends to influence the level and nature of private consumption and investment and the operations of the private sector of the economy, many of its actions will have very important effects.

WHAT ECONOMIC DEVELOPMENT PLANNING INCLUDES

Before adopting any measure, responsible government officials will consider its effects on governmental operations as well as on private consumption and investment and hence on the attainment of national goals. Presumably, they will specifically consider its effects on economic development. If one terms such analysis of individual measures economic development planning, then economic development planning is practiced, badly or well, by virtually every government in the world. If the term is to have a distinctive meaning it must include much more than this. As it is used in this volume, it includes also a set of more complex activities designed to see that the combined effect of all governmental measures affecting economic activity is optimum. For convenience these elements in development planning are numbered in the paragraphs which follow.

1. The first is the screening of individual proposals. While the merits of an individual project cannot be determined fully except in relation to all other projects, some may be so clearly desirable or disadvantageous that they can be approved or rejected when considered in isolation.

2. As a second step, economic develop-

ment planning involves considering whether the facilities and services planned by each agency of the government include those needed to complement the projects of other agencies, and whether the services and facilities planned by the government as a whole include those needed to complement anticipated private economic activity. For example, will transportation, communication, power, and water supply be adequate to serve the anticipated expansion in private production and to serve growing cities? Are teacher training facilities sufficient to provide teachers for the new schools being built? Where efficient complementarities are not present the planning officials must induce the revision of plans necessary to bring them about.

3. Taking such complementarities into account rather than considering single projects in isolation, planning officials must also evaluate the relative desirability of all components not only of anticipated government activity but also of private consumption and investment. Even if each proposed government program is advantageous, the various public and private programs complement each other efficiently, and anticipated government plus private demand for the goods and services to be produced is great enough to provide full employment but not so great as to threaten inflation, changes in some of the government or private plans may be desirable. Some proposed government programs may be less advantageous than some possible projects which are not included in the plans submitted to planning officials. Even though the entire highway construction program is regarded as beneficial, it may be desirable to reduce it somewhat to free resources for use in increasing the school construction program or some aspect of the community development program. Similarly, even though anticipated private economic activity seems desirable to the persons making the expenditures, changes may seem to be in the interest of the entire population. For example, anticipated private investment in luxury apartment buildings may seem less advantageous than expansion of housing construction for the lower income market; and expanding some proposed governmental activities at the expense of certain anticipated private activities, or the reverse, may seem desirable. Increasing the school construction program may seem more advantageous to the people of the country than constructing the luxury apartment buildings, or, on the other hand, leaving enough funds and incentive for private investment so that a private textile factory is built may be more important than constructing an olympic stadium or a new highway. Good planning must then include proposals for the substitution of one government program for another or for measures to induce changes in private economic activity.

It is worth while to note that the decision to increase governmental activity at the expense of private consumption or investment, or the reverse, cannot be made merely on the basis of a general view of the relative desirability of governmental and private activity. Even though a given society has opted for a highly socialized state of affairs, so long as there is any private sector some increase in the production of the kinds of goods and services provided by that sector may be more advantageous to the public than increases in governmental activity; on the other hand, even if only a minor role has been assigned to government, some increases in government services may be more advantageous than any increases in private production. The choice must be made by evaluation of the relative desirability of a small change in private expenditure and the specific public services being considered.

Increased government purchases of goods or services when the country's productive capacity is fully utilized will result in a reduction of private purchases through an inflationary process if the government does not reduce them through tax increases. Hence a choice between government and private spending is inescapable. However, to some persons any governmental decision concerning the relative desirability of various increases or decreases in private investment and especially in private consumption seems entirely arbitrary. Moreover, the concept of such governmental control seems objectionable. Thus, although the proposition is shocking only when put in general terms, just as Molière's Monsieur Jourdain was surprised to find that he had been talking prose all his life, the question merits brief discussion. The heart of the argument for private economic activity and a free market, it is argued, is that these institutions permit consumers to choose the goods and services which will give them the most satisfaction and draw production into the activities for which there is the greatest demand. Does not the concept of governmental measures designed to influence choices by individuals or firms contradict the purposes of private production and a free market?

Of course it does not. If judiciously carried out, such measures compensate for certain inadequacies of the market. One of the major inadequacies is that the market serves whoever has income to spend, without any regard for the distribution of the income among individuals. If poor men offer enough money to induce the production of hoes, the market will provide hoes; if a wealthy man offers enough to induce the production of a yacht, it will provide the yacht.

In every society equality of income distribution has a moral appeal, yet it is appreciated that the opportunity to earn a higher income is a necessary inducement to efficiency in production and to innovation in methods of production and the production of new goods. There is no assurance that the market will result in a distribution of income that balances these two criteria in a satisfactory way, and in every society in one way or another,

mainly by fiscal measures but also in other ways, the government achieves the balance that seems most suitable to the public or at least to the groups who control the government.

Governmental decisions concerning private consumption and investment are of course not usually decisions concerning specific consumer goods or specific investment projects. More commonly they are decisions to cause or permit a relative increase in the income and hence expenditures of one rather than another income class or occupational group, or to adopt measures facilitating one rather than another general type of private investment. However, even decisions concerning the private production or use of specific goods may be desirable. For example, even though the accumulation of high incomes is deemed socially desirable because of the incentives which the possibility provides, certain specific restrictions on the freedom of high-income individuals to spend their incomes as they choose may also be socially advantageous. For example, the use of foreign exchange to finance the import of materials for luxury apartment buildings may compete with its use to finance the import of materials for low-cost housing or of equipment needed for industrial production. Also, refusing permission for construction of the apartments may cause the investors to turn instead to projects whose immediate benefit to the society is deemed greater. Consequently it may be thought that the dulling of incentive resulting from restrictions on luxury expenditure is more than offset by the gains from the alternative production made possible. For reasons such as these, in some developing countries—notably India—all investment requires government licenses. The government has added to the veto of the market its own veto on all investment decisions.

It should be noted, however, that there is a cost. Unless the opportunity to spend income in satisfaction-giving ways is present, the incentive to obtain it is dulled. (This is a problem not merely of private enterprise economies; it exists in socialized economies as well.) Therefore it should not automatically be assumed that goods which will benefit only a high-income class are less advantageous than goods which benefit lower income classes. But the restrictions on private expenditures in every society, and the reweighting of the relative prices of various goods which the government accomplishes through tax and other measures, indicate the almost universal agreement that in many specific cases direct interference with the private market, in addition to measures which affect the distribution of income, increases the general welfare. For these and other reasons[1] in practice every government interferes with the operation of the market in many respects, by use of the various types of instruments mentioned earlier in this chapter, and individuals of every political persuasion approve one or another type of interference.

4. Efficient development planning also includes proposing measures to increase or reduce the prospective level of aggregate demand for goods and services if it promises to be too low or too high. As a basis for judgment concerning the matter, the planning process must include estimating how high the level of economic activity during, say, the coming year will be. Will total government employment and purchases from private industry plus private production for export or for sale to consumers plus private investment (*a*) be just enough to employ all of the country's workers and all of the productive capacity of its factories, shops, farms, and mines; (*b*) leave some unemployment and idle capacity (or some unemployment of labor even though there is no idle capacity); or (*c*) result in a demand for labor and goods greater than the country's total productive capacity can meet? Making such judgments requires that the planning officials, in addition to consider-

ing the total of proposed government expenditures, must also estimate how great private consumption, investment, and exports will be. Planning therefore involves acquiring a great deal of understanding of the processes of private production even though the government intends to influence its level not by any direct controls but only by fiscal and monetary measures.

If they judge that aggregate demand will be too low, the planning officials must decide by how much to increase government activity, by how much to stimulate an increase in private consumption or investment, and what fiscal and other devices to use for the latter purposes. In making these decisions the planning officials must make all the types of choices between government and private production and among various sorts of increase in private production discussed in paragraph 3 above. Similarly, in deciding how to decrease aggregate demand, if the total seems larger than the economy can meet, they must make the same complex set of decisions.

Shortages of three types may set limits on the production of an economic system: labor, productive capacity, and foreign exchange. If there is unemployment both of laborers and of productive capacity, and if sufficient foreign exchange is available to finance the imports needed for added production, a simple increase in demand through an increase in government expenditures or a decrease in taxes can result in full employment. If there is unemployment of labor even though the country's productive facilities are fully in use, labor-intensive projects—projects using little capital equipment but much labor—may be the only way of providing added employment in the short run. And even if both laborers and productive capacity are idle, if foreign exchange is scarce there may be difficulty in stimulating an increase in production. Planning officials must then ration imports in the way that will be the least possible obstacle to expanding production and in ways that will encourage a shift from the use of imported materials to domestic materials. Except in the most fortunate of countries a shortage of foreign exchange occurs when a development program increases the demand for imported machinery, equipment, and materials. The classical solution is devaluation of the currency, by which all imports become more expensive relative to domestically produced materials. If for reasons of national pride or for other reasons a country chooses not to devalue, the devices by which the government endeavors to capture all the foreign exchange earnings of its exporters and those by which it controls the use of the foreign exchange become important in its development planning.

5. One aspect of the choices among alternative uses of productive resources which planning officials must make is of such especial importance that it merits separate mention. This is the determination of the shares of the country's production to be devoted to investment (government plus private) and consumption (private consumption plus the current services of government) respectively. It is an oversimplification to state that the share of the nation's production devoted to investment determines the rate of economic growth. Other factors, notably the amount of effective innovational entrepreneurship and good business management manifested by private business managers and government officials alike, are equally important. Yet the decision concerning the rate of investment has the crucial importance of determing how great a flow of resources will be available to those public and private entrepreneurs. Involved are decisions between expanding the current services of government and its capital expenditures, between holding taxes low to permit relatively high private consumption and raising them deliberately to check consumption, simultaneously using the flow of tax revenues either to finance government investment or to extend a relatively large flow of credit to effective private entrepreneurs or both. The decision concerning the appropriate rate of investment will therefore be central in many planning operations.

THE PLANNING PROCESS

To make the best possible decision concerning each of the many interrelated factors involved in economic development planning may seem an impossibly complex process. So it is if one thinks of an ideal set of decisions which can be proven superior to any other possible set. However, such perfection is a fantasy. The goal of planning in the real world is to make as good a set of decisions as sensible men can make in view of the complexity of the problem and when they have developed an efficient procedure for considering the relevant factors.

Actually, when the process of planning is divided into a series of steps, it no longer seems impossibly complex, even though the magnitude of the task looms large.

THE NEED FOR PLANNING

The need for planning arises because labor and productive resources are scarce relative to the demands upon them. If there were enough productive capacity to provide everything desired, there would be no need for choice or planning. Goods and services and the labor and productive resources to produce them are scarce in any country, even the wealthiest. Hence in the technically most advanced countries, even for example in the United States, although the term *planning* is not usually applied to governmental processes the government must coordinate its actions and policies so that they will have the most advantageous impact on the nation's economic activity.

The political leaders of economically underdeveloped countries, however, are most apt to be acutely aware of the need to plan. Among the urgent purposes of an underdeveloped country is to increase its ability to produce, and its leaders are likely to feel intensely a need to take positive actions toward this end.[2] Moreover, quite apart from this intensity of feeling on the part of national leaders, there are two purely objective reasons why planning is especially important in newly developing countries. One such reason is that in a society where change in the past has been little and slow, where resources are scarce or have not been developed, and where an effort is now being made to obtain rapid change, the need for seeing that the various governmental measures fit together sensibly and have the desired impact on development is much more urgent than in a country whose institutions have long been adjusted to continuing change.

The other is that national unity may be weak in a newly developing country, and development plans may become an integrating force, drawing the people of the country toward national unity as they are drawn into the development effort. This effect is not likely to be achieved, however, merely by the preparation of a blueprint for development by a group of national planners; it requires a sense that the desires and purposes of individuals and of localities and regions are being recognized and given their place in a national program.

The machinery of government inherited from colonial administration is not fully adapted to planning and executing measures for development. (This is true even if the colonial power sincerely desired to develop the region, and much more surely if it did not.) Neither is the machinery inherited from a traditional independent government which was not interested in development. Therefore, when a new government interested in development appears

in any country, some changes must be made. What adjustments are necessary and advantageous for the purposes of economic development? This is a question to which this volume seeks answers.

SOME TERMINOLOGY

Two bits of terminological information will be useful to the reader as he turns to the case studies. One relates to the length of period a development plan covers. Plans are classed as long-range, medium-term, or annual plans, depending on whether they look ahead for ten years or more, for a period of at least two years but less than ten, or for a single year. The only long-range or "perspective" plan discussed, that of India, is for fifteen years. While it purports to establish a framework within which the shorter term plans may be fitted, it has not in fact been important in Indian planning. Medium-term plans are typically for no more than five years. By way of exception, Burma's and Iran's multiyear programs encompassed longer periods, and the Nigerian program, initially planned for five years, was extended to six. Annual plans are necessary if developmental expenditures form part of the governmental budget, since one year is the budget period. Each of the countries discussed except Japan, where formal planning has little relationship to action, and Iran, where development expenditures have their own source of finance, has its annual plan.

The other matter of terminology useful to keep in mind relates to the distinction between a plan, a program, and a project. In accordance with common usage, in this volume the word "project" will be used to refer to the smallest unit of development activity—a single school, a factory, a road between two towns. A "program" is a set of related projects—for example, a school building program or a program of community development. The term "plan" is sometimes used to refer to an aggregate larger than a program but smaller than the entire national scheme for development. Thus the improvement of education may be termed a plan.[3] However, "plan" is also commonly used to refer to the entire complex of development activity contemplated for a year or a multiyear period, and "program" is often used interchangeably with plan in this sense, or alternatively to refer to the governments, share in the plan. If the distinction between project and program is kept in mind, the various uses of program and plan will rarely be confusing.

NOTES

1 An added justification for government interference with the private market is that some types of production injure individuals not associated with it, in ways for which they cannot obtain compensation from the producer. Examples are the erosion of farm land on the plains which may result if the timber is stripped from the mountainside above, or the dumping of industrial refuse in a river which may interfere with its use by persons living downstream. In such cases only government regulation can prevent public injury from activity in which the profit motive would lead a private producer to engage. There are many such cases. To maximize the public welfare, the government must forbid or limit the production or penalize the producer by an amount sufficient to compensate the injured parties, leaving it for the producer to decide whether in this case the activity is profitable.

An injury caused by someone else's productive activity for which compensation cannot be obtained on the market is termed an *external diseconomy*. The opposite case, that of an *external economy*, is that in which the production benefits individuals in addition to those who buy the products, so that the public may benefit even though a private producer cannot profitably engage in the activity. An example is education. Literacy benefits not only the boy who obtains it but also many other persons with whom he deals throughout his life. In such cases the optimum solution often is for the government itself to provide the activity since a private producer cannot afford to furnish as much as is in the public interest.

2 Almost every country which seeks to develop will be able to obtain aid for this purpose from the economically advanced countries either directly or through international agencies. Such aid, however, will never be enough for the purpose; most of the resources which are to be devoted to the development program must be provided from within the country itself. Moreover, even if an unlimited amount of external aid were available, most of the necessary programs could be carried out only with the use of materials and skills available only in the country itself. Hence if economic growth is to be attained, a significant fraction of the country's own productive resources must be allocated to this purpose.

3 For these uses of the three terms, see, for example, United Nations, *Programming Technique for Economic Development* (Bangkok, 1960), p. 33.

Growth and Anti-Growth
J. R. Hicks

We are living in an age of growth. The Growth Rate of the GNP is now no private concern of economists; it is the

J. R. Hicks, "Growth and Anti-Growth," *Oxford Economic Papers*, 18 (November 1966), pp. 257–269 Reprinted by permission of the Clarendon Press, Oxford.

business of Ministers of State to foster it; political parties hurl it at one another. Economists, indeed, have a particular responsibility for it, for it was from their theories that the idea was derived, and it is by their calculations that it is measured. They have launched it into public discussion; their continuing concern with it is apparent from the writings that appear, almost every month, in almost every economic journal in the world.

I have myself made some contributions to that literature; but it is not my intention, in this paper, to go on with what I have been doing in that direction, or to put in another way what I have already said in my latest book. What I want to do is to stand back a bit; to try to see this growth-mindedness, and its consequences, in some perspective.

It is not by any means necessary that economics should be growth-minded. I can indeed myself remember a time when it was not growth-minded at all. I remember listening to a course on Principles, that was given as LSE in 1926–1927 by Hugh Dalton. He began by setting up objectives (derived, of course, from Pigou). (1) The National Income should be as large as possible; (2) it should be divided as equally as possible; (3) the efforts and sacrifices needed to produce it should be as small as possible; (4) they should be divided as equally as possible; (5) it should fluctuate over time as little as possible. And that was all. Nothing about it having a high growth rate! And when we (myself and my contemporaries) began to get our teeth into this sort of thing, it wasn't the omission of growth on to which we picked. We got excited, for instance, about inter-personal comparisons (and perhaps it may be allowed that when we were asked to contemplate an "equal" division of efforts and sacrifices we had some justification); but it was not until much later that what now looks like that glaring omission of growth forced itself upon our attention. We were quite happy to be *static* in most of our economics; even when we turned to the "Trade Cycle" (as we were forced to do, by events, after 1929) our concern was for *stability*. Even the problem of the Cycle seemed, for quite a while, to be just a matter of keeping the *price-level steady*.

How economists have passed from that state of mind into the very different atmosphere which is revealed by their current writings is an interesting question; I shall have something to say about it before I have done. But for the moment I want to go further back. The "static" state of mind, which I have been describing, was not original to economics. It was itself the product of an evolution. We are, I think, helped to get the perspective which I am trying to attain if we consider a little how it came in.

First of all, when did it come in? There can be little doubt that it is characteristic of what is generally called "neo-classical" economics, the economics that was taught in Britain and in America, in Austria, in Sweden, and at Lausanne, between (say) 1870 and 1930. One must not (of course) exaggerate. There are two chapters on "Economic Progress" at the end of Marshall's *Principles*; but they are really rather perfunctory. There is a chapter on Accumulation of Capital at the end of Wicksell's *Lectures*, but it is just tacked on at the end of his important work. They are there but the spotlight is not on them. And in Walras, Pareto, and the Austrians there is even less.

When we go further back, to the "classical" economists proper, there is a great change. The modern growth theorist does find stuff that interests him in Adam Smith and in Ricardo, such as he does not find in Marshall and Marshall's contemporaries. It is fair to say that classical economics is actually, from one aspect, an Old Growth Economics, which has something of the same relation to modern Growth Economics as Greek geometry to modern mathematics. In the neo-classical epoch, it was just put to bed. Why was it put to bed? What happened to it? Could it happen (for the awful thought can hardly be suppressed) that modern Growth Economics might get put to bed in much the same way?

Why were the classical economists

interested in growth? To a thoroughly growth-minded person that may seem to be a stupid question, but in the light of what I have been saying it is clearly a question that we ought to ask. For if the classical economists were interested in growth, and their successors (as we have seen) were much less interested, there must have been some reason for the former interest which in the latter period had disappeared, or seemed to have disappeared. A general interest in growth, just because it is a good thing (if it is), could not play box and cox like that. So we ought to ask why the classical economists were interested; when we have found the answer it may help us to deal with the other question: why has the interest come back again?

If we ask Adam Smith why he cares about growth, he will tell us:

It is in the progressive state, while the society is advancing to the further acquisition, rather than when it has acquired its full complement of riches, that the condition of the labouring poor, of the great body of the people, seems to be the happiest and the most comfortable. It is hard in the stationary, and miserable in the declining state. The progressive state is in reality the cheerful and the hearty state to all the different orders of society. The stationary is dull; the declining melancholy.[1]

The picture that he has in mind, put rather formally, is like this. There is a "natural" or normal level of wages which works very like the normal price of a commodity. If the actual wage is higher than the normal wage, the supply of labour will be tending to increase; if it is lower, the supply of labour will be tending to diminish. But it takes a long time for supply to adjust to demand, so that a condition in which the wage is above the normal level can go on for a long time. In the "progressive state" the demand for labour is increasing, and in view of the lag this means that wages are, and can for

quite a long time remain, above normal. This, he thinks (and we may agree with him in thinking it), is a nice state of affairs. As for the other "orders of society," I suppose he would say that profits must also be in some sense *above normal*, or the supply of capital would not be increasing, as it must be if the economy is to be progressive. But there are snags about that, as further discussion was to show.

You will notice that in Adam Smith's progressive economy, the supply of labour is increasing. This is tiresome, in that the increasing supply is a threat to the surplus of wages above normal, otherwise, however, it is not important. For Smith is writing before Malthus; the size of population is not, in his model, a thing he cares about. His stationary state ("dull" as it may be) can arise at *any* level of population. He would have been quite at home with a Growth Equilibrium, such as is the delight of our optimistic contemporaries, in which growth is unimpeded by the fixity of any factor of production.

Before Ricardo wrote, Malthus had exploded his bombshell; so the level of population is no longer a matter of indifference to him, as it could be for Smith. But though Ricardo's theory incorporates this Malthusian element (so that it has been labelled "pessimistic" in contrast with Smith's "optimism"); and though it is so much more subtle theoretically than the Smith version; nevertheless I believe that on this question of the attitude towards Growth they are quite close together. With one qualification, which I shall mention in a moment, Ricardo could have subscribed to the whole of that passage from the *Wealth of Nations* that I quoted. For him also it was the progressive which was the "cheerful and hearty" state: the state which it should be the object of policy to keep going, as long as that could be done at all.

The difference between them is simply that Ricardo had a clear idea of a mechanism by which the progressive state was liable to move into stationariness, a point on which Smith had been rather vague. That there was some such "equilibrating" tendency, Smith must certainly have also held; even for him, there must have been a sense in which increasing population would, in some long run, cause wages to revert to an "equilibrium" level. But why should it do so? He had nothing but vague phrases about society having attained its "full complement of riches." But what does that mean? He did not explain.

Ricardo did explain—or thought he had explained. What was missing in Smith was the Law of Diminishing Returns. Land is a fixed factor; if labour goes on increasing, even if capital is increasing with it, the marginal product of the variable factors must diminish—in whatever proportion they are combined. Wages cannot be reduced below their "normal level" without bringing the expansion to a halt; if one sets that constraint upon wages, diminishing returns means a falling rate of profit. There is some size of population, in any given technical conditions, at which the rate of profit will be reduced to *its* normal level. Once population has reached that figure, there can be no more accumulation and no more increase in population; though if Ricardo had heard of the Cobweb Theorem, he could have made our flesh creep by describing a cobweb path to equilibrium, through cycles of Pestilence and Famine.

But Ricardo is not being pessimistic; not (say) any more pessimistic than those contemporary writers who advise us of ways of putting off the Day of Judgment of the Atom Bomb. His Stationary State is not attractive; but it is a horror that can be put off, by wise policy, by taking good advice, into the almost indefinite future. By developing foreign trade, by the exploitation of the almost limitless resources of the extra-European world, the Ricardian apocalypse is indefinitely (or almost indefinitely) postponable. And what better incentive

to virtue than certainty—but indefinitely postponable certainty—of Hell Fire?

Ricardo is so fascinating that one can hardly stop oneself talking about him; but I must stop. For it is after Ricardo that the really interesting things, from my present point of view, begin to happen. Ricardo did not know about them, but he almost did. For the last thing he ever wrote, on the day when he was stricken down by his fatal illness, was a letter[2] in which he corrected an essay written by the seventeen-year-old son of his friend James Mill—John Stuart Mill.

It is John Mill who is the key character in my story; it is he who killed the old Growth Economics and paved the way for the Static Epoch which was to follow.

Though he is commonly regarded as the last representative, the final summing-up of classical economics, he was in some quite essential ways the creator of neo-classicism. (There are other ways in which that view can be defended, apart from that which concerns us here; but I must stick to my particular theme, on which I have quite enough to say.)

It was Mill's contention—and it is evident that the idea occurred to him very early—that this Smith–Ricardo doctrine, of the only decent existence being that of the progressive, growing, economy, in which capital and population were increasing more or less *pari passu*, was quite wrong. It was the increase in population that was the Devil; by birth control that could be exorcized. Mill, even in his early years, was a great believer in birth control; he became famous, or notorious, for his "neo-Malthusian" propaganda before he had written any of his books. As the poet put it:

There are two Mr. Mills, too, whom those who
    like reading
What's vastly unreadable, call very clever;
And whereas Mill senior makes war on good
    breeding
Mill junior makes war on all breeding
    whatever. [3]

Lots of people have propagandized for birth control; many have needed much courage to do so. Mill had that courage, but he had more. For he drew the logical consequence.

If population can once be controlled, there is no need for the economy to go on expanding, in order that wages should be above the subsistence level. Instead of land being *the* fixed factor, so that (as in the Ricardian stationary state) surplus production is swallowed up in rent, it is labour that becomes the fixed factor, so that surplus production can be made to go, at least in large measure, to wages. This is an altogether different, and far more agreeable, picture. The Stationary State is no longer a horror. It becomes an objective at which rational policy should be *aiming*.

So much could be said by Mill, simply as economic analyst; but Mill was much more than an economic analyst, and he did not stop there. The chase of capital after population revolted him, not simply for the Malthusian reason of its effects upon the food supply; there were other things too. Perhaps I may be allowed to read you a famous passage (I shall follow the text of the first—1848—edition of the *Principles*) since it is essential to my argument, and it may be better appreciated when it is set against the background against which I have been trying to set it.

I cannot (he says) regard the stationary state of capital and wealth with the unaffected aversion so generally manifested towards it by political economists of the old school. I am inclined to believe that it would be, on the whole, a very considerable improvement upon our present condition. I confess I am not charmed with the ideal of life held out by those who think that the normal state of human beings is that of struggling to get on; that the trampling, crushing, elbowing and treading on each other's heels, which form the existing type of social life, are the most desirable lot of human kind, or anything but the disagreeable symptoms of one of the phases of industrial progress. The northern and middle states of America are a specimen of this stage of civilization in very favourable circumstances; having, apparently, got rid of all social injustices and inequalities that affect persons of Caucasian race and of the male sex, while the proportion of population to capital and land is such as to ensure abundance to every able-bodied member of the community who does not forfeit it by misconduct. They have the six points of Chartism, and they have no poverty; and all that these advantages seem to have done for them is that the life of the whole of one sex is devoted to dollar-hunting, and of the other to breeding dollar-hunters. This is not a kind of social perfection which philanthropists to come will feel any very eager desire to assist in realising.[4]

Mill, of course, did not confine these views of his to such rhetorical passages; they influenced the whole structure of his work. What were later to be regarded as "equilibrium positions" became more important for him; the "path to equilibrium" became less important. The designing of the objectives at which one was aming moved into the centre of attention. It was not so important to be in a hurry to attain those objectives; it might indeed be a bad thing to be in too much of a hurry. The objectives that he had in mind were essentially static; he would have hated to set up as an objective the maximizing of a growth rate.

It is not easy to trace the direct influence of these views of Mill's on the next generation; but that they did have a great influence, even if it was an indirect, or unconscious, influence seems to me hardly doubtful. After all, we do know that Mill's book was read very widely. From 1848, at least until 1890, it was the book from which people in Britain learned their economics; and it was widely read (much more widely than Marshall ever was) in other countries too. There was much that must have been soaked up from Mill, even by people who did not realize from where they were getting it. There are several sorts of intellectual tendencies traceable in the next half-century (and longer) which become intelligible if they are interpreted in those terms.

I cannot attempt to follow this out in detail; I must confine myself to one aspect—the distributional side. A radical or a Socialist who had learned his economics from Mill, or from those who had learned from Mill (at however many removes) would naturally have been more concerned with the static problem, of the workability of a system with a more equal distribution of income *once it had been attained*, than with what he would have considered as mere incidents upon the path to his New Jerusalem. It was the objective itself, not the road to the objective, which became the centre of his interest. This holds, I think, for the professional economists, for Wicksell and Pigou, and for the Dalton to whom I was referring; less (indeed) for Marshall, who set a value upon striving as against attainment which had more to do with the Protestant Ethic than with his economics. But it certainly also holds for those who were concerned with distributive economics less professionally; for the Fabians (who took their name from *not* being in a hurry) and for the other saints and prophets of the British Labour Movement. It was the division of the cake (as Ramsay MacDonald[5] put it), not the increase in its size, which was their concern. They, like the contemporary economists, belonged to the Static Epoch.

But what (you will be asking) about Marx? I am no Marxologist. I can only conjecture how he fits in. I think that Schumpeter was right when he said that Marx was the last of the Classical Economists: that is to say, from my present viewpoint, he was the last representative of the Old Growth School. His general picture of the slowing-up of the progressive economy he took from Ricardo; but since he refused to accept Malthus, he had to find another route by which growth was "inevitably" to pass into stationariness, or Capitalism into Full Communism (to

use his terms). Whether or not the "concentration mechanism" which he invented for this purpose, will perform the function that he allotted to it, is not a thing which it is necessary for me here to discuss; for the relevance of Marx to my present topic (and I agree that he has a relevance) seems to me to be different. The interesting thing about Marx is his perception that the passage from the one state to the other (whatever they may be called) must imply some deep structural changes: changes not only economic, but social and political as well. When he tried to describe those changes, he fell (as was natural enough, considering his background) into crude revolutionism. But he had posed a problem which—in some form or other—has to be faced.

II

All I have said so far, lengthy as it has been, is no more than preface to my main inquiry, which concerns a more modern age. But without this preface, I could not expect you to see what my question is. When one is living in the world of the New Growth Economics, it is hard not to take it for granted. In order not to take it for granted, one must contemplate the world as it was without it. Only then can one stand back enough to ask oneself how it has come about.

I can distinguish several reasons for it, some good, some not so good. They are quite separate, and it will be well to keep them separate.

There is one with which it will be convenient to begin, since it ties on with what I have just been saying about Marx.

The Russian Revolution was an uncomfortable accident for Marxism, since it took place in a country which on Marxist principles was far from ready for it. Russia had not passed through the "last stage of capitalism"; the political revolution had occurred (for political, not for economic reasons) but the economic revolution was not ready; it had to be delayed. Thus Communism, in power, was obliged to stimulate capitalism: to take to itself the striving, the "pushing and elbowing," which in opposition it had abhorred. "Accumulate! Accumulate!": the maxim that Marx had associated with capitalism, became the maxim of those who claimed to be his followers. Maybe that was only a phase; perhaps it is only now, fifty years later, that Russia is ready for Consumer Sovereignty, or for what they might call, in their language, a Dictatorship of the Proletariat.

I have been putting the point in Marxist, or quasi-Marxist, language; but I would not deny that there was something which lay behind, and which is equally expressible in other ways. One of the reasons which have led to the rise of the New Growth Economics was the discovery (made in Russia, but also made in many other countries as well as in Russia) that the gains that could be got by mere redistribution were disappointing. The rich may have (or may have had) a large proportion of the National Income, as statisticians measure it; but much of that "income" will vanish when it is taken from them, and even if it did not, it would not go far when spread among the relatively poor, just because there are so many of the latter. It was only (to speak of this country) when statisticians got down to National Income calculations (Bowley, 1911) that the point could be realized; even then, of course, it took time to sink in. When it did, it became apparent that the raising of real wages—the effective raising of real wages—could not be accomplished, to any great extent, by redistribution. Granted that the State was doing what it could to redistribute, it was to Labour's interest that production should increase as fast as possible; so Labour, in a sense, became a convert to Growth.

I say "in a sense" for there are compli-

cations. Not even a Socialist economy can avoid the choice between consumption and investment: between consumption now and consumption in the future, or what may lead to consumption in the future. Under capitalism, this opposition in entwined with the opposition between capital and labour; under Socialism, and under the Quasi-Socialism which is the typical economic form of the twentieth century in so-called non-Communist countries, the same opposition reappears, in another form. Not everyone would make the choice between present and future satisfactions similarly; but under Socialism, and under Quasi-Socialism, it has to be made centrally, by those who rule, for those who are ruled. It can hardly be doubted that those who rule (by whatever right they rule) tend to have a bias in this matter; merely because they have to concern themselves with their chances of maintaining themselves as rulers *in the future*, they tend to have a bias towards the investment side. Their interest tends to be growth-oriented; more growth-oriented than the average interest of those whom they rule. To overcome the opposition which they thus engender, they have, in the first place, the power of propaganda. To set an extra value upon growth, through the power of propaganda; to set up a tide of opinion, against which those with a relative preference for present consumption have to pull; these belong to the secrets of government—the *arcana imperii*—of the Socialist State. They are exploited under Socialism and under Quasi-Socialism; but under Quasi-Socialism, where the means of resistance are stronger, they need reinforcement. Resistance can still be overcome, even when it is expressed (as it often is) in a strong Trade Union movement; or if not overcome directly, it can still be cheated—by Monetary Inflation.

That—all that—is just one of the reasons why economists are now concerned with Growth Economics; there are others also.

I have so far been thinking of a single

country, by itself; but it is of major importance that there is a corresponding pattern internationally. The statisticians have got to work on international income statistics, just as they did (a generation earlier) on the income statistics of some particular nations; the comparability of these statistics is still bad, but they have revealed the inequality between rich and poor nations, even making people think that we know more about it than we do. Consciousness of the inequality has grown, but a willingness to meet it by redistribution has not grown with it. This is partly for the same reason as applied internally, that the numbers of the poor are so vast; but there is a further complication, in that the poor have different governments from the rich, and they set a high value on their national independence. A world government, imbued with Socialist prinples, would be unacceptable to the richer countries, since for them it would be so impoverishing; but it would be unacceptable to the poorer countries also, since to them it could only appear as a reimposition of Colonialism in another guise.

There is therefore nothing for it, for the poorer countries, but to seek for their own "development," assisted by such crumbs of "Aid" as the richer countries are willing to spare, and as they themselves are willing to accept. They call themselves "developing" countries, but the only meaning that can be given to that courtesy title is that development is more important for them than it is for others. That is true, but it is not true that they have, or are likely to have (save in exceptional cases), any outstanding achievement in the way of development. How can they? Just because they are poorer, the sacrifice of present for future satisfactions is harder for them. It is not at all surprising that they find it so hard to force their growth rate. Growth-mindedness, in the richer countries, is (from this point of view) an enemy of the poorer countries; it causes the gap to widen, instead of narrowing, as

on the principles we profess it should be doing.

But at this point we encounter other issues. There is a further argument in favour of striving for a high rate of growth —in the richer countries—which I have not mentioned. This striving, it will be maintained, is necessary to these countries in order that they have a high level of activity (or employment); and high activity in the richer countries is favourable to the poorer countries, since it keeps up the demand for their products. It is accordingly maintained that if growth in the richer countries were damped down, though the gap between rich and poor would not be widened, it would not be narrowed. The poorer countries would in fact be absolutely worse off, since the rate of growth which they would attain would be even smaller than it is at present.

Some such argument as this is frequently implied in the case that is made for striving for a high rate of growth in the richer countries. But it is a nasty argument; we should look at it, and its implications, very closely before we accept it.

One must distinguish, in the first place, between GNP per head and total GNP. It is the gap between GNP per head in the rich countries and in the poor countries which is the international inequality; in order that is should be reduced the growth rate in GNP per head in the poorer countries must be the larger. This could happen, even if the growth rates of total GNP were the same, provided that the rate of increase of population were smaller in the poorer countries (instead of being, as it is, rather the other way round). The deduction, from this, that it is particularly important for the poorer countries to control their populations, is commonly drawn; and I have certainly no desire to question it. But I am not so sure that it should be looked at in this *comparative* manner. For if the thing is looked at in that way, it seems to follow that it does not matter if the rich countries allow their own populations to increase very freely; and that is a deduction which I think we should have learned from Mill to be very reluctant to accept.

Yet in terms of modern economics there is force in it; more force than Mill could have seen. It was, I remember, my own impression when I first read the *General Theory of Employment* (and I do not need to rely upon memory, for it is set down in black and white in the review of Keynes which I wrote for the *Economic Journal*) that Keynes had provided a strong argument for the desirability of increasing population, even within a single country, which the Old Growth School had left quite out of account. "We have to realize (I then wrote) that we can have too much, even of the economic virtues. It was indeed a happy age which could think the contrary; but the nineteenth century could only afford Ricardo (I meant the monetary system of which the principles were laid down by Ricardo) because it sinned so luxuriantly against Malthus."[6] It does appear from Keynes that increasing population—the expectation of increasing adult population—works to keep up the marginal efficiency of capital and so tends to prevent an economy from lapsing into unemployment stagnation. At the time when Keynes wrote (and when I was writing) the upward surge of population which had characterized the nineteenth century seemed to have spent itself; this, it was very commonly thought, was a factor making for the Depression then experienced.

Things look very different now; but the point which Keynes (and his interpreters) were making still has something in it—it has got to be worked in. And when the matter is looked at internationally, as we have been trying to do, there is another point that seems to tell in the same direction. If the GNP of the richer countries is rising, largely by increase of population, it is likely that their demands for primary products will be increasing more or less *pari passu*; but such increase is likely to

be less, or less reliable, if their "growth" is a growth in income per head, without increase of population. Thus in the former case there is more likely to be a movement of the terms of trade in favour of primary producers; many of those who benefit will be primary producers in the poorer countries; these will accordingly find it easier to develop; international inequality may accordingly be reduced.

These points are valid, but what do they imply? Both in relation to this last point, and to the Keynes point, we must be careful to look far enough ahead. Population is a long-run matter; when we are thinking about the effects of population movements it is the year 2000, not the year 1967, on which we should be fixing our eyes. It is inevitable, now, that we should regard the short-run as important, more important than it was treated as being by the economists of the Static Epoch. But we can still learn from them that it is important to consider where we are going; the Path to the objective is not the only thing that counts.

I would therefore like to conclude by asking you to consider two alternatives. It may well be that we shall do worse than either of these alternatives, for in both of them I shall make the optimistic assumption that population growth in the poorer countries (or in most of the poorer countries) can somehow be controlled. I must make that assumption, for if I cannot make it, the long-run prospect before the World (or at least before those countries) is very depressing indeed.

My two alternatives differ by what is assumed about population growth in the richer countries. In one of them I assume that the increase continues, in the richer countries, much as it tends to do at the present. There should then, in those countries, be a high Marginal Efficiency of Capital; there should thus be no difficulty in maintaining high employment; their demands for primary products should continue to expand. The terms of trade of the primary producers should thus be rather favourable; and they should have prospects of development financed by the profits which they get from their exports. It is nevertheless likely, on this alternative, that they will remain, for the most part, primary producers; for not much capital will be available for them, from the richer countries, whose savings will largely be absorbed in providing for their own increasing populations. This (call it alternative A) is one thing that might happen.

Under Alternative B, the populations of the richer countries do not expand, or do not expand appreciably. There will then be more danger of Keynesian stagnation; it will be harder to maintain a high level of employment; it will, at least, not come about, as in the other case, more or less automatically. The terms of trade will also be less favourable to primary producers. All these things make Alternative B look much less attractive. Yet the fact that there is a less urgent demand for savings in the richer countries means that there can be more to spare for the poorer countries; it should be possible for them to get capital on easier terms. And as for the terms of trade turning against primary producers, that matters to the poorer countries only so long as they are predominantly primary producers. Under Alternative B (remember that we are thinking of a long run) they should not remain as predominantly primary producers. Their chances of industrialization, with the easier capital that should be available to them, should be greater. That is how things should work out under Alternative B.

I fully admit that Alternative B is the harder to realize. Alternative A requires no substantial change in institutions; it would almost work itself. If Alternative B were to develop its potentialities, it would require to be organized. Without appropriate organization, savings would run to waste in inactivity, or be absorbed (I fear we must say) in national armaments or in

moon-shooting; but the organization that is required is not impossible to devise. Surely this is the direction in which we ought to be looking.

That, I am sure, is what Mill would have said. May I let him have the last word?

There is room in the world, no doubt, and even in old countries, for a great increase of population, supposing the arts of life to go on improving, and capital to increase. But even if innocuous, I confess I see little reason for desiring it. The density of population necessary to enable mankind to obtain, in the greatest degrees, all the advantages both of co-operation and of social intercourse, has, in all the more populous countries, been attained. A population may be too crowded, though all be amply supplied with food and raiment. It is not good for man to be kept perforce at all times in the presence of his species. A world from which solitude is extirpated is a very poor ideal. Solitude, in the sense of being often alone, is essential to any depth of meditation or of character; and solitude in the presence of natural beauty and grandeur, is the cradle of thoughts and aspirations which are not only good for the individual, but which society could ill do without. Nor is there much satisfaction in contemplating the world with nothing left to the spontaneous activity of nature; with every rood of land brought into cultivation, which is capable of growing food for human beings; every flowery waste or natural pasture ploughed up, all quadrupeds or birds which are not domesticated for man's use exterminated as his rivals for food, every hedgerow or superfluous tree rooted out, and scarcely a place left where a wild shrub or flower could grow without being eradicated as a weed in the name of improved agriculture. If the earth must lose that great portion of its pleasantness which it owes to things that the unlimited increase of capital and population would extirpate from it, for the mere purpose of enabling it to support a larger, but not a better or happier population, I sincerely hope, for the sake of posterity, that they will be content to be stationary, long before necessity compels them to it.[7]

When Mill wrote that, there were no motor-cars.

NOTES

1 *Wealth of Nations*, Book I, ch. 8 (Cannon ed., vol. i, p. 83).

2 Ricardo, *Works* (ed. Sraffa), vol. 9, p. 385.

3 Thomas Moore, *Ode to the Goddess Ceres*. I cannot understand why Mr. Packe (*Life of Mill*, p. 58) has to be so haughty about the fun of this outstanding political poet.

4 *Principles of Political Economy*, Ashley ed., p. 748, Toronto ed., vol. 3, p. 753–754.

5 In his *The Socialist Movement* (Home University Library).

6 *Economic Journal*, 1936, p. 253.

7 *Principles*, Ashley ed., p. 750, Toronto ed., vol. 2, p. 756.

Economic Theory and Development Policy[*]
Hla Myint

Both economic theory and development economics are getting highly specialised nowadays. A specialist in a branch of economic theory cannot hope to keep up with the highly technical development in other branches of economic theory. Similarly, a specialist in a particular aspect of economic development or on a particular group of underdeveloped countries cannot hope to keep up with the vast outpouring of publications in other fields of development economics. The proliferation and sub-division of development economics is most dramatically shown by the many periodicals which devote themselves entirely to some particular aspect of the subject, such as development finance, development agriculture and so on.

But, it seems to me that precisely because of this trend towards specialisation, there is some need, in the universities at least, for a general practitioner to act as a middleman between different specialised fields of development economics and also between development economics and general economics. Such an economist

Hla Myint, "Economic Theory and Development Policy," *Economica*, 34, No. 134 (May 1967), pp. 117–130.

* The text of an inaugural lecture given at the London School of Economics on December 1, 1966.

should try to acquire a good working knowledge at least, of the broad economic dimensions and the basic features of the situation, in a wide range of underdeveloped countries. His aim should be to try to apply to existing economic theory in a more realistic and fruitful way to suit the varying conditions of the different types of underdeveloped country. An equally important part of his job would be to try to prevent serious misapplications of economic theory, whether of the orthodox type or the newer modern theories, to the underdeveloped countries.

This way of looking at a general development economist as a middleman between the tool-makers and the tool-users bring me face to face with the perennial controversy: how far are the existing tools of economic theory applicable to the underdeveloped countries? There are many distinguished economists[1] who would be impatient with my proposal to start from the existing theoretical framework and try to improve its applicability to the underdeveloped countries in the light of accumulating experience and factual knowledge. They would say that the existing "Western" economic theory is so intimately bound up with the special conditions, problems, and preconceptions of the industrially advanced countries that large portions of it have to be abandoned before we can come to grips with the problem of the underdeveloped countries.

These economists have advanced three main types of criticism against the existing economic theory.

First, they question the "realism" of trying to apply the standard models of theoretical analysis meant for the advanced countries to the different economic and institutional setting of the underdeveloped countries. I have no quarrel with this line of criticism. In fact I shall be giving illustrations of other types of lack of realism in applying economic theory to the underdeveloped countries which are not mentioned by the critics. But it seems to me that this is not an argument for abandoning existing economic theory but merely an argument for trying to improve its applicability.

Second, the critics question the "relevance" of the static neo-classical economics concerned with the problem of allocating given resources within an existing economic framework to the problem of promoting economic development in the underdeveloped countries, which is concerned with increasing the amount of available resources, improving techniques and generally with the introduction of a dynamic self-sustaining process of economic change, disrupting the existing framework. Here again I agree that we do not possess a satisfactory dynamic theory for studying development problems. In fact, I would go further and say that the recent developments in the theory of dynamic economics in terms of the growth models are not very relevant and are not meant to be relevant for the underdeveloped countries.[2] But I do not accept the conclusion which the critics have drawn, viz. that the static theory of efficient allocation of given resources is irrelevant for the underdeveloped countries. I shall come back to this point.

Third, the critics maintain that the orthodox economic theory is inextricably bound up with preconceptions and biases in favour of the orthodox economic policies of *laissez-faire*, free trade, and conservative fiscal and monetary policies. They believe that these orthodox economic policies are generally inimical to rapid economic growth, which can be promoted only by large-scale government economic planning, widespread protection, import controls, and deficit financing of development programmes, if sufficient external aid is not available. Thus they propose that large chunks of existing economic theory, particularly the orthodox neo-classical theory, should be abandoned to pave the way for the adoption of these new development policies.

There are two questions here. The first is the general question whether the new policies are always more effective than the orthodox policies in promoting economic development in the underdeveloped countries. The second is the more specific question whether there is an unbreakable ideological link between orthodox economic theory and orthodox economic policies so that if we wish to adopt the new development policies we must necessarily abandon much of the existing theory.

The underdeveloped countries vary widely among themselves and I, therefore, find it difficult to accept the general presumption that the new policies will always be better for their economic development whatever their particular individual situation. Later, I shall give some examples where the orthodox type of economic policies have in fact been more effective in promoting economic development than the new-style development policies. However, I have chosen as the subject of my lecture today, not the general debate on the rival merits of the orthodox and the new development policies but the relation between economic theory and development policy. I have done this partly because I feel that such a general debate without reference to a concrete situation generates more heat than light and partly also because it has been rapidly overtaken by events. Whether we like it or not, it is no longer an open question whether the underdeveloped countries should choose the orthodox or the new type of development policies. One after another, they have already made their choice in favour of the new policies which have now become a part of conventional economic wisdom. Accepting this as one of the facts of life, the more immediately relevant question seems to be the second question, viz. whether large parts of orthodox economic theory have now become obsolete because the underdeveloped countries wish to plan for rapid economic development.

I shall argue that this is not so; that on the contrary, the orthodox economic theory assumes a greater significance in the context of the new "progressive" development policies. I shall show that even if development planning is to be regarded as new and radical policy, the *theory* underlying development planning is, technically speaking, quite orthodox and conventional. Similarly, I shall show that the orthodox theory of international trade can be made to support more liberal and generous trade and aid policies towards the underdeveloped countries, if we choose to use it in this way. What I am saying is not new. It is merely a restatement of the familiar doctrine that economic theory is "ethically neutral" and can be made use of in the more efficient pursuit of the economic objectives to be chosen by the "value judgments" of the policy maker.

However, let us start from a closer look at the question of "realism" in applying existing economic theory to the underdeveloped countries. Some critics speak of "existing theory" as though it were contained in a modern textbook like Samuelson. Properly speaking, it should include the whole corpus of Western economic theory, offering a wide choice of theoretical models, ranging from those of the older economists writing at earlier stages of economic development to the highly complex and abstract models of contemporary economic theory. To my mind, a very important cause of lack of realism arises from the wrong choice of theoretical models to be applied to the underdeveloped countries. In much the same way as the governments of the underdeveloped countries succumb to the lure of the "steel mills" embodying the most advanced and capital-intensive type of Western technology, many development economists have succumbed to the lure of the intellectual "steel mills" represented by the latest and most sophisticated theoretical models. This is where I believe the greatest mischief has been done. This is why I have always maintained that a good development economist should also be something of an applied historian of economic thought.

If it is unrealistic to apply highly sophisticated theoretical models meant for the complex economic structures of the advanced countries to the simpler economic structures of the underdeveloped countries, has this been corrected by the new theories of development and underdevelopment which are specially meant for the underdeveloped countries? Looking at these new theories which became popular during the 1950s, such as the "vicious circle," the "take-off," or the "big push," it does not seem to me that these have stood up any better to the test of realism. The weakness of these new theories is that they try to apply to all the underdeveloped countries a composite model of *the* underdeveloped country incorporating in it certain special features of some one or other type of underdeveloped country. The "vicious circle" theory assumes poverty and stagnation caused by severe population pressure on resources; the "take-off" theory assumes the pre-existence of a fairly high level of development in the political, social and institutional framework; the "big push" theory assumes both and also an internal market large enough to support a domestic capital-goods sector. By the time we have incorporated all these special features into a composite model, the number of the underdeveloped countries to which this model might apply becomes severely limited to one or two countries such as India and possibly Pakistan.

The limitations of these new theories of development, particularly the "vicious circle" theory, can be illustrated by looking at the broad dimensions of the economic performance of the underdeveloped countries during the decade 1950–1960. During that decade, compared with the 4 per cent. average annual growth rates for the advanced Western countries, the gross domestic product of underdeveloped countries as a group has grown at the average annual rate of 4.4 per cent., giving them a growth in *per capita* incomes of a little over 2 per cent. per annum.[3] This may or may not be very much, but the really interesting thing is that some underdeveloped countries have been growing at a faster rate than the average, say between 5 and 6 per cent., while others have been barely able to keep up with their population increase. Thus instead of the earlier *simpliste* view according to which all underdeveloped countries are caught up in a vicious circle of stagnation and population pressure, we are led to the question why some underdeveloped countries grow faster or slower than others.

When we try to answer this question, we become greatly aware of the differences between the underdeveloped countries, in size, in the degree of population pressure on natural resources, in the conditions of world demand for their exports and in their general level of economic development and political stability. These differences by themselves will explain quite a lot of the differences in the growth rates among different underdeveloped countries. If in addition we want to say something about the influence of development poli-

cies, we shall have to choose a fairly uniform group of countries where the basic social and economic differences are small enough for us to isolate the effect of economic policy.

To illustrate, let me take the concrete example of the post-war economic development of Southeast Asia. This will also serve to illustrate the dangers of generalising about development policies, particularly the danger of assuming that the new "progressive "development policies will always promote faster economic growth than the orthodox economic policies.

The five countries I have chosen, Burma, Thailand, the Philippines, Indonesia, and Malaya, form a fairly homogeneous group. In contrast to India or China, they are not only much smaller but also do not suffer from any great pressure of population. They do not have to contend with food shortage and have much more elbow room in respect of natural resources to allow for the working of economic incentives. They are also similar in the general level of social and economic development and moreover have common exports such as rice, timber, and rubber. Yet the rapid postwar economic development of Thailand, the Philippines, and Malaya contrasts sharply with the economic stagnation of Burma and Indonesia. By 1960, both Thailand and the Philippines doubled their pre-war gross national product (in real terms) combined with a considerable growth in import-substituting industries, while the gross national product of Burma and Indonesia rose by a bare 11 per cent. above the pre-war level, much slower than their rate of population growth during the same period. Malaya, starting at a somewhat higher *per capita* level than the others, has also enjoyed economic prosperity which compares favourably not only with Burma and Indonesia but also with Ceylon to which her economic structure is similar in many aspects.

These large differences in the rates of economic growth are closely related to the rate of expansion in the exports of the two groups of countries and, since they have common exports sharing the same world market conditions, the differences in their export performance must be traced largely to the domestic economic policies which have affected the supply side of their exports. Here, broadly speaking, the first group of countries with the faster rates of economic growth, viz. Thailand, Malaya, and the Philippines, have pursued the more orthodox type of economic policies with a greater reliance on market forces, private enterprise, and an outward-looking attitude to foreign trade and enterprise; while Burma and Indonesia lean heavily on economic planning and large-scale state intervention in economic life combined with an inward-looking and even hostile attitude towards foreign trade and enterprise.

More specifically we may note the following. (i) Thailand and the Philippines have very successfully used market incentives to encourage their peasants to bring more land under cultivation and expand production both of export and domestic food crops, while the Burmese peasants have been depressed by the operation of the state agricultural marketing board which has used peasant agriculture simply as a milch cow for government investment in state enterprises in manufacturing industry and social overhead capital. (ii) Thailand and the Philippines have encouraged their domestic entrepreneurs to set up new manufacturing industries through protection and subsidies, while Burma and Indonesia have tried to do this by state enterprises which have failed, amongst other reasons, because of a shortage of entrepreneurial ability among the civil servants. Here it may be noted that all these Southeast Asian countries suffer from the fear of being dominated by the Chinese or the Indian entrepreneurs who are or were prominent in small or medium scale enterprises in light manufacturing indus-

tries. Thus one may say that Burma and Indonesia have chosen to substitute Indian and Chinese private enterprise by indigenous state enterprise while Thailand has absorbed the Chinese entrepreneurs into her own business class and the Philippines have successfully substituted Filipino private entrepreneurs for them. This problem has yet to be solved in Malaya. (iii) Malaya, Thailand, and the Philippines have offered a stable economic climate to Western enterprises both in the traditional plantation and mining sectors and in the new manufacturing sector and have benefited from a considerable inflow of private foreign capital, while Burma and Indonesia have discouraged fresh inflow of private investment by nationalization and other hostile policies. (iv) Malaya and Thailand have pursued conservative monetary and fiscal policies and their currencies have been strong and stable, and the Philippines tackled her balance-of-payments disequilibrium successfully by devaluation in 1962. In contrast Burma and Indonesia have tried to solve their balance-of-payment problems arising out of deficit financing and domestic inflation through an intensification of inefficient and hurtful import controls, which, combined with pervasive state interference at all levels of economic activity, have throttled most of the promising infant industries.[4]

It is not for me to judge the ultimate rightness or wrongness of the economic nationalism and the anti-Western attitude of Burma and Indonesia contrasted with the more pro-Western attitude of Malaya, Thailand, and the Philippines. But at the conventional level at which economists judge development policies, it seems to me that in the case of Southeast Asia at least that the orthodox type of economic policies have resulted in a more rapid rate of economic development during the post-war period than the newer "progressive" development policies. How far is the Southeast Asian experience applicable to other underdeveloped countries outside the region? I think that it may be of some relevance to the other smaller and less densely populated export economies, notably in West Africa. There, also, expansion in the exports of primary products still offers the most promising engine of economic development both as a source of foreign exchange earnings to finance the new import-substituting industries and, even more important, as the method of drawing the under-utilised natural resources of the subsistence sector into the money economy. But these conclusions in favour of the orthodox policies are likely to become weaker as we try to extend them to less similar types of country, particularly to large overpopulated countries like India. But conversely it would be equally unrealistic to try to apply the Indian model to the smaller export economies.

Let me now conclude my remarks on the "realism" of applying economic theory to the underdeveloped countries by drawing attention to the dangers of trying to be too different from the standard models of economic analysis. These arise from selecting the "queer cases" in the standard Western models of analysis and in taking it for granted that these exceptions to the standard case must automatically apply to the underdeveloped countries because they are so different from the advanced countries in social values and attitudes and institutional setting. Such for instance is the famous case of the "backward-sloping supply curve" of labour attributed to the underdeveloped countries by many writers, who nevertheless speak also of the "demonstration effect" and "the revolution of rising expectations." Such also is the belief that the people of the underdeveloped countries, being more communally minded, will take more easily to co-operative forms of economic organization, despite the fact that writers on the co-operative movement in the underdeveloped countries frequently complain about the lack of co-operative spirit and the excessive individualism of the people. Yet another example is the generalisation that the people of the underdeveloped countries naturally lack entrepreneurial ability, irrespective of the economic policies followed by their governments. Here, if one were to tell the politicians of the underdeveloped countries that their people are lazy, stupid, lacking in initiative and adaptability, one would be branded as an enemy: but if one were to rephrase these prejudices in another way and say that they lack entrepreneurial capacity, one would be welcomed for giving "scientific" support for economic planning. To take just one more example, there is the hoary belief that peasants in the underdeveloped countries do not respond to economic incentives, while agricultural economists have been accumulating abundant evidence to show that peasants do respond to price changes by switching from one crop to another or by bringing more land under cultivation. The real problem is how to introduce new methods of cultivation which will raise productivity: this is a difficult practical problem, but in principle it is little different from, say, the problem of introducing new methods to raise productivity in British industry.

This is where I think that a closer co-operation between economics and other branches of social studies is likely to prove most useful, both in getting rid of questionable sociological generalisations and also in tackling the more intractable problems of analysing social and economic change.

Let me now turn from the "realism" to the "relevance" of the existing economic theory to the underdeveloped countries. The problem of promoting rapid economic development in these countries may ultimately lie in the realm of social and economic dynamics of the sort we do not at present possess; and there is nothing in my argument to prevent anyone from launching into new dynamic theoretical approaches to the underdeveloped countries. But in the meantime it is dangerously easy to underestimate the significance to the underdeveloped countries of the orthodox static theory of the allocation of given resources. The affluent Western economies with their steady rates of increase in productivity may be able to take a tolerant attitude towards misallocation of resources. But the underdeveloped countries are simply too poor to put up with the preventable wasteful use of their given meagre economic resources. In particular, they can ill afford the well recognized distortions of their price system such as the excessively high levels of wages and low levels of interest rates in their manufacturing and public sectors compared with those in the agricultural sector, and the over-valuation of their currencies at the official rates of exchange. Having to bear the brunt of low earnings and high interest rates discourages the expansion of agricultural output both for export and for domestic consumption and this in turn slows down the overall rate of growth of the economy. Higher wages attract a large number of people from the countryside to the towns but only a small proportion of this influx can be absorbed because of the highly capital-intensive methods adopted in the modern import-substituting industries. This aggravates the problem of urban unemployment and the problem of shanty towns which increases the requirements for investment in housing and social welfare. The scarce supply of capital tends to be wastefully used both in the government prestige projects and in private industry because of the artificially low rates of interest. This is aggravated by the over-valuation of currencies and import controls in favour of capital goods which positively encourage the businessmen who are fortunate enough to obtain licences to buy the most expensive and capital-intensive type of machinery from abroad.

These then are some of the glaring sources of waste which can be reduced by a better allocation of resources. Now I should point out that just because the orthodox neo-classical theory is concerned with the efficient allocation of *given* resources, it does not mean that the theory becomes unimportant in the context of aid policies to increase the volume of resources available to the underdeveloped countries. On the contrary, a country which cannot use its already available resources efficiently is not likely to be able to "absorb" additional resources from aid programmes and use them efficiently. That is to say, a country's absorptive capacity for aid must to a large extent depend on its ability to avoid serious misallocation of resources. A similar conclusion can be drawn about an underdeveloped country's ability to make effective use of its opportunities for international trade. If we find that a country is not making effective use of its already available trading opportunities, because of domestic policies discouraging its export production or raising the costs in the export sector, then we should not expect it to benefit in a dramatic way from the new trading opportunities to be obtained through international negotiations.

This is a part of the reason why I have suggested that orthodox economic theory, instead of becoming obsolete, has assumed a greater significance in the context of the new "progressive" policies for promoting economic development in the underdeveloped countries. Let me illustrate this argument further by examples from development planning theory and from recent discussions about the appropriate trade and aid policies.

I think that a great deal of confusion would have been avoided by clearly distinguishing the *policy* of development planning and the economic *theory* which underlies development planning which is, as we shall see, only an appliction of the traditional theory of the optimum allocation of the *given* resources. This confusion was introduced during the 1950s when it was the fashion to try to make out the case for development planning mainly by attacking the orthodox equilibrium and optimum theory. At the macroeconomic level, there were theories of deficit financing trying to show how economic development might be accelerated by forced saving and inflation or by making use of "disguised unemployment" for capital formation. More generally, the theories of the "vicious circle," the "big push," or "unbalanced growth" tried to show, in their different ways, the desirability of breaking out of the static equilibrium framework by deliberately introducing imbalances and disequilibria which would start the chain-reaction of cumulative movement towards self-sustained economic growth. Ironically enough, when the underdeveloped countries came to accept the need for development planning and asked how this might be done efficiently, it turned out that the economic theory required for this purpose was basically nothing but the traditional equilibrium and optimum theory.

Thus according to the present day textbooks on development planning,[5] the first task of the planner is to test the feasibility of the plan at the macroeconomic level by making sure that the aggregate amount of resources required to carry out the plan does not exceed the aggregate amount of resources available. That is to say, deficit financing and inflation are to be avoided and this is to be checked at the sectoral level by seeing to it that the projected rate of expansion of the services sector does not exceed the possible rate of expansion in the output of commodities by a certain critical margin. The next task of the planner is to test the consistency of the plan at the sectoral and microeconomic level to make sure that the demand and supply for particular commodities and services are equated to each other and that there is an equilibrium relationship between different parts of the economy, not only within any given year, but also between one year and another during the whole of the plan period. Finally, if the plan is found to be both feasible and consistent, the task of the planner is to find out whether the plan adopted is an optimum plan in the sense that there is no alternative way of re-allocating the given resources more efficiently to satisfy the given objectives of the plan.

If this standard formulation of development planning is accepted, then there is no fundamental theoretical difference between those who aim to achieve the efficient allocation of the available resources through the market mechanism and those who aim to achieve it through the state mechanism. Both accept the optimum allocation of resources as their theoretical norm and their disagreements are about the *practical* means of fulfilling this norm. In any given situation, they will disagree how far planning should be "indicative" or "imperative," that is to say, how far the task of allocating resources should be left to the decentralised decision-making of the market or to the centralised decision-making of the state. But technically speaking they are using the same type of economic theory, viz. the extension of the orthodox neo-classical theory, in the pursuit of their different practical policies.

From a theoretical point of view the great divide is between those who believe on the one hand that economic development of the underdeveloped countries can be promoted in *an orderly manner* by a more efficient allocation of the available resources which is assumed to be steadily expanding between one period and another through good management of domestic savings and external aid, and those who believe, on the other hand, that only sudden disruptive and *disorderly* changes such as social revolutions and technical innovations can bring about economic development. Now this second revolutionary approach to economic development may well be the correct approach for some underdeveloped countries. But it is difficult to see how this can be incorporated into the planning approach. Development planning is by definition an orderly approach: on the other hand, genuinely far-reaching and disruptive social changes cannot be turned on and turned off in a predictable way and incorporated into the planning framework. Those who advocate the necessity of breaking out of the static equilibrium framework by deliberately introducing imbalances and tensions are in effect advocating at the same time the need to break out of the planning framework. Thus one may advocate social revolution now and planning later, but one may not advocate social revolution and planning at the same time without getting into serious contradictions. Further, it should be pointed out that the revolutionary approach to economic development is by no means the monopoly of the critics of the private enterprise system. The case for *laissez-faire* can be made, not on grounds of static allocative efficiency, but on the ground that it imparts a "dynamism" to the economy by stimulating enterprise, innovation, and savings. Schumpeter's picture of the disruption of the existing productive framework through a process of "creative destruction" by innovating private entrepreneurs is a well-known illustration of this type of revolutionary approach to economic development.

Let me conclude by illustrating how the orthodox theory of international trade may be used in support of more liberal or generous trade and aid policies towards the underdeveloped countries. There is still a considerable amount of prejudice against the export of primary products in the underdeveloped countries. To some extent this has been overlaid by the more pro-trade views which have gained ground since the United Nations Conference on Trade and Development. The views which are now accepted by most underdeveloped countries may be summarised as follows. (i) While the underdeveloped countries should be allowed to protect their domestic manufacturing industries in any way they think fit, they should have preferential treatment or freer access to the markets of the advanced countries for their exports of primary products, semi-processed products and fully-manufactured products. (ii) More aid should be given to supplement the trade concessions, but there should be less tying of aid to imports from the donor country and also less tying of aid to the specific projects chosen and managed by the donor country.

Now it is possible to find a variety of opinions among the orthodox-minded economists on the question of giving aid to the underdeveloped countries. There are some who are against aid-giving either because they fear that this would lead to a misallocation of the world capital resources or because of the various undesirable political and sociological side effects of aid. For instance, Professor Bauer has recently argued that the material benefits which an underdeveloped country might obtain from aid would be swamped by the deleterious sociological and political effects, such as the development of a beggar mentality and the growth of centralized power which would pauperise the aid-receiving country.[6] On the other hand, not all orthodox economists are against aid-giving. In this connection, I should mention the name of the late Professor Frederic Benham, who wrote what I consider to be the best book stating the case for aid-giving.[7] These individual views aside, the standard orthodox economic theory would say something like this on the subject: how much aid the rich countries should give the poor countries should be decided by "value judgements" based on moral and political considerations which are beyond the scope of economic analysis. But once it is agreed that a certain amount of aid, say 1 per cent. of the national income of the rich countries, should be given, economic analysis can be used to show how this given policy objective can be carried out in the most efficient way. By a familiar process of reasoning, orthodox theory would say that this could be most efficiently carried out by free trade for both the aid-givers and the aid-receivers. For the aid-givers, the more efficient allocation of their resources through free trade would enable them to spare the 1 per cent. of their income they are giving away with the least sacrifice. For the aid-receivers, free importation of goods at cheaper prices than could be produced at home would maximise the value of the aid they received. Further, if the aid resources are to be invested, the more efficient choice of investment opportunities under free trade would raise the returns from investment.

Thus from the point of view of orthodox trade theory the one-way free-trade plus aid for which the underdeveloped countries are asking is less efficient than two-way free trade plus the same amount of aid. This is likely to be so even when the need to protect the "infant industries" has been conceded.[8] But if the underdeveloped countries insist on adopting what it considers to be the less advantageous option, then the orthodox trade theory can still say something useful within this restricted framework: and what it has to say is in support of opening the markets of the advanced countries more freely to the products from the underdeveloped countries and in support of the untying of aid.

Take the rather protracted debate about "reciprocity," on the question whether the advanced countries should give trade concessions to the underdeveloped countries without getting back some *quid pro quo*. In support of one-way free trade the champions of the underdeveloped countries usually appeal to moral considerations such as not having the same rule for the lion and the lamb and the need for a double moral standard when dealing with unequal trading partners. The advanced countries, on the other hand, tend to argue that while they do not expect "reciprocity" from the underdeveloped countries, they would like other advanced countries to give similar concessions to the underdeveloped countries before they commit themselves. Professor Harry Johnson[9] has recently reminded us that these arguments, based on the mercantilistic view of trade, have entirely overlooked the point that according to the theory of comparative costs the gains from trade consist in having cheaper imports. By allowing free imports from the underdeveloped countries, the consumers in the advanced countries already would have gained from trade by being able to buy these imports more cheaply: thus there is no need to ask for a further *quid pro quo*.

Basing himself entirely on the orthodox trade theory, Professor Johnson has argued that the United States would gain by a unilateral removal of trade barriers to the products from the underdeveloped countries without waiting for other advanced countries to follow suit. Similarly, he has shown that the official figures for the United States aid to the underdeveloped countries would be very appreciably reduced if the goods and services given under tied aid, notably aid in the form of agricultural surpluses, were revalued at world market prices under free-trade conditions.

These seem to me to be very good illustrations of how orthodox trade theory can be used in support of more liberal trade and aid policies, if we choose to do so. What has given flexibility to the theory is the much-maligned postulate of the "ethical neutrality" of economic theory. The champions of the underdeveloped countries tend to look upon it with great suspicion as a sign of an underdeveloped social conscience on the part of those who adopt it. But I hope that I have shown it to be no more objectionable than the notion of a constrained maximum.

Finally, the question of how far aid should be tied to the specific projects to be chosen and managed by the donor country raises fundamental issues of how far we consider the underdeveloped countries to be competent to run their own affairs without a benevolent supervision from the advanced country. Here we come at last to the "presumptions" and "preconceptions" of the orthodox economists which conflict sharply with those of the planning-minded economists. One important presumption of the liberal orthodox economists which I believe in, is that the underdeveloped countries can best educate themselves for economic development by being allowed to make their own mistakes and learning from them, and that without this painful process of self-education and self-discipline they are not likely to acquire the degree of competence required for economic development. I think this runs contrary to the implicit or explicit philosophy of the present-day administrators of aid. They would like to make up for the underdeveloped countries' lack of "absorptive capacity" for aid by insisting upon tighter planning and supervision of their economic affairs by economic and technical experts from the advanced donor countries. Ultimately, then, we have two philosophies about aid-giving to the underdeveloped countries. The liberal orthodox view is to give an agreed amount of aid to the underdeveloped countries and then to leave it to them to use it freely in any way they think fit, to learn from their mistakes, and to take the consequences of their action. According to this view the advanced countries can only guarantee the amount of aid but not the rate of economic development of the underdeveloped countries which must to a large

extent depend on how they use the aid. One further implication of this view is that, since the underdeveloped countries differ so much in their circumstances and capacity to benefit from mistakes, it would be unrealistic to expect an equally fast rate of economic development for all the underdeveloped countries. The alternative view which pervades thinking at present is that the advanced countries should take the responsibility of guaranteeing a politically-acceptable target rate of economic growth for all underdeveloped countries and, if this cannot be achieved by the latter countries' own efforts, the advanced countries should be prepared not only to increase the total volume of aid but also to increase the planning and supervision of the use of this aid so that the peoples of underdeveloped countries may enjoy economic development in spite of themselves.[10] Obviously the underdeveloped countries cannot insist on freedom to use aid in any way they like and at the same time insist that the advanced countries guarantee a minimum target rate of economic growth for them all. Ultimately they will have to choose the one or the other. I, with my orthodox liberal inclinations, hope that they will choose the former.

NOTES

1 For example, G. Myrdal, *Economic Theory and Underdeveloped Regions*, 1957; also his *An International Economy*, 1956; D. Seers, "The Limitations of the Special Case," *Bulletin of the Oxford Institute of Economics and Statistics*, May 1963.

2 Cf. Sir John Hicks, *Capital and Growth*, Oxford, 1965, p. 1.

3 United Nations, *World Economic Survey*, 1963, Part I, p. 20.

4 For a fuller treatment, see my article, "The Inward and the Outward Looking Countries of Southeast Asia and the Economic Future of the Region," Symposium Series II, *Japan's Future in Southeast Asia*, Kyoto University, 1966.

5 See, particularly, W. A. Lewis, *Develop-*

ment Planning, 1966; A. Waterson, *Development Planning: Lessons of Experience*, Oxford, 1966; and W. B. Reddaway, *The Development of the Indian Economy*, 1962.

6 *Two Views on Aid to the Developing Countries*, by Barbara Ward and P. T. Bauer, Institute of Economic Affairs, Occasional Paper 9, 1966.

7 F. Benham, *Economic Aid to Underdeveloped Countries*, 1961.

8 For one thing, the import controls practised by the underdeveloped countries are too indiscriminate and bound up with short-run balance-of-payments considerations to give selective protection to the promising infant industries; for another, the correction of the distortions due to the imperfections of the domestic market may require other forms of government intervention than protection. See my paper (ch. 9) in R. Harrod and D. C. Hague (eds.), *International Trade Theory in a Developing World*, 1963; and H. G. Johnson, "Optimum Trade Intervention in the Presence of Domestic Distortions," in *Trade, Growth and the Balance of Payments*, Economic Essays in Honor of Gottfried Haberler, Amsterdam, 1965.

9 H. G. Johnson, *U.S. Economic Policy Towards the Less Developed Countries*, Washington, D.C., 1967.

10 For example, contrast I. M. D. Little and J. M. Clifford, *International Aid*, 1965, p. 192, with H. G. Johnson, *op. cit.*, ch. 4.

Summaries

Stephen Enke, "Economists and Development: Rediscovering Old Truths," *Journal of Economic Literature*, 7 (December 1969), pp. 1125–1139.

In this very interesting article, Stephen Enke, who has earned a reputation as a development economist, discusses the relevance of some of the old development theories to modern development problems. He begins by emphasizing the point that theoretical contributions in this area have at best been limited and reiterates his belief that less developed countries must strive for total agrarian revolution if their planning efforts are to succeed to any degree. He goes on to say that these countries can never experience sustained economic growth to any extent unless they first succeed in greatly lowering their birth rates and also accept the fact that many of their traditions and institutions will change radically as a result of this technological progress.

Enke concludes his article with the following remark about rediscovering old truths: "Economists who practice development are also reverting to a much earlier role, becoming more concerned with alleviating poverty, the quantity and quality of population, and the incidence of local institutions and cultures. Many old truths are being rediscovered. Altogether the 'Decade of Development' has been a sobering ten years."

Sid Mittra, "The Simulatrics of a Developing Economy: Some General Considerations," in *Simulatrics and Development Planning* (Bangkok: U.N. Asian Institute for Economic Development and Planning, 1969), pp. 14–28.

In this monograph, which is based on the seminars conducted at the United Nations in 1965, Mittra critically discusses the present and future roles of simulatrics in modern economic theory. He defines simulatrics as the act of simulating a real-world situation by using the computer and applying the technique of econometrics.

There are two distinct advantages in using simulatrics as a planning technique. One of these results from the speed and accuracy with which modern computers can perform myriad calculations. The other advantage results from the fact that computers print out a step-by-step operation of numerical values of important variables, starting from a given set of initial conditions and working through a set of constraints imposed upon a computerized model.

Mittra explains in his paper the operational aspects of simulatrics and outlines the goals of a "good" simulatrics model. He also points out the distinct advantages of such a model. Mittra concludes with a discussion of the major contributions that can be made by simulatrics. This technique is making it possible for simulatricians to simulate national economies and to improve data collection and analysis pertaining to these economies.

Alexander K. Cairncross, *The Short Term and the Long in Economic Planning* (Washington, D.C.: Economic Development Institute, 1966), 30 pp.

In this lecture delivered at the Economic Development Institute in 1966, Cairncross is concerned with "What limitations on long-term planning does the need to make short-term adjustments impose? And conversely what limitations on short-term policy are necessary in order to take account of long-term trends and plans? What administrative machinery is calculated to secure the right balance between long-term and short-term considerations? What division of responsibility between departments is desirable in order to marry short-term and long-term planning effectively?"

In his treatment of the subject of economic planning, the author never loses sight of the fact that his objective is to enlighten the students interested in planning and development. Cairncross, therefore, discusses such complicated ideas as conflicts of aims in the short and the long term, the preservation of equilibrium, and the creation of new machinery for planning with great care. He concludes his lecture thus: "What seems to me unhealthy . . . is to think of economic co-ordination exclusively in long-run terms, and still more to think of it as satisfactorily discharged through the periodic preparation of a document called the Plan . . . Of course, long-run development is highly important. Economists to whom the long run is meat and drink (even if it is the death of them) are only too well aware of its importance. But to get to the long run you have to survive the short."

Bibliography

Irma Adelman *et al.*, "Economic Development. Instruments and Goals in Economic Development," *American Economic Review*, 59 (May 1969), pp. 409–426.

V. V. Bhatt, "Some Notes on Balanced and Unbalanced Growth," *Economic Journal*, 75 (March 1965), pp. 88–97.

Douglas F. Dowd, "Some Issues of Economic Development and of Development Economics," *Journal of Economic Issues*, I (September 1967), pp. 149–160.

Denis A. Goulet, "Ethical Issues in Development," *Review of Social Economy*, 26 (September 1968), pp. 97–117.

Nicholas Kaldor and James A. Mirrlees, "A New Model of Economic Growth," *Review of Economic Studies*, 29 (June 1962), pp. 174–192.

Robert I. Rhodes, "The Disguised Conservatism in Evolutionary Development Theory," *Science and Society*, 32 (Fall 1968), pp. 383–412.

T. W. Swan, "Economic Growth and Capital Accumulation," *The Economic Record*, 32 (November 1956), pp. 334–343.

14
ECONOMIC POLICY

Proponents of the free-market system contend that any deliberate attempt by policy makers to influence the free-market forces will create economic imbalances and distortions and retard economic growth in the long run. Many contemporary economists, however, do not believe that a free-market system is a viable one. They argue that all nations face certain economic problems and that the application of a judicious economic policy by their policy makers is essential if they are to solve—or even mitigate—these problems.

The first selection in this part is a survey by a group of professional economists of economic policy objectives and the tools which can be used to achieve these objectives. In the second article, Stahl comments on the art of economic forecasting. In the next article, Adams develops a framework for analyzing the interrelationship between inflation, unemployment, income, and economic policy. In the final selection, Spencer presents two different views on inflation versus the unemployment dilemma.

What Constitutes Economic Policy?
E. S. Kirschen *et al.*

A. ECONOMIC POLICY

By "policy" in this book we mean action taken by the Government in pursuit of certain aims. The aims of Government policy are sometimes summed up in a single phrase, such as "the general good of the country," or "the welfare of the population"; this general aim is made up of a multiplicity of rather more meaningful subsidiary aims—such as the aims of preserving law and order, of guarding the freedom of expression and choice, of re-

E. S. Kirschen *et al.*, "Definitions," in *Economic Policy in Our Time* (Chicago: Rand McNally and Co., 1964), pp. 3–18.

ducing social tensions, of defending the country from outside attack, of raising the population's standard of living, and of making adequate provision for health and education. We must also recognise that Governments in our countries were elected Governments, and that one of their aims was to keep the electors' support.

All these aims have, to a greater or lesser extent, an economic aspect. The standard of living is obviously an economic matter; but the other aims, too, usually require some kind of Government intervention in economic affairs. Preparations for defence or expenditure on health, for instance, require that resources are diverted from directly productive uses.

Economic policy, therefore, is the economic aspect of Government policy in general: it is the deliberate intervention of the Government in economic affairs in order to further its aims. In pursuit of these aims, Governments have tended to set for themselves certain specific objectives which can be stated in economic terms, and which in principle are capable of measurement (either ordinal or cardinal). The next section of this chapter gives a systematic presentation of these objectives. We do not in this book attempt a systematic classification of aims (since this would take us too far from the subject of economic policy). Consequently we do not discuss in detail which particular aims are served by which particular objectives.

In the first part of the book we treat the Government, by and large, as a single unit; it is the entity which has the right of coercion, whose duty it is to provide for collective needs, and which is held responsible for measures of economic policy. It comprises the Central Government (including the Central Bank) the local authorities,[1] and the social security agencies where these are State-organised.[2] We only discuss the relationships between these main constituents of Government when it is necessary for the understanding of particular instruments. In most countries there are other public bodies—such as nationalised industries—which sometimes act as agents for Government economic policies; insofar as they do this, the measures they take are included in this study. But insofar as they have their own economic policies, these policies are excluded, together with the policies which may be pursued by firms, interest groups or individuals.

In the second part of the book, we no longer treat the Government as a single unit; for we are concerned to disentangle the processes of decision, and to discover who the policy-makers were. In chapters VIII to X, therefore, we narrow down the definition of Government to the Ministers;

and we discuss separately the importance of Parliament, the political parties, the Administration (or civil service), interest groups, the Courts, and foreign or international influences.

There are some international organisations—for instance, the European Economic Community—which can have their own economic policy, and can in certain circumstances overrule the economic policy of a member Government. These supra-national economic organisations are treated in the same way as Governments, in part III.

To put its economic policies into effect, the Government either alters certain economic quantities (such as Bank rate or tax rates), or makes changes in the economic structure (such as nationalisation). These economic quantities which the Government can change, or these types of intervention in the economic structure, we call instruments. The Government's main policy problem is to select, from a wide range of instruments, the ones which will, in its opinion, most nearly achieve its objectives. The use of an instrument does not normally bring about changes in objectives directly: it operates on other economic quantities. For instance, a Government may have expansion of production as its objective. It may choose to increase private consumption, investment, or exports, and to effect these increases it can select from a large number of possible instruments—such as a guaranteed minimum wage or export subsidies. Section E of this chapter analyses and classifies the various types of instruments. Finally, the use of a particular instrument on a particular occasion we call a measure.

B. THE OBJECTIVES

The dividing-lines which this analysis of economic policy requires, between aims, objectives, instruments, and measures, are necessarily somewhat arbitrary—as are all such divisions between means and ends. In producing our classification of objectives, we tried to find the one which was most useful in showing up the important differences in the policies of our nine countries. The classification has been derived partly from the analysis of actual economic policy in these countries, and it takes into account the objectives which the various Governments themselves have stated from time to time. It also uses the various systematisations which have been prepared by other economists.

A short list of the objectives is given below, together with a short description of the components, where appropriate.

The list is followed by a discussion of the extent to which they can in fact be quantified (section C) and then by a longer discussion of each item (section D). To keep our analysis as near as possible to actual experience, we have tried to use in the list phrases which were in fact commonly employed to describe the objectives; this means that sometimes the objective is defined in terms of the state which it is hoped to reach (full employment), and sometimes in terms of the direction in which it is hoped to move (improvement in the balance of payments). A more formal definition of the objectives is given in the Appendix to this chapter.

OBJECTIVE	SHORT DESCRIPTION
Mainly Short-Term (Conjunctural)	
1. Full employment	This includes both the short-term objective of reducing cyclical unemployment and the long-term objective of reducing structural and frictional unemployment.
2. Price stability	This has also been mainly a short-term objective (though some countries by the end of the period were beginning to regard it more as a long-term problem).
3. Improvement in the balance of payments	This includes both the short-term need to protect the gold and foreign exchange reserves and long-term objectives, such as a structural change in the proportion of exports or imports in national expenditure.
Mainly Long-Term (Structural) Major	
4. Expansion of production	This is concerned with the long-term promotion of economic growth.
5. Improvement in the allocation of factors of production	This objective comprises (a) Promotion of internal competition (b) Promotion of coordination (c) Increase in the mobility of labour within countries (d) Increase in the mobility of capital within countries (e) Promotion of the international division of labour

OBJECTIVE	SHORT DESCRIPTION
6. Satisfaction of collective needs	Collective needs are grouped under the following heads: (a) General administration (b) Defence (c) International affairs (d) Education, culture, and science (e) Public health
7. Improvement in the distribution of income and wealth	This is concerned both with direct changes in the distribution of income (brought about, for instance, by taxation) and also with changes brought about indirectly—for example, by social security systems. It includes any deliberate changes in either direction towards or away from greater equality. It also includes the redistribution of wealth—by death duties, for example—as well as of income.
8. Protection and priorities to particular regions or industries	This includes both the protection given to a particular industry which may be threatened by home or foreign competition, and the industrial or regional priorities arising, for example, from a national plan.
Minor	
9. Improvement in the pattern of private consumption	This includes any changes which the Government wishes to bring about in the pattern of personal consumption. The Government may wish in some instances to prevent consumers from buying what they would like to buy (deterring them from buying alcohol, for example), and in other instances it may wish to make it easier for them to do so (by consumer advisory services, for instance).
10. Security of supply	This is concerned with the safe-guarding of essential supplies.
11. Improvement in the size or structure of the population	Government intervention in matters of emigration, immigration, or the birthrate is included here.
12. Reduction in working hours	This includes both the reduction of the working week and any increase in statutory holidays.

We kept the number of objectives as small as possible, subject to two conditions. First, it had to be possible to subsume all measures of economic policy under the heading of one or other of the various objectives. Secondly, if we found that very different sets of policies were aiming at one broad objective, then we subdivided the objective. For instance, we thought the promotion of competition should be kept separate from the promotion of coordination—although they can both be grouped together under the general objective of the improvement in the allocation of factors of production. They need to be kept separate because we want to know the relative importance of each in the economic policies of different countries.

The objectives are divided into two groups: mainly short-term and mainly long-term. This is because it is of interest to examine separately the various methods used in the different countries to counteract short-term cyclical fluctuations, and the methods used to pursue longer-term economic policies. However, all the short-term objectives have long-term aspects as well. For instance, the objective of maintaining full employment was most commonly a short-term cyclical problem; but Governments have also had long-term full employment objectives, of reducing structural unemployment, for example. The longer-term objectives are divided into major and minor ones. If, in the years we are surveying, most countries have had an objective and most countries considered it important, then we have classed it as a major objective—otherwise as a minor one.[3]

We have already referred to the danger (on page VI of the Introduction) that this systematisation may make Government policies appear to have been much more logical than in fact they were. Part II of this book goes into this question more fully; here, it is only relevant to say that our standard list of objectives could not possibly include all the various economic objectives which may have been in the mind of some particular Minister in one or other of the nine countries at some time. At various times some people have elevated to the rank of objectives such things as the balanced budget, the reduction of the national debt, or the preservation of a particular exchange rate. These and others

like them are discussed in the chapters on instruments which follow and in the country chapters; we consider them as constraints on the use of instruments.

The objectives are not, of course, independent of each other. Some are complementary—when the achievement of one helps the achievement of another; some conflict. We discuss these interrelationships to some extent in chapter IX (page 221)—though our discussion is limited; for a full analysis would require agreement on the results of particular policies, and this agreement we have not attempted to reach (page VII).

When the word improvement is used, this only implies that the change that was intended was an improvement in the judgement of the Government which took the measures, and nothing more. An improvement in income distribution, for example, is not necessarily a move towards greater equality. It could be the opposite.

C.   QUANTIFICATION OF OBJECTIVES

When Governments pursued these various objectives, how far did they have specific figures, or quantities, in mind? The answer varies according to the objectives.

For some of them, most Governments did have some figure or figures in mind, which acted as a kind of "norm" in their thinking about the objective. This "norm" was something accepted in a general kind of way, not only by the Government but usually also by the opposition parties and impartial observers. For instance, in the United Kingdom any Government would have been seriously worried if unemployment rose above 3 per cent, or if an annual rise in prices was much above 4–5 per cent; and to the extent that these figures were exceeded, it was generally agreed in the country that the Government had failed to achieve full employment and price stability.

Most Governments probably had some explicit norm of some kind in mind (which varied between countries, and within countries at different times) for six out of twelve objectives: for full employment, for price stability, for the improvement in the balance of payments, for the expansion of production, for the reduction in working hours, and also—to some extent at least—for the improvement of income and wealth; for many Governments had either a minimum wage or a minimum scale of national assistance, and this was the main part of their policy for the redistribution of incomes.

For the other objectives (and also in some countries for those just mentioned) there was generally speaking no "norm" in the sense that there was a generally agreed figure for the desirable range of values for that objective. In these cases, the measures actually taken can be considered as an indication of the quantification of objectives implicit in the minds of the policy-makers. For most of these objectives Governments did in fact come to some quantitative decisions about relative priorities—they decided, for instance, how much they were going to spend in fact on roads or hospitals; or perhaps they decided—in the field of improvement in the pattern of private consumption—how much they would like to increase milk consumption or to reduce alcohol consumption.

There are difficulties about this approach of inferring a quantification of the objectives from the measures actually taken—particularly for the objective of the improvement in the allocation of factors of production. We have attempted in the Appendix to give some indication of ways in which these quantifications might be made.

D. DESCRIPTION OF OBJECTIVES

1. Full Employment

Governments have been mainly concerned, under this heading, with the objective of preventing and reducing short-term cyclical unemployment, caused, for example, by a decline in exports or by the ending of an investment boom. But some have also had long-term policies which were specifically directed to reduce unemployment which is not cyclical: for instance, frictional unemployment—unemployment due to the delay in matching vacancies with the unemployed who are capable of filling them; or structural unemployment—for instance, unemployment due to the decline of a particular industry, or to the fact that industry is moving away from a particular region.

Because of the incidence of frictional unemployment, policies were not directed to the complete elimination of unemployment. Government objectives in the nine countries have varied. Some countries have a more comprehensive definition of unemployment than others, and so, with the same real unemployment, the published figures are different. Further, some countries have substantial problems of structural unemployment which they could not hope to eliminate in the short-term. Finally, Governments have varied in the relative importance they have given to the objective of removing cyclical unemployment and the conflicting objective of price stability.

Consequently the definition of full employment—the level at which further anti-cyclical action against unemployment is considered unnecessary—has varied considerably, and Governments have been content to take no further anti-cyclical action with unemployment percentages ranging from $1\frac{1}{2}$ to 5 per cent of the working population. Further, some Governments have tended to pay regard, not only to the unemployment figures by themselves, but also to the relationship between the unemployment and vacancy figures.

2. Price Stability

This objective is concerned with maintaining general stability of prices (usually measured by the retail prices index); it does not of course mean that every individual price should remain stable. Some economists have considered that stable wages and falling prices would be preferable to stable prices and rising wages. But no post-war Government has in fact had a more ambitious objective than price stability. None of the nine Governments considered here has in fact been successful in maintaining stable prices for a period longer than a few years[4]; and it is probably true to say that most Governments would consider that they had achieved "price stability" if they kept the average annual rise as low as 1–2 per cent a year. This is because they considered that this objective conflicted with other objectives, in particular with the expansion of production and with full employment, and Governments have usually tended to consider these other objectives as more important than complete price stability. Throughout most of our period, most Governments have tended to regard price stability as a short-term problem: the tendency to rising prices was something to be corrected by "conjunctural" policies. More recently, an increasing number of Governments have begun to regard this tendency as a long-term problem which may require structural or institutional changes in the economy.

3. Improvement in the Balance of Payments

Short-term balance of payments policies have usually had as their object the maintenance of a "satisfactory" stock of gold and foreign exchange: for it is normally a fall in these gold and foreign exchange reserves which has been the sign prompting the Government to rapid action.[5]

Most countries define their reserves as the Central Bank's holdings of gold and convertible currencies. In addition to gold, the two currencies which have in fact been used as reserve currencies in the post-war period have been the dollar and the pound sterling. Some countries included their credit with the European Payments Union in the period when the Union was functioning, and some did not.

The level which countries have regarded as satisfactory has varied considerably from country to country.[6] Clearly the position is different for countries such as the United States and the United Kingdom, which, because their currencies are reserve currencies, consequently had large short-term liabilities. Some countries have become accustomed to high levels of reserves in relation to imports and other countries to low levels. In some countries, also, the level of reserves considered desirable has varied, according to whether stocks of materials were high or low. But most Governments had some level in mind —a level which may have changed from time to time—below which they did not wish the reserves to fall. Further, many countries tended to take some action if the reserves were falling faster than a certain rate from whatever level.

Some countries have aimed to reduce the rate at which their reserves were rising— partly because they considered that their export surplus was becoming inflationary, and partly because other countries were protesting that their own reserves were being run down too fast.

Some countries, in addition to the short-term difficulties with their exchange reserves occasioned by the trade cycle, have also had a long-run need to improve the proportion of their output which is exported. In some countries there have been fairly precise long-term balance of payments objectives, such as a balance of payments surplus of a certain size, either on current account alone or on current and long-term capital account together.

There have been other long-term balance of payments problems as well—such as the problem of changing the regional pattern of exports, for instance by increasing the proportion going to dollar markets. These long-term objectives have needed rather different instruments from the short-run objective of stopping the fall in the exchange reserves. For instance, new institutions have been established, such as institutions to guarantee export credit, and import saving industries have been encouraged.

4. Expansion of Production

This is an objective which has been increasing in importance in recent years. It can be defined as a satisfactory rate of growth in the real national product, either absolutely or per head of the population.

Some countries have set themselves specific target rates; this has become increasingly the fashion in recent years. Further, some international bodies have set targets for groups of countries; the Organisation of European Economic Co-operation, for instance, in 1952 set a target for member European countries of a 25 per cent increase in real national product over five years (1951–1956) and its successor body, the Organisation for Economic Cooperation and Development, set a target of 50 per cent over ten years (1960–1970).[7]

To attain this general objective, Governments have tried a number of different policies. They have considered it important to maintain and raise the proportion of national resources which goes into productive investment. They have also taken steps to encourage technical progress, in particular by increasing the facilities for technical education and also by subsidising industrial research. Some have, on occasions, aimed to raise the proportion of the population engaged in productive work—for instance, by directing expansion towards areas with high unemployment, or by encouraging workers to immigrate

from other countries. Some have experimented with various forms of central planning.

5. Improvement in the Allocation of Factors of Production

This includes a number of policies which can, from the economist's point of view, logically be grouped together, but are here separated out so that separate comparisons can be made. For all five sub-divisions, precise quantification is difficult.

(a) PROMOTION OF INTERNAL COMPETITION. The Government is here concerned to promote competition between individual firms or entrepreneurs—frequently by legislation or other measures against monopolies or restrictive practices.

(b) PROMOTION OF COORDINATION. Here the Government is concerned to reduce the disorder and the waste of resources which competition, in certain circumstances, is alleged to create. For example, in many cities there are restrictions on the number of bus companies which can run buses through the streets, on the grounds that free competition would lead to traffic chaos. In the same way, local monopolies tend to be granted to gas, electricity, and water companies. One of the main instruments used to bring about coordination is nationalisation. Town and country planning can be considered as another example of Government coordination: so also is the redistribution of agricultural land.

(c) INCREASE IN THE MOBILITY OF LABOUR, WITHIN COUNTRIES. This is concerned with facilitating movement of labour from one job or one area to another. The mobility of labour can be increased by the institution or expansion of labour exchanges, for example, and by the provision of grants and other facilities to encourage labour to move from areas of heavy unemployment to areas were there are more employment opportunities.[8]

(d) INCREASE IN THE MOBILITY OF CAPITAL, WITHIN COUNTRIES. The mobility of capital can be increased, for example, by the improvement of the capital market, or by steps to enable capital to flow to small and medium-sized businesses.

(e) PROMOTION OF THE INTER-NATIONAL DIVISION OF LABOUR. Governments here are concerned to encourage and promote international specialisation. This includes the encouragement of the free movement of goods (by reducing trade barriers, for example) and of services ("invisible" transactions). It includes, too, moves towards the free movement of labour between countries—either employees or self-employed, and towards the free movement of short-term or long-term capital.

6. Satisfaction of Collective Needs

This objective concerns the steps taken by the Government to meet those needs of the population which they cannot or prefer not to satisfy themselves, individually, in the open market. This Government intervention has economic implications because it normally results in resources being diverted from one use to another. In some countries more needs are classed as collective than in others; and some Governments may consequently take a larger proportion of the national income in taxation in order to meet them. This proportion can be treated as a rough measure of the extent to which needs are met collectively rather than individually. In this field it is difficult to quantify Government objectives except by the amounts that they actually spend. Governments are constrained on the one hand by the constant demand for higher standards, in, for example, education and health services, and on the other hand by the

need to keep public expenditure from rising too fast.

The satisfaction of collective needs can be grouped under the following heads:

a. General administration (including justice, police, fire protection, flood control, etc.)
b. Defence
c. International affairs
d. Education, culture and science
e. Public health

Only that Government expenditure which provides collective facilities of some kind is considered as fulfilling this objective. We have considered that the objective of Government social security expenditure, for instance, is mainly to improve the distribution of income; and the objective of expenditure on housing is also either to improve income distribution or to change the pattern of private consumption.

7. Improvement in the Distribution of Income and Wealth

The objective here is a redistribution in whichever direction the Government considers it should be redistributed. In most instances, the Government has taken measures to reduce the gap between high and low incomes. During the period covered in this book Governments have not in general been mainly concerned to make the tax structure more progressive; in most countries this had already been done before or during the war. But a number of measures were taken to improve the relative position of the low wage earner or the pensioner, for example.

On a few occasions some Governments have taken measures which increased the gap between high and low incomes; they have for instance taken the view that managers and scientists were taxed too heavily and have reduced the tax on people in the appropriate income brackets.

Policies which aim at a fairly broad redistribution of income between major social groups are considered as aiming at this objective; policies which aim more narrowly at improving the relative position of a particular industrial or regional group —such as farmers, coal-miners, or the inhabitants of Southern Italy—are considered under the next heading: protection and priorities to particular regions or industries.

The objective of changing the distribution of wealth, rather than income—by redistribution of property, for instance—is also included here.

8. Protection and Priorities to Particular Regions or Industries

The definition of this objective is the provision for an industry or region, or a particular group of entrepreneurs or workers, of incomes higher than those they could obtain in a freely competitive national or international system. This protection may take various forms, such as the imposition of a tariff on foreign produce or a subsidy to the industry to enable it to survive.

Sometimes Governments have before them some quantitative indication of the amount of protection which should be given to a particular industry—sufficient, for instance, to bring the price of the imported commodity level with that of the home product. On other occasions there is no quantitative guide.

This objective also covers the case where, for instance, a Government give some priority to a particular industry or region as part of a national plan, with no particular intention of protection.

9. Improvement in the Pattern of Private Consumption

Governments take action under this heading when they consider that they can judge consumers' needs better than the consumer can himself. For instance, most Governments discourage the drinking of alcohol by high taxation; some Governments encourage the provision of satisfactory housing by subsidising it; others

subsidise milk. Social security payments may be intended to increase the consumption of medical services. Cultural subsidies do the same sort of thing.

Governments may also intervene to protect the consumer in various ways—for instance, by hire purchase legislation or by the imposition of quality standards. They may also help the consumer to get what he really wants—by consumer information. Measures of decontrol, such as the abolition of consumer rationing, may also be said to improve the pattern of private consumption.

10. Security of Supply

The objective here is to ensure supplies of essential primary products. Some Governments have required industries to keep certain stocks of such commodities as wheat, for example, or oil; other Governments have built up strategic stockpiles themselves. In the early part of the period, Governments made long-term contracts with supplying countries with this objective in view. In some countries measures have also been taken for the preservation of natural resources: for instance, measures to preserve forests or to restrict the rate at which home supplies of petroleum are tapped.

11. Improvement in the Size or Structure of the Population

Not many countries have had a conscious population policy. In those countries which have had one, Governments have often been concerned with the promotion of emigration. For instance, the Netherlands Government has considered that their population was likely to become too big for the country, and has encouraged emigration. Most countries have an immigration policy; some were mainly concerned to encourage the immigration of skilled workers, others to restrict immigration. Some other countries encouraged a high birth rate—by measures such as family allowances, for example.

12. Reduction in Working Hours

Here again, not many Governments have a conscious policy of reducing working hours: this has normally been left to negotiation between unions and employers. The Governments which have intervened in this matter have done so either by increasing the number of days which employers must grant as holidays, or by reducing the length of the working day or working week.

E. THE INSTRUMENTS

An instrument is defined here as something which the Government itself can change in order to produce an economic effect. It may be an economic quantity, such as the Bank rate, or it may be a part of the institutional framework, such as the rules which regulate the behaviour of entrepreneurs—for instance, a change in the legislation about restrictive practices. An instrument, therefore, in our terminology is the means by which the objective is pursued.

The classification of instruments used here is one that is fairly common in economic analysis. They are grouped in the following five families:

1. Public finance
2. Money and credit
3. Exchange-rate
4. Direct control
5. Changes in the institutional framework

These five families of instruments are discussed briefly below: they are discussed more fully in the separate chapters of part I which are devoted to them.

1. Public Finance

This set of instruments covers most income and expenditure of the Central and local Governments. Government expenditure is largely devoted to the objective of the satisfaction of collective needs.

On the income side, changes in individual taxes can obviously influence the distribution of income or the structure of private consumption, or can be used, for example, through the encouragement of investment to help to bring about expansion. Further, Government income and expenditure are used, together, as an instrument aimed to affect the total economic situation; in particular the Government may decide to increase or reduce the total Budget surplus or deficit, in order to stimulate or restrain the economy as a whole. But all Government lending and borrowing is included, together with transactions in the Government's existing debt, in money and credit.

2. Money and Credit

This set of instruments includes those which serve to make it either more difficult or easier for persons, companies, or Governments to borrow money; they include, for instance, measures designed to change the rate of interest or to increase or reduce bank advances. Measures of persuasion are included, as well as legal controls. A few instruments are included in this family which could also be considered as direct controls—such as hire purchase controls and direct instructions to the banks to limit advances to a certain sum; it is clearly more appropriate to consider these controls in money and credit.

All Government debt operations—both new borrowing and lending and operations in existing debt—are included here.

3. Exchange-Rate

This is one instrument and not a set of instruments. Its use covers both general revaluations and devaluations and changes in the exchange-rate for particular transactions, or changes against particular currencies. It also includes any change in the type of exchange-rate system.[10]

4. Direct Control

This is defined as the fixing by the Government of prices, quantities, or values, generally by fixing maxima or minima. These instruments include any absolute prohibition, such as making the export of capital illegal. Usually direct controls were imperative, with the force of the law behind them. But sometimes the Government had used techniques of persuasion; and these are included here, in so far as they are not included in money and credit.

Sometimes the persuasion has been so strong, with the threat of statutory measures if it was not complied with, that it virtually amounted to an order. At the other end of the scale, persuasion was on some occasions little more than mild suggestion. The setting up of any major new machinery or institution for exercising direct control is discussed under "changes in the institutional framework"; the operation of the machinery or institution after it is set up is included here.

5. Changes in the Institutional Framework

Some of the changes in the institutional framework alter the basic system within which other instruments are used: for instance, a substantial change in the banking system. Some do not affect the other families of instruments, but have a direct bearing themselves on the process of production: for instance, anti-cartel legislation. There is a third category: changes which create new international institutions, and which therefore limit the freedom of national Governments.

The dividing line between changes sufficiently large to be considered a change in the institutional framework and changes within the existing framework is necessarily an arbitrary one. Only fundamental changes are considered under this heading; small changes are considered elsewhere, in the appropriate families. For instance, the decision to impose indirect taxes on a new range of goods would not be considered an institutional change big enough to be included here. On the other hand, the creation of a tax on the value added counts as a change in the institutional framework.

F. MEASURES

A measure is the use of a particular instrument at a particular time in order to promote one or more objectives: for instance, the decision to raise Bank rate on a certain day, or to reduce income tax in a particular budget.

The removal of a measure—for instance, the removal of a price control—is also a measure. If the measure is removed simply because the objective it was introduced to serve no longer depends on such controls being retained or because the measure itself turns out to be increasingly unpopular or tiresome no new objective is introduced in our analysis. On the other hand, if the removal is due to a conflict between the first objective and some other objective, then this other objective is considered as the objective of the removal.

In some instances, enabling legislation is passed which permits a Government to take action at a later date if it wishes; on other occasions there are a succession of preliminary Parliamentary steps to a particular measure. If the passing of the enabling legislation, by itself, has significant economic effects, then it must be considered a measure in its own right. Otherwise, the measure is discussed when the Government takes action.

NOTES

1 Only major changes in local government policy are considered; it would not be possible to deal with every minor matter.
2 See chapter II, page 31.
3 When in any particular country one of the major objectives in our standard list was a minor one, or vice versa, this is noted in the country chapter in Vol. III.
4 With the exception of Germany from 1952 to 1955.

5 There have been occasions when Governments have been disturbed in the short-term about the balance of payments, although the reserves were not falling. For instance in 1959 the United Kingdom Government took some action to restrain home demand in the interests of the balance of payments, although the reserves were rising at the time; this was because it was only the inflow of short-term money which was leading to a rise in the reserves and the balance of payments on current and long-term capital account was in substantial deficit.

6 In some countries, part of the stock of gold has to be held as backing for the internal monetary circulation, and so cannot strictly be regarded as part of the stock available for meeting a payments deficit.

7 The first is equal to 4.56 and the second to 4.14 per cent a year.

8 This does not mean that all Governments are necessarily concerned to increase the mobility of labour as much as possible. In some circumstances, labour may become too mobile, and the high turnover of labour increases industrial costs.

9 Any measures which are designed to alter the relative purchasing power of different income groups are considered to aim at this objective; thus, for example, subsidies on items of working class consumption, although they do not strictly speaking redistribute income, have the same effect in practice.

10 Though, strictly speaking, such a change might be considered as a change in the institutional framework.

Economic Forecasting
Sheldon W. Stahl

Forecasting is defined as "calculating or predicting some future event or condition, usually as a result of rational study and analysis of available pertinent data." Economic forecasting, in particular, which attempts to predict the future course or level of economic activity, has become relatively commonplace. Despite the current abundance of forecasts, it should be noted that both the increased efforts in the field of economic forecasting and public awareness of these efforts and their results are of fairly recent origin. Although there may be general recognition that any kind of economic planning, whether by private business firms, governmental units, or consumers, involves making certain assumptions about the future, the analyses of business conditions made prior to the economic depression of the 1930's were confined largely to theoretical probings

Sheldon W. Stahl, "On Economic Forecasting," Federal Reserve Bank of Kansas City, *Monthly Review* (January 1968), pp. 16–22.

into the causes of cyclical change. Empirical evidence or data based on observation were not readily available, and the kinds of economic data which did exist were not very reliable. A consequence of this paucity of accurate and timely economic information was the absence of any major concerted activities in economic forecasting.

With the calamitous economic circumstances of the 1930's, World War II, and the postwar problems of economic adjustment, increased attention was focused on the manner in which the economy worked and, as a corollary, the probable causes and effective controls of fluctuations in business activity. The development and publication of a formal system of national income and product accounts for the United States provided the economist with an important tool for research and analysis in the field of business conditions. Continual refinement of economic theory and the growth of econometrics, in which economic theory is integrated which mathematics and statistics, have added another dimension to economic forecasting.

With a growing volume of literature devoted to the subject, and at a time when the annual volume of short-term forecasts of the economy reaches peak levels, it is useful to look behind the actual forecasts themselves to view several fundamental questions related to economic forecasting. Despite the fact that the practice of forecasting has grown enormously in recent years, the forecasts are the end product of a variety of analytical approaches, rather than the result of a single technique. In this article, some of the more commonly used techniques in short-run aggregate economic forecasting will be discussed. Before proceeding to a discussion of methodology, however, consideration will be given to both the objectives and the problems inherent in attempts to predict the future of the economy.

FORECASTING OBJECTIVES

While forecasts dealing with the future behavior of a specific industry, or of a particular sector of the economy, are of limited interest, those which deal with the general level of activity for the economy as a whole interest a much wider audience. For the private sector of the economy, such forecasts are indispensable as an aid in dealing with questions such as the magnitude and timing of new investment outlays, the probable terms of new collective bargaining agreements, consumer spending plans, and so on. In the case of governmental units, and especially at the Federal level, knowledge of the current and future state of business conditions is also of vital importance. The Employment Act of 1946 explicitly charges the Government with the responsibility for formulating and implementing public policies designed to promote stable economic growth and maximum purchasing power and employment. To insure the maximum likelihood

of realizing these objectives, knowledge of the expected future course or behavior of the economy is needed so that public policy—monetary and fiscal—may be shaped and reshaped as evolving economic circumstances may dictate. Additionally, the progressive nature of much of the Federal tax structure means that the volume of tax receipts is highly dependent upon the level of aggregate economic activity. Any changes in the performance of the economy affect those receipts. Therefore, the whole budgeting process is related intimately to the reliability of forecasts of the overall level of economic activity.

From the preceding observations, two fundamental objectives of economic forecasting emerge. First, forecasting attempts to determine the direction of economic movement, especially the timing of any probable change in direction. This function is frequently referred to as locating cyclical turning points. The second objective is to provide some estimate of the probable magnitude of any changes in the movement of the economy. Even though the objectives of forecasting are reasonably clear, some of the problems inherent in achieving those objectives make the task difficult.

A LOOK AT SOME OF THE PROBLEMS

Perhaps the most fundamental problem facing the economic forecaster is that which relates to the nature of the economy itself. The U.S. economy is decentralized; the decisions which determine the level and direction of overall economic activity spring from a myriad of sources, public and private. However, the sum of all the individual decisions made in such an economy may not necessarily add up to a definitive answer regarding the future path of the economy. The reason for this is that each individual decision which is made in the private or public sector of the economy relates to and is, in turn, affected by all other decisions. If the circumstances which underlie a given decision or set of decisions should change, or have been incorrectly anticipated by the decision-makers, the aggregate outcome may be quite different than would be supposed by a simple summing-up process.

The notion of change suggests a second kind of problem for the forecaster. The U.S. economy is not only decentralized, it is highly dynamic as well. The constancy of change almost insures that the future behavior of economic activity cannot be predicted with unerring success. To be sure, there are many functional economic relationships and institutional arrangements which may be relatively constant or which change very slowly over time. One of the basic premises which underlies almost all efforts at forecasting is that there are certain continuities present in the economy over time, and that the future is related partly to past behavior. It is also true that the economy is being subjected continually to change with new institutions evolving to replace older ones, and with new forces which affect the behavior of business activity being introduced at the same time older forces are receding or being withdrawn. The growth of collective bargaining, for example, and the emergence of large and powerful unions have brought about fundamental changes in the wage-bargaining process, as well as in the degree of flexibility of wages to differing levels of economic activity. The rapid growth of employment in the government sector of the economy relative to the goods-producing sector in recent years similarly has added an element of stability to overall employment levels. To a degree, this increased stability helps to insulate the total economy from the efforts of a slowdown in activity in the private sector.

It was suggested earlier that knowledge of the future behavior of the economy was needed to allow for the shaping and reshaping of policy decisions, to maximize returns in the private sector, and to bring about desirable public goals such as the attainment of stable economic growth for the economy. This consideration raises a third problem for the forecaster: the effect of the forecast itself on the behavior of the economy. For example, assume the forecaster sees the period ahead as one which might be characterized by an unsustainably high level of aggregate demand with all the problems of resource availability and inflation attendant to such a situation. Once this forecast was made public, the result might be changes in private and public economic decisions with regard to spending, production, investment, and so on, which would alter the course of the economy's behavior and render the forecast invalid. Conversely, the forecast might be self-generating as people outbid each other in the market for the available resources and goods and services. Obviously, the more influential the forecaster, the greater this problem tends to be. But it should be noted that, to the degree that the forecast causes changes to be made which serve to improve the economy's performance, the net cost to the forecaster becomes a net benefit to the economy as a whole. Few forecasts, however, thus far have achieved such import that alterations in business plans follow in their wake. In addition, few forecasts are offered without a host of qualifying assumptions accompanying them to cover a variety of situations which the forecaster must consider before making any meaningful judgment. This point will be developed further in discussing forecasting techniques.

Finally, it should be recognized that the behavior of the economy in any future period is determined by noneconomic as well as economic considerations. Changing demographic factors, social factors, or political factors all exert their impact on the economy; yet, economic forecasters have no special expertise in making judgments about these matters. Thus, the area within which the economic forecaster works is circumscribed by a number of constraints over which little control may be exercised. Within this area the forecaster attempts to make meaningful judgments about the future.

TECHNIQUES OF FORECASTING

Opinion Polls

Probably one of the most commonly used approaches to short-term forecasting involves the use of opinion polls. Simply stated, this technique involves questioning many people regarding their opinions of the probable course of business in the period ahead. Implicit in this approach is the notion that, while the opinion of one respondent may carry little weight, the opinions of many respondents added together may, in fact, provide substantive indications of the future path of the economy. The more responsible polls exercise considerable care in selecting the sample population to be surveyed, and include representatives of business and industry, government, and academic groups. However, these polls too often ask only for the respondents' appraisals of general business conditions rather than specific questions dealing with areas in which they may possess more intimate knowledge. In addition, to the extent that the individual assessments of the economic outlook are developed by using readily available or public sources of information, they do not represent an independent response, and averaging such responses fails to improve their analytical merits. Finally, even if such polls took account of all their inherent shortcomings, they would still only serve as very rough indicators of the future direction of movement of the economy, while supplying little or no information on the magnitudes of change involved.

The More Specific Survey

If the general opinion poll is not specific enough to be of value in assessing the economy's future performance, a more recent analytical tool is the survey designed to elicit specific information on future plans, commitments, or intentions of representatives of various sectors of the economy. Rather than focus attention on the respondents' attitudes about future business conditions for the whole economy, this type of survey requests specific information on the respondents' own areas of specialization. Growth of these newer types of surveys has paralleled the growth and refinement of statistical sampling procedures and improved methods for collecting and summarizing data.

Although the more specific survey possesses distinct advantages over the opinion poll approach discussed earlier, it relates only to various sectors of the economy rather than the whole economy. However, the various sectors are interrelated. The consequences of spending decisions made in the consumer sector do have an impact on the investment and spending plans of the business sector. And both these sectors affect, and are in turn affected by, taxing and spending decisions made by various levels of government. Thus, the integration of survey results from the different components of the economy has enhanced the ability of short-term forecasters to more accurately judge the future.

One of the most well-known anticipations surveys is that conducted by the McGraw-Hill Publishing Company relating to business capital spending plans for new plant and equipment. At the Government level, the Department of Commerce and the Securities and Exchange Commission also survey business intentions to spend for new plant and equipment. For more than a decade the National Industrial Conference Board has surveyed capital appropriations of the 1,000 largest manufacturing corporations in an effort to gain advance knowledge about the course of capital spending. Most sizable companies prepare annual capital budgets which give indications of spending intentions. These intentions become actual expenditures by means of specific appropriations, and the Conference Board survey measures these appropriations as an added way to determine the expected magnitude of a key component of total investment spending.

In addition to surveying plant and equipment spending plans, the Department of Commerce regularly looks into manufacturers' sales and inventory expectations. The Bureau of the Census periodically examines consumers' spending plans and perhaps the most well known of the consumers' surveys is the *Survey of Consumer Finances* conducted annually by the Survey Research Center of the University of Michigan. The latter survey attempts to measure the attitudes of consumers rather than the actual volume of consumer purchases which might be forthcoming in the period ahead. In this respect, it varies from surveys of business plant and equipment spending or inventory spending plans.

One of the more important sources of information dealing with the spending plans of a major sector of the economy is not a survey in the same sense as those already discussed, but should be mentioned because of its extreme importance to overall economic activity. This is the Federal budget and the appropriations data issued by the Federal Government. The information contained in the budget, as well as the data on future spending plans or intentions which arise from specific surveys, are valuable additions to the forecaster's knowledge, but they are human decisions and are always subject to change. They should be considered only as an aid to forecasting rather than as a self-sufficient method.

The Leading Indicators Approach

Since economic forecasting has as its overall object the prediction of future levels of economic activity, any measure which can point out ahead of time what is going to happen to the economy would be most valuable to the forecaster. The earlier paragraphs which dealt with surveys or opinion polls noted that these were attempts to gain information about the future behavior of the economy through general or specific questions dealing with attitudes, intentions, or expectations regarding the period ahead. The leading indicators approach differs from this technique in that it makes inferences about the future of the economy on the basis of information dealing with the economy in the present. It does this by singling out and analyzing various measures of economic activity which move in the same fashion as does the overall economy, but which do so in advance of general economic activity.

This approach is an integral part of the business cycle concept of economic activity. It relates to the view that the U.S. economy has been characterized by recurring periods of rising economic activity followed by periods of declining economic activity, and that this basic pattern of upswing and downswing is more or less a permanent characteristic of the economy. Because the leading indicators tend to move up or down in advance of the economy as a whole, observing or tracking their progress may provide insights into such questions as the probable direction of economic movement, its time dimension, and other considerations.

This technique evolved largely under the sponsorship of the National Bureau of Economic Research, with a pioneering effort by Wesley C. Mitchell and Arthur F. Burns which led to a study published in 1938 entitled "Statistical Indicators of Cyclical Revivals." This study suggested some 21 indicators which the authors felt would help to confirm an upswing in aggregate economic activity. The list included not only "leaders "but "coincident" indicators as well—that is, direct measures of aggregate economic activity or measures which move at roughly the same time as the overall economy. From that time, work on such indicators has continued and the efforts of the Bureau have resulted in an expanded set of leading and coincident indicators, as well as the addition of a group of "lagging" indicators to the basic series. The latter indicators usually reach turning points at some time after aggregate economic activity has turned up or down.

Since October 1961, the Bureau of the Census, in its monthly publication "Business Cycle Developments," has published data on various economic time series including updated information on all of the National Bureau's leading, coincident, and lagging indicators. Examples of the leading series—now numbering 36— include data on average hours of production workers in manufacturing, manufacturers' new orders for durable goods, housing starts, corporate profits after taxes, and the index of stock prices of 500 common stocks. The 25 coincident indicators include nonagricultural employment, industrial production, current dollar gross national product (GNP), and retail sales. Included among the 11 lagging indicators are plant and equipment spending, unit labor costs, and instalment credit.

Within the framework of business cycle analysis, the indicators approach provides the forecaster with a means of making judgments about the movement of the economy. Using this frame of reference, analysts may study and interpret the behavior of the various time series insofar as they may shed light on the current state of the business cycle. Once the judgment has been made about the current stage of the business cycle and its relative rate of change, based on the performance of the indicators to date, further conclusions may be drawn about the remaining life and magnitude of the upswing or downswing on the basis of the various indicators' present and past relationship to the business cycle. To the degree that the business cycles framework accurately describes the behavior of the economy, the indicators approach is an invaluable tool in probing the future. However, to the extent the economy's performance over time departs from the business cycle reference frame, at best it may prove to be an unfruitful exercise, and at worst a misleading venture. In any event, by recognizing the bounds within which this kind of approach may be pursued, the forecaster may acquire another important analytical tool.

Model Building

In a very real sense, the model building approach to short-term economic forecasting represents the logical synthesis of all the techniques which have been discussed in this article, as well as many other approaches which were not included. It involves the construction of an analytical vehicle which reduces the real world to a simplified model. It omits enough detail so that the model is workable and understandable, while at the same time it retains enough meaningful variables so that it can provide substantive answers to the real world questions it is attempting to solve. Model building incorporates lead-lag relationships between economic variables which have persisted over time; it makes use of attitude surveys and surveys of anticipation such as those referred to earlier for inventories or for new plant and equipment. It is comprehensive and is carried on in terms of the components of the GNP, using time-series data and mathematical and statistical tools to generate quantitative estimates of the GNP and its components at some future period.

If the preceding remarks suggest that model building must inevitably result in the best estimates of the future performance of the economy, this inference should be drawn only after certain precautionary observations have been made regarding the inherent capabilities of the model.

Although this technique demands a certain discipline from its practitioners by forcing them to tightly organize in a logical and consistent fashion their judgments about how the economy functions, it should be recognized that a model can tell us nothing about the future that has not been previously fed into it. Because the results derive almost wholly from the assumptions or judgments about significant economic variables and their functional relationships over time, they will be no more valid nor useful in predicting the future than was the original intellectual process used in developing the model.

There is also an inherent danger that a model which lacks flexibility may fail to perform successfully in an economic environment characterized by rapid change. Explanatory variables and functional relationships, which pertained in an earlier period, may become less pertinent in explaining the behavior of the economy in the near-term future. It is at this point that that the element of judgment plays a key role. Not only must the model builder be aware of what forces have shaped the economy's performance up to the present, he must appraise and continually reappraise the changes in economic institutions, and in functional relationships between economic variables over time to assure that

the data which are fed into the model are significant and relate to the real world he is attempting to describe. In an economy such as ours, this is no small task.

A FINAL NOTE

The subject of economic forecasting is one which deserves far more consideration than could be given in this article. Although the objectives of forecasting may be readily discerned, the problems which confront those who would judge the future are numerous and not easily disposed of. The techniques discussed here, as well as those which were not discussed, represent attempts to introduce qualified judgments about the future in the place of existing uncertainty. The model building approach to economic forecasting has much to commend it, especially the rigor and discipline it imposes upon those who would utilize this technique. It has obvious limitations, however. Despite the fact that it represents the furthest advance in the field of forecasting—an effort to integrate the better parts of the other techniques of forecasting with quantitative methods—much additional work remains to be done. For the foreseeable future, economic forecasting is likely to remain neither an art nor a science, but an amalgam of both.

Economic Policy and National Income[*]
John Adams

Keynes in the *General Theory* [2] and standard interpretations [1] [3] acknowl-

John Adams, "The Phillips Curve, a 'Consensual Trap,' and National Income," *Western Economic Journal*, 6 (March 1968), pp. 145–149.

* The author wishes to thank E. Ray Canterbery for his assistance at all stages in the preparation of this paper.

edge that inflationary pressures can arise before an economy reaches full employment. Actual money wage changes occurring as full employment nears have been estimated for the United Kingdom by A. W. Phillips [5], whose name has been attached to an assortment of inflation-unemployment trade-off curves. In the

United States analogous estimates of schedules of wage or price inflation and labor unemployment have been made by Paul Samuelson and Robert Solow [6] and G. L. Perry [4].

This paper designs an elementary framework for analyzing the interconnections of inflation, unemployment, income, and economic policy. Its main intent is to develop a theoretical construct that bridges the long-existing gap between the Phillips curve and Keynes' national income model. First, we list the sometimes forgotten structural and institutional elements supporting the Phillips schedule. Next we link public opinion and political pressures to an inflation-unemployment schedule through use of a device called the "consensual trap." Finally, we demonstrate how all these factors—prices, employment, and the political process—affect national income determination.

A brief reference to the structural and institutional milieu affecting relationships among prices, wages, and unemployment illustrates the *ceteris paribus* conditions behind the Phillips curve and also identifies the forces public policy must modify if the national inflation-unemployment trade-off is to be improved in response to public preferences.

The labor market is, of course, far from being perfectly free. Labor mobility, the heterogeneity and adaptability of the labor force, sex and race discrimination in employment, immigration policy, and governmental programs (minimum wage legislation, unemployment insurance, wage guidelines) cause the overall unemployment-wage pattern to vary. The labor union and its pervasiveness are institutional parameters. As an approximate generalization, the more unionization, the greater the strength of unions in concentrated industries, and the more wage-centered the union's goals, the weaker the connection between national unemployment levels and specific wage demands. The lure of high profit levels ordinarily incites

greater wage-increase pressure. Any modification of these labor-providing, wage-setting institutions will tend to shift the association between unemployment and wages.

A number of factors affect the connection between wages and general prices, the pace of productivity being the most important. It is generally assumed that the faster the progress of technology the faster may wages rise without forcing the general price level upwards. Also, firms in heavily-concentrated industries are in a favorable position to correct prices for wage gains; and, they may well overreact. Anti-trust enforcement, informal or formal price and wage controls emanating from the public sector, and suasion are some of the policy ploys that may break existing wage-price ties.

The direction of influence is not always from wages to prices; the cost of living also affects wage demands. Price rises for whatever reasons tend to increase wage requirements regardless of employment conditions. These elements help to explain why Perry finds that trade-offs differ among sectors of the economy. Such findings provide some hope, perhaps in vain, that economic policy can improve the price-unemployment trade-off.

Figure 1 shows a representative inflation-unemployment trade-off curve, *PC*. The institutional setting is assumed unchanged. Monetary and fiscal policy is never neutral, even when active responsibility is temporarily abdicated; governmental actions therefore decide what levels of unemployment and inflation on the *PC* curve the economy must endure, given the prevailing business environment.

Inflation, which to the public and public official alike is best embodied in the behavior of the consumer price index, is calibrated on the vertical axis and the unemployment rate is on the horizontal. As the economy must be somewhere on the *PC* curve, the point representing full

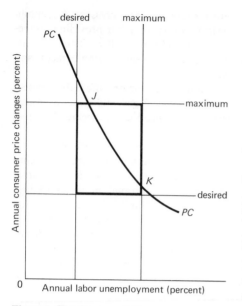

Figure 1. **The Consensual Trap**

employment with stable prices (0, 0) is a meaningless target for monetary and fiscal policy. If office-holding is contingent on public opinion, the task of elected officials is to trade off inflation and unemployment in such a way that the public is reasonably contented. Not needing to press for an ideal unique solution such as (0, 0), policy formulators merely strive to achieve a consensus wherein most of the people are more or less satisfied.

The public does hold strong preferences about inflation and unemployment. These sentiments are transmitted to their representatives via several channels, none of which is infallible; also, legislators and administrators are capable of displaying minds of their own. As even the most independently minded policy makers are not totally immune to public influence in a representative democracy, however, the effect of public opinion about prices and employment is to draw a "consensual trap" around economic policies.

The consensual trap, shown as a heavily lined rectangle in Figure 1 is a consequence

of four different opinions. The sides of the consensual trap are the median responses to questions designed to draw out preferences on desired and sustainable levels of inflation and unemployment. Half the distribution of opinions thus lies on either side of each edge. These constraining boundaries can be estimated for the nation, special groups, or regions by elementary polling devices.

The top horizontal edge of the trap signifies the maximum rate of inflation most persons will bear for any substantial length of time. Underneath is a parallel line that indicates the amount of price change most would actually *prefer* to experience. This line is above the horizontal axis because the public has some knowledge that to demand no inflation is unrealistic and because some persons may reasonably expect to gain in real terms as a consequence of the redistributive effects of general inflation. The other two sides of the consensual trap illustrate bounds on policy freedom set by majority preferences about the maximum unemployment thought bearable and the level of unemployment thought desirable. The desired level is not necessarily the full-employment point since the total elimination of unemployment can be viewed by some persons as unattainable or unwarranted.[1]

Because of the political constraints summarized by the consensual trap, some portion of the PC curve must always fall within the consensual trap and political forces will inevitably operate to keep the economy at or inside points J and K on PC. Within the trap public officials are free from wholesale censure on grounds of economic policy failure. While there are no majority public pressures resulting from dissatisfaction, some groups would still favor a positive program to move the economy's operating point towards the southwest corner of the trap, where majority satisfaction is maximized. Political actions to shift PC towards this goal may be anticipated. Thus the public's representatives can avoid negative reactions by judicious manipulation of fiscal and monetary measures, but positive acclaim could flow from achieving the more difficult task of structural-institutional reform, altering the constants behind the given Phillips curve.

Exactly how permanent are the boundaries of the consensual trap and what conditions determine desired and maximum levels of price changes and unemployment remain unanswered questions. The position of the estimated *PC* curve itself, the tone of public pronouncements by authoritative figures in or seeking

power, the degree of education in economic affairs, and expectations warrant further examination. Another assumption of the simple model is that desires of the public will be proportionately reflected in pressures on politicians and that politicians respond equitably. This is unrealistic to the extent that some groups have greater impact on the centers of power.

The *PC* curve and this consensual trap may be employed to supplement the analysis of income determination. The result is that full employment will not ordinarily be the goal of fiscal and monetary policies.[2] The equilibrium income, or what

Figure 2. The PC Curve, the Consensual Trap, and National Income Determination

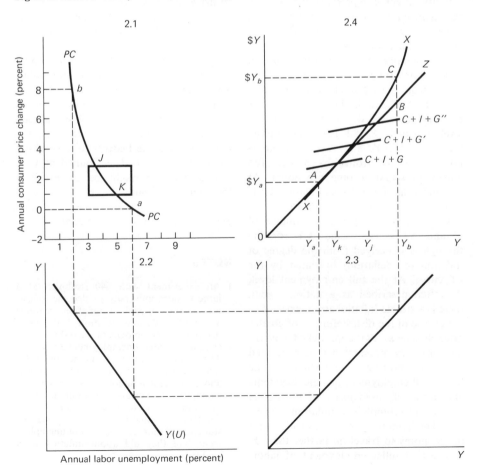

turns out to be a range of equilibrium national incomes, will usually be found *below* the full employment state. Figure 2 combines a *PC* curve, the consensual trap, and a standard income determination diagram. The upper lefthand coordinates contain a *PC* curve and a consensual trap, which uses values taken from the experimental results mentioned earlier. Below, income is shown as a declining function of unemployment. On the upper right is a Keynes-type aggregate demand diagram with modifications as described below.[3]

On the *PC* curve lie two points of interest in the process of income resolution. Point *a* indicates the level of unemployment associated with complete price stability. Point *b* represents the full-employment level and the associated rate of price change. In the test sample these are: $a(6, 0)$ and $b(2, 8)$. Dashed lines trace the other diagrammatic reference points of these pairs. Income levels Y_a and Y_b follow from the six and two per cent rates of unemployment. In Diagram 2.4 these two income levels define the no-inflation level of income (Y_a, \$$Y_a$) and full-employment income (Y_b, \$$Y_b$). At Y_a there is no price effect from any source and money and real income are equal. At any higher level of income, inflation exists in the amount shown by the *PC* curve. Beyond Y_a and A on OZ the equality of Y and \$$Y$ ceases. Line XX running through A is derived from the degree of inflation (or deflation) indicated by the *PC* curve. At the full employment level, Y_b, often described as a national goal, there is a sizable inflationary interval, BC.

Because of the distastefulness of greater price changes as Y_b is approached, governmental policy measures will be restrained by public pressures somewhere to the left of full-employment income. Segments and eventually a majority of the public will begin to complain as inflation accelerates. The bounds of consensus will permit the economy to travel no farther than Y_j in quest of fuller employment of labor.

On the other hand voters would not allow movements toward price stabilization that would push the economy lower than Y_k. The range of tenable income positions is thus delimited by the arc *JK*, that part of the *PC* curve inside the consensual trap. Satisfaction about the gains and losses of inflation and unemployment determine a range of incomes from Y_j to Y_k in which government policies will keep the economy. The economy is unlikely to operate at either the zero inflation or full-employment positions. And in recent years it has not.

Institutional policies designed to affect *PC* will also shift *XX*. The ill-fated wage and price guidelines, for example, represent an attempt to move *PC* southwest and to drive *XX* down to *OZ*.

Every relationship in Figure 2 can be estimated with a modicum of difficulty and uncertainty; the consensual trap is an operational concept. The technique could readily be applied to the general public and special interest groupings. Regular collection of this information would greatly reduce the need for baseless speculation by the President and his advisers, the Congress, and the Federal Reserve about what people want. The Council of Economic Advisers might be an excellent location for a continuing study of trade-offs among economic objectives and people's valuations of those goals.

NOTES

1 An experiment with 640 freshmen at a large Eastern university yielded the following results: maximum inflation bearable 3 per cent, desired inflation 1 per cent, maximum unemployment bearable 6 per cent, and desired unemployment 3 per cent. The median selection of points on a *PC* schedule was 3.5 per cent unemployment and 3 per cent inflation, thus suggesting a willingness to sustain maximum levels of inflation in order to reduce unemployment. Another set of questions confirmed that the students felt more strongly about unemployment than they did about inflation as a problem.

2 It is emphasized that not all policy-making institutions favor the same point on the *PC* curve. As examples, the Federal Reserve may be close to *K* whereas the President's Council of Economic Advisers may prefer to point close to *J*.

3 *G, G′*, and *G″* are used with fixed *I* and *C* to illustrate varying governmental policies. These *G*'s influence the level of income as well as the accompanying inflation-unemployment combination on *PC*.

REFERENCES

1. R. A. Gordon, *Business Fluctuations*, 2nd ed. New York, 1961.

2. J. M. Keynes, *The General Theory of Employment, Interest and Money*. New York, 1936.

3. R. C. O. Matthews, *The Business Cycle*, 2nd impression. Chicago, 1962.

4. G. L. Perry, "The Determinants of Wage Rate Changes and the Inflation-Unemployment Tradeoff for the United States," *Rev. Econ, Stud.*, Oct. 1964, *31*, 287–306.

5. A. W. Phillips, "The Relation Between Unemployment and the Rate of Change of Money Wage Rates in the United Kingdom, 1861–1957," *Economica*, Nov. 1968, *25*, 283–299.

6. Paul A. Samuelson and Robert M. Solow, "Analytical Aspects of Anti-Inflation Policy," *Am. Econ. Rev., Proc.*, May, 1960, *50*, 177–194.

The Relation Between Prices and Employment
Roger W. Spencer

Monetary and fiscal authorities are currently confronted with the task of simultaneously slowing price increases and maintaining employment growth. Policies directed toward the achievement of both objectives are affected by the policymakers' understanding of the underlying factors influencing prices and employment (or unemployment). Two principal views on this issue have emerged in the past decade. One stresses the short-run "trade-off" between prices and unemployment, and the other emphasizes the absence of a stable long-run relationship between varying rates of anticipated price changes and the level of unemployment. The short-run, for purposes of this analysis, is a period in which the relevant economic

Roger W. Spencer, "The Relation Between Prices and Employment: Two Views," Federal Reserve Bank of St. Louis, *Review*, March 1969, pp. 15–21.

factors do not fully adjust to expectations, while the long-run is a period in which the values of actual and anticipated variables coincide.

This article discusses these two views of the relation between prices and employment without delving excessively into the theoretical complexities of the relation. For expositional purposes, the two views are discussed separately, because the literature tends to be divided into these two groups. The purpose of the article, however, is to demonstrate that the differences between the two views stem primarily from the emphasis on short-run vs. long-run considerations rather than from diametrically opposing theories or models. Whether the short run or the long run is emphasized has substantially different implications for stabilization policy. These different implications are discussed in the concluding section of the article.

THE SHORT-RUN TRADE-OFF VIEW

High levels of unemployment in this country have generally been associated with slowly changing price levels, while low levels of unemployment have usually been accompanied by rapidly rising prices. These observed relationships have prompted attempts to explain price variations through changes in unemployment relative to the labor force. The Trade-Off View does not focus on unemployment as a determinant of prices directly, however. It holds that unemployment and the rate of change of unemployment influence money wages, and wage changes, in turn, bring about changes in the level of prices.

A. W. Phillips' study of the relation between wages and unemployment in England is generally considered the point of departure for most recent investigations into the trade-off controversy.[1] Phillips constructed a "trade-off curve" between the unemployment rate and wage changes, which indicated that wages in Great Britain rose rapidly when unemployment was declining and slowly when unemployment was rising. The "Phillips curve" was drawn to reflect a relationship between wages and unemployment, but other analysts have maintained that a similar relationship holds between prices and unemployment.[2] They have assumed or observed that the factors which influence wages similarly influence other prices, or that wages are a principal independent determinant of prices.

Those analysts who follow Phillips in stressing a trade-off between wages or other prices and unemployment have found several factors besides employment pressures which apparently determine wage changes. Factors most often included in this group are profits, productivity, and the cost-of-living. Employment pressures, however, remain the primary explanatory variable.

Factors Influencing Wage-Price Changes

The unemployment rate reflects the state of the demand for labor, a demand which is derived from the demand for goods and services. In a period of rising labor demand, employers attempt to attract workers from one another, thus bidding up wage rates. Additional labor may be obtained by attracting, through higher pay, such "secondary" or "reserve" workers as housewives, students, retired persons, or those already holding one job. The ability of workers to obtain large wage gains may be increased in periods of rising demand for goods and services when employers are especially anxious to avoid strikes. Profits are usually higher and inventories are often at lower levels when demand is high; consequently, employers probably exhibit less resistance to wage demands at such times.

A state of falling demand for goods and services and labor is reflected in a higher unemployment rate. According to Phillips, "...it appears that workers are reluctant to offer their services at less than the prevailing rates when the demand for labour is low and unemployment is high so that wage rates fall only very slowly."[3]

Changes in both profits and consumer prices are positively associated with changes in wages in the Trade-Off View. Workers often use high earnings reports and cost-of-living advances to improve their bargaining position. Some labor groups have cost-of-living escalator clauses written into their wage contracts.

No general agreement relating productivity and wage changes can be found among those who favor the Trade-Off View. Statistical studies have produced conflicting results.[4] Analysts have found insignificant, significantly positive, and significantly negative relationships between productivity and wage changes. Consequently, for purposes of analysis, productivity is generally assumed to increase at some constant rate. Analysts then can focus on the effects of changes in other variables, particularly unemployment, on wage rates.

Most observers who emphasize the Trade-Off View relate money (nominal) wage changes to the above explanatory variables through regression analysis. If all but one of the explanatory factors are held constant, a relationship between one variable—usually the unemployment rate—and wages can be depicted graphically. The resulting curve slopes downward from left to right, and is usually shaped similar to the rounded "L" determined by Phillips. (See Figures 1 and 2.) The non-linear shape suggests the existence of a critical high-employment range. According to Levy, "That price inflation, rather than reduced unemployment, is the main result of any expansionary policy after the economy has reached a *critical* high employment range, is a basic inference from traditional economics which is rarely questioned."[5]

The critical high-employment range may be defined as that range in which the number of employment vacancies are approximately equal to the number of workers seeking employment.[6] By this definition, excess demand in the labor market exists when the number of vacancies exceeds the number of job seekers, and there is an excess supply of labor when the number of workers seeking employment exceeds the number of vacancies. Excess demand causes wage rates to rise rapidly in the former case, and excess supply in the latter case tends to slow the rate of wage increase. Labor demand and supply factors may vary from sector to sector, but there is some evidence that a close tie exists between the ". . .aggregate unemployment rate and unemployment among various subgroups in the population."[7]

The Stability of the Phillips Curve

An issue of particular importance to policymakers is the stability of the prices (wages)-employment relationship. Most Trade-Off View studies, by holding constant those factors other than unemployment which determine wages, do not stress fluctuations within a Phillips curve, shifts of the curve itself, or changes in the critical high-employment range. These studies, which rely heavily on regression analysis, often imply that the economy is operating on a single curve, and stabilization actions directed toward guiding the economy to some point off the curve may prove unsuccessful. Such studies, strictly interpreted, indicate that the Phillips curve is a stable relationship.[8] This implication is refuted by Michael Levy, who found that "during the post-war years, the basic (Phillips curve) relationship for the U.S. economy between wage rate advances on the one hand, and the unemployment rate, the corporate profit rate, and cost-of-living increases on the other, has been highly unstable."[9] [Italics omitted]

Although the relationship may be technically unstable, a plotting of the wage and price changes and the unemployment rate reveals that Phillips' hypothesis —regarding the association of declining unemployment with rapidly rising wages (prices), and rising unemployment with slowly changing wages (prices)—has been generally observable over the past sixteen years. A simple correlation between two variables, as given here by a plotting of points on a two-dimensional graph, does not demonstrate causality, however. The relationship between the rate of change of manufacturing wages and the unemployment rate for the 1953–1968 period is plotted in Figure 1. The curve, which is similar in shape to the curve determined by Phillips, has been arbitrarily drawn to fit the data from 1961 to 1968, a period of uninterrupted economic expansion.[10] The shape of the curve would be altered

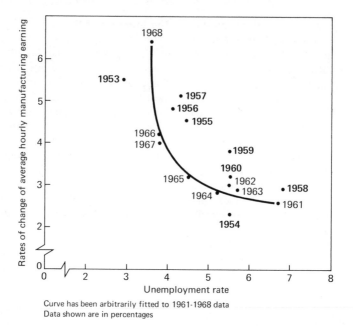

Figure 1. Rates of Change of Manufacturing Wages and Rates of Labor Unemployment

Figure 2. Rates of Change of Consumer Prices and Rates of Labor Unemployment

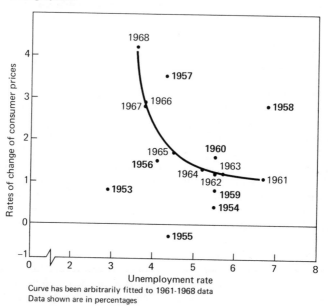

to some extent if fitted to the 1953–1960 period. For the sixteen-year period, the curve would be shifted slightly to the right.

Graphical trade-off analysis usually focuses on the wages-unemployment relationship, but it has also been extended to the prices-unemployment relationship as has been done in Figure 2. The overall fit for the sixteen-year period would not be as satisfactory as in the previous chart, but there is a close parallel for the past eight years. In some earlier years, sharp price increases occurred at varying rates of unemployment. Unemployment averaged slightly above 4 per cent of the labor force in the 1955 to 1957 period, more than 5 per cent from 1959 to 1960, and a little less than 4 per cent in the 1965 to 1968 period. This evidence suggests that the critical high-employment range has varied, perhaps reflecting the changing nature of the labor force in particular and the economy in general.

Phillips curves derived from regression analysis are based on rather specific assumptions, and the shape can vary substantially when minor modifications of the behavioral assumptions are made, as illustrated by the two following examples. A basic curve derived by George Perry relating consumer prices and unemployment was constructed from an equation in which prices were allowed to respond freely to market pressures. By assuming instead that half of the price increases were autonomous, Perry found that the curve, fairly steeply sloped in the first instance, became relatively flat. In fact, the slope of the curve was less than half of that calculated originally.[11]

Ronald Bodkin[12] determined a near-horizontal linear relation between wages and unemployment. Rees and Hamilton,[13] utilizing the same data and nearly the same assumptions as Bodkin, found a much steeper curve. Their results precipitated the remark:

Our final caution is that we have been astounded by how many very different Phillips curves can be constructed on reasonable assumptions from the same body of data. The nature of the relationship between wage changes and unemployment is highly sensitive to the exact choice of the other variables that enter the regression and to the forms of all the variables. For this reason, the authors of Phillips curves would do well to label them conspicuously "*Unstable. Apply with extreme care.*"

This conclusion implies that the usefulness of such statements as "... 4 per cent unemployment is consistent with a 2 per cent rate of inflation if profit rates are at 11.6 per cent..."[14] is limited by the validity of the assumptions which underlie the model.

Characteristics of the Trade-Off View

The chief characteristics of the Trade-Off View might be summarized as:

1. The relation between money wages and unemployment is stressed, rather than the prices-unemployment relation.

2. Money wage changes are assumed to be a primary, if not the primary, determinant of changes in prices of final goods; consequently, changes in prices of final goods follow wage changes.

3. The relevant variables are specified in nominal rather than real (or price-deflated) terms.

4. The basic relationships are established by the use of regression analysis using observed data.

5. The relation between rates of wage or price changes and the unemployment rate may be represented by a line which curves downward on a graph from left to right.

6. The rationale behind movements along the Phillips curve, rather than shifts of the curve itself, is stressed. The policymakers attempt to attain the point on the curve which seems least undesirable.

7. The time units and period covered by the analysis are specified in terms of months, quarters, or years. Phrases such

as "the length of time required for the factors to reach their long-run values" are not found in the Trade-Off View.

THE LONG-RUN EQUILIBRIUM VIEW

The Long-Run Equilibrium View considers the trade-offs between wages or prices and unemployment as transitory phenomena, and that no such trade-off exists after factors have completely adjusted to the trend of spending growth. In the short-run there can be a discrepancy between expectations and actual price or wage changes, but not in the long-run. After the discrepancies between expected and actual values have worked themselves out, the only relevant magnitudes are "real," or price-deflated ones.

To illustrate the view, consider the following hypothesized sequence of events in the upswing of a business cycle, beginning with an initial condition of significant unemployment. Monetary or fiscal actions may start an upturn of business activity. Spending occurs in anticipation of a continuation of the price levels which had prevailed in the downswing. Employers begin actively seeking workers to accommodate the rising demand, but wages increase only moderately since a large number of unemployed are seeking jobs. Output and employment rise more rapidly than wages or prices. The remainder of the scenario is outlined by Milton Friedman:

Because selling prices of products typically respond to an unanticipated rise in nominal demand faster than prices of factors of production, real wages received have gone down —though real wages anticipated by employees went up, since employees implicitly evaluated the wages offered at the earlier price level. Indeed, the simultaneous fall *ex post* in real wages to employers and rise *ex ante* in real wages to employees is what enabled employment to increase. [The non-technical reader may wish to substitute "anticipated" for "*ex*

ante" and "actual" for "*ex post*."] But the decline *ex post* in real wages will soon come to affect anticipations. Employees will start to reckon on rising prices of the things they buy and to demand higher nominal wages for the future. "Market" unemployment is below the "natural" level. There is an excess demand for labor so real wages will tend to rise toward their initial level.[15]

As real wages approach their original level, employers are no longer motivated to hire workers as rapidly or bid up wages so much as in the earlier portion of the upswing. Moreover, rising wages may encourage employers to utilize more labor-saving equipment and relatively fewer workers. As the growth of demand for labor slows, the unemployment rate declines to its "natural" level. Economic units come to anticipate the rate of inflation, and are no longer misled by increases in money income—the so-called "money illusion." The unexpected price increases which accompanied the original expansion of total demand and production caused a temporary reduction of unemployment below the long-run equilibrium level. Only accelerating inflation—a situation in which actual price rises continue to exceed anticipated rises—can keep the actual unemployment rate below the "natural" rate.[16]

Inflation has not been allowed to rise uncontrolled for sustained periods in this country, so little empirical evidence can be amassed to support the contentions that no permanent trade-off exists. In other countries such as Brazil, however, it has been found that sustained inflation does not generate continuous employment gains; in fact, recessions and high unemployment rates have occurred as secular inflation continued. Unanticipated price increases have, in those countries as well as in the United States, generated increased temporary employment, just as unanticipated declines in the rate of price increase have caused temporary rises in unemployment. But if inflation is "fully and instantaneously discounted, the

Phillips curve becomes a vertical line over the point of 'equilibrium unemployment.' This is the rate of unemployment where wage increases equal productivity gains plus changes in income shares. The unemployment–price stability trade-off is gone."[17] In other words, there is no particular rate of price change related to a particular rate of unemployment when the price changes are fully anticipated. Unemployment shifts to its equilibrium value and is consistent with any rate of change of prices. A low rate of unemployment can no longer be "traded-off" against rapidly rising prices, nor can a high unemployment rate be "traded-off" against slowly changing prices.

Costs of Information

A modified version of the Long-Run Equilibrium View is framed in terms of costs of obtaining information about job opportunities. When the demand for labor is low, the costs to a worker of discovering the state of labor demand are relatively high because employers are not actively seeking workers by publicizing extensive lists of vacancies. Employers are not as likely to absorb job training and transfer costs as they are when aggregate demand is rising. When labor demand rises and employers begin bidding up wage rates to attract additional labor, the costs of information, training, and transferring are lowered to employees. The lower costs mean that employees will not have to search as long for acceptable employment, and the shorter the search time, the lower rate of unemployment. Rising wages are accompanied by a declining unemployment rate.[18]

A reversal of stimulative policies will generate declining demand for labor. Some workers will accept smaller wage increases or reduced wages, but others will prefer to leave their jobs to seek employment at their former money wage rates. They expect prices and wages will remain at their earlier, higher levels. Prices and output will have fallen, however, and the high real wage rate will have stimulated employers to lower the quantity of labor demanded, thereby raising search costs to those workers who leave their jobs to seek employment elsewhere.[19] Higher search costs and lower money wage rates will be accompanied by rising unemployment. When workers realize that demand and price increases have slowed, they will be willing to accept the lower money wage rates and unemployment will stabilize at the "natural" level. For the stabilization to occur, however, no money illusion can exist. Anticipated wage (or price) changes must equal actual wage (or price) changes.

The costs-of-information approach combines the two factors determining the equilibrium rate of unemployment—the structure of real wage rates as determined by labor demand and supply, and "imperfections" within the labor market.[20] Bottlenecks, labor and product market monopolies, positive costs of information, training, and transfers create "imperfections" in the labor market. In other words, all markets are not cleared instantaneously and without cost. At any point in time the degree of the so-called "imperfection" within the labor market will vary, depending on transactions and information costs; correspondingly, the "natural" rate of unemployment will vary.

Enactment of policies oriented toward eliminating or reducing market imperfections (adjustment costs) will cause the short-run Phillips curve to shift to the left and down. Policies which increase these costs move the short-run Phillips curve upward and to the right. Different forces are at work at different times, causing the curve to shift frequently. Expectations of higher prices will cause the curve to shift upward, and expectations of lower prices move the curve in the opposite direction. The optimal stabilization policies, therefore, would be those which would reduce market adjustment costs and expectations of higher prices.

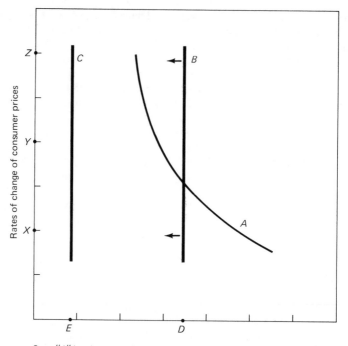

Curve "*A*" is a short-run prices-unemployment relationship.
Vertical line "*B*" is the long-run relationship between prices (fully anticipated
  regardless of the rate of change) and the "natural" rate of unemployment,
  "*D*", before reduction of market "imperfections."
Vertical line "*C*" is a similar long-run relationship between prices and
  unemployment after assumed reduction of labor and product market
  imperfections.

Figure 3. Hypothetical Relationships Between Prices and Unemployment

Enactment of such policies would at first move the short-run Phillips curve to the left and downward, and in time, as expectations are fully realized, cause the curve to become a vertical line over the "natural" rate of unemployment.

A hypothetical, long-run relationship between prices and unemployment is presented in Figure 3. Point *D* represents the "natural," or equilibrium rate of unemployment before market imperfections or adjustment costs are reduced. Curve *A* represents one of many possible short run Phillips curves that exist before price changes are fully anticipated. After the rate of inflation becomes fully discounted,

the unemployment rate will shift from some point beneath curve *A* to point *D*, regardless of whether prices are rising at some slow rate, *X*, or a rapid rate, *Z*. The shift may occur along any of an infinite number of Phillips curves. The vertical line above point *D* indicates that no economic units—workers or employers, sellers or consumers, borrowers or lenders —are surprised by price changes. If programs to reduce labor and product market imperfections are implemented, vertical line *B* will shift, after a transitory period, to the left. Vertical line *C* represents the new long-run relationship between prices and employment above point *E*.

Characteristics of the Long-Run Equilibrium View

The principal characteristics of the Long-Run Equilibrium View might be summarized as:

1. The relationship between all prices and unemployment is emphasized, rather than the wages-unemployment relation.
2. Changes in selling prices usually precede changes in the prices of productive agents.
3. The relevant economic factors are specified in real rather than nominal terms.
4. Because of the lack of data on accelerating inflations, expectations of price changes, and the "natural" rate of unemployment, the analysis is generally accomplished through abstract reasoning rather than empirical testing.
5. The relation between the long-run rate of price or wage changes and the unemployment rate is a vertical line over the equilibrium rate of unemployment.
6. The long-run relationship and reasons for observed shifts of the Phillips curve are stressed. The authorities do not have to choose as a target some fixed relationship between prices and unemployment on a Phillips curve, but can attempt to move the economy off a short-run curve. In the long-run, they can seek any trend in prices desired without a sacrifice in terms of foregone employment or production.
7. The time period of the analysis is not specified. In the long-run, the actual values of the relevant economic variables equal the expected values, while in the short-run, they do not.

POLICY IMPLICATIONS OF THE TWO VIEWS

Unemployment declined from 5.2 per cent of the labor force in 1964 to 3.5 per cent in 1968. The annual rate of increase in consumer prices rose from 1.3 per cent to 4.2 per cent for corresponding years. These data indicate, according to the Trade-Off View, that stabilization authorities must decide to accept either high rates of price increases in order to maintain low unemployment rates, or adopt deflationary measures and accept relatively high levels of unemployment. Only significant reductions of imperfections within the product and labor markets could prevent employment declines in the face of deflationary policies.

Proponents of the Long-Run Equilibrium View point out that even in the absence of structural improvements, monetary and fiscal policies need not be limited by a short-run trade-off between prices and employment. Continuation of expansionary developments will generate either (1) a high, steady rate of inflation which will eventually become fully anticipated and confer no net additional employment benefits (unemployment will gradually return to its "natural" rate), or (2) an accelerating rate of inflation which will permit unemployment to remain below the "natural" rate. Neither expansionary policy alternative appears economically or politically desirable. Deflationary actions would produce increased unemployment (as expectations of price changes are slowly revised) but only temporarily, according to the Equilibrium View. As soon as a new price trend becomes stabilized and fully anticipated, nominal and real wages will coincide, and unemployment will fall to its "natural" rate. An inflationary policy is neither a necessary nor a sufficient condition for the attainment of high levels of employment. Since price expectations seem to change only slowly, actions to reduce the rate of inflation should probably be applied gradually to minimize the transition cost in terms of reduced output and increased unemployment.

Both views recognize the merits of structural measures in complementing monetary and fiscal actions. Policies which reduce the costs of obtaining employment information, improve labor mobility and skills, and eliminate product and labor market monopolies will lower the optimal level of unemployment. Adoption of such policies would improve the short-run dilemma faced by monetary and fiscal authorities and enable them to shift their long-run unemployment target to a lower level.

NOTES

1 A. W. Phillips, "The Relationship Between Unemployment and the Rate of Change of Money Wage Rates in the United Kingdom, 1861–1957," *Economica*, Vol. XXV (November 1958), pp. 283–299.
2 See, for example George L. Perry, *Unemployment, Money Wage Rates, and Inflation* (Cambridge: The M.I.T. Press, 1966), p. 107. Perry states that "the factors affecting wage changes have been analyzed on the assumption that the wage relation is central to an understanding of the inflation problem."
3 Phillips, p. 283.
4 See Ronald G. Bodkin, *The Wage-Price-Productivity Nexus*, (Philadelphia: University of Pennsylvania Press, 1966), pp. 143–151, for a discussion of such studies as well as Bodkin's own regression results.
5 Michael E. Levy, "Full Employment Without Inflation," *The Conference Board Record*, Vol. IV (November 1967), p. 36.
6 Edmund S. Phelps points out that labor union behavior and the existence of "unemployables" may partially account for the fact that excess demand in the labor market seldom appears to exist, that is, ". . . vacancies almost never exceed unemployment." See "Money-Wage Dynamics and Labor-Market Equilibrium," *The Journal of Political Economy*, Vol. LXXVI (July/August 1968), p. 686.
7 Perry, p. 25.
8 Stability exists, technically, when the parameters computed for various time periods appear to be drawn from the same underlying population.
9 Levy, p. 37. Levy's conclusion is based on a statistical technique ("the Chow test") designed to test the degree of stability among relationships.

10 The 1961 to 1968 curve for the United States mirrors more closely the relationship found by Phillips than do other possible subsets of the sixteen observations. Moreover, the fitting of the curve to the last eight years emphasizes the present position on the "low unemployment–rising wages" portion of the curve. Annual data were used in keeping with Phillips' original work. The problems inherent in using annual data in the Phillips curve relationship are well known. ". . . we regard the construction of a plausible Phillips curve from annual data for a long period as a tour de force somewhat comparable to writing the Lord's Prayer on the head of a pin, rather than as a guide to policy. This is because it is highly probable that the relationship has changed during the period. . .and because of the large changes in some of the variables that take place during the course of a calendar year and are blurred in the annual data." Albert Rees and Mary T. Hamilton, "The Wage-Price-Productivity Perplex," *Journal of Political Economy*, Vol. LXXV (February 1967), p. 70.
11 Perry, p. 68.
12 Bodkin, p. 279.
13 Rees and Hamilton, p. 70.
14 Perry, pp. 108–109.
15 Milton Friedman, "The Role of Monetary Policy," *The American Economic Review*, Vol. LVIII (March 1968), p. 10.
16 Phelps, pp. 682–683, provides a comprehensive listing of several authors and their variations of the "anticipated inflation" thesis. Also, see: Charles C. Holt, "Improving the Labor Market Tradeoff Between Inflation and Unemployment" (Working Paper P-69-1, The Urban Institute, Washington, D.C., February 20, 1969).
17 Henry C. Wallich, "The American Council of Economic Advisers and the German *Sachverstaendigenrat:* A Study in the Economics of Advice," *The Quarterly Journal of Economics*, August 1968, pp. 356–357.
18 The cost of information analysis is derived from studies by George J. Stigler, "Information in the Labor Market," *Journal of Political Economy*, Vol. LXX (Supplement: October 1962), pp. 94–105; and Armen A. Alchian and William R. Allen, *University Economics*, 2nd ed., Chapter 25 (Belmont, Calif,: Wadsworth Publishing Company, Inc., 1967). Also see Armen A. Alchian, "Information Costs, Pricing, and Resource Unemployment" in a forth-

coming issue of the *Western Economic Journal*.

19 The Committee for Economic Development points out that "slow adjustment to unexpected price increases may increase employment as prices accelerate, but this slow adjustment may also cause an increase in unemployment as the rate of price inflation slows. The temporary trade-off is a double-edged sword." *Fiscal and Monetary Policies for Steady Economic Growth*, a statement on National Policy by the Research and Policy Committee of the Committee for Economic Development, January 1969, p. 40.

20 The Equilibrium View maintains no monopoly over discussions of the relevance of labor market structure; indeed, Lipsey's rigorous reformulation of Phillips' original view was predicated to a large extent on the importance of unemployment among different sectors of the economy. See R. G. Lipsey, "The Relation between Unemployment and the Rate of Change of Money Wage Rates in the United Kingdom, 1862–1957: A Further Analysis," *Economica*, Vol. XXVII (February 1960), pp. 1–31. On the whole, however, it seems that the Equilibrium View, which stresses the reasons for the changing nature of the short-run Phillips curves—varying expectations and cost-of-information—is the view in which structural considerations should be discussed.

Summaries

Arthur M. Okun, *Policies for Sustaining Prosperity*. Address given before the 1969 Stanford Business Conference, San Francisco, February 19, 1969.

In this highly provocative speech delivered by Okun in 1969 as a private citizen after having served for several years as chairman of the Council of Economic Advisers, he demonstrates a high sensitivity to social, military, political, and industrial complexities which make the task of maintaining economic growth and stability extremely difficult. Okun begins his speech by emphasizing that the Nixon administration has a clear commitment to high employment and full prosperity. He then points out that, if full employment were the only national goal sought by the administration, that goal could be reached easily, although such an achievement would inevitably create widespread inflation. However, in reality, the administration's economic policy embraces more than one goal; hence, it must aim at achieving all of these goals simultaneously.

In his speech, Okun discusses the major shortcomings of the economic policies of the Johnson administration. In his judgment, our ability to achieve reasonable price stability, along with full prosperity, depends not only upon the judicious application of monetary and fiscal policies but upon other economic measures (such as voluntary price and wage controls) as well. Thus, Okun says, "Combining prosperity and price stability will require an intensive battle against inflation waged by all groups of Americans on a great many fronts."

James Tobin, "Unemployment and Inflation: The Cruel Dilemma," in Almarin Phillips and Oliver E. Williamson (eds.), *Prices: Issues in Theory, Practice, and Public Policy* (Philadelphia: University of Pennsylvania Press, 1967), pp. 101–107.

In this article, James Tobin concerns himself with the so-called "Phillips curve" dilemma. A .W. Phillips, a noted British economist who developed the concept of a trade off between unemployment and price inflation, shows that, in any economy, the rate of change of money wages is inversely related to the rate of unemployment, with prices stabilizing at some moderately high level of employment and rising more and more as unemployment declines. If this is true in the case of the United States, then our society must face the dilemma of either unemployment or inflation.

Discussing the Phillips curve dilemma, the author says it "is in a sense a reincarnation in dynamic guise of the original Keynsian idea of irrational 'money illusion' in the supply of labor. The Phillips curve says that increases in money wages—and more generally, other money incomes—are in some significant degree prized for themselves, even if they do not result in equivalent gains in real incomes. Empirical support for this view is found in statistical variants of the Phillips curve where the elasticity of money-wage increase with respect to price increases is generally found to be smaller than 1.0."

In his article, Tobin makes some suggestions for solving these dilemmas. His first suggestion is that the nation's policy makers try to shift the Phillips curve downward so that inflation is associated with low unemployment. His second suggestion is that the policy makers undertake a set of long-run measures in order to make labor and product markets more competitive. A third suggestion of his is that an attempt be made to increase the capital-labor ratio. Tobin concludes that all three approaches must be taken simultaneously. In the short run, the guideposts are the only tool we have. For the long run, however, we must start on the difficult structural reforms needed to dissolve the unemployment-inflation dilemma.

Bibliography

Daniel H. Brill, "Can the Government 'Fine Tune' the Economy?" Paper presented on February 28, 1963, before the Washington Chapter of The American Statistical Association, pp. 1–16.

G. Corry and D. Laidler, "The Phillips Relation: A Theoretical Explanation," *Economica*, 34 (May 1967), pp. 189–197.

Sheldon W. Stahl, "The Phillips Curve: A Dilemma For Public Policy: Inflation Versus Unemployment," Federal Reserve Bank of Kansas City, *Business Review*, January 1969, pp. 11–16.